Also by James B. Stewart
THE PARTNERS
THE PROSECUTORS

SIMON & SCHUSTER

NEW YORK   LONDON   TORONTO

SYDNEY   TOKYO   SINGAPORE

James B. Stewart

DEN
of
THIEVES

SIMON & SCHUSTER
SIMON & SCHUSTER BUILDING
ROCKEFELLER CENTER
1230 AVENUE OF THE AMERICAS
NEW YORK, NEW YORK, 10020

LIBRARY OF CONGRESS CATALOGING-IN-PUBLICATION DATA
    DEN OF THIEVES / BY STEWART, JAMES B.
        P.   CM.
        INCLUDES BIBLIOGRAPHICAL REFERENCES AND INDEX.
        1. INSIDER TRADING IN SECURITIES—UNITED STATES.   2. INVESTMENT
BANKING—UNITED STATES—CORRUPT PRACTICES.   I. TITLE.
HG4910.s683   1991
364.1'68—DC20   91-28819
                                                                    CIP

For Jane, my sister;
Michael, my brother;
and for Kate

Contents

And Jesus went into the temple of God, and cast out all them that sold and bought in the temple, and overthrew the tables of the moneychangers, and the seats of them that sold doves.

And said unto them, It is written, My house shall be called the house of prayer; but ye have made it a den of thieves.

MATTHEW 21:12–13
King James Edition

Cast of Characters

As crime on Wall Street neared its climax, late 1985.

At KIDDER, PEABODY & CO., New York
Martin Siegel, investment banker
   Ralph DeNunzio, chief executive
   Al Gordon, chairman
   John T. Roche, president
   Robert Krantz, counsel
   Richard Wigton, head of arbitrage
   Timothy Tabor, arbitrageur
   Peter Goodson, head of M&A
   John Gordon, investment banker
   Hal Ritch, investment banker

At IVAN F. BOESKY CORPORATION, New York
Ivan F. Boesky, arbitrageur
   Stephen Conway, investment banker
   Lance Lessman, head of research
   Michael Davidoff, head trader
   Reid Nagle, chief financial officer
   Setrag Mooradian, chief accountant

At DREXEL BURNHAM LAMBERT INC., Beverly Hills
Michael R. Milken, head of high-yield securities
   Lowell Milken, lawyer
   Richard Sandler, lawyer
   James Dahl, salesman
   Gary Winnick, salesman
   Warren Trepp, head trader

Terren Peizer, trader
Cary Maultasch, trader
Bruce Newberg, trader
Charles Thurnher, accountant
Lorraine Spurge, administrator
Lisa Ann Jones, trading assistant

AT DREXEL BURNHAM LAMBERT INC., New York
Dennis B. Levine, investment banker
Fred Joseph, chief executive
Donald Engel, consultant
Stephen Weinroth, investment banker
David Kay, co-head of M&A
Leon Black, co-head of M&A

AT GOLDMAN, SACHS & CO., New York
Robert Freeman, head of arbitrage
Robert Rubin, future co-chief executive
Frank Brosens, arbitrageur
David Brown, investment banker

AT LAZARD FRÈRES, New York
Robert Wilkis, investment banker
Randall Cecola, analyst
Felix Rohatyn, investment banker

AT SHEARSON LEHMAN BROTHERS, New York
Ira Sokolow, investment banker
J. Tomilson Hill III, co-head of M&A
Steve Waters, co-head of M&A
Peter Solomon, investment banker

AT BANK LEU, Nassau, the Bahamas
Bernhard Meier, banker
Bruno Pletscher, banker

At Merrill Lynch & Co., New York
Stephen Hammerman, general counsel
Richard Drew, vice president, compliance

Major investors
Carl Icahn, corporate raider and future chairman of TWA
John Mulheren, head of Jamie Securities
Henry Kravis, principal, Kohlberg Kravis Roberts Inc.

At Wachtell, Lipton, Rosen & Katz, New York (counsel for Goldman, Sachs)
Martin Lipton, partner
Ilan Reich, partner
Lawrence Pedowitz, partner

At Paul, Weiss, Rifkind, Wharton & Garrison, New York (counsel for Michael Milken and Dennis Levine)
Arthur Liman, partner
Martin Flumenbaum, partner

At Williams & Connolly, Washington, D.C. (counsel for Michael Milken)
Edward Bennett Williams, partner
Robert Litt, partner

At Cahill, Gordon & Reindel, New York (counsel for Drexel Burnham)
Irwin Schneiderman, partner
Thomas Curnin, partner

At Fried, Frank, Harris, Shriver & Jacobson, New York and Washington (counsel for Boesky)
Harvey Pitt, partner
Leon Silverman, partner

AT MUDGE ROSE GUTHRIE ALEXANDER & FERDON, New York (counsel for Siegel; later at Fried Frank)
  Jed Rakoff, partner
  Audrey Strauss, partner

AT ROBINSON, LAKE, LERER & MONTGOMERY, New York (public relations advisors for Michael Milken)
  Linda Robinson, partner
  Kenneth Lerer, partner

AT THE UNITED STATES ATTORNEY'S OFFICE, New York
  Rudolph Giuliani, U.S. attorney
  Benito Romano, deputy to Giuliani, future U.S. attorney
  Charles Carberry, assistant U.S. attorney, future head of fraud unit
  Bruce Baird, assistant U.S. attorney, future head of fraud unit
  John Carroll, assistant U.S. attorney
  Jess Fardella, assistant U.S. attorney

AT THE SECURITIES AND EXCHANGE COMMISSION, Washington, D.C.
  John Shad, chairman
  Gary Lynch, chief of enforcement
  John Sturc, assistant chief of enforcement
  Peter Sonnenthal, attorney
  Leo Wang, attorney

Prologue

Martin A. Siegel hurried through Washington, D.C.'s, National Airport and slipped into a phone booth near the Eastern shuttle gates. For years now, phone booths, often at airports, had served as his de facto offices. He complained often about his long hours and frequent absences from his wife and three children, but the truth was that he thrived on his pressure-filled life as one of the country's leading investment bankers.

May 12, 1986, had begun much like any other day. He had flown that morning from New York to Washington to visit a major client, Martin Marietta, one of the country's leading defense contractors. A few years earlier, he had helped Marietta fend off a hostile takeover bid from Bendix Corporation, and the deal had launched Siegel's star. He became one of the country's most sought-after takeover strategists.

The visit to Marietta had gone smoothly, with only one disturbing note. The company's chairman, Thomas Pownall, was upset about a recent insider-trading case. Pownall was set to testify as a character witness for Paul Thayer, a former deputy secretary of defense in the Reagan administration, who had been charged with insider trading for leaking top-secret information he gleaned while a director of Anheuser-Busch to, among others, his Dallas mistress. Pownall, along with most of corporate America, had been stunned. He had often done business with Thayer at the defense department, and the two men had become friends. "It's unbelievable, isn't it?" he had remarked to Siegel.

Siegel had nodded and quickly pushed any thoughts of Thayer aside. Handsome as a movie star, tanned, fit, Siegel, at 38, had recently moved to Drexel Burnham Lambert Inc., the powerhouse junk-bond firm. He was ready to vault to even greater stardom.

Now Siegel dialed his office in New York. It was just after 2:45 P.M., and he wondered what the stock market was doing. He hated

13

being separated from his array of sophisticated news-delivery mechanisms, from computer screens to wire services.

His secretary, Kathy, briefed him quickly and then started ticking off the many calls that needed to be returned that day. Suddenly a rapid series of bells rang at the Dow Jones ticker tape just outside Siegel's office, a signal that a major news announcement was imminent.

Kathy moved to the ticker and gasped as the headline emerged. "SEC charges Drexel Burnham Lambert official with insider trading," she read aloud.

As Kathy waited for the ticker to resume its account, Siegel felt his almost perfect world collapsing. Everything he had worked for all his life. His $3.5 million compensation and his $2 million bonus he earned when he moved to Drexel from Kidder, Peabody & Co. earlier that year. The astoundingly lucrative mergers-and-acquisitions practice he was melding with Michael Milken's junk-bond money machine. The blue-chip clients, like Martin Marietta, Goodyear, and Lear Siegler, that were now flocking to use Drexel's and his services. The house on the beach in Connecticut, with its own tennis courts and swimming pool. The four-bedroom cooperative apartment in Manhattan's exclusive Gracie Square. The helicopter rides to Manhattan. The glowing newspaper and magazine profiles.

Suddenly the image of arbitrageur Ivan Boesky, once Siegel's confidant and mentor, flashed before him and he felt a sudden terror. He thought Boesky might have him murdered.

"Oh my God!" Kathy exclaimed as the ticker resumed. "It's Dennis! It's Dennis Levine! He's been arrested!"

Siegel told his secretary to keep reading. "The SEC charged Dennis Levine, a managing director of Drexel Burnham Lambert Inc., with insider trading in connection with an alleged scheme to buy and sell securities based on non-public information gained through his employment as an investment banker for a period of five years," she continued. "Drexel Burnham said it will cooperate fully with the SEC in the investigation . . ."

Dennis Levine. Dennis Levine was the investment banker in the office next door. Siegel broke into a sweat. All he could think was this: A gun had been pointed at his head, the trigger had been pulled, and miraculously, the bullet had killed Dennis Levine instead. Overweight, overeager, self-promoting, ineffectual Dennis Levine.

In the Beverly Hills office of Drexel Burnham Lambert it was just before noon Pacific time, the peak of the trading day. Michael Milken sat at the center of a huge, X-shaped trading desk, his loyal traders and salesmen radiating out along the axes. As he avidly scanned the trading data on his computer screen, he reached for his two ringing phones— one for each ear.

This was the epicenter of the new economic order, the capital of the junk-bond empire that Milken had created. "Hey, Mike," called out one of the traders as the Levine news came over the wire. "Look at this." Just weeks before, Levine had debuted at Milken's hugely successful 1986 junk-bond conference, the "Predators' Ball," hosting a breakfast on mergers and acquisitions. Milken paused in his phone conversation, glanced at the news on his computer screen, then resumed work as though nothing had happened. "It's like a bad car wreck," one of the salesmen shrugged. "You slow down for a couple of days and then drive fast again." Nothing could stop the Drexel juggernaut.

Ivan Boesky, the legendary arbitrageur, emerged from the conference room at his Fifth Avenue offices and walked down the hall, trailed by several of his employees. Suddenly Jeffrey Hennig, one of Boesky's traders, rushed out of his office waving a piece of ticker copy. He shouted toward Boesky, "Did you see this about Dennis Levine?"

Boesky stopped abruptly and turned. "Dennis who?" he asked.

"Levine," Hennig replied. "Here." He showed Boesky the ticker tape announcing the SEC's charges against Levine.

Boesky read the item quickly, then handed it back. "I've never heard of him," he said, walking briskly away.

Years later, looking back on that day, Siegel realized he had been wrong. The bullet that killed Levine killed him, too. It killed Ivan Boesky. It killed Michael Milken.

The same bullet shattered the takeover craze and the greatest money-making boom in Wall Street's history, and it exposed the greatest criminal conspiracy the financial world has ever known. The Greed Decade may have taken four more years to play itself out, but after May 12, 1986, it was doomed.

Even now it is hard to grasp the magnitude and the scope of the crime that unfolded, beginning in the mid-1970s, in the nation's markets and financial institutions. It dwarfs any comparable financial crime, from the Great Train Robbery to the stock-manipulation schemes that gave rise to the nation's securities laws in the first place. The magnitude of the illegal gains was so large as to be incomprehensible to most laymen.

Dennis Levine, the small fish, confessed to $12.6 million in insider-trading profits. Ivan Boesky agreed to pay $100 million in forfeitures and penalties; no one pretends now that that is anywhere near the total of his illegal gains over the years. And then there is Michael Milken, whose crimes were far more complex, imaginative, and ambitious than mere insider trading. In 1986, Milken earned $550 million in salary and bonus alone from an enterprise that had been tainted with illegal activity for years. When he finally admitted to six felonies, he agreed to pay $600 million—an amount larger than the entire yearly budget of the Securities and Exchange Commission.

Nor were these isolated incidents. Only in its scale and potential impact did the Milken-led conspiracy dwarf others. Financial crime was commonplace on Wall Street in the eighties. A common refrain among nearly every defendant charged in the scandal was that it was unfair to single out one individual for prosecution when so many others were guilty of the same offenses, yet weren't charged. The code of silence that allowed crime to take root and flourish on Wall Street, even within some of the richest and most respected institutions, continues to protect many of the guilty.

To dwell on the ill-gotten gains of individuals, however, is to risk missing the big picture. During this crime wave, the ownership of entire corporations changed hands, often forcibly, at a clip never before witnessed. Household names—Carnation, Beatrice, General Foods, Diamond Shamrock—vanished in takeovers that spawned criminal activity and violations of the securities laws.

Others, companies like Unocal and Union Carbide, survived but were nearly crippled. Thousands of workers lost their jobs, companies loaded up with debt to pay for the deals, profits were sacrificed to pay interest costs on the borrowings, and even so, many companies were eventually forced into bankruptcies or restructurings. Bondholders and shareholders lost many millions more. Greed alone cannot account for such a toll. These are the costs of greed coupled with market power—power unrestrained by the normal checks and balances of the free market, or by any fears of getting caught.

Nor should the financial implications of these crimes, massive though they are, obscure the challenge they posed to the nation's law-enforcement capabilities, its judicial system, and ultimately, to the sense of justice and fair play that is a foundation of civilized society. If ever there were people who believed themselves to be so rich and powerful as to be above the law, they were to be found in and around Wall Street in the mid-eighties. If money could buy justice in America, Milken and Drexel were prepared to spend it, and spend it they did. They hired the most expensive, sophisticated, and powerful lawyers and public-relations advisors, and they succeeded to a frightening degree at turning the public debate into a trial of government lawyers and prosecutors rather than of those accused of crimes.

But they failed, thanks to the sometimes heroic efforts of underpaid, overworked government lawyers who devoted much of their careers to uncovering the scandal, especially Charles Carberry and Bruce Baird, in the Manhattan U.S. attorney's office, and Gary Lynch, the head of enforcement at the Securities and Exchange Commission. Their efforts did not succeed perfectly. The pervasiveness of crime on Wall Street after a decade of lax enforcement sometimes overwhelmed their resources. Not everyone who should have been prosecuted has been, and mistakes were made. Yet their overriding success in prosecuting the major culprits and reinvigorating the securities laws is a tribute to the American system of justice.

This is the full story of the criminals who came to dominate Wall Street, how they achieved the pinnacle of wealth, power, and celebrity, and how they were detected and brought to justice. Despite the intense publicity that accompanied the charges against them, very little of this story has been made public. Milken, Boesky, Siegel, and Levine, by pleading guilty to reduced charges, avoided full public trials. This account is based on over four years of reporting, including scores of interviews, the review of voluminous documentary records, grand jury and other transcripts, lawyers' interview notes, and notes of various participants. In an era that purported to glorify free-market capitalism, this story shows how the nation's financial markets were in fact corrupted from within, and subverted for criminal purpose.

At the most basic level, American capitalism has flourished because everyone, rich and poor alike, has seen the marketplace reward merit—enterprise, innovation, hard work, intelligence. The securities laws were implemented to help protect that process, to guard the integrity of the markets and to encourage capital formation, by providing a level playing field on which everyone might pursue their fortunes. Violations of the securities laws are not victimless crimes. When insider traders gain windfall stock profits because they have bribed someone to leak confidential business secrets, when prices are manipulated and blocks of stock secretly accumulated, our confidence in the underlying fairness of the market is shattered. We are all victims.

Above the Law

BOOK ONE

1.

Martin Siegel, the youngest member of the class just graduated from the Harvard Business School, reported for work at Kidder, Peabody & Co.'s Manhattan headquarters at 20 Exchange Place in August 1971. That morning, the 23-year-old Siegel wandered through the halls looking at the portraits of Henry Kidder, Francis Peabody, Albert R. Gordon, and others that hung above the Oriental rugs and slightly threadbare carpets. Siegel tried to absorb the images of this strange and rarefied world of old money and discreet power.

He didn't have much time for reflection. He and his new wife hadn't even unpacked before he was thrown into a day-and-night project to win some new underwriting business from the Federal National Mortgage Association. Siegel's partner on the project made little impression on him, except for his name: Theodore Roosevelt IV, or maybe V; Siegel could never remember which.

In 1971, with the Vietnam War still raging and spurring opposition to the Establishment, few top students were going to business school, let alone Wall Street. Siegel, one of the top graduates in his Harvard class, had had his pick of nearly every major investment bank and securities firm. He had applied to 22; all had shown interest.

Kidder, Peabody, with about $30 million in total capital, barely ranked in the country's top 20 investment firms. In the hierarchy of Wall Street, Kidder, Peabody was in the second-tier, or "major" bracket. It didn't rank in the elite "special" bracket with Salomon Brothers, First Boston, Morgan Stanley, Merrill Lynch, or Goldman, Sachs.

Though the winds of change were apparent in 1971, Wall Street was still split between the "Jewish" and the "WASP" firms. At an earlier time, when major corporations and banks had discriminated overtly against Jews, Wall Street had rewarded merit and enterprise. Firms like Goldman, Sachs, Lehman Brothers, and Kuhn Loeb (made up historically of aristocratic Jews of German descent) had joined the ranks of the most prestigious WASP firms: Morgan Stanley—an outgrowth of J. P. Morgan's financial empire—First Boston, Dillon, Read, and Brown Brothers Harriman. Giant Merrill Lynch Pierce Fenner & Smith, something of an anomaly, had once been considered the "Catholic" firm. Kidder, Peabody remained firmly in the WASP camp. Siegel was the first Jew it hired in corporate finance.

Siegel was looking for variety and excitement. Only investment banking offered the prospect of an immediate market verdict on a new stock issue or the announcement of a big acquisition. He had narrowed his choices to three firms: Goldman, Sachs, Shearson Hayden Stone, and Kidder, Peabody. A Goldman recruiting partner phoned, and asked, if Goldman made him an offer, would he accept? Siegel didn't commit. Shearson Hayden Stone offered him the largest salary— $24,000 a year.

Kidder, Peabody offered only $16,000. But Siegel saw unique opportunities there. The firm was full of old men, but had a roster of healthy blue-chip clients. Siegel envisioned a fast climb to the top.

Kidder, Peabody's aristocratic aura appealed to Siegel. One of America's oldest investment banks, it was founded in Boston as Kidder, Peabody & Co. in 1865, just before the end of the Civil War. Early on, Kidder raised capital for the railroad boom, primarily for the Atchison, Topeka & Santa Fe. Its clients also included two stalwarts of establishment respectability, United States Steel and American Telephone & Telegraph.

The modern Kidder, Peabody was dominated by Albert H. Gordon, the son of a wealthy Boston leather merchant, and graduate of Harvard College and Business School. In 1929, when the firm was devastated by the market crash, Gordon, a young bond salesman at Goldman, Sachs, stepped in with $100,000 of his own capital. Along with two partners, he acquired the firm in 1931.

The indefatigable Gordon, a physical-fitness fanatic with limitless energy and impeccable Brahmin bearing, moved the firm's headquarters to Wall Street from Boston and set about building a roster of clients. He had an advantage: Kidder, Peabody's reputation, in sharp contrast to many of its rivals, had remained remarkably unsullied in the aftermath of the crash.

The shock of the crash and the Depression had set off a reform movement in Congress culminating in Senate hearings conducted by special counsel Ferdinand Pecora beginning in 1932. Through Pecora's withering cross-examination of some of Wall Street's leading investment bankers, the American public learned about insider trading, stock-price manipulation, and profiteering through so-called investment trusts. Most of the abuses uncovered involved information bestowed on a favored few and withheld from the investing public. It was not only information that directly affected stock prices, such as the price of merger or takeover offers, but information that could more subtly be turned to a professional's advantage: the true spread between prices bid and prices asked, for example, or the identities of buyers of large blocks of stock and the motives behind their purchases.

In the wake of widespread public revulsion and populist fury, Congress passed historic legislation, the Securities Act of 1933 and the Securities Exchange Act of 1934. A new federal agency, the Securities and Exchange Commission, was created to enforce their provisions. Congress deemed the enforcement of its new securities laws to be so important that it enacted corresponding criminal statutes.

By separating banking from securities underwriting, the raising of capital, and distribution of stocks, bonds, and other securities, the securities acts set the stage for modern investment banking. Under Gordon's guidance, Kidder, Peabody concentrated on its underwriting function. The firm was a pioneer at opening branch offices in U.S. cities. The idea was, as Gordon liked to put it, to "sell your way to success."

Through most of its history, Kidder, Peabody was a tightly controlled partnership, with Gordon personally owning most of the firm and its profits. When the firm incorporated in the 1960s, the ownership changed little; Gordon simply became the firm's largest shareholder. He was parsimonious about bestowing ownership stakes on the firm's executives.

Kidder, Peabody prospered, if not spectacularly, under Gordon's conservative leadership. Determined to avoid another capital crisis, Gordon insisted that Kidder's executives plow their earnings back into the firm. This gave the firm the capital to survive the sudden drop in trading volume and profits that struck Wall Street in 1969. A Kidder vice president, Ralph DeNunzio, served as vice chairman of the New York Stock Exchange and helped arrange the merger of such old-line houses as Goodbody & Co. and du Pont. DeNunzio became chairman of the stock exchange in 1971, the same year Siegel graduated from Harvard Business School.

Martin Siegel's lineage was modest in contrast to that of the leaders of Kidder, Peabody. His father and an uncle owned three shoe stores in Boston, outlets that relied on American suppliers and catered to middle-to-working-class tastes. In the late sixties and early seventies, the stores were devastated by chains benefiting from national advertising and low-cost foreign suppliers. This was painful for Siegel, who had never seen anyone work so hard for so little as his father. As a kid growing up in Nadick, a Boston suburb, he had almost never seen his father, who worked seven days a week, often spending the night in the city. Unlike his classmates' fathers, Siegel's father never played ball with him.

Siegel wasn't good at sports in school; he started first grade a year early, so his physical development lagged behind his classmates'. But starting as a freshman in high school, he excelled academically. He thought he wanted to be an astronaut. When Siegel was accepted in his junior year of high school for a work-study program at Rensselaer Polytechnic Institute, a science and engineering college, he became the first member of his family ever to attend college. He continued to do well academically even while working part-time, and entered a master's program in chemical engineering in 1968. He knew he'd never become rich toiling as an anonymous engineer in a corporate laboratory, so he applied to Harvard Business School and was accepted for the class entering in September 1969.

The turmoil sweeping American campuses during the late sixties had had remarkably little effect on Siegel, but at Harvard, he was caught up in the antiwar movement after the U.S.–led invasion of Cambodia in 1970 and the killings of students at Kent State by the Ohio National Guard. He participated in an antiwar sit-in in Harvard Yard and smoked marijuana cigarettes a few times. Still, he was annoyed when students managed to get that year's final exams canceled. He took his anyway, exercising an option to take the exams at home and submit them by mail.

For his senior thesis, Siegel tackled the mounting woes of his father's shoe store business. His solution: The stores should be transformed into specialty high-end boutiques, catering to wealthy, fashion-conscious women. This would avoid the growing competition in the rest of the market. Siegel's father agreed in principle, but then his brother, who did the buying for the stores, had a heart attack. His father didn't have the eye or instincts for high-fashion retailing, but Siegel's thesis earned "distinction-plus," Harvard's equivalent of A +.

On the Fourth of July 1970, Siegel married Janice Vahl, a music student from Rochester he'd met two years earlier. After Siegel accepted Kidder, Peabody's offer, he and Janice moved to New York, paying $212 a month for a modest one-bedroom apartment on Manhattan's East 72nd Street.

Siegel took naturally to Wall Street and investment banking; his energy and drive were, as he had predicted, a breath of fresh air at Kidder, Peabody. DeNunzio, now Kidder, Peabody's chief operating officer, seemed early on to have taken favorable notice of his new employee. He too came from a modest background and seemed far more comfortable with earthy sales and trading types than he was with upper-crust investment bankers.

Siegel began working on some merger-and-acquisition transactions, since no one else at Kidder, Peabody was eager to get involved. Hostile takeovers bore an unsavory taint. They generated bad feelings, especially toward those who represented the attackers. This sometimes alienated other clients. Many of the WASP investment banks and law firms preferred to leave such work to the other firms, many of them Jewish.

None of this bothered Siegel. His first takeover deal came just after the passage of the Williams Act, which spelled out new procedures to protect shareholders from coercive takeover tactics. The deal was an unsuccessful bid by Gulf + Western's acquisitive Charles Bluhdorn, a longtime Kidder, Peabody client, for the Great Atlantic & Pacific Tea Co. Bluhdorn, who was close to DeNunzio, praised Siegel's work, and DeNunzio made sure that Siegel was assigned to another major client, Penn Central's Victor Palmieri. In 1974, recognizing the dearth of expertise in the area, Siegel wrote a textbook on mergers and acquisitions for use within Kidder, Peabody; it was hailed by his colleagues. In only two years, he was promoted to an assistant vice president.

As Siegel's career took off, trouble developed in the rest of his life. His father's business continued to worsen; Siegel flew to Boston almost every weekend to help. His marriage suffered. Janice sang with the Bel Canto opera in New York and wanted to pursue a musical career. Siegel, who had no interest in opera, gave her little support. In February 1975 they separated.

Shortly before, his father's bank and principal lender had pulled the plug on the Siegel shoe business. Robert Siegel's company filed bankruptcy. The once-proud and energetic retailer became, at 47, a broken man. He tried selling real estate; that didn't work out. He tried doing house repairs. Finally he landed a job selling roofing at Sears. Siegel watched with alarm as his father seemed to give up on his own life. He noticed the older man beginning to live vicariously through the sons and daughter he had once never had time for.

Siegel was haunted by the possibility that something similar might happen to him. He vowed he would never wind up a broken man.

. . .

After his father's misfortune, Siegel plunged even more completely
into his work, frequently logging 100-hour weeks. Emulating Gordon,
still titular head of the firm, he embraced physical fitness. One of his
contemporaries at the firm, a former all-American wrestler named
Scott Christie, put him through a fitness regimen at the New York
Athletic Club. At one point, Christie, Siegel, and John Gordon, Al
Gordon's son, were standing in a corridor at the firm when Siegel
boasted that he could do 50 push-ups in a minute. Christie squeezed
Siegel's bicep and rolled his eyes skeptically. "Come on, Marty." With
that, in his shirt and tie, Siegel dropped to the floor. He did the 50
push-ups in less than a minute.

Handsome Martin Siegel became Kidder, Peabody's golden boy.
He bought an Alfa-Romeo convertible and a beach house on Fire
Island, a popular resort off Long Island. He became socially poised and
gregarious. DeNunzio, awkward and physically unprepossessing himself, shrewdly recognized in Siegel a talent for getting and nurturing
clients, DeNunzio's major weakness. He made Siegel a full vice president in 1974, and soon Siegel was reporting directly to DeNunzio.
When Kidder, Peabody client Gould Inc. made a cash tender offer for
a valve manufacturer around Christmas 1975, DeNunzio assigned Siegel to work with the legendary Lazard Frères financier Felix Rohatyn,
who was representing the target company. Siegel was reticent at first;
he was in awe of Rohatyn. Then, during a meeting, Rohatyn excused
himself to use the bathroom. Siegel thought, "My God, he's human!"
There was no reason Siegel couldn't become a legend himself, like
Rohatyn.

In April 1976, takeover lawyer Joseph Flom (a founder of Skadden, Arps, Slate, Meagher & Flom) invited Siegel to give a presentation
on "identifying takeover targets" at a panel discussion. Siegel was
flattered, though he knew it didn't take much to be an expert. Anyone
who'd handled even one post–Williams Act deal was considered quali-
fied.

Siegel was even more flattered when he met the other participants:
Ira Harris, one of Salomon Brothers's leading investment bankers;
Robert Rubin, a fast-rising star at Goldman, Sachs; John Shad, head of
E. F. Hutton; Arthur Long, the leading proxy solicitor; Theodore
Levine, an enforcement attorney at the SEC; Arthur Fleischer, a promi-
nent takeover lawyer at Fried, Frank, Harris, Shriver & Jacobson; and,
seated right next to Siegel, Flom's principal rival in the takeover bar,
Martin Lipton, a founder of Wachtell, Lipton, Rosen & Katz.

Collectively, the panel's expertise covered the emerging field of
hostile takeovers, a field that was to transform the face of corporate

America to a degree that none of them then dreamed possible. American industry had undergone other periods of industrial consolidation, most recently in the sixties, when the fad to diversify had led many large companies into mergers, generally financed with stock during that decade's great bull market. Those acquisitions were mostly friendly. Earlier, the monopolistic corporations of the Morgan era had been produced by numerous mergers (some of them not-so-gently coerced by the great financier himself). None of these kinds of deals were really comparable to the hostile takeover boom that began in the mid-seventies and surged in the eighties, however, except in one key respect: they offered enormous opportunities to profit on the stock market.

Siegel noticed that Lipton was scribbling notes furiously while others made their presentations. Then, when Harris's turn came to speak, Lipton shoved the notes in front of him, and Harris virtually read his presentation. So this was how the M&A "club" worked, Siegel thought.

After Siegel's presentation, Lipton stayed behind to compliment him. After this, the two talked frequently about M&A tactics and exchanged gossip. They made an unlikely pair; the glamorous Siegel and the portly Lipton with his thinning hair and heavy dark-framed glasses. But Siegel recognized Lipton's mastery of the field and became an eager student.

Lipton and Flom had developed a new and lucrative retainer arrangement with their clients. Companies who wanted to ensure the firm's availability in the event they became the target of a hostile bid paid the lawyers a substantial retainer fee each year. In the event that they were attacked by another client of either Lipton or Flom, the attacking client agreed in advance to waive any conflict-of-interest, with the understanding that the lawyers would defend the target company.

Scores of major corporations eventually signed on with Lipton and Flom, even as some established bar members cringed. These lawyers billed strictly by the hour, eschewing even contingency fees. The Lipton and Flom retainers, since they didn't necessarily require work, were more like an insurance policy. The establishment viewed the advance waiver of conflicts with distaste. Yet clients themselves seemed unfazed, a measure of the clout Lipton and Flom could wield.

Siegel began to think Kidder, Peabody should begin to make similar deals. By the time of the panel discussion in 1976, he had become convinced that the merger wave was going to continue, even grow. Bigger rivals, such as Morgan Stanley, Salomon, and First Boston, were already developing reputations for their M&A offensive capabilities. Siegel thought Kidder, Peabody could carve out a niche on the defensive side.

He began to visit potential corporate clients, selling what he called the "Kidder, Peabody tender defense product." He argued that, with only seven days—as provided by the Williams Act—in which to react to a hostile takeover bid, companies had to be prepared in advance with carefully thought-out defensive strategies. This meant retaining Kidder, Peabody—and paying a lucrative retainer like those paid to Lipton and Flom—to ensure preparedness and the firm's availability. Lipton introduced Siegel to leading figures in the close-knit M&A community, and lent his prestige to Siegel's plan.

Siegel's real boost came in May 1977, when *Business Week* hailed him as the leading takeover defense expert. After describing his success in several large deals, the article also mentioned in passing that he was so good-looking he was considered a "Greta Garbo heartthrob." The article included a photograph, and suddenly Siegel was deluged with requests from women seeking dates. Siegel was amazed that the story, which wasn't given major play in the magazine, conferred such instant status and legitimacy. Kidder, Peabody's copiers went into high gear, sending out copies to prospective clients.

From 1977 on, Siegel called personally on 200 to 300 clients a year. His targets were midsize companies (typically those doing from $100 to $300 million a year in sales) that weren't being adequately serviced by the bigger investment banks. These were the companies most vulnerable to a hostile offer from a larger company. Siegel's product sold. He eventually had 250 corporations paying Kidder, Peabody an annual six-figure retainer.

His main competition came from Goldman, Sachs, the much larger, more powerful firm that had also decided to stake out takeover defense work as its special preserve, albeit for somewhat different reasons. At the time, Goldman had made it a policy to eschew the representation of hostile bidders. With the most enviable roster of large corporate clients on Wall Street, Goldman didn't want to risk alienating them by representing anyone who might be construed as a raider. Traditional investment banking services for these established clients were the bread and butter of its lucrative business.

Siegel loved beating Goldman out of a client. In 1977, Peter Sachs, then head of M&A at Goldman, flew out to the West Coast to meet with Steve Sato, the chairman of Ivac Corporation, a medical equipment manufacturer that had just become the target of a hostile attack by Colgate Palmolive. Sachs, according to the chairman, boasted of the "Goldman prowess." When Siegel went to see Sato, he spent most of the time listening to Sato's goals for the company. The chairman was of Japanese descent. Although Siegel had never eaten raw fish in his life, he joined Sato at his home for sushi. In awarding him the business, Sato told Siegel, "I can't believe that you actually listen. All Goldman told me was how great Goldman is."

Siegel found that his most effective tactic was to let Goldman make its presentation, which typically emphasized that Goldman could get the best price if the target company were sold. Then Siegel would step in. "Hire me," he'd urge. "I'll do my best to keep you independent. I want you as a future client." In fact, most of the companies ended up being sold, given the weak positions of most takeover targets, and Siegel's pitch often couldn't compete with Goldman's size, dominance, and reputation for quality. But Siegel's message frequently convinced the targets' managements that he had their interests at heart—instead of the investment banking fees to be reaped if the company had to be sold.

In 1977, Siegel invented a brilliant but controversial tactic that also endeared him to scores of corporate managers—the golden parachute. The golden parachute, essentially a lucrative employment contract for top corporate officers, provided exorbitant severance payments for the officers in the event of a takeover. Supposedly, the contracts were intended to deter hostile takeovers by making them more expensive. In practice, they tended to make the officers very rich.

DeNunzio was thrilled by Siegel's success, even though Siegel was working so hard and traveling so much that he rarely saw him. DeNunzio ran Kidder, Peabody in the paternalistic way he had learned from Gordon, usually setting salaries and bonuses singlehandedly. In 1976 Siegel earned over $100,000, then considered a princely sum, especially for someone only 28. In 1977, Siegel was made a director of Kidder, Peabody, the youngest in the firm's history with the exception of Al Gordon, who had owned the firm.

Soon after, DeNunzio called Siegel into his office. "Marty, you're a bachelor," he said. DeNunzio paused, and Siegel didn't know what was coming. "You've got an Alfa-Romeo convertible and you've got a house on Fire Island. It's too much." What was he getting at? Siegel assumed DeNunzio meant that his style was too racy for some of Kidder, Peabody's clients, or perhaps the other directors, but DeNunzio wasn't more explicit and Siegel couldn't be sure.

"There's a nice house for sale across the street from me in Greenwich," DeNunzio continued. Greenwich was the WASPiest, whitest, most exclusive suburb in Connecticut, a bastion of country clubs and conventional respectability. It was also filled with some of the dullest, most straitlaced people Siegel knew. In addition, he couldn't see living right under DeNunzio's watchful eyes.

But Siegel went out to look at the house. Afterward he got into the offending sports car and drove on Interstate 95 for exactly one-half hour. He found himself in Westport, and called a realtor from a pay phone. He'd been thinking of selling the Fire Island house anyway. The realtor took him to an old house on a small river north of town, and Siegel loved it. He bought it, and spent his weekends fixing the place up.

Siegel told DeNunzio that he was heeding his advice and buying a house in Connecticut. It was in slightly bohemian Westport, not in Greenwich. "A half hour from you is about as close as I can take," Siegel joked.

Later, when he moved to a far more lavish home right on the coast, Siegel sold the Westport house to CBS News anchor Dan Rather.

One day, not long after he had bought the house in Connecticut, Siegel's secretary told him he had a call from an Ivan Boesky. He knew Boesky only as another arbitrageur, one of the many who were calling him now that he was developing a reputation in the M&A crowd. But Siegel also knew that Boesky was a trading client of Kidder, Peabody. He took his call.

Siegel was impressed with Boesky's market acumen, his knowledge of takeover tactics and stock accumulation strategies. They became friends though they didn't actually meet for some time. In the peculiar world of Wall Street, close friendships can develop entirely on the telephone. Gradually Siegel began to see Boesky as someone he could discuss strategy with, bounce ideas off of, gossip with. He needed this information since he had no Kidder, Peabody arbitrageur to turn to. The firm had traditionally shunned arbitrage, and had no department. DeNunzio and Gordon believed arbitrageurs were unsavory, tried to get inside information, and gave rise to conflicts of interest within the firm.

Yet arbitrageurs like Boesky were becoming increasingly important to any investment banker involved in M&A. Historically arbitrageurs had traded to take advantage of price discrepancies on different markets, such as London and New York. It was conservative, nearly risk-free trading yielding small profits. But they had become progressively more daring, first buying heavily stocks that were the subjects of announced takeover bids, betting the deals would go through; eventually they started buying stocks they only suspected would be the targets of takeover bids. When they guessed right, the profits were huge.

Evaluating the effects of these massive purchases of rumored or real takeover stocks had become a crucial part of Siegel's job. Arbitrageurs were also fonts of information, from clues to the other side's tactics, to rumors of impending bids that could be used to attract defense clients.

Arbitrageurs tended to be crass, excitable, street-smart, aggressive, and driven almost solely by the pursuit of quick profits. Their days were defined by the high-pressure periods between the opening and closing bells of the stock exchange, during which they screamed orders into phones, punched stock symbols into their electronic terminals, scanned elaborate screens of constantly shifting data, and placed phone calls to every potential source of information they could imagine. After work, they tended to blow off steam by carousing in bars like Harry's, just across Hanover Square from Kidder, Peabody, or, if they'd had a good day, in expensive Manhattan restaurants.

One day in 1979, Siegel confided to Boesky that he'd fallen in love. The affair was threatening to become a minor scandal at Kidder, Peabody.

In the late seventies, the first wave of women business school graduates reached Wall Street's shores. Jane Day Stuart turned heads at Kidder, Peabody on the day she first swept through the corporate finance offices. A Columbia Business School graduate, she was smart, blonde, thin, personable, stylish, and married.

Kidder, Peabody had long maintained an unspoken policy against office affairs. A fling with a summer employee had damaged another investment banker's career. But in late 1978, Stuart and her husband were divorced. Shortly after, Siegel and Stuart played tennis. By August 1979, they were living together. When colleagues tried to warn Siegel, he brushed them aside, saying he wasn't interested in firm politics and didn't care whether he ever ran the firm.

When Henry Keller, head of corporate finance, learned of the affair, he went to DeNunzio, prompting speculation that DeNunzio would bring the relationship to an abrupt halt. DeNunzio did nothing. Unknown to many, DeNunzio's son, David, was also having an affair at the firm. DeNunzio's tolerance was interpreted as a sign of the times and a measure of Siegel's clout. DeNunzio also seemed relieved that Siegel's bachelor days appeared to be numbered.

Some of Stuart's friends and relatives in Baltimore warned her against marriage to someone Jewish, even someone as nonreligious as Siegel. But she was headstrong and in love, even though some of her male colleagues speculated unkindly that she was using her business acumen to trade up the marriage ladder. She and Siegel were quietly married in May 1981 and began drawing up plans for a new, larger house in Westport.

Soon after their marriage, Boesky called to invite Siegel and Jane Day to his house in Westchester County for dinner. It was Boesky's first social invitation to the Siegels, a small dinner for three couples: Boesky and his wife Seema; financier Theodore Forstmann, who numbered Boesky among the investors in his partnership, and his date; and the Siegels. Siegel decided to bring along a copy of his house plans to show the Boeskys.

Following Boesky's directions, the Siegels drove north from Manhattan for about 45 minutes, through the exclusive towns of Bedford and Mount Kisco. The area is one of large estates, wooded rolling hills, and some pre-Revolutionary houses. Few of the large houses are visible from public roads, and the Boesky house is set so far back in its 200 acres of property that visitors sometimes got lost winding through the maze of driveways and service roads leading from the entrance gates.

The Siegels pulled into the drive between large pillars and a gatehouse and stopped as a security guard parked in a pickup truck waved them to a halt. Siegel went over to the guard, introduced himself, and was cleared for entry—but not before he was startled to see the blue-black steel of a large pistol in a holster strapped to the guard.

As they approached the house, the Siegels were awed. Behind a cobblestone courtyard rose a massive, red-brick Georgian-style mansion. The estate had previously been owned by Revlon founder Charles Revson. In the distance, past formal gardens studded with Greek statuary, was a large pool house. On one side was a large pool, on the other a sunken indoor squash court, and at the side, a tennis court with a bubble that could be inflated in winter for indoor play.

The Siegels were greeted at the entrance by Seema Boesky, an attractive, talkative brunette who immediately struck them as warm and friendly. She led them through rooms decorated in traditional style with beautiful wallpaper, elaborate moldings, rare Aubusson carpets, and expensive antique furniture. The walls featured what looked to Siegel's untrained eye like serious art; Seema, it turned out, was an enthusiastic collector of American paintings and antiques. They continued through the gardens and pool house, where the carpeting was embossed with a large, intertwined monogram, *IFB*.

Boesky was a gracious host, dressed impeccably as always in a black three-piece suit and white shirt that complemented his year-round tan. Asked why he wore the same suit every day, Boesky once replied, "I have enough decisions in my life already." Boesky's silver-blond hair was clipped and neatly parted. His prominent cheekbones and piercing eyes could make him look driven, even gaunt, but he was relaxed and affable as a dinner host, tending constantly to his guests and eating little himself.

Jane Day mentioned their house plans, and Seema exclaimed, "You've got to have a big kitchen. I'll show you mine." The Boesky kitchen was larger than the Siegels' entire Manhattan apartment. Siegel was impressed by the signs of wealth. Boesky must have been far more successful at arbitrage than even Siegel had realized. Siegel decided that he wouldn't show the house plans he'd brought along. They now seemed embarrassingly modest.

Later, after dinner, Siegel took Boesky aside and mentioned that he'd noticed that the guard at the estate entrance carried a pistol. "It's loaded," Boesky replied. "In my business, you need security."

Lance Lessman peered across the desks of the small research department in Ivan F. Boesky Co.'s offices in Manhattan's financial district. Inside Boesky's own glass-enclosed corner office, he could see his boss's eyes roving, first toward the trading floor where his buy and sell orders were executed, then toward Lessman's research area. Suddenly Boesky's eyes locked on his.

The intercom on Lessman's desk crackled to life. "Who's buying," Boesky barked.

Lessman frantically scanned his computer screen, looking for big price and volume movements in individual stocks in order to figure out what had caught his master's interest.

"Who's buying?" Boesky practically screamed. "Why the fuck don't you know?"

Now intercoms sprang to life all over the office. Every desk had a speaker connected to a central control panel manned by Boesky himself. He could activate individual speakers or throw open the system for office-wide announcements. Now he had everyone on line.

"I want service. I want service," he repeated in ever louder and more demanding tones. "Who's buying? I want it now. Who's buying?"

Lately Boesky had been even more testy than usual. A few weeks earlier that year, 1981, Boesky had shocked the office with an abrupt announcement: He was liquidating Ivan F. Boesky Co., taking out all of his profits.

The Hunt silver panic and resulting stock market plunge had hit

Boesky hard, and he had decided to cash out with his remaining profits. He wanted to take advantage of the favorable long-term capital-gains tax rates available to partners liquidating their interest. But, to get the rates, he needed someone to keep the firm going. His recent efforts to force his top lieutenants to take over the remains of the partnership and assume all its liabilities had led to screaming matches. When they balked, he fired them. During a short period that year, Boesky had lost his two top strategists, his head trader, and his head of research.

Few people really expected Boesky to be out of arbitrage for long. Despite the Hunt setbacks, he had been a phenomenal success. Ivan F. Boesky Co. had opened in 1975 with $700,000 from Boesky's mother-in-law and her husband. Now the firm's capital had grown to nearly $90 million. Arbitrage was Boesky's life. His earnings had brought him the estate in Westchester and a Manhattan townhouse. A chauffeured limousine drove him into town every morning. His efforts had also finally brought him the grudging respect of a father-in-law who had believed his daughter had married beneath her.

Boesky seemed to share his father-in-law's disdain for his own family and background. He constantly tried to burnish his résumé and family connections in conversations with New York colleagues. He often implied that he had graduated from Cranbrook, a prestigious prep school outside of his native Detroit, and the University of Michigan. Others assumed he had attended Harvard, since Boesky made so much of his Harvard Club membership. He said his father ran a chain of delicatessens in Detroit.

During Boesky's childhood, his family lived in a spacious Tudor-style house in what was then considered a nice, upper-middle-class neighborhood. Ivan's father, William, had emigrated from Russia in 1912, and owned a chain of several bars, called the Brass Rail, rather than delicatessens (his uncle's business). To boost profits, the Brass Rails introduced topless dancing and strip shows. In the eyes of many, the bars hastened the decline of their neighborhoods.

Boesky worked hard while he was in school, selling ice cream from a truck. He was picked up repeatedly by the local police for staying in business past the 7 P.M. curfew imposed by his license. He did attend Cranbrook for two years, though he didn't graduate. His academic record there was undistinguished, but he excelled at wrestling, starving himself to lower his weight category and driving himself to the point where he could do an astounding 500 push-ups. He was constantly in the gym with his best friend, an Iranian exchange student named Hushang Wekili. As a sophomore, Boesky won the school's Craig trophy as outstanding wrestler.

Boesky often used wrestling analogies to describe his work as an arbitrageur. "Wrestling and arbitrage are both solitary sports in which you live or die by your deeds, and you do it very visibly," he told reporter Connie Bruck in a 1984 *Atlantic Monthly* interview. In wrestling he also found a metaphor for life. "There are times when I really feel like dropping, but I don't, and that kind of summoning up, I think, is what I learned [from wrestling]. . . . There are plenty of opportunities in life to be beaten down. People feel beaten, demolished, demoralized, and they give way to it. I don't."

When Boesky chose a corporate logo for his new arbitrage operation, he had engravers copy his Cranbrook wrestling medal, showing two classical Greek men, nude, in a wrestling hold. It became the symbol for Ivan F. Boesky Corp., and Boesky was immensely proud of it. Not everyone shared his enthusiasm. "It looked like something from Caesars Palace," was one employee's comment.

After Cranbrook, Boesky transferred to inner-city Mumford High (immortalized by Eddie Murphy in *Beverly Hills Cop*). He never graduated from college. He did course work at Wayne State University in Detroit, the University of Michigan, and Eastern Michigan College, but he left for Iran, partly to be near his friend Wekili, just before graduating. Exactly what Boesky did in Iran remains a mystery. He later testified that he worked for the U.S. Information Agency, teaching English to Iranians. But USIA personnel records for the relevant period make no mention of any Ivan Boesky. Boesky told Siegel in one of their early conversations that he had worked in Iran as an undercover agent for the CIA.

After returning from Iran, Boesky enrolled at Detroit College of Law, a low-prestige law school that didn't require a college degree for admission. He graduated five years later, in 1964, after twice dropping out. When Boesky was 23, his father made him a partner in the Brass Rails. Boesky was rejected by all the law firms he applied to for a job.

Boesky's desultory record made it all the more surprising that he caught the eye of Seema Silberstein, whose father, Ben, was a wealthy Detroit real estate developer. But colleagues say it was Seema who fell in love with and tracked after Boesky after meeting him in June 1960. A relative of hers, a federal district court judge, hired him for a one-year clerkship. Boesky and Seema were married soon after and had their first child, Billy. When a Cranbrook wrestling teammate working at Bear, Stearns in New York told Boesky about arbitrage, he decided to make his fortune on Wall Street. Colleagues recall Boesky's feeling that Detroit was too small and confined for his ambitions.

Boesky's father-in-law installed Ivan and Seema in an elegant Park Avenue apartment. Boesky landed a job as a trainee at L. F.

Rothschild that lasted a year. He moved to First Manhattan, getting his first taste of real arbitrage trading, then shifted to Kalb Voorhis. He promptly lost $20,000 in a single position and was fired. Boesky was contemptuous of a firm that put any store in the loss of such a paltry sum. After a brief period of unemployment and a foray into venture capital, he joined a small member firm of the New York Stock Exchange, Edwards & Hanly. Remarkably, given his employment history, limited experience, and track record, Edwards & Hanly gave Boesky carte blanche to establish and run an arbitrage department.

Boesky made a splash in the small world of arbitrage almost immediately. Using maximum leverage, buying on margin constantly, he managed to convert Edwards & Hanly's modest capital into $1 million- and even $2 million-dollar positions, large enough to actually move individual stock prices from time to time. He was considered audacious and bold. Once, for selling stock short that he hadn't actually borrowed prior to the sale (and thus further boosting his leverage), he was sanctioned by the SEC and fined $10,000. Some of Boesky's tactics contributed to the demise of Edwards & Hanly. By 1975, the firm was bankrupt.

Tired of begging for a position at a prestige firm, Boesky decided to open his own operation, devoted primarily to arbitrage. He stunned his fellow arbs by actually taking out advertisements in *The Wall Street Journal,* seeking investors and extolling the profit potential in arbitrage—the last thing members of the "club" wanted others focusing on, fearful that it would attract more competition. Boesky boldly allocated just 55% of the operation's profits to the investors, keeping 45% for himself. He did, however, assign investors 95% of any losses. He didn't attract enough capital to meet his ambitions. It was his wife's family's money that gave him enough to go forward.

From the first day of Ivan F. Boesky Co. in 1975, Boesky arrived at work by limousine. If he needed something fast, he wouldn't hesitate to pay private couriers. He dressed in what he deemed the image of the successful Wall Street financier: his signature three-piece black suit, starched white shirt, and gold chain dangling from the vest pocket. It looked like a Phi Beta Kappa key.

Boesky didn't waste money on the firm itself. It was housed in a single room in an aging Whitehall Street office building. The room was so small that a stock exchange auditor ordered Boesky to move into larger quarters. He hated his employees to leave their desks during lunch, so he picked up the tab for lunch orders delivered to the office, imposing a $5-per-person limit.

One of his first employees was an accountant hired to manage the firm's "back office." The son of an Armenian immigrant, Setrag Mooradian had worked at Oppenheim, Appel, & Dixon, known in the arbitrage community as OAD. The firm, more than any other, specialized in arbitrage accounting. Though he didn't tell Boesky, Mooradian had been severely sanctioned for violating capital requirements. It had made it hard for him to get a job, and he was always grateful to Boesky for hiring him.

Boesky told Mooradian to be at work every morning promptly at 7 A.M., when his own limousine would pull up to the building entrance. If Boesky wasn't going to be in the office, he'd call in at 7:01; if no one answered, he'd fly into a rage. Once, years later, Boesky called in when a fire drill was in progress. No one answered the phone immediately. The next day a memo appeared on everyone's desk. "Yesterday, at 3:15 P.M., I called in," the memo began. "My phone rang 23 times. I understand there was a fire alarm. Certainly, I don't want you to risk your lives. But I extend my appreciation to those of you who stayed behind."

Boesky disliked the idea that his employees might take a day off. He never came into the office the Friday after Thanksgiving, when most Manhattan offices are reduced to skeleton staffs. But no one else was allowed the day off. Boesky checked attendance by calling so many times—in some cases, as many as 10 times to a single employee—that the others in the office figured Boesky might as well have come to work. He also refused to hand out paychecks until after 3 P.M. on Fridays, after banks had closed. When employees complained, he explained that he didn't want the "disruption" of his staff dashing out to cash and deposit checks in the middle of the day. But they suspected he wanted the extra interest that would accumulate over the weekend.

Almost from the beginning, Boesky screamed at everyone regularly. After several such incidents, Mooradian asked Boesky to stop yelling. "I'm the boss," Boesky replied. "I'm allowed to yell." Boesky expected Mooradian to work routinely until 9 or 10 P.M. Once his wife found him still up at 5:30 A.M. trying to complete work Boesky had demanded. "He can't keep this up," Mooradian told her. But as the years went by, Boesky seemed to need less and less sleep and became even more demanding. A favorite tactic was to call Mooradian with a complex question. "I'll get back to you," Mooradian would answer. "I'll hold," Boesky would reply.

Boesky sometimes spent the workday at his estate. Near the "Wall Street" sign he had placed on a lamppost on one of the roads was an office complex with secretaries and all the electronic market and communications gear he needed to stay in constant touch with the market. "Can you believe that husband of mine?" Seema asked Mooradian. "He always dresses in a business suit to go to the office on his own property."

One morning Boesky's employees arrived at the office to discover a Wierton terrier puppy scampering about the premises. Boesky had bought the pet as a surprise for Seema, but she had banned the terrier from the house. So Boesky said the dog would live at the office, and his chauffeur, Johnny Ray, could take care of it at night and on weekends. Soon Boesky and the puppy were inseparable. He even took the dog along to meetings with investors.

Just a week later, Lessman and others heard a shriek from Boesky's office. They rushed in to discover a stricken look on Boesky's face. The puppy looked confused. In a pile right in front of Boesky's desk, on his spotless beige carpeting, the dog had demonstrated convincingly that it wasn't yet housebroken. Boesky wiped up the mess. No one ever saw the dog again.

Boesky had other idiosyncrasies, namely, his eating habits. Some days it seemed as though he ate nothing, as if he were still training for a wrestling weigh-in. For breakfast, he liked to order a single croissant. He would pick at it, then eat a single flake. One colleague recalls that once, when Boesky took a normal bite, he said, "Ivan, you little pig." Boesky looked startled and put it down.

Boesky often invited prospective investors in his partnership for lunch in the private dining room in his office. One afternoon Meshulam Riklis, the chairman of Rapid-American Corporation who bankrolled a film career for his much younger wife, Pia Zadora, was scheduled for lunch. Boesky had his people call ahead to find out what Riklis liked to eat, then ordered a lavish spread from the 21 Club. At the table, Boesky fretted that Riklis didn't seem to be enjoying the food.

"I'm due at the gym in a few hours," Riklis explained. "I have to work out with a personal trainer."

"Why work out?" Boesky asked. "Relax. Eat more."

Riklis paused. "Ivan, you have no idea what it's like to be married to a younger woman." But Riklis proceeded to eat merrily, and he invested $5 million in Boesky's partnership. Boesky ate a single grape.

As he had vowed, Boesky "retired" in early 1981, liquidating his interest in Ivan F. Boesky Co. Having failed to persuade any of his senior employees to take over (most had been fired or quit), he had recruited an arbitrageur from Morgan Stanley, Steve Royce, to take over the entity, renamed Bedford Partners. The largest investor was Seema, who rolled about $8 million of her share of Boesky Co. into the reconstituted partnership. Though Boesky had none of his own money in Bedford, he was on the phone to Royce every day, usually six to eight times, making investment decisions as though he were still in charge.

Boesky set about almost immediately raising money for a new arbitrage partnership, Ivan F. Boesky Corp. As a corporation rather than a limited partnership, the new entity had a more complicated ownership structure, divided between common stockholders and pre-ferred stockholders. Investors received mostly preferred stock, and the profits were allocated heavily to the common stockholders (Boesky, principally) and the losses to the preferred holders.

Boesky enlisted Lessman, one of the few holdover employees from the earlier company, in his endless quest for investors' capital. Boesky's limousine took them to countless meetings with wealthy individuals and people who represented deep pockets, seeking invest-ments of a minimum $2 million. In addition to the projected returns based on investors' performance in the prior partnership, Boesky of-fered a unique advantage: direct access to him. He promised to pass on market intelligence that the investors would be free to use in their own portfolios.

The campaign wasn't all that successful, despite the impressive rate of return Boesky had amassed for his previous investors. One day Lessman dared to suggest that the allocation of profits and losses turned potential investors off. "The deal stinks," Lessman said. Boe-sky glared.

Lessman also tried to invest some of his own money in the new corporation, telling Boesky that he had recently inherited about $500,000 and wanted to put it in the company. Boesky offered him the same stiff terms he was offering other outsiders. "But I'm working for you," Lessman protested. "Why can't I earn my share of the profits?"

Boesky's face tightened, his voice changed. "I don't need your lousy half million," he said icily.

"Then why do you need my twenty-five percent of the profits?" Lessman rejoined.

"Get out!" Boesky screamed, chasing Lessman out of the office and slamming the door with a crash.

In the end, the corporation was launched in 1981 with less than $40 million, far less than Boesky had hoped for. Boesky, Lessman, now head of research, and Michael Davidoff, a trader Boesky hired away from Bedford Partners, set up shop in an unused partner's office at the Manhattan law firm of Fried, Frank, Harris, Shriver & Jacobson, where Boesky's principal lawyer, Stephen Fraidin, was a partner. Even in those close quarters, Boesky liked to boast that no one knew every-thing about his operation except himself. He deliberately kept even his own employees off guard.

Lessman was instructed to answer Royce's calls and share his research with him. Late one evening, Royce called and said, "Ivan wants your position" in a particular stock. Lessman pulled it up on his computer screen and told Royce. Boesky called Lessman soon after, and Lessman mentioned in passing that Royce had called and he'd disclosed the position. There was silence on the line. Then Ivan screamed, "I should fire you for this. Don't ever give away a position again."

"I thought Royce was in the firm," Lessman answered as Boesky slammed down the receiver.

Soon after, Royce called Lessman again one night seeking a stock position. Lessman refused, saying he'd been ordered by Boesky not to talk. The phone rang again. This time Boesky reamed out Lessman for failing to answer Royce's question. Finally Royce called asking for Boesky's position in Marathon Oil, then a potential takeover target; this was highly sensitive information. Lessman, anxious not to be caught in the middle, gave Royce an answer, but greatly understated the true position.

Then Boesky called from a dinner party. Lessman proudly told Boesky that Royce had pumped him for information, and that he'd deliberately misled him. "You asshole!" Boesky shouted. "You're making me out to be a liar!" Boesky himself, it turned out, had given Royce inconsistent but equally misleading information. Lessman's head was spinning. Why would Boesky lie to someone managing his own wife's money?

Soon after, Lessman had to call Boesky one evening at home in Bedford, and Boesky's eldest son, Billy, answered.

"It's Lance," Lessman said in a weary voice. "Your dad's really beating up on me."

Billy's reply made a deep impression on Lessman. "Seriously understand about my father," Billy said in a somber tone. "He is stark raving mad."

I. W. ("Tubby") Burnham II led his new recruit, corporate finance head Frederick H. Joseph, through the crowded trading floor of Drexel Burnham & Co. on Joseph's first day of work in 1974. There was someone, Burnham explained, that he wanted Joseph to meet right away, someone who just might help Joseph realize his outsize ambitions for his new firm.

Joseph, then 41 years old, a well-built former amateur boxer with graying hair, had landed the Drexel corporate finance job with an audacious claim: "Give me fifteen years," he had said. "I'll give you a firm as powerful and successful as Goldman, Sachs."

The proposition then seemed ludicrous, calling for nothing less than a revolution against the status quo on Wall Street. In 1974 Goldman, Sachs was at Wall Street's pinnacle. That year, Drexel Burnham had total revenues of just $1.2 million. Its capital was thin. The stock market was in a slump. And despite the illustrious Drexel name, Drexel Burnham barely ranked as a second-class citizen on Wall Street.

Drexel Burnham was essentially Burnham & Co., a retail-sales-oriented brokerage firm founded in 1935 by Tubby Burnham, a grandson of the founder of the I. W. Harper distillery, and a few remnants of old-line Drexel Firestone, which traced its lineage from the illustrious Philadelphia Drexel family and the unabashedly anti-semitic J. P. Morgan empire.

In 1971, Burnham & Co. merged with Drexel—an odd match. Burnham was mostly Jewish, filled with rough-and-tumble traders who survived on their selling skills. Drexel, by contrast, had an old-line aversion to hard sales tactics and a steadily dwindling roster of corporate clients who increasingly opted for firms with more aggressive distribution networks. Drexel was tottering, surviving largely on its reputation and its historical status as a major-bracket firm. Indeed, Tubby Burnham sought out Drexel as a merger partner primarily to hoist his company out of the submajor bracket and attract more underwriting work.

When Burnham visited the chairmen of Goldman, Sachs and Morgan Stanley, the eminent firms whose blessing and goodwill the merged firm would need to survive in the still-clubby world of Wall Street, they gave their approval on one condition: The venerable Drexel name had to come first, regardless of the true balance of power in the firm. Hence Drexel Burnham & Co. was born.

The survivors of the two firms still mostly shunned one another, even now, three years after the merger. As they walked through the firm, Burnham told Joseph that when he first met the head of Drexel at the time of the merger, he'd asked how many of the firm's more than 200 employees were Jews. He was told that there were a total of three. One, Burnham said, was the man he wanted Joseph to meet: Michael Milken.

Joseph shook hands with the intense, slender young man with dark, deep-set eyes. Joseph wondered briefly how someone like Milken had ever ended up at Drexel Firestone, but otherwise Milken didn't make much of an impression. They didn't work directly together. Joseph headed the more upscale investment banking area, and Milken

was the head of convertibles and noninvestment-grade securities, later
dubbed the high-yield department. He reported to a longtime Burnham trader, Edwin Kantor, and, as far as compensation was concerned,
directly to Burnham.

To encourage Milken, who complained that he'd always been
treated as a second-class citizen by the starched-shirt Drexel WASPs,
Burnham let Milken set up his own semi-autonomous bond trading
unit. In 1975, he gave Milken a compensation arrangement crafted to
provide strong performance incentives. Like all Wall Street firms,
Drexel paid relatively low salaries, and most employee compensation
came in the form of bonuses. But Milken's bonus arrangement was
unusually generous. Milken and his group of employees were awarded
35% of all the firm's profits attributed to their activities. Milken was
given the discretion to allocate the money among his people, keeping
whatever remained for himself. Burnham also gave Milken additional
"finder's fees" of 15% to 30% of the profits attributable to any business brought into the firm by Milken or his people. Burnham paid out
35% of profits to the people actually doing the work and up to 30%
of the profits to whomever landed the client. The firm kept as little as
35% to cover overhead and the partners' share of profits. The system
for compensating Milken was a closely guarded secret at the firm.

Over the year or so after they first met, Joseph and Milken came
to know each other reasonably well, mostly because Milken was eager
to generate finder's fees by calling Joseph with tips for potential new
corporate finance business.

Joseph wasn't a snob, but at first he tended to associate Milken
with the Burnham trading crowd, many of whom knew little about the
world beyond the hustle of their native Brooklyn or Queens. Joseph
himself came from a modest background, growing up in Roxbury, a
blue-collar neighborhood in Boston. His father drove a cab for a living,
and his parents were Orthodox Jews. But Joseph had acquired a veneer
of sophistication as a scholarship student at Harvard College and then
Harvard Business School. He had joined E. F. Hutton & Co., hired by
John Shad (future chairman of the Securities and Exchange Commission), and made partner in only four years. He had moved to Shearson,
helped negotiate its merger with Hayden Stone, and been named chief
operating officer, the firm's second-ranking position.

Drexel was a big step down from Shearson, but Joseph had
wanted to get back into hands-on investment banking, and he had a
dream of building a powerhouse firm from scratch and being identified
with it for posterity. Joseph had seen enough of the changes sweeping
Wall Street to believe that practically everything about the old order
was vulnerable. At Drexel, however, he was certainly starting low.

Drexel's corporate finance department consisted of 19 people; Joseph promptly dismissed seven of them. His first year, the department's entire bonus pool was a measly $15,000.

Joseph felt he had to overhaul the whole culture of the firm. Soon after arriving, he hosted the first of what became annual dinners for new recruits at Windows on the World atop New York's World Trade Center. He felt he had to build integrity as he instilled the drive to succeed in these new investment bankers. "You will be tempted," he warned his audience. He mentioned their access to confidential information about clients' business plans, stock and debt offerings, merger plans. "If you act on that temptation, you will be caught. I guarantee it. They will take your shoelaces. And here at Drexel, we won't give you the time of day."

It didn't take long after their initial meeting for Joseph to realize why Burnham was so eager for him to meet Milken. Milken wasn't just another trader at the firm. He was, in fact, one of the highest-paid employees. Starting with $2 million in capital in 1973, he was generating astounding 100% rates of return, earning bonus pools for himself and his people that were approaching $1 million a year. And he was doing it in an area that Joseph knew little about and considered distasteful: high-yield, unrated bonds.

The American bond market is dominated by two giant bond-rating agencies, Moody's and Standard & Poor's, who for generations have guided investors seeking to gauge the risk in fixed-income investments. The value of these investments depends on an issuer's ability to make promised interest payments until the bond matures, and then repay the principal. Top blue-chip corporate debt for companies like AT&T or IBM is rated Triple A by S&P. Companies with weaker balance sheets or other problems have correspondingly lower ratings. Some companies are deemed so risky that they receive no rating at all. Interest rates on corporate debt fluctuate with market rates for U.S. Treasuries and the perceived risk of the issuer, so the lower the debt rating, the higher the rate a company must pay in order to attract investors.

In the midseventies there wasn't all that much low-rated and unrated debt around, and investors, by and large, wouldn't touch it. The big investment banks weren't interested; it was too hard to sell, too risky for the firms' reputations, and tended to alienate the mainstream, top-rated issuers. Much of the high-yielding debt around was once-rated paper of companies that had fallen on hard times (so-called "fallen angels" in the parlance of Wall Street). Milken had been drawn to this obscure backwater of Wall Street.

Unlike Joseph, Milken had grown up in a comfortable, upper-middle-class home. Encino, California, a town in the San Fernando Valley north of Los Angeles, had a sizable Jewish population—the synagogue was near the Milken home —but was about as homogeneous as the rest of rapidly growing Southern California. Milken's father was an accountant. Starting at age 10, Milken helped his father, sorting checks, reconciling checkbooks, later helping with tax returns. From the first grade, Milken had dazzled his classmates by doing complicated multiplications in his head.

Milken thrived at Birmingham High School in nearby Van Nuys, where he graduated in 1964. Birmingham students were almost all middle-class whites. Many of their parents, like the Milkens, had migrated from the industrial Midwest and East. They loved sports, embraced the surfing craze and bouffant hairdos, were crazy about the Beach Boys, and drove their cars endlessly around town. Milken was full of energy, more academically oriented than most, eager to be accepted by his classmates. He was elected a cheerleader, the next best thing to being a sports star. He was active in student government and was voted most popular. He dated a pretty, vivacious classmate, Lori Anne Hackel, whom he'd met in his seventh-grade social studies class. Other classmates included future movie star Sally Field and Hollywood super agent Michael Ovitz.

The University of California at Berkeley was an abrupt change for Milken. By the time he graduated in 1968, it was the epicenter of the student antiwar and counterculture movements. Milken, comfortably in the mainstream in high school, was suddenly a misfit. He was a member of a mostly Jewish fraternity, Sigma Alpha Mu, when fraternities were out of favor. He didn't drink, smoke marijuana, or use LSD. He majored in business administration rather than the more-fashionable sociology or psychology, and he studied hard. He was named to Phi Beta Kappa. His social life, for the most part, focused on Lori, who was also studying at Berkeley. They married right after graduation.

Soon after, Milken and Lori moved to Philadelphia where Michael enrolled in the University of Pennsylvania's prestigious Wharton business school. Milken worked summers and part-time during the school year at Drexel Firestone's Philadelphia office (a predecessor firm had been headquartered in Philadelphia). After graduating with all A's, Milken stayed at Drexel, commuting from a Philadelphia suburb, Cherry Hill, N.J., to Drexel's Manhattan headquarters. He seemed remarkably unsophisticated about Wall Street's pecking order, largely oblivious to considerations of prestige. He didn't have any real familiarity with the Morgan Stanleys or Goldman, Sachses of the world.

Milken was unfazed by the tradition that held that promising business graduates went into investment banking—corporate finance, not sales and trading. At Drexel, Milken started in research and then asked to moved to sales and trading, where he gradually focused almost exclusively on the low-rated and unrated securities that would become his hallmark.

Years later, the myth grew up and was cultivated by Drexel that Milken was a "genius" who discovered the profit potential of what became universally known by the pejorative name "junk" bonds. But Milken never made any secret of the fact that the intellectual underpinnings of his interest in low-grade bonds was provided by others. W. Braddock Hickman had done a landmark analysis of low-grade and unrated bonds that Milken read while still at Berkeley. In a thorough analysis of corporate bond performance from 1900 to 1943, Hickman had demonstrated that a diversified long-term portfolio of low-grade bonds yielded a higher rate of return, without any greater risk, than a comparable portfolio of blue-chip, top-rated bonds. A later study of bonds from 1945 to 1965 reached the same conclusion.

Later, in his early conversations with Joseph, Milken, a genius salesman, constantly preached his gospel of high-yield securities. Joseph was intrigued; he asked for a copy of Hickman's study. Milken kept talking. The only problem with low-grade debt was its lack of liquidity, he argued. Most of Drexel's customers were still unwilling to invest their assets at higher yields, but Milken began to make some headway. He countered investor reluctance and risk aversion with meticulous research into the underlying business prospects of as many low-grade issuers as he could handle. He amazed Joseph with his grasp of arcane aspects of various businesses, all aimed at predicting a company's ability to make its interest and principal payments when due.

It was an enormous task; virtually no research on these companies was being done on Wall Street, where research departments focused almost exclusively on stocks of widely traded companies. Milken was handling all his own research, carrying bulging briefcases of research reports and other data on his long commutes to and from Cherry Hill. He used his findings to persuade investors to gamble on high-yielding securities that Milken believed would make their payments and were, as a result, undervalued.

Some of Milken's prospects were also potential corporate clients for Drexel. Insurance companies with large pools of assets were especially eager to invest profitably. Joseph went along with Milken on countless visits to spread the gospel of high-yield. At each stop, Milken ran through his arguments: The bond market was too risk-averse; a well-diversified portfolio would provide a better return; liquidity was growing as more companies heeded Milken's message; and returns would comfortably exceed the risk premium. It was a simple, effective message. Increasingly, it worked.

Among Milken's early big successes was a group of wealthy, mostly Jewish financiers who had acquired insurance companies. None was a member of the Wall Street establishment. They didn't worry about the stigma associated with low-grade paper, and they liked Milken's new ideas. Saul Steinberg, Meshulam Riklis, and Carl Lindner became early converts, and Lindner, a non-Jew from Cincinnati, even became something of a father figure. As their annual returns met or exceeded Milken's predictions, they became increasingly heavy backers of Milken and clients of Drexel. For his part, Milken showed no concern that Lindner was a target of an SEC investigation, had never graduated from high school, was shunned by Cincinnati society, and was viewed as a pariah by many on Wall Street. Or that Steinberg had wrested control of Reliance Insurance Co. and waged an unsuccessful hostile attack on giant Chemical Bank that had enraged the establishment banking world and its investment banking allies. Or that Riklis started as a poor Israeli immigrant who had made his money in movie theaters and liquor. They had all been rebuffed on Wall Street at various times. They would never forget that Milken sought them out as clients.

By early 1977, Milken's operation controlled a remarkable 25% of the market in high-yield securities. It was really the only firm maintaining an active market-making operation with an eye toward enhancing the liquidity of the market. (A market-maker is a key to liquidity, assuring a holder of a security that it will buy it whenever the holder wants to convert it into cash. The market-maker, in turn, resells the security, keeping as its profit any difference between the "buy" and "sell" price it obtains. The New York Stock Exchange and the NAS-DAQ over-the-counter market are simply institutionalized market-making organizations, which provide the additional service of published trading prices.) Other banks, such as Lehman Brothers, the market leader in high-yield bonds, would underwrite some new issues and husband those it had previously underwritten, but this was mostly a service to existing clients; other firms weren't interested in being active market-makers.

So Milken became, in effect, the market for high-yield bonds. He had an incredible memory, and he knew who owned what issues, what they had paid, their yield to maturity, and who else wanted them. Increasingly, his clients developed such confidence in his research and market acumen that when he urged them to invest in a particular issue, they did. They didn't care about the absence of published prices, or what Milken's spread was—as long as they made money. And no one except Milken and a handful of his colleagues knew the pricing structure of this market—including the increasingly high spreads between the buy and sell prices.

Milken could thrive to the extent he did, in part, because his market was almost entirely unregulated. His operation dealt almost entirely in what is known as "secondary offerings." In such transactions, a large insurance company may decide to unload a large bond position it acquired from the original issuer; it might have Drexel buy the block of bonds, then reoffer them to its network of bond buyers. Such offerings don't have to be registered with the SEC, and there is no published listing of the price at which such offerings are made. The world of junk bonds were the financial equivalent of the early days of the American frontier; a rough justice was extracted from the weak by the strong.

One day a salesman in Drexel's midtown Manhattan office, Gary Winnick, bought some of Milken's bond inventory for one of his clients. Winnick earned one-eighth of a point on the spread, or the difference between the price the customer paid and what Milken charged him (A "point" means a basis point, or one one-hundredth of a cent per dollar of a bond. One-eighth of a point on the spread in a $1 million purchase represents about $125.) Winnick was furious to learn that Milken's spread had actually been 30 points, and that Milken had kept 29⅞ for himself. Winnick was astounded that Milken would be so greedy. They were, after all, colleagues. Winnick went to Milken's boss, Kantor, and complained. But Kantor did nothing. Already, by 1976, Winnick concluded, Milken was making too much money for anyone to discipline him.

For Milken, the transaction was just another trade, and the more one could squeeze out of the person on the other side of the trade, the better. For years to come, his colleagues on the trading desk would watch in amazement at the pleasure, even glee, that Milken displayed when he squeezed an extra fraction of a point out of an unwitting trader. Only in trading could superior knowledge be wielded to extract profits with such immediate satisfaction. Few ever got the better of Milken, because he gambled only with superior knowledge; when someone did, Milken went out and tried to hire him. Warren Trepp, for example, was the head fixed-income trader at Dean Witter when he sold short some real estate investment trust securities. One of Milken's people was on the other side of the trades. The REIT values dropped severely, causing serious losses for Milken and generating a big profit

for Trepp. Milken ordered his people to get the name of the Dean
Witter trader, then went out and lured him to Drexel. Trepp became
Milken's own head trader.

As Milken's business grew, so did Joseph's, if not at so spectacular a rate. Joseph moved quickly to improve the quality of investment
bankers at Drexel, hiring several people he had earlier recruited to
Shearson, among them John Kissick, Herbert Bachelor, Fred
McCarthy, John Sorte and David Kay, whom he put in charge of an
infant mergers-and-acquisitions department. And he hired an arrogant, chubby, headstrong young business school graduate, Leon Black.
Black's father, the head of United Brands, had been caught in a scandal
while Leon was at Harvard Business School and had committed suicide
by jumping from his office window.

In an effort to give Drexel an "edge" at attracting investment
banking business, Joseph had decided to target certain growing industries and smaller companies neglected by the major investment banks.
Drexel started building up its research coverage for over-the-counter
stocks, even though research brought no immediate profits to the firm.
The group managed to do enough deals that, by 1977, the corporate
finance bonus pool reached $1 million.

That same year, Joseph called Milken, explaining that a client,
Texas International, needed to raise capital but was already so highly
leveraged with debt that it would never get an investment rating. Could
Drexel do a public high-yield issue, underwritten by Drexel and mar-
keted directly to the public—an original new issue, in other words,
rather than the secondary offerings that were the mainstays of Drexel's
practice?

Milken said he'd try. He proceeded to sell the $30 million issue
easily, with a whopping underwriting fee of 3%. Milken went on that
year to do six more issues for companies that couldn't otherwise get
capital. At about the same time, he sold the idea of the first high-yield
mutual funds, allowing small investors to invest in a diversified portfolio of junk bonds. Milken's dream of liquidity was close to fruition.
The mechanism for a revolution in finance was in place, right under the
noses of the Wall Street establishment that had disdained low-grade
debt.

Winnick, meanwhile, had moved at Kantor's behest to the high-
grade bond desk in Drexel's downtown offices. He also traded some of
Milken's high-yield products and he quickly became Drexel's top-
producing salesman outside the high-yield area. He worked long hours.
One Friday night he mentioned to Milken that he and his wife were
looking at houses in Westchester County that weekend, and Milken
said somewhat cryptically, "Don't buy anything." Shortly after, he

asked Winnick to work for him—in Century City, adjacent to Beverly Hills, in distant California.

Milken's then two-year-old son, Gregory, had health problems, and Milken's father had cancer. The decision to move surely wasn't made just because Milken wanted a healthier climate and wanted to be close to his family and childhood friends, though those were factors. It was already obvious that Milken's success had little to do with Drexel, and that Drexel's success had everything to do with Milken. The hapless Burnham, the firm's titular head, knew little outside the increasingly unprofitable retail brokerage area; his shrewdest move had been to recognize Milken's potential and give him a long leash. Kantor was even less of an influence, an old-fashioned trader baffled by the computerized math and sophisticated strategies being developed by a new generation. Milken had no interest in wrangling with their likes for political influence.

Why not simply move, using Drexel as an umbrella, but effectively setting up an autonomous operation that would be under his total control? As Milken confided in Winnick and others, he had every intention of using the California base to expand junk bonds into virtually every profitable area, from underwriting and trading to mergers and acquisitions. Junk bonds were simply a fresh way to raise capital—capital that could be employed to serve any of an investment bank's traditional functions. As long as his compensation structure stayed in place—and no one at Drexel would dare to challenge it—the bulk of the firm's profits would end up under his control. Already, his employees in New York were making so much more money than anyone else at Drexel that all of them volunteered to move.

Milken and his family bought a house once owned by Clark Gable and Carole Lombard in his hometown, Encino. Milken opened for business in small offices on the Avenue of the Stars in Century City in 1978 with 15 Drexel employees, including Winnick. The offices were already too small when they moved in; Milken sat with Trepp, his head trader, at his side. He was within earshot of all his traders and salesmen throughout the trading day.

With Milken in control, everyone conformed to his standards. The workday began promptly at 4:30 A.M. (7:30 A.M. in New York) and continued until 8 P.M. (11:00 P.M. in New York). Phones rang constantly. With his two phones, Milken often carried on multiple conversations at once. There was a cacophony on the trading floor, with questions and comments constantly shouted. After the market closed (at 1 P.M. California time), Milken scheduled meetings, racing from one conference room to another. All were filled with clients hoping for direct access to him.

Milken was sometimes in the office before the scheduled opening. When his employees arrived at 4:30, they'd often find his notes on their desks, outlining their day's agenda.

In 1981 Milken found a sales counterpart to Trepp, someone who was as good at selling as Trepp was at trading. He was James Dahl, and on the surface he had little in common with Milken or others at Drexel. Dahl was a WASP, though not a product of the Ivy League establishment but the son of a struggling real estate broker in a lower-middle-class neighborhood of Miami. He graduated from Florida State University in Tallahassee with honors and won a scholarship to the university's business school, earning an MBA. He was handsome, with longish blond hair, green eyes, a tan that gave him a Beach Boys aura, and a dazzling smile.

Milken rarely gave any signs that such qualities mattered to him, but colleagues say he seemed fascinated by aspects of Dahl he lacked— as if the hiring of Dahl demonstrated conclusively that he could attract someone who at least looked like the embodiment of the American dream, a kind of Robert Redford of the bond world. After a series of 5 A.M. interviews, first in Los Angeles and then over breakfast at the Plaza Hotel in New York, Milken had asked Dahl about his wife, how many children he hoped to have, what he did in his spare time, his family background, and what his father had done for a living. He never asked him where he went to school, or how he'd fared academically.

Evidently Milken had concluded that Dahl had the fundamental qualities he was looking for: a real hunger to make money, and a commitment to family values. Dahl was out of work at the time, having passed through Citibank, Lehman Brothers, and a recently defunct trading subsidiary of First Penn Bank. Then he had moved to Trading Company of the West, which also failed. He'd returned to Florida, when a mutual friend arranged the introduction to Milken. Despite the track record of some of his employers, Dahl had done well for himself, earning $450,000 at the Penn Bank subsidiary. Milken hired him at $20,000 a month, with a promise that he'd sit next to the boss.

With Dahl, as with all his employees, Milken demanded total commitment and allegiance. No one left the office to eat; meals were catered every day for breakfast and lunch and often for dinner as well. To prevent any distractions, Milken hired several women to pick up dry cleaning for his traders and salesmen, go to the post office, wait at their houses for repairmen and deliveries, and take care of pets. Soon after he first came aboard, Dahl, still adjusting to the time change, started to leave the office after the markets had closed on a Friday.

"Where are you going?" Milken asked sharply.

"I'm tired, and I'm going home to read research reports," Dahl replied.

Milken was appalled at such a lack of stamina. "Read here, then go home and take a nap," he said. Dahl meekly returned to his desk.

On another occasion, Dahl was leaving the office after learning that his mother had been diagnosed with cancer. "Where are you going?" Milken again demanded.

Dahl said he was worried, his aunt and uncle had both died of cancer, he wanted to visit his mother. Milken looked disgruntled. "When are you going to be back?" he asked. He did not express any concern or sympathy.

A few years later, when Dahl's wife went into labor prematurely and the baby died after two hours, a devastated Dahl was at his desk the next morning, determined that Milken wouldn't notice his grief. He had learned that Milken expected nothing less.

No one had much private life. Ironically, given the lip service Milken paid to marital fidelity and family values, the intense, hothouse atmosphere kept employees away from their families and spawned intra-office affairs between traders and secretaries, including one between Trepp and Milken's own administrative assistant, Jeannette. Milken seemed oblivious until they announced their engagement.

One of the office's secretaries kept a diary detailing her sexual encounters with men in the office. One of the most talked-about entries described in lurid detail how she gave one salesman fellatio and used drugs. Such incidents were commonplace. Some of the trading assistants in the office even had breast implants, paid for by Drexel salesmen and traders.

On one occasion in 1984, Milken's employees hired a stripper to celebrate his birthday. She arrived during trading hours, shed all of her clothing while dancing around Milken's desk, then leaned toward him shaking her ample breasts in his face. Just then, Milken's phone rang. It was a client wanting to do a trade. To escape the stripper, Milken ducked down under the desk, still gripping his phone. The stripper followed him on hands and knees as Milken completed the trade.

Milken rarely socialized with others in the office and, indeed, spent little time with his own wife and his two sons and daughter, though he did show up for important sporting events and school occasions and coached his sons' basketball team. On a family trip to Hawaii, Milken rented three suites in the hotel: one for him and Lori, one for the children, and a third that functioned as his office. He worked every day of the vacation from 3 A.M. until 8 A.M. Hawaii time, while the markets were open in New York.

With rare exceptions, Milken only left his desk during work hours for nonbusiness reasons once a year, when he took his wife to lunch on their wedding anniversary. He usually ate at his desk, mostly junk food. He never seemed to get any exercise. Even during off hours, he was usually in his home office; calls there, even late at night and on weekends, were answered promptly. On the rare occasions when he did attend parties, he seemed awkward. At birthday parties, he spent most of his time playing with the kids.

Milken was a perfectionist and could be relentlessly critical, questioning a trade over and over, fixating on a fraction of a point. He'd ask the same question over and over, badgering a trader to make the point that the trader had been foolish or stupid. But after Trepp demonstrated to Milken that he'd been right in five disputed trades, he told Milken to "stop nagging me," and for the most part Milken did.

Dahl once asked Milken why he criticized so much and never praised anyone. "There's not enough time in the day to sit around praising each other," Milken sharply replied. "We don't need to talk about our successes. We only need to talk about our failures."

In this atmosphere, what might seem ordinary gestures of kindness elsewhere seemed memorable. Once, when Winnick was getting ready for a rare vacation to Italy, Milken sent him a bon voyage package and a note telling him to have a great trip. When they moved to the Los Angeles area, Milken extended personal loans to nearly all the employees so they could buy nice houses. When Dahl and his wife celebrated their wedding anniversary in Palm Springs, they were greeted with a large bouquet and a card reading, "Happy Anniversary. Mike and Lori." Milken made a hospital visit and offered financial help to the dying brother of a member of the office's support staff.

Trepp was constantly amazed at Milken's obsession with squeezing more profits out of trades, and frequently had to remind him that securities dealers' guidelines permit only a 5% markup. Milken's power over the market was so complete that he frequently tried to mark prices up as much as 25%. One of Trepp's responsibilities as head trader was to sign the trading tickets; when Trepp saw what he considered an egregious ticket, he bounced it back to Milken. But at times, Milken did the trades anyway and someone else forged Trepp's initials; he doesn't know who.

On at least four occasions, Trepp threatened to quit over what he considered serious trading improprieties. He had loud fights with Milken, and in each case, Milken backed down. Milken never fired anyone. He was obsessed with the notion that anyone who left would reveal his secrets, the scope and success of his money-making activities.

The pressure took its toll, in varying degrees. Peter Ackerman was hired initially as a trader, but Milken's relentless criticism reduced him on one occasion to tears. Ackerman quit trading, and focused increasingly on cultivating clients, functioning more as an investment banker for Milken. He became so sycophantic toward Milken that others resented him. His nickname was "the Sniff," because, in the words of a colleague, "his nose was always up Mike's ass."

Trepp began smoking four packs of cigarettes a day. Another trader took to chewing rubber bands; another developed a serious drinking problem. Bruce Newberg, deemed a brilliant technician by many in the office, had to start taking blood pressure medication. One day Newberg started raving hysterically when his phone line went dead during an important conversation with a client. It turned out that he had chewed through the phone cord.

Winnick developed a reputation as the office hypochondriac, sometimes checking himself into the Scripps Institute in San Diego because he thought he had brain tumors and other serious ailments.

In perhaps the saddest case, Cary Maultasch developed serious psychological problems and had to see a psychiatrist. Milken allowed him to move back to New York, where he became Milken's liaison with Drexel's headquarters—in effect, a Milken mole. Maultasch continued to handle trading for Milken; at the end of each day he shredded the records on Milken's orders so no one in New York would see the details of Milken's operation.

Milken didn't like the time his traders and salespeople spent trading for their own accounts. This was a major reason that the office formed various investment partnerships to take advantage of investment opportunities Milken encountered. He banned personal trading, but allowed each employee to invest up to an allocated amount in the partnerships. Within the office, employees could rank themselves on the "A" team or "B" team depending on the size of their partnership allocation. Some favored employees, such as Ackerman, even received partnership interests as part of their compensation. In some cases, Milken made large personal loans to employees so they could afford to invest the full amount of their allocation.

Soon after Dahl's arrival in California, Milken invited him to his home in Encino, where Milken took a rare break and lounged with Dahl by the pool. Milken told Dahl that the partnerships would make him rich. But he warned him not to live lavishly, and told him he shouldn't buy a large house, at least not yet. He said there would be plenty of time and money to do that later.

Such promises had to be accepted at face value, since access to partnership information was tightly restricted. No one knew in ad-

vance where the money would be invested. The office's computer runs
were altered so that no one but Milken was privy to the partnership
trading activity.

The compensation for all of this, of course, was money. While
their incomes had hardly reached the stratospheric levels they would
in the mid-eighties, the Drexel employees in Los Angeles were earning
five times what most of their counterparts earned on Wall Street. Dahl,
for example, topped $1 million in only his second year in Los Angeles.
Milken himself, though no one knew it at the time, earned a staggering
$45 million in 1982.

In keeping with Milken's admonitions, however, there was little
to suggest to anyone outside the office that such riches were being
earned. Although Trepp bought a white Rolls Royce Corniche convertible, Milken didn't want him to drive it to the office. Milken himself
lived comparatively modestly. His wife wore the same simple black
velvet dress to the Christmas party every year. Milken drove a slightly
battered yellow Mercedes; he sold it to Dahl when it had 80,000 miles.
When Armand Hammer, the famed industrialist who became one of
Milken's and Drexel's most important clients, visited the office, Milken
served him coffee in a Styrofoam cup. Decorations in the office consisted of some framed Olympics posters.

Milken, by his own design, made no impression whatsoever in the
Hollywood social orbit or even business and professional circles. His
reading consisted almost exclusively of research reports, prospectuses,
and other financial documents. Milken struck his colleagues as remarkably unworldly, knowing little about art, literature, politics, or even
current events outside of his immediate concerns.

Winnick, Dahl, and some of the other traders had read a Robert
Ludlum thriller, *The Matarese Circle*, published in 1979. They were
struck by Milken's resemblance to one of the main characters. The
book is classic Ludlum, a wildly improbable but suspenseful tale of
world conquest through multinational corporations. At the center of
this conspiracy is a brilliant, driven financier, fixated on his vision
of world control. His name is Guiderone, but he is known throughout
the book as "the shepherd," because he was born a Corsican shepherd.
His followers are so loyal they willingly sacrifice their lives to carry out
his vision of world conquest.

"I've heard of him," says one of the book's characters. "A
modern-day Carnegie or Rockefeller, isn't he?"

"More. Much more," replies another. "The Geneens, the Lu-
cases, the Bluedhorns [sic], the wonderboys of Detroit and Wall Street,
none of them can touch Guiderone. He's the last of the vanishing

giants, a really benign monarch of industry and finance. . . . I suppose you could call it the definitive story of the American dream."

Milken's disciples in Beverly Hills began referring to him as "the Shep," and the nickname stuck. Winnick gave Milken a copy of Ludlum's thriller, curious to see how Milken would react, whether he would see any resemblance in himself to the book's central character. But so far as he could tell, Milken never read it.

For many of the Beverly Hills employees, life in the office took a turn for the worse when Milken's younger brother, Lowell, joined the operation in 1979. Lowell, a lawyer, had been a partner in the Los Angeles law firm Irell and Manella, where he specialized in tax law. Milken had a relationship with his younger brother that was both intensely competitive—he seemed obsessed with beating him in tennis—and highly protective. Lowell was brought in, colleagues say, to relieve Milken from overseeing all the partnership activity and to handle tax issues. Others in the operation were struck that Milken would only trust a member of his immediate family for such a task.

Lowell seemed as driven as his brother, but he never showed flashes of warmth as Milken sometimes did. He had a lawyerly mind that struck the freewheeling traders as cold and anal. Lowell did little to mix with others. He installed a separate door in his office so that he didn't even have to walk through the trading floor. His office was grandiose by Drexel standards, with custom wood paneling and expensive art. If someone other than Milken walked into his office, Lowell would conspicuously turn the papers on his desk face down. Some of the traders would mockingly do the same whenever Lowell walked near their desks. In a typically crude stab at humor, they would also grab their crotches when Lowell's back was turned, imitating one of Lowell's nervous gestures.

Never one to miss a profit opportunity, Lowell helped arrange a move of Drexel's West Coast office from the Century City complex to Beverly Hills—into a building owned by Lowell and Milken on Wilshire Boulevard just off Rodeo Drive. It was a shrewd investment. Drexel rented the space from them, bestowing lucrative tax advantages in the process. And the location was almost certain to appreciate in value. Just down the street from the elegant Beverly Wilshire Hotel, it was also just around the corner from chic boutiques like Giorgio and Bijan.

But the interior of Drexel's building could have been miles away from the glitz and glamour, as far as Milken was concerned. Here Milken had installed a large X-shaped trading desk. He sat at the center, within easy range of his growing number of lieutenants arrayed along the four branches of the X. The desk was equipped with the latest high-tech communications and trading data, but the office decor remained spartan. Only the address—9560 Wilshire Boulevard, Beverly Hills—had cachet.

After Lowell arrived, he distributed sealed white envelopes to about a dozen employees. In them were loan statements, citing the amount Milken had loaned them for their houses, the accumulated interest, and a demand for immediate repayment. From then on, Lowell was viewed as Milken's hatchet man. Others in the office traded malicious stories about Lowell, including accounts of his relationship with his wife.

One afternoon in 1981, Milken was at work at the trading desk when he fainted and keeled over. Trepp, Dahl, Winnick, and others near him were horrified, fearful that their meal ticket had suffered a heart attack. They immediately shouted for Lowell. Lowell emerged from his office, looked at the unconscious and prostrate Milken, then turned around and went back into his office, closing the door without saying a word. The traders were dumbfounded. Milken soon revived, suffering no long-term effects from the mysterious incident.

Whatever the tensions, however, they seemed minor compared to the money being generated by the Milken operation. Milken made it a point to ensure that every employee made more money each year than he or she had the year before. By and large, Milken's people found something they genuinely liked about Milken.

Curiously, given how driven most of them were to earn large sums, it was clear to them that money alone held little interest for Milken; it was what that money could do. One day, chatting with Winnick, Milken said that one of his dreams was to boost his net worth by a factor of ten, from $3 billion, say, to $30 billion. Then, turning to the sweeping view from Century City across western Los Angeles toward the Pacific Ocean, he asked, "What do you think it'd cost to buy every building from here to the ocean?"

Milken might have realized those goals simply by continuing his lucrative dominance of secondary issues and new junk-bond issues. In Los Angeles, he had assembled a network of junk-bond customers that dwarfed his earlier sources in New York. Among the closest to him was Thomas Spiegel, the head of Columbia Savings and Loan. Spiegel venerated Milken. He worked the same arduous hours, and his office walls soon had numerous photos of Milken and his wife, posing with Spiegel at restaurants, at parties.

Charles Keating, the head of burgeoning Lincoln Savings and Loan, was another key link. Keating and Milken often discussed their families, and reinforced the importance each placed on family connections as the only true bonds in life.

But the closest of all was probably Fred Carr, the head of Executive Life Insurance Co. Carr was smart, one of the first to embrace Milken's theory of junk-bond opportunities, and an early and enthusiastic backer. To the amazement of others in the office, Milken would examine copies of Carr's and Drexel's portfolios every Friday afternoon, then, without consulting Carr, freely trade positions between the two accounts. By contrast, Milken made no secret of the fact that he thought Charlie Knapp, head of Financial Corporation of America, was a "moron."

Milken wasn't content with simply assembling the awesome buying power that large savings and loans and insurance companies offered, especially now that federal deregulation had opened up so many new opportunities in the savings and loan business. Junk bonds, in and of themselves, were enormously lucrative. But they could be harnessed to an even more potent force. Milken could see clearly what was beginning to happen on the American financial landscape. He heard about it from clients like Carl Lindner and Saul Steinberg. The big money was in the struggle for corporate control, in mergers and acquisitions and, increasingly, in a variation that seemed even more promising to Milken: the leveraged buyout, in which a public company was taken private. With corporate control went power.

It was clearly just a matter of time before Milken, having quietly nurtured his financing network into a huge money-spewing engine, burst upon the takeover scene. Then, Milken often told Trepp, there would be no deal that he couldn't do, no company so big that it need not fear his power. "We're going to tee-up GM, Ford, and IBM," he told Trepp in tones of almost grim determination. "And make them cringe."

2.

Robert Wilkis gazed across the crowded room high in Citicorp's Manhattan headquarters. Never before had he seen such a concentration of young WASPs. Had they all gravitated to banking like salmon following the instinct to swim upstream? The 1977 welcoming cocktail party had underscored his sense of isolation and difference. He had just shaken the hand of Citicorp's chairman, the legendary Walter Wriston. But Wriston had hardly noticed him; he was too busy looking at the plastic name tag of the next new employee in line. Wilkis sighed and headed back to the bar for another drink.

Then he spotted someone who looked even more out of place than he felt. The guy was standing by himself. Unlike the others, most of whom looked like former Ivy League athletes, he was overweight with longish hair and a dark moustache. Wilkis moved closer and saw the name printed on his name-plate: Dennis Levine.

"What's a nice Jewish boy like you doing in a place like this?" Wilkis asked. The two men started comparing notes but discovered they had little in common besides a Jewish upbringing. Wilkis was tall and thin, and, for all his insecurities, he had compiled an enviable résumé. Before joining Citibank's prestigious world banking group where he concentrated on high-profile international lending, he had worked at the World Bank. He'd also spent a summer at the U.S. Treasury doing research on major economic issues. Wilkis was worldly and sophisticated, having lived abroad and traveled extensively. He was a Harvard grad, married to a Cuban-born woman, and he spoke five languages fluently: French, German, Italian, Arabic, and Hebrew.

Levine, by contrast, worked in an area of the bank called "corporate counseling." Not even Levine seemed to understand the group's function, but he had plenty of free time and tried to insinuate himself into other corporate work. Levine had been born and raised in a Jewish middle class area in Queens. He had traveled little and his academic record at Baruch College, a part of the City University of New York, had been undistinguished.

Levine and Wilkis found a lot to talk about. Their offices were just down the hall from each other's in Citicorp's headquarters at 399 Park Avenue. Wilkis suspected he would be seeing more of Levine. There was something about him—a warmth, perhaps, an almost palpable longing to be liked—that made an immediate impression.

Wilkis's premonition was quickly borne out. The following week, early in the day, Levine dropped into Wilkis's office and asked what he was working on. Before Wilkis could answer, Levine said, "Let's go have coffee."

"I can't," Wilkis replied. "I've got to get this stuff out to a client."

"Oh, fuck your clients," Levine said, then grinned wickedly and walked out.

Wilkis was taken aback. He was responsible almost to a fault, a function, he often thought, of the orthodox Hebrew schooling he endured growing up in Baltimore.

The next day Levine was back, upping the ante. "Let's skip work after lunch," he proposed. Wilkis was appalled. Levine added, "You know you're bored."

Wilkis was indeed bored, and ambivalent about his life and career. He was 28 years old (three years Levine's senior), and before attending Stanford Business School, had never envisioned a job on Wall Street. Politically, he'd always been left-wing, and he still thought of himself as very liberal. After graduating from college, he'd taught handicapped children in the Boston public school system.

He had sought access to a higher-paying career by applying to business school, but once enrolled, he hated it. He was angry at himself for being there, for selling out. He nearly flunked accounting and he was contemptuous of many of his classmates, dismissing them as "morons" who "actually wanted to become accountants." He feared that he, too, would have to become a drone to survive. The experience, though he ultimately did well, was a blow to his self-image.

By the time he graduated in 1977, his wife was pregnant. His mother was getting a divorce and had financial problems. He was broke. Classmates were landing lucrative jobs, and when Citicorp offered him one, he grabbed at the opportunity. He had vague ideas about doing something in the international-relations arena.

But Citicorp so far had been dreadful. The big bank was a coat-and-tie version of the army, and he was in boot camp, surrounded by manuals of rules and regulations prescribing nearly his every move. His work environment was impersonal. No one besides Dennis Levine showed any interest in socializing with him. But Levine's interest proved intense.

Levine was by turns ingratiating—"You really went to Harvard and yet you'll talk to me?" he'd ask with mock sincerity, conspiratorial—"You know, we're just nice Jewish boys in a hostile, WASP environment," belligerent—"Screw the system! Screw the boss!" he'd exclaim, and philosophical. He called Wilkis a "left-wing pinkie commie." "You know your problem, Wilkis?" he'd ask. "You worry too much about the 'gray' areas in life. That's where we're different. I have clear-cut goals. You don't."

Wilkis had rarely met anyone so single-minded about his career. Levine said that as a young student at Baruch, he had come across a book called *The Financiers*, about the workings of the investment banking world. He was dazzled by passages describing these bankers' lifestyles, their expensive clothes and tailor-made suits, their cars and estates. Levine had never known that world existed.

Levine had grown up in Bayside, a Queens neighborhood of cookie-cutter brick bungalows that could have served as the opening credits for "All in the Family." He was the youngest of three sons; his mother had never gotten over the heartbreak of having her daughter die at age five. Levine's father, Philip, had his own business selling aluminum and vinyl siding. Philip Levine didn't trust banks, didn't want any records of his financial dealings, which he believed would be used against him by the Internal Revenue Service. He didn't even have a checking account and kept his life savings in cash under his bed.

Dennis excelled at nothing in high school, though he was reasonably popular with a small group of friends, some of whom he hung out with in Queens after graduating. Then, depressed at the idea of spending his life in the neighborhood, he applied to tuition-free Baruch College, quickly distinguishing himself from his classmates by wearing a jacket and tie to class almost every day. He ingratiated himself with his professors, certain that these "contacts" would be necessary to vault to Wall Street. During his senior year, Levine applied to every investment bank on Wall Street—and was rejected by them all. He blamed it entirely on his lack of a "white-shoe pedigree," and he was bitter.

Wilkis, on the other hand, considered himself cultured and literate; his primary interest was the great books. He'd never felt any prejudice because he was Jewish, and he didn't view the world as hostile. Yet he empathized with Levine. Levine's mother had died suddenly while Levine was in college; so had Wilkis's father. Over and over, Levine played on the theme that, working together, he and

Wilkis could triumph. Probably most of all—despite his wife, Elsa, and a new daughter—Wilkis was lonely.

One day Levine told Wilkis he'd met a young woman named Laurie Skolnick. He startled Wilkis, who was sensitive to feminist issues, by saying he intended to "own her." Wilkis later attended their wedding. Laurie was blond, pleasant, and Jewish, and believed, she said, in a "traditional" marriage: Levine would earn a living and she would raise a family. She spoke with a pronounced New York City accent. Wilkis didn't tell Levine, but he was appalled by the wedding reception, which he considered a vulgar display of bad taste. As far as he could tell, most of Levine's friends were involved in drugs. This was a world light-years removed from that of Wilkis and his Harvard-trained friends.

Oddly, the experience only seemed to heighten his empathy for Levine. Wilkis felt somehow that he was rescuing Levine. On their increasingly frequent outings, Levine came to share his deepest thoughts and aspirations. One evening he told Wilkis, in a somewhat cryptic tone, "I knew after I was bar mitzvahed that there was an inside track and information was the key." And he would often tell Wilkis his "dream of dreams: the euphoria, the omnipotence of reading on September 12 the *Wall Street Journal* of September 13."

Wilkis gave these musings relatively little thought. Levine seemed to be making little progress up the ladder of information. Not surprisingly, given his attitude and frequent absences from the office, Levine wasn't promoted the following year when he and Wilkis's class of new employees came up for review. Wilkis was. His new position included access to a junior executive dining room rather than the run-of-the-mill employee cafeteria. Levine was beside himself, constantly begging Wilkis to take him as his guest. And then Levine asked Wilkis to break the bank's rules: to get him an identification card that would get him into the dining room on his own. Despite some trepidation, Wilkis got him the I.D.

Shortly after being passed over at Citibank, Levine applied for jobs again at 25 New York investment banks. He got one positive response. This time he was actually hired by Smith Barney, Harris Upham & Co. He called Wilkis the first week of his new job with a stock tip.

"Just buy it," Levine insisted. "Don't ask any questions." Wilkis bought a couple of hundred shares, and soon after, the stock rose dramatically. "See, Bob," Levine said. "I'm going to take care of you."

Levine's opportunities to glean inside information were soon curbed when he was assigned to the Paris office of Smith Barney. Wilkis was envious of the assignment. He actually wanted international work, and would have viewed Paris as a plum. Levine had little or no interest in foreign affairs. In France, he worked on Eurobond syndications, selling Eurobond offerings to European clients, which required him to travel throughout Europe, visiting its financial capitals. He and Laurie lived in a spacious apartment owned by Smith Barney on the Avenue Foch in the fashionable 16th Arrondissement of Paris. But in frequent phone calls to Wilkis, Levine did little but complain, especially about his wife.

"She's getting in the way of my career," Levine griped. Laurie, wrenched from her comfortable Queens existence, felt isolated in Paris. She was miserable, and ended up in a hospital. Levine wasn't much happier himself. He was frustrated at being out of the "deal flow" in Smith Barney's New York office. Even though, as a junior corporate finance employee, he'd done little there besides spreadsheet analysis, he'd boasted to Wilkis that he knew practically every deal underway in the office. He said he had mastered the ability to read documents on colleagues' desks upside-down.

Wilkis left Citibank, taking a job at Blyth Eastman Dillon, one of the old, established WASP firms, because it was starting up a new international merchant bank. Wilkis had the idea that the new unit would finance development projects in Third World countries, but the whole thing had gotten enmeshed in an internal power struggle at the firm. Wilkis complained to Levine that he wasn't traveling, wasn't accomplishing anything he'd hoped for. Levine countered that Wilkis should forget about international work and get into M&A.

"I don't understand you," Levine said angrily. "You want to help the niggers and the spics? Why do you want to do this Third World crap?" Then his tone shifted. "Bob, you're my friend. I only want you to do well. You're so naïve. Wall Street is going to eat you up. No one cares about this left-wing shit of yours. They'll use you. You've got to think of yourself, your family. You've got to do more to help your mother." It was another variation on Levine's us-against-the-world view. "I'm the only one you can trust," Levine concluded.

But soon after, Wilkis defied Levine's advice, accepting a job in the international department of Lazard Frères, the small but prestigious investment bank whose best-known banker is Felix Rohatyn. Levine continued to chide Wilkis about his career path, but increasingly he was focusing on his own progress, or lack of it, at Smith Barney.

Whenever Levine was in New York from Paris, he'd drop in on J. Tomilson Hill III, agitating for assignment to M&A. Hill had come to Smith Barney from First Boston, one of the biggest firms in M&A. He was urbane, polished, well-educated. He dressed meticulously, in elegant well-tailored suits, and slicked his hair straight back from his scalp. While he struck some as cold, even arrogant, he impressed clients as experienced, efficient and professional. When he arrived, Smith Barney had recently merged with Harris Upham—another combination forced by the end of fixed commission trading. Historically, Smith Barney had been strong in retail brokerage and research. Like Burnham & Co., it had experienced a sharp decline in the profitability of those businesses. Harris Upham was strong in municipal finance and tax-exempt bonds. Neither firm had much of a corporate finance department, let alone an M&A department. Hill had been brought in to create one.

Hill needed people for his new department, and he found Levine to be a healthy change from the Harvard and Stanford grads who, in his view, thought they were God's gift to the world. Hill thought Levine was a hustler. He'd gone to city schools, and Hill figured if he'd gotten this far, he must be doing something right. Levine held out the promise of what Hill called "hybrid vigor."

Hill checked with Levine's superiors in the Paris office. They described him as aggressive, "hungry," someone who wanted to move fast. They said he had a very outgoing personality, loved new business situations, and seemed to have a facility with clients. He didn't hesitate to pick up the phone to schmooze with existing clients or cold-call new ones. It was an appealing profile.

Finally, during the summer of 1979, Hill granted Levine's wish and brought him back to New York to work in M&A. Levine was ecstatic. He and Wilkis celebrated at a Manhattan restaurant. "Who's paying?" Levine asked Wilkis. "You are? Oh, good. Waiter? We'll have the Chateau Talbot '71." Levine was eager to show off his newfound knowledge of fine French wines. As he and Wilkis toasted his return, Levine leaned over to confide in Wilkis. "I'm playing like the big boys now," he said with an air of mystery.

"What's that mean?" Wilkis asked.

"For a guy who went to Harvard, you're not very bright," Levine said. "Can't you figure it out? I'll give you a hint. What mountains are in Europe?" Levine paused, as Wilkis looked baffled. Finally, Levine divulged his secret. "Bob, I'm all set up. I've got a Swiss bank account."

Wilkis was still puzzled; he thought only gangsters had Swiss bank accounts. "So what?" he asked.

But Levine refused to say more. "If you don't get it, I'm not going to spell it out." He seemed disappointed at Wilkis's lack of enthusiasm.

Levine had a glaring weakness, however, that soon became apparent once he started work in the M&A department: his math skills were dismal. M&A work requires detailed calculations of discounted cash flow. Various kinds of valuations of business segments are necessary to arrive at the correct price for often huge transactions. Most of this work is done by junior M&A people. But Hill noticed that Levine invariably organized his team so that someone else had to do the math. Levine was a fast talker, and cut a swath through the fledgling department; but increasingly Hill sensed that Levine was, in his terms, a "bullshit artist."

Hill quietly asked around, trying to find out who was doing what on various deals. In Levine's case, he learned that much of the math work was being handled by a young summer intern from Harvard Business School, Ira Sokolow. Unlike Levine, Sokolow was quiet and studious, meticulous almost to a fault, a perfectionist. Eager to make a good impression, Sokolow was easy prey for Levine: he'd work late at night, on weekends, whatever it took to complete Levine's assignments. Sokolow never complained.

Hill finally called Levine in. "You're not fooling me," Hill told him, adding that he wouldn't advance in the department until he had mastered these basic skills.

"But my role is more important," Levine countered. "Anybody can do that."

"Dennis, you want to run before you can crawl," Hill insisted. "You have to pay your dues. Most professionals can react swiftly and wisely in a crisis because ten–fifteen years ago, they did spreadsheets late into the night."

But Levine paid him little heed. That year, at his bonus review, Hill told him he'd be earning about $100,000, including his regular salary. Levine was furious that he wasn't the top-paid associate at his level of seniority. "Dennis, you're not treating this like someone who wants to learn," Hill told him. "You seem to think the world is full of fools. You are sadly mistaken."

Levine complained to Wilkis that Smith Barney was full of white-shoe mediocrities who didn't appreciate him, especially Hill, his boss. "Hill is anti-Semitic," Levine told Wilkis.

"That's ridiculous," Wilkis replied. "He just doesn't like you."

Levine seemed obsessed with his bonus. He constantly sought out Hill, asking whether he'd reevaluate him, whether he'd cured his defects, wondering why he wasn't advancing faster. Though Levine pestered him far more than anyone else in his department, Hill, by and large, considered Levine's interest to be a healthy one. It showed Levine was aggressive. M&A was a business, he believed, that required people who were driven. What worried him slightly was Levine's own inflated view of his skills and contributions.

Then Levine scored what he considered a triumph. While others in the department concentrated on their spreadsheets, Levine began focusing on what he called "identifying opportunities." One afternoon he rushed into Hill's office with some shreds of ticker tape, noting that trading in a particular company's stock seemed unusually active. "Let's call and pitch the defense," he told Hill. "This company looks like it's going to get an offer."

Hill did some research and concluded that the company did look somewhat undervalued and could be a likely takeover target. He called the company and suggested that it could use some advice in anticipation of an unfriendly bid. While Smith Barney wasn't retained, Hill began regular conversations, helping the company interpret spurts in its stock price and trading volume. Sure enough, the company did get a takeover offer, and Levine was ecstatic. While Smith Barney wasn't assigned the defense work, it was hired to do a "fairness opinion" on whether the proffered bid represented the company's true value. For that relatively modest assignment, which Levine attributed entirely to his early intelligence, Smith Barney earned a healthy $250,000.

Levine now saw himself as a profit center. He began following the tape constantly, looking for similar trading surges that might signal an accumulation in anticipation of a takeover. He badgered Hill, demanding a bigger bonus, emphasizing the importance of the new role he was creating for himself. Thus, he was even angrier at his next bonus review when he again failed to get the top bonus, and was told by Hill that he wasn't being promoted to vice president, as were others at his level of seniority. "I'm disappointed," Hill bluntly told him. "You aren't developing into a complete investment banker."

For Levine, the experience only reinforced his view that without extraordinary measures, he was never going to realize his grand ambitions. Not that he was particularly surprised. As he told Wilkis constantly, he was convinced that everyone was using inside information to get ahead; the game was rigged. At their frequent lunches, or walks through Central Park, Levine told Wilkis that nearly all the partners in Smith Barney's Paris office had Geneva bank accounts, and frequently traveled to Switzerland on weekends. Even Hill, he alleged, was swapping inside information with an investment banker at Dillon, Read. Levine was convinced Hill also had a secret trading account. "I could bring Hill down with what I know," Levine boasted, without ever being more specific. (Hill has never been accused of any misuse of confidential information.)

One afternoon, on one of their walks, Levine asked whether Wilkis might be able to get him information about pending deals at Lazard which would help him identify targets and land business for Smith Barney. Or, he continued, he could use the information to trade in his Swiss account. It wouldn't be detected. No one would suspect that Levine would have any advance knowledge of deals that his own firm wasn't involved with. He paused to gauge Wilkis's reaction, then continued. "You could do this too with information I could give you from Smith Barney. It's easy. All you need is the right setup. You could get rich, get out of Wall Street. You could go to Nepal, become a Buddhist monk. Isn't that what you want?"

Now all of Levine's insinuations about the Swiss bank account made sense. On some level, Wilkis had known what was going on, but he had preferred not to focus on it. Now he asked whether Levine was using his Swiss account to trade on inside information. Levine nodded yes, looking Wilkis directly in the eye. He'd opened an account with just under $40,000 at Pictet & Cie. in Geneva just before returning from Paris, he explained. Since then, he'd traded in four Smith Barney deals, admittedly in small amounts so as not to attract attention. Still, his account had grown to over $100,000.

Wilkis was apprehensive. He knew that at both Lazard and Smith Barney, employees could be fired even for opening a brokerage account without telling the firm so the trading could be monitored by compliance departments. And there was no doubt that insider trading was a crime. "It's illegal, Dennis," Wilkis said. "I'm scared."

Nonetheless, Levine had shrewdly recognized that he ran little risk in revealing his secret to Wilkis. Wilkis felt even closer to him. His friend had entrusted him with a secret that could be used to destroy him. Levine's fate was now in Wilkis's hands, and Wilkis was flattered. Also, the germ of an idea had taken hold in Wilkis's mind. He didn't like his work at Lazard any better than he had at Blyth or Citibank. Maybe he could get rich, as his friend was suggesting—and get out of Wall Street for good.

On one of their walks, Wilkis asked Levine about his trading profits. "How do you pay your taxes without giving away your trading?"

Levine gleefully recognized that he had Wilkis on his baited hook. Wilkis's thinking was shifting from the ethics of the scheme to the chances of getting caught.

"You dumb fuck!" Levine exclaimed. "You don't pay taxes! That's part of the beauty of this. All you need is a setup. I'll explain it all for you." And he did, mapping out the procedures for creating shell corporations with nominee directors to conduct anonymous trading, as well as bank secrecy provisions in the Caribbean, where many Swiss banks had branches protected by Swiss secrecy laws.

It all seemed so easy. For several weeks, Wilkis thought of little else but Levine's proposal. It was true, he rationalized, that everyone on Wall Street seemed to be turning confidential information to their advantage. What was the real harm? Didn't the legitimate work he was doing often enrich the investment bankers with little or no corresponding social good?

Levine's scheme also seemed foolproof. His trading would be anonymous, and he wouldn't trade in any deals that could be traced directly to him or his firm. He'd have to trust Levine, of course, but hadn't Levine trusted him? Once they were in the scheme together, neither could implicate the other without destroying himself. In his constant calculations of risk and reward, the risks seemed minimal.

In November 1979, Wilkis persuaded Elsa to take a vacation to the Bahamas. She would have much preferred Miami, with its large Cuban-born population. He withdrew all his savings—$40,000 in cash—and stuffed it into a suitcase. They flew to Nassau. The weather was terrible during their entire stay.

If the trip was a failure as a family vacation, its real mission was easily achieved. Wilkis followed Levine's instructions to the letter. He incorporated as a Bahamian corporation he named Rupearl; he used an alias and introduced himself as "Mr. Green." Rupearl's officers and directors were all nominees of Wilkis; its assets were his $40,000 in cash. He interviewed at three different branches of major Swiss banks, finally settling on Crédit Suisse. No one looked askance at his arrangements. By the end of the vacation, he was "set up," in Levine's words.

Wilkis, isolated in Lazard's international area, hadn't been paying much attention to what was going on in corporate finance or M&A. Now he began to listen, to develop contacts with other investment bankers, and to pass on everything to Levine. Levine, in turn, passed information from Smith Barney to Wilkis.

Wilkis was nervous at first, afraid that the weak link in the scheme was the possibility that his relationship with Levine might be detected. So Levine suggested that they speak in code, using false names when they called or left messages. Wilkis became "Alan Darby"; sometimes Levine used the same name, or "Mike Schwartz." Using codes was fun; it gave their insider-trading scheme the aura of a Hardy Boys escapade. Soon they were engaged in conversations so riddled with codes they would have seemed ludicrous to any listener.

Levine—"Mr. Darby"—would call on the phone. "Hi, Bob. We've got to talk company business." Company business meant the trading scheme. "I'm taking a peck at Jewel" meant Levine was accumulating a modest position in Jewel Companies. "Textron is looking OK" meant Wilkis should pay more attention to that situation, gleaning additional information for Levine.

Some of their code names displayed a certain wit. John Fedders, then head of enforcement at the SEC, was known as "the air conditioner" because of his surname. Levine's nemesis, Hill, was called "the three sticks," lampooning what they deemed a pretentious use of the Roman numeral III at the end of his name.

Lazard was much more active in mergers and acquisitions than Smith Barney, and now Levine tried repeatedly to get hired there. Wilkis did what he could to help, even conducting mock job interviews with his friend. Although Levine was interviewed several times for jobs at Lazard, no one was interested. The rejections only fueled his desire to trade on information from Lazard. "They fucked me over," he told Wilkis. "I'll make them pay."

Levine was impatient with the flow of information Wilkis was providing. In May 1980 he called Wilkis and, after the requisite codes, mentioned that "Wally says Lazard is busy." Wilkis was startled. Earlier that year, Levine had intimated that he was cultivating a source within Wachtell, Lipton. Levine had often boasted that his relationship with Wilkis would be just the beginning; he envisioned a ring of information sources including collaborators at the key investment banks and at the two big merger law firms, Wachtell and Skadden, Arps. The more disparate the sources of information, Levine reasoned, the less likely any pattern would emerge in their insider trading, and the more money they'd make.

Wilkis wondered if "Wally" had been ensnared by Levine, but knew better than to pursue the matter on the phone. "We've got to get busy," Levine continued. Now that he knew something was afoot at Lazard, Levine wanted Wilkis to find out what it was. He'd even been pressing Wilkis to break into Lazard offices and look through files, and he renewed his plea. "It's easy," Levine said. "Go through the desks."

Wilkis shuddered at the prospect. "I can't do it, Dennis," he insisted. "It's too risky."

"Then I'll have to do it myself," Levine said impatiently. "I'll meet you at your office tonight."

Levine arrived around 8 P.M. It was a Friday evening, and the Lazard offices were deserted. Levine seemed relaxed, in command. He began sweeping through the offices, going through papers on desks, opening drawers and files, examining the diaries and Rolodexes of partners he knew. He even stopped to admire a cache of Cuban cigars in partner Louis Perlmutter's office.

Wilkis was petrified, hovering in the corridors while Levine searched, anxiously looking toward the entrances. How would he explain this if someone came in? Suddenly he heard a noise at the door and saw the knob turn, and his heart leaped. "Dennis," he whispered, trying to alert him. But it was a cleaning woman, who passed them without showing any interest.

Finally Levine found what he wanted: a cache of documents outlining the acquisition of Kerr-McGee, a large oil company, by the French oil giant Elf Aquitaine. If it happened, it would be the largest takeover ever, a tremendous opportunity to profit from inside information. Levine quickly copied the documents and returned them to the file. "See how easy this was?" Levine laughed as he and Wilkis fled the offices for the weekend.

Levine was thrilled with his haul from Lazard. Besides the documents on the Elf Aquitaine bid, he had found, and photocopied, a seating chart showing the position of every investment banker at Lazard. Now, armed with as little as a tip from "Wally" about who from Lazard was working on a still-secret matter, he could target the exact desk likely to hold confidential documents identifying the target and suitor, minimizing the time needed for the theft. And Levine was confident that he was about to fully ensnare "Wally" in the scheme.

Ilan Reich hurried across Manhattan's Grand Army Plaza. The square in front of the Plaza Hotel, bustling with Saturday shoppers, seemed like the crossroads of the Western world. Reich took up a position under the Plaza's multicolored flags, flapping in an unusually warm late-March breeze.

Reich paced nervously, wondering just what he was getting himself into. He'd been a lawyer at Wachtell, Lipton less than a year, but he was already making over $40,000, more than just about any other associate with his seniority in New York. Why was he risking his career? Before he could think further, Levine was at his side, all smiles, all reassurances. He even remembered to ask about Reich's family.

The two men walked across 59th Street and went into Central Park, strolling past a small lake, and sat down on a bench overlooking the ice-skating rink. Late-morning skaters swirled around the rink; the Plaza loomed in the distance, towering above bushes and trees just turning green.

Reich had promised Levine inside information on the phone the previous day, but now Levine didn't push. He reminded Reich that the scheme was foolproof; he promised to handle all of Reich's trading in an account that wouldn't even bear the young lawyer's name. He'd start Reich with $20,000, and execute the same trading strategies he was using himself. Whenever Reich wanted cash, all he had to do was ask. Levine would pass it on to Reich.

Reich seemed convinced. He told Levine that a secret takeover bid was in the works for a large American oil company, Kerr-McGee. Reich wasn't working on the deal, but its size had generated much attention and comment at Wachtell. It was going to be the first hostile takeover bid ever to top the $1 billion mark. Wachtell was working with Lazard, which had been retained by Elf Aquitaine to explore the possibility of a bid for Kerr-McGee. Now it looked like the deal was going forward. He thought Levine would be dazzled by the intelligence.

Reich was wrong. Levine played the moment as high drama, putting his arm over the back of the bench and leaning toward Reich. "I know," Levine said gently, smiling at Reich. He proceeded to reel off financial data he'd absorbed from the purloined Lazard documents, proving that he already knew even more about the transaction than Reich did. Reich was astonished. Levine must have been right when he said everybody was already spreading inside information! Levine reassured Reich that the Kerr-McGee tip was the kind of information that could be useful to them, but that Reich would have to do better. He'd have to be discreet, but he needed to gain access to confidential information that wasn't already the subject of rumors.

Levine's technique worked beautifully. Reich had always been competitive, struggling constantly to catch up to his older brother Yaron. As he left Levine in the park, Reich vowed that he'd prove himself to his new partner. He'd produce better, more useful information the next time. Once Reich set his mind on something, he'd almost always achieved it.

Law review at Columbia, for example. Yaron, a year and a half older than Ilan, had excelled at Columbia Law School, and was chosen for the prestigious law review on the basis of his high first-year grades. Ilan's grades were good, but not as good as Yaron's. He entered the writing competition for those students not chosen on the basis of grades. He didn't make it. In a virtually unprecedented effort, Ilan entered the writing competition again a year later, as a second-year student. Yaron helped him write his entry. This time he was chosen.

Like Wilkis, Reich had grown up in an orthodox Jewish home. His father was born in Poland and emigrated to Israel before World War II, moving to the U.S. in 1950. He earned a comfortable living as an optometrist, and the family lived in a middle-class Jewish neighborhood in Midwood, Brooklyn. Ilan's mother earned a PhD and taught English at City University. Reich attended a yeshiva where half of each day was spent studying religion. Apart from Judaism, academic performance was the most important of the family's values.

Reich was socially awkward. He had made few friends at Columbia, spent weekends at home, and studied hard, leaving no time for any extracurricular activities. When a girlfriend broke off with him after his freshman year, he felt suicidal, and began seeing a psychiatrist. He became increasingly estranged from his family, discarding their orthodox Jewish values without any clear sense of what might replace them.

Reich had been new at Wachtell when he first met Levine. He had been working full-time at the firm less than a month when, in October 1979, he was assigned to the friendly acquisition of one cement company by another. It was fairly routine work. Wachtell represented the acquiring company's investment bankers, Smith Barney. During a break in negotiations, Reich noticed one of the Smith Barney bankers who was working the group of less than a dozen lawyers and bankers, shaking hands, chatting, seeming to know everyone by name. Finally he reached Reich. "Hi, I'm Dennis Levine," he said.

Several months later, in March 1980, Reich answered his phone and was surprised to hear Levine on the other end. "Hey Ilan, it's Dennis Levine. Let's have lunch." Reich was flattered by the invitation. No one ever asked him to have lunch.

Reich had a great time at the lunch. He loved discussing deals, and Levine seemed to hang on his remarks, complimenting him on his M&A judgment and his acumen. Levine told Reich about his own family background, his wife, his frustrations at Smith Barney. Levine's confessions resonated with Reich, who had just gotten married himself. He understood Levine's family milieu, and he often felt frustrated and underappreciated at Wachtell.

Levine told Reich that he had big ambitions: he planned to earn from $10 million to $20 million fast, then set up his own operation, maybe as a corporate raider. Then he, Levine, would have the lawyers and investment bankers like himself and Reich working for him.

"How are you going to make that kind of money?" Reich asked.

Levine leaned forward. "There's a lot of money to be made in information," he said. "Look at the arbitrageurs. They're trading in it. Look at investment bankers. Everyone's doing it." He paused. "Wachtell is really a clearinghouse" for some of the most valuable information, he said. "You could make a lot of money with that information if you shared it with me."

The tone of the conversation had suddenly shifted. Reich looked gravely at Levine. He knew what he wanted, and he knew it was a crime. He protested half-heartedly that he was too junior at the firm to have much access to the intelligence Levine would need. He hoped Levine would just drop the subject; he didn't want to lose his new friend. But Levine insisted that Reich would be valuable and said that the scheme would be virtually risk-free. "I'll think about it," Reich finally conceded.

Levine called Reich often, assuring him that he knew all about Swiss secrecy provisions and the mechanics of trading through foreign nominee accounts. When Reich protested—he knew that even nominee accounts have at least one piece of paper with the name of the real owner on it—Levine volunteered to maintain an account for Reich in Levine's name. They had lunch again; Levine flattered Reich about his prowess at deals. He underscored his refrain that "Everyone is doing it," repeating the allegation he had made to Wilkis that Tom Hill was trading on deals leaked by others. "I riffled through his desk," Levine claimed. "I've got copies of Hill's trading records to prove it."

Later that same week, Reich heard about the Elf-Kerr-McGee planning. He called Levine. "I've got something you'll be interested in," he said. Levine cautioned him to say no more on the phone. After learning of the Elf plans for Kerr-McGee from both Wilkis and Reich, Levine thought he had a sure bet, and he invested in Kerr-McGee stock. Ironically, the French government ended up dissuading Elf from pursuing such a large, hostile bid against an American company. Nothing happened. Kerr-McGee's stock price dropped, and Levine had to sell at a loss. The whole thing made Reich even more anxious; he felt he had to make it up to Levine.

Levine's other trades in his Pictet account, while relatively modest, had nonetheless shown a remarkable correlation to announcements of merger activity. When Pictet officials reviewed Levine's trading activity shortly after his Central Park outing with Reich, the pattern was clear: Levine took positions in stocks just before announcements of mergers and takeovers. The bank ordered his trading halted and told Levine to close his account. But the bank did nothing to alert any authorities of its suspicions. And Levine had no trouble shifting his account.

As he had advised Wilkis to do, Levine flew to the Bahamas on Memorial Day 1980. He interviewed a number of Swiss banks, with the exception of Crédit Suisse. For obvious reasons, he didn't want anyone comparing his and Wilkis's trading. He finally settled on Bank Leu International—Switzerland's oldest bank, which had only recently expanded into international operations and was eager to provide its services to wealthy foreigners trading in U.S. securities.

Levine had polished his scheme. He told Bank Leu officials politely but firmly that he would communicate his trading instructions by collect phone call. He would identify himself as "Mr. Diamond," (Diamond was his mother's maiden name), and the account should be maintained solely under that code name. He wanted fast, efficient execution of the orders, which should be spread among a variety of brokers. He wanted no communication with the bank except in person or unless he initiated it by collect phone call. They should hold all records and account statements at the bank. Would that be acceptable?

It was acceptable. Levine filled out a routine new account application, listing his real name and address, 225 East 57th Street; his profession, "banker"; awarding his father a power of attorney. He signed it with his real name. A photocopy of his passport photo was stapled to the form so that bank employees could identify him if he wanted to make cash withdrawals. Even by Swiss banking standards, Levine's emphasis on privacy seemed extreme. One of the Bank Leu officials, Jean-Pierre Fraysse, wrote a memo to the file after opening the account, noting that "Mr. Diamond" seemed "obsessed by security" and that trading in his account would bear close watching. Several days later, $128,900 was wired into his new account at Bank Leu in two separate transfers. Just over half came from Levine's defunct Pictet account, suggesting modest gains on his earlier efforts at insider trading. The other $60,000 came from Levine's father, Philip, who had taken the money from under his bed and given it to his son as a "loan."

Levine's first big score came a few months later. Reich, eager to rehabilitate himself with Levine, came through with a surefire deal in September. A Wachtell client, Jefferson National Life Insurance, was going to be acquired in a friendly transaction by a larger insurance company. Levine was impressed; he took almost everything he had in the Bank Leu account and bought 8,000 shares of Jefferson National stock on September 24. As Reich had anticipated, the merger was announced two days later. Jefferson's stock price climbed. Levine sold immediately, making a fast profit of over $150,000.

None of this interfered with Levine's trading on his own deals at Smith Barney. He badgered Hill to assign him to more M&A transactions, and finally Hill put him on a tender offer by Tyler Corporation, a longstanding Smith Barney client, for Reliance Universal Inc. Levine, in defiance of all the Smith Barney trading restrictions, brazenly bought 5,000 shares of Reliance on April 7, 1981, less than a week before the deal was announced. He earned over $45,000 on that trade.

Reich rapidly became Levine's most valuable source. He kept up a reliable flow of information, always calling to invite Levine for lunch. Sometimes they'd meet at restaurants, other times they'd just grab slices of pizza and talk as they walked along busy midtown sidewalks. Levine loved the arrangement: when he traded in non–Smith Barney deals, he didn't feel constrained to take small positions. His profits swelled. Most of the tips he also passed on to Wilkis.

Reich was still ambivalent. When Levine invited him to a dinner party at his apartment where others from the "game" would be present, Reich was furious. He said that he didn't want to know the identities of other collaborators, and didn't want them to know him either. He worried that Levine was getting careless. By this time, he'd concluded from their many conversations about takeovers that his partner wasn't all that bright.

Levine sensed his reluctance. He tried to draw Reich further into the scheme. He encouraged him to set up his own trading account and urged him to withdraw some of his accumulated profits. Levine told Wilkis at one point that he was tempted to take a wad of hundred-dollar bills and throw them at Reich during one of their lunches. Levine wanted Reich to taste real money to motivate and excite him.

Reich continued to resist, but Levine was also becoming less dependent on his Wachtell source. During the summer of 1981, he made more progress in assembling a ring of collaborators. Ira Sokolow, the promising young investment banker who had worked with Levine the previous summer at Smith Barney, had graduated from Harvard and had gone to work at Lehman Brothers Kuhn Loeb. The firm had an active M&A practice. Levine invited him to lunch.

The script was the same as with Reich and Wilkis. Levine emphasized that "everybody" was trading on inside information and that his scheme was foolproof. He offered Sokolow an arrangement similar to his deal with Reich. Levine would handle the trading; Sokolow would get a cut of the profits. Sokolow, bored with the tedium of his early investment banking assignments at Lehman, proved to be the easiest convert. He still looked up to Levine from his days as a summer intern. He readily signed on and began providing information.

At one of their lunches, Sokolow reported to Levine that he had a close friend, a lawyer, working at Goldman, Sachs in the firm's mortgage department that he'd like to bring into the game. Levine was thrilled at the prospect of a mole in Goldman; he promised Sokolow a cut of the trading profits for his friend, too, but cautioned him not to reveal the friend's identity, even to him. Sokolow's source's code name would be "Goldie." He would prove an even more fruitful source, cheerfully riffling through Goldman partners' "in" boxes for clues to pending merger deals. Levine taunted Wilkis, pointing out how much more effective the other members of the ring were proving to be. "Lehman," Levine gleefully reported to Wilkis, "is an animal! He's devoted. He's committed." He added caustically, "Unlike you."

Later that year, 1981, Levine got the career break he'd been hoping for.

Eric Gleacher, head of M&A at Lehman Brothers, glanced down at the résumé of the investment banker he was scheduled to interview, halfway pleased to see it wasn't the usual Ivy League hot shot. Gleacher is an intense, hard-driving banker. He'd attended Western Illinois University in the small town of Macomb.

When Levine arrived, dressed in his best dark pin-striped suit (as coached by Wilkis), he went straight to the point. "I want a better firm than Smith Barney," he said. "Smith Barney is second-tier; Lehman Brothers is the big leagues. I've always wanted M&A but I couldn't get a job." Gleacher glanced again at the résumé, noting the almost stereotypically Jewish urban background. "I only went to Citibank to get a credential: I really wanted Wall Street," Levine pressed.

Gleacher was impressed by Levine's candor. Lehman Brothers had a history of hiring people who didn't fit conventional molds; the firm was proud of its willingness to take risks. Gleacher had hired Steven Rattner, for example, a reporter from *The New York Times* with no investment banking experience whatsoever, and in Gleacher's view, he had turned into a star. Lehman had taken a chance on Gleacher himself, hiring him right out of business school.

Lehman was anxious to expand its overworked M&A department. Levine at least had some experience and had been recommended by Sokolow. They'd bring him in at the bottom at a low salary—less than $50,000 a year—and take a look. If he was great, he'd be rewarded at bonus time. If not, he could at least process deals. Gleacher saw no downside. After Levine had been interviewed by several other people in the department, Gleacher made him an offer with the title of full vice president, the rank he'd been denied at Smith Barney. Levine accepted eagerly.

He couldn't wait to tell Wilkis about his new job. He wasn't worried that Sokolow was already at the firm; they'd still need Sokolow's access to deals Levine wasn't involved in. And he relished the prospect that he'd "throw it up in Hill's face," as he told Wilkis. When the encounter finally happened, Levine was subdued, having decided that he shouldn't burn bridges to anyone in the relatively small world of M&A. He came into Hill's office, sat down, and simply said he was leaving for a job at Lehman Brothers. Hill was neither surprised nor concerned. After their frank discussion at Levine's previous bonus review, he hadn't really expected Levine to stay. He didn't make Levine a counteroffer, and wished him well.

A few weeks earlier, on October 30, Levine had flown to the Bahamas, charging his airfare to his Smith Barney expense account. He'd opened another account at Bank Leu even more secretive than his first, using a Panamanian corporation he'd created with nominee directors. Nothing about "Diamond Holdings" suggested that Levine was the beneficial owner. He had transferred the growing funds from his individual account to the new corporate entity's. He had also taken the opportunity to withdraw $30,000 in $100 bills, which he had stuffed into a plastic shopping bag for transport back to the U.S. He carried it around with him, spending the cash on restaurants, clothes, taxis, gifts. The cash seemed to give him confidence. It was, he told Wilkis, his "walking-around money."

Gleacher liked to haze his new recruit. Soon after Levine arrived at Lehman, Gleacher called him into his office and announced that a Lehman client was about to make one of the largest tender offers in history. Levine had never heard of the target. Gleacher wanted Levine to find an example of a similar tender offer. Levine was at a loss. He rushed around the office, frantically looking for help. Suddenly Gleacher, known as "the colonel" for his stern military bearing, appeared at his office door, looking at his watch. "You've got 30 minutes, Dennis," he called out. "It is absolutely critical that you produce this."

A half hour later, Levine—flushed, sweating, looking stricken—told Gleacher he hadn't been able to find any precedent. He hadn't even been able to identify the target company or its lines of business. As he spoke, a small crowd of Lehman investment bankers quietly gathered outside Gleacher's office. "Jesus, Levine!" Gleacher shouted. "Can't you do anything?"

With this, the onlooking bankers burst into laughter, none louder than Peter Solomon, the Lehman partner whose office was next to Levine's. Gleacher had made up the whole thing.

Levine laughed along with the others, and complained only to Wilkis. In only a matter of months, he became the buffoon of Lehman's M&A department. Gleacher concluded that Levine was all but worthless in any conventional investment banking sense. His analytical skills were weak; he couldn't pull the structure of complex deals together. He wasn't even particularly well organized. His defects were even more glaring at Lehman than they had been at Smith Barney. And the deals were bigger and more frequent.

Young investment bankers at Lehman depended on more senior people to assign them work. Levine was popular in the office. His affable demeanor, his often vulgar jokes, his eagerness to be liked, were, for many, a refreshing change from the arrogant, sophisticated demeanor of so many of his counterparts. Some of the other bankers referred to him as *"bubeleh,"* a Yiddish term meaning something like "sweetie-pie" in English. He was constantly running to get partners coffee or sodas. But popularity wasn't getting him assignments.

Then, just four months after Levine's arrival at Lehman, a memo was circulated: Lehman was bringing in the head of M&A from another firm as a partner. The new partner was Tom Hill. When Levine saw the memo, he grabbed a notebook from a desk and threw it as hard as he could against a wall. He was still furious that night when he spoke to Wilkis. He vowed that he was going to "destroy" Hill.

Hill was no more impressed with Levine than he had ever been. He never enlisted him in any of his deals, but relied on Sokolow, whom he cautioned about his friendship with Levine. Sokolow warned Levine to "watch out" for Hill.

Then Reich came to Levine's rescue. In early August 1982 he called Levine with a lunch invitation, indicating he had information. Wachtell, he explained to Levine when they met, was representing a private investor group, Dyson-Kissner-Moran Corporation, which was putting together a bid for Seattle-based Criton Corporation.

Levine raced back to the office and went straight to Gleacher, looking as if he were about to burst. There was heavy activity in Criton stock, he told Gleacher, saying his "reading of the tape" suggested a tender offer was imminent. Gleacher was skeptical. No one else at Lehman had heard any rumors. There was modestly higher volume in the stock, but hardly anything major. "We've got to pitch the defense," Levine insisted. "There's going to be a bid." Gleacher shrugged and told him to go ahead and make contact with Criton.

Much to Gleacher's surprise, Levine came back triumphant. Criton was sending its general counsel to New York to interview investment bankers for a possible defense. Levine had gotten an appointment for Lehman.

Now Gleacher began to take the matter seriously. He met with Criton's general counsel and landed the business. Gleacher and Levine, as well as Sokolow, who was enlisted to handle the serious valuation work, flew to Seattle to meet with the company chairman. Later, Gleacher met alone with John Moran, leading the buyout group. Using Lehman's valuations, Gleacher managed to get Moran to boost his bid substantially, to $46 a share. Criton capitulated, happy at the rich price, and the deal was announced. For little more than one day of intense work, Lehman's investment banking fee—traceable directly to Levine's tip—was $2.5 million.

Suddenly the buffoon was a hero. Gleacher arranged for Levine to have a Quotron computer terminal so he could monitor trading activity in scores of stocks at once. He would get immediate news announcements, and wouldn't have to bother with the actual ticker tape. With a 30-foot cord on his telephone, Levine could roam as he worked the phone, broadening his circle of arbitrageurs and other potential sources of deal intelligence. And Levine was freed from the analytical work he hated, and encouraged to spend his time trying to generate new clients. His colleagues on the same level of seniority resented this, but Levine was happier than he'd ever been. He was carving out a niche in investment banking that had not existed before: he was someone who used information to hustle clients.

Levine had other reasons to celebrate the Criton deal. On August 17, a week before the deal was announced, and even before he had approached Gleacher about landing Criton as a client, Levine had bought 27,000 shares of Criton. His trading profit was his largest yet, $212,628.

Levine was quick to grasp the implications of his Criton score. The beauty of "the game," he told Wilkis, was that it could be played two ways. He could trade on the information, and he could also use it to land clients for Lehman.

Stardom, however, depended on keeping his ring of informants together, and there were problems. Reich had been the first to waver. He was torn between the thrill and the remorse.

Then Reich got a jolt at his firm. On a Wednesday morning in early September 1981, every partner, associate, paralegal, and secretary in Wachtell's offices was called into a meeting to be briefed on the shocking news that a 37-year-old Wachtell partner, Carlo Florentino, had been arrested, charged with insider trading, and dismissed by the firm. Florentino had amassed $600,000 in an E. F. Hutton account using his own name, trading in deals he had learned about at the firm.

Reich knew his arrangement with Levine was far more sophisticated, but the news was still terrifying. He decided to stop passing information to Levine. He even went so far as to mislead Levine about two deals, hoping Levine would lose so much that he'd stop. "This may be risk-free, but it's also return-free," Reich said sarcastically to Levine at one of their lunches. But Levine couldn't be stopped. He assured Reich that they'd learned from their mistakes and would do better. Reich tried not returning his phone calls. Finally, in August 1982, Reich broke the news that he wanted out of the arrangement. He didn't want any of the money that Levine tried to press on him. But, he assured him, he wanted to remain friends.

"Can you believe it?" Levine complained to Wilkis, "Wally wants out!"

"Don't push him," Wilkis advised. Reich and Levine continued their lunches, but the flow of inside information dried up.

Soon after, Wilkis got a bad scare of his own. That summer, Jean-Pierre Fraysse at Bank Leu had mentioned to Levine that the bank's brokers had received an SEC inquiry about trading in some of the same stocks that "Mr. Diamond" had bought and sold in his account. Levine dismissed the SEC inquiries as routine monitoring. Fraysse was well aware of the uncanny timing of many of Mr. Diamond's purchases, but had done nothing to discourage him. He now suggested that Mr. Diamond might want to slow down his trading, and spread his buying out more, at least temporarily. Levine ignored those suggestions, confident of the secrecy of his account; soon thereafter, he bought his huge stake in Criton.

Wilkis's bank, Crédit Suisse, had also heard from its brokers about the SEC's interest, and had notified Wilkis. Wilkis took the news to Levine, who told him, "Just tell them to lie. It's routine." But Crédit Suisse was not so blasé, nor nearly so amenable as Bank Leu had been. The bank's Bahamas chairman, Dr. Joseph Morger, called Wilkis and told him he wanted Wilkis to waive his rights to bank secrecy. The suggestion chilled Wilkis. He said he'd come to the Bahamas to meet with bank officials.

Morger was tall and stern, an old-style Swiss banker. He was the dean of the Bahamas banking establishment. He had Wilkis's trading records on the desk in front of him when Wilkis arrived.

"You work at Lehman Brothers?" he began sharply. The correlation between Wilkis's stocks and Lehman was obvious.

"No," Wilkis replied uncomfortably.

"That's curious." Morger paused. "For all this trading, you certainly haven't done very well, have you?" Indeed, Wilkis had showed an almost uncanny ability to trade on the tips that ended up losing money and investing only small amounts in the winners. Morger folded the papers and looked at Wilkis. "Take your business elsewhere."

Wilkis was terrified. He withdrew $40,000 in cash and had the bank wire the rest to his law firm in New York. He wanted nothing more to do with Swiss banks. The whole scheme was crazy. Here he was risking his career, his reputation, and he could have been making as much money investing in bonds at the 16% interest rates that were available. He had a wife and two children. He couldn't live with the anxiety. He resolved to confront Levine.

Back in New York, he called Levine and made a rare visit to his office. He hurried in, looking agitated, closed the door, and sat down. "It's over, Dennis. It stinks. Laws are being broken." He was near tears. "I'm not made for this."

Levine was calm. "That's too bad, Bob," he said. "The game's been good to me. I have a million dollars now. I'm where I want to be." Levine leaned over on the desk. "How are you doing at Lazard? Are they taking care of you?" Levine knew the answer, of course. Wilkis wasn't doing particularly well. He was stuck in international when the big money was in corporate finance and M&A. His self-esteem had been slipping.

"The game is fun, Bob, it's easy," Levine continued. "The government is stupid. Nobody with any brains is in that operation. They only make thirty grand, if that." Levine gauged the impact of his words, then leaned back and pulled open a desk drawer. He took a small paperback book and threw it at Wilkis. "Go down to the Cayman Islands."

The book was a compact airline flight guide. Wilkis stared at it, then looked at Levine. Something had changed in their relationship. It was Levine who now seemed poised, self-assured, and Wilkis who needed him.

A week later Wilkis arrived in the Cayman Islands. He deposited $86,000 in cash in his new account, also code-named "Rupearl," at the Bank of Nova Scotia.

3.

West 67th Street between Central Park West and Columbus Avenue is one of Manhattan's prettiest tree-lined blocks, home to one of the city's venerable eateries, the Café des Artistes. Ivan Boesky arrived at the restaurant in 1976 to meet, for the first time, a young Wall Street trader named John Mulheren. In keeping with the restaurant's genteel, old-world character, nearly all of its male patrons wear jacket and tie, as, of course, did Boesky.

Mulheren showed up in a bright knit polo shirt and khaki trousers. Tall and solidly built, with tousled sandy-colored hair and a friendly Irish countenance, he looked, at age 27, like an overgrown college kid. He'd shown up for his job interview at Merrill Lynch, where he was now helping to develop an arbitrage department, in a variation of the same outfit, and the casual look had become his trademark. Not even arm-twisting by Salim B. "Sandy" Lewis, the Merrill Lynch official who hired him, could get him to wear a suit for a night on the town, not even with Boesky, whom Lewis had deemed a genius. Mulheren and his wife Nancy entered the crowded restaurant, joining Lewis and his wife and Boesky and Seema. There was little in Mulheren's own middle-class Catholic background that he felt Boesky could identify with; but Boesky quickly showed an almost obsessive interest in the new techniques Mulheren was applying to arbitrage. Mulheren had become, in only a few years, one of Wall Street's savviest traders of stock options, a subject Boesky knew much less about. Options trading permits much greater leverage than buying stock on margin. Leverage was like catnip to Boesky, and he was mesmerized by the possibilities inherent in Mulheren's strategies.

Mulheren was a whiz at options trading and analysis, even though he'd had an unremarkable academic record as a political science major at Roanoke College, a small liberal arts college in Virginia. Looking for a job after graduation, he had only landed on Wall Street because his wife baby-sat for an official at a now-defunct firm. There he had dazzled his colleagues by developing one of the first computer programs for options analysis. He had been recruited to join Merrill Lynch by Lewis and no less a personage than Merrill Lynch's chairman, Donald Regan, the future White House chief of staff and secretary of the treasury under President Reagan.

Mulheren was also intrigued by Boesky. Mulheren had always considered himself to be something of a nonconformist and a renegade, but even he had to concede that Boesky was peculiar in a big way. When the Café des Artistes waiter came to take their order, Boesky said he hadn't decided and that the others should make their selections. Then Boesky ordered: "I'll have every entrée." The waiter's pen stopped in midair. Boesky repeated his order. "Bring me each one of these entrées."

Mulheren glanced at his wife, raising his eyebrows slightly. Seema chatted on as though nothing unusual had happened. Mulheren wondered whether this was how rich people ate.

When the food arrived, the waiter wheeled a table next to them. On it were the eight featured dishes of the day. Boesky looked them over carefully, circled the table, took one bite of each. He selected one, and sent the rest back.

Boesky only picked at his food. Mulheren was relieved that he didn't have to pick up the check.

But the dinner launched a close professional relationship, and a friendship, between Boesky and Mulheren. When Mulheren and Nancy had a belated wedding reception for 500 people a year later at their home in Rumson, N.J., Boesky was present. The Mulherens went to the bar mitzvah of Boesky's eldest son and the bat mitzvah of his daughter.

Soon after the dinner, Lewis went to work with Boesky—but less than a year later, he had fallen from favor with the arbitrageur, and Boesky ordered Lewis out of his offices. They argued over $250,000 in disputed earnings. Boesky called Mulheren to ask him what he should do. "Pay him the money, Ivan," Mulheren said. "What does it matter?"

Boesky thought for a moment. "I can't," he said. "It's not the money I care about, it's the principle."

"Don't give me that crap," Mulheren replied. "The money *is* your principle."

Soon, however, $250,000 would seem a pittance to both Boesky and Mulheren. America was on the eve of the greatest takeover boom in its history, one that would bring both of them riches they'd never dreamed of.

The causes of the boom were probably as much psychological as financial, though many economic explanations have been offered to explain the sudden, almost frenzied effort to buy existing companies rather than create new ones. Throughout the 1970s, investors had focused on company earnings, and the corresponding price/earnings ratios, as a measure of value. With an economy ravaged by post-Vietnam War and OPEC-induced inflation, high tax rates, and soaring interest rates, profits had been meager. So stock prices stayed low even as inflation pushed the value of income-producing assets ever higher.

Coupled with low-priced assets was the tax code's very generous treatment of interest payments on debt. Corporate dividends paid on stock aren't deductible; interest payments on debt are fully deductible. Buying assets with borrowed funds meant shifting much of the cost to the federal government. The election of Ronald Reagan in 1980 sent a powerful "anything goes" message to the financial markets. One of the first official acts of the Reagan Justice Department was to drop the government's massive ten-year antitrust case against IBM. Bigness apparently wasn't going to be a problem in the new era of unbridled capitalism. Suddenly, economies of scale could be realized in already oligopolistic industries such as oil, where mergers wouldn't even have been considered in the Carter years.

What really fueled the takeover boom was the sight of other people making money, big money, by buying companies and selling them. When the former secretary of the treasury (under Nixon and Ford) William Simon bought Gibson Greetings in 1982 and then resold it sixteen months later at a profit of $70 million (investors earned 100 times their initial investment), Wall Street couldn't stop talking. Suddenly "cash flow," needed to support interest payments or "asset value" in the event of a breakup of a company, became the bywords of valuation, replacing the quaint, dated notion of earnings. Corporate raiders began to emerge, realizing that just about anybody could buy a company, slash expenses or break off pieces ruthlessly, and then unload the assets at a huge gain. The next best thing to buying and selling companies, and much less risky, was to be the investment banker, lawyer, or arbitrageur standing by as the money changed hands.

In 1981, when Conoco, then America's ninth-largest oil company, was acquired by du Pont for a staggering $7.8 billion, the takeover frenzy really started to kick in. The deal, the biggest in history by far, involved no less than four competing suitors—Dome Petroleum, Mobil, the Seagram Co., and du Pont. All needed armies of investment bankers and lawyers. Practically every major firm on Wall Street was eventually swept in. It was an arbitrage dream: Conoco's stock traded at under $50 when the imbroglio began in May with a hostile bid from Dome of $65. It rose steadily before du Pont finally won the bidding in August, offering $98 a share.

For an arbitrageur, there was almost no way to lose money on such a deal, but Boesky's performance, drawing on every bit of intelligence at his disposal, was awesome. He drove his lawyers at Fried, Frank, led by Stephen Fraidin, to produce research on legal questions, including complicated antitrust issues with respect to Mobil. He was on the phone constantly to Mulheren and other arbitrageurs, watching volume and trading patterns in the stock, sniffing out clues for the next, invariably higher bids. And he backed his information with money, throwing everything the young Boesky Corporation had into Conoco stock, using maximum leverage. Had he miscalculated, the firm could have been ruined. As it turned out, Boesky doubled his capital in that single deal, earning profits of nearly $40 million. It was an intoxicating experience for Boesky and his colleagues.

Mulheren had also thrived in the new environment. He had always dreamed of making a lot of money, and having people say "He made it honestly." His dream, it seemed, had come true, even before the Conoco windfall.

At Merrill Lynch, Mulheren had become a multi-millionaire before he was 30. In 1980, he bought a sprawling Victorian house on the waterfront in exclusive Rumson, New Jersey, previously occupied by Francis Cardinal Spellman; it had been bequeathed to the Church by a wealthy parishioner. His mother told Mulheren he was spending too much money. "How do you know I'm spending too much money," Mulheren said, "if you don't know how much money I have?"

"It's $400,000!" she exclaimed. "That's too much money!"

Mulheren moved his operations to Spear Leeds & Kellogg, the largest specialist firm on the New York Stock Exchange, which also had an active trading and arbitrage operation. Spear Leeds occupied the former Lawyers' Club on lower Broadway in Manhattan, and Mulheren installed his trading desk directly under a huge Gothic stained-glass window.

He reveled in the pleasures that money brought him. He gave away large amounts, to his alma mater, Roanoke College, to local charities, and to any other charity he was asked to benefit. He made it a policy: If anyone asked him to give, he would, no questions asked. Mulheren and his wife adopted five children, three of them with learning disabilities. He bought a local beach club, a 6,000-acre farm in the mountains of Virginia which he stocked with a herd of buffalo, and a winter home in Fort Lauderdale. Sometimes he commuted to Wall Street in his sleek power speedboat, docking at the South Street Seaport. He hunted, he collected antiques, he took up jet-skiing and snow skiing. By the early 1980s, he had reached the point where he couldn't even say for sure how much money he made; it was all handled by accountants and lawyers. He simply told them to stop him if he was spending too much. They never did.

Mulheren also delighted in his role as the enfant terrible of the arbitrage and trading communities. He loved to do battle with the arbs, most of whom he considered fat and lazy, and boasted that he usually "ate them for lunch." One of his favorite pranks was to initiate heavy buying or selling about a half hour before a major market announcement, such as an antitrust court ruling that might make or break a merger deal, was due. In fact, Mulheren would have no idea about the outcome, but the sudden activity coming across the tape would suggest that he had advance knowledge. Arbs would go crazy, especially Boesky. "What did you find out?" he'd ask breathlessly. "What do you know?"

"Nothing," Mulheren would calmly reply. "I just did this to fuck people's minds."

"You're insane!" Boesky would scream. "You're so juvenile." Then he would hang up. Mulheren would roar with laughter.

On days when the market was weak, he loved to start dumping large arbitrage positions, knowing it would drive down the stock prices and torture other arbs sitting on large positions. Other arbs would flood him with calls, seeking information; generally he ignored them. Then, when he began to see some panic selling on their part, he'd step back in and rebuild his position at lower prices.

Mulheren made it a point never to talk to investment bankers. He thought they were arrogant, pompous, and of little use to him. Either they'd lie to him, which was worthless, or they'd give him inside information, which was illegal. Once he got a message that Siegel had called. He ignored it. He also shunned the press.

Boesky was different. Mulheren shared information with Boesky to an extent he would allow with few other market professionals. The two of them spoke nearly every day, and Mulheren always returned Boesky's calls. Almost from the time they'd first met, Mulheren had wanted Boesky to like him. Beneath his rebelliousness, Mulheren had always wanted to be liked by most people. It made him feel good to give Boesky information. Over time, Mulheren had become a major trader for large blocks of stock, so he often knew the identity of major buyers and sellers. This was invaluable arbitrage information, since the identity of buyers often suggested whether a hostile bid might be in the works or whether it was a staid purchaser, like a state retirement fund, unlikely to provoke any action. And Boesky still relied on Mulheren for options expertise. Boesky rewarded Mulheren, in turn, by steering much of his trading through Mulheren's firm, which therefore earned the commissions on the trades. Boesky became the firm's largest customer.

Yet their conversations were rarely about personal matters. Boesky thought everyone was motivated by one thing: money. Occasionally Boesky mentioned his children—his youngest, twins, had learning disabilities like some of Mulheren's children—but he never discussed what he really cared about in life. He didn't even discuss his sex life. That was unusual. In Mulheren's experience, everyone on Wall Street talked about their sex lives. Once, after a new water amusement park had opened near Mulheren's home in New Jersey, he told Boesky, "Ivan, I'm going to come kidnap you and take you down a water slide." There was dead silence.

Still, Boesky could be considerate. One Friday, with his wife in Florida with the kids, Mulheren was talking to Boesky on the phone, and Boesky insisted on having a car pick him up and drive him to Mt. Kisco for dinner. The other guests were Manhattan politician Andrew Stein, composer Jule Stein, comedian Alan King, and their wives. Boesky took Mulheren, a car buff, out to the garage to show him his new Rolls Royce Silver Cloud convertible, parked alongside his vintage Rolls Royce Phantom Five limousine.

On another occasion, Mulheren was having serious problems in his marriage, and confided in Boesky that he was contemplating divorce. "Don't," Boesky said. "Why don't you talk to my lifelong friend, Hushang Wekili? I've known him since I was fourteen. We went to school together. It's a very close relationship." Mulheren and Wekili met in the Palm Court of the Plaza Hotel. Wekili was slender, well-mannered, European-looking. He quizzed Mulheren about his marriage and personal life. "There are always conflicts," he said soothingly. "There are better solutions than divorce." Mulheren took his advice.

In May 1982, T. Boone Pickens, one of the first of the big-time raiders, launched a hostile tender offer for Cities Service, another huge oil company, and it seemed like Conoco all over again. Several weeks later, Gulf Oil launched its own friendly bid of $63 a share as a "white knight" rescuer for Cities Service, which agreed to be taken over to escape the clutches of Pickens. Boesky plowed an amount equal to all his firm's capital—$70 million, 90% of it borrowed—into Cities Service stock, and confidently settled back for the bidding frenzy and profits he'd experienced in Conoco. Lance Lessman, handling the research, thought it was a deal "I'd put my grandmother in."

Late on Friday, August 6, Lessman saw Boesky stride out of his office, a look of alarm on his face. He told Lessman he'd just heard a rumor that Gulf, citing antitrust concerns, was withdrawing from the Cities Service deal. The New York Stock Exchange had just closed, but trading in Cities Service stock on the Pacific Stock Exchange (which stays open until 4:30 P.M. Eastern time) and on the so-called private "third market" was ominous; the stock was plunging, dropping $4 to $8 a share.

The microphones around the office came to life. "Put all engines on max," Boesky shouted. The traders rolled into action, frantically calling West Coast market-makers such as Jefferies & Co. to try to find buyers for some of the huge Boesky position or to try to hedge the position. Then an announcement came clattering over the ticker, confirming the worst: Gulf was pulling out! All buying interest evaporated. Boesky was stuck with a huge stake that had just plummeted in value. Worse, margin calls were already pouring in, demanding full repayment of the money borrowed to buy the shares.

Boesky Corporation was in dire straits. It had nowhere near the cash to meet the margin calls, even if it liquidated all its other stock holdings. Worse, Boesky had $20 million in unsecured loans from banks: $5 million each from Chase Manhattan and Chemical banks, and $10 million from two European banks. The loans were callable, for any reason, and the banks would almost certainly get wind of Boesky's crisis. Then there was the New York Stock Exchange and the SEC. While much would depend on the price of Gulf stock when trading resumed on Monday, in all likelihood Boesky would be insolvent and in violation of regulatory capital requirements. The firm might be liquidated.

When he left the office that night for emergency meetings with the lawyers and accountants, Boesky was pale but calm and uncharacteristically quiet. His mood worried Lessman, who called him at home in Mt. Kisco that night. Surprisingly, he seemed collected, even dignified in defeat. "That's the game," he said. "That's how it goes." Lessman, trying to make him feel better, pointed out that the investment had been a sound one: Gulf's antitrust problem was insignificant, clearly just a pretext for a change of its mind. Lessman said, "It's like you decided to cross the street. The light was green, you walked—and then a building collapsed on you." Boesky seemed to like the analogy. He had Seema get on an extension and Lessman repeated it.

On Monday morning, Cities Service stock didn't open for trading because of an "order imbalance"; there were too many sellers and no buyers. The New York Stock Exchange specialists, who make markets in the listed stocks, weren't going to open trading until they knew they had a price that would attract buyers. That price depended, in large part, on what Boesky would do. Would margin calls force a massive liquidation of his position, driving the ultimate price even lower? At Boesky's offices, the suspense was palpable. Every position except for Cities Service was liquidated. Then everyone hovered around the ticker and watched their computer screens waiting for an opening price. Opening price "indications" dropped steadily, from $50 to $45, then even lower. Anything below $30 a share, they knew, would probably wipe them out.

With his own and his firm's fate hanging in the balance, Boesky embarked on a diplomatic offensive. Accompanied by his top lawyer, Fraidin, his outside accountant, Steven Oppenheim, and Setrag Mooradian, he called first on the four banks, urging—begging—them not to call in their loans. It was a delicate mission, since he didn't want to unduly alarm them by noting that calling the loans would render him insolvent. But Boesky was at his best, calm, articulate, confident that the investment in Cities Service stock would ultimately pay off. He managed to buy time.

Then the group traveled to the stock exchange to meet with regulators.

"What if the stock opens at $45?" an exchange official asked.

Mooradian did some hasty calculations. "We're OK," he replied.

"What about $40?"

"It's tight," Mooradian conceded.

"How about $30?"

Mooradian could see that Boesky was annoyed by the official's highhanded tone and 20-questions approach. "Look," Mooradian said, exasperated, "if the stock opens at zero, we will be out of business. And so will everyone else on the Street." The official curtly told them that they would be expected to meet the exchange's capital requirements and would get no special dispensation.

The group returned to Boesky's offices to wait. Finally, with only a half hour of trading left in the day, Cities Service stock opened—at $30, less than half of what Gulf had offered! At that price, no one knew for sure whether Boesky was insolvent, but the situation was dire. Boesky had to unload stock. Like so many times before, he was on the brink of failure.

There was only one person he thought he could turn to: John Mulheren. Like most arbitrageurs, Mulheren had a big position in

Cities Service, but he had had the foresight to hedge much of it through options trading, so he was in nowhere near the straits that Boesky was in. Boesky called Mulheren midafternoon that Monday.

"We have a major problem here," Boesky said, sounding grim. "Can you help us?"

"Well, what's the problem? I know you have a loss," Mulheren replied. Even though Boesky did most of his trading through Spear Leeds—Boesky was the firm's largest customer—Mulheren didn't have access to Boesky's positions, which were kept in confidence within the firm.

"I have to sell stock," Boesky said, without explaining the depth of the problem. Mulheren thought that Cities Service looked attractive at the new levels, so after consulting the firm's position, he said he'd take a million shares. Boesky balked, hesitating to sell once he realized Muheren wanted that much, but then agreed out of necessity to sell a block of 400,000 shares at just below $30 a share.

Within an hour, Boesky was back on the phone. "We are having major problems here," he said, asking to meet with Mulheren and his partners at Spear Leeds after the close of trading. "Think of some way I can get out of this position I have and meet requirements, because they tell me I'm having requirement problems." Boesky was beginning to sound desperate.

"Okay," Mulheren agreed. "I'll see what I can do."

Mulheren met with his partners, who were concerned for several reasons. The collapse of Boesky, given his huge positions, might trigger a selling panic that could damage Spear Leeds. And Boesky was the firm's largest client, so they had an interest in keeping him solvent.

At about 4:30 P.M., Boesky, Oppenheim, Fraidin, and Mooradian arrived, along with a stock exchange official.

"Can't you straighten this out?" Oppenheim asked Mulheren.

"I don't know any way out of this," Mulheren replied.

"Well, I've got a way to straighten it out," Oppenheim continued, turning to Boesky. "I've got the solution in my briefcase."

Oppenheim opened his briefcase, took out a Japanese ritual suicide knife, and handed it to Boesky. Boesky didn't laugh.

Three intense hours later, however, they had crafted a solution. Mulheren worked out a complicated series of options trades that had the effect of shifting any losses on further declines in Cities Service stock to Spear Leeds. That way, Boesky didn't need to liquidate the remainder of his position, sparing the market further selling pressure. In return, Mulheren gained the right to over half the profits from any gains in Boesky's Cities Service position. The stock exchange official agreed that the exchange would keep Boesky from being forced into liquidation, and that the arrangement should satisfy capital requirements.

Mulheren's and Boesky's faith in the underlying value of Cities Service stock proved correct. Despite the Gulf withdrawal, the Pickens bid had put the company "in play"—as Wall Street described companies that, once targeted, had little recourse but to capitulate or find a rescuer. Just two weeks later, Occidental Petroleum stepped in with a $58-a-share bid for Cities Service, and the stock price soared. Mulheren and Spear Leeds eventually made nearly $10 million from their Boesky rescue mission; Mulheren was hailed at the firm as a hero. The crisis cost Boesky an estimated $24 million in losses, or about a third of the firm's assets.

Boesky seemed briefly chastened by the brush with disaster. "You know," he told Mooradian as they were going over the books at the end of the month, "months like this teach you to be humble." He had Mooradian assemble some records relating to the deal and put them in a file to be labeled "Chartreuse." He told Mooradian to tell no one of the file's existence. He never mentioned it again, however, and eventually Mooradian threw it away.

The Cities Service debacle, however, did have a profound impact on Boesky. He felt strongly indebted to Mulheren; in Boesky's view, a favor of such magnitude was the true measure of friendship. He called Mulheren after the deal, and said, "I can't believe you did this for me." Soon after, he asked Mulheren if he would act as a co-trustee for his children's trust funds. Mulheren accepted; it was clear that, given the store Boesky set in his children, the offer was a tribute. Mulheren felt good about it. He was proud of being, as he put it, a "standup guy."

But Boesky had come, once again, to the brink of failure. He must have sensed that his nine lives were running out; not even his wife's family would tolerate yet another debacle, particularly at their expense. What maddened Boesky was that he was not at fault. No one could have predicted Gulf's about-face. Boesky's reasoning had been correct throughout, yet he had nearly been destroyed by events beyond his control.

The Friday night that Cities Service stock collapsed, the Boeskys had had a previously scheduled dinner party at the Mt. Kisco estate for Mulheren and several of his partners at Spear Leeds and their wives. Over cocktails in the pool house, the talk had turned to the debacle in the market, and Mulheren had said, "I hope this market doesn't break. It might kill us all." Seema had cut off the conversation. "As far as I'm concerned, this is never going to happen again." She repeated emphatically, "Never again."

Mulheren, knowing that much of the capital in Boesky's company was Seema's, had assumed that she meant she wasn't going to let Boesky risk so much money on a single deal.

But Boesky had other ideas. It was never going to happen again, all right. There were ways to control, even eliminate, the risk. There was no referee hovering over him to enforce the rules, as there had been in wrestling. He'd bounce back again, this time for good.

The very next week, even before the Occidental Petroleum bid rescued the arbitrage community from the Cities Service trauma, Boesky picked up the phone and called Martin Siegel.

"Hi, Marty," Boesky said, sounding casual and relaxed, giving no hint that he had just barely saved his firm from collapse, or that he was issuing an invitation that would change their lives irrevocably. "It's time you thought about joining the Harvard Club. Why don't we meet there for a drink?"

Earlier that year, in June 1982, Siegel had invited Boesky to play tennis at the recently completed house that had been built to his and Jane Day's plans in the exclusive enclave called Greens Farms. It was modern, fitted with gray wood vertical siding, with huge two-story plate-glass windows framing views of the pool and the sound behind it, where Siegel had recently taken up jet-skiing. Off to one side was something Siegel had always wanted, his own tennis courts nestled in some pine trees just off the beach.

A pink Rolls Royce turned into the driveway. It pulled quietly into the parking area, and a smiling Boesky emerged carrying his tennis racket and, Siegel noticed with some curiosity, a leather pocketbook, the kind some European men carry. The purse wasn't to his taste at all, but Siegel complimented Boesky on his shiny new car. "Seema gave it to me," he said.

Siegel had arranged a tennis outing for Boesky, Samuel Heyman, a former prosecutor turned successful real estate developer who was eyeing the burgeoning mergers-and-acquisitions arena, and another businessman. Heyman also lived in Greens Farms, practically next door to Siegel, in an enormous stone Georgian mansion. Heyman used his lawn for helicopter landings, and often gave Siegel rides into Manhattan.

That afternoon, the four played a series of round-robin singles matches. Heyman won. Boesky, though a gracious loser, was far and away the worst, which surprised Siegel because Boesky seemed obsessed with turning his sons into tennis champions. He had hired a coach.

After lunch, the others left and Siegel walked Boesky back to his car. There were things to discuss. Siegel was worried about the financial health of Kidder, Peabody and, more specifically, about his own merger practice. The deals on the street were getting bigger and bigger. Kidder, Peabody's client base of midsize companies was getting left behind. In 1981, Siegel had heard reports that United Technologies was about to make a bid for Carrier Corporation, but when he had pitched a defense to Carrier, the company chose to honor its long-term relationship with Morgan Stanley, a firm it believed had more muscle than Kidder, Peabody.

Worse, Siegel felt he was being gradually eased out of the lucrative M&A club led by lawyers Marty Lipton and Joe Flom. Lipton was still steering clients his way, and he sent clients to Lipton, but none were really big deals. Flom, Siegel feared, was definitely cutting him out of the loop in favor of firms like First Boston and Morgan Stanley. Siegel had asked Flom what the problem was. "They want to stick with their traditional investment bankers," Flom said. Siegel told Boesky about his anxieties.

"Why don't you come work with me?" Boesky asked. "Think about it."

Even as he complained to Boesky, Siegel was the undisputed young star of Kidder, Peabody. He was made the centerpiece of the firm's efforts to recruit top business school graduates. In what became an annual event, business students working at Kidder, Peabody for the summer spent a full day at the new Siegel spread in Connecticut, swimming, windsurfing in the sound, and playing round-robin tennis matches, all followed by a lavish catered dinner.

His wife had given birth that spring to their first child, a girl. With his attractive wife, adorable baby, and a house and grounds that were practically a self-contained country club, the none-too-subtle message was "Come to Kidder, Peabody and the life of Marty Siegel can be yours." Siegel was 34.

On the firm's organization chart, he was still officially assigned to the firm's corporate finance department, but in truth, Siegel had eclipsed them all and now dealt directly with DeNunzio. DeNunzio seemed to prefer the arrangement; it kept everyone else off balance. At the end of 1981, DeNunzio had called in Siegel for his bonus review. Siegel's salary was $80,000, so bonus was the bulk of his compensation.

"What do you want?" DeNunzio asked. "What do you think you deserve?"

What Siegel actually thought he deserved was a chunk of Kidder, Peabody stock, but that isn't what he told DeNunzio, whose 7% stake made him the firm's single largest shareholder apart from Al Gordon. DeNunzio determined who was required to sell and buy stock; this control over the firm's ownership structure was the ultimate source of his power. DeNunzio had been stingy about awarding Siegel stock, preferring less competent but loyal, older allies. So to figure out what he thought was fair compensation, Siegel looked at the firm's results and his own contributions. Then he calculated the rise in value of DeNunzio's shares and asked for the same amount.

In 1981 the figure came to $526,000, and DeNunzio gave it to him, no questions asked. It made Siegel the highest-paid officer in the firm. He was the only one given his own dial-a-cab account, with access to a car and driver whenever he wanted it.

Still Siegel was increasingly anxious. Besides his worries about the M&A business and Kidder, Peabody's decline, his expenses seemed to be soaring. The land and house in Connecticut had set him back almost $750,000. Now Jane Day needed full-time help with the baby, and the family required a larger Manhattan apartment. He and Jane Day had looked at three- and four-bedroom apartments in the neighborhoods consistent with DeNunzio's image of Kidder, Peabody—Fifth Avenue, Park Avenue, or Sutton Place. It was clear that an appropriate apartment was going to cost another $1 million. Suddenly he felt like he was having trouble making ends meet on more than half a million dollars a year—even though, in fact, his income was more than adequate.

He was also feeling the pressure of his work. The intense, high-stakes combat of a hostile takeover pumped him up with adrenaline, he'd be putting in hundred-hour weeks, then it would end. Suddenly he'd feel despondent and lethargic. He'd go to bed by 9 or 10 P.M. He suffered from mild allergies, and began taking Nyquil cold medicine in steadily increasing doses. Some nights, he downed 7 to 10 ounces of the remedy. At the end of every deal, he grew more nervous, wondering if it was the last.

This was how he was feeling when Boesky called with his invitation.

The Harvard Club of New York City, a distinguished landmark on West 44th Street designed by McKim Mead & White, is independent of Harvard University, though it admits only Harvard graduates and faculty members, and holders of faculty-level appointments. Boesky had gained admission through the most arcane route imaginable: he donated heavily to Harvard's least-known graduate school, the School of Public Health, and had been named to the school's board of overseers, a "faculty-level" appointment. He had bought his way into the club.

And he was enormously proud of his Harvard affiliation. The Harvard Club, with its dark paneling, somber portraits, Oriental carpets, and crimson drapes, offered the establishment respectability he craved. It made little impression, however, on Siegel as he pushed through the double doors leading to the popular grill room.

Siegel, who almost missed Boesky's table in a murky corner of the room, ordered a beer; he had a low tolerance for alcohol. Boesky chatted aimlessly, talking about his squash game, encouraging Siegel to take up the sport. They could play together at the Harvard Club. Then, gradually, Boesky segued to Siegel's financial pressures. He encouraged him to talk, as he had before, about his anxieties, about the M&A business, about the stodginess at Kidder, Peabody, and about his mounting expenses. Boesky renewed his job offer, but Siegel begged off. "I could make some investments for you, maybe do something to help your father," Boesky went on.

"I've been almost a consultant to you," Siegel responded. "Clients pay a lot for that kind of advice." He could see himself supplementing his income by becoming some kind of off-the-books consultant for Boesky, while continuing his work at Kidder, Peabody. It would be simple. He had, in fact, given Boesky all kinds of insights into the strategies of M&A deals, his own and others. Boesky agreed that Siegel's insights had considerable value and that he'd be willing to pay. Then he took the conversation one fatal step forward:

"If you put me in situations with plenty of lead time, I'd pay for that, too," Boesky said.

On a certain level, Siegel could think of this as an innocent suggestion. He could identify likely takeover targets based on his experience and expertise at what qualities made companies vulnerable. On the other hand, there could be no doubt that they were crossing a line. Plainly Boesky was asking for inside information. They even discussed the fact that Boesky's trading on Siegel's tips too close to an actual bid might attract suspicion; he would have to be tipped off well in advance. "I'd, like, negotiate a bonus at the end of the year," Siegel said. Boesky nodded.

Nothing more was said. There was no more talk of money, or how Boesky would pay Siegel. The conversation drifted into other matters.

At his peak, arbitrageur Ivan Boesky controlled $3 billion worth of stock-purchasing power, enough to strike terror into almost any corporation with a single phone call. "Greed is all right," he advised graduates of the University of California in 1985, coining a slogan for a decade.

From his X-shaped trading desk in Beverly Hills, Michael Milken ruled a junk bond empire that, by 1986, boasted $125 billion in new issues, nearly a ninefold gain in just a decade.

He was the most powerful man in American finance—and one of the richest, with earnings in one year of $550 million. "We're going to tee-up GM, Ford, and IBM," he told a colleague, "and make them cringe."

3

The 200-acre Boesky estate in Westchester County featured a Georgian-style mansion, an inflatable tennis bubble for indoor play, and adjoining squash courts. Carpeting was embossed with the monogram "IFB." Boesky later filed an application to remodel the mansion into a replica of Monticello, Thomas Jefferson's home.

4

Few people knew the real Boesky, not even his wife, Seema. He dreamed of being a "latter-day Rothschild," as he told one of his employees. But he also led multiple secret lives. He told one confidante he'd been a CIA agent in Iran. His constant companion was a mysterious Iranian, Hushang Wekili, who earned a $1 million salary for no visible work. Boesky was shadowed by armed bodyguards. "In my business, you need protection," he told a visitor.

5

At a conference on Latin American debt in Tijuana, Mexico, Milken spoke in front of his own larger-than-life image. He was hailed as a "genius" and a "king," the man who could solve everything from the Third World debt crisis to the savings and loan crisis to the balance of payments problem.

6

Martin Siegel was Kidder, Peabody & Co.'s "golden boy," one of the country's leading investment bankers, the symbol of a new era on Wall Street. He was the man who had everything, yet worried that everything wasn't enough. Even as he was being lionized in the press—*Business Week* called him a "heartthrob"—he embarked on a double life of clandestine meetings and briefcases of cash.

Though he wasn't identified, Dennis Levine (third from right) was featured in Lehman Brothers's 1983 *Review* with colleagues from the firm's mergers-and-acquisitions department. The photo was later used by investigators in a photographic "lineup." Employees at Bank Leu in the Bahamas identified Levine as their mysterious customer, "Mr. Diamond."

rederick Joseph, who became Drexel's hief executive, vowed to make the firm into rival of Salomon Brothers and Goldman, achs. Against what seemed impossible dds, he succeeded. But he couldn't believe at Milken, the man who'd made it all possi- le, would destroy everything he'd built— ntil it was too late.

Kidder, Peabody & Co. chairman Ralph DeNunzio staked the firm's future on Siegel's performance, and his gamble paid off. When he learned that at least part of Siegel's success stemmed from inside information from Goldman, Sachs, he said only two words: "Protect yourself."

Assistant U.S. Attorney Charles Carberry, head of the securities fraud unit, secured the guilty pleas of Dennis Levine and Ivan Boesky. One of the best-liked lawyers in the office, he quit after his arrests of three top arbitrageurs backfired.

10

Manhattan U.S. Attorney Rudolph Giuliani (left) brought new life—and hardball tactics—to a nearly moribund office. When crossed by the SEC, he threatened to derail the whole Milken case. But he presided over the most effective crackdown on Wall Street since the passage of the securities laws. Bruce Baird (right) became one of his top lieutenants.

11

12

No one worked longer and harder to bring the Wall Street criminals to justice than Gary Lynch, chief of enforcement at the Securities and Exchange Commission. He was so demoralized by press criticism of the $100 million Boesky settlement and guilty plea that he nearly resigned. But he rallied his staff. "We are engaged in what may be the most important thing we will ever do in our lives," he said.

13

Though he had always shunned the press, Milken found it increasingly difficult to avoid camera crews after news reports revealed that he was under investigation. On his right is Ralph Ingersoll, of Ingersoll Publications, a major Milken client and an ardent champion of Milken's innocence. Ingersoll, chosen to represent Milken's case in an appearance on ABC's "Nightline," made a hapless figure on television, bungling the lines scripted by the Milken public relations machine.

14

15

Lisa Ann Jones ran away from home and found riches working for Milken in Beverly Hills. But she proved too loyal for her own good. After she lied to protect Milken, she was slapped with a perjury indictment. She became the first Drexel employee convicted in the scandal, and the first to go to jail.

John Mulheren was Boesky's best friend on Wall Street. When he learned that Boesky had implicated him in the scandal, Mulheren, a manic-depressive, loaded a small arsenal of weapons into his car—and set out to kill Boesky. One of the few alleged conspirators to go to trial, he was convicted, but won on appeal.

The press barrage that accompanied the announcement of Boesky's agreement to plead guilty made him, overnight, a national symbol of greed. When he entered his guilty plea in April 1987, he seemed gaunt and thin. He had hoped to escape the press by slipping out a side door of the federal courthouse, but camera crews had staked out every entrance. They stampeded when he appeared, trampling over parked cars to reach him.

After pleading guilty and cooperating with prosecutors, Dennis Levine was sen- ¹⁷
tenced to three years in prison at a White Plains, New York, courthouse in March
1987. He agreed to pay $11.6 million in fines and penalties. "Through the informa-
tion he has provided, an entire nest of vipers on Wall Street has been exposed," the
sentencing judge said. Levine's wife, Laurie, is at the left, and one of his lawyers,
Martin Flumenbaum, is between them.

Milken managed a wan smile as he arrived at the courthouse to enter his plea of not guilty to a 98-count indictment in April 1989. His wife, Lori, is at his right. Directly behind him is one of his chief public relations spokesmen, Kenneth Lerer, who is flanked by Milken lawyers Martin Flumenbaum, on Lerer's right, and Arthur Liman, partially obscured on Lerer's left. Behind Lerer is Lowell Milken, Milken's brother, who was also charged in the indictment.

Milken hired the most powerful public relations team ever fielded by an individual criminal defendant. One of his leading strategists was Linda Robinson, a Ronald Reagan supporter and former acupuncture specialist who brought Republican-style "attack" politics to the public relations field. She wielded enormous influence, both in her own right and through her powerful husband, American Express chairman James Robinson, pictured on her right at a charity gala. Milken's legal and public relations costs were so steep that Drexel, which paid the bills, put Milken on a "budget" of $1.2 million a month.

20

Milken's first encounter with a potentially hostile audience came at a Congressional hearing convened by Congressman John Dingell in April 1988. On the advice of his counsel, legendary trial lawyer Edward Bennett Williams, seated on Milken's left, Milken invoked the Fifth Amendment and refused to answer questions. Williams died later that year, and Milken attended his funeral in Washington, covering his face with his hands and weeping.

Arthur Liman, pictured at Milken's left, stepped into the void left by Williams's death and became Milken's principal lawyer. Best known for his role in the televised Iran/Contra hearings, Liman disdained talk of settlement and portrayed Milken as a "national treasure." Sycophancy reigned in the Milken camp, with Milken's advisors mostly telling Milken what he wanted to hear.

21

In anticipation of the possibility of a jury made up largely of minorities, Milken launched a campaign to recruit support in the black community. He hailed Jesse Jackson as a "close friend" at a party for black junior high school students in Los Angeles. Here, Milken hosts a Variety Charities circus benefit in Los Angeles.

22

23 For a time, Milken managed to keep potential witnesses in "his tent pissing out," as Williams had put it. But, one by one, they defected into the government camp. The first major loss was James Dahl, left, the "Robert Redford of the bond world" and Milken's top salesman. Milken stopped speaking to Dahl and banished him to another floor in Beverly Hills. But he couldn't stop Dahl from testifying against him. Dahl was followed by Terren Peizer, lower right, a trader who liked to give Milken "high fives" on the trading desk but who had secretly kept incriminating documents which he handed over to prosecutors in exchange for immunity. Most damaging was Setrag Mooradian, upper right, Boesky's accountant. Mooradian had kept records of the secret arrangement between Boesky and Milken.

25 Working undercover, Boesky secretly taped Milken during a meeting in Boesky's suite at the Beverly Hills Hotel, above, the pink landmark in which Boesky had acquired a controlling interest. Unknown to Boesky, Milken had been tipped off that Boesky would be recording him. Still, Milken made incriminating comments and later said he hadn't been "careful enough."

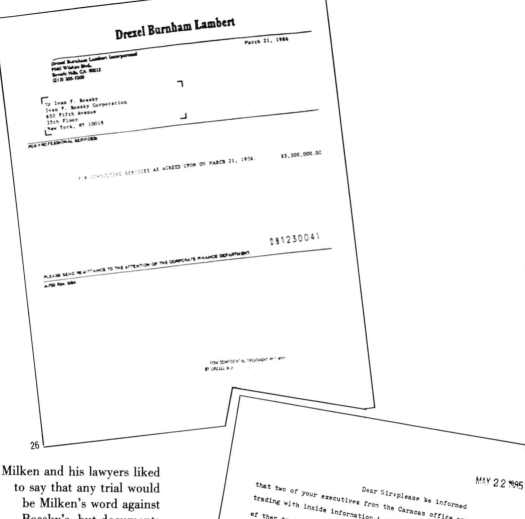

Milken and his lawyers liked to say that any trial would be Milken's word against Boesky's, but documents corroborated Boesky. Above is a copy of a phony Drexel invoice for $5.3 million in "consulting services"—in reality, a payoff in the illegal Boesky/Milken conspiracy, and an Achilles heel in the Milken defense. Below is a copy of an anonymous letter from Caracas sent to compliance officials at Merrill Lynch that triggered the investigation of Levine and, in turn, the entire Wall Street scandal.

28

Richard Wigton, right, was handcuffed and paraded across the trading floor at Kidder, Peabody after being implicated by Siegel, who'd once been his "advisor" in Kidder's secret arbitrage department. Wigton showed no emotion throughout, even when charges against him were dropped in one of the most embarrassing setbacks for the government. His lawyer, Stanley Arkin, is on Wigton's right.

Goldman, Sachs stood staunchly behind Robert Freeman, its partner in charge of arbitrage, even as evidence mounted that Freeman had entered into a wide-ranging insider-trading conspiracy with Siegel. Freeman eventually pleaded guilty to one felony after admitting that Siegel had tipped him to a development in the Beatrice deal with the cryptic words "Your bunny has a good nose." Ironically, Siegel didn't remember the incident.

29

Siegel was vilified by former colleagues on Wall Street for cooperating with the government and endured what seemed an interminable exile as he waited to be sentenced. But eventually his cooperation paid off. The judge hailed his candor and sentenced him to just two months in prison. He hurried from the courthouse with his wife, Jane Day, after hearing the sentence.

30

Judge Kimba Wood, a recent Reagan appointee to the federal bench, was assigned Milken's case. Despite her gentle demeanor, she demolished Milken's plea for leniency.

Milken was sentenced to ten years in prison in November 1990. He agreed to pay $600 million in fines and restitution.

They finished their drinks, shook hands outside on 44th Street, and parted in the warm summer night.

The more Siegel thought about it, the more an arrangement with Boesky made sense. His advice really was worth a lot of money. And Boesky's tips and favors were important for his own clients, too. He often needed Boesky to take positions, to get some buying pressure into a stock, to get a price moving, even to put a company in play, softening it up for a raid by one of Siegel's clients. He needed an edge if he was going to be able to compete with the likes of Morgan Stanley and First Boston.

And the venture seemed risk-free. Siegel wouldn't ever do any trading; no records could be traced to him. And Boesky himself couldn't be caught. He was the biggest, most successful arbitrageur in town. He traded everything—whatever Siegel gave him would blend in. The government would never be able to prove that a professional arbitrageur was trading on inside information, and certainly not Boesky. Boesky was too smart to run any risks.

Siegel didn't act immediately on Boesky's invitation. On August 26, 1982, just days after the meeting at the Harvard Club, Bendix Corporation, led by the mercurial William Agee, launched a $1.5 billion hostile takeover bid for Martin Marietta, the big defense contractor. Siegel was retained to lead Martin Marietta's defense.

The Bendix attack attracted a great deal of media attention. Agee was a household name after his highly publicized intra-office affair with and marriage to Mary Cunningham. But even more important, the contest quickly became the most freewheeling, hard-fought takeover battle ever, in large part because of the bold strategy for saving Martin Marietta adopted by Siegel. In the process, Siegel was hailed as a genius, both by the press and within the takeover community. Any slippage in his status within the M&A club was reversed. Kidder, Peabody suddenly ascended to the top of Lipton's and Flom's recommended lists.

Siegel's innovative defense technique is now known as the most audacious of defense strategies, the "PacMan" defense, named after the once-popular video game. In the PacMan defense, the target turns on its attacker and tries to devour it. Siegel didn't actually invent the PacMan concept, but few in or around Wall Street had heard of it before this, and it had never been tried on such a scale.

Siegel warned Agee that unless the bid were withdrawn, Martin Marietta would retaliate by moving to take over Bendix. Siegel knew that for the ploy to work, he had to demonstrate to Agee and the world at large that the threat was credible.

One afternoon, preparing his counterattack, he thought suddenly of the conversation with Boesky at the Harvard Club. This was the perfect opportunity! He needed Boesky now, as much as he ever had. Ordinarily, the stock of the acquiring company in a takeover bid drops, due to the anticipated costs and drain on earnings, while that of the target rises sharply. So any rise in Bendix's stock would send a powerful message that something unusual was afoot. Siegel wanted some buying action to push up the price and volume of Bendix stock. Nothing would make the threat credible to Agee faster than word that arbitrageurs—Boesky especially—were amassing unfriendly positions. At the same time, Siegel could do something for Boesky.

Siegel called Boesky. He cleared his throat, then said in a hushed tone, "My view is, we're going to do this PacMan defense. Buy Bendix stock." He had a moment of anxiety—he shouldn't risk leaking that kind of information by telephone; what if Boesky's phones were tapped?—but he was quickly consumed by the excitement of the battle. As he watched the tape, he saw instant signs of Bendix buying, and the price rose just as he had expected. Soon Wall Street and the media were rife with speculation that Martin Marietta was about to counterattack with a credible bid.

Just about everyone was persuaded but Agee. He didn't back down, forcing Martin Marietta to make good on its threat with its own $1.5 billion bid, and forcing the price of Bendix stock higher. The competing bids seriously weakened both companies. Bendix, wounded, triggered a bidding war between Allied Corporation and United Technologies, ultimately won by Allied. To the extent there were any victors, a financially-weakened Martin Marietta was hailed as the winner. It had maintained its independence against considerable odds. For that, thanks and public praise were given to Siegel.

Boesky earned $120,000 in profit on the Bendix position he took at Siegel's behest. In the scale of Boesky's trading, it was a trivial sum. But it was satisfying on a far more fundamental level: it had proven to be a risk-free return.

When Siegel called at the end of the year, asking for $150,000 as his "bonus," Boesky was willing. Siegel had calculated that his out-of-pocket cash expenses—the baby's nanny, housekeepers, and the like—were running at a clip of $85,000 a year. He hadn't given Boesky any inside information after Bendix, nor did he know just how much Boesky had made on his Bendix position. But he thought his contributions for the year, including all the legitimate advice he'd given Boesky, were worth $150,000. He felt just as if he were negotiating his bonus with DeNunzio.

"How do you want it?" Boesky asked.

"Cash," Siegel replied.

"That's something of a problem," Boesky said. "Isn't there another way? Can't I invest this for you, maybe in real estate?"

Siegel insisted that the payment be in cash. He didn't want any hassles, and he didn't want anything that could be traced.

Boesky reluctantly agreed. "Give me some time to work this out."

Several weeks later, after the Christmas holidays, Siegel jumped out of a cab and went through the revolving door on the east side of the Plaza Hotel. It was a midafternoon in January 1983. As instructed by Boesky, Siegel waited in the ornate belle epoque lobby of the hotel, not venturing into the adjacent Palm Court, where a string quartet would soon be playing salon music for ladies having tea. Siegel looked about, then felt a chill as he spotted the man he was certain was the courier.

He was almost a parody of a character out of a spy novel. He had dark skin and a powerful, muscular build. Boesky had said he knew the courier from his days in Iran; Boesky had also said he was a CIA agent. Could Siegel trust him?

The lobby wasn't crowded, and the courier easily identified Siegel. He approached him with some deliberation.

"Red light," the courier murmured as he approached Siegel.

"Green light," Siegel replied, as Boesky had instructed. The man handed Siegel the briefcase.

Siegel went straight to his apartment on East 72nd Street. He closed the door, put down the briefcase, and quickly undid the clasps. There, in neat stacks of $100 bills tied with Caesar's Palace casino ribbons, was the money.

Siegel stared at it. Everything had gone without a hitch. It was his money now; he'd earned it. He ought to feel great! Instead, he felt ill. He sat down and put his head in his hands, waiting for the nausea to pass.

4.

"Give me Milken," the familiar voice demanded of Milken's secretary. Sue Cochran replied that Milken was busy. "Quit lying to me," the caller practically shouted. "Don't give me that bullshit. Tell him to pick up the goddamn phone."

It was Boesky again, yelling and cursing. Cochran and her colleague Janet Chung hated answering his calls. He accused them of lying when he didn't get through immediately. If Milken were busy, which he usually was, Boesky would call every two or three minutes, working himself into a frenzy. When the secretaries wilted under the abuse, Warren Trepp or someone else might try to help. But Boesky would talk only to Milken.

By late 1983 Boesky and Milken were talking by phone two or three times a day. Their schedules meshed perfectly. When Boesky got to his New York office at 7 A.M., Milken was arriving in Beverly Hills at 4 A.M. They were in the habit of calling each other first thing, and they seemed to derive satisfaction from knowing that they were busy strategizing while most of their rivals were still in bed. Each boasted to the other that he slept no more than three or four hours a night. Milken encouraged Boesky's grandiose dreams, dreams that might be realized with Milken's money.

Like many of Boesky's close relationships, this one had begun on the telephone. Boesky had met Milken through Stephen J. Conway, a former investment banker at Drexel in New York. In 1981, a headhunter had called Conway at Drexel, saying he'd been retained by a major arbitrageur who wanted to hire an investment banker. "Who's the arb?" Conway asked. The headhunter said he couldn't reveal his identity. "If it's Ivan Boesky, maybe I'm interested," Conway said. "If not, forget it."

Numerous meetings between Boesky and Conway ensued. "I've already succeeded as an arb," Boesky explained. "The big opportuni-

ties are going to be in leveraged buyouts and strategic positions."
Boesky had already had access to some of those opportunities: he was
a major investor in the LBO fund run by Theodore Forstmann, and
Forstmann was an investor in Boesky Corporation. He was also close
to Henry Kravis, the driving force behind Kohlberg Kravis Roberts,
then in its infancy as an LBO firm. Doing LBOs, he explained, would
help him "diversify," so "I wouldn't have all my eggs in one basket."

Boesky saw himself becoming a "merchant banker"—a British
term for an investment banker who acquires stakes in companies; he
thought the term conferred respectability. Boesky claimed he had no
interest in the unsavory practice of "greenmail," in which a large,
hostile stake is accumulated in a company hoping to scare management
into buying out the raider at a premium price.

Conway signed on; he was intrigued at the thought of working for
someone who might turn into the next Boone Pickens or Carl Icahn.
His colleagues at Drexel were pleased: Conway could be counted on to
steer business to his former employer.

Indeed, to put his ambitious plans into effect, Boesky needed
much more capital—and Drexel seemed the perfect source for it. The
capital base in his arbitrage operation, always smaller than he had
hoped for, had been decimated by the Cities Service crisis; he wasn't
even financing his routine arbitrage activity on the scale he had
wanted. Conway talked to David Kay, head of M&A at Drexel, who put
him and Boesky in touch with Stephen Weinroth, in corporate finance,
who in turn consulted with Milken in Beverly Hills. Boesky was dazzled
by the fact that Drexel could get him $100 million, more than twice
what he had been able to raise to launch Boesky Corporation.

When Boesky made his pilgrimage to Drexel's Beverly Hills
office, he stayed in his usual splendor at the Beverly Hills Hotel.
Boesky kept his own suite on the first floor and maintained his tan by
the pool, where he had use of a private cabana. From this secluded
vantage, he could gaze past the sparkling water, the gardens and palms,
to the broad sweep of the pink hotel. This was his domain. He and
Seema owned a controlling interest in the hotel.

Like so much in his life, the Beverly Hills Hotel had come to
Boesky through his wife's family. His father-in-law, Ben Silberstein,
had died in 1979, leaving large portions of his real estate fortune in
equal parts to Seema and her sister, Muriel Slatkin. One of the crown
jewels in the Silberstein empire was the Beverly Hills, acquired in
1954.

The Beverly Hills Hotel was no ordinary real estate property.
Built in the thirties, it soon became a Hollywood nerve center, with
stars around the pool and agents and producers in the nearby Polo

lounge. Katharine Hepburn swam here, fully clothed, after a tennis game. Norma Shearer "discovered" Robert Evans here. Fernando Lamas was a regular; more recently, Eddie Murphy did flips off the board.

After Silberstein's death, ownership of the hotel was divided equally between Seema and Muriel, with a crucial 5% stake in the hands of other relatives. Boesky went after the small controlling stake, recognizing that a comparatively small additional investment would give him and Seema a controlling interest tantamount to outright ownership. In 1981, Boesky succeeded in snapping up the minority shares in Vagabond, the Silberstein corporation that owned the hotel, forever alienating the unwitting Muriel, who learned too late that her sister and brother-in-law had gained absolute majority control at her expense.

Vagabond didn't have impressive earnings, but it had valuable assets, cash flow, and a conservative balance sheet. It was the kind of vehicle that—with Milken's aid—Boesky could use to vault beyond the ranks of arbitrageurs into the world of corporate chieftains. Vagabond, later renamed the Northview Corporation, would be the vehicle through which the money would be raised. Some of the proceeds would also be allocated to Boesky's arbitrage activities.

Boesky was so immediately dazzled by Milken and Drexel that, in Lance Lessman's view at least, he refused to focus on the terms of Drexel's huge cash infusion. There was, to begin, Drexel's typically large cut of the proceeds. This was understandable, given that no one else on Wall Street was competing for the business. But then there was the interest rate—a whopping 17%. Moreover, Drexel, as it often did in such cases, extracted warrants giving it the right to buy an equity stake in Vagabond/Northview. Lessman worried that the high interest rate would put enormous pressure on the operation to earn huge arbitrage returns to make the interest payments. And the equity stake could give Drexel enormous influence over fundamental decisions affecting the business.

There was also the risk inherent in having an investment banker with a financial interest in an arbitrageur—an incentive to leak confidential information. This went unmentioned by Lessman, who knew better than even to raise the subject. But he did air his other reservations to Boesky, who brushed them aside impatiently. After all, now that he had Siegel as a "consultant," he didn't worry about earning large arbitrage profits; indeed, the Siegel arrangement fueled his hunger for additional capital. "Who else could we go to?" Boesky responded to Lessman. "We don't have any choice."

At Drexel, Fred Joseph was somewhat concerned. He was used to calls from arbitrageurs—they phoned him constantly when he was involved in a transaction—but not arbitrageurs who were also generating fees for Drexel. He warned everyone in corporate finance to make sure they didn't let anything slip with Boesky, who wasted no time testing Drexel's "Chinese wall." He called Joseph almost immediately to pump him for information about a pending deal. Joseph lied, saying, "I don't know; I'll check and get back to you." He made sure he got back to Boesky with the answer only after the information Boesky sought had otherwise been made public. Boesky's calls to Joseph tapered off, then stopped altogether. But that hardly mattered, once Boesky was talking regularly to Milken himself.

After Boesky got the $100 million Vagabond/Northview financing in mid-1983, the Boesky-Milken financial connections became intertwined at a dizzying pace. Milken agreed to undertake private placements of high-yield notes for Boesky Corporation totaling $110 million; a rights offering for Cambrian & General Securities, an English closed-end fund which Boesky had acquired as a vehicle for European operations and for additional investing in U.S. takeover situations; and a $67 million European issue for Farnsworth & Hastings, an offshore, Bermuda-based investment vehicle Boesky created and named after an intersection in his Detroit boyhood neighborhood. Most of Boesky's capital was now Milken-generated.

Boesky came out to Beverly Hills regularly, overseeing his interest in the hotel. A measure of his developing closeness with Milken was a rare dinner invitation to the Milken home in Encino. At a later dinner with several Milken colleagues, Lori Milken complained about Boesky, saying she was put off by his cold, arrogant manner. "I never want him in the house again," she told her husband.

On one of Boesky's visits to Beverly Hills, Milken was too busy to see him and instructed James Dahl, his top salesman, to talk to him. "Tell him what you know about S&Ls," Milken said, "because Ivan is interested in buying one." Instead, Boesky pressed Dahl about whether he knew anyone who'd be interested in buying Gulf stock, in which Boesky was then acquiring a position. Boesky would guarantee them against any losses and share any profits. Dahl was taken aback: it was an open invitation to get into an illegal "parking arrangement," in which Boesky would conceal his true ownership by having someone else buy and pretend to own the stock. Dahl told Milken of the incident the next day. "Don't pay any attention to Ivan," Milken said, blithely dismissing the matter. "He's a flake."

Others complained about Boesky, too. Lowell Milken, in particular, developed an almost instant aversion, and warned his brother, who paid no attention. "Drexel backs winners, and Ivan Boesky is a winner," Milken would say. But Boesky was about to learn the true cost of Milken's backing.

Another "winner" in Milken's camp was the eccentric Miami financier, Victor Posner, one of the country's original corporate raiders. Nothing about him or his tactics did anything to burnish the raider image. He had a reputation for acquiring a controlling stake in a company, plundering it, then letting the minority shareholders worry about the consequences, sometimes as extreme as bankruptcy.

Posner, 64 years old, was the son of a Russian immigrant. He had made his fortune in real estate in the thirties and forties, installing himself and his business interests in Victorian Plaza, a fading Miami Beach resort hotel he decorated in questionable baroque taste. Outside his 17th-floor office were a pool table and pinball machines. Posner never graduated from high school; he speaks with a blue-collar Baltimore accent. His primary vehicle for corporate raiding was Sharon Steel, which he acquired in 1969; other Posner entities in a complicated maze of cross-ownership arrangements included NVF, DWG, Pennsylvania Engineering, APL, and Royal Crown.

Throughout his career, Posner displayed little reverence for regulatory constraints. Soon after its acquisition by Posner, Sharon was directed to invest $800,000 of its cash in securities of Posner's DWG Corp. The SEC filed suit, charging self-dealing; the charges were settled, with the Posner entities neither admitting nor denying guilt. Other SEC investigations were eventually launched, but no charges were filed.

Until the SEC intervened, Posner had Sharon pay for many of his personal expenses (and those of two of his children), including housing, limousines and drivers, servants, vacations, even groceries—all deemed corporate perquisites. Even when his companies lost money, Posner, his relatives, and members of his entourage lived lavishly. In a year that Sharon lost over $64 million, Posner earned $3.9 million in Sharon salaries and bonuses alone. His son Steven, installed as Sharon's vice chairman, got more than $500,000. And they had use of the corporate yacht and the corporate jet.

But what many who knew Posner well found most distasteful was his appetite for teenage girls. In the latest, most eyebrow-raising example, his new mistress was the daughter of his former one, who became his public relations spokeswoman.

Posner had come to Drexel through one of Drexel's main client-getters, a corporate finance holdover from Burnham & Co., Donald "Donny" Engel. Outgoing, affable, Engel had the flair that many stiffer

investment bankers lacked. He didn't pretend to great financial sophistication, but he was street-smart and quick to spot a potential client.
He knew that the key to many client relationships was their personal
lives, not their business. He came to know virtually everything about
the lives of his clients, including their problems with their wives and
mistresses. He wasn't judgmental. On the contrary, he shared many of
their appetites. Among Drexel's important clients, Engel was given
credit for landing Ronald Perelman, Nelson Peltz, Jerome Kohlberg,
Gerald Tsai, Irwin Jacobs, and the Haft and Pritzker families.

Engel found a kindred spirit in Milken. They referred facetiously
to the wealthy establishment as "the white guys." They didn't care
much about them. For Drexel, they wanted clients like Herb Haft, a
man whose blow-dried, cone-shaped snow white hair made him look
like a character from "Star Trek." Scoffed at by most of Wall Street,
Haft had been poor, and he was hungry, with "fire in his belly," as
Engel liked to say. Engel liked clients who were short, unhappily
married, and insecure. This was his profile of the ideal raider-client.

Engel and Milken knew how to manipulate the egos and insecurities of this particular type, born losers who were always looking to go
their rivals one better. They had to be the best, the biggest, the richest.
In Engel's view, there were only two things that motivated these
clients: the next deal, and the next sexual conquest. This was simply
human nature.

Not everyone at Drexel was as comfortable with this approach as
Milken. Engel was praised for bringing in new business, but his nickname was "the Prince of Schlock." He was known as the "house
pimp," willing to arrange dates for important clients, such as William
Farley of Farley Industries. Asked to speak to new Drexel investment
banking associates on the topic of generating new business, Engel
offered this wisdom: "Corporate America likes women. Find a hooker
and you'll find a client."

Victor Posner eventually became one of Engel's biggest clients,
and Engel became the go-between for Posner and Milken. In the
mid-1970s, even before the move to Beverly Hills, Posner had begun
investing in Milken's junk bonds. By the early eighties he could be
counted on to buy whatever Drexel-issued paper Milken steered in his
direction.

But Joseph had fundamental reservations about Posner. He
asked one of his top corporate finance people, Stephen Weinroth, to do
an analysis of the raider's financial structure. The results were alarming: Posner had stopped holding annual meetings at most of the companies he controlled and was increasingly delinquent in reporting
financial results. His own compensation, including what he earned

from his private companies, was even more outsized than his public disclosures: a total of $23 million in 1984. And none of the companies was doing well. As Weinroth put it, Posner was turning "gold into dross." Drexel's reputation would only suffer if it was marketing issues that went bad.

Posner had big plans to use Sharon to make forays at other companies. At its peak, Sharon had stakes in over 40 firms. Posner would put them in play and buy them out or acquire them for his empire. He broke them up and sold pieces if necessary. To do this, he needed vast amounts of additional capital, far more than could be generated through earnings, even in a good year for the steel industry.

One frustrating Posner foray was a run at a New York-based construction company, Fischbach Corporation. Posner thought the company could be merged nicely with his Pennsylvania Engineering. In 1980, Posner had acquired over 5% of Fischbach's stock. He filed a Schedule 13-D with the SEC disclosing his position, and proceeded to threaten Fischbach with a hostile takeover. But Fischbach had fought back, threatening litigation on antitrust and other grounds. Posner had been forced into signing a standstill agreement that he now bitterly regretted. Under the agreement, he promised not to buy more Fischbach stock unless someone else mounted a raid on the company or filed a 13-D disclosure showing ownership of more than 10% of Fischbach's stock.

Posner brought the situation to Milken and Drexel, saying he was determined, nonetheless, to wrest control of Fischbach. He wanted Drexel to underwrite a debt issue for Pennsylvania Engineering; he would use the proceeds to buy Fischbach—once he solved the standstill problem. Milken must have realized that he had the market power to give Posner what he wanted, with millions in fees as his and Drexel's reward.

Soon after, in December 1983, Executive Life Insurance Co. filed a 13-D with the SEC, conveniently revealing that it had acquired a 13% stake in Fischbach. This was enough to trigger the end of the standstill agreement. Executive Life, it happens, is run by Fred Carr, one of Milken's earliest backers and the owner of a huge portfolio of Milken-generated junk bonds. Carr depended on Milken to make markets and maintain liquidity in those holdings. He was the kind of Drexel client who generally did what Milken told him to, and, in any event, there was little risk in the Fischbach stake. Milken knew, even if Carr didn't, that Posner was going to take over the company eventually.

Whatever Posner, Milken, and Carr expected, they apparently made a major miscalculation—albeit a highly technical one. Because

Executive Life is an insurance company, it reports stock positions on a Schedule 13-G, and isn't required to file a 13-D. Fischbach warned Posner that it would sue for a judgment that the standstill remained in effect because Executive Life should have filed a 13-G. The standstill agreement provided for termination only in the event of a 13-D filing. Whatever the merits of that argument, it would at least succeed in throwing the whole matter into court, buying Fischbach needed time. Not even Milken could sell securities with unresolved litigation threatening their investment potential. Posner and Milken were enraged.

Milken evidently decided to take matters into his own hands. He got on the phone to Boesky. As usual, Milken's call was put straight through. Boesky got on the line immediately. He listened carefully. Milken was asking him—"instructing him" might be a better description—to acquire a large stake in Fischbach. After all, given the recent financings, Boesky owed Milken a favor.

Milken had chosen Boesky as the vehicle for freeing Posner from the standstill agreement. He directed him to begin accumulating Fischbach stock and convertible debentures, slowly, in small blocks so as not to attract undue attention. Milken assured Boesky that he expected an announcement by Posner to boost the share price, giving Boesky a profit. If that didn't happen, Milken would guarantee Boesky against any losses. It seemed a no-lose proposition, so Boesky started buying on May 4, 1984. He stopped, at the behest of the Milken operation, when he came near the 10% threshold. Then, on July 9, Boesky bought a 145,000-share block of Fischbach directly from Milken's high-yield department. Boesky crossed the triggering threshold and filed a false 13-D disclosure statement with the SEC, making no mention of Milken's interest in his position or that he had been guaranteed against loss.

Ordinary observers would have assumed, wrongly, that Boesky had a real interest in Fischbach. They would have suspected an imminent takeover bid, by him or by someone else. A 13-D is intended to protect investors by revealing publicly that a large stake—anything over 5%—has been accumulated in a company. Everyone is put on notice that a takeover bid might be in the offing, and the investor filing the 13-D is required to disclose the purpose of the investment, including whether additional purchases are contemplated. Stock prices often rise on news that a 13-D has been filed, since they often precede a takeover offer. Because 13-Ds are relied on so heavily by investors, lying on a 13-D form is a crime.

This can hardly have caused Boesky much anxiety. There had been few prosecutions for 13-D violations. He was more upset that, despite Milken's confident prediction, the share price of Fischbach kept going down, dropping from the mid-30s when Boesky began buying, to the mid-20s. Boesky kept getting assurances from Milken's people in Beverly Hills that he'd recoup his mounting losses.

To make sure, Boesky called Mooradian, his chief recordkeeper. Earlier, Milken had ordered Boesky to take a large position in Columbia Savings and Loan, another of Milken's reliable buyers and sellers of junk bonds. He hadn't explained the request, but he'd promised to reimburse any losses—and he wanted credit for any gains. Boesky had obliged. In effect, Milken thereby created a secret ownership interest in one of his major clients. At the time of the Columbia purchases, Boesky had asked Mooradian to create one of his mysterious files, like "chartreuse," that he wanted no one else to know about. This one Mooradian identified with a red tie and a label, "Special Projects." Now Boesky told him to keep track of their positions in Fischbach stock, their costs of carrying it, and any trading profits and losses realized. He wanted it all collected in the "Special Projects" file. As the price of Fischbach stock drifted steadily lower, Mooradian's calculations showed Boesky with growing losses.

An increasingly impatient Boesky finally wrote to Milken on Nov. 28. "Dear Mike," he began. "Enclosed you will find a self-explanatory list of information through and including Nov. 27, 1984." The letter continued, cryptically, "I think it will be appropriate to resolve all of the enclosed." Milken responded by arranging a series of trades that resulted in profits to Boesky, demonstrating anew his awesome power over the junk-bond market. The trades typically involved thinly traded securities where Milken had huge discretion to set the price. But the trades didn't nearly offset what were now huge losses for Boesky.

Meanwhile, the scheme had achieved Milken's purposes: the standstill was broken when Boesky crossed the 10% level. Fischbach conceded as much by abandoning the lawsuit over Executive Life's shares and bowing to what was now inevitable. Posner and Milken were free to go forward.

But the prospect of financing a major Posner acquisition was alarming to Joseph and Weinroth. Joseph sent Weinroth and another corporate finance executive out to Beverly Hills to talk Milken out of doing a Fischbach takeover for Posner, who was now under investigation for tax fraud. At first Milken resisted, arguing a refrain frequently heard at Drexel: "If Drexel doesn't do this deal, First Boston will." Gradually, however, he seemed to come around. He praised Weinroth, saying the report on Posner was good work. When he left, Weinroth felt he had killed the Fischbach deal. He had no way of knowing that Milken was already inextricably intertwined in Fischbach. Milken's

attention to Weinroth's presentation had been little more than a cha-
rade.

The very next week, preparations in Beverly Hills for the Fischbach deal went forward as though Weinroth's trip had never happened.
Weinroth, dismayed, went to Joseph, who called Milken. Milken was
adamant that the deal proceed. Milken cited the success Posner had
had with his earlier acquisitions and told Joseph he also valued
Posner's "information flow."

Joseph offered only token resistance, despite Fischbach's declin-
ing earnings and stock price. He managed to rationalize the deal on the
grounds that Fischbach had a strong market share. Joseph did insist
that the proceeds of any offering be used solely for Fischbach stock, not
other Posner activities. He also succeeded in modifying the terms of
the offer slightly. But no one at Drexel close to the situation was fooled:
Milken, not Joseph, was calling the shots.

Pennsylvania Engineering raised $56 million in February 1985 in
a Drexel-led private placement of high-yield notes. Nothing was said
about the Milken-Boesky arrangement, of course; no one would have
bought the securities had they known they were part of an illegal
conspiracy. As it was, not even stalwart Milken clients were willing to
buy all the notes. A large position was unloaded on one of the firm's
captive clients, Dort Cameron III, a former Milken employee and
protégé who had moved to a Bass family investment partnership where
he traded in Milken-backed issues. Drexel itself absorbed most of the
rest, adding it to its own inventory of junk bonds. Drexel's fee for the
private placement: $3 million.

The scheme subsequently played out just as Milken had planned,
without a hitch. Some months later, Boesky quietly sold his Fischbach
stake for the equivalent of $45 a share on the London Stock Ex-
change—even though Fischbach shares were trading at less than $40
a share in New York. Boesky still suffered a loss, by his calculations,
of approximately $5 million on the gambit, but he was assured that
would be reconciled at a later date. No buyer, of course, was identified
when Boesky disclosed the sale in a routine SEC filing. It would have
taken a patient and lucky detective to sift through the thousands of
SEC disclosures and discover that Pennsylvania Engineering reported
buying precisely the same amount of Fischbach stock and debentures
that Boesky sold, at the same price, using proceeds of the Drexel
offering. As Milken must have surmised, no one noticed the correlation.

It was noticed at Drexel, of course, even in New York. On its face,
the transaction made no sense: why would Posner pay Boesky an

above-market price, when he could simply buy stock in the open market? Weinroth and others wondered uneasily whether Boesky had been promised he'd get out of the position at his cost, and if so, who had made what promises to whom. They discussed the possibilities, but let the matter drop. No one wanted to ask Milken about it.

Milken's triumph was complete when, later that year, Fischbach announced the identity of its new chairman: Victor Posner. He promptly brought his own management style to the company, inflating his own salary, siphoning off assets, and laying off workers at the once-thriving business. Its results steadily worsened.

In the scheme of things, the Fischbach capitulation attracted little notice outside of a handful of arbitrageurs and investment bankers on Wall Street. But those who did witness the events were awestruck by Milken's performance. Posner, on his own, had locked himself into an impossible position. But then Milken had stepped in, bursting those constraints, bringing Fischbach to its knees. This was power, and Fischbach occupied only a small corner of Milken's imagination. At the same time he was masterminding the Fischbach triumph, he was also steering Posner through another nettlesome takeover stalemate, this one involving a bigger, tougher adversary: National Can Co.

Posner had been building up his position in National Can, a large Chicago-based packing company, for years. By 1981 his 38% stake made him the company's largest shareholder by far, but he claimed he was buying only for investment purposes. Then, in late 1983, about the time the Fischbach maneuvering began, National Can announced a routine note offering that would raise $100 million. The offering would be underwritten by National Can's customary investment banking firm, Salomon Brothers.

There was rage in Beverly Hills. Nothing brought out the competitive fire in Milken more than the prospect of a rival getting a piece of business that he thought was his. Drexel would do the National Can offering. If not, National Can could share the fate of other Posner victims.

Posner contacted National Can's management and, for the first time, intervened directly in their running of the company. He said he was unhappy at the prospect of Salomon handling the bond offering. He wanted National Can's officers to meet with Drexel. Agreeing to the demands of their largest shareholder, National Can executives met with Drexel's Engel and others in Chicago several times that December, and Drexel proposed its own offering. But the Drexel plan called for interest costs a full percentage point higher than what Salomon was offering. There was no defensible reason for choosing Drexel over

Salomon; Posner was obviously pressuring National Can into the Drexel orbit.

National Can's executives resisted. Posner bluntly proposed that either National Can buy out his position at a huge premium—"greenmail"—or join with him in a Drexel-led leveraged buyout in which he would end up owning 80% of the company, but management would also have a 20% stake. Posner didn't need to mention, of course, that an alternative was for him simply to take over the company and throw management out.

Never in their careers had National Can's management, led by its revered chairman, Frank Considine, a pillar of the Chicago business establishment and a paragon of down-to-earth Midwestern values, encountered such ugly, nakedly aggressive tactics –all triggered by a routine bond offering. In conversations with Considine and National Can's chief financial officer, Walter Stelzel, Posner constantly threatened them. Even though Posner's 13-D filings had never mentioned that he was part of a group with common interest in National Can's stock, he repeatedly told National Can's officers that over 50% of the company's stock was in "friendly" hands—in the hands of shareholders who would do as Posner told them. With the gravest trepidation, sensing no alternative, National Can committed itself to pursuing the leveraged buyout with Posner.

Drexel moved into high gear, structuring a buyout at $40 a share, or about $410 million. Posner would end up in control of the company, after earning a big profit on the shares he'd already acquired at prices far lower than $40. It would be enormously lucrative for Drexel; on top of its investment banking advisory fees, it would raise over $150 million in Milken-led junk bonds, skimming off its usual percentage, or about $5 to $6 million in financing fees alone.

And this wasn't all. The true extent of Milken's gains were concealed in the closely guarded partnership accounts in Beverly Hills. The Milken-led investment partnerships, originally launched to free his junk bond people from worrying about their own investments, had been thriving, moving Drexel-underwritten junk bonds in and out of their portfolios at large spreads, buying positions at favorable offering prices that quickly soared once trading in the bonds began after the offer. One of the first of the office's partnerships was named Otter Creek. It was launched in 1979, and among its participants were Milken, his brother Lowell, and favored employees in Drexel's Beverly Hills operation, a total of 37 people. Participation was limited to Milken's entourage. Everyone was instructed not to mention the partnerships or their financial results to anyone in New York, for fear that such disclosures would ignite jealousies. Not even Joseph knew the scope of their activities. When Weinroth asked who was participating in the West Coast partnerships, a member of the Milken circle told him it was none of his business. Trading was monitored only in Beverly Hills, not by Drexel's compliance department in New York.

Prior to the National Can dealings, Otter Creek had invested almost exclusively in junk bonds and related securities, such as warrants and convertible debentures, never in common stocks. But the partnership's trading records show a huge stake of 54,200 shares in just one publicly traded company as of December 1983: National Can. These were undoubtedly some of the "friendly" shares Posner mentioned so often when threatening National Can.

National Can finally agreed to go along with the Drexel-financed leveraged buyout over the Christmas holidays. This was highly sensitive information likely to cause an immediate stock market reaction, so it was to be held in the strictest confidence by those privy to the news. Yet, on January 3, 1984, just days after the decision was made, and before any public announcement, Otter Creek bought another 10,000 shares of National Can.

On January 5, National Can's board met and agreed to pursue the buyout plan. That very same day, exhibiting uncanny market timing, Otter Creek bought 21,300 more shares of National Can. It added 2,000 shares two days later. The decision to buy the shares was purportedly made by Otter Creek's management committee, headed by Milken's brother, Lowell.

Average daily trading volume in National Can was only about 4,000 shares. The sudden surge, with a corresponding increase in the share price, triggered immediate concern on the part of National Can's management and directors that word of the proposed buyout was leaking into the marketplace. So National Can, on January 12, rushed out a public announcement that it was contemplating a Drexel-led leveraged buyout proposal. Predictably, the stock price surged on the news.

The Otter Creek trading just days before the announcement was so blatant that it triggered an insider-trading investigation by the New York Stock Exchange. Drexel dragged its heels responding to requests for information about Otter Creek, doing everything possible to throw the exchange's investigators off the scent, calling Otter Creek's trading an "unsolicited transaction" in a "nondiscretionary account." After repeated questions, Drexel finally acknowledged that the investors in Otter Creek were Drexel employees, but then made what seems to be a deliberate misstatement, saying there was no other connection between Otter Creek, Drexel, and National Can, when Drexel was at that very moment financing the leveraged buyout.

The investigation made a mockery of any notion of compliance at Drexel: the exchange's inquiries should have triggered an internal investigation as to why Drexel employees were trading in a stock of a client about to undergo a leveraged buyout. Instead, Drexel covered up. After all, the person in charge of compliance in Beverly Hills reported to Lowell, who was involved in the partnership trading. But Drexel's approach succeeded: the exchange eventually abandoned the investigation, concluding in a final report that Otter Creek had "no known connections to National Can." Incredibly, it apparently never dawned on the exchange that Otter Creek was made up of the same people who were financing the National Can buyout.

Posner, in the end, never got National Can, but he was rescued by Milken nonetheless. With Posner's financial empire teetering by mid-1984, suffering from the overleverage and bad management that had concerned Joseph and Weinroth even before Fischbach, the banks slated to be involved in the National Can deal pulled out. Considine frantically tried to put together his own financing for a leveraged buyout, but it was really no contest. Milken simply shopped National Can to his other loyal clients, offering them the chance to seize the company in Posner's stead, sure that they would top any bid Considine could muster.

Carl Icahn eyed National Can seriously, even taking a large position, but eventually demurred. Ultimately another Milken protégé, Nelson Peltz, bought the company. Drexel, raising a total of $595 million for Peltz, made even more in financing and investment banking fees than it would have had Posner carried through with the original plan. Who bought the National Can bonds used to finance the takeover from Milken? A familiar list, including Fred Carr's First Executive Corporation; Thomas Spiegel's Columbia Savings and Loan; and Meshulam Riklis, Carl Lindner, and Ronald Perelman.

As for Otter Creek, it quietly sold its National Can position into Peltz's tender offer for $3.8 million, for an enormous trading profit. The partnership earned nearly a half million dollars on the January 1984 trading alone. Thus, in a pattern that would be repeated, what appears to be insider trading became inextricably intertwined with coercing a public company into a Drexel-financed change in ownership.

Back in New York, Fred Joseph, still head of corporate finance, knew nothing about Otter Creek or its trading in National Can. Milken still reported to Kantor, and Kantor to Linton, Drexel's chairman. But Engel did work for Joseph, who couldn't deny that Engel's relationship with Posner was proving to be lucrative for Drexel. Even better, Engel had become fast friends with another member of the Milken entourage, Ronald Perelman, the head of a holding company called MacAndrews & Forbes that was becoming ideally positioned as a vehicle for Drexel-backed maneuvers. But Drexel's compliance officers had brought Joseph some trading records that resurrected all of his apprehensions about Engel's ethics and judgment. The trading of a Drexel salesman who, Joseph knew, was a close friend of Engel's, smacked of insider trading on a deal Engel was involved in. Joseph wouldn't tolerate this.

Joseph ordered Engel into his office, along with the salesman. He was angry. The records showed the salesman had been buying the stock when the transaction looked like it was going through, and then sold just before an announcement that the deal had fallen apart. Engel, Joseph knew, had been privy to these developments. "Explain this exceptional timing," Joseph ordered. Engel remained calm, denying there was anything improper. "It was just a coincidence," Engel insisted. The salesman backed him up. Joseph felt they were lying. "Pray to God there's not another 'coincidence' like this," Joseph said sternly, his disbelief obvious. "If there is, I'll fire you both. You'll be dead meat."

Within weeks, Weinroth told Joseph that he'd learned from a client that Engel had "borrowed" $65,000 from a Drexel client, had executed a promissory note, and hadn't reported the transaction to anyone at the firm. Joseph was disgusted. There wasn't any formal rule, but it should have been obvious that one of the firm's investment bankers should not be financially beholden to a client; it could affect the investment banker's judgment and objectivity. Joseph called Engel in and fired him on the spot.

Engel went straight to Milken. He protested that the client actually owed him $100,000, that the $65,000 only partly made up that debt, and that Weinroth had gone to Joseph in an effort to get rid of him. Milken called Joseph and demanded that Engel be reinstated. Engel was "useful," Milken argued. Milken, Joseph knew, put a huge premium on selling, and Engel could "sell" clients in ways that, however distasteful to Joseph, seemed to work. It crossed Joseph's mind that Milken put little premium on ethics or integrity. But how many traders did?

With Milken up in arms, Joseph felt he had to compromise. He wouldn't relent on the firing, but Milken proposed that Engel become a "consultant" to Drexel, a "finder," as he put it. Engel would be compensated, as he had been, based on a percentage of the fees generated by clients he brought into the firm, ranging from 4% to 20%.

Joseph insisted that Engel couldn't hold himself out as a representative of Drexel, but otherwise gave in.

It was a crucial compromise on a matter of integrity. The fig leaf of Engel's "consultancy" fooled no one inside or outside of Drexel. Milken had triumphed over Joseph, saving one of his loyalists. Engel moved his office to the third floor of the Manhattan town house used by Perelman as his headquarters. To reach Engel by phone, callers dialed the Drexel switchboard. With his new consulting arrangement, Engel earned more money from Drexel than he ever had as one of its employees. And he became even more intensely loyal to Milken.

Late in 1983, David Kay, head of M&A at Drexel, had sauntered into Joseph's office, in high spirits, dressed as usual in a European-cut suit, looking tanned from a recent trip to Beverly Hills. "We're doing great," Kay said, ticking off the fees generated from his department. But Joseph wasn't so impressed.

"Let's look at those numbers," he said. Drexel's revenues, swollen by the success of Milken's bond operations, had grown rapidly to nearly $1 billion, a tenfold increase since Joseph had come to the firm. "You only did ten percent of our revenue, or about one hundred million dollars," Joseph told Kay. "At most firms, M&A is accounting for 30% to 40%."

"You're an asshole," Kay replied.

Joseph wasn't being entirely fair to Kay. Because of the exponential growth in Milken-generated revenues, no other department at Drexel was contributing the share of revenue that similar departments did at other Wall Street firms. Joseph wanted to diversify; he knew that overdependence on one person, one line of business could be dangerous in the boom-and-bust cycles of Wall Street. But what could he do? Every time corporate finance, M&A, or any other department managed to show some gains, Milken far outstripped them.

After his conversation with Kay, Joseph thought a lot about the role of M&A at the firm. The big firms, those like Morgan Stanley and Goldman, Sachs that Joseph had promised he would equal or surpass in fifteen years, were becoming ever more prominent in the M&A area. But Drexel had something they didn't: Michael Milken. He could be the "edge" that Joseph was always seeking. The Posner experiences had shown how closely aligned the Milken money machine and an M&A practice could be.

Over the years, Joseph had turned to a management guru named Cavas Gobhai, a Bombay-born consultant who ran two-day, intensive sessions with businessmen intent on brainstorming and "expressing themselves." In November 1983, Joseph convened another encounter session with Gobhai, a session aimed at finding ways to vault Drexel into the forefront of the burgeoning M&A field. In a significant acknowledgment of where Drexel's power now resided, the meeting was held at the elegant Beverly Wilshire Hotel, just down the block from Milken's headquarters.

A group of 11 Drexel bankers was invited. Milken had four slots; he brought Trepp, Ackerman, and Bob Davidow. From New York, Joseph brought Kay, Leon Black, John Kissick, Herbert Bachelor, and Fred McCarthy. The group quickly concluded that Drexel needed an M&A "star" to attract major clients. They listed Bruce Wasserstein at First Boston, Eric Gleacher at Lehman Brothers, and, fresh from his success in Martin Marietta, Martin Siegel, who they ranked first on their list. It was an interesting exercise, but in truth, no one in the room thought any of the candidates would give any serious consideration to an offer from Drexel.

But the group had more intriguing ideas. The big companies were fueling the M&A boom only because they were the ones with big money and borrowing power. Drexel had demonstrated that you didn't need the money if Drexel could come up with it for you. A Posner armed with a $1 billion war chest was just as formidable as a blue-chip company with $1 billion in cash and borrowing power. Shareholders, especially the arbitrageurs who poured into stock of companies involved in takeover bids, could care less where the money came from— as long as they got paid.

The group took this thinking one step further. What if Drexel hadn't actually raised the money, but promised that it would? The firm could issue a "highly confident" letter, a formal pledge from Drexel that it was "highly confident" it would raise the money promised in a takeover bid. As long as Drexel always followed through on the promise, the letter would be as good as cash.

Obviously, large companies with access to bank loans and the credit markets wouldn't switch to a substitute so ephemeral as a Drexel letter. But what about people who didn't have any options? There was one area in particular that, Drexel knew from experience, was very difficult to finance: the hostile tender offer. Banks shunned them, as did investment banks like Goldman, Sachs. The group talked about the negative publicity associated with them, and the risks to Drexel if the firm became even more closely identified with the likes of Posner. Milken had no reservations, and even the more cautious Joseph thought the firm could take the heat. If Drexel were to thrive, it really had no choice. And its reputation was hardly so sterling that a hostile raid or two would do much to tarnish it.

Joseph and his colleagues returned to New York, spreading the word around the firm to be alert to the possibility of hostile deals. But the big push, he decided, would come at the upcoming high-yield bond conference. There, Joseph and Milken would unveil their new strategy for transforming the world of hostile takeovers.

The high-yield bond conference had begun small, in the late 1970s, two years before Milken moved his operation to the West Coast. The market had been in a slump at the time, and Milken had been in one of his rare demoralized states. He complained to Joseph that he couldn't get any buyers to listen to his message about the profit possibilities in low-rated paper. "Get me some clients," Milken begged.

Joseph had the idea of a conference bringing together some of his corporate finance clients, the kind of companies that would typically issue unrated debt, and some of Milken's network of buyers. The meeting was hardly a rousing success. Joseph could only muster three companies, and Milken managed to attract only seven or eight buyers. But on a cold rainy day in March, they had the meeting in a Drexel conference room. Milken spoke with fervor about the potential of junk bonds, as though he had an audience of hundreds.

The next year was only slightly more successful: 50 people showed up. In 1979, Milken moved the conference to the Beverly Hilton Hotel in Beverly Hills. The dinner on Friday night, meant to be the social high point of the two-day session, was a fiasco. Ten minutes before guests were to be seated, Drexel executives were handed lists of the corporate and institutional clients who were to be seated at their tables. They were supposed to greet them and steer them to their assigned seats. Most had never met before, so they couldn't recognize them. People had to sit at random. The food—greasy quiche and pu pu platters with chicken and beef on sticks—had everyone searching for extra napkins. There was no entertainment except a dry speech by the chairman of Sun Chemical.

Afterward, Engel came up to Milken. "These CEOs are used to doing things in style," he said. "The hors d'oeuvres were disgusting and dinner was chaos." Milken was only too happy to give Engel responsibility for planning the next conference.

At Engel's direction, the 1980 conference was done with greater style at the more upscale Beverly Wilshire Hotel. It began Tuesday night and ended Saturday morning, as would all the future conferences. Engel invited existing clients, potential clients that Milken thought should issue debt, bond buyers, and institutions deemed potential bond buyers. Executives of companies that already had issued low-grade debt were featured as speakers, praising the rejuvenative powers of junk.

At the Friday-night dinner, the food and seating arrangements were vastly improved. But the speakers, a panel of academics and a pollster, were dull. Many of the 175 guests dozed off.

By 1984, however, the high-yield conference had come of age. Over 800 people, a capacity crowd, attended the gathering, held at the Beverly Wilshire. Milken was the official host, the star of every session he attended. He spoke about junk bonds and broader, grander themes: job formation, education, and the scarcity of human capital. They were themes he would repeat in countless speeches for years afterward, and his minions hung on every word, as though Milken the bond salesman had metamorphosized into a worldly philosopher for the eighties.

Engel now had a staff of eight people, but Milken himself approved the 1984 conference in every detail, even the seating arrangements. Nothing was left to chance. Barry Diller, the head of 20th Century–Fox who'd defected from Paramount Pictures, couldn't be seated near Martin Davis, the chairman of Gulf + Western, Paramount's parent. Roger Stone, head of Stone Container, a junk-bond issuer, was seated near representatives of Fidelity, the mutual fund that was a huge buyer of Stone's bonds. Client service was taken to new lengths: when an institutional junk-bond buyer asked for a mirrored ceiling and walls in his hotel room, Drexel had them installed.

The Friday-night dinner for 1,500 had to be moved to the Century Plaza Hotel. This time no one fell asleep. Instead of the dreary economist or pollster, a giant screen was unfurled, the lights were dimmed, and a video "commercial" appeared, starring Steve Wynn and Frank Sinatra. Then Milken and Wynn came onstage and into the spotlight. "You guys don't know how to do commercials," Milken kidded Wynn.

"Oh yeah?" Wynn replied. "Let's have an expert decide."

With that, Sinatra himself came striding onstage, brandishing a fistful of cash. "Here you are kid," Sinatra said, handing the money to Wynn. "Buy yourself a few bonds." The audience roared its delight as Sinatra launched into a 45-minute medley of songs.

The Sinatra appearance cost Drexel $150,000. But it was a pittance compared to the billings eventually generated by clients, and by people who became clients, as a result of the conference.

A year later, at the 1985 gathering, Joseph looked out over the packed ballroom and marveled at the turnout. The conference had been moved back to the Beverly Hilton to accommodate the huge crowd. Over 100 issuers of Drexel-backed junk bonds were scheduled to make presentations. Joseph moved from the head table to the podium for one of what he and Milken referred to as their "brief commercial interludes," an opportunity to pitch Drexel to the assembled throng.

This was the moment to tout the firm's new shift into the takeover arena. "We've been working on ways to finance the unfriendly takeover," Joseph said as the audience listened raptly. He explained the concept of the "highly confident" letter that had been discussed at the November strategy session. "We think we've solved the problem; we believe we can do it," he said. Joseph elaborated on his own philosophy: Companies should belong to those willing to take risks— in other words, to Drexel's clients rather than to public shareholders. That's what capitalism was all about. Anyone with Drexel's backing could buy a company. "For the first time in history, we've leveled the playing field. The small can go after the big," Joseph concluded.

He wondered if the full import of what he'd said had sunk in. But afterward, in the men's room, he overheard two conference participants. "Did you hear what Fred said?" one asked. "Yeah. Wow!" said the other. "It's awesome."

With the new emphasis on hostile takeovers, the conference that year was dubbed the "Predators' Ball." The sobriquet proved as hard to suppress as the term *junk bonds,* and it stuck to all subsequent high-yield conferences.

Later that afternoon, Joseph and Milken held an M&A session, and Milken estimated that the attendees combined could muster $1 trillion in buying power. Practically every raider, would-be raider, and raider specialist was there. Carl Icahn gave a presentation. Sir James Goldsmith, the legendary Anglo-French financier, asked questions, as did Carl Lindner. Publishing magnate Rupert Murdoch added his thoughts, with more comments from Boone Pickens, the Texas oil raider, and Joe Flom. There was also a healthy dash of glitz. For its presentation, Mattel, a Drexel client, paraded buxom models dressed in full-size counterparts of Oscar de la Renta's new line of Barbie doll evening gowns.

But the real action unfolded in a far more private setting, in Bungalow 8, situated in the lush tropical gardens of the Beverly Hills Hotel. Bungalow 8 is the largest of the hotel's bungalows, with three bedrooms, a living room, dining room, and private terraces.

Bungalow 8 had become the nerve center of the conference, the site of the most feverish dealmaking and the pursuit of other fantasies. It was Engel's abode each year. He had begun hosting the Thursday-evening cocktail party in 1983. Only selected clients were invited, giving the parties instant cachet within the Drexel client orbit. Beautiful young women, mostly aspiring actresses and models, mingled with the wealthy businessmen. Wives were banned, though they could attend the lavish dinner that followed at Chasen's restaurant. Few did.

Drexel corporate finance officials begged Engel to invite their clients. Clients themselves would plead with Engel. "I know I've paid $50 million to Drexel in fees this year and I think I should be invited to the party," was a typical refrain. By 1985, competition was fierce.

That Thursday evening, the select converged, greeted by the affable Engel. Joseph's attention was momentarily diverted by some of the dazzling young women mingling in the crowd. He'd been assured that none of them were prostitutes. After all, who needed to pay attractive women to attend a cocktail party with a collection of the world's richest men? One of Drexel's biggest clients, Carl Lindner, had already had Joseph check out a young woman who'd caught the eye of Lindner's son; Joseph had been assured she was a respectable doctor's daughter, a personal friend of one of Drexel's directors. Joseph had said he wouldn't tolerate the loose mores of the old Burnham & Co., especially now that Drexel was moving onto center stage.

But those thoughts quickly vanished, for far more important matters were brewing that night in Bungalow 8. Boesky was in a corner talking quietly with Icahn; Sir James was in a group with Pickens and Flom. Murdoch and Lindner were chatting with Kay and Engel, the affable host. Within only a few weeks, Pickens would launch his bid for Unocal, Peltz would bid for National Can, Sir James would attack Crown Zellerbach, and Farley would go after Northwest Industries— all with Drexel financing.

A sense of electricity had begun moving through the conference crowd, even outside Bungalow 8, as imaginations were released by the prospect of Drexel-generated billions. The excitement climaxed at the Friday-night dinner. The crowd rocked to the strains of "Ghostbusters": "Who ya gonna call when you want money fast? Call Drexel," went the lyrics. Then the screen vanished and Diana Ross, dazzling in a sequined gown, stepped into the spotlight as the evening's surprise star. She sang a medley of Motown hits and managed to change outfits twice.

Most participants were suitably impressed. Yet a few doubts remained. "What you don't know is if you have a watershed in American business," one participant that year told the *San Francisco Chronicle,* "or a South Sea Bubble."

5.

Wilkis answered the phone in his office at Lazard Frères. It was the first call of the morning and, not surprisingly, it was Levine. "Don't work today," he began.

"Dennis," Wilkis replied wearily, "you know I can't." Wilkis was amazed that Levine had so much free time; nothing had really changed since his days of playing hookey at Citibank.

"Then let's have lunch," Levine continued. "We'll go to the River Cafe."

Wilkis agreed. "Let's have lunch" meant, of course, that Levine wanted to talk about "the game." Nowadays, they never discussed it on their office phones. They used pay phones if they had to, or better yet, met in person.

At the time, in mid-1984, no place in New York was "hotter" than the River Cafe, an elegant, exorbitantly expensive restaurant located on a barge tethered to the Brooklyn waterfront. Restaurants had suddenly become the new theater for rich New Yorkers, most on expense accounts. They were the places to see and be seen, to display the latest fashions, to impress each other with the ability to get the right table.

Levine loved the trendy spots, loved using his "walking-around money" to secure the best tables. That afternoon he got a table with a stunning view of the Manhattan skyline across the East River and waited for his friend. "I'm testing your loyalty," Levine began when Wilkis arrived. "Are you paying?"

Wilkis nodded, feeling he had no alternative.

"Good."

Wilkis could easily afford it. He'd recently visited the Cayman Islands for the first time since shifting his account, and his bankers had been all smiles. In little more than a year, his account showed gains of well over 50%.

Levine ordered a bottle of expensive Bordeaux and looked im-
ploringly at Wilkis. "Bob, there's something I want to know," Levine
began. "Are you seeing me because you're really my friend? Or do you
only come because I give you information?"

"Cut the crap, Dennis," Wilkis replied, uncomfortable at the
sudden sentimentality. "Let's talk about the game."

But Levine seemed to want to talk about anything else. He loved
to complain about his wife, and invited Wilkis to do the same, but
Levine's crude, even vicious remarks made Wilkis uncomfortable. "I
hate to go home," Levine would say. "I can buy any babe you want."

Levine took a similar approach to just about anything Wilkis
brought up. For the first time, Wilkis was beginning to enjoy life in
Manhattan, going to concerts, operas, and bookstores, meeting people
with similar interests. None of this interested Levine. "Fuck it if you
can't buy it," was his standard line.

Levine loved to regale Wilkis with tales of injustices he endured
at Lehman Brothers. Peter Solomon "loved him," he said, but nearly
everyone else discriminated against him. Lehman was "old money," he
explained. Wilkis was puzzled. "I don't get it. Aren't they Jewish?"

"They're German," Levine answered. "They're just as bad as
WASPs."

After a while, Levine turned to the real purpose of the lunch.
"We have to talk," he said, seriously.

"What about?" Wilkis asked.

"Relax, Bob," Levine replied, drawing out the conversation even
more, prolonging the suspense. "Have a brandy." Only when the
vintage brandy arrived did he come to the point.

"Wally's incredible," he said. "So is Goldie."

Wilkis squirmed. He knew he hadn't been contributing much.
He had gleaned advance word of United Technologies' bid for Bendix,
near the end of the takeover battle that had brought Martin Siegel to
fame. That had netted Levine over $100,000 in profit on a 20,000-share
trade less than a week before the bid. But the big scores had come from
others: Levine had made over $800,000 on a Lehman deal, a Litton
Industries bid for Itek Corporation, trading on information from his
own firm. Sokolow had leaked the details of that transaction, and
Levine had incautiously bought a whopping 50,000 shares just five days
before the bid was announced. Levine had also made nearly $150,000
on the acquisition of Simmonds Precision Products Inc., a Goldman
client, by Hercules Inc.

"I've been keeping score," Levine continued. "Here's Goldman,
here's Wally. Wilkis, you're in the red."

Wilkis felt a stab of anxiety. Had he become dispensable? For all his discomfort with the relationship, Levine was still his closest friend. The game bound them together at a level of intimacy he had experienced with no one else. He truly believed that Levine cared for him. Levine seemed in frequent need of reassurance that Wilkis was his friend.

But there was an even stronger element. Wilkis had to admit that he loved the thrill of gambling on takeover bids. He liked the tension when things looked tentative and the exquisite pleasure when the bid came through and the stocks soared. These triumphs gave him an overarching sense of superiority. The money itself seemed increasingly irrelevant; unlike Levine, Wilkis didn't want to walk around with cash bulging from his pockets. He'd withdrawn almost none of his mounting trading profits.

Levine exhorted Wilkis to try harder to learn what was going on at Lazard, but made it clear he wasn't going to cut him off—at least, not now. "I have to have someone to help me keep my deals straight," Levine said, explaining that that could be Wilkis's role. "Your memory frightens me sometimes," he continued. Wilkis had almost photographic retention. "I only hope the tables don't turn and I come up against you. You know more about me than I do."

Wilkis took comfort from the fact that, for better or worse, his life was now almost inextricably linked to Levine's. Levine confessed that the game was almost the only thing that mattered to him. It was "the holiest of institutions," he said.

Wilkis returned to Lazard with new determination to serve Levine better.

Despite all of Levine's complaints, his stature at Lehman Brothers had been increasing as the takeover boom gained momentum and the firm was gradually beset by internal turmoil, chronicled in the best-selling *Greed and Glory on Wall Street*. As the earthier traders, led by Lewis Glucksman, had gained the upper hand in their battle with the more patrician investment bankers, led by Peter G. Peterson, other investment bankers fled the firm. Levine's seniority increased accordingly. Gleacher, who'd hired him, left in late 1983 for Morgan Stanley, after Glucksman bypassed him to install Richard Bingham as head of M&A. Levine had maneuvered himself into the office right next to Bingham's. He argued that his intelligence-gathering was so vital that he had to be close to the department head to "report the breaking news."

In the summer of 1983, Levine managed to grab the ball during a Lehman-backed bid by Clabir Corporation for HMW Industries Inc., a defense contractor and weapons manufacturer known for its deadly cluster bombs. Clabir was a client of Lehman investment banker Steve

Waters, who tapped Levine to be his number-two man on the deal. Levine in turn asked Sokolow to handle some of the analysis. The comparatively low-profile, roughly $100 million deal soon had an illustrious Wall Street cast: Siegel represented the target, HMW; Reich was assigned to the deal by Wachtell, so he was actually working with Levine; and the two biggest factors in the outcome of the bid were arbitrageurs Boesky and Robert Freeman at Goldman, Sachs, who amassed huge positions in HMW.

Levine, his extra-long phone cord trailing him as he paced about the office, soon staked out a role talking to the arbs and working the street for information about Boesky's and Freeman's intentions. Waters let Levine do his thing, amazed at the way information spread in this new era of dealmaking. Sometimes he'd mention something to Siegel, his counterpart on the other side, and within an hour his phone would ring with calls from Boesky and Freeman, who would already know what he'd just told Siegel. Other investors, of course, were privy to none of this, but no one gave much thought to whether securities laws were being skirted; it all fell into a broad "gray area."

Boesky and Freeman played vital roles in the HMW drama, illustrating the new central position of arbitrageurs. HMW initially resisted Clabir's bid, but Waters thought he could get a friendly deal at the right price. Boesky and Freeman, however, had amassed such a large block of HMW stock between them that the company's attitude was almost irrelevant. Indeed, it was Siegel, capitalizing on his relationship with the arbs, who persuaded Boesky and Freeman to work together, using their large combined shares to hold out for a high price. He persuaded them to file a 13-D disclosure which would acknowledge that they were acting as a group.

What mattered, therefore, was the price at which Boesky and Freeman would sell. Waters and Levine visited Freeman at his office at Goldman, Sachs, asking him point-blank, "What do we have to do to get you to sell?"

Obviously Clabir was going to have to raise its bid, and the higher the ultimate price, the more Lehman would earn in fees. Clabir chairman Henry Clark lived in Greenwich, Connecticut. One Sunday evening, Levine offered to drive Waters up for a meeting at Clark's house. Levine pulled up to the curb outside Waters's apartment building in a sleek new top-of-the-line BMW, which startled Waters. He guessed the car cost nearly $50,000, far more than any car he owned. "It's a present for my wife," Levine told him.

At the meeting, Clark was proving obstinate, seemingly indifferent to the sophisticated financial projections Waters was prepared to explain. But Levine startled him. "Come on, Henry," he said. "Raise your bid. If you change your offer, I'll kiss you."

Suddenly Clark had a twinkle in his eye. "Dennis, I'll change the offer if you *don't* kiss me." And he did raise the bid.

Levine was flush with the success of that minor triumph, and Waters had to admit Levine's unorthodox approaches struck a chord with some clients. But Levine's gambit was quickly eclipsed when Kohlberg Kravis Roberts, encouraged by Siegel, entered the bidding for HMW. Clark had to raise his bid repeatedly, ultimately offering $47 a share.

Finally Waters, at Lipton's and Reich's behest, called Boesky and Freeman, offering to drop the tender offer and buy out the arbitrageurs' stakes. Just as they hoped, the prospect of losing a bid for the whole company led HMW into a merger agreement: within five minutes, Siegel called Waters, seeking to negotiate a friendly deal.

Though it looked like a defeat on the surface, the deal was considered another triumph for Siegel. His shrewd handling of the arbs and encouragement of KKR had forced Clabir to raise its price numerous times, ultimately leading to a transaction at a level that was more than three times the price at which HMW had been trading before the bidding contest. Ironically, in what later could be deemed a sign of the times, the only real loser in the process was the ostensible winner. Clabir never successfully absorbed its new acquisition and lost enormous amounts of money. HMW had to be sold, and Clark was ultimately ousted.

Levine considered Clabir a personal triumph, but he hadn't impressed everyone. Waters was under no illusions about Levine's analytical capabilities, even though he acknowledged some of his strengths. Siegel was even less impressed. Levine started calling him, sounding him out about going to work at Kidder, Peabody. Siegel interviewed him, but the session only confirmed his distaste for Levine. Levine didn't get an offer. But Siegel had been impressed by Sokolow and offered him a job.

Sokolow called Gleacher for advice. He said he had offers on the table from Kidder, Peabody and Goldman, Sachs. Gleacher encouraged him to accept the Goldman bid, but for reasons he never explained, Sokolow stayed at Lehman, continuing to feed Levine information about his deals.

In November, participants in the Clabir deal gathered for a lavish closing dinner at the 21 Club, long a favorite with investment bankers and chief executives. The dinner gave Levine an opportunity to work on his shaky relationship with Reich, who, though he had remained reasonably friendly, had cut off the flow of inside information in late 1982.

Levine was still determined to have a source inside Wachtell, Lipton, but he'd followed Wilkis's advice and hadn't leaned on Reich. At the dinner, however, he played his card, moving to the table where Reich was sitting with Wachtell colleagues and raving about his old friend's performance. He went so far as to say the deal couldn't have been completed without Reich's innovative ideas. Reich was obviously pleased; later that evening Levine maneuvered him aside and whispered, "We ought to get together again." Soon the two were having lunch on a regular basis.

Levine had chosen a propitious time to renew his attentions. Despite his brilliance in the Clabir deal, Reich felt underappreciated at Wachtell, Lipton. He was billing about 3,000 hours a year of work to clients, an astounding rate. Yet, at his annual review in late 1983, Reich was stunned by some negative criticism. He'd done little to disguise his contempt for the routine work law-firm associates were expected to perform, but partners thought he'd gone too far when, earlier that year, he'd openly read a newspaper at a meeting with a client he deemed dull. The man had complained to the firm. Reich was warned that he was developing a reputation as a prima donna, unwilling to pull his oar.

He was furious after his evaluation. He vowed to "show" them by making partner in 1984, after a mere five years as an associate. He plunged into his work even more vigorously, seething with resentment.

He was also having troubles in his marriage, and was contemplating divorce. Levine, as he had with Wilkis, drew Reich further into his orbit by sharing his own marital woes and underscoring his notion that Wachtell, Lipton didn't appreciate him and wouldn't reward him. It wasn't hard for Levine to lure "Wally" back into the fold as a full-fledged participant in the game. That spring and summer, Reich proved a gold mine of information, tipping Levine, who in turn tipped Wilkis, to six imminent deals, including a proposed transaction involving G. D. Searle, on which Levine reaped over $600,000 in illegal profits.

But by far the most thrilling coup for Levine and Wilkis was a bid by American Stores for Jewel Companies, a large Chicago-area food chain. In March, not long after their relationship revived, Reich had tipped Levine to the fact that American Stores was preparing a bid for Jewel in the neighborhood of $75 a share. Wachtell, Lipton was representing American Stores, so Reich had access to details of the planning. Levine plunged into one of his largest gambles, investing well over $3 million to buy an enormous stake of 75,000 Jewel shares.

Then nothing happened. Despite reassurance from Reich, Levine's anxiety mounted. He'd never risked so much on a single transaction. He began to talk up the possibility of a bid for Jewel with his arbitrage contacts, hoping that a surge in price and trading volume would put some pressure on American Stores to make an announcement, but no one seemed to be taking the bait. The stock was listless. So Levine and Wilkis hatched a scheme to get news of a possible bid into the press—a time-honored tactic used by investment bankers to try to get companies "in play." They felt sure they could use the press as a catalyst for speculative trading in Jewel stock.

They chose the *Chicago Tribune* as their vehicle; any news reported in its well-read business section would quickly be picked up by the rest of the financial press. Chicago was removed from Wall Street; there was little danger of any vigorous inquiry into the leaks. So Wilkis called the *Tribune*, and asked to speak with an M&A reporter. Without revealing his identity, he passed on the tip that Jewel was in negotiations to be acquired by American Stores. The *Tribune* reporter promptly checked out the tip with Jewel's chairman, who scoffed at the idea of a merger. Nothing appeared in the paper.

A few days later, Wilkis called with more specific information that the reporter could check out: the chairmen of the two companies had had a secret meeting to discuss the proposed deal at a Denver hotel. The reporter was able to confirm the information, and the *Tribune* reported that the talks had taken place and that American Stores was prepared to make an unfriendly bid for Jewel, then trading at about $44 a share, at as high as $75 a share.

The gambit worked just as Levine and Wilkis had planned. The *Tribune* article set off a flurry of buying on Wall Street, and the two companies announced their merger just a month later. Both Levine and Wilkis made their biggest profits of the game—in Levine's case, more than $1.2 million. Their leak had proven so effective that they now anonymously sent reporters copies of actual deal memos they'd stolen involving Boise Cascade, another takeover they were trying to help along. Even more exciting than the money was the thrill. The partners felt omniscient. Using information, they could actually take events into their own hands. Levine was going beyond his dream, reading *The Wall Street Journal* the day before it appeared. He was making the news.

Reich, however, was again having doubts and bouts of self-loathing. In August, he leaked details of a Warburg Pincus & Co.–led leveraged buyout of SFN Companies to Levine, who promptly bought stock (reaping profits of more than $100,000). But SFN proved to be a watershed in Reich's career at Wachtell for unrelated reasons. The family controlling 30% of SFN's stock was opposing the Warburg Pincus bid. The effort looked doomed. Then Reich discovered an arcane "fair price" provision governing the company: family members were precluded from voting their shares against the bid. Two days after Wachtell, Lipton unveiled Reich's discovery, the family capitulated.

The client was ecstatic, and Reich was a hero within the firm and, more important, in the eyes of Lipton. Suddenly Reich's vow of making partner seemed attainable. With the decisions only about two weeks away, he went to a top partner, James Fogelson, asking, "Have you heard about SFN? Do people appreciate me?" Fogelson, somewhat cryptically, said he shouldn't be talking to Reich about his partnership chances, but assured him that he was appreciated. Reich smelled partnership in the air. Moreover, he'd patched up his problems with his wife; she was now pregnant with their second child.

SFN was Reich's last leak to Levine. As before, he stopped returning Levine's calls. He wanted out of the relationship, but didn't want to confront Levine directly, fearful that he might succumb to emotional blackmail. Finally he agreed to meet Levine for lunch at a hamburger place on First Avenue in the upper 40s. Reich briefed Levine in detail on his tactics in SFN, eager to deflect the conversation from the inevitable discussion of the game. Levine went through his ritual complaints about Lehman, but this time Reich didn't echo them with his own laments about Wachtell. On the contrary, he told Levine he thought he had a good chance of making partner that year.

As they walked back toward their offices after lunch, Reich told Levine he was getting out. "It's bad, Dennis. It's wrong," Reich said. He said he was filled with anxiety and felt sick every time he leaked information.

Levine accepted the decision stoically. He told Reich his "account" was up to $300,000, and offered to pay him. "Don't you want your money?" Reich didn't. Levine promised to hold it for him, and Reich said he didn't ever want it. In Reich's mind, not taking the money was as close as he could come to expunging the whole experience from his life.

A few weeks later, the Wachtell, Lipton partners convened for their annual meeting and the selection of new partners. Reich was practically paralyzed all day, sitting at his empty desk, turning idly from one task to another but accomplishing nothing. He kept getting up to walk by Lipton's office, checking to see whether he'd returned from the meeting. Finally his phone rang, and Lipton's secretary summoned him.

When he walked in, the outcome was obvious from the smile of genuine pleasure on Lipton's face. "Congratulations," Lipton said, rising to shake his hand. "You made partner." Reich, bursting with pride, rushed back to his office to phone relatives and friends. That night he and his wife dined at an elegant French restaurant, Le Cygne. Reich, loath to drink since reading an article suggesting that alcohol killed brain cells, indulged. He was intoxicated from the wine and by his own good fortune.

Reich's loss was a blow to Levine. That summer, 1984, had been extraordinarily successful, with his insider-trading profits totaling well over $2 million. As Reich left the picture, Wilkis's determination to provide better information had begun to pay off. That summer, Wilkis had learned of a Lazard-backed bid by the Limited for Carter Hawley Hale Stores, the big California-based department store chain. The deal brought Levine over $200,000 in profits, even though the takeover bid ultimately failed. Afterward, Wilkis took steps to increase the information flow even more.

In 1983, about the time Levine was wrapping up the Clabir deal, Wilkis had finally managed to get transferred out of international and into the corporate finance mainstream at Lazard. He was assigned to a leveraged buyout and some divestitures of parts of companies. That year, Wilkis had gotten to know a young Lazard analyst named Randall Cecola, who, Wilkis noticed, was constantly hanging around a Quotron machine, punching up stock symbols. He must be trading actively, Wilkis thought. Otherwise he wouldn't be so interested in the stock market. Cecola seemed, on the surface, to have little in common with Wilkis. He was a fresh-faced Midwesterner with little exposure to either high finance or high culture. But Cecola and Wilkis, both Upper West Siders, began walking home together, usually cutting through the southwest corner of Central Park.

Cecola was the oldest of three sons; the youngest was retarded, he told Wilkis. His father had abandoned the family when he and his brothers were young and his mother had worked hard to make ends meet. Cecola spoke often of his need for more money to pay for business school and to help his family. One evening, at La Cantina, a Mexican restaurant on a lively stretch of Columbus Avenue, Wilkis started pouring out his whole story, the way he'd opened a foreign account and traded on Levine's information. He even told Cecola about his ring of informants. It was a relief to unburden himself to someone other than Levine, and Cecola was not only enthusiastic, he told Wilkis he'd already begun using inside information to trade stocks in an account in his girlfriend's name. Wilkis said he'd front Cecola $10,000, using it to trade in an account he'd maintain for Cecola's benefit. He'd learned from Levine's experience with others in the ring that it would be best to maintain control of Cecola's trading.

Cecola told Wilkis that he was already at work on a top-secret deal that would be a perfect trading opportunity: Lazard was working for Chicago Pacific Corporation on a bid for Textron, the big conglomerate.

Wilkis called Levine that night. He felt he'd proved himself, landing a new recruit with access to a deal flow, just when the loss of Reich threatened the scheme's profitability. Levine was elated, and wasted no time taking advantage of the hot new information about Textron. He bought 51,500 shares; Wilkis bought nearly 30,000. Levine also tried to capitalize on the information to enhance his reputation at Lehman.

Once his own purchases were made, Levine went to see Steve Waters, who had some dealings with Textron and knew its president, Beverly Dolan. Levine was in a high state of excitement, telling Waters he knew a hostile bid was in the offing and that Lehman should pitch Textron to get a defense assignment. Levine had visions of duplicating his coup in Criton. Waters was initially skeptical. "How do you know?" Waters asked. Levine was vague, saying only that he had an "anonymous source." Waters asked to see figures on Textron stock's price movement and trading volume. The information persuaded him that something might very well be going on.

Waters arranged a call to Dolan, with Levine also on the line. He told Dolan that Levine had information suggesting that Textron was about to become the subject of an unsolicited tender offer, and urged him to consider defensive countermeasures. But Dolan didn't sound unduly alarmed; he said he hadn't heard anything like that himself, but would be interested if Waters and Levine came across any more intelligence.

Just two weeks later, Levine's forecast proved uncannily accurate when Chicago Pacific made its tender offer. Levine was bitterly disappointed when Lehman was snubbed by Textron, which hired Morgan Stanley for its defense. But he was partly consoled by his own trading profits of more than $200,000.

Wilkis earned about $100,000 in profits on his stock. But there was a hidden cost: Levine and Wilkis's large purchases—a total of nearly 100,000 shares—and the fact that word of the Textron bid had apparently been leaking all over Wall Street, had contributed to inordinate trading volume and price movement in Textron stock before the Chicago Pacific bid was announced. The situation was so extreme that routine monitoring by the stock exchange triggered an investigation into Textron trading by the SEC.

The SEC lawyers, following the usual procedure, interviewed participants in the deal for clues as to how information may have spread. Dolan told them that his first indication of a bid was the phone call from Waters and Levine. The SEC subpoenaed the two investment bankers shortly after the deal announcement.

Sokolow was worried when he heard that Levine had been subpoenaed, but Levine was unconcerned, brushing aside Sokolow's warnings. "I've never done this sort of thing before," he told Waters. "What do I say?"

"Tell them what you know," Waters said, unconcerned. He'd participated in many such interviews over the years.

"Should I tell the truth?" Levine asked casually.

This took Waters aback. "For God's sake, yes!" he replied. "Of course you do. You're under oath."

Levine testified on November 14, 1984, just a few weeks after the deal was announced. He later laughed about it with Wilkis, boasting about how easy it had been to dupe the "pansy" SEC lawyers. Under questioning from SEC lawyer Leonard Wang, Levine lied repeatedly and flamboyantly, seeming to warm to the task as he embarked on a convoluted explanation for his prescience. He denied trading stocks in any brokerage accounts he controlled, and denied having any offshore accounts. As for the Textron bid, he offered this account: He'd been sitting in the reception area of Drexel Burnham Lambert one day, when he overheard a conversation between two men "dressed in pinstripes, gray suits, just like us. They both had briefcases." The men dropped the names of Lester Crown, a name Levine claimed to recognize as a director of Chicago Pacific, as well as others involved in the bid. "I then overheard what I would consider as garbled," Levine continued, "where they said something about a 13-D filing, the words Skadden, Arps and First Boston, and also 'fireworks in Rhode Island,' which is a direct quote." Levine claimed to have deduced that Chicago Pacific would make a hostile bid for Textron from the identity of Crown and the fact that Textron happens to be headquartered in Rhode Island—something Levine also claimed to know off the top of his head.

The explanation was both self-aggrandizing, making Levine out to be some kind of deductive genius, and utterly preposterous. Moreover, Levine couldn't provide any corroboration of his visit to Drexel's reception area. It wasn't in his calendar, and he claimed that the person he was there to visit had been out. Wang knew Levine was lying. Rarely in his years as an SEC interrogator had he heard a lamer explanation. But why? With nothing to connect Levine to any trading, or to any leaks to people who did trade, and without a witness to contradict Levine's account, the investigation went nowhere. It was eventually closed without any action.

For Levine, the brush with regulators only seemed to heighten the excitement of the game, and his sense of his own strength.

In at least one respect, Levine's testimony about how he deduced the Textron bid was correct: he had recently had occasion to visit Drexel Burnham Lambert. The firm, rebuffed by all the "stars" it had earlier targeted to complement Milken, had, perhaps inevitably, begun considering Levine.

Levine had consulted a professional "headhunter" at a recruiting firm earlier in 1984, shortly after the strife-ridden Lehman Brothers was acquired by Shearson/American Express. His résumé began circulating discreetly on Wall Street. Furious about the merger, Levine told Hill that "his dream had always been to be a Lehman partner, and now they've taken that away." "My birthright," he said, has been "taken from me."

Shortly after the merger, each department was asked to submit a list of people who should be considered for the rank of "managing director," the equivalent of partner at the now publicly traded firm. Waters, Hill, Bingham, Peter Solomon, and other top people in the M&A department met to draw up their list, and briefly, very briefly, considered including Levine's name on it.

The fact that Levine was even considered said more about the internal climate at the firm than about his colleagues' assessment of Levine's talents. Shearson Lehman was thought of as a new playing field, and former Lehman partners felt they should cast their net wide in considering possible managing directors. They had also realized that there was an opportunity to elevate many of their ranks; it was obvious Shearson wanted to stop the flow of Lehman talent to other firms.

But no one had changed their assessment of Levine's weakness in fundamental investment banking skills—not even Solomon, his biggest supporter. Levine was credited with landing some business, but everyone was expected to be a business-getter; Levine's achievements didn't stand out particularly. Moreover, his attitude and posturing had alienated many of the younger members of the department. So Levine was quickly discarded as a possibility. Indeed, Sokolow had much better reviews, and was dropped from the list only because of his youth.

Levine was stunned. He complained bitterly to Wilkis, and began badgering Solomon, who tried to reassure him, promising that he'd be reconsidered later in the year. At that time, Shearson Lehman again failed to elevate him to managing director. But the firm did value him, promoting him to senior vice president and giving him a bonus of $500,000 on top of his base pay of $75,000.

By the standards of anything but deal-crazed Wall Street, it was a princely sum, an amount few of Levine's 33-year-old peers from Queens had even dreamt of. But Levine greeted the news with contempt. A half million dollars, in his eyes, wasn't nearly enough to support his newfound standard of living.

From the outset, Levine had preached to other members of the ring that their spending, consumption, and lifestyles should be modest, so as not to raise questions about their incomes. But he had begun violating his own strictures almost immediately, first with his withdrawals of "walking-around money," and later with purchases of ever more extravagant status symbols.

His top-of-the-line BMW had already raised colleagues' eyebrows, and that was only the beginning. Levine and his wife became regulars at many of Manhattan's most expensive restaurants. Levine usually paid in cash. He also bought her a diamond necklace. His father, Philip, received a new Jaguar. Levine began frequenting expensive, snobbish art galeries, where he was an easy target for sharp and sophisticated dealers. He bought works by Picasso, Miró, and Rodin.

He also spent $500,000 to acquire the ultimate Manhattan symbol of having "arrived": a large Park Avenue co-op. The building he chose, on the east side of the wide boulevard, is rich with gothic detailing and occupies almost an entire block. Its interior courtyard is accessible through imposing wrought-iron gates. This embodiment of prewar bourgeois respectability hardly reflected Levine's own taste, but he wasted little time in remaking the apartment in his image.

Levine hired an architect and interior decorator, and out went the architectural detailing. The apartment was gutted, and sweeping curved walls were installed. Glass blocks separated the dining room from one of the bedrooms. Bleached oak floors were laid. Sybaritic new bathrooms were created, along with a dazzling high-tech kitchen or, rather, two kitchens: Levine had the first one ripped out when it didn't suit him.

Reich, who lived in an old brownstone on the West Side, was flabbergasted at the transformation and the extensive high-tech gadgetry. Levine obviously loved his new surroundings, despite his frequent, contemptuous references to his "fag" decorator. His favorite detail was a large color television set that, at the push of a bedside button, rose from its hiding place in a custom-made bureau. The renovation cost $500,000, enabling Levine to boast, accurately if indiscreetly, about his "million-dollar" apartment.

Paying for all of this necessitated much more frequent visits to Bank Leu in the Bahamas, trips Levine often described to colleagues as gambling jaunts. His bankers often had to scramble to muster enough $100 bills, the currency Levine insisted upon. During 1984 alone, Levine withdrew $200,000 in March, $200,000 in July, and $90,000 in December. He appears to have spent all of it.

By the time Levine got the bad news that he was being promoted only to senior vice president, he was already prepared to abandon Shearson Lehman. As the deal flow had steadily increased during the year, other firms were becoming almost desperate for investment bankers with even a modicum of experience in M&A, and Levine's headhunter at Hadley Lockwood found his once-lackluster résumé to be in high demand. Nearly all the top investment banks were at least willing to consider hiring Levine; even Gleacher, now at Morgan Stanley, tried to recruit him.

But almost from the outset, Levine had his eyes on Drexel. He had his first contacts with the firm in March, and, he reported to Wilkis, "They love me." Drexel, he said, was a "license to print money." All the firm really needed was "a great banker" like himself to complement the Milken West Coast operation. He envisioned hobnobbing with Sir James Goldsmith and Ronald Perelman, a prelude to the day when Levine himself would step onto the stage as a major corporate raider.

Hadley Lockwood did a custom résumé for Levine specifically targeted at Drexel. It was almost a parody of the emerging values of the times: "Dennis describes himself as a person who truly loves to do two things," it began, "do deals and make money."

Drexel, the résumé went on, was "tailor-made" for Levine's "aggressive" deal skills and "new business-generation capability." And it made a virtue of Levine's weak academic record and lack of broadening activities: "Having graduated from schools that do not generally produce investment bankers, Dennis has had great difficulty fighting his way into the major bracket. In the process, he has become something of a workaholic who rarely touches down for an interview except on the shortest of notice, and even then often has to cancel."

The pitch struck just the right tone for David Kay, Drexel's head of M&A. Levine reported an immediate affinity for Kay, who, unlike Gleacher or Hill, seemed to have much in common with him. What had often come across to others as a phony heartiness, boastfulness, and self-aggrandizement, seemed to Kay to be the very hallmarks of "star quality"; Kay went so far as to describe Levine as "flawless." When Kay made some checks on Levine, he was particularly impressed that both Lipton and Flom, the preeminent takeover lawyers, gave Levine enthusiastic recommendations.

Eventually Levine had offers from Morgan Stanley and First Boston, too. But he recognized that competition was almost nonexistent at Drexel, and the potential vast. He negotiated a package that gave him a base salary of $140,000 and a thousand shares of Drexel stock, with a minimum guaranteed bonus his first year of $750,000. He could collect $200,000 of this bonus as an advance when he arrived at Drexel for work. For its efforts in promoting Levine, Hadley Lockwood's fee (paid by Drexel) was $267,000.

Levine, typically, hadn't accepted immediately; he had tried to use the Drexel offer as further leverage at Shearson Lehman. He went to see Waters and unveiled the Drexel offer, emphasizing that he'd be a managing director there and would be paid more than a million dollars. "This is a terrific chance," he said. Waters wasn't impressed. Indeed, the Shearson Lehman managing directors had recently decided that, in the wake of all the turmoil within the firm, they needed to emphasize collegiality and a commitment to the firm over self-interest. Levine was the antithesis of this. "We're not going to do that for you, Dennis," Waters had responded. "Maybe you should take it."

Levine celebrated his move to Drexel with another extravagant purchase. One sunny weekend morning, Gleacher was enjoying a stroll through Central Park when Levine came rushing up, smiling and seemingly excited to see him. "You've got to see my new car," he said, steering Gleacher back toward Fifth Avenue. There, parked at the curb, was a bright red, low-slung, two-seat Ferrari Testarossa. Levine had paid $105,000 for it. Gleacher wasn't a car buff, but Levine insisted he get in for a ride. He pressed hard on the accelerator and roared down the avenue, flattening Gleacher into his seat. He gleefully reported to Wilkis that he'd "scared the shit" out of his former boss.

Levine arrived for work at Drexel on February 4, 1985. When Drexel's Fred Joseph ran into Peter Solomon soon after, Solomon told him he was "furious" that Drexel had "stolen" his protégé. Joseph just smiled, taking Solomon's obvious anger as a high compliment.

Kay, eager to get Levine on the fast track to stardom, immediately assigned him to what would be Drexel's first foray into the world of junk bond–backed hostile takeovers, a plan by Drexel client Coastal Corporation to acquire American Natural Resources Co. (ANR), a gas pipeline company. Using one of its "highly confident" letters, Drexel planned a lightning-fast strike with an all-cash tender offer of $60 a share.

On February 14, just 10 days after starting at Drexel, Levine used a pay phone to call Bernhard Meier, the Swiss banker who was now handling the "Mr. Diamond" account at Bank Leu. He told Meier to buy an astounding 145,000 shares of ANR, using almost the entire balance of his account, over $7 million. He cautioned him to spread the buying among several brokers so the size of the trading wouldn't attract attention.

Levine similarly wasted no time in pursuing his own brand of investment banking, immediately spending much of his time canvassing his Wall Street sources for rumors and tips that might lead to new business, and maintaining his ties to his network of arbitrage sources. He reassured Coastal executives in early strategy sessions that ANR was increasingly vulnerable because more and more of its stock was moving into the hands of arbitrageurs, who weren't interested in longterm investments in the company and would be eager to sell into a tender offer for fast profits. Levine staked out a role for himself, keeping in constant touch with arbs for any developments that might affect planning.

Ivan Boesky had, heretofore, never taken any calls from Levine, even though Levine had been so anxious to make an impression on the arbitrageur that he had sent him, anonymously, copies of the Elf/Kerr-McGee documents he and Wilkis had stolen from Lazard. Boesky had never heard of Levine before he moved to Drexel. Now Kay and other contacts of Boesky's at Drexel were touting Levine as the new star who'd beef up Drexel's M&A capacity. If Levine's move to Drexel achieved nothing else, it was notable for moving Levine into the small orbit of people with access to Boesky.

On the phone, as he had with many others, Boesky began by parrying and probing with Levine, seeking hints of any bid in the offing, trying to gauge the investment banker's attitudes about ANR, a stock Boesky had already accumulated. Boesky must have been amazed at the ease with which he was able to get Levine to reveal confidential aspects of the impending bid. Levine was desperate to make a favorable impression on Boesky, recognizing how important access to him could be for his career at Drexel, and he began phoning the arbitrageur at regular and frequent intervals, often 20 times a week. Levine asked for nothing in return for what he knew was valuable information, but Boesky instinctively reciprocated with market information about other traders, gleaned from his own sources, such as John Mulheren.

Boesky's trading records in ANR suggest that Levine was passing on information to a remarkable degree, since Boesky increased his stake in the company right after nearly every significant—and supposedly confidential—development in Coastal's strategy. Eventually

Boesky had amassed 9.9% of ANR's shares, requiring a public disclosure of the dates and amounts of his purchases.

With trading so heavy in ANR stock, Coastal rushed out an announcement of its tender offer in early March. After initially struggling to stave off the bid, ANR succumbed two months later and agreed to accept Coastal's offer. Levine, having bet nearly all his profits, made nearly $1.4 million. Boesky earned over $3 million.

The preannouncement trading had been so massive, so brazen, that all the stock-watch monitors buzzed at the stock exchange and the SEC. The computers, however, were of little help in actually proving there was any insider trading. Investigators made even less progress than they had in the Textron case; this time, they didn't even get to the point of questioning Levine, a deal participant, before they abandoned the investigation for lack of good leads.

Even as he reaped his massive illegal profits and breached his client's confidences, Levine had proven himself on his first hard-fought, high-profile transaction at Drexel. Kay was impressed with Levine's ability to gather market intelligence. He was convinced he had the star Drexel needed.

ANR was Levine's biggest score to date, but it was soon eclipsed. Even as his new post at Drexel put him in close proximity to a potentially far more lucrative deal flow than the one he'd seen at Shearson Lehman, his ring of informants kept him amply supplied with other trading opportunities. The scheme was working as Levine had dreamed it would. In March, "Goldie" leaked word of an impending leveraged buyout of McGraw Edison. In April, Cecola tipped Wilkis that Houston Natural Gas had retained Lazard to handle a merger with Internorth, another pipeline company. Wilkis passed the information on to Levine, who again bought through Meier, indiscreetly characterizing the as-yet-unannounced transaction as a "sure deal." In May, just after the Coastal merger, Sokolow at Shearson Lehman—now having "recruiting" lunches with Levine, according to Levine's expense accounts—tipped Levine to R. J. Reynolds's impending mega-bid for Nabisco Brands.

Levine again wagered almost everything he had, buying 150,000 shares of Nabisco on May 6. Less than a month later, with hectic trading plainly indicating the existence of leaks, an anxious Reynolds announced its bid. Levine's profit was $2.7 million.

Celebrating with Wilkis over dinner at a Manhattan steakhouse, Palm Too, Levine couldn't resist telling Wilkis that there was now a new component to the ring. "I tipped the Russian on Nabisco," Levine confided to a surprised Wilkis. From his remarks about the importance of "the Russian," Wilkis knew exactly who Levine meant. It made him nervous; involving someone the size of Boesky was vaulting their conspiracy to an entirely new level, one more likely to attract scrutiny.

Levine was reassuring, saying they could ultimately get more out of "the Russian" than vice versa. In any event, since ANR, Levine had curried favor with Boesky by passing on deals generated within his ring. He didn't know the size of Boesky's positions, but he knew Boesky had traded actively—and made millions.

The pattern of leaks had become so consistent that Levine and Boesky met to formalize their arrangement. Levine had baited the hook and secured his access to Boesky by initially offering the information for nothing in return; now he wanted profit participation. As he had done with Siegel, Boesky proposed that the two meet at the Harvard Club. There and in subsequent meetings, they plunged into much tougher negotiations than Siegel had engaged in. Rather than some ill-defined promise of a "bonus," Levine wanted a precise measure for calculating his share.

Despite his high regard for his own negotiating abilities, Levine seems to have gotten a worse deal than Siegel did. Eventually, Levine and Boesky agreed on two separate formulas: Levine was entitled to 5% of Boesky's profits on a stock if Levine's tip led to Boesky's initial purchase. If Boesky already held a position, but Levine's information proved useful, Levine would receive 1% of Boesky's profits. And Boesky extracted a tough concession: Any losses he incurred acting on Levine's tips would be deducted from Levine's share of the profits.

Once, Levine would have rushed to tell Wilkis everything about his new conquest. Now, however, he shaded the facts to the point of falsehood. "It's unbelievable," Levine confided on one of their midday walks, as he told Wilkis about the meeting with Boesky at the Harvard Club, "but Ivan offered me $1 million in cash. Any way I want it. He owns everybody. Gleacher, Wasserstein. But I refused it," Levine said.

Wilkis was skeptical. "That doesn't sound like you," Wilkis said sardonically.

"I'd much rather have the Russian owe me," Levine shot back, "than own me."

Even as Levine was dazzled by his conquest of Boesky, he had set his sights on a new and grander role model. That year, 1985, Levine attended his first Predators' Ball, where he basked in the afterglow of the successful Coastal/ANR transaction. Kay and other Drexel officials touted Levine as their new star, and introduced him to an array of Drexel's big-money clients. He finally met Boesky face to face. But the one who made the greatest impression on him, he told Wilkis repeatedly, was Sir James Goldsmith, who gave a speech at the conference.

Few men could outwardly have had less in common than the

Queens-bred Levine and the worldly Anglo-French financier. Sir James was one of the few early raiders to have powerful intellectual and ideological underpinnings for his pursuit of fortune. He was impatient with the ennui of the old European order, hated the entrenched "corpocracy" of complacent corporate management, and believed passionately in meritocracy and free markets—all, at the time, wildly unconventional ideas in his native Europe. He had assembled a far-flung empire, often through hostile takeovers, ranging from French publishing (he owned the influential weekly *L'Express*) to the Grand Union grocery chain to European foodstuffs manufacturers and American forest tracts and natural resources. None of this made much of an impression on Levine, however. He coveted Sir James's lifestyle.

Sir James had a wife, a former wife, and a mistress, and had even vacationed simultaneously with his two families, shuttling back and forth by boat between the Italian peninsulas where each was housed. His Manhattan townhouse, with its marble floors, antique furniture, damask wallpaper, and art and statuary, was the embodiment of Old World taste, money, and refinement. He owned or rented equally palatial houses in London and Paris, the Costa del Sol, Sardinia, and Barbados, and later launched construction of a lavish estate on the Pacific coast of Mexico. He was gracious, disarmingly polite, friendly, and open to the unconventional. Levine arranged a vacation in Barbados; he excitedly told Wilkis after returning that he'd gotten a good look at Sir James's estate. He started imitating some of Sir James's mannerisms. Wilkis thought it was ridiculously pretentious, but still an improvement over Levine's usual crass demeanor.

One of the deals generated at the bond conference was a Drexel-backed bid by Sir James for Crown Zellerbach Corporation, a huge forest-products and paper company based in San Francisco. Sir James had already accumulated a substantial stake in the company, which had rebuffed his approaches about a friendly acquisition. Levine was thrilled when Kay tapped him to head the Drexel M&A team on the deal. (Financing, of course, stayed under control of the Milken operation on the West Coast.)

After Sir James launched his bid, Crown Zellerbach began negotiations to be acquired by a "white knight" rescuer, Mead Corporation, another paper company. Mead, Crown Zellerbach hoped, would keep the company whole, rather than breaking it up and selling off pieces as threatened by Sir James. Mead agreed to buy the company at a substantial premium, $50 a share, and arranged to buy Sir James's large stake to end the hostilities and complete the transaction. Levine had already built a healthy stake of his own in Crown Zellerbach stock, trading as usual on inside information. Now, in anticipation of the

Mead deal, Levine called Bank Leu to arrange another large purchase of Crown Zellerbach shares, spending a total of about $4 million. Boesky also took a big position, and Levine was thrilled to be able to impress Sir James by lining up Boesky's support and arranging for Sir James to buy Boesky's stake.

The day Mead's board was meeting in Dayton, Ohio, to approve the deal, Sir James hosted a celebratory luncheon in his elegant town-house dining room, with food prepared by his staff and served on Limoges china with rare wines, both red and white. Levine was in a jovial mood, and Sir James seemed to enjoy his high spirits. Several others involved in the bid were also there, including Roland Franklin, an aide to Sir James, and George Lowy, a partner at Cravath, Swaine & Moore, the firm representing Mead. During lunch, Lowy excused himself to take a phone call from Mead.

When he returned, Lowy looked sheepish. "You won't want to give me dessert," he said to Sir James, announcing that, in a surprise move, the Mead board had rejected the Crown Zellerbach acquisition, dashing the company's hopes for a white knight rescue and the lucrative buyout of Sir James's position. The decision, once announced, was certain to cause Crown Zellerbach stock to plunge. Sir James was remarkably nonchalant, shrugging and announcing that he would simply proceed with his own hostile bid. He insisted Lowy stay and enjoy the rest of the meal.

In striking contrast, Levine suddenly turned "gray" at the news, Franklin noticed. Levine's mood plunged, and he left at the earliest opportunity. He ran, panicked, to a pay phone, and ordered Bank Leu to liquidate his large position. "He must be calling his broker," Sir James observed after Levine had rushed from the room. He smiled, and everyone laughed at the prospect. No one took it seriously.

By calling his broker when he did, Levine avoided a big loss in his trading account, and emerged with a small gain. Sir James eventually completed his takeover of Crown Zellerbach, despite a vigorous defense. While Levine was lauded by Kay for his work within Drexel, Sir James showed scant interest in furthering his relationship with Levine.

Levine's honeymoon at Drexel was coming to an end. Soon he was again in a familiar mode, complaining to Wilkis that he wasn't sufficiently appreciated. He hated Leon Black, he said, the obnoxious fellow M&A strategist, whom he referred to as "the fat slob." Black, Levine claimed, was the only banker in New York who had any influence with the firm's real power center in Beverly Hills. And he complained that Drexel, unlike Shearson, was all finance-driven. The West Coast operation was bringing in all the M&A and corporate finance business, which meant that his share of the bonus pool would be correspondingly smaller.

Wilkis, eager to leave Lazard, feeling that his career was going nowhere, wished Levine would complain less, and help *him* get a job at Drexel. But Levine seemed increasingly uninterested in Wilkis's future. Although Wilkis managed to get an interview at Drexel, his cerebral approach and more reserved demeanor didn't seem to be what the firm was looking for, and he didn't get an offer. Wilkis blamed Levine for not going to bat for him. Finally, on his own, Wilkis did get an offer from E. F. Hutton. He seemed thrilled—until Hutton told him he'd have to take a routine lie-detector test for prospective employees.

Wilkis broke into a cold sweat, terrified that he'd have to lie about a foreign bank account and his illicit trading. He begged Hutton to exempt him, saying it was demeaning, an imposition. But Hutton insisted. A Lazard colleague who overheard some of Wilkis's pleas asked him why he was upset. "Everybody has done something," Wilkis said. "Everybody's stolen something." The day before he was scheduled to take the test, Wilkis broke out in hives from head to toe.

But in the event, he took the test and passed without incident. In the typically cursory examination common at the time, there were no questions he couldn't answer truthfully. He was asked about drug use, but not insider trading.

At Hutton, Wilkis seemed finally to find his niche. He felt he was treated as a seasoned professional, an important member of an M&A team that, while not a major force, was growing. He celebrated the new job by buying a Park Avenue apartment to rival Levine's, and again began to consider distancing himself from his best friend.

At dinner with Wilkis and his wife, Levine would drone on, bragging about his exploits at Drexel. Laurie Levine would gaze dreamily into space, but the evenings drove Wilkis's wife to distraction, and she begged not to continue them. Wilkis also lost his Lazard source, Cecola, who completed his analyst program at Lazard and left that fall for Harvard Business School. "Can't you throw me some bones while I'm at business school?" Cecola had pleaded, eager to keep up his trading. Wilkis couldn't see recruiting another source, and he didn't want to compromise his work at Hutton. In any event, Levine was drifting away from him, increasingly preoccupied with a world that offered riches and glamour that Wilkis could never rival.

At Drexel, after having worked there for just 10 months, Levine had his first bonus review with Kay, an event he'd anticipated by working up a departmental profit calculation, demonstrating his own contribution to the bottom line. He'd made no secret of the fact that compensation was extremely important to him, frequently reminding

Kay that "I want to become as wealthy as one can get" and that he wanted "to make more money every year than I did before." Kay saw such attitudes as a plus, and thought they typified star qualities in the M&A business. At their session, Kay reviewed Levine's work during the year, telling Levine he felt he could be "relied upon to take a transaction and work on it at the highest level of confidence." Then, feeling certain that he was about to bestow on Levine a sum that exceeded even Levine's measures of his own abilities, Kay said, "Your bonus for 1985 is . . . one million dollars."

"That," Levine replied, "is an insult." He stood up and stalked out of Kay's office.

6.

"Let's have coffee," Siegel said to Boesky on the phone, using their new code to indicate he wanted a meeting. Siegel now insisted they meet in person; he worried that Boesky's phones were tapped. With all Boesky's CIA talk, and after his recent experience with the exotic courier, Siegel thought anything was possible. He walked the few blocks from Kidder, Peabody to Water Street, then paced back and forth. He wondered briefly what he'd say if he encountered anyone he knew. It was winter, January 1983, not a time of year when one would ordinarily go for a stroll around the block.

Boesky soon emerged from the lobby of his office building at 55 Water Street and hurried toward Siegel. As they walked, Siegel explained that Kidder, Peabody had been retained by Diamond Shamrock Corporation, a large chemical and natural resources company, to explore the acquisition of an oil company. While nothing was definite yet, Siegel had been shown a list of possible acquisition candidates, and a likely target was a comparatively small oil producer, Natomas Co.

Siegel thought that Natomas fit into the Boesky scheme in two important ways: If Boesky started buying the stock now, months before any transaction was likely, the trading would be so far in advance as to elude any monitoring for possible insider trading; Siegel himself wasn't even certain there would be a deal. Of course, Boesky wasn't the only one who would profit if he started buying now. Siegel wanted some buying pressure to show in Natomas's stock. He wanted to soften up the company for the possibility of a friendly overture from Diamond Shamrock, and the best way to do that was to convince Natomas that it was "in play," likely to be the target of a much less attractive hostile takeover bid.

The men turned off Water Street, walking toward the East River in a largely deserted section of Manhattan south of the South Street Seaport. Talking quietly, glancing around occasionally to see if they were being observed, Siegel laid out Diamond Shamrock's plans, urging Boesky to begin buying slowly, and warning him of the possibility that the deal wouldn't be consummated.

Shortly thereafter, Boesky started buying. Things went smoothly until, in March, Diamond Shamrock briefly decided to scrap the deal because it was having trouble raising money for the acquisition. Boesky nearly panicked, but Siegel reassured him, urging him to hold on to his position.

Ultimately, the money for the acquisition was raised through a stock offering, and the deal was closed in May. By then, Boesky had built up an enormous position, though he never disclosed to Siegel exactly how much he was buying, or at what prices. Siegel wouldn't let him discuss any aspect of his position on the phone. Only while reviewing data for the merger did Siegel note, to his amazement, that Boesky had acquired over 800,000 shares. Boesky's total profit on the deal came to $4.8 million. That, Siegel thought, ought to ensure his generosity later on.

Siegel soon had another opportunity to serve Boesky and his own client, as well. In September, Gordon Getty, the eccentric heir to the J. Paul Getty fortune, called. He was dissatisfied with the way Getty Oil was being run. Siegel thought he was likely either to launch a bid for the company himself, probably with other allies, or to sell his stake to someone likely to acquire the entire company.

The stocks of companies controlled by family interests are often depressed by an expectation that they can't be taken over, so any news of disaffection in a powerful family is eagerly sought by arbitrageurs. Siegel leaked the news to Boesky, who bought some Getty options, later disposing of them at a profit of $220,000. Boesky later played the deal for even more profits, as first Pennzoil and then Texaco made bids for Getty. Some estimated that Boesky's Getty profits were as high as $50 million.

Siegel tried to tailor his leaks to what he perceived as the interests of his clients. He kept far more information secret than he gave Boesky. Boesky pressed him for more leaks, even offering to put money for Siegel in a European account. "Ivan, I'm not interested in that," Siegel had replied. "I'm not going to flee the country, for God's sake." Boesky kept trying, offering to invest in real estate for Siegel, even going so far as to offer to hire Siegel's father.

Perhaps the most striking example of Siegel's failure to tip Boesky came when Brown-Forman Distillers Corporation launched a cash tender offer for Lenox Inc., a maker of fine china. Lenox retained Siegel, who helped pioneer, during the course of the deal, one of the most effective antitakeover techniques of the eighties: the "poison pill." The poison pill was largely the brainchild of takeover lawyer Martin Lipton, but Siegel had contributed significantly to its evolution. The pill, now widespread in corporate America, is used to make a hostile takeover prohibitively expensive by giving shareholders exorbitant rights if such an attempt is launched. Lenox, for example, tried to save itself by developing a pill giving its shareholders the right to buy Brown-Forman stock if Brown-Forman launched a bid.

The deal was an arbitrage challenge because Lenox fought back. After surging initially, its stock price dropped back. The situation moved into litigation, making the outcome even more uncertain. Many arbs panicked and sold, but Boesky continued buying. On the very day that Lenox decided to capitulate after all and accept a higher bid from Brown-Forman, Boesky bought a huge stake of over 62,000 Lenox shares. He ultimately owned about 9% of Lenox and made about $4 million on the deal.

Other arbitrageurs were amazed and jealous; rumors began circulating on Wall Street that Boesky had to have a source of inside information. No one, it was reasoned, could be so consistently prescient, especially in a deal with the peaks and valleys of a Brown-Forman/Lenox. Yet it was one of the deals in which Siegel didn't breach his client's confidence. Until almost the very end, Lenox wanted to fight. And Siegel thought the poison pill defense would actually succeed. He advised Boesky not to buy the stock. When the Lenox board suddenly capitulated, Siegel became convinced that Boesky had had another source of inside information on the deal.

In another instance, Boesky called Siegel, saying he'd gotten some confidential information on Gould Inc., a client of Siegel's. Siegel suspected Boesky had gotten the information from a Kidder, Peabody institutional broker in Boston named Donald Little. Little, an avid polo player, handled a lot of trading for Boesky and was a close friend through polo circles of William Ylvisaker, the chairman of Gould. Boesky asked Siegel to confirm the information, but Siegel lied, saying he didn't know.

Late in December 1983, the two met to discuss Siegel's "bonus." Siegel reminded Boesky of how valuable his information had been in the Natomas and Getty deals, and they also discussed at some length other advice Siegel had given, such as his estimates of valuation on a Utah pipeline. Though this was hardly as valuable as inside information, Siegel thought it was only fair to be compensated for that too; he rationalized what he was doing by seeing his relationship with Boesky as a sort of "consulting" arrangement. Finally Siegel asked for $250,-000. He didn't make any elaborate calculations; he knew Boesky had scored big in Natomas, and, though the Getty situation was still unfolding, he assumed Boesky stood to make a lot on that deal, too. Siegel simply approached the matter as he did his bonus at Kidder, Peabody, and $250,000 was what he thought was "fair."

It was also what Siegel thought he needed. His own salary and bonus that year, a substantial $733,000, was actually less than he'd made the year before. He'd bought a four-bedroom cooperative apartment on Gracie Square, just across from the New York mayor's mansion, for $975,000, and the repair work and redecorating were just beginning.

Boesky readily agreed to the $250,000—the sum represented a tiny fraction of his own profits on Siegel's information—and the cash drop was arranged. Again Siegel stood in the lobby of the Plaza Hotel, watching for the swarthy courier. The same code words, "red light" and "green light," were repeated, and the briefcase was handed over.

When Siegel returned to his apartment, he counted the money, again wrapped in Caesar's Palace ribbons, and found that a substantial amount was missing—taken, he assumed, by Boesky's courier. In one stack of bills, instead of the hundreds he had requested, were one-dollar bills. The total only came to $210,000. He felt cheated.

Siegel arranged another meeting, and confronted Boesky, saying the courier was stealing. Boesky was indignant. He swore the courier was someone he could trust, someone who wouldn't skim any of the cash. Siegel shrugged, deciding it wasn't worth pressing the argument. Still, a deal was a deal. He vowed to himself that next year he'd increase his demands, assuming that 15% to 20% would end up in someone else's pockets.

Within months, Boesky was making more money than ever, mostly from a deal that didn't involve any information from Siegel: Gulf Oil, Boesky's old nemesis, the company that, by abruptly pulling out of the Cities Service deal, had nearly ruined him. Texas oilman T. Boone Pickens, the corporate raider and Drexel client, had disclosed a large stake in Gulf in September, about the time Boesky received his first Getty tip. Eventually, with Drexel's backing, Pickens launched a partial tender offer for the huge oil company. It scared Gulf enough to drive it into the arms of a white knight rescuer, Standard Oil of California (Socal), in what became history's largest merger at the time. The deal rocked Wall Street by its sheer size, and demonstrated the power of a Drexel-backed raider.

The deal also added substantially to Boesky's riches. He began tracking Pickens's purchases, checking regularly with Mulheren for news of large trades, and continuing to buy steadily himself as the maneuvering continued into 1984. As he had done before, Boesky was willing to risk a huge percentage of his capital, ultimately acquiring a stake of about 5 million Gulf shares. This time the Gulf splurge had a happy outcome, at least for Boesky. A bidding war broke out, with one bidder being Kohlberg Kravis Roberts, advised by Siegel. Siegel didn't give Boesky any inside information, even though he knew all the details of KKR's planning. But when the Socal acquisition went through—after some suspense-filled days while Congress contemplated antitrust action against the combination—Boesky earned an estimated $65 million in profits.

To celebrate, Mulheren, who also profited handsomely on the deal, threw a lavish party for about 25 of his arb friends who'd ridden the Gulf deal to its lucrative conclusion. Mulheren had decorated the tables with centerpieces of Gulf service station products with the familiar orange Gulf Oil trademark. As expensive wines, cocktails, and brandies flowed, Mulheren rose and addressed the group. "I have some good news for you," he said. "James E. Lee [the defeated chairman of Gulf, whose decision to pull out of Cities Service had enraged so many arbs] has decided to join us and bury the hatchet. He wants to put this whole thing behind him." With that, Mulheren gestured, and in came a trained monkey dressed in bright blue overalls with the Gulf logo. Boesky roared until he had tears in his eyes. He liked the monkey so much that he later hired the primate for a party of his own.

The fiscal year that ended in March 1984 was a very good one for Boesky. After losing $13.7 million the previous fiscal year because of the earlier Gulf fiasco, he earned an extraordinary $76.5 million. It was surely more than the former Detroit ice cream salesman, having come so close to bankruptcy so many times, had ever expected to earn. Boesky moved his operations to lavish new offices in midtown Manhattan, at 650 Fifth Avenue, that had been occupied by the Pahlevi Foundation, which administered the fortunes of the shah of Iran before he was overthrown. The mysterious Hushang Wekili accompanied Boesky, gaining his own office, salary, and bonus. The bonus reached $1 million a year—despite the fact that no one else who worked with

Boesky could figure out what he did. Conway, Lessman, Mooradian, and others learned, however, to confide in Wekili.

In contrast to the spartan conditions in Boesky's earlier operations, the new offices were lavish, decorated with help from Seema. The corridors were marble, with soft etched-glass panels and sculpture. Boesky's own office was huge, with snow-white carpeting and white walls, and views of Central Park and midtown's glittering office towers.

Most amazing was the electronic gadgetry that made his earlier microphone command system seem primitive. In addition to speakers, each researcher and trader now had a desktop television on which Boesky could project his image. At his own desk, Boesky had a large-screen television divided into two sections. On the upper screen he could project any image, including his own. The lower part of the screen was divided into sixteen sections. TV cameras trained at each trader and researcher transmitted their images into those sections. Boesky could hear and see each of his employees at all times. Any unexplained absence, even a trip to the bathroom, would be immediately detected. There were other toys: Boesky's telephone switchboard contained 160 direct phone lines to Mulheren, Milken, arbs, stockbrokers, researchers at other firms, traders, and the like. Electronic ticker tapes flashed across the walls of his office, and a digital clock displayed times in zones around the globe.

The move to midtown had little effect on Boesky's relationship with Siegel. When Siegel had information to impart, he still called with the invitation to have coffee. But now they actually did have coffee, at a Pastrami 'n Things delicatessen just across 52nd Street from Boesky's new address. This humble venue, boasting Formica-topped tables, open containers of ketchup and relishes, and fake plants, was Boesky's choice: he saw no reason to squander his wealth on expensive coffee. And Siegel thought it unlikely that anyone there would recognize either of them.

In spring 1984, Carnation Co. retained Kidder, Peabody and Siegel to discuss the sale of a large block of Carnation shares. Siegel inferred that Carnation would be sold; management agreed Siegel should try to get the highest price. He arranged a meeting with Boesky and discussed the situation, and Boesky began accumulating a large Carnation position that summer. Predictably, Carnation's stock price rose.

By August, Boesky's buying of Carnation had become so heavy, and had attracted so many copycats, that the New York Stock Exchange intervened. Carnation was asked whether it had any explanation for the sudden rise in price and trading volume of its stock.

Carnation knew, of course, of the supposedly secret talks about its plans to sell a block of stock, but was genuinely baffled by the stock market activity. In public statements that violated the exchange's and SEC's disclosure requirements and typified corporate America's own willingness to dissemble, Carnation announced that "there is no news from the company and no corporate developments that would account for the stock action." Several weeks later, Carnation said that it knew of "no corporate reason for the recent surge in its stock price" and said flatly that it was "not negotiating with anyone."

The announcements panicked many arbitrageurs on Wall Street, but not Boesky. Siegel encouraged him to ignore Carnation's public statements and keep up the buying pressure. And in any event, Boesky knew from other sources that a takeover was likely. Boesky took advantage of drops in Carnation's stock price to increase his stake. "This is Getty all over again," Siegel assured Boesky.

In fact, it was better than Getty: cleaner, shorter, and more profitable. The old-line Carnation, one of America's most familiar and trusted brand names, succumbed to a friendly merger offer from the giant Swiss food conglomerate Nestlé. For Boesky, the deal was his single biggest score on information from Siegel: $28.3 million, or roughly half of Boesky's total profits in the deal.

The huge score again left other arbs jealous and incredulous. Wall Street had never before seen a string of arbitrage successes to rival Boesky's: Natomas, Lenox, Getty, Gulf, and now Carnation. The massive size of his positions had earned Boesky the envious nickname "Piggy." Increasingly, Mulheren found himself defending Boesky's reputation when others complained and hinted that Boesky had to be using illegal information. "Come on," Mulheren would say. "Can't you just admit that someone's smarter and better than you are?"

One afternoon Boesky called and asked Mulheren to take charge of a fund-raising dinner. The dinner would honor Boesky himself, and benefit the Jewish Theological Seminary, a prestigious scholarly institution near Columbia University in Manhattan. Mulheren had never detected any genuine interest on Boesky's part in Judaism, but he knew Boesky gave to the seminary, probably to impress his wealthy Jewish investors. "Ivan, you know I don't like to run things. Can't I just give you a check?" Mulheren asked. He always made a point of donating to any charity a friend asked him to support. Boesky paused for a moment; then, sounding dejected, almost like a child, he said, "No one else will."

Mulheren sighed and agreed to do it. He twisted Carl Icahn's arm until he agreed to be co-sponsor and between the two of them they managed to sell all the tickets. Given the widespread feeling of hostility and jealousy toward Boesky, it wasn't easy, but the event raised nearly $500,000 for the seminary. The dinner was a gala black-tie affair; even Mulheren donned a dinner jacket and bow tie. Boesky's mother came from Detroit. She struck Mulheren as a sweet, dignified lady, showing a Jewish mother's pride and concern for her son. After Mulheren introduced her, he said to the guests, "I know why you're really here tonight. You're here because you can't believe Ivan Boesky actually has a mother." The audience roared.

Even within his own staff, there was incredulity over Boesky's mounting success. Lessman, the head of research, knew that neither his nor anyone else's research had led Boesky into these positions. Yet he didn't sense any pattern; he didn't notice Kidder, Peabody's involvement in a disproportionate share of the deals. In the midst of his boss's hot streak that year, Lessman learned that Kidder, Peabody and Siegel were representing a target company in a takeover situation they'd taken a position in. He knew Boesky and Siegel spoke on the phone often, so he went to Boesky with the news. "I just learned Kidder's in the deal," Lessman said, proud of his intelligence. "Why don't you call Marty Siegel and see if you can get some help?"

"What do you mean by that?" Boesky asked sharply, looking angry. "Why would Marty Siegel talk to me?"

"I mean, you're tight with him, aren't you?" Lessman said. "You could . . ."

Boesky cut him off. "Get one thing straight. There's no special relationship between this firm and Marty Siegel. Now get out."

Rather quickly, a more ominous warning shot crossed Boesky's bow, one that also sent cold shivers down Siegel's spine. Up to this point, despite his enormous success, Boesky had attracted surprisingly little attention from the nation's financial press. During the summer of 1984, however, a *Fortune* magazine reporter, Gwen Kinkead, had begun work on a major feature story. Boesky rarely returned reporter's phone calls, but he had granted Kinkead an interview, albeit one in which he refused to discuss any of his trading and wasn't forthcoming even about trivial details of his life.

Siegel knew the article was in the works; the reporter left a message with his secretary. When he returned the call, however, Kinkead was out, and she never got back in touch with him. Siegel assumed she was simply looking for a comment from him on Boesky. During the last week of July, however, Siegel was surprised when Boesky called to warn him of an unfavorable "reference" in the article to Boesky's relationships with Kidder, Peabody and First Boston.

Siegel was aghast. "This is very bad," Siegel said angrily. "It's bad for you and it's bad for me."

Boesky seemed unconcerned. "You're overreacting," he said, saying there was really nothing new in the article and that it was just a "followup" to a *Los Angeles Times* article that had also referred to Boesky's connections to the two investment banks. This agitated Siegel even more. The *L.A. Times*! He hadn't even heard about that. Was this turning into an avalanche of bad news reports? He knew how sensitive his business was to the press.

Siegel wanted to break the news to DeNunzio himself, before it came out in the magazine. DeNunzio reacted with concern but wasn't overly troubled. He certainly didn't ask Siegel if there might be any truth to the article. They called Peter Goodson, the nominal head of M&A, to assess the potential damage to the firm's merger practice, and decided it would be minimal. Rumors swirled around Wall Street all the time. But they were greatly relieved that First Boston was also mentioned.

The following Monday, Siegel rushed to the newsstand to buy *Fortune*'s August 6 issue. Much of the article was innocuous, focusing on Boesky's great financial success and aspirations, though it did contain some unflattering characterizations and details of his early background. Deep in the story, however, were two paragraphs that horrified Siegel: "Boesky's competitors whisper darkly about his omniscient timing," the passage began, "and rumors abound that he looks for deals involving Kidder Peabody and First Boston. Boesky vehemently denies using inside information. . . ."

Then the article touched on a particularly sensitive matter. Boesky's "moves—and those of Kidder, Peabody and Forstmann Little— fascinated Wall Street when Pargas, a Maryland liquid gas distributor, was being chased last year by the wealthy Belzberg family of Canada." The incident involved some of Boesky's closest relationships: with Siegel, who had talked with Boesky about Pargas, but who hadn't—*he didn't think*—given him any inside information; with Teddy Forstmann, the founder of Forstmann Little, who often talked with Boesky; and with Mulheren, for whóm the Belzbergs were a major client and backer. Siegel knew that information about movements of the Belzbergs was routinely passed from Mulheren to Boesky.

"On the day after the Belzbergs told Pargas of their tender offer, but before any public announcement," the article continued, "Boesky bought 35,000 shares of Pargas. . . ." The obvious implication, though entirely circumstantial, was that Boesky had inside information on the Belzberg bid—probably through Pargas, which pointed toward Siegel.

The story went on to say that Boesky had unloaded a huge amount of Pargas stock before Forstmann Little's announcement that it would reduce its own bid for Pargas caused the stock price to plunge.

This pointed to the possibility that Forstmann had leaked his plans to Boesky ahead of time; Siegel himself had suspected as much. Boesky's response, as quoted by Kinkead: "I have no comment on any trading. We buy and sell securities every day, always properly. We have superb counsel always advising us."

Siegel was panicked. How could this have happened? His worst fear was that his relationship with Boesky might be detected, and now here it was in black and white in a national publication. The message wasn't lost on Wall Street. Lessman's friends began referring in jest to Siegel as Boesky's "executive VP in charge of Kidder, Peabody."

Later that August, Siegel got a call from Robert Freeman, the powerful head of arbitrage at Goldman, Sachs. For years, Siegel had been talking on the phone to Freeman almost every day. Freeman and Siegel had become close, chatting at first about deals their firms were involved in, then increasingly about sports, philosophy, and their salaries and aspirations. Freeman had moved his family from New Jersey to exclusive Rye, N.Y., and told Siegel all about the large house he had bought near the prestigious Apawamis Country Club. Siegel thought of Freeman as a telephone "pen pal."

Freeman was urbane, soft-spoken, measured, personable. He had majored in Spanish at Dartmouth College, and gone on to Columbia Business School, then to Goldman. He learned arbitrage at the side of Robert Rubin, who went on to become co-head of the firm. Goldman's legendary chairman, Gustave Levy, had himself been an arbitrageur, one of the deans of the field on Wall Street. Freeman was named a partner in 1978, and his advice was increasingly sought by other partners in the firm as arbitrage assumed a growing role in the outcome of mergers, recapitalizations, and other major corporate transactions.

To protect its reputation, Goldman had established a strict Chinese wall between the arbitrage department and the rest of the firm. It circulated "restricted lists"—confidential lists of clients involved in pending investment banking activities. Arbitrageurs and others in the firm were forbidden to trade in the stocks of these companies. Freeman frequently complained to Siegel about all the deals he couldn't trade because of Goldman's role in them.

Like Boesky, Freeman was also indispensable as a source of market intelligence and news of deals outside of Goldman. He had an enviable position in a tightly knit circle of established arbitrageurs. Indeed, Siegel had long suspected "club" members of sharing information. The beauty of such an arrangement was that, even though one arb might be restricted from trading because of his firm's involvement, the other members wouldn't be. They were free to trade, on condition that they share similar information with the others.

Somehow, Siegel knew, such information was finding its way into the marketplace in advance of market-moving corporate announcements. Anyone could see the trading volume and price increases, and it wasn't hard to trace the identity of the purchasers. A whole cottage industry grew up on Wall Street consisting of self-styled arbitrageurs who simply tracked the trading patterns of the club members, blindly buying and selling in copycat fashion.

The Carnation deal was in full swing when Freeman called, reinforcing Siegel's suspicions about the arbitrage community. Freeman mentioned that he knew Boesky owned a million shares of Carnation. Siegel was doubly astounded, both by the magnitude of Boesky's position—he had had no idea how heavily Boesky had invested—and by the fact that Freeman knew. Obviously, there were no secrets in the Boesky organization, at least when it came to powerful arbs like Freeman. No wonder rumors were appearing in the press. Siegel's mind raced as Freeman talked on. Then he heard something that gave him another stab of anxiety: "You should be careful," Freeman said. "There are rumors that you're too close to Boesky."

"I'm not talking to him anymore," Siegel blurted out. "I used to."

Freeman's comment was the last straw. Siegel vowed that the Carnation disclosure would be his last. He had to distance himself from Boesky, fast. Otherwise he'd be dogged by rumors forever.

Then, just when he thought the *Fortune* incident was over, Siegel received a call from reporter Connie Bruck, who was at work on another profile of Boesky, this one for *The Atlantic*. She had read both the *L.A. Times* articles and the *Fortune* piece, and was prepared to mention Siegel by name as the subject of the rumors. Siegel begged her to keep him out of the article, to no avail. He went again to DeNunzio to warn him, saying that something had to be done. Something was. When Bruck turned in her manuscript with the reference to Siegel, she was told by lawyers for the magazine that the article would not be published unless she deleted the material about Siegel. She protested, but they were adamant. The article appeared in the December issue, with no mention of the Siegel rumors. Only later did Siegel learn that Kidder, Peabody's lawyers had intervened, threatening suit if the offending material wasn't dropped from the manuscript.

For the rest of the year, Siegel remained determined to sever his ties with Boesky. His almost daily phone contacts with Boesky fell off dramatically. He gave him no new inside information. And yet, as the end of the year approached, and despite all the anxiety, Siegel began to contemplate his year-end "bonus." Even for Siegel, it was hard to make a rational case that he really needed the money. He had had a terrific year in 1984, and his legitimate salary and bonus at Kidder, Peabody had crossed the $1 million mark; he was paid $1.1 million in cash and Kidder, Peabody stock. Still, the renovations on the apartment were costing more than he expected, approaching $500,000. And he had earned the "bonus," after all, with the incredibly valuable tips and insights. Why shouldn't he share in Boesky's outsize profits?

In January 1985, Siegel and Boesky settled down again at Pastrami 'n Things. As he had vowed, Siegel upped his request to cover the anticipated skimming. He asked for $400,000, expecting to realize about $350,000. With that cash, he could pay off all the building contractors on the apartment. Boesky readily agreed; the value of the Carnation tip didn't even have to be discussed. But this time Boesky had a new plan for the cash drop-off. He didn't want to risk another transfer in the Plaza lobby.

Boesky instructed Siegel to be at a pay phone booth at 55th Street and First Avenue precisely at 9 A.M. Siegel would pick up the receiver and pretend to be making a call. While he was on the phone, the courier would stand behind him as though he were waiting to make a call. He would place a briefcase by Siegel's left leg, then disappear. Siegel thought this scheme sounded even more ridiculous than the Plaza plan, like something out of a bad spy novel, but Boesky was insistent.

Siegel arrived at the pay phone early on the appointed date. To kill time, he sat down at a table in the window of a coffee shop across the street. As he sipped his coffee, he spotted someone who had to be the courier: a swarthy man with a briefcase milling about the small plaza where the pay phone was located. He was wearing a black pea coat.

Then Siegel saw someone else. About a half block up the street, he spotted another dark-skinned man walking back and forth on the sidewalk, keeping an eye on the man Siegel suspected was the courier. Siegel started to feel panicky. What was going on? Was someone else involved? Suddenly all of Siegel's fears about Boesky and his reputed CIA involvement surged to the fore. "They're going to kill me," Siegel thought. That was the reason for the bizarre plan to have the courier come up behind him: he was going to be murdered. Siegel finished his coffee, paid the check, and fled, stranding the courier with the briefcase filled with cash.

The same day, soon after Siegel arrived at his office, Boesky called. "How did it go?" he asked.

"Nothing went," Siegel answered.

"Why not?" Boesky sounded disturbed.

"There was more than one person there," Siegel explained. "Someone was watching."

"Of course," Boesky exclaimed. "There always is. I want to make sure they deliver."

Siegel was astounded. Boesky didn't trust his own courier.

Boesky insisted that Siegel repeat the exercise at the phone booth. "I've gone to all the trouble to get this cash, you might as well take it," Boesky argued. Siegel was wary, but he couldn't bring himself to disengage. After holding Boesky off for several weeks, he gave in. This time the hand-off went without a hitch. As usual, some of the money had vanished, but Siegel didn't even bother mentioning it to Boesky. "This is the last time," Siegel vowed to himself. He didn't intend to keep living in fear.

In Siegel's mind, the scheme was over, the last payment made. Siegel stopped calling Boesky entirely, and when Boesky called, he was evasive, busy, eager to get off the line. It didn't take Boesky long to realize what was happening.

One afternoon, as Siegel took Boesky's call but then tried quickly to end the conversation, he sensed a softening in Boesky's tone, a genuine sadness. "What's the matter, Marty?" Boesky asked quietly. "You never want to talk to me. You never call anymore. I never see you.

"Don't you love me anymore?"

His relationship with Boesky was not the only reason for Siegel to panic at the appearance of the *Fortune* article. Even as he was trying to disengage from Boesky, Siegel was trading insider information with his other telephone friend, Freeman—even as Freeman was warning Siegel about rumors of impropriety in Siegel's relations with Boesky. The Freeman relationship was motivated not by Siegel's need for cash, but by Kidder, Peabody's.

Despite appearances, Kidder, Peabody was a firm in trouble, heavily dependent on Siegel for its profits. Even as its traditional sources of revenues, like brokerage and underwriting commissions, dried up, the firm disdained new profit opportunities. Kidder, Peabody had no arbitrage department of its own. Unlike virtually every other Wall Street firm, it didn't trade for its own account. Al Gordon, and after him DeNunzio, believed that trading for a firm account blurred a firm's duty to its clients' interests. Firms without such scruples were also generating some of the biggest profits—firms like Goldman, Sachs, which had always had a major arbitrage operation, and even Morgan Stanley, which had more recently embraced such market opportunities.

DeNunzio was dubbed the "ostrich" by some of the younger bankers at Kidder, Peabody. When new lines of business were proposed, he'd routinely ask whether this was a business that Kidder, Peabody "needed" to be in to serve its clients. The answer was rarely yes. Meanwhile, the firm's capital stagnated as rivals' grew by leaps and bounds, enabling them to finance enormous projects from their capital bases. Kidder, Peabody was still relying on its retail brokerage network and distribution capacity, an increasingly cumbersome, archaic, and unprofitable way to raise capital. The retail brokerage network was actually losing about $30 million a year.

If that weren't bad enough, Kidder's carefully burnished reputation had been seriously besmirched in March 1984. Peter Brant, a smooth, socially ambitious young stockbroker featured in magazine advertisements touting Kidder, Peabody, admitted to an insider-trading scheme. He became the government's chief witness in the most sensational insider-trading case in years: the trial of R. Foster Winans, a reporter for *The Wall Street Journal*, who had written the paper's influential "Heard On the Street" column and leaked the contents of the column to Brant in advance.

The case attracted enormous publicity; it lifted the lid on a sensational tale of an alcoholic society lawyer, homosexual lovers, and clandestine meetings at chic restaurants and polo clubs. No one else at Kidder, Peabody was implicated, and the firm tried to downplay the matter, but Robert Krantz, the general counsel, proved a hapless figure on the witness stand. Kidder, Peabody's compliance procedures appeared laughably inept.

The trial and attendant publicity made it even more imperative for Kidder, Peabody to find new sources of revenue. Earlier, DeNunzio and Gordon had met and taken a liking to a tall, boyishly handsome young Rhodes Scholar named Timothy L. Tabor. Tabor had some accounting experience and an Oxford patina that appealed to the two men, and they hired him as a consultant reporting directly to DeNunzio. His title was vice president in charge of planning.

After reviewing the firm's operations and their profitability, or lack thereof, Tabor concluded that Kidder, Peabody's very survival depended on its embracing new profit opportunities. He concluded that the firm had no choice but to begin aggressively trading for its own account. It would have to establish an arbitrage department. Tabor volunteered to join the new operation himself. He claimed to have done some options trading for his own account, but otherwise he had no experience whatsoever in arbitrage, and little knowledge of trading.

DeNunzio, still reluctant, followed Tabor's advice while trying to avoid the appearance of doing so. He assigned the young consultant to a senior trader named Richard Wigton, the nominal head of institutional sales. Wigton was a former credit analyst who had spent most of his career at Kidder, plodding from one job to another, attracting neither attention nor embarrassment. He was portly, kindly, and dull. Everyone at the firm called him: "Wiggie."

As a trader, Wigton had begun "piggybacking" trades of some of the firm's shrewder clients—simply buying and selling whatever he saw in their trades—and he had eked out some profits. On the basis of that flimsy track record, DeNunzio told him to begin an arbitrage department for Kidder, Peabody. A clerical employee from the firm's library was sent down to work as an arbitrage clerk. That was it.

DeNunzio called Siegel into his office to explain the arrangement, cautioning him that he wanted no one outside the firm to know of the department's existence. He said he was worried how their clients would react.

Siegel knew and liked Wigton, but thought he would be almost hopelessly inept in any arbitrage capacity. He knew almost nothing about Tabor except that he seemed totally inexperienced and had just arrived at the firm. Then DeNunzio dropped a bombshell. He wanted Siegel to be their "advisor," to be responsible for them. And no one else was to know. Siegel groaned.

At the time, March 1984, he was embroiled in the Gulf Oil bidding, representing KKR. When antitrust opposition to Socal's acquisition of Gulf surfaced in Congress, and arbs and other investors began to get nervous, causing Gulf's stock price to fall, Siegel decided to test his new arbitrage advisory status. He called Wigton and Tabor and told them to start buying Gulf stock. "The values are there," he said, based on his study of Gulf's earnings and assets for KKR. He dismissed the antitrust threats. "This company is going to get taken over by somebody. It's a no-brainer." By Kidder, Peabody standards, Wigton and Tabor amassed a huge position—200,000 shares. (By contrast, Boesky had a position of about 4 million.) When the Socal deal finally went through, Siegel was hailed as an arbitrage genius. Kidder, Peabody's profit was $2.7 million. DeNunzio was thrilled, lavishing praise on Siegel for his insight. Siegel felt terrific. Arbitrage was so easy! He'd suspected he could be good at it. He felt he was making another important contribution to the firm.

No one seemed to recognize how perilously close Siegel had come to breaching the usual notion of a Chinese wall separating arbitrage from other activities at an investment banking firm. Siegel hadn't used any confidential information gleaned in his role as a financial advisor to KKR in the Gulf deal. But he had come close.

One afternoon, Robert Freeman called Siegel, as he did almost daily, and mentioned that he liked the stock of Walt Disney Co., adding that he owned a position for his own trading account. Corporate raider Saul Steinberg had taken a large position in Disney stock, and there had been speculation in the arbitrage community that Steinberg would make a bid. The Texas Bass family, known for its shrewd investments, also had amassed a huge stake. Freeman strongly implied, without actually saying so, that he was in direct contact with Richard Rainwater, the financier credited with much of the Bass family's success.

This, Siegel assumed, was how arbitrage in the "club" worked—tips, hints, nods, mutual connections, relationships based on reciprocal favors, all of which stopped just short of the actual passing of inside information. Why bother, when anyone could establish the reliability of a tip without having to say how the information was obtained or where it came from?

Siegel called Wigton and Tabor and told them to load up on Disney stock. Soon after, in June 1984, "greenmail" rumors coursed through the market, suggesting that, instead of bidding for the whole company or keeping it in play, Steinberg was going to be bought out by Disney. Siegel immediately called Freeman, who reassured him. "No way," Freeman said. So Kidder, Peabody held onto its large stake, and Siegel hurriedly left the office to catch a flight to Cleveland, where he had a meeting scheduled with a client.

As soon as he got to the Cleveland airport, he called his office, and was sickened by the news: Steinberg had, in fact, taken greenmail. His takeover threat was over. Disney stock had plunged. Worse, Wigton and Tabor had been caught totally unawares. Kidder, Peabody's loss on the Disney position was already bigger than the $2.7 million it had made on Gulf. Siegel was stunned. So much for his being an arbitrage "genius."

The next morning Siegel got on the phone to Freeman. He was furious, even more so when Freeman told Siegel that he had sold his own position before the news was made public. "Why didn't you tell me?" Siegel fumed. "You put me in that stock, you had the information, and you didn't let me know?" Siegel was incredulous; he couldn't believe Freeman would jerk him around like that.

Freeman seemed genuinely concerned. He said he didn't realize Siegel had taken such a big position and, besides, he had tried to call Siegel with the information, but Siegel had been on a plane to Cleveland. Siegel was slightly mollified, but the loss still hurt. He didn't know how he'd explain it to DeNunzio, especially since there had been so many rumors that greenmail was in the offing. Yet Kidder, Peabody, on Siegel's advice, had held its entire position.

Several days later, a Friday, Siegel spent the day working at his desk in his Connecticut home. He had calmed down sufficiently from the Disney incident to call Freeman, and the two were chatting again about market and M&A developments as though nothing had happened. Siegel, without really giving the topic much thought, steered the conversation to a large Goldman client, Continental Group, a packaging company which was then the subject of a takeover bid from Sir James Goldsmith. Siegel asked Freeman whether he thought Sir James's bid would hold up.

Siegel expected something helpful but not explicit, given that Goldman, Continental's investment bank, was actively involved in plotting Continental's strategy. Perhaps Freeman knew nothing about Continental, since Goldman supposedly had a strict Chinese wall between arbitrage and investment banking. Instead, Freeman said, "It doesn't matter. They'll sell the company anyway."

Siegel was astounded. Coming from a partner in the firm representing Continental, this sounded like inside information. He hung up the phone and gazed out over the late-spring panorama of the Connecticut coast. He knew that, in his conversation with Freeman, they had just crossed an unspoken line. He also knew that he could easily make it right by simply not acting; insider trading requires trading on the information. But he also thought that, after the embarrassing Disney loss, Freeman owed him a favor. Wasn't this how the arbitrage network worked?

Siegel picked up the phone and called Wigton and Tabor, suggesting they buy Continental stock. Much to his annoyance, they balked. They were still grumbling about Disney. Siegel raised his voice and told them he'd just gotten off the phone with Freeman. He repeated to them, word for word, exactly what Freeman had told him about the company's intent to sell. "Now do you understand?" he asked. They did, and dutifully began buying.

About a week later, Siegel again asked Freeman about Continental. Freeman was in high spirits. "I get to play corporate finance," Freeman said. "I get to do what you do, Marty." Then Freeman brazenly crossed the line of inside information. He explained that a close friend of his, a sometime corporate raider named David Murdock, was being lined up by Goldman as a white knight for Continental. Freeman spelled out details of the Murdock plan, and said he was advising Murdock. Now Siegel was getting inside information from both the Continental side, to which Freeman was privy at Goldman, and the Murdock side. Siegel called Wigton and Tabor and urged them to buy more Continental stock.

Sir James increased his bid, causing a nice run-up in the stock price, and Siegel again called Freeman. "Don't worry, we'll pay more," Freeman assured Siegel. Kidder, Peabody bought even more stock, eventually amassing a position of 25 million shares, its largest holding ever.

Within Kidder, Peabody, only two people other than Siegel, Wigton, and Tabor were allowed to see the arbitrage position sheets: DeNunzio and John T. "Jack" Roche, Kidder, Peabody's president, a weak manager installed by DeNunzio. After the Disney losses, DeNunzio became increasingly concerned about the size of the firm's gamble on Continental, and finally called Siegel into his office for an explanation.

DeNunzio looked anxious and was perspiring, as he often did when feeling stress. How could Siegel risk so much of the firm's capital? How could he be so confident? Finally, Siegel blurted out the truth: "This information is coming from Bob Freeman." DeNunzio, of course, knew who Freeman was. He paused, looking grave, then said just two words: "Protect yourself." He had no further comments about the size of the Continental stake.

The Continental deal climaxed on June 29. Murdock made the highest bid, $58.50 a share, topping Sir James at $58, and Tenneco, a large conglomerate, at just over $55. The Murdock bid was accepted at a special, closed meeting of Continental's board at approximately 4 P.M. The news became public when it appeared on the Dow Jones ticker just before 5:30 P.M., but Siegel didn't have to wait for a public announcement of the good news. Freeman had called more than an hour before the public announcement, less than 20 minutes after the board reached its supposedly confidential decision.

Wigton and Tabor cashed in Kidder, Peabody's shares for a profit of $3.8 million, more than recouping the Disney losses. Everyone was jubilant. Siegel's reputation was restored, though DeNunzio now knew, of course, that Siegel's success wasn't based on "genius" alone. Roche patted Siegel on the back, saying "You're keeping the firm alive."

Siegel realized that Freeman had made sure he would recover the earlier losses, for which he must have felt responsible. Now he felt he could trust Freeman; he was an honorable man. Siegel found he loved the high of the arbitrage gambles. He liked being the recipient of information, not the donor. The process seemed so much safer, the likelihood of detection so remote as to hardly be relevant.

He continued to milk the Freeman connection, but to make sure

Kidder, Peabody's level of trading didn't attract attention, either by regulators or within the firm, Wigton and Tabor placed their orders through third-party brokers, such as Boyd Jefferies, a Los Angeles broker who had built a business around such private transactions. He was the leading player in what was known as "third-market" or "off-market" trading. The beauty of the arrangement was that no trading records would directly link Freeman's phone calls to Siegel to any trading by Kidder, Peabody. Wigton liked to refer to the tactics as "hiding our hand."

Freeman wasn't told the scope of the Kidder, Peabody trading. DeNunzio still insisted that Kidder, Peabody's arbitrage department be kept secret. Siegel told Freeman that he was trading for his own personal account. He was surprised when Freeman told him that he, too, was trading actively in his personal account and in accounts maintained for the benefit of his children.

Arbitrageurs at major firms were usually strictly barred from trading in their own accounts because of the temptation to put their own interests ahead of the firm's, buying and selling in their own accounts first, in a process known as front-running. He was sure that Goldman must ban such activity. Freeman blithely brushed Siegel's inquiry aside. "When I stop trading for Goldman, I turn to my own accounts," Freeman explained.

Not surprisingly, Freeman soon demanded a quid pro quo—one that made Boesky's payoffs look like a pittance. At the time of the Continental deal, Siegel and Freeman were involved in two other potential big acquisitions: Waste Management, the giant waste disposal concern, was considering a possible bid for SCA Services, a smaller company in the same business and a Siegel client. Goldman, Sachs's client Rupert Murdoch was eyeing a bid for a large forest products concern, St. Regis Paper Co.

During June, Goldman, Sachs, at Freeman's behest, had taken a massive position in SCA after Waste Management sent a letter force-fully proposing a friendly acquisition, a technique known to arbs as a "bear hug." The letter was made public. SCA was a client of Kidder, Peabody and Siegel, and immediately put up resistance. The first line of defense was potentially deadly: there were antitrust problems that might cause the government to block the proposed acquisition.

Given the size of Goldman, Sachs's position, word of antitrust problems caused Freeman great anxiety, and he called Siegel at home in Connecticut. "Marty, you've got to help me with SCA," Freeman said. "Is this antitrust threat real?"

Siegel tried to avoid leaking inside information, talking in general terms about the companies' options, but Freeman pressed, and finally Siegel abandoned the attempt at discretion. He told Freeman details of SCA's defense plans, and said the antitrust defense was largely a ploy to get a higher offer. "This company is going down," he reassured his friend, encouraging him to increase his position.

As the SCA deal evolved, Siegel and Freeman gradually developed a kind of code to make the transmission of information less explicit. Just before Browning Ferris, another waste disposal company, entered the fray with its own bid, Siegel told Freeman: "This thing is really going to trade." Freeman realized, of course, that a price rise was imminent.

On Monday, August 13, SCA announced that it was entertaining offers from companies besides Waste Management, and the stock soared on rumors that Browning Ferris was making a higher bid. The previous Thursday and Friday, Goldman had purchased over 70,000 SCA shares. It bought another 57,000 shares Monday before SCA's announcement sent the stock price soaring.

After that sudden price rise, Freeman worried that the market had gotten too euphoric about the prospects for a higher bid. He wondered whether he should unload some of Goldman's position and called Siegel again. "What do you think of the price of the stock?" Freeman asked. Siegel decided to be coy.

"What do you mean?" he asked. But with so much at stake, Freeman was in no mood for games.

"You know what I mean," he testily replied.

"It looks fine to me," Siegel obliged, knowing that "fine" would be understood as encouragement to buy more SCA stock. Over the next few days, Goldman bought an additional 123,500 shares. Eventually Waste Management did top Browning Ferris's bid, the antitrust problems were resolved, and Goldman had made one of its biggest arbitrage scores of the year, earning a profit of many millions.

The ball was now in Freeman's court; he owed Siegel information, and St. Regis seemed the ideal vehicle for repayment. St. Regis had been in play for most of 1984. Sir James Goldsmith, in his quest for forest products concerns (which would culminate in his bid for Crown Zellerbach), had nibbled early in the year. Alarmed, St. Regis had turned to its investment bankers at Morgan Stanley, who in turn contacted another big paper company, Champion International, a Goldman client, about the possibility of a white knight rescue. St. Regis stock was put on a so-called "gray list" at Goldman. The gray list at Goldman and other firms had been developed as a more confidential version of the firm's restricted list, which prohibited trading in the stock by the firm's officials and employees. Restricted lists, circulated widely within the firm, had proven too liable to leaks. So gray lists were distributed only to a handful of top officials.

Eventually, St. Regis bought out Sir James's stake in another greenmail transaction, and the threat of takeover seemed to dissipate. Talks with Champion ended, and Goldman removed St. Regis from its gray list. Then talks resumed on June 27. The new threat came from Goldman, Sachs's client Rupert Murdoch. Murdoch and the Bass family (advised again by Freeman's friend Rainwater) announced publicly that they'd acquired large stakes in St. Regis.

Freeman hadn't been entirely candid with Siegel when he had told him he always finished trading in Goldman's account before trading in his own account and those of his children. On July 16, Champion and St. Regis signed a confidentiality agreement as they examined each other's financial results in anticipation of a merger. At that point, of course, Goldman, Sachs officials couldn't trade in the stock of either company. Yet the next day, Freeman bought 15,000 St. Regis shares for his own accounts at prices ranging from $43 to $45 a share. The very next day, Murdoch announced a tender offer for St. Regis at $52 a share. The compliance department at Goldman, which should have reviewed such trades by Freeman, proved as somnolent as Kidder, Peabody's or Drexel's. The low-prestige compliance officers at Goldman wouldn't dare challenge the trading of a powerful partner like Freeman. Goldman was hardly unique in that respect.

Several days later, St. Regis formally rejected the Murdoch bid, dashing market hopes for a quick surrender. The next day, however, encouraged by information Freeman leaked, Kidder, Peabody began building its St. Regis stake, continuing with steady purchases until the end of July, when Champion announced a $2 billion bid for St. Regis.

Inside information was only a small part of the alliance between Siegel and Freeman. Their relationship was useful in other ways, too. Earlier in the St. Regis deal, St. Regis's investment bankers at Morgan Stanley had promised Siegel they wouldn't "shop" any Champion bid to other potential suitors (meaning they wouldn't try to leverage the Champion bid to start a bidding war). Siegel, through his market sources, learned that in spite of their promise Morgan Stanley was using Champion to try for a better deal that would, not coincidentally, result in a higher fee for Morgan Stanley. Siegel promptly informed Freeman, who took the information straight to John Weinberg, the head of Goldman, Sachs. Goldman confronted Morgan Stanley, and Champion insisted on signing a definitive agreement to merge that very night. Kidder, Peabody also used the information to add over 100,000 St. Regis shares to its holdings.

News of the Champion/St. Regis agreement to merge appeared on the Dow Jones ticker the next morning. Both Kidder, Peabody and Freeman cashed in their St. Regis shares for enormous profits.

Siegel was feeling euphoric. Wall Street was beginning to boom, and he was at the center of the action. He was even beginning to lose his anxiety that each deal would be his last. America was regaining its confidence and exuberance. Freeman had just been out to Los Angeles for the 1984 Summer Olympics, hailed as an American triumph. He called Siegel one day as the SCA transaction was reaching its lucrative conclusion. "I've got to hand it to you," Freeman said approvingly. "You really know how to trade information."

Then came the *Fortune* article. Suddenly Siegel was haunted by Freeman's words. Just as he vowed to distance himself from Boesky, Siegel determined to stop the flow of inside information between himself and Freeman. He'd continue talking—he liked Freeman, and the relationship was too valuable a source of legitimate market intelligence to break off altogether—but he wouldn't give him anything confidential. After all, the Kidder, Peabody arbitrage department had already succeeded beyond anyone's wildest dreams. With accumulated profits of over $7 million, it was suddenly one of the top profit centers in the firm, less than a year after its creation. He, Wigton, and Tabor didn't have to do another trade for the rest of the year in order to be hailed as heroes. It was just a sideline to his main business anyway.

Siegel felt a great sense of relief. He'd saved Kidder, Peabody for at least another year. He could stop feeling like a criminal.

Hal Ritch settled into his desk chair in his Kidder, Peabody office and braced for a bad morning. That summer, 1984, he was working closely with Siegel on the same SCA deal that figured so prominently in the Siegel-Freeman relationship. The day before, he had misunderstood something Siegel said and inadvertently passed the error on to someone at Merrill Lynch. Siegel had flown into a rage, storming into Ritch's office and yelling so loudly he'd had to close the door.

That sort of behavior was anathema to Ritch. Though a few years younger than Siegel, Ritch seemed to embody the old Kidder, Peabody. He was blond, a Stanford and Wharton graduate, thoughtful and considerate almost to a fault. At his annual review, Siegel had criticized him for being "too nice."

Even before coming to work at Kidder, Peabody, Ritch had been good friends with John Gordon, Al Gordon's son, who shared a secretary with Siegel. When Siegel first tried to recruit Ritch, Gordon warned him to stay away. Not only did Gordon resent the fact that Siegel's work always took priority; he told Ritch he believed Siegel to be a "dark force." Siegel's obvious ambition and sometimes rough edges had alienated Gordon. Then, after Siegel married Jane Day, Gordon changed his mind. He told Ritch he thought Siegel was mellowing, turning into a decent fellow, and that he saw no reason now why Ritch shouldn't come to work with him at Kidder, Peabody.

The shouting incident upset Ritch. He wondered whether Gordon's optimistic reassessment of Siegel's personality hadn't been premature. But the next day Siegel appeared in his doorway looking almost sheepish. "Are you okay?" he asked Ritch, who said he guessed he was. "I'm sorry," Siegel said. "I was upset. I shouldn't have yelled." Ritch felt better.

But Ritch did worry sometimes about Siegel. Ritch lived in Greenwich, Connecticut, not far from Freeman's house in Rye, and Ritch and Freeman often shared a ride into the city. Ritch liked Freeman. One morning, as they drove into the city, they discussed the movie *Kramer vs. Kramer*. Ritch thought Freeman seemed very sensitive to the divorce and family issues raised by the film. Ritch knew Freeman was in arbitrage, but he didn't seem anything like other arbs, most of whom Ritch regarded with distaste. Freeman was about to get out of the car at 60 Water Street when he turned to Ritch and said quietly, "Tell Marty Siegel, don't talk to Ivan." Before Ritch could ask him anything, Freeman was gone.

Ritch wondered what Freeman meant. Why didn't he tell Siegel himself? Ritch sat close enough to Siegel to know that Freeman called Siegel two or three times a day. "Bobby's on the phone" was a constant refrain, and he knew Bobby was Freeman. And in any event, why would an arb criticize someone for talking to another arb? Isn't that what arbs did?

Then Ritch read the *Fortune* article, which caused quite a stir at Kidder, Peabody. Freeman again told him, "Marty Siegel had better watch himself. This looks bad." Ritch finally raised the subject with Siegel. "Don't talk to Ivan, Marty," he said. "He's bad news." Siegel insisted there was nothing to be concerned about. The *Fortune* article was "horseshit," he told Ritch.

Ritch believed him. Scrupulously honest himself, he didn't believe Siegel would cross any lines of impropriety with an Ivan Boesky. Still, he knew something was afoot at Kidder, Peabody. Despite the secrecy with which Wigton and Tabor's arbitrage operation was shrouded, hints of it were leaking out. For one thing, it wasn't any secret that their trading profits had soared, and no one believed Wigton and Tabor alone were capable of producing such results. Proximity to Siegel had led Ritch to realize that, at the very least, he was involved, looking over their shoulders, perhaps offering insights drawn from his M&A experience.

Then Siegel confirmed all his suspicions, actually showing him, briefly, a copy of all Kidder, Peabody's arbitrage positions, and boasting about how well they were doing. Ritch was shocked by the size of the positions and the amount of money at risk. "You can't have Wigton in charge of this," he argued. "He's incompetent. You've got to hire a professional arb." He recommended someone he knew from Dean Witter. Siegel talked to him, but later told Ritch he didn't want to hire him. "We can't put Wiggie out to pasture," Siegel said. "He's a team player." Ritch was skeptical that Siegel was that loyal to Wigton. Something else had become clear to him: Siegel was having fun with arbitrage, and he didn't want anyone else interfering.

This worried Ritch. While he was at Dean Witter, the firm had established an arbitrage department, and he'd been involved in its creation. Before beginning any trading activities, Dean Witter had hired two separate law firms, Shearman & Sterling and Kidder, Peabody's outside counsel, Sullivan & Cromwell, to prepare directives on how arbitrage could be safely separated from investment banking. Now he'd figured out that Kidder, Peabody was engaging in arbitrage trading, and the firm didn't even have a Chinese wall, the minimum requirement both law firms had insisted upon.

Ritch didn't feel he could go to Siegel. In any event, due to the structure of the firm, Siegel wasn't even officially in the M&A department, so Ritch's titular boss was Peter Goodson. Ritch went to Goodson. "I know there's arbitrage going on, Peter," he told him. "This is dangerous. Something's got to be done. I was involved at Dean Witter, I could help. But Siegel can't be involved. We've got to have a Chinese wall."

Goodson adopted a posture of concern. "You're right, Hal," he said. "It's very troubling. I'm going to write Ralph [DeNunzio] a memo on this."

But Ritch knew the arrangement continued as before; he frequently overheard Siegel on the phone trying to cajole Wigton and Tabor into various trading positions. So he went to Goodson again, complaining that nothing had changed. Goodson admitted he'd never written a memo to DeNunzio, or put anything in writing about Ritch's concern. "I talked to Ralph about it, though," he said, sounding as though that relieved him and Ritch of all further responsibility in the matter. "You know," Goodson continued, "Marty's getting a little stale. He's tired of pitching tender retainers. This arb stuff is good for him to manage." Ritch felt there was nothing further he could do. After all, Goodson was a director, and so was Siegel. They ought to know what they were doing.

During the SCA deal, Ritch put in especially long hours. Siegel often wanted to be at home in Connecticut with his wife, who was pregnant with twins. Siegel had boasted to Ritch and John Gordon that they were fraternal twins, requiring two separate sperm, as though that suggested that Siegel was unusually potent. Gordon thought the remark showed tremendous insecurity on Siegel's part.

Because they were involved in the deal, Ritch and Gordon paid unusually close attention to trading in SCA stock, and they were repeatedly amazed by the timeliness of purchases by Goldman. When they saw records of Goldman's huge purchases just before Browning Ferris's surprise bid, Gordon said, "Holy shit! How could they be that bright?" They speculated together about the possibility of a leak, though it never occurred to them that Siegel might be exchanging information with Freeman. They simply wouldn't have believed it. Still, Siegel made Gordon uneasy.

Kidder had decided that Siegel, as the firm's major star, ought to belong to one of New York's exclusive clubs, where he could mingle with the corporate chieftains Kidder, Peabody needed to attract as clients. Siegel always professed to loathe such clubs—their homogeneity, snobbishness, and old-fashioned values. But if he had to join one, he wanted one of the best. On some level, he coveted the establishment acceptance that membership would confer.

So he asked John Gordon to intervene on his behalf at the River Club, an extremely exclusive, WASPy dining club located on the ground floor of River House, a cooperative apartment building next to the East River on 52nd Street. The River Club had been founded by members of the Rockefeller family, some of whom lived in River House, and had become a magnet for the East Side social and business establishment. Among the few Jews admitted was Henry Kissinger.

John Gordon's father, Al, was a pillar of the club, and the two had begun to float the possibility of membership for Siegel. The prospect had met with a distinctly cool reception. The word *Jewish* was never mentioned, but the Gordons could easily tell that it was a problem, one exacerbated by the publicity Siegel had received as an M&A specialist. "Isn't he an M&A wheeler-dealer?" asked one member, his tone conveying his contempt. Another mentioned that he understood Siegel to be "a hard-sell artist." John Gordon backed off, fearful that too enthusiastic an endorsement of Siegel could damage his own reputation.

Another member had been roundly criticized for bringing up the name of corporate raider Ronald Perelman, who, it went without saying, was rejected out of hand. Now Gordon himself was beginning to share the doubts of others. After the SCA situation, he would occasionally assure Siegel that he was continuing to press his case. But his effort was, at best, halfhearted.

Siegel finally did join another club, the far less prestigious Union League Club on Park Avenue. His membership was short-lived. He found it unbearably dowdy. When members voted to continue excluding women, despite pressure from the New York State attorney general, Jane Day was outraged. Siegel was only too happy to drop out in protest. DeNunzio's effort to mold Siegel in the image of the old Kidder, Peabody was doomed.

As 1985 began, Siegel was preoccupied with the twins, a boy and girl, who were born in March and quickly filled the extra rooms at the Gracie Square cooperative. His own M&A practice was thriving as the pace of deals, defying all predictions, continued to quicken. He hoped that Wigton and Tabor would be able to build on the previous year's arbitrage successes on their own, with minimal guidance from him, but his hopes were soon dashed.

Wigton and Tabor, on their own, were only allowed to invest up to $1 million. If a takeover deal had already been announced, lowering the risk (and the profit potential) they could go up to $5 million. Even so, they were losing money. They had to have an "edge," they kept telling Siegel. He was all too aware that they expected the edge to come from him.

By the spring, Siegel was starting to feel desperate. DeNunzio was continuing to wring his hands about the firm's financial performance. Siegel felt the pressure to produce information for Wigton and Tabor, but he held back. He couldn't bring himself to beg Freeman for more.

Siegel and Freeman remained in almost daily contact by phone, part of the whirlwind of information-sharing that linked Wall Street professionals like Boesky, Mulheren, Sandy Lewis (the arbitrageur who had introduced Mulheren to Boesky), and others. Toward the end of March, Freeman mentioned an investment firm named Coniston Partners, formed by a former White, Weld investment banker named Keith Gollust, and two others.

Freeman knew Gollust through one of his best friends, James Regan, who headed a maze of investment partnerships, including Princeton-Newport Partners based in Princeton, N.J. There have always been large numbers of private investment partnerships on Wall Street, but rarely have they thrived as they did in the 1980s. Virtually anyone could start such a partnership, raising capital from wealthy investors much as Boesky had done, and invest it, extracting a management fee and a percentage of any profits.

Siegel had never heard of Coniston, which had begun by investing in undervalued, closed-end mutual funds. Coniston had begun to pressure management of the funds, which had led to proxy fights and takeover threats on a broader and far more lucrative scale. At the time Freeman mentioned Coniston to Siegel, it was all but unknown and had little credibility as a would-be corporate raider. Freeman, however, vouched for them and said they were a force worth watching.

Even now, Freeman told Siegel, Coniston was building up a large position in Storer Communications, a cable television and broadcast concern, with an eye toward a possible bid for the company. Freeman was amassing his own stake in Storer, both in Goldman's account and in his personal accounts, amounting to about 3% of the company's stock. "They're serious," Freeman said of Coniston's intentions to force some kind of major transaction.

Siegel considered it a typical conversation. He had an image of Freeman sitting alongside a rushing stream of information, plucking what he wanted like a bear fishing salmon. Still, Siegel wondered: How was Freeman privy to sensitive information about Coniston's plans for Storer? Finally Siegel asked him. "I'm very close to the people buying the stock for Coniston," Freeman replied. Freeman didn't mention the names of Princeton-Newport or of his friend and former Dartmouth classmate James Regan. Regan was doing the buying for Coniston, and he was "piggybacking" on Coniston, buying for a Princeton-Newport account. All stood to reap huge profits should Storer be sold.

It didn't even occur to Siegel to suggest to Wigton and Tabor that they, too, buy a stake in Storer, though that may have been Freeman's hope. It's possible he wanted to create buying pressure to soften up Storer for some kind of buyout proposal. Instead, Siegel immediately saw the possibility of a bigger role for Kidder, Peabody. Siegel had talked often with Henry Kravis at Kohlberg Kravis Roberts since representing KKR in its unsuccessful bid for Gulf. He knew Kravis was looking for a buyout. The more he heard about Storer, and the more he reviewed Kidder, Peabody's own research on the company, the more vulnerable he thought it looked to a well-financed buyout bid.

On April 15, Siegel called Freeman, mentioning that he thought he'd show KKR some data on Storer, curious to see if Freeman had any objections. He didn't mind at all, so Siegel called Kravis, who said, "Great, can we get a meeting?" Siegel promptly called Dillon, Read, Storer's traditional investment bankers, and they got together for preliminary discussions of what a transaction with KKR might look like. When Siegel talked to Freeman again, he was surprised to learn that he already seemed to know everything that had happened at the meeting.

Siegel told Freeman he was now representing KKR, and the two discussed strategy. Storer wasn't yet signaling it would welcome a friendly bid, and KKR hadn't yet embarked on any unfriendly raids. Both Siegel and Freeman were hoping KKR would, and they strategized about what might be done to force a bid. They talked about the possibility of a "bear hug" letter, in which KKR would propose a friendly buyout but simultaneously convey the threat of a hostile bid if the friendly deal were spurned. It was the usual dialogue between investment banker and arbitrageur, one that yielded clues to what was likely to happen without involving the disclosure of any secret plans.

Then, the following weekend, Freeman called Siegel at home in Connecticut. Freeman sounded beside himself. He couldn't stand the suspense, he said. He had to know: Was KKR going to make the bear hug? The day before, Kravis had agreed to Siegel's suggestion that he make what Siegel termed a "teddy bear pat," a very mild form of the bear hug in which the threat was deliberately left vague. Siegel knew that if he answered Freeman's question and Freeman traded, they would again cross the line of legality he had vowed to respect. But he also felt that letting Freeman know was in the interest of his client. Freeman was one of Storer's largest shareholders, and he could help pressure Storer into reacting favorably to a KKR approach. Siegel answered: Yes, KKR would send the letter.

Armed with that supposedly secret information, Freeman embarked on a Storer buying spree, adding over 74,000 shares to Goldman's already huge stake on April 17. Freeman's assistant in the department, Frank Brosens, also snapped up 2,000 shares for himself (an investment of close to three-quarters of a million dollars). As Siegel had assured Freeman it would, KKR made its bid on April 19. The next day, somewhat to Siegel's disappointment, Storer rejected the approach, issuing a letter to shareholders urging them to turn down any offer from KKR. Freeman called Siegel soon thereafter. "Don't worry," he reassured Siegel. "We'll squeeze the board, Coniston, [Gordon] Crawford, and me. You come back with another approach." (Freeman and his allies, however, never filed any SEC disclosures that they were acting as a group.)

Siegel went back to Kravis, and they added some warrants to buy stock at a later date as a sweetener for the deal. Siegel went back to Freeman, who wasn't happy. He wanted a higher bid. "This is the bottom line," Siegel said. "We're not going up on this." KKR made its revised offer on April 22.

Then Storer threatened to throw a wrench in all of their plans. It again rejected the KKR bid, offering shareholders a recapitalization plan instead, but one that was hard to value. With Freeman and Regan continuing to buy Storer stock and options, Coniston announced it would launch a proxy fight to thwart Storer's recapitalization plan and force Storer into the hands of the highest bidder.

Freeman and Siegel continued to stay in close touch on the Storer affair, even as it moved into the stalemate of a drawn-out proxy fight. Then, about July 4, rumors swirled that yet another bidder was about to surface for Storer. Freeman warned Siegel, who immediately passed on the valuable information to Kravis, who was attending the British Open tennis matches at Wimbledon. A week later, a company called Comcast launched its own bid, and Freeman called Siegel. "Will KKR compete with Comcast?" Freeman wanted to know. Siegel assured him it would. He believed Kravis wouldn't mind his leaking the information. He'd told Kravis in general about his conversations with Freeman, and though Kravis never endorsed leaking inside information, he had agreed that it was in his interest to keep the pressure on Storer. Freeman was now so privy to secret information that he might as well have been a member of the KKR team.

Finally, late in July, as the bidding reached levels no one had expected, Freeman called again. "I've got a large personal position" in Storer, he said (though by now that was obvious to Siegel). "I've just sold the August 90 calls at two dollars." (Selling the calls is a bet that the final price won't go above a certain level—in this case, the strike price of the call, $90, plus the option price, $2.) "Did I do the right thing?" Freeman asked.

Siegel knew the final, secret price KKR was bidding. Somehow, Freeman had hit it exactly: it was $92. "It sounds good to me," Siegel said, and Freeman gave a satisfied chuckle. Siegel had no way of knowing just how many millions of dollars Goldman, Freeman, and his network of friends and contacts like Regan, Gollust, and Coniston Partners had just earned; but he knew that the profits were vast, since the network wielded a combined capital that went way beyond anything that even Boesky could muster.

KKR was delighted with Siegel's performance. It bought Storer for cash and stock valued at $92 per share and, despite the rich price, Storer became one of the firm's most successful buyouts.

After this battle, Siegel once again felt that Freeman owed him something in return. Without his making a conscious decision, Siegel's resolve to stop the information exchange with Freeman had eroded. Their arrangement had simply picked up where it left off. Freeman soon had ample opportunity to pay Siegel back.

Freeman had gained considerable stature within Goldman, and was now being included in top-level strategy sessions for some of the firm's most important clients, such as Unocal, the target of the latest oil company raid by Boone Pickens. In what soon became one of the most bitter, hotly contested takeover battles ever, Goldman defended Unocal. Peter Sachs, Goldman's head of M&A, often spent two to three hours a day consulting with Freeman about the situation. Freeman had valuable insights into how various defense alternatives would be interpreted by his colleagues in the arbitrage community. While such communications tended to undermine any notion of a Chinese wall, Sachs had no way of knowing that Freeman might betray Unocal's confidence.

Shortly after Siegel first leaked details of KKR's bid for Storer, Siegel mentioned that he'd taken a position in Unocal. Freeman assured him there'd be an "economic solution"—meaning value would be realized for shareholders—so Siegel had Wigton and Tabor increase the size of their position. When Freeman leaked the details of Unocal's plan to create a separate master limited partnership of some of its oil-producing properties, Siegel urged them to buy more.

Many of Freeman's tips to Siegel in Unocal showed how important seemingly arcane details of financial transactions can be in the hands of sophisticated investors. As part of its defense, Unocal offered to buy back 50% of its stock at $72—but none of Pickens's stake—leaving the stock it didn't buy to fall to whatever price the market would support. Word of the plan sent panic through the market, because Pickens was likely to sue. Siegel was en route from Dallas to Tulsa at the time, and when he got into the airport, he called Wigton and Tabor, who were frantic, given the huge size of Kidder, Peabody's position in Unocal. So phone records wouldn't show a direct call to Freeman's office, Siegel called his secretary, who connected him to Freeman's office. "Don't worry," Freeman said. "It doesn't matter. We [Unocal] are going to buy the stock anyway in the partial tender." That meant that even if a court said Pickens had to be included in the share buyback, Unocal would go forward (as eventually happened.)

Siegel immediately hung up and called Wigton and Tabor. Knowing now that the tender offer would proceed, he suggested a strategy to sell calls to lock in their profit on the half of the position that wouldn't be subject to the offer. (Wigton and Tabor actually bought puts, the right to sell Unocal at a fixed price, which implemented the same strategy.)

When he hung up, Siegel felt elated. He knew the Unocal battle was nearing a climax, and now he had guaranteed a huge profit for Kidder, Peabody using Freeman's information. He'd more than re-

couped all of Wigton's and Tabor's losses, and the department would
be well on its way to another big year, maybe even better than the one
before. The pressure on him from DeNunzio would ease off. Siegel felt
the same surge of adrenaline he'd sometimes felt in his dealings with
Boesky.

Siegel was stuck in the Tulsa airport until he could get a flight
back to New York, and he was bursting to share the good news. So he
got back into a phone booth. Recklessly, he called DeNunzio at home.
He told him about everything, including the call to Freeman, and how
they'd come up with the strategy to lock in their profits. DeNunzio
seemed thrilled. Siegel felt the warm comfort of a father figure's
approval.

Unocal's Goldman-crafted buyback gambit worked. After the
partial tender offer, the so-called pro ration factor—the percentage of
the shares tendered by each shareholder that would actually be purchased—had to be calculated based on the total number of shares
actually tendered. Freeman obligingly shared the supposedly confidential percentage so Siegel could precisely tailor Kidder, Peabody's
final options trading. It was like shooting fish in a barrel. "You guys
are all going to be happy," Freeman told Siegel, and he was right.

The Siegel-Freeman relationship continued through the year.
They talked constantly, often two or three times a day, and inside
information didn't even figure in most of their conversations. Their
dialogues were an increasingly seamless tapestry of mutually beneficial
information useful in recruiting clients, in triggering deals with reluctant parties, in getting higher sale prices and accompanying investment
banking fees, and in generating profits for their firms. It was all, of
course, a secret from the rest of the world.

The exchange of inside information also continued unabated.
Gray as the lines sometimes were, Siegel was almost never in any doubt
about when the line was crossed. He always felt at least a twinge of guilt
and anxiety. Siegel gave Freeman details of International Controls
Corporation's bid for Kidder, Peabody client Transway International;
Freeman told Siegel he had taken a big Transway position for his
children. While Goldman was involved in the Philip Morris acquisition
of General Foods, Siegel asked Freeman, "What do you think of the
stock? [General Foods]?" Freeman replied, "It looks good to me."
This meant that Siegel should buy it, which he did, through Wigton
and Tabor.

Freeman also gave Siegel details of Baxter Tavenol Laboratories'
bid for American Hospital Supply, and in the 1986 R. H. Macy leveraged buyout handled by Goldman, Freeman told Siegel that the market had overreacted to rumors that Macy would lower its offering price:

Macy was lowering its price, but to a smaller extent than the market expected. The financing was secure.

Freeman was similarly generous with information about R. H. Macy when Boesky called him, asking the same questions as Siegel. Freeman assured Boesky the financing would be secure. In any event, Boesky had yet another source inside Goldman, Sachs on the Macy deal, someone in the firm's real estate area.

Such leaks were all too common, making a mockery of any notion of a fair marketplace. Participants were rarely as explicit in their leaks as Freeman and Siegel; they knew it wasn't necessary. Nor did they reveal all that they knew. Meanwhile, Siegel continued to rationalize much of what he gave Freeman as being in his clients' interests.

Nowhere was this more apparent than in the Beatrice deal, the biggest LBO ever, 1985's deal of the year. It was the pinnacle of Siegel's work for KKR, the deal that established KKR as the premier leveraged buyout force in the country, a name to be feared. It was also a deal shot through with illegal and questionable behavior by Wall Street professionals.

Beatrice was KKR's first "hostile" deal. KKR had always considered its approaches friendly, working with management to take a company private or entering a hostile takeover battle as a white knight rescuer. In the case of Beatrice, however, KKR, advised by Siegel, had joined forces with Donald Kelly, a former Beatrice chairman. If Beatrice resisted KKR's embrace, KKR would acquire the company, oust its current management, and install Kelly and his team in their place. The plan was such a sharp departure that KKR's senior partner, Jerome Kohlberg, soon withdrew from the partnership that bears his name, citing "philosophical differences" with his partners, cousins Henry Kravis and George Roberts.

Despite Kohlberg's reservations, the bid went forward. Freeman was soon amassing huge positions for himself, for his children, and for Goldman. He was in his usual daily contact with Siegel throughout the deal, but Siegel stopped short of conveying inside information. At times, it seemed as though Freeman didn't need information from Siegel; his stature had reached the point where he could simply pick up the phone and talk to Kravis himself. On Halloween, for example, after John Mulheren unloaded a fourth of his huge Beatrice holdings on rumors that the KKR bid was encountering problems, Freeman called Kravis and asked him why the stock was dropping. "Everything is fine," Kravis told Freeman. In this exceptionally valuable communication, Kravis added, "We're not pulling out." Minutes later, Freeman went on a Beatrice buying binge, adding 60,000 shares and hundreds of call options to his holdings.

Beatrice's board eventually succumbed to KKR's final November 1985 bid of $50 a share. Soon thereafter, KKR learned from its investment bankers at Drexel, who were arranging the financing on the deal, that they couldn't finance the deal at $50. The price would have to be lowered or the financing restructured. There were obvious market implications. The decision was supposed to be so confidential that not even Siegel was told. Arbitrageur Richard Nye, a New York socialite and member of the inner circle of establishment arbitrageurs, showed uncanny prescience, disposing of his 300,000 shares of Beatrice the very next day. Later that day, Freeman and Nye talked on the phone. Freeman also called Kravis.

The next morning, January 8, 1986, as soon as the market opened, Freeman unloaded his entire option position. Shortly after, Morris "Bunny" Lasker, a well-known member of the New York Stock Exchange, and yet another member of the "club," called Freeman to report that there was trouble with KKR's bid. Freeman, in turn, called Siegel to confirm the information. Siegel couldn't—because the first he knew of it was from Freeman.

Siegel was astonished. There truly were no secrets these days on Wall Street. Here he was the investment banker and advisor to Kravis, and he didn't even know the financing had run into trouble. It only confirmed his darkest suspicions that his own breaches of confidentiality were hardly isolated examples: the exchange of inside information on Wall Street was becoming an epidemic. Siegel called KKR to get details of the problem.

Soon after, Siegel called Freeman back. "Your bunny has a good nose," Siegel said, amused by his own play on words. It was all the confirmation Freeman needed. That afternoon, Freeman sold 100,000 Beatrice shares and 3,000 calls (which represented the right to buy an additional 300,000 shares), all at enormous profits.

The terms of the KKR bid were soon modified along the lines Siegel had confirmed. Though the terms were less favorable to shareholders—the cash portion was reduced from $43 to $40—Beatrice had little choice but to accept the revised offer, and did so. Beatrice stock declined accordingly. Freeman would have made large profits on his massive Beatrice stake in any event, but Siegel's confirmation saved him an enormous sum, boosting his earnings on that deal into the stratosphere.

Because of Siegel's role in the deal, Kidder, Peabody's arbitrage operation didn't participate in the Beatrice windfall. Still, 1985 had been another amazingly successful year for Wigton and Tabor. The department's total profit, even after deducting a disproportionate share of the firm's overhead and expenses, was more than $7 million. Now that they had repeated their first year's success, some of the skepticism within the firm had worn off. Although estimates of Wigton and Tabor's innate skills remained low, the plethora of deals that year had made it seem as though anybody could make money in arbitrage simply by throwing money at any takeover announcement that came across the ticker tape. And, in truth, they probably could.

But Siegel knew the truth about Kidder, Peabody's arbitrage prowess. Like a drug habit, the thrill of arbitrage success always carried with it the immediate craving for and anxiety over the next "fix," the next takeover bid, and the need for inside information to provide the "edge." The thrill of the sure bets was fading even as the pressure to perform rose. Siegel knew he had rescued the firm for another year— but could he start all over again, with the same renewed pressure, simply because the calendar turned over to 1986? Increasingly, he dreaded the prospect.

Early in 1985, while awaiting the birth of his twins, Siegel had picked up a copy of *The New York Times* and seen the huge tombstone ad Drexel took out when it completed the Coastal/ANR deal. "They're a power if they can raise this kind of money," Siegel had thought to himself. Now he could see it happening. He could see the powerhouses arrayed against him: especially Drexel, with its amazing ability to raise billions almost overnight, a feat Kidder, Peabody could never duplicate. It was no wonder that, on deals like Storer and Beatrice, where it had been Siegel's imagination and resourcefulness that persuaded Kravis to go forward, Drexel got the lucrative financing assignments, leaving Siegel to collect only the investment banking advisory fee. In Storer, for example, Kidder, Peabody earned $7 million, while Drexel got $50 million. Other rivals, like Goldman and Morgan Stanley, were building their capital bases and clout even as Kidder, Peabody struggled with its still-unprofitable brokerage operations. Siegel felt like he was carrying the entire firm on his own shoulders, and he didn't know how much longer he could go on before something in him broke.

Late in 1985, about bonus time, he went in to see DeNunzio. His own compensation wasn't the issue. For 1985, DeNunzio recognized Siegel's contribution to the firm—including the arbitrage profits—by awarding him a cash bonus of $2.1 million, nearly double what he'd made before. But Siegel wasn't elated; he was despairing. A negative article in *Institutional Investor* had only reinforced his fears that Kidder, Peabody, as an institution, was drifting toward crisis. He pleaded with DeNunzio. "Ralph, I can't keep this up," he said. "I can't be the only engine for this firm. I only have so many hours in the day. I'm bringing in all the profits and revenues." Siegel told DeNunzio he'd reached the conclusion that Kidder, Peabody could only survive by merging with another firm. DeNunzio looked stunned and depressed by the mere notion of Kidder, Peabody's loss of independence. He hadn't reached the pinnacle of his professional career to preside over the firm's demise. Siegel despaired that he'd ever make DeNunzio face reality.

For the first time, Siegel had begun to contemplate the once unthinkable: He would escape, fleeing Kidder, Peabody for a strong, healthy, progressive firm. He had to get out of arbitrage; he knew his involvement was wrong. Yet he knew he couldn't extricate himself at Kidder, Peabody as long as Wigton and Tabor were the only alternatives.

Feeling furtive, Siegel agreed to meet Michel David-Weill, the courtly head of Lazard Frères, for breakfast at the elegant Carlyle Hotel on Manhattan's Upper East Side. He settled into a comfortable banquette, shielded from view by a sumptuous arrangement of fresh flowers, and David-Weill talked of the virtues of a firm like Lazard for an investment banker with Siegel's star status, mentioning how Felix Rohatyn had thrived there.

Suddenly Siegel remembered the day, years before, when as a young investment banker he'd been assigned to a deal with Rohatyn. That day, he'd believed for the first time that he had it in himself to become another Rohatyn. Instead, he was leading a secret life of crime.

But now the vision came back to him. He'd leave Kidder, Peabody for a new life, one without Boesky, Freeman, Wigton, or DeNunzio dragging him back into the mire. With his reputation and celebrity within the world of takeovers, he could go anywhere. When the history of the eighties on Wall Street was written, Siegel wanted to be at its center: in the role of a statesman.

7.

John Mulheren pulled on his sweat socks, tied his shoelaces, and headed out onto the exercise floor of the HEAR Institute, a sports fitness clinic in Red Hook, N.J., not far from his home in Rumson. Mulheren was determined to get himself back into shape. He hated the idea of sinking into a middle-aged bloat.

Beside him, rock singer Bruce Springsteen was doing a bench press. Springsteen looked great, Mulheren thought. The last time he'd seen him, Springsteen had looked like any other 35-year-old guy, fairly slender and a little paunchy. Now he looked like a trimmer Rocky Balboa. Mulheren didn't know Springsteen very well, but seeing the transformation made Mulheren even more disgusted with himself.

Like Marty Siegel, Mulheren had been feeling under pressure to generate big profits for his firm, Spear Leeds. So far, 1984 had been a rollercoaster year; he'd done well at the start, with the Gulf deal, then he'd had a terrible spring, and he'd surged ahead again during the summer. But Mulheren felt himself slipping toward a dark state of mind. It had taken years for him to face it, but he knew he was a clinical manic-depressive. He was almost always "high." His energy was tremendous, he needed little sleep, and he did many things—from drinking to partying to stock speculating—to excess. The drug lithium helped control his moods but, in what he'd come to recognize as four-year cycles, he sometimes plunged into black, self-destructive moods that lasted several days. At those times, he constantly contemplated suicide. That summer, he felt such a mood approaching. Increasingly, he was losing interest in showing up for work at Spear Leeds.

Then, one August afternoon, he heard his wife Nancy scream. He rushed out to her and saw in the pool the submerged body of his 18-month-old adopted son. When Mulheren, who had once worked as a lifeguard, pulled the child from the water, he wasn't breathing. He applied mouth-to-mouth resusitation, gently, taking care to avoid collapsing the infant's lungs. He succeeded in removing the blockage, and the Mulherens rushed the child to the hospital. In four days he was back to normal.

The harrowing rescue had a profound impact on Mulheren. He felt that if he hadn't been at home that day, his son would have died. The next day he went into Spear Leeds's offices and told his partners, "I'm not going back to work."

With time suddenly on his hands, Mulheren plunged into his fitness campaign, and discovered that he and Springsteen had a good deal in common. For one thing, they were among the few 35-year-old men in Rumson who could spend most of the day in the gym. They didn't have to get up early, either. Springsteen liked to stay up late, and Mulheren hardly slept at all. Mulheren loves music; he had been a fan of Springsteen long before the singer-songwriter became a national sensation. Mulheren was even an early champion of rap music. Like Mulheren, Springsteen threw himself into activities with enthusiasm. He, too, considered anything worth doing worth doing to excess. So they took up jet skiing in the Atlantic Ocean, just offshore from the beach club Mulheren had bought as an investment. They took their families and went skiing in the Rockies. Soon Mulheren considered Springsteen his best friend.

The day after Mulheren quit Spear Leeds, he had gotten a call at home from Boesky. "What did you do that for?" Boesky asked gruffly. He didn't seem sympathetic to Mulheren's explanation; he must have been anxious over the loss of a source of market intelligence, just at the time Siegel was beginning to pull away. Mulheren didn't hear from Boesky again until rumors surfaced that a Pickens deal was in trouble. Boesky called Mulheren, convinced that Mulheren was talking to his friend Pickens. "What's going on?" Boesky demanded. "I don't have any idea," Mulheren replied, the deal far from his mind. Boesky yelled, insisting that Mulheren was in contact with Pickens.

Other Wall Streeters called Mulheren regularly, urging him to return to work. Alan C. ("Ace") Greenberg, the head of Bear, Stearns & Co., made a strenuous effort to hire Mulheren. But Mulheren turned them all down, preferring to dabble in real estate and cavort with Springsteen. When Springsteen started to prepare for his 1985 "Born in the U.S.A." tour, however, Mulheren started getting restless. Springsteen would soon be out of town and unavailable. Mulheren started to miss the highs of his old business.

The wealthy Belzberg family offered to set him up in his own partnership, and Mulheren couldn't resist. He began raising money for his return, eventually amassing $65 million in capital for a new firm,

Jamie Securities—an acronym for John A. Mulheren and his partner, Israel Englander. He contacted Boesky, who gave him some fundraising suggestions. Mulheren kept Boesky informed about who his new limited partners would be. Boesky was suddenly his friend again, and the ingenuous Mulheren was as eager to please him as ever.

When Jamie Securities opened for business in July 1985, Mulheren immediately heard from Boesky, who knew that his friend had a big pile of fresh capital that he hadn't yet put to work in the market. Boesky told Mulheren he was "raising cash" and wanted to sell Mulheren some stock. Would Mulheren take some, and if so, how much? Mulheren, eager to oblige, said he'd buy $10 million worth.

So Boesky had his head trader, Michael Davidoff, follow up with a call. "Ivan said you'd do us a favor," Davidoff began, then asked Mulheren to buy 330,000 shares of Unocal from Boesky. He agreed.

"Okay," Davidoff continued. "I'm going to sell it to you and I might want to buy it back. And you'll be held harmless. You won't lose any money." Suddenly Mulheren got the picture: Boesky wanted to "park" his Unocal position with him, making it look as if Mulheren owned it. Boesky, however, would continue to bear the risk of any losses and would realize any profits. Mulheren didn't like the smell of this.

"You can stop right there," Mulheren said. "I don't do those trades. If I'm not at risk of the market, I will not do the trade."

"Okay, thanks a lot, let's do the trade," Davidoff replied, eager for the transaction. Later, as Unocal stock sagged and Mulheren showed a loss of hundreds of thousands of dollars on the position, one of his colleagues asked why he kept it. "It's a favor for Ivan," Mulheren replied. "Don't worry about it."

Despite such requests, Mulheren didn't really feel used by Boesky. In his view, Wall Street was one big network of interlocking favors. Services were routinely paid for with what were dubbed "soft dollars"—the exchange of mutual favors. If Mulheren wanted to repay Boesky for a useful tip, he steered more business through Seemala, Boesky's broker-dealer operation that traded on the New York Stock Exchange.

When Boesky asked for favors, Mulheren didn't worry unduly about Boesky's motivation. But it was no secret that Boesky, given the enormous size of his positions and his insatiable quest for greater leverage, was constantly in danger of violating the regulatory net capital requirements.

Boesky and many arbitrageurs had always viewed the net capital requirements with thinly veiled contempt. His colleagues Conway and especially Mooradian, who had nearly lost his career after being disciplined for net capital violations, took the law much more seriously and tried to keep Boesky in compliance. They even went so far as to build in what they termed a "fudge factor" that overstated Boesky's actual leverage in order to try to keep him in bounds.

In 1985, however, with the pace of merger deals quickening, and the resulting increase in arbitrage opportunities, it was getting harder and harder to keep Boesky in compliance. Finally, that summer, Conway wrote Boesky an angry memo: "You have continued to show very small regard for our net capital position or the debt covenants under our loan agreements. . . . We are on a self-destruct course that will, in the extreme, make it impossible to raise new equity or debt capital. . . . You are risking everything and your reputation on a business strategy which can only be characterized as reckless. We must ratchet down the size of the portfolio as soon as possible. We must maintain minimum net capital at $15 million. . . . We are sitting on a time bomb that has only 18 days to go before the default provisions of the debt covenants come into effect. You must take action immediately."

Boesky could, of course, have solved the problem immediately by selling some of his positions. That, however, was anathema when the stocks were, he thought, still rising in value. So he had Davidoff call Mulheren again.

"We need a favor," Davidoff said.

"What's it in?" Mulheren replied.

"Well, I got a lot of stocks. You can take your pick." Mulheren settled on large positions in three stocks: Storer Communications, then in the later stages of its battle with KKR, Boise Cascade, an oft-rumored takeover target, and Warner Communications. It was understood that Boesky would buy them back sometime later. "We'll take the risk," Davidoff said, as he had with the Unocal position. "I told you before," Mulheren interjected, "I don't do those kinds of transactions. I'm a big boy and I take the risk because it's not legal if you do it that way."

Now Boesky's books, minus the positions taken by Mulheren, showed him to be in compliance with his regulatory and debt requirements. But Boesky still deemed the stocks parked with Mulheren to be "his," and he was particularly elated because Warner kept going up. When profits on Mulheren's Warner position reached $500,000, Davidoff called again. "This is really getting to be a problem," he said.

"Oh no," Mulheren replied. "It's getting to be a problem for you. It's a profit for me."

Davidoff was getting anxious. "You're not going to do anything for us on this?"

"I didn't say that," Mulheren replied. "I'm just telling you whose positions they are and I decide what happens here." When Mulheren finally sold the Warner position back to Boesky, he realized a profit of $1.7 million, which meant, in Boesky's view, that Mulheren owed him money.

Later in the year, after similar incidents with other stocks, Boesky called. Despite Mulheren's earlier claim that he owned the positions, the two were soon enmeshed in a discussion of how Mulheren would pay Boesky back.

"You know, you made all this money on these things. What's going to be worked out here? Michael [Davidoff]'s been talking to you."

"I know."

"Don't you think you owe us something?"

"I don't know. I don't know what I'm going to do," Mulheren replied.

"Well, would you write me a check?" Boesky asked.

"Under no circumstances," Mulheren shot back. "And I won't give you any money. I won't give you cash."

"Well, what do you mean?" Boesky asked.

"I'll do other things for you. I'll give you ideas. I'll do more brokerage for you. I'll do all kinds of soft things, normal return-of-favor things."

Boesky agreed, and over time, Mulheren was as good as his word. When Boesky sent brokerage bills to Mulheren for trading through Seemala, Mulheren had him inflate the invoices by a factor of ten. Other times he'd just add a lot of money to the payment. Eventually, Boesky was satisfied. The inflated payments stopped, though not the exchange of mutual "favors."

Not long after taking the Unocal position, Boesky called Mulheren asking for another kind of favor. "Born in the U.S.A." had vaulted Springsteen to superstardom. His tour had become the rock music event of the year, and his concert at Giants Stadium in the New Jersey Meadowlands had sold out instantly. Boesky wanted tickets for his kids. Even though they were now close friends, Mulheren had never asked Springsteen for free tickets to his concerts. He would not ever try to take advantage of Springsteen's celebrity.

"Ivan, I'm not going to Springsteen for tickets," Mulheren said. "That's not the kind of thing I'd ever do. But if you want tickets, I can get them through a scalper, and you'll have to pay. They'll be expensive."

"Just get them," Boesky said. "I don't care what they cost."

The next day Mulheren called to tell Boesky he'd gotten the tickets and Boesky could pick them up. "That's great," Boesky said.

"But my kids would really like to meet Springsteen. You could just fly Springsteen up to Mt. Kisco in your helicopter, and we could have dinner. Just you, me, the kids, and Springsteen. Then you could fly back. It'd just be for one evening."

Mulheren was appalled. "For God's sake, Ivan," he said. "He's not a trained chimpanzee."

———

It was a bleak Friday morning in early January 1985. As they gathered in the conference room for the daily morning meeting, many of Boesky's employees were looking forward to a quiet weekend after the previous week's round of New Year's parties. The meetings typically began at 9 A.M. and continued until 9:45, with Boesky issuing the day's trading instructions and research requests. The traders usually left before 9:30 to be ready for the market opening.

Boesky arrived promptly at 9 A.M., nodded curtly to his staff, and took a seat at the head of the oval table, a phone within easy reach. He began dispensing orders. Then, after about 20 minutes, Boesky's secretary, Ianthe Peters, appeared in the doorway behind Boesky, looking anxious. She knew Boesky hated to be interrupted. Intrusions were normally met with rage. "Mike's on the phone," she said. Boesky broke off his orders. "I'll take it," he said immediately.

Everyone in the room knew that "Mike" was Milken. The traders referred to him as "the Coast," but Boesky's secretary always called him simply by his first name. He was the only person who always got through to Boesky.

Boesky put his fingers to his lips and looked around the table, ordering silence. Then he picked up the phone. There were no pleasantries. Boesky said little, mostly indicating agreement with whatever Milken was saying. When he hung up, his eyes were gleaming with excitement.

"We're putting all engines on max," Boesky exclaimed, and everyone realized their hopes for a quiet day were gone. Boesky ordered Lessman to generate research on both Diamond Shamrock and Occidental. He ordered Davidoff and the traders to buy immediately as much Diamond Shamrock stock as possible while simultaneously selling short Occidental Petroleum. Davidoff plunged into action, eventually snapping up a whopping 3.5 million shares of Diamond Shamrock. He had more trouble shorting Occidental, managing to sell short only 19,000 shares.

Lessman wondered what was going on. What had Milken said to

Boesky? Neither stock had been on their research or trading lists before that morning. Something, he thought, was fishy. Before he could make much research headway, trading was halted in the securities of both companies at their request. Then they announced jointly that they were discussing a "possible business combination," and trading in the stocks opened. There was little market reaction; the announcement was too vague. Often, the shares of the company being acquired soar in price, while those of the company making the offer decline. But no one knew from the press release whether Occidental was talking about acquiring Diamond Shamrock, or vice versa. And sometimes "business combination" meant a stock swap, in which case, depending on the exchange ratio, the shares of both companies might stay the same. That didn't stop Boesky, who showed remarkable confidence in his strategy.

The day before, Ray Irani, Occidental's president and a Milken client, had interrupted a dinner meeting at which a merger of Diamond Shamrock and Occidental was in fact being discussed. He had called Peter Ackerman at Drexel, one of Milken's top aides. Other investment bankers were working on the deal, but Occidental had hired Drexel to examine the transaction and issue a "fairness opinion" assuring Occidental's board that the transaction was fair for shareholders.

Irani quickly briefed Drexel on the terms of the proposed deal, and a Drexel team arrived at Occidental's offices in Los Angeles the next morning to begin work on the opinion. The plan was for Occidental and Diamond Shamrock to merge through a one-for-one stock swap, meaning Occidental would exchange one share of its stock for each Diamond Shamrock share. Since, as of January 3, Occidental was trading at $26.75 and Diamond Shamrock at $17.75, the deal would be a windfall of $9 a share to Diamond Shamrock holders. Because of the dilution caused by issuing so many new shares, Occidental's share price would almost certainly drop.

Given the terms of the deal, it made perfect sense for Boesky to buy Diamond Shamrock and sell Occidental short. James Dahl, Milken's top salesman, who was sitting next to Milken at the trading desk in Beverly Hills, overheard Milken—before the deal's terms were announced publicly—tell Boesky to short Occidental and go long on Diamond Shamrock. Then he listened while Milken refined the strategy.

This wasn't just a friendly tip from Milken. He wanted to participate in the trading himself, despite the fact that Drexel, now working for Occidental, was obviously barred from trading. Milken and Boesky agreed that Boesky's Diamond Shamrock and Occidental positions would secretly be half-owned by Milken. This was the conversation that, unbeknownst to Milken, was being overheard on Boesky's end by everyone sitting in the conference room.

The deal, which appears to have been Milken's and Boesky's first overt collaboration in insider trading, proved star-crossed. What had seemed a slam-dunk profit opportunity soured the following Monday, when Diamond Shamrock's board voted down the deal. Soon after the secret board decision, Dahl noticed that Milken looked upset. Milken again picked up the phone and called Boesky. This time he practically screamed: "The deal didn't go through. We've got to get out of the position."

Boesky was apoplectic and frantically ordered Davidoff to dump the position. But it was too late in the day; the market closed at 4, and news that the deal had fallen apart was released at 4:18 P.M. Now every arbitrageur was trying to dump Diamond Shamrock.

That afternoon and the next day, Milken called constantly, complaining bitterly that Boesky was taking too long to get out. People in the office heard Boesky yelling back that it was Milken who'd gotten them into the mess. Davidoff finally talked to the frantic Milken himself, saying he was doing his best and giving him estimates of the losses they were suffering as Diamond Shamrock's stock dropped throughout the day.

Dahl heard Milken slam down the phone and complain that the department had lost more money on the Diamond Shamrock/Occidental transaction than it had made all month. Dahl was baffled; how could the high-yield operation have been hurt by the proposed Occidental merger? Milken explained angrily that the department held a position "off line" with Boesky, and that as a result, the department now owed Boesky another $10 million. Milken was in such a bad mood that Dahl knew better than to push the issue, but he was still confused. He went to Lowell Milken to find out what was going on, but Lowell brushed him aside. Milken brooded for the rest of the afternoon.

Increasingly, Dahl and others in the office were worrying about Milken, the stress in the office, and the effects it was having on them and their lives. Business was frantic; corporate finance in New York called constantly to see whether Beverly Hills could finance their deals. Milken seemed incapable of turning deals down; he always worried that Drexel might lose its dominance of the high-yield market. Already, they were embroiled in Pickens's foray at Phillips Petroleum, for which Milken had raised an extraordinary $2 billion in financing over a single weekend.

The atmosphere was tense. Milken was spending 14 hours a day on the trading desk. He developed dark rings under his eyes. For a six-month period, he actually called Jim Dahl "Tom"; Dahl was afraid to correct him. Dahl told Lowell that "Mike looks like shit," and Lowell said, "I'm worried about him, too."

One of Milken's problems was Boesky. Milken was now far more deeply in Boesky's debt than he'd even hinted to Dahl. Boesky and Milken had taken the exchange of "favors" to dangerous, previously unheard-of lengths.

During the spring of 1984, one of Milken's earliest and most important clients, Golden Nugget, the casino company headed by Milken's friend Stephen Wynn, secretly had begun accumulating shares of MCA Inc., the owner of Universal Studios. The goal was a possible takeover. By the end of July, Golden Nugget had acquired well over two million shares, and MCA's shares rose from about $38 to $43. By August, however, Wynn and Milken had decided the deal wasn't feasible. Golden Nugget wanted out of its huge position at the highest possible price, but if word leaked out, the share price would quickly plunge. Nevertheless, Wynn told *The Wall Street Journal* in October that Golden Nugget owned just under 5% of MCA and intended to hold the stock "for now."

It had been a tricky situation, and Milken had again called on Boesky for help. Boesky bought huge chunks of Golden Nugget's position at the high market price, and Milken promised to guarantee him against loss. Because of Boesky's interest, the continued high volume of trading, and the fact that Drexel was handling the accumulation, an MCA takeover seemed more likely than ever to close observers.

As other buyers stepped in in anticipation of a takeover, Boesky began selling his position in smaller trades so as not to attract attention. Boesky did sustain losses, but Golden Nugget got out at a high price, guaranteeing its continued loyalty to Milken. The scheme to mislead the marketplace worked like a charm.

Milken now owed Boesky for the MCA losses. He also owed the arbitrageur $8 million from the Fischbach deal. Boesky flew to Los Angeles, and the next morning he reminded Milken of their agreement. Milken turned him over to one of his colleagues, Cary Maultasch, who had begun keeping track of the Boesky positions. Milken told them to work out the balance due. In the meantime, Milken embarked on a series of transactions trying to narrow the difference.

Because of his extraordinary control over the junk-bond market, Milken could buy back securities at artificially low prices from Drexel clients who had no way of knowing their actual value; sell them to Boesky at a small profit; have Boesky resell the securities to Drexel at a much higher price; and in turn resell them to Drexel clients at still higher prices. This enabled Milken to repay Boesky millions of dollars, even while continuing to earn profits from his trading operation. Drexel clients, of course, were none the wiser.

Even after these maneuvers, however, Boesky still had a credit. At his request, Milken engineered another series of trades that generated artificial tax losses for Boesky. This time, it was American taxpayers who were cheated.

By May 1985 the slate was clean. It was a measure of Milken's extraordinary market power that, in less than six months, he could clandestinely repay Boesky more than $10 million without so much as writing a check. Both Milken and Boesky realized that they could use each other to achieve other ambitions: not only insider-trading profits, but far grander dreams of corporate conquest and control.

That spring, Milken, like Siegel and Freeman, was heavily involved in KKR's bid for Storer Communications. Henry Kravis, growing increasingly close to Milken and impressed with his fund-raising abilities, had hired Milken to arrange the financing for the bid, while retaining Siegel as his strategic advisor. Siegel never met Milken in the course of the transaction, but it was the first deal in which he worked closely with investment bankers at Drexel. Milken couldn't trade in Storer himself, of course, so he had Boesky take a position on Drexel's behalf shortly after he and his colleagues met to discuss financing for an increase in KKR's bid. This gambit went smoothly, and Boesky credited Milken with a gain of over $1 million when the shares, predictably, went up and were sold on instructions from Milken's high-yield department.

But trading on inside information, even a sure bet, yielded profits that were small potatoes compared to what Milken could earn from the takeover transaction itself. For the Storer financing alone, Milken earned a staggering $49.6 million in fees. He also gained equity interests in the future KKR-led Storer, which he dispersed in the myriad private partnerships that benefited himself, his family, and others in the high-yield department. He didn't tell KKR or Joseph at Drexel where the equity ended up; on the contrary, he told them falsely that it had been used to induce clients to purchase the debt. It seemed to Milken's colleagues that the Storer deal fueled his almost insatiable lust for more takeovers. If the market faltered, Milken had shown that he had the awesome power to step in and make things happen—his way.

This was amply apparent to everyone in the Beverly Hills operation just a few months after the Storer deal, when a delegation from Atlanta's Turner Broadcasting showed up for a visit with Milken. In many ways, Ted Turner was the kind of client Milken liked. The colorful owner of the Atlanta Braves and "superstation" WTBS, had recently founded a bold new cable broadcasting venture, Cable News Network. Turner was brash, irreverent, and rocked the establishment. Now he wanted to buy MGM/United Artists, in part for its library of film classics he could draw upon for a cable movie channel. MGM/UA, however, was far larger than Turner's company and, given Turner's own weak financial status, the prospect seemed almost laughable.

Milken assured Turner that Drexel could finance the deal. Both MGM and Turner hired Drexel to represent them—creating an extraordinary potential for conflict of interest, even though Milken promised Turner that he'd respect the confidentiality of any information Turner gave him.

Despite Milken's assurances, however, the deal began to look increasingly shaky. Even Milken's malleable bond-buying clients were balking at the terms, especially since both Turner's and MGM's financial conditions were deteriorating during the summer. The press began voicing skepticism: *The New York Times* reported on August 7, "Wall Street remained skeptical about Turner's ability to raise the money," and *The Wall Street Journal* noted on August 16, "Despite the Drexel [highly confident] letter, it remained unclear" how Turner would be able to support the huge amount of debt.

In August, Milken began directing Boesky to buy MGM stock, agreeing that they'd divide any profits or losses in half, with Milken's ownership kept secret. Milken was determined to complete the deal, though its terms did have to be restructured. The Boesky arrangement served at least two purposes: his purchases presented the illusion that an important arbitrageur believed the deal would go through, helping support the stock price. That, in turn, helped persuade Drexel clients that the bonds were a good buy. And, of course, Milken and Boesky made money off of Milken's knowledge that the deal would be restructured and completed, as it eventually was. The profit on the joint Boesky/Milken position was $3 million.

As with Storer, the trading profits were almost incidental. Milken and Drexel earned an extraordinary $66.8 million in financing fees for raising the $1.4 billion Turner needed for the transaction.

The double threat of Milken information and Boesky buying power may have reached its apogee in the takeover of Pacific Lumber Co., the country's largest owner of redwood forests, by Drexel client Maxxam Group Inc., a real estate developer whose rise had been fueled by Milken's junk bonds. MGM/UA had at least wanted a merger with Turner. Pacific Lumber, on the other hand, fought vigorously for its independence. Milken demonstrated the futility of its resistance.

Maxxam announced its bid for Pacific Lumber at the end of September 1985, and on the same day, retained Milken and Drexel to handle the financing. As soon as the bid was announced, Milken directed Boesky to begin massive purchases of Pacific Lumber shares in anticipation of higher offers and as a tactic to pressure Pacific Lumber into accepting the Maxxam bid. As before, Milken retained a 50% interest in Boesky's Pacific Lumber position. By October 22, when Pacific Lumber finally capitulated, Boesky had bought more than 5% of the company's shares, helping to drive up the stock price. Maxxam responded by raising its bid twice, on October 2 and 22, ultimately settling on $40 a share.

The Pacific Lumber trading netted profits of over $1 million. Since Boesky's buying arguably caused Maxxam to pay a higher price than it would have, it boosted the financing costs as well. Drexel earned a fee of $20.5 million and received 250,000 warrants to buy Pacific Lumber stock, an equity stake whose value was potentially far greater. Boesky's SEC disclosures in the deal, of course, made no mention of the true ownership in the position. Indeed, the perception that it was the feared arbitrageur Boesky who was amassing its shares had been one of the factors that caused Pacific Lumber to capitulate.

Pacific Lumber, under Maxxam control, soon aroused the ire of conservationists by felling tracts of redwood forest to meet its debt obligations.

Even as the Pacific Lumber deal was underway, Milken wielded similar tactics to drive Harris Graphics into the arms of an acquirer, a feat all the more profitable because Milken himself was one of the principal shareholders in Harris, and thus reaped enormous profits from the takeover.

Harris had been created in 1983 when an investor group in which various Milken and Drexel partnerships figured prominently acquired the printing division of Harris Corp., then offered shares to the public. The partnerships held about 1.2 million shares acquired for $1 a share at the time Harris Graphics was formed. Original investors in the Drexel deal also included Fred Carr, the Executive Life official who had played a role in Fischbach, and Saul Steinberg, the important Milken client who headed the Reliance Group. Leon Black, the investment banker in Drexel's New York office, was a member of the Harris Graphics board.

In May 1985, Harris Graphics management, needing to raise capital, settled on a secondary offering of stock, which, while in the long-term interests of the company and its shareholders, would have the immediate effect of diluting the holdings of the Drexel/Milken partnerships. Even as Drexel was retained to handle the offering, Milken apparently determined that it would never take place. Instead,

Harris Graphics would be sold whether it liked it or not, cashing out the partnerships at huge profits.

Milken and his colleagues in Beverly Hills immediately started shopping Harris Graphics to clients who might be used to mount a bid for the entire company, including Boesky. On May 22, the eve of the day the secondary offering was supposed to take place, Harris Graphics management learned, much to their surprise, that a takeover bid appeared imminent. That same day, Milken ordered Boesky to start buying Harris Graphics stock and to continue until he'd amassed a stake of more than 5%. Then Boesky could file the required SEC disclosures, revealing to the world that Harris Graphics was "in play." Boesky immediately did as instructed and, as in their other gambits, Milken retained a half interest in Boesky's Harris Graphics stake.

In the wake of the informal takeover bid, and sudden buying in its stock, Harris Graphics had to scrap its secondary stock offering. The first prong of Milken's master plan had been achieved. But the takeover bid Harris management had learned about was illusory. A real buyer had to be found, and Milken ordered his most persuasive salesmen into action. They focused on AM International, another Drexel client with interests in the printing business. Meanwhile, at Milken's behest, Boesky kept the pressure on, increasing his stake to over 8%. Pressure also came from Steinberg, who began amassing a position that would grow to more than 5%. He, too, filed SEC disclosure documents. Now Harris Graphics had not one but two potential raiders breathing down its neck.

Not surprisingly, when AM finally made a "friendly" bid of $22 a share, Harris Graphics management all but rushed to embrace it. For Milken, the profits rolled in: the Milken/Drexel partnerships could now be cashed out at profits of more than $30 million. Boesky earned $5.6 million on the Milken-directed stock accumulation, and Drexel earned $6.3 million. Harris Graphics was destroyed as an independent company, becoming just another cog in the much larger AM.

By now, Milken and Boesky were deeply intertwined in what was a sweeping criminal conspiracy. Taken together, the ventures were practically a catalogue of securities crimes, starting with insider trading, and including false public disclosures, tax fraud, and market manipulation, as well as a slew of more technical crimes. What was breathtaking about the scheme, however, was not just the variety of crimes, or their frequency. It was how the crimes meshed to achieve ends more ambitious than anything even contemplated by the drafters of the securities laws. The crimes were mere way stations toward outcomes, such as hostile takeovers, that were, on their face, perfectly legal.

That was the exquisite beauty of the scheme. It was a far more valuable relationship than anything Boesky had forged with Siegel or Levine, and it seemed even more foolproof. No outsider could possibly grasp its dimensions. There hadn't been so much as a hint of regulatory concern. And within the scheme, no one knew but Boesky and Milken. Milken could never betray Boesky, because Boesky could quickly implicate him. Though they often argued, sometimes yelling at each other, Boesky was comforted by their mutual dependence.

Another aspect of the relationship was becoming clear to Boesky, however. Milken was the engine of their profits. He, after all, was the one privy to the deal flow and the confidential plans of Drexel's clients. Boesky, increasingly, was little more than an order taker, a source of additional capital, and a front for Milken's larger designs.

Sometimes Milken told Boesky to take positions in particular securities, and sometimes Boesky extended his leverage by having Milken take positions for him. They traded at an ever-increasing pace, in Greentree Acceptance, Ensearch, National Health Care, Hospital Corporation of America, Centrust, Mapco, ABC, and CBS. Milken remained the dominant force.

The mounting number of stocks was causing headaches for Boesky's chief accountant in New York, Set Mooradian. He was constantly having to update the ledgers in his red-tie "special projects" folder. Boesky kept giving him more positions to enter or change, and he demanded regular updates on the net positions. "This is just between you and me," Boesky would frequently emphasize in his phone calls from the palatial new midtown office to the downtown quarters where Mooradian and the rest of the operations staff had stayed. "Don't tell anyone else about it."

After the flurry of activity in Pacific Lumber and Harris Graphics, Boesky had told Mooradian to finish the update of the file. "We've got to settle up with Drexel." Mooradian's ears perked up. It was the first time he'd ever heard Drexel connected to the "special projects" file. But he didn't attach any significance to the information.

In May Mooradian left for a long-awaited vacation, staying at his brother's condominium in Pompano Beach, Florida. He groaned when the phone rang and he was told Boesky was calling. Boesky always called him while he was on vacation, and he hated it. He never got a day's peace. "Is that schedule I asked for finished?" Boesky demanded without any preliminary civilities.

"Ivan, I'm on vacation," Mooradian pleaded.

"I don't care. We've got to get this done."

So Mooradian called his office, saying someone had to fly down to Florida with the red tie folder. Maria Termine, a young employee, volunteered, and she and Mooradian spent a day with the profit and loss statements on all the Boesky/Milken stocks spread out on the kitchen table. Boesky told Mooradian to work out any discrepancies with someone named "Thurman" in Drexel's Beverly Hills office. When Mooradian called, he learned there was no Thurman, but there was a Charles Thurnher. Boesky never got his name right. Thurnher, who kept similar records for Milken, would relay Drexel's calculations, and they tried to reconcile disagreements, which were numerous. They were far from having finished by the end of Mooradian's vacation.

Both Mooradian and Thurnher found themselves frequently confused. Mooradian would ask Boesky, who'd say only, "It's fifty percent mine and fifty percent theirs. Talk to Davidoff." But Davidoff knew even less. Did Boesky mean 50% ownership for the entire period, or only some of the time? When trouble developed on the Beverly Hills end, Thurnher told Mooradian, "I've got to talk to Mike."

By the end of the year, the statements still couldn't be reconciled, and Boesky was continuing to pressure Mooradian to come up with a bottom line. Mooradian told Boesky he couldn't make any more progress with Thurnher over the phone. He'd have to meet with him. Boesky was about to leave for Beverly Hills himself, so he suggested that Mooradian join him.

Mooradian was thrilled at the chance for a trip to California. He took his wife, Rusty, and stayed over a weekend. They reveled in the glamorous surroundings of the Beverly Hills Hotel, even though they couldn't get a table in the hotel's Polo Lounge. They languished in the dining room while the celebrities and movie moguls and agents in the Polo Lounge had the staff scurrying to satisfy their every whim. That changed dramatically after Boesky stopped by their table one evening. From then on, the Mooradians were treated like royalty. Mooradian later told friends that the visit was "the high point of my life." He didn't mind the fact that Boesky ignored them for the rest of their stay, traveling to Drexel's Wilshire Boulevard offices in a limousine while Mooradian took a cab.

Mooradian never met Milken, the man he thought of as the "junk-bond king." But he liked Thurnher and his secretary, and they settled down in a conference room to try to make sense of the increasingly complex series of transactions and records. "That fuckin' Ivan," Mooradian said at one point, "he kept me in the dark on this."

"I know how you feel," Thurnher replied. "Mike does the same thing to me."

As Thurnher produced copies of various trading records, they realized that some of the cost calculations were different. Drexel, which could borrow money at low brokers' call rates of 7% to 8%, had figured a much lower cost of carrying the large positions. Boesky's costs were higher, in part because of the high interest rates on the Drexel-issued debentures that were an important source of Boesky's capital, more in a range of 13% to 14%. They realized that by harmonizing the cost of carry calculations, most of the differences could be worked out. Whatever minor differences remained, one thing was clear: given the big gains on the jointly owned positions that Boesky took at Milken's behest, Boesky owed Milken millions of dollars—and Milken wanted every penny of it repaid.

The debt was a pittance in the context of the growing magnitude of Milken's business. The year 1985 was a watershed in the history of corporate control, when Drexel's "highly confident" letters and junk-bond prowess made the transition from novel but untested weapons into the most potent forces Wall Street had ever witnessed. The 1985 Predators' Ball had been the prelude to a series of hostile corporate attacks that left investors reeling: Pickens's bid first for Phillips Petroleum, then for mighty Unocal; KKR's assaults on Storer, then Beatrice; Ronald Perelman's conquest of venerable Revlon; Rupert Murdoch's acquisition of Metromedia; and, at the end of the year, a lightning-fast, $6 billion bid by GAF chairman Samuel Heyman for one of America's blue-chip industrial companies, a component of the Dow Jones average, Union Carbide. For that bid, Milken raised $5 billion in financing in a matter of days.

The juggernaut was moving so fast that even the U.S. Congress took notice, floating proposals to curb the tax deductibility of junk financing and holding public hearings on the threat to Unocal. Drexel, relatively naïve to the world of politics, hastily began courting support from legislators and put together its own political action committee. But despite all the bluster and rhetoric, Drexel and Milken had little to fear from Washington in the heyday of the Reagan administration's free-market, antigovernment intervention policies.

As Milken careened from triumph to triumph that year, he seemed, to those around him, a changed man. He had always eaten his lunches off of paper plates with his traders and salesmen. Now he instructed the caterers to serve him his lunch on china, and he often ate alone or with Lowell in Lowell's sumptuous office. Milken's appearance changed, too. He obtained an expensive new toupee, so skillfully done that it was imperceptible to all but knowledgeable observers. It looked like natural curls, and gave him a more stylish, youthful look. Milken had often shown up for work wearing mismatched socks; now he wore well-tailored suits and French cuffs. With Thomas Spiegel, his close friend and client at Columbia Savings, Milken bought a Gulfstream IV state-of-the-art private jet. He and Spiegel also began frequenting trendy, celebrity-filled restaurants, like Bistro Garden and Morton's. Milken hired a bodyguard and started coming to work in a chauffeured limousine.

The hiring process also changed. Before, Milken would bring candidates out to Beverly Hills, where they'd meet just about everyone in the office. Anyone could veto the applicant. This system helped maintain a sense of collegiality among the employees. Now, however, only one opinion mattered: Milken's. People complained that they didn't see the point of spending an hour or two with job applicants, only to have Milken dismiss their objections. One of Milken's most controversial hirees was his own brother-in-law, Allen Flans, a dentist who had married Lori Milken's sister. Flans knew little about the securities industry. Milken assigned Flans to Dahl, and told Dahl to train him.

Dahl quickly realized the assignment was hopeless. As far as he could tell, Flans contributed almost nothing to the operation. Flans would typically order two of the free lunches, eat one, wrap the other up, and take it down to his car. He wouldn't return for several hours, and colleagues occasionally saw him napping in the car. Flans earned more than $5 million in one two-year period.

Then there were Milken's boyhood friends, such as Harry Horowitz, who'd grown up with Milken in Encino. First Horowitz worked as a computer expert, spending millions on equipment that had to be replaced when it turned out to be the wrong kind. Then Horowitz got assigned to the junk-bond conferences, and later dabbled in lobbying and Milken charitable activities.

More worrisome, in the eyes of some, was Richard Sandler, who'd played with Milken at Sandler's mother's backyard camp. Sandler was a lawyer who installed his office right inside Drexel's, and appeared to work exclusively for Milken and the Milken family. His chief qualification seemed to be blind devotion to Milken. Some referred to him contemptuously as "the real estate lawyer," though they took care not to alienate him. Sandler was frequently closeted with Lowell.

The partnerships were also a source of discontent. Gary Winnick, in particular, had become suspicious of Milken's insistence that everyone was being taken care of even as he refused to reveal details of what the partnerships owned and what people's shares of them were. One day Winnick called Dahl into his office and said, "I'm going to show you something that will make you sick." Somehow Winnick had gotten a copy of a master partnership list, and it showed more than 40 accounts in the names of Milken, his wife, his children, and other relatives.

Winnick confronted Milken, who was affronted that anyone in the department would dare complain. Soon after, Winnick told Milken he was leaving. Milken accepted his resignation, and graciously offered to help finance a new fund for Winnick to run. "We'll put a fund together like KKR and you'll run it," Milken offered. They raised $1 billion, and Winnick launched Pacific Asset Holdings.

Winnick was soon disabused of the illusion that he'd escaped Milken. When Bear, Stearns brought him a potential LBO that interested him, Ackerman called from Drexel to tell him to forget about doing any deal that didn't come from Milken. "It's our fund," Ackerman said arrogantly. "We won't let you invest" in the Bear, Stearns deal. Winnick's capital simply became another pool for Milken to manipulate for his own ends.

Others also complained after warrants from the Beatrice deal were cashed in. The proceeds turned out to be far less than expected, and some of the employees summoned the courage to complain at a department meeting. Milken said he was "outraged" that anyone would complain, but he promised he'd have Lowell provide an explanation. None ever appeared. The truth was far worse than Milken dared admit.

Milken had extracted the Beatrice warrants (the right to buy Beatrice stock at a low price) from KKR by arguing that he needed to offer them to clients as an inducement to buy the Beatrice junk bonds. Instead, Milken had kept almost all the warrants for Drexel, lodging the bulk of them in his and his family's partnerships. Those warrants, originally purchased for 25¢ each, now represented the right to acquire over 22% of Beatrice—an interest worth $26 a share, for a staggering total of over $650 million. The explanation for the small payouts to employees was that Milken had kept most of the proceeds for himself and his family. Had the employees known, there probably would have been open rebellion.

In addition to preliminary calculations of bonuses and partnership shares, the end of the year always brought a flurry of Milken-directed trading designed for tax purposes. With clients like Columbia Savings, the trades looked suspiciously like "parking" to create phony tax losses.

One day Alan Rosenthal, one of the original salespeople who'd accompanied Milken to California, came up to his boss at the trading desk and, laughing, showed him a copy of a parody of The Wall Street Journal, called The Bawl Street Journal. "Listen to this," he said, reading one of the paper's headlines out loud as others in the office gathered. "Drexel Burnham's Michael Milken is the latest figure to be indicted in New York City's Parking Violations scandal. Although

Milken has not been to Manhattan in years, his violative parking practices leave no doubt as to his involvement."

Everyone laughed, until they noticed that Milken wasn't smiling. "Alan," he said curtly, "get that piece of crap out of my sight."

———————

Reid Nagle, a young, clean-cut savings and loan official from New Jersey, glanced impatiently around the gloomy interior of the Harvard Club, then looked at his watch. It was almost 3 P.M. on a late summer day in 1985. Ivan Boesky had promised to meet him at 2.

Nagle had been approached nearly a year before by Stephen Conway, Boesky's chief operating officer, for advice on the possible acquisition of a savings and loan. Now Boesky had called and said he was interested in talking to Nagle about a job. Boesky had been vague, but referred to developing a financial services business within his Northview corporation.

The club was practically empty. Suddenly the double doors swung open and Boesky came hurrying toward Nagle. "I'm sorry I'm late," Boesky said. "I've only got ten minutes."

The two moved to out-of-the-way seats. Nagle was still trying to figure how someone with his credentials might fit into an arbitrage operation, so he asked Boesky why he was interested in him. Boesky quickly dismissed talk of arbitrage, saying arbitrage no longer offered the challenges he was seeking. "Then what is your objective?" Nagle asked, puzzled.

"Where have the great fortunes been made?" Boesky asked in reply, and then answered his own question. "Real estate, oil, financial services." Then Boesky gazed past Nagle, toward the wall bearing oil portraits of distinguished Harvard graduates. "I want to be a latter-day Rothschild." By the time Boesky finished his discourse, the 10 minutes had stretched into an hour.

Nagle was suitably awed by his encounter with Boesky, who had never been so celebrated as he was that summer. Profiles in magazines and newspapers had made him well known nationally, but his quest for fame and, even more fundamentally, respectability, had led him to publish a book and embark on a national publicity tour. At the same time, his scheme with Milken was running at full tilt.

The title of Boesky's book, *Merger Mania*, (the subtitle was *Arbitrage: Wall Street's Best-Kept Money Making Secret*) was arguably the most intriguing line in the volume. "I considered whether to talk about the behind-the-scenes maneuverings and smoke-filled rooms, but I decided I wanted to do a serious book on arbitrage," Boesky told *The Wall Street Journal. Merger Mania* was a dry-as-dust treatise on technical aspects of arbitrage. The 242-page book, which Boesky said he'd been working on for three years, presented arbitrageurs as models of skill, foresight, and industry. "Undue profits are not made; there are no esoteric tricks that enable arbitrageurs to outwit the system," Boesky concluded piously.

The book received mostly respectful reviews, and helped Boesky polish his image as an academic: he was appointed to the faculty of the New York University business school and he became a lecturer at Columbia University; these were credentials he would mention with increasing frequency. Boesky received so many speaking invitations that he had to turn many down. It wasn't unusual, when he did appear, for him to be greeted with a standing ovation.

In these appearances, Boesky portrayed himself as more than an arbitrageur. He coined a new phrase, *venture arbitrage*, for the practice of buying large blocks of stock as a tactic to pressure companies into buyouts or takeovers. Yet, perhaps unwittingly, he also displayed flashes of self-doubt. In June, during his book tour appearances in Washington, Boesky was asked by a *Washington Post* reporter, David Vise, what motivated him. "You already are a wealthy man. What are you chasing?" Vise asked.

"Well, I sometimes say casually that I was given the God-given gift of being a horse that's kind of good at running around a track," Boesky explained. "I don't know any other way. I don't know how to be a milk horse and I don't know how to go to pasture, so I just keep doing what I was allowed to have the good fortune to do well and try to do it better and better and better." Then he offered a curious premonition: "As far as whether my system or formula will continue to work or not, the jury is still out. It's quite possible that tomorrow you'll see my epitaph and it will be something like 'News pending. Stop trading.'"

Boesky's vehicle for achieving his new ambitions was going to be a savings and loan: Financial Corporation of Santa Barbara. Milken and Dahl had brought the possible acquisition to him, excited by the potential in the newly deregulated savings and loan industry. Previously restricted to taking deposits and making home loans and other real estate loans, savings and loans had been liberated to invest anywhere. They attracted deposits with high interest rates. For depositors and savings and loans owners, risks were minimal because the government insured all deposits up to $100,000. It seemed almost as if the government wanted S&L owners to speculate.

To pay such rates, the savings and loans had to generate even higher returns with their own investments. Junk bonds, with their higher rates, seemed ideal. Milken and Drexel had already transformed once-sedate institutions like Centrust, Columbia, Financial Corporation of America, and American Savings into huge buyers of its junk bonds. Boesky and Financial Corporation of Santa Barbara could be a similar vehicle.

For Boesky, always in search of capital for his arbitrage plunges, an S&L offered unlimited funds. But whatever Boesky's own plans for the capital, Milken and his team could, with some confidence, predict where most of the money would end up: invested in high-yield bonds chosen by Milken. That was the price his clients paid for continued access to Milken.

Nagle was invited to a meeting of what Boesky had begun calling his "merchant banking" group at the Elbow Beach Hotel in Bermuda. Boesky flew in by private jet, accompanied by his usual entourage: Conway; Steve Oppenheim, Boesky's accountant at Oppenheim, Appel, Dixon; and Stephen Fraidin, his lawyer from Fried, Frank. Boesky took over the hotel's Presidential Suite for his own accommodations and for their meetings.

Nagle, for one, was dubious about the venture. He pointed out to Boesky that California law still restricted the amount of S&L assets that could be invested in common stock; he wouldn't have the unlimited leverage he dreamed of. Moreover, Nagle thought Santa Barbara's financial position was bad and getting worse. Conway glared at Nagle: he was determined finally to do a deal.

Boesky listened politely, but seemed unfazed. Guided by Drexel, he'd already acquired 10% of Santa Barbara, and had options through Northview to increase his ownership to 51%, all with Drexel-provided financing. Santa Barbara, Boesky insisted, would establish him as a "merchant banker."

Milken quickly bent Boesky and Santa Barbara to his will. Shortly after completing the agreement to purchase 51% of the shares, Boesky told Santa Barbara that it had to improve its performance before the acquisition could proceed. His formula for improvement: purchasing a huge portfolio of junk bonds chosen by Milken. He told the S&L to purchase "up to $284 million of funds" in "high-yield corporate bonds." The S&L's board could hardly ignore its largest shareholder and soon-to-be owner. It met with Milken and Dahl in Beverly Hills and bought a total of more than $250 million worth of junk bonds over the next eight months, all of them purchased through the Milken operation.

But Boesky's dream of owning Santa Barbara was destined to be foiled: even in the freewheeling climate of the age of Reagan, regulators balked at the idea of S&L deposits being invested in an arbitrage operation that, by its very nature, would be highly speculative. They didn't reject Boesky's application for approval to take control, but they never approved it. It simply languished. Meanwhile, Santa Barbara had its huge portfolio of junk bonds.

Conway wasted no time in trying to interest Boesky in other acquisitions. He knew Boesky envied Icahn's conquest of TWA and other companies, and felt he could play in the same leagues. He nearly bid for Scott & Fetzer, a household products concern, and even acquired a large position and made an informal offer to the company, subject to financing. But Conway couldn't persuade Drexel to do the financing; Drexel's evaluation of the company's worth was more conservative than Conway's. Legendary investor Warren Buffett, head of Berkshire Hathaway, eventually bought the company.

They looked at Kirby Vacuum Cleaners; All-Steel, a maker of office furniture; a small railroad in Louisiana. In each case, Boesky found a problem. And if that problem was solved, he'd find another. Conway became increasingly frustrated. "There's never perfect information in a deal," he told Boesky. "There's always a risk." Conway concluded that Boesky didn't have the fortitude or confidence to be another Icahn. He seemed jealous of the raiders, but he was terrified of failing, afraid that the others would scoff. Boesky worried constantly, he told Conway, about overpaying. Conway felt Boesky's credibility with Drexel was ebbing. David Kay had agreed at the outset that Drexel would shop opportunities and provide research if Boesky later used Drexel as its advisors and financiers. Drexel would more than recoup any expenses in the eventual financing and merger fees. This was standard at most Wall Street firms; virtually no one paid for research directly. But obviously, Drexel's incentive to offer deals diminished as Boesky kept finding reasons not to do anything.

On one of the deals, Conway said, "Ivan, if you don't like this company, just say so now. Don't put my people through this bullshit. Don't take two to three months of our time. Morale suffers when you say no for no good reason."

Boesky rationalized his failure to act, often suggesting that the proposed deals weren't big enough or grand enough to suit his ambitions. He wanted visibility, and he wanted some glamour. Media properties seemed the right vehicle. *U.S. News and World Report* had interested him; it was for sale, and the magazine also owned some valuable real estate in Washington, D.C. Boesky's friend Martin Peretz, a big investor in his partnership, had bought *The New Republic* magazine, and Boesky admired the prestige and cachet that ownership of a national publication conveyed. But he was far too cautious in his pursuit, and was handily outbid by Mortimer Zuckerman, a real estate developer with similarly outsized ambitions. Boesky even talked about helping finance a new satiric monthly magazine, *Spy*. But *Spy* got off the ground without Boesky's help.

Then an intriguing opportunity surfaced. Boesky's longtime friend, Icahn, suggested that Boesky look into the shares of Gulf + Western, a force both in Hollywood, with its Paramount Pictures unit, and in publishing, with Simon & Schuster. Both businesses appealed strongly to Boesky's escalating ambitions, and Icahn told Boesky he thought Gulf + Western shares were "significantly undervalued." Boesky began amassing a position, stopping at just under the 5% level that would require public disclosure.

He remained in close contact with Icahn, who also owned a large stake in Gulf + Western. Together, they had just under 10% of the company, making them formidable shareholders. So Icahn suggested that the two of them, "as two shareholders," visit Martin Davis, Gulf + Western's chairman. Boesky obtained an opinion from his lawyers that he and Icahn weren't a "group." If so, they would have had to make a public disclosure of their holdings and their intentions.

Davis had been dealing with Icahn as a Gulf + Western shareholder for years. They had first met in 1983, soon after the death of Charles Bluhdorn, Davis's predecessor at G + W. It had been an acrimonious encounter, with Icahn looking for short-term gains, and Davis committed to building the company over the long term. Over the years, Davis had developed a grudging respect for Icahn. He had come to believe that his word was good.

Boesky was another matter. The arbitrageur had wormed his way into a meeting with Davis just a few months earlier. Davis had been helping raise money for the restoration of New York's famed Carnegie Hall, and had sent a fund-raising letter to Boesky. Icahn had called shortly after. "You dumb bastard," Icahn said, half in jest. "Ivan'll use this as an excuse to meet you." Sure enough, Boesky went to Icahn, saying he wanted to make a donation to Carnegie Hall—and that he wanted to hand the check personally to Davis. So Icahn dutifully arranged a meeting. Davis took an almost instant dislike to the arbitrageur, an impression little changed by what he deemed the paltry size of Boesky's check—$5,000.

But now that Boesky had become a shareholder as large as Icahn, Davis felt he had no choice but to meet with them. He invited them to dine with him on September 5 in his private dining room atop the Gulf + Western building at the southwestern corner of Central Park. Davis made Boesky's bodyguard check his weapon with Gulf + Western's own security guards. Boesky didn't like that, but otherwise he lavished praise on Davis, saying he thought Gulf + Western to be an "exceptional company." Davis he described as an "exceptional manager" and an "outstanding manager." Davis was immediately suspicious. Boesky was laying it on too thick, and Davis found it obnoxious.

That evening, in the wake of all the praise, Boesky and Icahn proposed a leveraged buyout in which the company would be taken private, with Icahn and Boesky owning it, along with management. Davis would remain as chairman, they assured him. With G + W stock in the low forties, they were prepared to offer $52 a share, an amount, Boesky said, that could leave Davis with "$100 million in your pocket."

Davis was appalled. "You'd be raping the shareholders," he exclaimed. Davis deemed the proposal to be little more than an attempt at bribing him to sell the company at a low price. Boesky agreed that it was a lowball bid, but seemed unfazed. "You'd be my partner," Boesky said, as odious a prospect as Davis could imagine.

Davis prudently said he'd consider the suggestion. Unlike many chairmen of public companies, he'd often said his principal goal was to increase shareholder value, and he wouldn't reject takeover bids out of hand. Too many managements were stealing companies through LBOs at scandalously low prices, however, and he wasn't about to join their ranks. He told Icahn and Boesky that he liked running a public company, and wanted to keep it that way. He phoned Boesky soon after, politely rejecting their suggestion for a leveraged buyout.

Icahn and Boesky persisted, meeting again with Davis on October 1. This time they had more detailed financial projections, but Davis was firm. Although the meeting began just before 8 P.M. and lasted for three hours, he didn't offer them anything to eat. He said he'd made up his mind, and didn't want to take the company private.

Soon thereafter, on October 3 Boesky's friend John Mulheren paid Davis a visit. Davis had never met Mulheren, who arrived wearing an open-necked plaid shirt and cowboy boots. Davis thought he looked like a lumberjack. In an effort to insinuate himself into any bid for Gulf + Western, Mulheren told Davis, "You can't trust Boesky. Trust me. I'll be your eyes and ears."

Mulheren assured Davis that he didn't own any stock in G + W and wouldn't buy any. But Davis didn't trust Mulheren any more than he did Boesky. He feared Mulheren would pass information about Davis's reaction to the buyout proposal to his wealthy investors, and, despite his promise to distance himself, even to Boesky. He thanked Mulheren and declined.

Icahn and Boesky reviewed their options. Boesky told Icahn they should accumulate still more stock to increase the pressure on Davis.

But Icahn told Boesky—and Davis—that he wouldn't do that without Davis's consent. Boesky called Davis, and this time the lavish praise and warmth were conspicuously absent. He threatened to go up to 9.9%, adding "I want two seats on the board." Davis was firm. "That's not going to happen. You're not welcome. Period."

Boesky paused briefly, and said, "Then buy me out." He asked for $45 a share; the stock had closed that day at $44. "Absolutely not," Davis replied. "When the stock trades at $45, I'll entertain the possibility of buying you out." The company had recently announced a plan to buy back its own stock, but Davis wasn't about to pay greenmail, which was what Boesky and Icahn now wanted.

Boesky did nothing. He had already been shaken by a far more public takeover defeat. Earlier in the year, representatives of Accuracy in Media, a conservative media watchdog group led by Senator Jesse Helms, had called on Boesky, seeking support for their effort to threaten CBS with a hostile takeover. Boesky had found the prospect ludicrous, but started thinking about the prestigious network. He concluded that the Federal Communications Commission probably wouldn't stand in the way of a hostile takeover bid, but knew he couldn't muster the capital to launch a multibillion-dollar takeover on his own. If he could amass a large stake, however, perhaps as much as 15%, he could at least put CBS "in play." Surely others lusted for such a crown jewel. He'd heard that Ted Turner was interested. And he'd seen how easily he and Milken had driven Pacific Lumber and Harris Graphics into the arms of hostile suitors. Perhaps he'd emerge with a prestigious seat on the network's board. Boesky began to accumulate shares, asking Milken to buy for him, too.

When Boesky filed his SEC disclosures, however, hoping to strike fear into the heart of CBS, the network fought back vigorously and decisively. CBS's chairman, Thomas Wyman, wouldn't even dignify Boesky's purchases with a face-to-face meeting, much to Boesky's disappointment. CBS's lawyers at Cravath, Swaine & Moore filed a blistering lawsuit, charging that Boesky was overleveraged and had violated net capital requirements to acquire his stake.

Boesky looked grim the day the lawsuit was filed. He suspected a traitor; how else could Cravath and CBS have zeroed in on such an Achilles' heel? Boesky couldn't possibly subject his operation to discovery by CBS's lawyers. He couldn't risk discovery of the Milken dealings. Boesky caved in immediately. Desperate to negotiate a truce that would end the lawsuit, he signed a standstill agreement promising not to acquire any additional shares of CBS, and began to unwind his position.

Now, bloodied in his runs at both CBS and Gulf + Western,

Boesky was stuck with his huge Gulf + Western stake. His CBS position could easily be sold at a profit; improved operating results and continued takeover speculation had pushed the stock price substantially higher, and he had a nice profit. But Gulf + Western's had declined.

As the weeks went by, Gulf + Western stock did rally, reaching $44 by mid-October. So Boesky called Mulheren. "I like Gulf + Western," Boesky told him. "I wouldn't pay more than $45 for it, and it would be great if it traded at $45."

"I understand," Mulheren replied. Usually when Boesky said he "liked" something, Mulheren could count on big gains. So he started loading up on Gulf + Western, driving the price up further. One of his assistants asked him why he was buying the stock, and Mulheren replied, "I don't know. Ivan likes the stock." It was enough of an explanation.

Finally, in large part because of Mulheren's buying, the price reached $45. Moments later, Mulheren saw a 6.7 million-share block sale of Gulf + Western cross the tape at $45. He realized Boesky had bailed out, selling his stake to G + W, leaving Mulheren with his large new position. Far from "liking" the stock, Boesky had been pushing the price up so he could bail out more profitably. "The son of a bitch," Mulheren said out loud, to no one in particular.

By late 1985, Boesky seemed farther than ever from his dream of being a latter-day Rothschild. So he turned again to the only person who could vault him into the front ranks of American financiers: Michael Milken.

The two had been discussing ways to increase Boesky's capital for more than a year when, in the wake of the CBS and Gulf + Western failures, Boesky told Milken he wanted to go forward with plans for the largest arbitrage capitalization in history. As they had discussed previously, Boesky would wind up his existing partnership, Ivan F. Boesky Corporation, and raise $220 million in contributions from limited partners. Then Milken would raise $660 million in proceeds from the sale of junk bonds. This would be buying power on a scale Boesky had hardly dreamed of—an arbitrage operation with nearly $1 billion in capital. Leveraged at three to one, Boesky would have the unfettered power to invest $3 billion! Even the biggest and most powerful corporations would quake at his approach.

Further dependence on Milken was part of the price. This quickly

became clear to Conway. Early in 1986, Merrill Lynch approached
Conway and Boesky with what seemed an almost risk-free opportunity:
Gulton Industries was under hostile attack from Mark IV Industries.
Goldman, Sachs, representing Gulton, was all but begging Boesky to
come in as a white knight for the company, which could be had for less
than $50 million. Conway studied Gulton and its operations, and
decided that even the cautious Boesky could be sold on this investment. He told Boesky the deal was "as close to perfect as you can get."
The board of Northview, the Boesky vehicle for the bid, met and
approved the acquisition.

Then, just when Conway thought they'd cleared all the hurdles,
Boesky asked him, "Should I call Mike Milken and ask him what he
thinks?"

"No!" Conway exclaimed emphatically. This wasn't a Drexel
deal—Merrill Lynch was going to handle the financing, since it had
shopped the company to Boesky—so Conway knew Milken would try
to derail it. "Don't talk to him, Ivan," Conway pleaded. "He'll just
leave you with a bad taste about this, and you'll get all kinds of vague
doubts." Conway emphasized that he'd be "very unhappy" if Boesky
went to Milken on this.

"Well, at least let me sleep on it," Boesky said.

The next morning, with Merrill Lynch ready to proceed, Boesky
called Conway into his office. "Mike isn't sure it's a good deal," he said.
Conway was stunned. Milken couldn't possibly know as much about
the company as Conway did. It was now obvious, Conway thought, that
Boesky wouldn't pee without Milken's consent. "Forget about merchant banking," Conway said angrily, and stormed out. He submitted
his resignation soon after, having never done a deal for Boesky.

Nagle, hired to help in the merchant banking operation, was
pressed into service to help Boesky raise his $220 million share of the
big new Milken/Drexel financing. They called on the Belzbergs, Riklis,
London investor Gerald Ronson, chairman of Heron International,
singer Paul Anka, and real estate developer Peter Kalikow. At each
stop, Boesky launched into his standard sales package on the beauties
of arbitrage. He touched on its history, invoked the name of Gustave
Levy at Goldman, Sachs, how great fortunes had been amassed but
never made public. He said the new Drexel financing provided previously unheard-of opportunities. "This is leverage," he exclaimed in
summation. "This is the stratosphere."

Discussions usually moved quickly away from the arcane details
of arbitrage. Kalikow, for example, had photographs of private jets on
his office wall, and he and Boesky launched into a detailed discussion
of the features they wanted in their next planes. The Belzbergs, on the

other hand, were into boats, and they showed pictures of their favorite yachts.

By and large, investors reacted enthusiastically. The largest single investor—and in Nagle's view one of the most mysterious—was Jeffrey Picower, who invested $28 million. Nagle had no idea where Picower's money came from; he occupied an unmarked office suite in an anonymous Manhattan tower.

Other investors included Gould Inc., a company Boesky knew through Kidder, Peabody broker Don Little, who had its pension fund invest $5.7 million; the British Water Authority Superannuation Fund; Lincoln National Life Insurance; Interallianz Bank of Switzerland; Northern Trust Co.; Milton and Joseph Dresner, New York investors; and Martin Peretz.

But the reaction at Drexel to the proposed Boesky financing was distinctly cool. Stephen Weinroth, the investment banker who'd tried to dissuade Milken from backing Posner in Fischbach, now trained his sites on Boesky. Fred Joseph told Weinroth to keep an eye on the financing transaction; it raised some very tricky issues, given that Boesky's main business was arbitrage.

Weinroth had an immediate reaction against the deal. Boesky's financial statements were virtually meaningless; his big stock positions could change in the course of a single trading day. There was no way potential investors could evaluate his holdings. Boesky didn't even want to provide quarterly reports identifying his positions, which he deemed confidential information. If there was a scandal, investors could be wiped out.

Drexel hired a private detective to investigate Boesky, but he turned up nothing beyond a few SEC inquiries that had been satisfactorily resolved. Still, Weinroth thought he'd succeeded at persuading Joseph and others at Drexel to turn down the deal. Then, in November 1985 after the CBS and Gulf + Western fiascos, Boesky and Milken began pressing for a closing.

Opposition to Boesky had also coalesced in Beverly Hills. One of Milken's top aides, Peter Ackerman, warned that he thought too much money was being put into Boesky's hands. He couldn't effectively manage so much; he would be tempted to throw money at deals even before he'd analyzed them, Ackerman argued. Lowell Milken, who was closer to Milken than anyone, also opposed the financing. He didn't like Boesky and didn't trust him, he said. Dahl, too, lined up against the financing, arguing that if there was a sudden market drop, Boesky could be wiped out, along with investors in the bonds. When Dahl shared his reservations with Lowell, Lowell replied, "I don't know why the hell we're doing it, either. Go ask my brother."

Milken rejected all their arguments out of hand. "Drexel backs winners, and Boesky's a winner," he insisted once again, and that was the end of the discussion. What Milken didn't disclose was that he would be gaining a personal equity stake in Boesky's operation as part of the deal. It would bind Boesky even more closely to Milken.

Weinroth made an attempt to go over Milken's head and block the deal. He pleaded with Joseph to overrule Milken. Joseph could have, but didn't.

At first, the market acted like it would derail the deal even though Drexel wouldn't. One after another, even some of Drexel's most loyal bond buyers balked, saying they wouldn't invest in an arbitrage fund. Dahl, the master salesman, even despaired of being able to place the debt, and feared that Drexel itself would end up owning much of it. Weinroth, Dahl, and others did manage to persuade Milken to change some of the terms of the offering. Some restrictions had to be imposed. Boesky was furious that he was specifically barred from using the proceeds to purchase the Gulfstream jet he wanted. Boesky wanted unlimited leverage; he was held to three-to-one. He didn't want any restrictions on equity ratios; the debt required him to liquidate if the value of his assets sank below a designated level. Dahl enhanced his reputation as a legendary salesman by persuading Charles Keating of Lincoln Savings to buy $100 million of the debt. The closing of the $660 million offering, formally known as Hudson Funding, was scheduled for March 21, 1986. At the same time, Ivan F. Boesky Corporation would be liquidated and Ivan F. Boesky Limited Partnership would be born.

For their efforts on Boesky's behalf, Milken and Drexel earned $24 million in financing fees. Milken also was granted a $5 million equity interest in Boesky's operation (setting up the inherently dangerous situation where an investment banker actually owned an interest in an arbitrage operation). No one at Drexel outside the Beverly Hills high-yield department knew about this potentially lucrative provision. Now there was only one sticking point: the payment Boesky owed Milken from their whirlwind of illegal activities. With $660 million in the balance, Milken had all the leverage he needed. He calmly told Boesky there would be no closing until Boesky paid him what he owed.

In a flurry of phone conversations the morning of March 21, the very day of the closing, Boesky agreed to make the payment. But it was too late to cover it up in securities transactions, as they'd done before. Boesky sold Milken some real estate warrants and United Artists securities at below-market prices. But that still left a large amount outstanding: $5.3 million, according to Mooradian and Thurnher's calculations. Eager to lay the matter to rest so the closing would go forward,

Boesky did something he'd never done in the course of his illegal dealings with Milken: he told Mooradian to issue a check for $5.3 million, and to identify the payment as "trading commissions."

And there the matter might have rested, were it not for Boesky's accountants at OAD. The accounting firm was retained to peruse the books of Ivan F. Boesky Corporation and issue a so-called "comfort letter." While a comfort letter doesn't have the scope or stature of a full-blown audit, it is a representation by the accountants that everything appears to be in order and, as its name suggests, is designed to reassure investors in the new partnership. Ivan F. Boesky Corporation formally ceased existing at 4 P.M., when the stock exchange closed, and the accountants were present to take a last look at the final days of the corporation's existence.

Peter Testaverde, one of the OAD partners who handled the Boesky organization and was in charge of the Hudson Funding closing, was assigned to meet with Mooradian in a conference room to examine the most recent transactions. Testaverde was an old friend of Mooradian's and he expected the procedure to be routine. At about ten minutes past four, however, Testaverde spotted a $10,000 account payable. "What's this?" he asked Mooradian.

Mooradian looked at the ledger, and was momentarily confused; in the excitement of a $1 billion deal he hadn't paid much attention to anything so minor as a $10,000 bill. "I don't really know," he said.

"I'll need some documentation on this," Testaverde said.

"Oh come on, Pete," Mooradian replied, arguing that the sum was immaterial.

"I'll have to have some kind of backup, Set," Testaverde insisted. "I'm sorry."

Now Mooradian was agitated. "For God's sake, Pete," he said. "Why are you busting my balls on this?" Then, without thinking, he plunged ahead, saying what was really on his mind: "Why the fuck do you care about a little $10,000 when I've got $5.3 million sitting over here?"

A stunned silence fell over the room, and Mooradian wished he could pull back his words. After all, he hadn't actually made the payment yet, and he hadn't even had time yet to enter it into the books as an account payable. Of course, when he did make the payment later that day or the next, it would have to be accrued, but meanwhile, who was to know? By then, the whole deal would have closed. He prayed that nobody had paid attention, but he could tell from the look on Testaverde's face that the cat was out of the bag.

"What $5.3 million?" Testaverde asked, obviously alarmed.

"Uh, forget about it," Mooradian said. "Forget I ever mentioned this. We can't talk about it now." Testaverde gathered up his notes, put them in his briefcase, and started to leave. "No," Mooradian cried out, frantic at the thought that the closing was collapsing around him. "Don't go! We can work this out."

But when Mooradian confirmed that he had, in fact, a $5.3 million account payable for which he had no documentation, no bill, no invoice—nothing but Boesky's direction to make the payment—Testaverde left for his own office a block away. He said he couldn't go any further until he'd had a chance to confer with the senior partner on the Boesky account, Steven Oppenheim.

Mooradian waited in the conference room, chain-smoking, nearly paralyzed with anxiety. After what seemed like hours—but was really little more than 15 minutes—the phone rang.

"You stupid fucking bastard," Boesky screamed. "You stupid son of a bitch. What the hell are you doing?" Mooradian had never, in all his years with Boesky, heard him rant like this. Before he could respond, Boesky slammed down the phone. Moments later, it rang again. "You stupid fucking bastard," Boesky began again. Within the next hour, Boesky called four or five times. He screamed "You stupid fucking bastard" over and over, until it seemed permanently branded into Mooradian's mind.

Mooradian was devastated. He figured he wouldn't get any bonus. Worse, he'd probably be fired. For a guy like himself, with SEC sanctions behind him, finding another job would probably be next to impossible.

At the OAD offices, Oppenheim told Boesky that, without documentation, the firm wouldn't sign off on the comfort letter, which meant the deal wouldn't close. Once he calmed down slightly, Boesky got on the phone to Milken. He and Boesky hastily agreed that the $5.3 million payment could be for "consulting"; after all, Drexel had done a fair amount of research on various Boesky projects. Boesky returned to his accountants and lawyers, suddenly "recalling" that the huge payment had been for research and other unspecified consulting.

All agreed to go forward on the basis of Boesky's representation, with the understanding that documentation for the transaction would be promptly forthcoming. In Beverly Hills, Milken had his brother Lowell draft a letter explaining the payment as a consulting fee. Lowell Milken buttonholed Donald Balser, a low-level operations employee who happened to be nearby, and had him co-sign the letter.

Despite the highly suspicious maneuverings surrounding the large payment, Boesky's accountants and lawyers assured him that there wouldn't be any problems. Boesky visibly calmed down, though he didn't bother to call Mooradian. Only at about 7:30 P.M. did Nagle call Mooradian to relieve his misery. "Everything's all right," he said. "Drexel's sending a bill for investment advisory services. Ivan is cool."

Mooradian was so relieved that he didn't give the matter much further thought. He'd concluded from all his accounting work with Thurnher that Boesky and Milken were some kind of partners in something, so maybe Drexel had been doing some research. If so, of course, there wouldn't have been such a brouhaha, but who was he to ask questions? He'd gotten into enough trouble already.

An invoice from Drexel arrived three days later. It read "For consulting services as agreed upon on March 21, 1986, $5,300,000.00." The cover letter, from Thurnher, was brief and to the point:

> Mr. Boesky,
> Please send your remittance check for the attached invoice directly to me at the address listed above.

The address, of course, was in Beverly Hills, not in New York. Mooradian dutifully executed and sent the check.

Mooradian's deeper fears never materialized. The nearly $1 billion in proceeds from the sale of the partnership interests and the debt offering flowed in on schedule, making Boesky's the most heavily capitalized arbitrage operation in history. Mooradian not only wasn't fired, but he got his bonus: $350,000. He didn't resent the fact that others got far more that year: Davidoff, the head trader, got $1.5 million; Lessman got over $1 million; Nagle got $1 million, and so did Wekili, even though Mooradian had no idea what Wekili did.

Mooradian was just happy to have emerged with a job, especially with a firm that was now sitting on close to $1 billion of cash. "We're going to be rich! Our ship has come in," he exulted to his wife once he realized the deal would go through. But he never forgot the events of March 21, the pain and humiliation of the browbeating he took from Boesky.

8.

Jim Dahl took a deep breath and walked into the conference room for his annual salary review. This year, 1986, he was prepared to insist on more than Milken offered. He never knew the exact size of the high-yield operation's bonus pool, but he knew it had to be big. Other employees, such as Ackerman, had succeeded in wheedling large amounts out of Milken. This year, Dahl had been indisputably the top salesman, coming through even in the most difficult situations, as in the $100 million of Boesky debt he sold Charles Keating.

Milken went right to the point. "You're going to be paid $10 million this year," he told the 33-year-old Dahl. This was more than Dahl had ever dreamed of making, but he stuck to his resolution. "I really think I'm entitled to more," he insisted, ticking off his achievements. Milken listened sympathetically, but quickly disagreed. "Jim, I really can't pay you any more," he said in a soft voice, "or you'd be making more than me. Now that wouldn't be fair, would it?"

"I guess not," Dahl said. He was surprised at the low amount, but he guessed that Milken was plowing a larger share of the department's profits back into the firm than he'd suspected. Dahl now owned nearly 1% of Drexel's stock, so he admired Milken's apparent selflessness.

In New York, Fred Joseph was grappling with the issue of Milken's pay. That spring, Joseph had been elevated from head of corporate finance to chief executive officer when Robert Linton stepped down. In some ways Joseph hadn't wanted the promotion. *Institutional Investor* had just named him the best corporate finance manager on Wall Street, and he was enjoying himself, feeling he was accomplishing something as his department capitalized on the Milken phenomenon. He also liked having some free time to spend with his wife at their working farm in northwestern New Jersey.

Milken made no secret of his opposition to Joseph's appointment. He complained about it to Joseph, claiming Joseph was too important to him in corporate finance. Yet Milken, who could have placed anyone he chose in the top position, didn't offer any alternatives. He first suggested his own nominal boss, Edwin Kantor, but even he had to acknowledge that Kantor's wasn't the image the firm wanted to project. The personable Joseph was the nearly inevitable choice.

Drexel had soared even beyond Joseph's own ambitious projections. In 1986, Milken's high-yield department was entitled under Drexel's compensation formula to approximately $700 million in bonuses. Approximately half was attributable to finder's fees, allocated to Milken for referring clients to services elsewhere in the firm. By comparison, the corporate finance bonus pool was about $140 million, reflecting the disproportionate weighting of compensation and underlying power wielded by the Beverly Hills operation.

Once Joseph approved the overall bonus pool of $700 million, it was up to Milken to divide it up as he saw fit. Milken doled out about $150 million to his colleagues in Beverly Hills, including the $10 million he'd promised Dahl. But Milken didn't keep just $10 million for himself, as he'd implied. Nor did he plow the remainder into the firm's capital, as Dahl had surmised. Dahl had no way of knowing this at the time, but Milken bestowed $550 million on himself. That was more than the $522.5 million in profit that Drexel itself—the entire firm—had earned.

Yet Milken didn't think $550 million was enough. Milken was actually angry with Joseph about the size of the bonus pool.

Joseph was responsible, along with Milken, for allocating the finder's fees that formed such an important part of Drexel's compensation system. Each year, Joseph and Milken got on the phone to go over the fees, deciding who deserved credit for bringing which clients into the firm. There were usually anywhere from 150 to 200 such matters, and conflicting claims affected less than 20%.

The previous year, one of the finder's fees had never been resolved to Milken's satisfaction. Milken had insisted he was entitled to it. He admitted that another department deserved some of the credit for landing the client, but had argued that his personal contact had been the deciding factor. Joseph disagreed and refused to allocate the sum to the high-yield bonus pool.

As they neared the end of their review of the 1986 fees, Milken had again raised the issue. Joseph was amazed at the vehemence with which Milken argued the point. He wouldn't give in. Nor would he let the matter drop. He called Joseph repeatedly and they ended up arguing for hours, reviewing in minute detail the circumstances under which the client had come to the firm. Joseph didn't know where Milken found the time. Neither Milken nor Joseph ever backed down.

Milken wasn't paid, but he continued to insist that Joseph had cheated him. The amount at stake was $15,000.

Joseph dismissed the incident as a quirk in Milken's character. Milken had always been obsessive about his work, and apparently this trait extended to his earnings.

In any event, Joseph had more important matters on his mind. He'd staved off congressional outcries over the Unocal attack, and legislation to curb the use of junk bonds was languishing. The press had also discovered Drexel, and largely laudatory accounts of the firm began to proliferate, not only in the financial newspapers and magazines, but in general-interest publications. Most reporters liked the people at Drexel—the affable Joseph, his circle of advisors, and press relations people. They made for a terrific story of conflict and success, the old guard against the new.

Joseph shrewdly decided to court the press, throwing lavish semiannual luncheons. Milken, however, took the opposite tack. He refused all requests for interviews, was contemptuous of reporters, refused to return their calls even to say "no comment," and hated the thought of publicity. He maintained his invisibility to a surprising degree. Living on the West Coast helped. Milken never attended any of the firm's press luncheons in New York, which only heightened his mystique.

New large competitors were soon trying to emulate Drexel's success, developing their own junk-bond divisions, plunging into hostile takeovers and LBOs with growing abandon. Staid Goldman, Sachs negotiated the over $4 billion leveraged buyout of Macy's. Morgan Stanley, with Gleacher at the helm of M&A, had stunned the establishment by joining with Drexel on the conquest of Revlon by Ronald Perelman (lending a Drexel-backed hostile raid a respectability none had had before). Merrill Lynch moved aggressively, as did Shearson Lehman and, especially, First Boston, with its merger star Bruce Wasserstein.

Milken, determined not to cede any of Drexel's huge market share, competed ever more aggressively. Drexel threatened to break up pending Goldman, Sachs–led leveraged buyouts of Warnaco and National Gypsum with higher bids from Drexel clients backed by the Milken money machine. When Drexel wrested the business of Wickes Companies away from Salomon Brothers, an irate John Gutfreund, Salomon's chairman, sent one of his top lieutentants to see Milken in Beverly Hills. "If you don't stop this, we're going to fry you," the Salomon banker warned.

In the case of Staley Continental, the giant midwest corn processor, Drexel tried to bludgeon the company into a leveraged buyout.

Drexel had begun acquiring shares in Staley in late 1986, and a Drexel official called Staley's chief financial officer, Robert Hoffman, to indicate its interest in "establishing an investment banking relationship with Staley." Two days later, the Drexel official called again, saying "our guys" in Beverly Hills had acquired a "large position" in Staley's stock. Then Dahl called Hoffman, stating firmly that Drexel "wants to be Staley's investment banker." He said that Drexel owned 1.5 million Staley shares. Hoffman asked why Drexel hadn't filed required 13-D disclosure forms with the SEC. They're "bad for business," Dahl retorted, then suggested a Drexel-led leveraged buyout. "We can take Staley private in 48 hours," he boasted.

Hoffman was stunned, and rebuffed the suggestion. Later, Dahl called back, urging that they all meet at Drexel's New York offices to look over the numbers in a leveraged buyout. Hoffman again resisted, and this time Dahl became angry, arguing they should "sit down and talk" before "I do something that hurts you."

Staley looked like it might be about to suffer the fate of a Pacific Lumber, but Joseph intervened, rushing to calm the nearly hysterical Staley executives, assuring them that Drexel wouldn't take any hostile steps against Staley. He had to take similar steps with another victim of the high-yield department's hardball tactics, Winn-Dixie, a large Southern retail food chain. He worried that such tactics were getting out of hand. Joseph knew that with this level of competition, Drexel's dominance of the junk-bond market couldn't last forever.

Joseph had tried to build up other departments in the firm in his attempt to create a full-service giant like Goldman or Morgan Stanley. Under his brother, Stephen Joseph, Drexel's mortgage-backed securities department had thrived, becoming one of the top five such departments on Wall Street. In municipal finance, Drexel had moved almost into the top ten, from nowhere before. It was eighth in the trading of government securities. Its equity research department was highly respected. Yet none of these departments could rival Milken as an engine of earnings and growth. The more they improved, the faster Milken surged ahead of them.

This was causing growing tension between what were known internally as the East Coast faction, led by Joseph, Weinroth, and corporate finance head Herbert Bachelor, and the West Coast faction, led by Milken, which also included Engel, Kay, and Black in New York. The Milken camp criticized the performance of corporate finance, arguing that they weren't generating clients and were only riding the West Coast's coattails. They went so far as to urge Bachelor's ouster. Joseph wouldn't consider it. But he knew he needed at least one other "star," preferably more, in New York to help offset the growing dominance of the Milken camp. Dennis Levine was not going to fill the bill.

David Kay continued to praise Levine, but others at Drexel and outside the firm considered him something of an embarrassment. During the 1985 Pantry Pride bid for Revlon, Levine was the senior New York investment banker assigned to the deal. Yet Milken, who was handling the financing, insisted that others from Drexel be present, including Ackerman and Engel. While they were in a conference room with Perelman, Levine was usually outside on a telephone, sometimes all day. Every once in a while he'd dart into the room and repeat a rumor. Ackerman, in particular, found him embarrassing, telling others in Beverly Hills that he was a phony. Gleacher, who had once offered Levine a job, now dismissed the idea. In New York, Levine boasted to colleagues that Revlon was "his" deal.

So Joseph again began to recruit. Four years earlier, Drexel couldn't have dreamed of recruiting top-tier investment bankers. Now the idea didn't seem so farfetched. And Joseph had an idea: He would approach both Martin Siegel and Bruce Wasserstein, the two biggest M&A stars, and invite them to forge a powerhouse such as Wall Street had never seen, a power center in New York that could truly serve as a counterbalance to Milken in Beverly Hills.

This time, when Joseph phoned Siegel at Kidder, Peabody, he found a receptive listener.

Joseph first called Siegel in June 1985, and they agreed to meet. Joseph emphasized Drexel's growing capital strength, the financing capability that Kidder, Peabody sorely lacked, and the potential for extending Drexel's client base into Kidder's blue-chip, establishment territory. As things were developing, Joseph argued, Wall Street would soon be dominated by only a handful of capital-rich firms. Kidder, Peabody, it seemed increasingly obvious, wouldn't be one of them.

Within Kidder, Peabody, even Al Gordon, the firm's patriarch, had come around to the view that Kidder, Peabody should be sold. He was prepared to cash in his large stock position for enormous profits. But he was blocked by DeNunzio, who over the years had shrewdly bestowed stock on his own allies. He had recognized early on that a man like Gordon would almost inevitably clash with his hand-picked successor.

Others at the firm favored other solutions. Max Chapman, Jr., the head of fixed income and financial futures, had turned Kidder, Peabody into a major player in the field of index arbitrage and program trading (using options on broad market indices traded in Chicago and computer-driven trading strategies). He had become DeNunzio's heir apparent. DeNunzio had tried to set up a rivalry between Chapman and Siegel, but Siegel had told DeNunzio that he wasn't interested in administering the firm. "Don't tell Chapman that," DeNunzio insisted. Now Chapman, recognizing the need for more capital, wanted to sell a 20% minority stake in the firm, probably to the Japanese. This would raise capital and allow him to run a still-independent firm.

Other executives favored going public. This would allow them eventually to cash their shares in at market prices, and would preserve the firm's independence. Morgan Stanley had successfully sold part of itself to the public earlier that year. But Siegel and others doubted Kidder, Peabody could mount a successful stock offering, given its growing problems. Even if it did, it probably wouldn't stay independent for long; like any other publicly traded company, it would be vulnerable to a takeover bid. DeNunzio seemed content to let the factions fight among themselves, thus preserving the status quo he cherished.

Now, at the end of 1985, Kidder, Peabody faced a financial crisis that crystallized Siegel's thinking and caused him to despair for the firm's future. The firm was carrying a record year-end inventory of municipal bonds and other securities. In an effort to boost returns on those and other operations, the once-conservative firm, lacking a large capital base, had pushed itself into a highly leveraged position. Much like Boesky, it had fallen out of compliance with minimum capital requirements. It couldn't meet end-of-year cash demands; any default could be ruinous. The banks all said no. Kidder, Peabody's chief financial officer, Richard Stewart, spent New Year's Eve frantically phoning the firm's banks and traditional lenders. Only at 10 P.M. did he nail down a syndicate of foreign and U.S. investors willing to make short-term loans to carry the firm through the crisis. A measure of Kidder, Peabody's desperation was its willingness to pay exorbitant short-term interest rates of over 15%.

The firm scrapped its ambitious plan to expand its retail brokerage network. Stewart quit, partly in protest over the firm's undercapitalization, and moved to Merrill Lynch. There had been other defections of top executives. The head of municipal finance defected to First Boston. Yet DeNunzio was doing nothing.

As the year-end crisis continued, Siegel's talks with Joseph accelerated, and he signaled, for the first time, that he was leaning seriously toward accepting a Drexel offer. Even though Siegel would be joining Drexel as co-head of M&A (with David Kay and Leon Black) he would report directly to Joseph. But he still had to receive Milken's blessing.

Siegel flew to Beverly Hills in January 1986 and checked into the Beverly Wilshire Hotel, just down the street from Milken's offices. Milken spared Siegel the 4:30 A.M. interrogation most job applicants went through. Instead, he came to Siegel's suite in the hotel late in the afternoon, well after the markets had closed on the East Coast. Siegel had never met Milken before. He was immediately struck by the intensity of Milken's gaze, the tension and energy that seemed to emanate from his slight frame.

Siegel gestured for Milken to take a seat on the plush sofa, but Milken ignored him. He began talking rapidly, pacing back and forth in front of the seated Siegel. He moved rapidly from topic to topic, giving his view of the markets, elements of his standard spiel on junk bonds, and dwelling at some length on his views of money. "I don't want anyone keeping score" of what I make or of what other people make, he told Siegel. "If people here ever know how rich they are, they'll get slow and fat. You must never count your money; you have to keep driving yourself to make more."

Milken told Siegel that customers and clients had to be exploited financially as much as the market would bear. The issue, he insisted, wasn't how profitable they were. No margin was too large. "If our costs are here," he said, lowering one hand, "and the market will bear a price here"—he held his other hand high above—"then we should price our services here." He lowered the upper hand almost imperceptibly. "We've earned that spread. You price one penny below the competition, whatever the cost to you."

Milken told Siegel he'd just been meeting with Marvin Davis, the wealthy oilman who'd moved to Hollywood and bought 20th Century–Fox. "I'm bringing together all these pools of capital," Milken boasted. The buying power would be beyond anything the world had ever seen. His only challenge, he said, pausing momentarily to look at Siegel, "is finding people like you."

Milken left after 45 minutes, without having sat down. He had talked almost constantly and was so hyperactive that Siegel wondered whether he was on some kind of medication. After that meeting, Siegel thought of Milken as a kind of sun god. "Don't get too close, or you'll get burned," he warned himself.

That night, Siegel went out for dinner with the top executives from Carnation to celebrate their acquisition by Nestlé. Siegel had leaked the deal to Boesky, but his conscience felt unusually clear. With the move to Drexel, such sordid dealings would be behind him forever.

When he returned to New York, Joseph told Siegel that he'd passed muster in Beverly Hills. Over the next few weeks, they worked out the financial details. It went without saying, of course, that Siegel would be promised more than the $2.1 million he'd made for 1985 at Kidder, Peabody. Siegel also argued that his Kidder stock would have to be sold back to the firm at a price far beneath its true value, which was a hardship given the likelihood, in Siegel's estimation, that Kidder, Peabody would be sold soon.

Joseph was prepared to pay Siegel what seemed an exorbitant sum: a guaranteed base compensation of $3.5 million, a $2 million sign-on bonus, and a block of Drexel stock. Siegel valued the package at well over $6 million—three times his earnings at Kidder, Peabody. For Drexel, of course, the pay level was hardly out of the ordinary, even for investment bankers far less accomplished and well-known than Siegel.

The following Tuesday, the same day the *Challenger* space shuttle exploded, Siegel went down to DeNunzio's office and told him, for the first time, that he was in negotiations with Drexel. DeNunzio seemed shocked. He began to fidget and perspire. He begged Siegel not to make a decision until he'd had time to prepare a counteroffer.

Siegel was in no mood to wait, however. That Friday night, he visited Al Gordon at his apartment in Manhattan. Gordon was gracious, offering Siegel a drink, perhaps recognizing that the news made his own plan to sell the firm a much greater likelihood. After Siegel told Gordon he'd decided to join Drexel, Gordon's only comment was, "All good things must come to an end." Privately, however, he was more upset that Siegel was joining a firm like Drexel than he was over Siegel's departure. Gordon loathed Drexel and all it represented.

The next day, Siegel drove out to Greenwich to meet with DeNunzio at his home. DeNunzio had already heard from Gordon, and was furious that Siegel had gone to Gordon before completing their discussions. But DeNunzio's remonstrations had no effect on Siegel. The encounter was a painful one for him, but he held to his decision.

Siegel also felt he owed Boesky the call. Boesky seemed disappointed and hurt that Siegel hadn't consulted him about the decision.

Word of Siegel's decision to defect now coursed through the ranks of Kidder, Peabody, causing grave concern and, in some cases, near panic. John Gordon, who'd been with Siegel ever since Gordon arrived, was in San Francisco for the weekend when he heard the news from his father on Saturday night. He boarded a "red-eye" flight and came into the office Sunday for an emergency meeting of the corporate finance and M&A groups. Hal Ritch was there; Siegel had called him at home over the weekend to break the news, adding, "I'm not supposed" to recruit, but "I'll answer the phone." Ritch realized Siegel would be talking huge numbers, but rejected the idea out of hand. "I wouldn't work for those dirtbag liquidators," he said of Drexel. John Gordon, too, was disgusted. He thought everyone had gotten too money-conscious; that's all anyone wanted to talk about: the size of their bonuses. Loyalty was dead.

Kidder, Peabody's annual shareholders' meeting was held the following week. Even as he unveiled the firm's record 1985 profits, DeNunzio had to announce that Siegel was leaving. No one knew better than DeNunzio how large a percentage of those profits would be walking out the door with Siegel. DeNunzio, vacationing over the holidays at his Vermont ski house, had reluctantly recognized that without a star like Siegel, the firm could only compete on the basis of capital. Since the firm's capital was precariously low, he announced that Kidder, Peabody would "explore" sources of additional capital. Publicly, he explicitly rejected any notion that the firm would be sold. But he knew something had to be done, and fast—before it all came crashing down around him.

As the gloom darkened, Kidder, Peabody tried desperately to stave off more defections. For the first time in the firm's history, DeNunzio guaranteed that everyone would at least earn as large a bonus in 1986 as he or she had earned in 1985. But not everyone believed that would be possible. Just six weeks after Siegel's departure, on Good Friday, a crown jewel of the firm's corporate finance department, the high-tech group, quit en masse, also to go to Drexel.

For John Gordon, this was the last straw. He went to his father, saying he had to force DeNunzio to take bold action. The lack of leadership was "insane," he argued, concluding, "I'm going to leave the firm." The prospect that his own son might bail out of Kidder, Peabody was almost more than the senior Gordon could bear. He mustered all his still-considerable authority and went to see DeNunzio.

The result of Gordon's visit was all but inevitable. Within a few weeks, in late April, DeNunzio convened Kidder, Peabody's directors and announced, with tears in his eyes, that the firm would be sold to General Electric. GE paid $600 million for an 80% stake, leaving 20% in the hands of Kidder, Peabody officials who stayed at the firm, and promised to add an additional $130 million in capital. Al Gordon retired a rich man, selling his entire 6% stake for over $40 million. The Kidder, Peabody he had known was gone. But not even he could have forecast how fast its remnants would disintegrate.

Siegel was too busy at Drexel to dwell on the sale of his old firm, even though he realized that, had he stayed, his stock would have been worth millions. When he arrived, he'd been assigned an office directly adjacent to Levine's. He plunged into his new life as co-head of M&A with Black and Kay. He quickly discovered that there had been virtually no management of the department. Black worked on deals and cultivated his relationships with the West Coast; Kay, in Siegel's view, contributed little. Siegel instituted controls and procedures for dealing with issues like conflicts of interest, which, astoundingly, had never been formally addressed within the department at Drexel.

Siegel was unimpressed by the quality of people working with him. He knew Jeffrey Beck, one of Drexel's rising young stars who had worked with him on the Beatrice deal, and asked Black whether he should be brought into the M&A department. Black shrugged. "He's a congenital liar, but he can get you a meeting with anybody in the food industry." Siegel was appalled that a "liar" would be kept on the staff, and refused to hire him for M&A.

Siegel also held Levine's skills in low regard. At a Union Carbide meeting at the law offices of Paul, Weiss, Rifkind, Wharton & Garrison, Levine launched into a discourse on the subject of stock proration. It was obvious he had no idea what he was talking about, and Siegel saw Black and Ackerman, attending the meeting from Beverly Hills, roll their eyes in contempt. "He's no rocket scientist," Black said later, which Siegel deemed an understatement.

Siegel was also surprised by Levine's seemingly casual approach to his work. Levine was frequently absent or missing during the middle of the day, and often left early. One day Levine asked Siegel to "cover" for him for several days. "I've got to go scuba diving in the Bahamas," Levine said.

Given the talent vacuum, Siegel realized he'd be playing a bigger role in the department than he'd anticipated. He kept in close touch with many of his former Kidder, Peabody clients, anxious to see whether Drexel's notorious reputation would deter them from using his new firm. Much to his relief, most seemed eager to use Drexel's financing capabilities. Pan American, Strawbridge & Clothier, Carson Pirie Scott, Lear Siegler, Goodyear, Holiday Inn were some of the blue-chip companies that followed Siegel into Drexel's orbit. Their establishment aura lent Drexel a cachet it could never have obtained without Siegel. Siegel found himself working harder than ever, often putting in 20-hour days.

Joseph was delighted. His plan to meld Drexel's financing might with Siegel's expertise was working out more quickly than he had dared hope. Kay and Black, too, showed little concern that they were being upstaged by the charismatic Siegel. But Levine complained bitterly about Siegel's arrival. Levine was furious that he wasn't also made a co-head of M&A.

He even went so far as to meet with Boesky about the possibility of replacing Conway as head of merchant banking in the Boesky organization. At a lunch with Ilan Reich at the Water Club, Levine boasted that Boesky had offered him a $5 million signing bonus. He said Boesky told him he needed someone "tougher" than Conway, someone like himself.

The truth was somewhat more complicated. Actually, $5 million was the sum Levine claimed Boesky owed him as his share of the insider-trading profits Boesky had generated using Levine's tips. Boesky had countered with an offer of $2.4 million, which he conceded was owed Levine under the arrangement. If Levine were hired, the "bonus" would be a disguised method for making the payment. But the talks fizzled; Levine was far more valuable to Boesky as a source from within Drexel. So the talks continued periodically, with no resolution.

Despite Levine's continued lavish spending—more fine art, a house in the Hamptons—his insider-trading profits were tapering off. He made a modest amount trading on MidCon, a Drexel deal, but then his trading stopped. He had made total profits of well over $10 million, the goal he had once set for himself, and the ring was disintegrating, with Wilkis at Hutton and Cecola gone. Increasingly, Levine looked to the Boesky arrangement as the source of future profits. In February, Reich had Levine and his wife over to their Upper West Side brownstone, where he'd just completed a new kitchen. Reich's marriage had been rejuvenated, and he was thriving as a young partner at Wachtell. Even Levine was impressed. When he and Reich were alone, Levine told him, "You made the right decision" in pulling out of the scheme. Levine said his own career at Drexel was thriving, too. "It's almost enough to make an honest man of me." He laughed.

One day Siegel overheard Levine discussing confidential details of a Warnaco deal that Goldman, Sachs was working on, and he called Freeman. "You've got somebody over there in a ring with Dennis Levine," Siegel said. "I think I know who it is," Freeman replied, but didn't elaborate. Freeman reciprocated by warning Siegel that someone at Drexel was leaking details of a Drexel-backed MidCon merger. Siegel called Joseph, saying, "You've got a real problem on your hands."

Since moving to Drexel, Siegel had remained in close contact with Freeman, who continued to give him details of Goldman deals. Since Siegel was no longer responsible for arbitrage, however, he didn't trade on any of it. Moreover, true to the vow he had made when he left Kidder, Peabody, he stopped giving Freeman confidential information. When Freeman pressed him for details about Graphic Scanning, a Drexel deal in which Freeman had a large stake, Siegel insisted, falsely, that he didn't know, and referred Freeman to Kay.

The past seemed truly buried, except for one jarring note. One afternoon Levine sauntered into Siegel's office and, after shooting the breeze a few minutes, casually asked, "Where do you get your inside information? Boesky?"

Siegel froze. Would he always be haunted by his past? He tried to be equally casual. "I stopped dealing with Boesky years ago."

In April 1986, a ripple of anticipation washed over the more than 2,000 participants crammed into the main ballroom of the Beverly Hilton as curtains drew back for a screening of one of Drexel's "commercials," now a popular fixture of the Predators' Ball. As the strains of the "Dallas" theme song filled the room, Larry Hagman strode onto the screen, flashing a "Drexel Express titanium card." The card has "a ten-billion-dollar line of credit," J. R. drawled. "Don't go hunting without it."

Then came a spoof of the popular Madonna video, "Material Girl." A voice like Madonna's lip-synched "I'm a Double-B girl living in a material world," a double entendre referring to low-grade bond ratings and bra size. Madonna danced on the video screen and the chorus sang "Drexel, Drexel." The crowd roared with delight. When the spotlight fell on the conference's surprise entertainer, it was Dolly Parton.

Drexel, proud of its own new star, wanted Siegel front and center throughout the affair, but Siegel demurred. He'd only been at the firm a month and a half, and he didn't want to upstage veteran Drexel officials. Siegel declined the opportunity to host the M&A department breakfast, leaving that role to Levine, who boasted of Drexel's growing strategic prowess. But Joseph did persuade him to moderate a panel featuring takeover lawyer Flom and other lawyers discussing legal developments in the takeover field.

"You know me as a staunch defender of targets," Siegel began, reaching under the table and donning a white cowboy hat, symbolizing the blue-chip Kidder, Peabody. "Just because I've come to Drexel doesn't mean I've changed my views," he said with a twinkle in his eye as he reached under the table again and substituted a black hat for the white one.

Everyone laughed, even Siegel's establishment clients. Several of them, including the chairmen of Lear Siegler and Pan American, gave presentations at the conference. The corporate lambs were lying down with the lions.

And so were the politicians. Drexel had had no Washington office or registered lobbyists before 1985. Then, however, Congress had begun rumbling about hostile takeovers. During the Unocal raid, Representative Timothy Wirth, the powerful Colorado Democrat who chaired the Subcommittee on Telecommunications, Consumer Protection, and Finance, introduced a bill outlawing greenmail. Drexel, opposed to the measure, hired a former White House aide and opened an office in Washington. It retained Robert Strauss, former Democratic National Committee chairman, and John Evans, a former SEC commissioner, as lobbyists. Contributions from Drexel's political action committee rose from $20,550 in the 1984 elections to $177,800 in the 1986 elections.

At the 1986 Drexel bond conference, the once-critical Wirth was a featured speaker. Drexel executives gave $23,900 to his successful Senate campaign, and Wirth became a defender of junk bonds. His earlier attempt to prohibit greenmail went nowhere, and he didn't reintroduce it. Drexel invited other influential politicians to speak, including Senators Bill Bradley, Alan Cranston (the recipient of $41,-750 in Drexel money that year), Edward Kennedy, Frank Lautenberg, and Howard Metzenbaum. Most of them seemed as dazzled by the aura of megamoney as the lowliest pension-fund manager. For good measure, Drexel executives contributed $56,750 to Senator Alfonse D'Amato of New York, then chairman of the securities subcommittee.

"The force in this country buying high-yield securities has overpowered all regulation," Milken confidently told *The Washington Post*. The Milken creed on high-yield junk bonds, once an arcane topic of economic analysis, had become the gospel of the 1980s. Companies with conservative balance sheets began to feel foolish. Almost no one questioned Milken's premises anymore.

And who could argue with the numbers? Several academics, most prominently New York University professor of finance Edward Altman, issued studies showing that data through 1985 confirmed Milken's thesis that a portfolio of junk bonds yielded substantially higher returns with no greater risk than U.S. Treasuries. Altman became an eager proponent of Milken's views.

During the early and mid-1980s, Milken's highly leveraged clients seemed to show an amazing ability to stave off default, even when operating results were disappointing. In those cases, Milken simply "restructured," piling on a new and dazzling array of high-yield securities to replace the debt that was on the verge of default. The new tiers invariably pushed payments further into the future, giving the company more time to revive, and forestalling any rise in default rates.

That Milken could sell such restructurings—many of which, to anyone who studied the numbers, appeared obviously doomed—was not merely a tribute to the pervasiveness of his myth. It was a measure of the pliability of his captive clients, especially the savings and loans and insurance companies. By mid-1986, Milken's friend Tom Spiegel had loaded Columbia Savings and Loan with $3 billion of Drexel-generated junk; his crony Fred Carr's First Executive had a whopping $7 billion. More astoundingly, Milken himself would sit down at the end of the day and move chunks of securities in and out of their portfolios. No one minded as long as profits kept mounting.

Milken had other captive buyers. David Solomon ran his own money management firm, Solomon Asset Management, with over $2 billion in assets, most of it from employee welfare and pension plans. He had become one of Milken's earliest converts, and invested heavily in Milken high-yield products. Milken rewarded Solomon by making him a manager of a junk-bond mutual fund, the Finsbury Fund.

Finsbury's purchases of Milken products generated enormous commissions for Milken's high-yield department, some of which were owed to the Drexel salesmen who induced clients to buy into Finsbury. But Milken wanted all the commissions. So he ordered Solomon to reimburse him for the commissions he had to pay other Drexel salesmen. When Solomon refused, Milken threatened to have Solomon removed from his lucrative position as Finsbury's manager. Solomon capitulated.

Milken and Solomon, to recoup the commissions, simply inflated the price paid by Finsbury for junk bonds, and Milken pocketed the difference. Sometimes Milken helped generate phony tax losses for Solomon's personal trading account. Solomon evaded paying taxes on about $800,000 of income in 1985 alone. And Milken bestowed some equity from the Storer buyout on Solomon. Much of this scheme was illegal; ultimately, it was the Finsbury shareholders and U.S. taxpayers who were being cheated.

Milken hired a young salesman from First Boston, Terren Peizer, just to handle Solomon's accounts. In contrast to many others in the office, Peizer seemed the consummate Yuppie—well-dressed, fit, vain, with a sleek condominium apartment on the beach in Santa Monica with black leather furniture and high-tech stereo equipment. Peizer had been recommended by Solomon, and he quickly earned the resentment of others in Beverly Hills as he ingratiated himself with Milken and seemed to become his "pet." Milken installed Peizer at his left side on the trading desk; Peizer and Milken liked to give each other a "high five" when one or the other had vanquished someone on the other side of a trade.

One day Milken handed Peizer a blue-backed notebook, previously maintained by Alan Rosenthal, that kept track of the elaborate reckonings between Milken and Solomon. When Peizer asked about it, Milken told him, "Go ask Lowell. He'll explain it." Lowell did so, in several meetings with Peizer, in which Peizer dutifully took notes. It was Peizer's initiation into the dark underside of the Milken empire.

With Peizer in place, the illegal arrangements continued apace. The blue book functioned much as Thurnher's spread sheets did in the Boesky arrangement. Lowell oversaw the operation. No one complained; the scheme seemed undetectable to regulators.

Thus, in ways large and small, legal and illegal, the ordinary discipline of a free market of arm's-length buyers and sellers was undermined. The high-yield market's growth was limited only by Milken's ability to generate product—not by market discipline or independent decision-making on the part of buyers. In 1976, before Milken moved to Beverly Hills, junk-bond issues had totaled $15 billion. Now, in 1986, it was $125 billion—nearly a ninefold gain.

As for Milken's own personal wealth, public and private estimates at the time tended to hover around the $1 billion mark, placing Milken in the rare category of self-made billionaires. Yet this was very far from the truth. Milken made $550 million from Drexel in 1986. In addition, he (and the funds he controlled in the names of family members) probably earned at least that much from the Beatrice warrants alone. Milken and other partners received a distribution of $437.4 million from Otter Creek, the Milken-created partnership that had traded so presciently in National Can stock. Beatrice was only one of dozens of transactions in which Milken and his family gained valuable warrants and other equity interests, and Otter Creek was only one of more than 500 Milken-created partnerships. While such assets shift in value and are difficult to measure in any event, a closer and still conservative estimate of Milken's and his family's net worth by the end of 1986 would be $3 billion. In all likelihood, Milken had made himself one of the ten richest men in America.

No wonder Milken seemed so in command at the 1986 junk-bond conference. On Thursday evening of the conference, Fred Joseph walked down the garden path leading from the Beverly Hills Hotel to the secluded Bungalow 8 with Irwin Schneiderman, the Cahill Gordon & Reindel senior partner who was Drexel's chief legal advisor. The early April air was fragrant, yet bracing. Joseph had every reason to be in awe of Drexel's transformation, and proud of his own contribution. The firm had rolled back government challenges. It had vanquished the establishment. That year, Drexel handled a staggering $4 trillion in transactions. The firm had revenues of $5 billion. It had pretax net income of $2 billion. Drexel had agreed to lease a new 47-story, 1.9 million-square-foot skyscraper in Manhattan's World Trade Center complex which would be 49.9% owned by the firm, a fitting monument to its new stature. Drexel was now truly a rival to Goldman, Sachs and

Morgan Stanley. At this rate, those firms would inevitably be eclipsed. The fortunes and opportunities of Wall Street had proven as fluid as Joseph predicted when he came to Drexel just 10 years before.

As Joseph and Schneiderman approached the bungalow, Donald Engel's annual party was in full swing. Despite the selectivity of the guest list, hundreds of people were there, crowded into the bungalow's rooms and spilling out onto the surrounding terraces. Waiters carrying champagne and cocktails threaded their way through the crowd.

That year's guest list was practically a who's-who of self-made multimillionaires of the 80s: Merv Adelson, Norman Alexander, Henry Kravis, George Roberts, Boone Pickens, John Kluge, Fred Carr, Marvin Davis, Barry Diller, William Farley, Harold Geneen, Rupert Murdoch, Steve Ross, Ron Perelman, Peter Grace, Sam Heyman, Carl Icahn, Ralph Ingersoll, Irwin Jacobs, William McGowan, David Mahoney, Martin Davis, John Malone, Peter Ueberroth, David Murdock, Jay and Robert Pritzker, Samuel and Mark Belzberg, Carl Lindner, Nelson Peltz, Saul Steinberg, Craig McCaw, Frank Lorenzo, Peter May, Steve Wynn, James Wolfensohn, Oscar Wyatt, Gerald Tsai, Roger Stone, Harold Simmons, Sir James Goldsmith, Mel Simon, Henry Gluck, Ray Irani, Peter Magowan, Alan Bond, Ted Turner, Robert Maxwell, Kirk Kerkorian. Mingling with them were key Drexel corporate finance and bond salesmen, such as Siegel, Ackerman, and Dahl.

Boesky arrived, accompanied by two bodyguards. Siegel hadn't seen Boesky since March 1985, more than a year ago. He noticed Boesky was carrying his small purse, and then he noticed how tired and drawn Boesky seemed.

There were no women at Bungalow 8 this year. Siegel had told Joseph that he wouldn't participate in anything that involved procuring women, whether they were out-and-out prostitutes or not. Joseph himself had tried to ban the women after the 1984 conference, but Milken and Engel had opposed him. Milken, despite his own professed family values, insisted that "men like this sort of thing." This year Joseph had put his foot down. He assured Siegel and Schneiderman that he had ordered Engel not to invite any women to the bungalow, and Engel had reluctantly complied. But he made sure there would be beautiful women at the dinner afterward at Chasen's, even if wives also attended.

As Joseph moved through the rooms, illustrious raiders and corporate chieftains hurried to his side, praising the conference and exulting in Drexel's ascendancy. "If somebody bombed this room, the takeover era would be over," quipped one guest. And he was right.

Joseph looked over the crowd, and felt, for the first time, an almost palpable sense of the power that Drexel had unleashed. He turned to Schneiderman. "We can't let this go hog-wild," he said, struggling to be heard over the din of the party. "No one is going to let every company in America get taken over."

Boesky, his trademark black three-piece suit and watch chain concealed under cap and gown, looked out of sorts as he waited impatiently in the wings of Berkeley's Greek Theater, the outdoor amphitheater that serves as an open-air setting for the University of California's commencement ceremonies.

Rows of students filed into their seats, eagerly anticipating Boesky's address. The students of the university's business school, Milken's own alma mater, had chosen Boesky, by popular vote, to be their 1986 commencement speaker. The famous arbitrageur, lacking even a college degree, had flown to California that day, May 18, 1986, in a private jet. He was typically late, arriving halfway through the traditional dean's banquet that precedes the ceremony.

Before the speech, in a brief interview with the local paper, Boesky said he "didn't give a damn" what the students wanted to hear. What he planned to tell them, he said, was that "they must take the role that nobility played in ancient times, by becoming involved in the arts, politics, science and culture for the betterment of mankind."

After welcoming remarks by the dean, Boesky stepped to the podium, greeted by enthusiastic applause. He quickly demonstrated that he could be an excruciatingly dull speaker. He dwelled on platitudes about America as a land of opportunity and told of his own rise, a highly edited story of how the Detroit-raised son of immigrant parents had conquered Wall Street. Then, when it seemed as though he would lose his audience permanently, he galvanized the crowd with just a few sentences.

"Greed is all right, by the way," he said, raising his eyes from his text and continuing with what seemed like genuinely extemporaneous remarks. "I want you to know that. I think greed is healthy. You can be greedy and still feel good about yourself." The crowd burst into spontaneous applause as students laughed and looked at each other knowingly.

Boesky finished his talk and left the stage. He didn't stay for the rest of the ceremony. Nor did he attend the reception under the university's campanile, where the commencement speaker traditionally mingles with students, their families, and faculty. Boesky departed without conversing with a single student.

Back in New York, he seemed more irritable and moody than ever. His staff was struck by the fact that, despite the fresh infusion of nearly $1 billion, Boesky was doing practically nothing with the huge amounts of cash. The level of the firm's stock positions hadn't changed appreciably since the recapitalization and launching of the new partnership. Mooradian told others in the back office that he was worried about the high cash levels. "This isn't like Ivan," he said, but others did not share his alarm.

Boesky stayed in touch with Milken and others in Drexel's Beverly Hills operation, but he didn't seem to be pursuing any of the big "merchant banking" undertakings that he could now afford. With the final reconciliation of the $5.3 million payment, the pace of dealings between Milken and Boesky had tapered off. During April, Boesky did undertake two "favors" for Milken's high-yield department, manipulating the prices of Stone Container Corporation and Wickes Companies. In both cases, his actions enabled Drexel to go forward with lucrative deals. Boesky entered into these schemes with little enthusiasm and, apparently, little expectation of being reimbursed. He was simply obeying orders now. He too had become a captive of Drexel.

That summer, Lessman became concerned about Boesky's attitude and behavior. Boesky was hardly ever in the office, and when he was he seemed preoccupied. Mulheren owned a helicopter that he rented out, and Boesky was frequently taking it somewhere; no one knew its destination. He was often in Europe; he and Wekili had bought a house together in Théoule-sur-Mer, France, a village on the Côte d'Azur. Sometimes they were there together; other times Boesky called in from London or Paris, where he had paid $1.2 million for an apartment, or Hawaii, where he had purchased a condominium. He also spent long stretches in Los Angeles, presumably overseeing the Beverly Hills Hotel operation. But who really knew?

Though he maintained his tan, Boesky looked thinner than ever. He seemed to eat almost nothing, and obvious gaps appeared between his shirt collars and his neck. During the increasingly rare afternoons when he was in the office, he'd leave for the Harvard Club. Instead of the informal meetings he had always held there, he'd go to the locker room, don a heavy sweatsuit, wrap a towel around his neck, and sit alone in the sauna with the heat turned on high, sweat pouring off of him.

One morning Boesky came up to Lessman's desk and said, "Lance, I'm getting too old. I'm tired. I'm looking elsewhere. One day I'm going to drop the keys to this office on your desk, walk out of here, and never come back." Lessman was astonished. Boesky didn't seem to be joking. He looked grim. Lessman knew what a control freak

Boesky was; it was unthinkable that he'd let Lessman run his operation.

Boesky had filed an application for a zoning ordinance to permit the transformation of his mansion in Westchester into a larger replica of Monticello, Thomas Jefferson's home in Virginia. The plans called for a 48-foot dome that would conceal a sybaritic new master bedroom suite and a portico with four large columns. Then, he seemed to lose interest.

One day Boesky had Reid Nagle call his banker at Swiss Bank Corporation in Geneva and arrange a large transfer of cash to Wekili. On April 23, Boesky followed up with a letter. "Pursuant to conversations you have had with myself and Mr. Nagle of my office, I authorize you to transfer 1,785,800 S.F. from my account to your Geneva office in favor of Mr. Hushang Wekili. He will provide your Geneva office with instructions as to where and how these funds should be transferred." Nagle wondered what was going on.

On another occasion, Seema called. Boesky was out, and Lessman picked up the phone. Seema said it wasn't important, but then sounded wistful. "Ivan's away too much," she said. "I never see him." Lessman murmured sympathetically, but then she really surprised him. "We don't have any sex life."

Lessman had thought the Boeskys' marriage was pretty good. Seema had seemed actively involved in Boesky's life, though her visits to the office had diminished in the last two years. Lessman suspected Boesky had affairs, but he thought Seema had a healthy attitude about that. She'd once told him that her father told her that no man would ever be faithful. As long as the sexual involvements were just flings, that was all right.

Mulheren knew a little about Boesky's activities, too. His helicopter pilot sometimes flew companions to meet Boesky at Kennedy Airport, where they would board the supersonic Concord for flights to either London or Paris. Boesky installed a mistress in an apartment in the posh Stanhope Hotel on Fifth Avenue opposite the Metropolitan Museum of Art. The arrangement was supposed to be so secret that Boesky hired lawyers at Cravath, Swaine & Moore to handle the apartment transaction rather than his usual lawyers at Fried, Frank. But the apartment's decorator had told Seema. Boesky himself confided in no one, with the possible exception of Wekili, and neither Lessman nor Mulheren thought his private life was any of their business. It would always, they assumed, be shrouded in mystery.

The majestic *Queen Elizabeth II*, flagship of the Cunard line and the world's most sumptuous floating palace, stretched for what seemed

like blocks along the pier at Manhattan's West Side Passenger Terminal, drawing crowds of curious and admiring onlookers.

At the gangplank, a string quartet greeted guests with strains of
popular standards. Clowns entertained those waiting to board and
handed out balloons to children. Overhead billowed a huge banner,
MAZEL TOV, JENNIFER, ROBIN AND JASON. For the first time, at a cost
approaching $1 million, the *QE2*—the entire ship, with its crew of
1,000—had been rented by one person, Gerald Guterman, a real estate
developer and owner of the Stanhope Hotel, to celebrate the September 1986 bar mitzvah of his 13-year-old son, Jason. His daughters by
a previous marriage, Jennifer and Robin, were also, somewhat belat-
edly, celebrating their bas mitzvahs.

By the time the great ocean liner pulled out into the Hudson River
for its 46-mile, overnight "cruise to nowhere," one of Guterman's most
important guests, a fellow hotel owner and neighbor in Westchester, was
nowhere to be seen. Ivan Boesky had missed the sailing.

Then, above the welcoming strains of the Peter Duchin orchestra,
guests craned their necks on deck as a twin-engine helicopter came into
view, hovered over the ship, then descended to the sports deck helipad.
With the blades still turning, the cockpit door opened, and Boesky,
elegantly dressed in a tuxedo and black tie, stepped onto the deck. He
flashed a smile and waved as guests laughed and applauded. The
helicopter rose and roared off into the sunset, leaving Boesky to upstage his hosts.

Boesky joined other guests at the champagne reception and six-
course dinner, including roast lamb, beef Wellington with truffle
sauce, and Cornish hen with foie gras and wild rice, all prepared in the
ship's kosher kitchen. Masses of calla lilies and huge ice sculptures
decorated tables. Each of the three children cut into his or her own
towering, three-foot-high cake topped with sprays of fresh flowers as
the crowd sang "Happy Birthday." The next day, in addition to the
QE2's luxurious amenities, guests were entertained by a 51-member
troupe of mimes, musicians, and roving entertainers. Hair and makeup
stylists from the chic Manhattan salon La Coupe tended to the beauty
needs of Guterman's wife, Linda, and women guests. At the ceremony
itself, Rabbi Arthur Schneier praised Jason's parents. "In a home that
has everything, Linda and Gerry also stress to their children that which
gives us purpose in life."

The next day, on Sunday, Mulheren called Boesky at home.
Boesky had rented Mulheren's helicopter, and the pilot had called
Mulheren as soon as he got back. "You're not going to believe this,"
the pilot reported to Mulheren, "but Ivan had me drop him onto the
QE2." Mulheren was irate. "Don't ever do that kind of thing for him

again," he ordered. Mulheren knew the landing had been no emergency occasioned by Boesky missing the departure. The helicopter had been reserved well in advance. Boesky was seeking attention by flaunting his wealth.

Ivan got on the phone. "Don't ever use my helicopter again for a stunt like this," Mulheren said angrily. "Are you fucking out of your mind? Revolutions are made of this. People get put in gas ovens."

Boesky just chuckled. "You've got to admit one thing, John," Boesky said. "When I go, I go first class."

The next day, September 17, 1986, Boesky surrendered to federal authorities and became an undercover agent for the Department of Justice.

The Chase

BOOK TWO

9.

Richard Drew, vice president of the compliance department at Merrill Lynch, was puzzled by the letter on his desk. It had arrived that day, May 25, 1985, forwarded from the international division.

Dear Sir:
Please be informed that two of your executives from the Caracas office are trading with inside information. A copy with description of their trades so far has been submitet to the S.E.C. by separate mail.As is mantion on that letter if us customers do not benefit from their kno-leg,we wonder who surveils the trades done by account executives.Upon you investigating to the last consequecie we will provide with the names of the insider on their owne hand writing.

At the bottom of the letter were the names of two Merrill Lynch brokers, Max Hofer and Carlos Zubillaga, their Merrill Lynch account numbers, and a postscript: "mr. frank granados might like to have a copie."

The letter was so poorly written that an overworked compliance officer might easily have tossed it aside. Poorly paid, shunned by upper-level managers and partners, compliance officers were kept far from the center of the action. They were paid to maintain an appearance of self-policing in the securities industry—without actually insti-gating too many investigations.

Merrill Lynch, however, was more serious about compliance than most firms. Its general counsel, Stephen Hammerman, set the tone, insisting on thorough monitoring of customer and account-executive trading. Hammerman had built the largest compliance department on Wall Street, with a staff of 75.

Drew, a lawyer who'd spent 14 years monitoring trading at the New York Stock Exchange, had joined Merrill Lynch in 1981. He worked closely with another compliance official, Robert Romano, who had worked as a federal prosecutor and in the SEC's enforcement division, investigating insider trading.

Despite the grammar and spelling mistakes, the phrase "inside information" caught Drew's attention, as did other aspects of the Caracas letter. The writer's first language wasn't English, but he or she was reasonably sophisticated. He or she knew of the existence of a compliance department, knew the brokers' account numbers, and knew that Frank Granados was Merrill Lynch's regional director for Latin America.

Merrill Lynch brokers are required to trade through the firm, so Drew was able to access the personal account records for Hofer and Zubillaga. They were, in fact, brokers in Merrill Lynch's Caracas, Venezuela, office, but their trading activity wasn't extensive. In four or five instances, however, they had both traded in stocks that had suddenly risen sharply in price. The trades *were* suspicious. Drew didn't expect the inquiry to go very far, but he handed the letter and records over to one of his analysts, a young compliance officer named Steven Snyder.

Snyder scanned the records—Hofer's and Zubillaga's Merrill Lynch Cash Management Accounts—as Drew briefed him. "Oh shit," Snyder said at one point, interrupting Drew.

"What's the matter?" Drew asked, as Snyder pointed out debits for two CMA checks Zubillaga had written that very month. The amounts were $4,500 and $839.39, hardly startling, and the payee was someone named Brian Campbell. "I know that guy," Snyder said. "He's an institutional broker right here at Merrill Lynch."

Drew and Snyder were intrigued. Why would a broker in Caracas be writing a check to another broker in New York? Ordinarily in such matters, Snyder would have called Hofer and Zubillaga to ask for an explanation, but such inquiries are often easily deflected. So Drew ordered copies of the personnel files of the two Caracas brokers and Campbell, as well as Campbell's CMA account statements.

The next week, after they'd examined all the accounts, the officers realized they had stumbled onto something far more mysterious than they had at first suspected. Campbell was no longer working at Merrill Lynch, although Snyder's recollection had been correct. Campbell had been an institutional broker in Merrill Lynch's international division, and had left that February for Smith Barney. Zubillaga had also worked in the international division before moving to Caracas. In fact, Campbell and Zubillaga had been in the same Merrill Lynch training and orientation program in 1982.

Campbell's trading records were even more revealing. He had traded in precisely the same handful of takeover situations as Zubillaga and Hofer—one day earlier, in each case, suggesting that the trades were originating with Campbell. Campbell had also traded in several other situations that looked as if they were based on inside information—a total of eight, involving just 100 or 200 shares.

It looked as though Campbell had some source of information, so Drew and Snyder obtained a list of Campbell's clients, about 35 in all, and pulled up their trading records. Nothing struck them until they got to Campbell's biggest client: the Bahamas branch of Switzerland's oldest bank, Bank Leu International. All eight of Campbell's suspicious trades showed up in the Bank Leu trading accounts. When they examined them more closely, they found eight other suspicious trades. In only one case had Campbell's own trading preceded Bank Leu's; this suggested that Campbell was copying his client's orders. These were no longer small trades and profits. Bank Leu typically traded heavily, in 10,000-share blocks.

At each level of inquiry, the trading volume and amounts of money involved had mushroomed. With the addition of Bank Leu, the matter had reached a new level of seriousness. Drew and Snyder took their findings to Romano, who stepped in to pursue the investigation. Having exhausted Merrill Lynch's own internal records, Romano called Zubillaga and Hofer in Caracas, and ordered them to fly to New York for questioning.

They were apprehensive but cooperative, confirming much of what the compliance officials had already surmised. Zubillaga said that he and Campbell had been friends, and that Campbell would call periodically, suggesting they buy specific stocks. "This looks good," Campbell would say. "Maybe you should buy it." In return, Campbell wanted a percentage of Zubillaga's trading profits, which accounted for Zubillaga's checks. But Zubillaga hadn't kept the information to himself; he'd passed it on to Hofer, his office colleague, and to his own brother.

Merrill Lynch fired Zubillaga and Hofer. Not for insider trading—they appeared to be distant "tippees," unaware of the quality or source of the information. But Merrill Lynch barred any undisclosed shared ownership in securities positions, and the kickbacks to Campbell were deemed to be violations. The two Caracas brokers didn't know who wrote the anonymous letter. But they were only its first casualties.

There was little more that the Merrill Lynch officials could do. They did contact a Smith Barney lawyer, urging him to investigate Campbell and his trading for Bank Leu. The lawyer, however, told Campbell that Merrill Lynch was probing his trading. Merrill Lynch wasn't in a position to contact Campbell directly. The source of the takeover information must have been a Bank Leu client. Merrill couldn't pursue Bank Leu, which would protect the identity of its clients at all costs. At an impasse, Romano called the chief of enforcement at the SEC, Gary Lynch.

"Jesus," Lynch said, after Romano outlined the details of their investigation.

That was the last Romano, Drew, or Snyder heard for nearly a year. As far as they knew, the SEC was having no success at finding the mysterious source of the takeover information. As the takeover boom continued, generating ever more work for Merrill Lynch's compliance division, the curious letter from Caracas was all but forgotten.

When Romano called, Lynch had been head of enforcement at the SEC for just four months—four difficult months. Morale had been badly damaged when Lynch's predecessor, John Fedders, resigned in early 1985 after *The Wall Street Journal* revealed that he had physically abused his wife. To quell the scandal, SEC chairman John Shad had moved quickly to replace him. Lynch, the division's associate director, a 35-year-old lawyer who'd spent almost his entire career with the SEC, was the somewhat surprising choice. Some better-known outsiders had been considered: New York Senator Alfonse D'Amato lobbied for New York lawyer Otto Obermaier. Jed Rakoff and Robert McCaw, both prominent securities lawyers, were also candidates. But the staff was relieved that Lynch, one of their own, was chosen rather than some Reagan favorite, someone who might be too committed to deregulation to enforce the laws.

Lynch, by contrast, seemed the consummate civil servant. He kept his political views to himself. His colleagues considered him calm, restrained, decisive when necessary, and at times somewhat distant and aloof. His background was far removed from the high-pressure, big-money world of Wall Street.

The youngest of five children, Lynch had grown up in the countryside near Middletown, a small city in rural upstate New York near the Pennsylvania border. His father ran a small trucking operation and owned several other small businesses. Lynch was raised a Methodist. He graduated from Syracuse University and Duke University Law School. After graduation, he worked for a Washington, D.C., law firm for a year and then joined the SEC, looking for litigation and investigative work. Eventually he was named associate director of the enforcement division, and worked on the Foster Winans and Thayer insider-trading cases.

As the merger boom unfolded, Lynch was appalled by the persistent run-ups in stock prices on takeover rumors. Obviously, confidential information was leaking into the market on an unprecedented scale, to the detriment of investors who waited for public announcements. Average investors were becoming alienated and distrustful. Soon after Lynch assumed his new position, in April 1985, *Business Week* ran a cover story with the headline, THE EPIDEMIC OF INSIDER TRADING: THE SEC IS FIGHTING A LOSING BATTLE TO HALT STOCK-MARKET ABUSES. The article only underscored Lynch's own concerns. He vowed to step up insider-trading enforcement, to increase the staff assigned to it, and to follow up every lead vigorously. Public confidence in the markets, he felt, was at stake.

Without such determination, Lynch might very well have allowed Romano's lead to languish. When he received a copy of the mysterious Caracas letter, he didn't think that much of it. It seemed to be a routine complaint about brokers. Brokers weren't "insiders" in the conventional sense, and someone was always complaining to the SEC about their broker. But the Bank Leu angle held some promise. Bank Leu had figured in two other recent SEC inquiries, including the Textron case, neither of which had gone anywhere. So Lynch turned the letter over to John Sturc, his associate director and a dogged investigator and litigator, who put together a team. Among the lawyers assigned was Leo Wang, the same lawyer who had taken Levine's deposition in Textron.

What was most intriguing about the case was the large number of stocks involved: about 27 in the case of Bank Leu, about 16 in Campbell's account. Most insider-trading cases, even the sensational Thayer case, involved only a few stocks, often only one. The illegal trading is done by a company insider or immediate tippee with knowledge of only that company's transactions. Yet the staff knew that such isolated cases couldn't account for what seemed to be an epidemic of insider trading on Wall Street. Very few people are privy to as many secrets as seemed to be involved in the Bank Leu trading. Just about the only people with that kind of information are lawyers or investment bankers. Perhaps this case would finally take the SEC into the heart of a conspiracy that the staff had long suspected: a network of professionals with frequent access to the most confidential inside information.

Lynch, Sturc, and their colleagues concluded there were enough leads worth pursuing, and the SEC commissioners gave their routine approval to begin an investigation. On July 2, 1985, the SEC investigation, identified only by its case number, HO-1743, formally commenced. Armed with the agency's subpoena power, the lawyers set about looking for evidence.

Wang subpoenaed Brian Campbell and obtained his trading and phone records. In August, Campbell himself arrived at the SEC's offices in Washington, accompanied by a lawyer. Campbell—young, blond, self-assured—was a contrast to the stocky and often disheveled Wang. Campbell seemed a little tense, though not abnormally so, given the circumstances. Under oath, he answered questions for three full days.

Wang could tell from Campbell's phone records that the young stockbroker was in almost daily contact with a Bank Leu official named Bernhard Meier. The constant contact wasn't surprising; the bank was far and away Campbell's largest client. He had taken the Bank Leu business with him when he moved to Smith Barney from Merrill Lynch. "Did it ever occur to you at any time that Mr. Meier had access to inside information?" Wang asked.

"No, I had no knowledge of that, no," Campbell replied, adding that he never even had any "suspicion" or "indication" of inside information.

Wang asked Campbell about the times he bought stocks just before takeover bids. Campbell insisted (while acknowledging that the trades mirrored Bank Leu trading) that he had bought the stocks after doing his own research into the companies, not because of any inside information. Campbell said he told Meier he was copying some of the trades, but added that he had been "evasive" and hadn't mentioned any specific stocks to Meier.

Then Wang asked Campbell about a curious $10,000 check deposit that showed up in his bank records. The check had been drawn on Meier's Morgan Guaranty Trust Co. account in New York. That, Campbell testified, was a "loan" from Meier for a real estate venture. "Have you had any other business dealings with Mr. Meier?" Wang asked.

"No, I've not," Campbell said.

Then Wang asked Campbell about another client account that appeared to trade in the same stocks as Campbell and Bank Leu: BCM Capital Management. Campbell seemed increasingly uncomfortable. That, he admitted, was a company formed by a friend, a lawyer named Kevin Barry. Campbell himself had tipped Barry to the Bank Leu stocks. Campbell continued to insist, however, that he had no inkling inside information might be involved. The deposition ended.

Wang's instincts told him that Campbell was lying. Reviewing the testimony, Lynch agreed. Campbell was in almost constant contact with Meier at Bank Leu, and, given the pattern of takeover bids, Campbell had at least to suspect Meier had access to inside information. Campbell was also far more involved with Meier than he seemed willing to admit. BCM Capital Management, it seemed obvious, stood for the first initials of Barry, Campbell, and Meier. The three seemed to be copying the Bank Leu trades for BCM.

Pursuing Campbell and Barry, however, wouldn't lead the lawyers further "upstream" in what they now suspected was a fairly significant insider-trading scheme, given the number of stocks. Their goal had to be the original source of the intelligence, and for that, they were going to have to assault the formidable obstacle of Bank Leu, shrouded in centuries of Swiss secrecy traditions. The SEC lawyers decided to start simply, with a friendly, low-key phone call to Meier at his office in Nassau.

The phone call caught Meier by surprise, even though he knew the SEC was interested in the stocks Bank Leu had traded through Campbell, who had told him everything. At that point, Meier had talked to Dennis Levine, since Levine was the customer who'd initiated the trading. Meier anxiously told Levine about the SEC's interest in Campbell. Levine had not been concerned. He had called the inquiry routine and said it would go nowhere. But now Meier had the SEC on his own phone line, asking about 28 stocks that Levine had told him to trade. Meier stalled for time, saying the SEC would have to request information in writing. He said he'd have to consult counsel before deciding how to respond.

Meier was consumed with anxiety. He realized now that, despite Levine's instructions, he had steered too many trades through Campbell. He had also traded the same stocks in his own account, as had Campbell, and BCM had traded in the same pattern. Levine had warned them about this, too. No wonder the SEC was suspicious.

Meier rushed into the office of his colleague, Bruno Pletscher. Neither had any idea of how to handle the SEC. They decided to turn to Levine for advice. They couldn't call "Mr. Diamond" themselves. By the time Levine called them several days later, they'd received the SEC's written request for information on the 28 stocks. They described the situation to Levine, and insisted that he come to Nassau for a meeting. Levine agreed.

On his way to Bank Leu, Levine stopped off in Key Biscayne, Florida, to visit Wilkis, who had rented a house there for most of the summer; Wilkis came down from New York most weekends. He'd been looking forward to the long Labor Day weekend.

Levine briefed Wilkis on the latest developments. After Meier first told Levine of the SEC's interest in the Campbell trading, Levine told Wilkis, he'd turned to Boesky for advice. Boesky had recommended a lawyer named Harvey Pitt. "He's gotten me through hundreds of these," Boesky had told Levine.

"So you're retaining Pitt?" Wilkis asked, feeling queasy.

"No, don't be crazy," Levine retorted. "I'm getting the bank to retain him. We'll shut this down fast. I don't have anything to fight."

Wilkis wasn't reassured. He worried that Pitt would place the bank's interests ahead of his friend's. How did Levine know he could manipulate Pitt?

"You may have the right lawyer," Wilkis told Levine. "I don't know about the client."

Then Levine broke the more serious news that the SEC had sent the bank a written request for information about trading in 28 take-over-related stocks, all in Levine's Diamond account. "They want my records!" he exclaimed. "What do I do?"

Wilkis was petrified, but listened quietly as Levine spun out his strategy: to "keep the bank warm," and "hold their hands." He called Meier his "number three," and said he'd rehearse the nervous Swiss banker until he came across as a convincing stock picker. He'd get Drexel's research reports on the companies involved. Levine seemed to regain his confidence as he spoke. He left in a cheerful mood.

Levine arrived in Nassau on Labor Day weekend 1985. Poised and confident, he quickly took charge of the situation, belittling the SEC, calling them incompetent. "You don't have anything to worry about," he assured the two bankers—as long as they did what he told them.

Quickly, Levine briefed them on his cover-up plan. He told Meier to take responsibility for initiating the trades. "If you go to the SEC and tell them that you traded in these stocks on behalf of your managed portfolio," Levine explained, "you are the smart guys. You have decided to buy these securities and allocate them throughout your portfolio. The SEC can't prove the opposite."

Levine recognized that it might seem implausible to an SEC lawyer that someone of Meier's background and limited experience with stocks would be so skilled as to repeatedly and accurately identify takeover targets ahead of public announcements. But Meier was to insist that this was the case. Meier would testify that his own research suggested these companies as likely takeover targets. Levine assured Meier he would furnish him with appropriate research materials to back him up. The essential thing was to prevent any suspicion that a Bank Leu client was the actual source of the trading recommendations. Meier, as a bank official, would never be legally considered an insider.

Levine also recommended that the bankers hire a good lawyer to deflect the SEC. He suggested Pitt, a former SEC general counsel now in private practice with Fried, Frank, Harris, Shriver & Jacobson's Washington office. By the time Levine left, Meier and Pletscher felt greatly relieved. They briefed the Bahamas branch general manager, Jean-Pierre Fraysse, on the plan to deceive the SEC. "This seems to be the way to go," Fraysse agreed.

Harvey Pitt settled his bulging waistline into a banquette of the Polo Lounge in the Westbury Hotel in New York. The bearded, slightly disheveled, 40-year-old lawyer was a contrast with the tall, thin, impeccably groomed Fraysse, who was staying at the hotel and had flown to New York to meet Pitt in person.

Fraysse had called Pitt for the first time just after the Labor Day weekend meeting with Levine.

"Why did you call me?" Pitt asked Fraysse.

"Your reputation has spread," Fraysse said. "We've heard of you." Fraysse smiled politely, saying no more.

"Ah, the Swiss," Pitt thought to himself. It was obvious that Fraysse would say no more about how he had heard of Pitt.

Fraysse outlined the history of the bank's contacts with the SEC, and the men talked generally about SEC investigations. Fraysse seemed relaxed, then mentioned that because he was returning to Switzerland, Pitt would soon be dealing with Meier directly.

"He's a terrific portfolio manager," Fraysse said of Meier, setting up the cover story they'd devised with Levine. "He's very astute. He's done a terrific job for our clients."

Pitt was concerned when Fraysse mentioned the number of stocks on the SEC's list. Most SEC investigations he'd been familiar with dealt with only a single stock. Pitt thought he ought to come down to the bank in Nassau, but Fraysse said Meier was scheduled to be in New York a few days later, and would meet with Pitt then.

Pitt met Meier for the first time on September 18 at Fried, Frank's offices in lower Manhattan. The well-dressed Meier was calm, and seemed charming, worldly, and confident. His wife was an engaging and beautiful woman younger and taller than he was.

Tutored by Levine, Meier spoke at length about his stock-picking prowess, and his success at managing trading accounts for Bank Leu's customers. He insisted he'd bought the stocks in question on the "fundamentals," saying he had the research to back him up. When the meeting ended in midafternoon, the Meiers returned to their room at the Waldorf.

.   .   .

That same day, Peter Sonnenthal, one of the SEC lawyers assigned to the case, entered the cavernous art deco lobby of New York's Waldorf-Astoria Hotel. Passing quickly through the bustling lobby, he stopped at the registration counter.

"Could I have the room number of Bernhard Meier," Sonnenthal asked politely.

"We don't provide that information," the clerk replied.

"But I'm a government agent," Sonnenthal said.

The clerk still refused, so Sonnenthal grabbed a piece of paper and pen and hastily wrote out a makeshift subpoena demanding that the Waldorf-Astoria disclose Meier's room number. The startled clerk took the paper to a superior, and the hotel complied immediately. Meier was staying in room 2341, in the exclusive Waldorf Towers section.

Sonnenthal rode up the elevator, walked swiftly to Meier's room, and knocked. Meier, having arrived at the room only a short time before, opened the door unsuspectingly. Sonnenthal handed the startled banker an official U.S. government envelope containing two subpoenas: one calling for the bank's records, and another, ominously, calling for all of Meier's own personal trading records.

Meier was stunned, as much by the fact that the SEC had found him in New York as by the subpoenas themselves. (The SEC had alerted the U.S. Customs Department to watch for Meier. Customs in turn told the agency that Meier had entered the U.S., and had listed the Waldorf as his address.) At about 5:30 P.M., a frantic Meier called Pitt. His urbane façade was in shreds. Pitt, too, was now alarmed. These weren't the ordinary tactics of the SEC. The agency was playing hardball.

Pitt tried to calm Meier, to no avail. Terrified, Meier didn't leave his hotel room for the next three days.

After the frantic call from Meier, Pitt wasted no time. Four days later he was on a flight to the Bahamas with a Fried, Frank colleague, Michael Rauch. A team of lawyers from the firm had hastily analyzed the trading and stocks in question, compiling lists of people involved, looking for common denominators. This had turned up nothing. Pitt wondered if a ring of sources might be involved, but he dismissed the thought. It seemed too farfetched. The absence of any obvious source of the information lent some credence to Meier's story, though the number of stocks and the consistently prescient timing still looked suspicious.

Pitt and Rauch met with Meier, Pletscher, and Richard Coulson, an American expatriate and former lawyer at Cravath, Swaine & Moore who was advising the bank. Meier seemed to be in charge, although Coulson often spoke for the bank.

Pitt was skeptical of Meier's claims to be a stock-picker, but he hesitated to challenge his new client directly. Instead, he enumerated the perils of lying to one's own lawyer. "You may be afraid of telling the truth," Pitt suggested gently. "But we're very good lawyers. If you tell us the truth, the likelihood is that we can help you."

Coulson cut him off. "Bernie did the trading, and that's all there is to it," he said. "We'll take our explanation to the SEC, and that should be the end of this," he insisted. The bank offered to have Meier and others testify under oath to satisfy the SEC that the whole matter could be explained as shrewd stock-picking, waiving foreign jurisdictional problems.

The bank officials had no intention of changing their story—but they were worried. The publicity of an SEC enforcement action could be devastating to the bank's effort to build a business base in the U.S. Bank Leu wanted good relations with the SEC. At the same time, the bank was adamant in its refusal to reveal the identity of its clients or trading in individual client accounts. It was barred by Bahamas banking law from doing so, and such disclosures would violate the bank's long tradition of secrecy.

After they returned to Washington, Pitt and Rauch contacted the SEC and began laying the groundwork for Meier to appear. Eventually Pitt met with Wang, Sonnenthal, and other SEC lawyers working on the case.

The SEC lawyers were eager for some explanation of the trades. Pitt repeated the explanation approved by Coulson, insisting that Meier had made the investment decisions for a variety of the bank's managed accounts. There was no involvement of the bank's customers in the trades, so there couldn't be any insider trading of the kind the SEC obviously suspected, Pitt explained. In support of the bank's position, Pitt offered to produce bank documents, with the names of customers deleted. Meier would also testify. All Pitt asked was a little more time to gather the materials. The SEC lawyers could barely contain their skepticism, but reluctantly agreed.

Pitt himself hadn't had a chance to review the bank's documents supporting the story, and he wasn't about to sign an agreement providing for Meier's testimony without having seen them. Pitt also realized that this was possibly the bank's last chance to set the record straight, if its officials were lying. Given Pitt's representations to the SEC, it might already be too late.

At Bank Leu, Pletscher was wavering. He'd never been as closely involved with Levine as Meier, and his own piggyback trading had been modest. He'd earned only about $46,000 in total trading profits from Levine's information. Unlike Meier, he wasn't Levine's "number three." After the bank received the SEC's written demand for information, Pletscher had told Levine to stop his trading. Now Levine was badgering Pletscher to let him resume. "I could easily be earning 100% returns trading," Levine complained. "I hate sitting around and earning bank interest rates." He argued that a sudden suspension of trading looked suspicious. If Meier was such a good stock-picker, why wouldn't he continue to score? But Pletscher did not relent. Levine was causing them enough trouble.

On one visit, Levine brought a shopping bag bulging with Drexel research reports and other materials on the suspicious stocks. Meier and he set about preparing ex post facto research justifications for all of the trades. Levine also asked to review his account files at the bank. He was horrified to discover a photocopy of his passport, complete with his picture, and the signature card he'd filled out when he opened his first "Diamond" trading account at Bank Leu. There were also withdrawal slips that Levine had signed with his own name on the numerous occasions he'd made cash withdrawals. "Make sure you destroy these," Levine ordered the two bankers.

Evidently unaware that their actions could constitute obstruction of justice under U.S. law, the two bankers shredded Levine's passport copy and the original account signature card. They believed that all were obsolete anyway; Levine had shifted his account to his Panamanian corporation, Diamond Holdings. But Pletscher, without telling Levine, refused to destroy the withdrawal slips. He believed they were necessary to protect the bank in the event Levine ever claimed he hadn't received the cash. The cautious Swiss banker wasn't about to destroy withdrawal slips.

Finally, there remained the thorny issue of the "managed accounts," the linchpin of their explanation for the trades. If, as he was claiming, Meier had made all the investment decisions for the bank's managed accounts, it stood to reason that records would show the trades in numerous client accounts. Yet all the suspicious trades had occurred in just one account, Diamond Holdings. Even if the name of that account were withheld, the managed account alibi would lose credibility, and suspicion would focus on the single account and the identity of its owner. Levine was confident that the bank would never have to break down its trading into accounts for the SEC, but now Pitt and Rauch, the bank's own lawyers, were demanding individual account records to support Meier's story. Levine and Meier urged Pletscher to alter the computer records to create 10 fictitious accounts that would appear to have traded in the same stocks as Levine. Meier assured Levine they'd take care of the matter.

Again, however, Pletscher balked. Hans Knopfli, the chairman of Bank Leu's management board, had recently visited the Bahamas branch and had spoken with Meier and Pletscher about the SEC investigation. Meier told the high-ranking official that he'd reluctantly concluded he'd have to lie before the SEC.

"Mr. Meier, under no circumstances can you go to an authority and lie," the startled Knopfli had said. "This is a critical situation. I want you to do what is best for the bank. However, do not go and lie."

When it came to actually creating the false accounts, Pletscher couldn't bring himself to do it. He did make one alteration, however. Meier insisted that Pletscher expunge an entry from Meier's own account statement. The mysterious item was a $5,000 wire transfer from Meier's Bank Leu account to the Delaware National Bank in the tiny Catskill mountain town of Delhi, N.Y.

Pitt and his colleagues also pressed forward. They flew to Nassau to see the managed account records supporting Meier's story. The lawyers expected about 40 to 50 accounts, all indicating trading in the 28 stocks that figured in the SEC investigation. Accompanied by several paralegals, the lawyers checked into the Cable Beach Hotel.

Meier arrived just after lunch, carrying several large ring binders. When the lawyers eagerly opened them, they found only a handful of pages. They were mostly Meier's travel and entertainment receipts. Pitt was stunned, and angrily told Meier that these weren't the trading records they'd traveled to the Bahamas to see. Meier, looking uncomfortable, promised to be back the next morning with the account records.

This time he had trading records from 25 of the bank's accounts, but none of it involved the 28 suspicious stocks; none of it corroborated his story. Pitt struggled to maintain his composure. "We have two possibilities here. Either we have the wrong documents," Pitt told Meier, pausing for emphasis, "or we have the wrong story." Meier said nothing and, for the first time, looked crestfallen.

They were at an impasse. Suddenly Meier rose from his seat, went to the telephone, and called Pletscher. Since Meier spoke in Swiss German, the lawyers didn't understand; Pletscher, it seemed clear, was getting a tongue-lashing. Meier hung up, told the lawyers to wait, and left the room. Efforts to get further information proved fruitless, however. Coulson took over for Meier, and stonewalled.

The lawyers gave up and flew back to the U.S., more skeptical of their clients than ever. It was becoming obvious that one person had traded in 28 stocks in advance of takeover announcements. If so, this was history's largest insider-trading case.

The lawyers' suspicions were finally confirmed the following Monday, when Pitt and Rauch returned to the Bahamas and met with Hans Peter Schaad, Bank Leu's general counsel, who had flown in from Zurich. Meier and Pletscher had finally told Schaad the truth, and he had ruled out the possibility of any further lies.

"It is my understanding that there is one account for all this trading," Schaad announced to Pitt. "What do we do now?"

Given the degree to which they'd already been misled—not to mention the embarrassing representations they in turn had made to the SEC—Pitt and Rauch gave serious thought to withdrawing from the case. They felt their own reputations were at stake.

They agreed to continue if the bank promised to halt all trading in the account. They couldn't sanction what might be the ongoing commission of crime. Without unduly arousing suspicions, the bankers also had to agree to freeze the account assets. And they had to give Pitt and Rauch a complete, candid account of everything that had happened with respect to the account. The Bank Leu officials agreed, despite Meier's obvious discomfort, with one condition: they would not reveal the identity of the account's owner, referring to him only as "Mr. X."

Pitt, however, thought the bank's best hope was to exchange the identity of Mr. X for immunity for the bank and its officers. Whether such a deal would appeal to the SEC, of course, depended almost entirely on who Mr. X was. Schaad, still reluctant, finally agreed to divulge some details: Mr. X was an investment banker, and he worked at Drexel Burnham Lambert. Now Pitt realized the ramifications of the case.

Several days later, Meier invited Pitt to have dinner with him and his wife at the exclusive Lyford Cay Club, where he was a member. On the way, Meier tried to ingratiate himself with Pitt, explaining that the scheme wasn't his idea alone. "I don't want you to think the worst of me," Meier said.

Pitt couldn't resist taking advantage of Meier's conciliatory frame of mind. "We're going to have to know Mr. X's name eventually," he said. "Why don't you tell us?"

"You know the firm," Meier said.

"That's right, Drexel," Pitt replied.

"Do you know anyone at Drexel?" Meier asked. "Who do you know there?"

Suddenly Pitt remembered a dinner he'd attended less than two months before, in mid-October. Fried, Frank had been interested in doing more work for Drexel, especially in the takeover area, and one of Pitt's partners, Arthur Fleischer, had invited him and David Kay to dinner at Lutèce, one of New York's most expensive French restaurants. Kay had brought along his rising M&A star, Dennis Levine. Pitt didn't remember much about the dinner; it was a typical client-cultivation affair, with too much expensive food and wine and a sense of enforced camaraderie. Levine had made little impression. But he and Kay were practically the only Drexel investment bankers Pitt knew.

"David Kay?" Pitt ventured, and Meier shook his head no.

"Dennis Levine?" Pitt asked. Pitt knew immediately from Meier's expression that he had the right name.

"That's it," Meier said.

Since Levine had visited him in Key Biscayne, Bob Wilkis had developed insomnia. He was irritable with his wife and daughter, refusing to explain what the problem was. One evening he broke into tears, for no apparent reason. But then he pulled himself together. "I can't be selfish," Wilkis told himself. "I have to help Dennis through this."

Levine called him constantly, sometimes as many as 8 or 10 times a night. "Don't get upset," Levine kept saying. "It's routine. We're doing fine." Wilkis was reassured when Levine was invited by the SEC to appear at a roundtable discussion on takeovers.

That discussion turned, almost inevitably, to the topic of insider trading. Takeover lawyer Martin Lipton brought up the subject. "I think it would be worth the commission's while to look at the trading in some of the more notorious takeovers of the past two years," he said. "Only the commission has the power to get at the facts behind this, but I think there are enough instances . . . that it is something that ought to be looked at very closely."

Levine piously agreed. "The other thing is, I don't think you should limit your analysis of that phenomenon to the corporations' activities," he said. He even recommended that the SEC look into trading in Nabisco and General Foods—both stocks in which he himself had traded heavily on inside information.

"We've got nothing to worry about," Levine crowed to Wilkis after the discussion. "The SEC loves me." Levine received a thank-you letter from the SEC signed by John Shad, a letter he proudly showed off to numerous colleagues and to Meier and Pletscher. He asked Wilkis, "Would they feature me like this if I was in trouble?"

Gary Lynch looked out over the low Washington rooftops from the expansive windows in his corner office. Christmas was just a week away, but his mind was far from family shopping. He sensed that something important was about to unfold in the Bank Leu investigation. Late the previous week, Lynch had gotten a curious phone call from Harvey Pitt, who had insisted on meeting with Lynch personally. Lynch knew Pitt was an SEC veteran; he had worked under him when Pitt was the agency's general counsel. He knew Pitt wouldn't insist on the presence of the SEC enforcement director unless he had something important to divulge.

On December 17, Pitt and Rauch arrived at Lynch's office at 10 A.M. Lynch had invited the SEC lawyers most involved in the matter: Sturc, Wang, Sonnenthal, and Paul Fischer. Lynch shook hands with the Fried, Frank delegation, then seated everyone around a conference table in the office.

"What's on your mind?" Lynch casually began.

Pitt opened a binder and began to speak from prepared notes. He began by briefly reviewing the status of his negotiations on behalf of Bank Leu. Then he dropped his bombshell.

"I can't stand by my factual representations to you," he said.

Fischer practically exploded. "What? Then we've wasted a lot of time. You made specific representations . . ."

Pitt let Fischer go on, then unveiled, as delicately as he could, what he had in mind. Speaking hypothetically, Pitt suggested that the SEC lawyers "assume" that the trading in the suspect stocks had been initiated not by Meier, as he had previously represented, but by a single client of the bank, someone he identified as a "status player" on Wall Street. He knew that would whet the SEC staff's curiosity. If that were the case, he asked, would the SEC agree to prosecute only the bank's client, and not the bank or any of its officers? And would the SEC consider such an agreement even if it emerged that some of the bank's officers had piggybacked the customer's trades, and may have destroyed evidence at the client's behest? If so, Pitt said the bank would seek the permission of Bahamian authorities to disclose the customer's identity. Rauch added that any such agreement would have to be contingent on the Justice Department similarly agreeing not to prosecute the bank or its officers under any criminal statutes.

Lynch asked Pitt and his colleagues to step outside the office while he conferred with his SEC colleagues. At first, Lynch needed some convincing; but the SEC wasn't eager to get into protracted litigation over Swiss and Bahamian secrecy laws. Similar ventures in other cases had turned into legal quagmires.

Ultimately, everyone agreed to Pitt's deal. They realized that the "status player" had to be an investment banker or a lawyer, someone at the heart of the inside action. This could be the pivotal case the staff had been hoping for, the start of a major crackdown.

After less than a half hour, the Fried, Frank lawyers were invited back to the table. Lynch said that he thought a satisfactory agreement could be worked out. He explained that he had some problems including Meier in any immunity agreement, but Pitt was adamant about protecting all the bank's officers, and Lynch relented.

Pitt considered the meeting a success. Pletscher and Meier had placed Bank Leu in grave danger. Ironically, Levine's orders to destroy evidence had robbed the bank—and Levine—of a defense. Without the risk of U.S. prosecution for obstruction of justice, the bank could simply have acknowledged that a single customer had initiated the trading and invoked Bahamian secrecy laws to protect the customer's identity. The bank would have done nothing wrong, and at the very least, the SEC would have been tied up for years in Bahamian courts trying to force disclosure of the customer's name. That was no longer a viable option because of the destruction of evidence and the bank's vulnerability to obstruction charges.

As the lawyers put their papers back into their briefcases, Wang and Fischer couldn't resist pressing Pitt to identify the bank's customer. They were beside themselves with curiosity. But Pitt wasn't about to play his trump card so soon.

"Don't worry, you're going to get a big fish," he assured them.

Suddenly Sturc spoke up. "For what you're asking, he damn well better be a whale—Moby Dick."

St. Andrews Plaza is a tiny plot of pavement tucked behind Manhattan's towering Municipal Building and the federal courthouse on Foley Square. When lawyers in New York speak of St. Andrews Plaza, however, they mean one thing: the U.S. attorney's office, which has long been viewed as the most prominent, prestigious, and powerful outpost of the Justice Department. This is, in part, because of the office's jurisdiction (it is responsible for federal cases filed in Manhattan, the Bronx, and parts of southern New York State) and its proximity to the nation's financial center on Wall Street. Historically, the plaza has played host to a vast majority of the most sophisticated and complex financial cases, as well as to New York's organized crime and drug-trafficking cases.

Over many years and different U.S. attorneys, the office developed a reputation for caution, quality work, and unshakable integrity. The means were as important as the ends, even if that meant some potentially good cases were never filed. Even the youngest assistant U.S. attorneys were held to high standards. Publicity was shunned. Rudolph Giuliani had inherited this tradition when he was named U.S. attorney in 1983. He had wasted no time in casting off much of it.

Not since Thomas E. Dewey in the 1930s had Manhattan seen a U.S. attorney like Giuliani, one who had already forged a prominent national reputation. As associate attorney general, the number-three official in the Reagan Justice Department, Giuliani had been one of the administration's most visible spokesmen, appearing tirelessly on news and talk shows to address crime and law enforcement issues. Voluble, energetic, and openly ambitious, he arrived in New York eager to put his own stamp on the office.

He confronted an office badly in need of rejuvenation. Under his immediate predecessor, John Martin, Jr., the office had been largely coasting on its reputation. Its caution bordered on paralysis. The office's prominence had faded. Giuliani immediately shifted office resources and personnel into two areas guaranteed to attract media coverage—organized crime and drugs—and soon scored major victories. These were trumpeted with Giuliani's characteristic fanfare; press conferences at St. Andrews Plaza became routine occurrences. Giuliani even went so far as to embark on an "undercover" drug-buying expedition in the Bronx. No arrests resulted, but Giuliani turned the foray into a photo opportunity, posing for cameras clad in a black leather jacket.

Press coverage was almost uniformly positive, bordering on fawning. Giuliani argued that the office's visibility played an important role in deterring crime. It was hard to argue with success, and his office scored a series of impressive convictions. Its reputation grew stronger.

Giuliani brought to the office what many perceived as a Catholic, even Jesuitical view of the world, one marked by clear divisions between right and wrong, friend and enemy. He seemed to equate crime with sin, punishment with penance, cooperation with repentance. And he showed a willingness to take risks. "I'm not in this job to do the safe thing," he said in 1986. "If you never try to accomplish anything, you never fail. I'd rather fail."

Assistant U.S. attorneys quickly adapted to the new regime, some more comfortably than others. Many were invigorated by Giuliani's approach. Others worried. Decisions were now invariably accompanied by discussions of how the press would react. References were made to the office's new "cowboy" spirit. Coming from traditionalists, the term was mildly derogatory, implying a tendency to shoot first and ask questions later.

The fraud unit mirrored the changes in the office. The chief of the unit was Peter Romatowski, the prosecutor who had tried the Winans case, but Romatowski had already announced his resignation. His successor was a gruff, plain-speaking, overweight prosecutor named Charles Carberry.

Everyone in the office liked Carberry. He was smart, funny, and self-deprecating. His low-key professional approach and unquestioned integrity appealed to traditionalists. Like Giuliani, he was a product of Catholic schooling, and his view of crime and punishment was in keeping with his new boss's attitude. Carberry had grown up in New York, dropped out of Colgate University, and eventually graduated from St. John's University in Queens. He edited the law review at Fordham Law School, but was rejected when he first applied to the U.S. attorney's office. He worked for a year at Skadden, Arps before being hired on his second try.

When he had first spoken to Lynch about the Bank Leu investigation, after Meier was subpoenaed, Carberry hadn't been all that interested. Insider trading was not high on Giuliani's list of priorities. Indeed, the size of the securities fraud unit had actually shrunk as Giuliani shifted assistants into organized crime prosecutions. Carberry, by and large, had been disappointed by the fruits of the office's insider-trading cases. In a case involving a Morgan Stanley investment banker, a court of appeals had ruled that an investment banker or other fiduciary who leaks confidential information to someone else who actually does the trading is guilty of insider trading, and this had been a big step forward. But most of their convictions had been of what Carberry deemed "rogue" employees, mostly low-level printers and secretaries at law firms and investment banks. Carberry had mastered the securities laws and the markets to a degree unrivaled in the U.S. attorney's office. He knew insider trading was rampant, but he thought enforcement was better left to the SEC.

The Bank Leu situation, however, had piqued his interest. This appeared to be a far more systematic breach of confidentiality, one that posed a more fundamental threat to the integrity of the market. Several weeks after meeting with the SEC, Harvey Pitt and his colleagues visited St. Andrews Plaza to discuss criminal aspects of the situation. Romatowski, Carberry, and the Bank Leu lawyers crowded into Romatowski's office—soon to be inherited by Carberry—a room dominated by an old oak desk that has been handed down for years from one head of the unit to his successor. The prosecutors listened to Pitt and the SEC lawyers, then discussed the case with each other.

The prosecutors didn't see many risks in giving the bank immunity, which was what Pitt wanted. They might be criticized, but they knew that without the bank's cooperation, it could take years to determine the identity of the key customer—if, indeed, they would ever find it out. They had rarely had the opportunity to penetrate to the heart of an insider-trading scheme so quickly. And they were convinced, from what Pitt had told them, that the case against the customer would be far more important than any possible case against the bank. Giuliani authorized them to negotiate a grant of immunity, as did Justice Department officials in Washington. Carberry told Pitt and Lynch to go ahead with their agreement.

Negotiating the agreement between the bank and the SEC took months. The SEC insisted on a clause voiding the agreement if the bank failed, for whatever reason, to identify its customer. Pitt argued that the bank should be required only to make a "good faith" effort, and shouldn't lose its immunity if ordered by Bahamas authorities not to disclose anything. The SEC ultimately prevailed.

Then the Diamond account trading records had to be reviewed and analyzed. Pitt had to be able to confirm the identity of Mr. X. After all, he knew the name was Dennis Levine, but he couldn't be certain that it was the same Dennis Levine who worked as an investment banker at Drexel. At Rauch's suggestion, Pitt's staff conducted an extensive search for background information or a photo that would help confirm the customer's identity, but came up with nothing conclusive. Pitt didn't want to contact Drexel, for fear of alerting the firm to the investigation. Finally his staff obtained a copy of an old Lehman Brothers Yearbook with a photo of Levine. Pitt had his staff put together a photo "lineup," including Levine's photo with a series of other head shots. Pitt took the photos to the Bahamas, and had each bank employee with any contact with Levine look at them. "Can you identify Mr. Diamond?" he asked. Without exception, they pointed to the photo of Levine.

The SEC also wanted deposition testimony from Meier to strengthen any future case or injunctive action against Mr. X. Shaken since his subpoena at the Waldorf and by the intensifying investigation, worried about his relationship with Campbell and his own trading, Meier had arranged a transfer back to Switzerland. He was living in a suburb of Zurich. Pressed by Pitt for a written promise to testify, Meier was nervous. He said he'd consulted a lawyer of his own.

By the end of February, it was clear to Pitt that Meier, feeling secure in far-off Switzerland, was stalling. He finally gave him an ultimatum. "Look," he said, "either you're in this deal or not. We are cutting a deal with or without you." Pitt reminded Meier that he was risking the loss of immunity. Meier remained evasive, but then had his lawyer call. Meier was backing out.

The Fried, Frank lawyers were initially dumbfounded. Why would Meier abandon the deal when he was being offered immunity for a day or two of testimony? The answer seemed to lie in the mysterious wire transfer of $5,000 to a Catskill bank he'd had Pletscher expunge from his account records. The money, it turned out, was paid to a carpenter in tiny Delhi, N.Y., who did work on some buildings owned by Kevin Barry. It appeared to link Meier to BCM, and the additional trading of Campbell and Barry—all matters that were not covered by Bank Leu's immunity grant, and which Meier had never disclosed to Pitt. Meier had never seemed fully to trust the American lawyers or the American judicial system in which they functioned.

Fortunately, Pletscher, now based in London, was lined up as a substitute. Lynch finally forced a conclusion of the negotiations, saying he wanted to "stop this fascination with the process" and get the deal done. The agreement was signed at 10 P.M. on March 19. It called for the bank records to be turned over shortly thereafter, and for Pletscher's testimony in two weeks.

Carberry and SEC lawyers Wang, Sonnenthal, and Fischer flew to London, where they met Pletscher at Fried, Frank's London office. Pletscher testified for two full days, and proved to be far more forthright than the evasive and secretive Meier probably would have been. He described in detail "Mr. Diamond" 's obsession with secrecy, the manner in which he opened his account, the creation of the Panamanian corporation, the trading that preceded takeover bids, the cash withdrawals, and the shredding of the incriminating documents. Pletscher, an accountant by training, proved to have a precise memory. Though he never revealed Mr. Diamond's true name, referring to him only as "Mr. X," Pletscher said he was an investment banker living in New York City. The SEC had what it wanted, and even Carberry was impressed by the rapid progress of the case.

Now all that remained was the revelation of Mr. X's identity. Pitt turned his attention to the Bahamian secrecy issue. Much as it might like to, Bank Leu couldn't simply turn over Levine's name. Levine had threatened to sue them if they ever took that course; the bank also risked prosecution by Bahamas authorities.

The Fried, Frank lawyers settled on a bold strategy: they would approach Bahamian attorney general Paul Adderly directly, avoiding the publicity and delays of seeking a court order. On May 7, a delegation from the SEC and the the Justice Department, along with the U.S. ambassador to the Bahamas, and Pitt, Rauch, and their Bahamian lawyers arrived for an audience. Adderly seemed impressed by the presence of high-level representatives of the U.S. government, but angered Pitt by excluding him and Rauch from the proceedings.

Nonetheless, the approach they'd agreed upon seemed to make an impression. Lynch argued that the disclosure of securities trading records was not technically a revelation of "banking transactions" within the meaning of the Bahamian secrecy statute. The argument distinguishing stocks from other deposits and withdrawals seemed somewhat tortuous, but it had the crucial backing of Bank Leu itself. The attorney general indicated his tentative agreement. "This isn't banking, it's brokerage," he said, and Lynch eagerly agreed.

Two days later, Pitt received a copy of a letter containing the attorney general's opinion that to divulge the identity of the bank's customer would not risk prosecution by Bahamas authorities. Bank Leu's directors met and passed a resolution authorizing the disclosure.

The pieces were now all in place. On Friday, May 9, 1986, Pitt picked up the phone and called Lynch, who got on the phone immediately. Pitt didn't waste time with any preliminaries.

"Moby Dick," he said, "is Dennis B. Levine."

On Friday, May 9, 1986, just hours after his name passed from Pitt to Lynch, Levine arrived at the Gulf + Western tower in Manhattan for a gala buffet dinner and preview screening of the new Paramount production *Top Gun,* starring Tom Cruise. He had been invited because he'd helped represent Esquire Inc. in its acquisition by Gulf + Western. (Indeed, he'd traded on inside information in that deal.)

Ordinarily, this was the kind of glamorous event Levine loved, an exclusive gathering that underscored his own access to the rich and powerful and gave him the opportunity to schmooze with a corporate chieftain like Martin Davis. This evening, however, Levine was preoccupied with his increasingly troublesome dealings with Bank Leu. The day before, he'd phoned Pletscher, who had not taken his call; he'd been handed over to a lower-level employee, Andrew Sweeting.

"I want to transfer $10 million of my account to a bank in the Cayman Islands," Levine said.

Sweeting rambled, saying he really wasn't sure about the procedures for such a large transfer. Levine, irritated, said he'd have his Bahamian lawyer contact him with instructions. When Levine called

again with the instructions, Sweeting insisted on having them in writing. That was it. Levine decided he had had it with Bank Leu. He
vowed to get the written withdrawal order to the bank first thing
Monday, and stop dealing with the increasingly uncooperative Swiss
bankers.

Levine's request hadn't taken the Fried, Frank lawyers or the
bank entirely by surprise. When Levine's call was transferred to Sweeting, Pitt and Rauch were standing right behind the young banker.
They'd given him orders to stall if Levine tried to withdraw any money.

For months now, it had been obvious that Levine was becoming
apprehensive over the continuation of the SEC investigation and the
failure of his bankers at Bank Leu to derail the inquiry. He had also
been telling Pletscher about a new scheme he had hatched, what
Levine called his "genius plan." Pletscher hadn't quite followed the
details, but Levine's creation seemed to resemble a mutual fund. Levine would raise money, divide it into numerous accounts managed by
a Swiss banker, then have all the accounts trade on inside information
he furnished. The "genius" of the plan, Levine asserted, was that it
would provide the multiple accounts necessary to convince the SEC
that the trading was being orchestrated by a bank employee who was
a shrewd stock picker, rather than an insider trader. Lately, Levine had
also been strongly hinting that the "genius plan" might have to be
executed at a bank other than Bank Leu.

Now, almost with a sixth sense, Levine had decided to take his
money just as the government investigation was about to come to a
climax. With the revelation of Mr. X's identity, and the news that
Levine was trying to withdraw his money, Lynch knew that he and the
U.S. attorney's office had no time to waste. They couldn't let the $10
million out of the Bahamas, or they might lose it forever.

Lynch called Carberry, who in turn roused Thomas Doonan, an
investigator and special deputy U.S. marshal assigned to the fraud
unit. Doonan, in his late 40s, looks like an amateur boxer. Seven of his
relatives work in law enforcement. He and the lawyers worked around
the clock over the weekend, drafting civil injunction petitions to freeze
Levine's assets, preparing an arrest warrant. For simplicity, the warrant focused on obstruction of justice only, since the government had
the strong testimony of Pletscher providing probable cause for an
arrest. The lawyers briefed Doonan, who in turn signed a sworn affidavit setting out the facts in the case.

On Monday, May 12, Levine's written demand to transfer the $10
million arrived at Bank Leu, and the SEC promptly filed injunction
papers. The bank retained the money. Carberry and Doonan went
before a federal magistrate, who signed the arrest warrant. Doonan,

accompanied by Augie Kaufman, a six-foot eight-inch federal marshal, immediately left in search of Levine.

The pair went first to the Levine apartment on Park Avenue. Laurie answered the door, turning pale when Doonan identified himself and Kaufman as representatives of the Department of Justice. Levine had already left for the day, his wife said, but she promised to reach him and have him contact the U.S. attorney's office.

Quickly, the men left for Drexel's offices downtown, but Levine wasn't there either. He was, the marshals were told, meeting with Drexel client Ronald Perelman at Perelman's town house offices in midtown. But Perelman's office said Levine hadn't shown up for the meeting. Doonan returned to St. Andrews Plaza. Perhaps Levine's wife had warned him. Levine's name was immediately fed into computerized lists maintained by U.S. Customs. Should he try to flee the country, he would be restrained.

Events now moved at a fast pace. At 2 P.M., Lynch placed a courtesy call to Fred Joseph, whose secretary told him the SEC enforcement chief was on the line and it was urgent. Joseph listened in silence for about 10 minutes as Lynch revealed that, in the SEC's view, Levine had traded massively on inside information stolen from Drexel and others. Levine had apparently assembled a ring and bought information from other investment bankers, Lynch said. The SEC would be filing its charges and a request for an injunction momentarily, Lynch continued, adding that criminal charges were likely to follow as soon as Levine was apprehended.

Joseph was stunned. "Gary, it sounds like you've got him," he said. "If he did it, it's awful. What can I do? We'll cooperate totally."

At Lynch's request, Joseph ordered Levine's office, desk, and files sealed. Joseph immediately called Kay. "They're about to arrest Dennis," he told Levine's stunned mentor. Kay called Perelman's office, and also learned that Levine had never shown up for the meeting. John Shad, the SEC chairman, called Joseph soon thereafter.

"I'm sorry it's your guy," Shad said.

"Don't apologize," Joseph replied. "This is your job. We've often speculated that something like this could be going on and no one would ever detect it."

And then the news broke. At precisely 2:46 P.M., bells rang and tickers clattered into action in brokerage firms, trading floors, and newsrooms across America, as the headline appeared.

Levine surfaced briefly later that afternoon, calling Kay from a pay phone. He had to shout to be heard over the traffic.

"Dennis, they're looking for you," Kay said, his mind racing with questions.

"I know, I know," Levine shouted. "It's all a big misunderstanding. They're trying to fuck me over, ruin me. I haven't had any chance to explain. I haven't done a thing wrong."

"Dennis, shut up, stop talking," Kay advised. "You've got to get a lawyer."

"Who?" Levine shouted. Pitt was obviously out of the question.

Kay ticked off the names of Flom, Lipton, and Arthur Liman (of Paul, Weiss, Rifkind, Wharton & Garrison), whom he knew from takeover circles. As soon as Levine hung up, Kay called Joseph. "Dennis says it's all a misunderstanding," he said.

"He's full of shit," Joseph replied.

Doonan and Carberry were still in their offices about 5:30 that evening when Doonan's phone rang.

"Uh, this is Dennis Levine. I believe you're looking for me, and I think it would be a good idea if we met," Levine said, sounding remarkably unruffled given the magnitude of his plight. "I gather you have a subpoena for me, or something," Levine added.

Doonan urged Levine to meet him at St. Andrews Plaza as soon as possible. Despite the announcement of the SEC action, Levine had planned to attend a charity ball to benefit Mt. Sinai Hospital that evening, but agreed he'd stop by the U.S. attorney's office.

Levine drove down alone, in the BMW rather than in the even more conspicuous Testarossa, and parked the car on the nearly deserted street outside the office. At 7:30 P.M. he signed his name at the entrance.

Doonan met him at the sixth-floor reception area and escorted him to Carberry, who was seated behind the large desk in his office. Peter Sonnenthal, the SEC lawyer, had come up from Washington, and stood nearby. In contrast to the typically rumpled attire worn by Carberry, Doonan, and Sonnenthal, Levine was dressed in a stylish dark European suit, a yellow Hermès tie, and black Gucci loafers. He smiled ingratiatingly and tried to shake hands with Carberry as though he were being introduced to a prospective client.

Doonan quickly cut him off. "I have a warrant for your arrest," he said. "Mr. Levine, you're under arrest."

"You have the right to remain silent," Carberry began as Levine, stunned, turned ashen. Doonan ordered him to lean forward and put both hands flat on Carberry's desk, and Levine obeyed mechanically. Doonan frisked him, and told him to empty his pockets. Then Carberry displayed a few Bank Leu documents on the desk containing Levine's signature, and motioned for Levine to look at them. Levine saw then that, contrary to his instructions, Meier and Pletscher had not destroyed all the documents connecting him to the account.

"Do you want to cooperate?" Carberry asked. Levine said he wanted to talk to his lawyers. Doonan took him to the phone in the reception area and stood by as Levine called Arthur Liman, whom he had retained after talking with Kay earlier that day. Levine knew Liman from the Revlon deal, on which Liman had represented Revlon.

At one point the dazed Levine turned to Doonan while holding the receiver. "What's going on?" Levine asked. "What's happening to me?"

"You're under arrest," Doonan said again.

"I'm under arrest, for God's sake," Levine repeated into the phone.

As soon as Levine hung up, Liman called Carberry, asking him to release Levine for the night. Carberry refused, explaining that Levine could request bail at his arraignment the next day. Carberry was taking no chances. Arrests of prominent businessmen accused of white-collar crimes were often genteel affairs, with the accused agreeing to surrender at a convenient time and immediately posting bail. Carberry felt that white-collar criminals were too often coddled, however, in conspicuous contrast to the treatment meted out to less affluent defendants accused of more mundane offenses. And he felt there was real danger that Levine might flee.

It was nearly midnight when Doonan completed the processing and led Levine to the Metropolitan Correction Center, the federal prison adjacent to the U.S. courthouse on Foley Square.

Levine's main concern seemed to be his BMW. He told Doonan he was worried about leaving the car on the street overnight. Doonan obligingly took the keys and moved the car into the nearby municipal garage. He'd never driven such an expensive car.

At the MCC, Doonan signed a form promising to pick up Levine at 9 the next morning. Levine was led away and placed in a holding pen, where his cellmates for the night were two accused drug dealers. The next morning Levine looked tired and drawn, and Doonan wasn't surprised. In his experience, few people slept during their first night in the MCC.

Wilkis had buried all his worries about Levine by concentrating on his work at E. F. Hutton. He'd handled some relatively small deals of his own, and the head of the M&A department, Daniel Good, had all but promised Wilkis that he'd be made a managing director when he came up for consideration that year. Even so, following Levine's lead, Wilkis was leveraging his success. He'd contacted a headhunter, who was negotiating offers with two other investment banks, both at the managing director level. Wall Street was hungry for investment bankers with Wilkis's experience.

When the news of Levine's arrest broke on May 12, Wilkis was in a cab heading toward La Guardia airport for a flight to Omaha. When he got to the airport, he phoned the headhunter. Like everyone else on Wall Street that afternoon, the headhunter could talk of nothing but Dennis Levine.

"There may be an opening at Drexel," the headhunter said excitedly.

Wilkis was stunned, even though it was an event he had envisioned in his mind many times. He flew on to Omaha, but couldn't get over his sense of panic, and couldn't concentrate. That evening he phoned his wife, Elsa, who told him she'd seen Levine that afternoon. He'd picked up his son at the Episcopal School, an exclusive private school in Manhattan also attended by Wilkis's son. Levine had been glad-handing, working the crowd of mothers picking up their children, claiming "I've been framed." He almost seemed to be enjoying his sudden notoriety, Elsa said. It was more than Wilkis could take. Didn't Levine realize that their lives were at stake? He felt he had to get back and talk to him.

Pleading illness, Wilkis left Omaha and flew back to New York the next day. He immediately phoned Levine, who had been arraigned, pleaded not guilty, and posted $5 million in bail that morning. He had put up $100,000 in cash and pledged his apartment and shares in Drexel.

"You'd better come right over," Levine said.

Wilkis took a cab over to Levine's apartment. Laurie answered the door, looking as though she hadn't slept, her eyes red and swollen from crying. In contrast, Levine was casually dressed in athletic clothes and seemed cheerful, even excited.

"Jesus, Bob, can you imagine? They threw me in jail. Christ, I had notes and my phone book with Ivan Boesky's name all over it! I had nine hundred bucks in my pocket." But Levine was already hatching a plan.

"You'll get a lawyer in the Cayman Islands to claim he owns the account," Levine began, but Wilkis wasn't paying attention.

"It's too late, Dennis," he pleaded. "Don't you realize this? It's over."

Wilkis spent a tortured week, unable to sleep, unable to concentrate at work, not eating. He told his wife nothing about his own involvement, but she knew how close he was to Levine. She insisted he contact a lawyer, and Wilkis called a cousin at one of Baltimore's leading firms, Piper & Marbury. He didn't tell the whole truth, admitting only that he had had vague "dealings" with Levine that worried him. The cousin arranged for him to see a lawyer in New York on Tuesday.

Meanwhile, against his better judgment, Wilkis agreed to meet Levine again on Monday. To make sure they weren't bugged, they met at the garage on West 56th Street where Wilkis kept his car. They got in the car and drove aimlessly. Wilkis was so petrified that he'd be stopped by police that he barely drove 15 miles per hour.

"You look terrible," Levine began cheerfully. "Here I'm the one who's been in jail and you're the one who looks bad. None of this matters," he continued. "It doesn't matter as long as you're famous." He was impressed that *The Wall Street Journal* had run a front-page story on him, complete with an artist's drawing, the previous Thursday. He told Wilkis to pull over to the curb by a corner newsstand, and hopped out of the car.

"I hear I'm on the cover of *Newsweek*," he said, and moments later returned brandishing the latest issue. But he was disappointed. He was featured in the cover story, headlined "Greed on Wall Street," but the illustration showed hands grabbing at a pile of money—not Levine. Levine's picture was deep inside the magazine.

"I'm ready to turn myself in," Wilkis said once Levine had finished with the magazine. "What do they know?"

"I don't know," Levine said.

"Has my name come up?"

Levine again said he had no idea, adding, "Don't get a lawyer. I've got the greatest lawyers in the world and we're going to fight it. I'm sealed up like a tomb." Levine continued, "If I talked, the Russian would put a bullet through my head. Now you, you couldn't handle this. You'd snap. But not me. I'm a stand-up kind of guy."

Then Levine unveiled a new plan. Levine would confess, and implicate Wilkis as a source of some of the information. But he'd conceal the fact that Wilkis traded on inside information in his own foreign bank account. "We'll go to jail. It will be one of those country-club prisons. We'll be roommates, we'll play tennis, and get a tan. Then we'll retire to the Cayman Islands, and live off of your money," Levine said.

"Dennis, where does this lead?" Wilkis asked in despair.

The next day, Wilkis broke down with the lawyer recommended by his cousin, confessing his crimes. "I don't want to fight," Wilkis said. The lawyer promptly referred him to a criminal lawyer, Gary Naftalis, a former assistant U.S. attorney and a partner at the New York firm Kramer, Levin, Nessen, Kamin & Frankel. Wilkis told Naftalis the whole story, sobbing periodically, including details of his own account and his recruitment of Randall Cecola. Naftalis sternly ordered Wilkis never to talk to either Levine or Cecola again.

After so many years, however, Levine's hold couldn't be so easily broken. When Levine called soon after, Wilkis took the call, though he tried to resist.

"Dennis, it's not good to talk," he said, but Levine pressed on with more plans for their eventual escape to the Cayman Islands. Wilkis cut him off.

"The newspapers are focusing on the cover-up. They're acting like that's worse than the trading. I won't get involved. I'm never going to talk to you again."

Levine seemed stunned and hurt by Wilkis's reaction. "Oh Bob," he said, "you mean after everything we've been through, this is it?"

Yet Wilkis called Levine on Memorial Day, and again the following Friday, telling him he just wanted to see how he was doing.

"I'm holding up," Levine said, but his spirits seemed to be waning. He seemed near despair, asking Wilkis to take care of his wife if he went to prison. He was especially emotional on Friday.

"I love you like a brother," he told Wilkis repeatedly. "I'll be ruined financially," he continued. "I don't give a fuck about the business. I've done all the big deals, fuck them. But I'm ruined. I won't see my son's bar mitzvah." For the first time in his contacts with Wilkis, Levine seemed near tears.

Wilkis told Naftalis nothing of his exchanges with Levine, nor of another phone call. Two days after Levine's arrest, Wilkis had heard from Cecola, the Lazard associate he'd recruited into the ring. "Do we have anything to worry about?" an anxious Cecola wanted to know.

"I do," Wilkis replied. "My life is probably over. But I'll protect you." Cecola said he was going to be in New York soon, since he'd be working that summer at Dillon, Read; Wilkis promised they'd get together.

Cecola arrived on June 4. Wilkis attended what was supposed to be a festive dinner for Hutton's M&A department, but couldn't eat. Already thin from jogging, he'd lost 15 pounds since Levine's arrest, and he looked emaciated. He'd begun seeing a therapist. As soon as he could get away, he left and took a cab to a restaurant at 77th Street and Broadway, where he met Cecola. The two walked east into Central Park, where they'd be shielded by the darkness.

"Do I have to worry?" Cecola asked anxiously.

"Dennis Levine knows who you are," Wilkis said ominously.

"But they can't prove anything, can they?" Cecola asked. "You'll cover for me, won't you?"

"Randy, my life is over," Wilkis said wearily. "I hope you don't get involved in this, but I won't lie. I can't commit perjury."

Cecola paused. "You could position the truth," he said.

"Randy, it wouldn't do any good. Levine knows all about you."

"Look," Cecola said, "if you deny what he says, and I do, it's two against one."

"I'm sorry, I won't lie," Wilkis insisted. The two trudged in despair out of the park.

The next day was the last day of classes at The Brearley School, and Wilkis's daughter Alexandra, an exceptionally talented young pianist, was being honored at an assembly. When he arrived at the auditorium, Wilkis realized suddenly that he couldn't take his place among the other parents. Instead, he stood at the back. As the program began, he began to cry. Through his tears he could see his daughter, glowing with excitement at the school year's end, a picture of innocence. Now he was going to ruin her young life. He fled from the room.

Ilan Reich's phone had rung at about 5 P.M. on May 12. "Have you heard about Dennis?" a friend of his at Goldman, Sachs asked breathlessly. "He's been charged with insider trading. It's on the tape."

Reich was stunned. He had been expecting to see Levine that very evening at the Mt. Sinai benefit. He hung up, then dialed the firm's library, asking for a copy of the ticker item. In a taxi on the way home that evening, he began to reconstruct the dealings with Levine he'd tried so hard to repress. He didn't panic; the events all seemed too remote. And he took comfort from the fact that he'd never taken any money.

But now anxiety was building. Each night, he ran out to get *The New York Times* at 10 P.M., as soon as the earliest edition arrived at his newsstand. He was up early in the morning to buy *The Wall Street Journal*, scanning for any hint that the investigation was widening. He had no contact with Levine.

Several days later, Reich flew to Los Angeles for a client meeting, and the tension and anxiety reached the breaking point. He began to fantasize about his detection and public disgrace. All of his old anxieties and insecurities were rekindled, threatening to overwhelm him. Hardly conscious of what he was going to do, he rented a car and began driving aimlessly around Los Angeles, finally ending up on a winding cliffside road high above the Pacific Ocean. Reich came quickly around a turn, accelerated, then aimed the car toward the edge of the cliff.

Only at the last moment did thoughts of his family save him from suicide. He braked, turned sharply back onto the road, and stopped.

He slumped over the wheel, gulping. Somehow, he vowed, he'd fight his way out of this.

When he heard the news of Levine's arrest, Sokolow rushed to meet David Brown, the Goldman, Sachs investment banker he'd recruited into the scheme, at Brown's apartment. Sokolow had taken $125,000 in cash payoffs from Levine, a tiny fraction of the millions in profits his tips had generated. Of that, Sokolow had paid Brown $27,500. Panicked, the two young men took what was left of the cash they'd received from Levine, ripped it into small pieces, and flushed it down the toilet.

Once Siegel recovered from the shock of learning that the SEC had charged Levine rather than him with insider trading, he left the phone booth at National Airport and boarded a shuttle flight for New York. After he was back in his Kidder, Peabody office, he returned a phone call from Bob Freeman at Goldman, Sachs.

"He's obviously in a ring," Freeman said of Levine. "Who do you think's in it?"

They speculated about various possibilities, and then Siegel dared broach the unthinkable: "You don't think he talked to Boesky, do you?"

"Oh no, not a chance," Freeman said firmly. "Ivan Boesky would never talk to a Dennis Levine."

Late on the afternoon of Levine's arrest, not long after Boesky told his employees that he'd never heard of Levine, Mulheren called him.

"What's the definition of an arb?" Mulheren asked.

Boesky said nothing, and Mulheren plunged ahead with the punch line.

"Someone who's never seen, heard of, or talked to Dennis Levine!"

Mulheren burst into laughter. On Boesky's end, there was silence.

10.

By no means was Dennis Levine's $10 million nest egg safely under government control. The restraining order freezing his assets, obtained on May 12, was temporary. The SEC also had to obtain a preliminary injunction at a federal court hearing less than two weeks later, demonstrating that it had a real case against Levine. The freeze gave the SEC its principal leverage with Levine, handicaping his efforts to lead a normal life and even making it difficult for him to pay his lawyers' fees. His lawyers at Paul, Weiss promptly attacked the freeze, gaining the right for Levine to have access to a $300,000 account at Citibank for personal expenses and legal fees. Martin Flumenbaum, a Paul, Weiss partner working with Liman and known for his tenacious, combative style, told the court that "the government has no prima facie case, the government will not be able to make its showing, the government will not be able to come up with its proof on this in this court on Thursday."

Flumenbaum's challenge spurred the SEC lawyers. They worked frantically before the hearing, obtaining depositions and affidavits from Levine's former employers at Smith Barney, Lehman Brothers, and Drexel, establishing that Levine did have access to confidential information. They gathered and analyzed the Bank Leu trading records and even retained a handwriting expert, who confirmed that the handwriting on Levine's Smith Barney job application matched that on the Bank Leu withdrawal slips.

SEC lawyers tried to question Levine, both in person and in writing, but his lawyers instructed him to invoke the Fifth Amendment and refuse to answer on grounds that it might incriminate him. Levine defied a court order to produce an account of his finances, including the total of $1.9 million in cash he'd withdrawn from the Bank Leu account over the years. The SEC subpoenaed Levine's wife, his father, and his brother, who had allegedly accompanied him on some of the trips to the Bahamas. Curiously, the Levine family members also invoked the Fifth Amendment. Philip Levine even took the Fifth Amendment when asked his wife's maiden name—which turned out to be Diamond, Levine's alias at Bank Leu. The SEC staff wondered what the family members had to hide.

On May 21, the day before the preliminary injunction hearing, Lynch received his first call from Arthur Liman, asking for a 10-day postponement and hinting at a willingness to begin some kind of settlement talks. Lynch bluntly refused. Liman seemed taken aback. Given his reputation as one of the country's premier trial lawyers, he evidently expected a certain deference.

"I don't see why not," Liman retorted sharply. "This should be a no-brainer for you."

Lynch felt his ire rising. He'd never met Liman, but this approach was patronizing and insulting.

"I'll do what's appropriate," Lynch said icily. To make matters worse, Lynch soon received a call from Ira Sorkin, the SEC's New York regional enforcement director, who was an acquaintance of Liman. "Liman's upset," Sorkin said, as though that were Lynch's fault. "He doesn't know you." Lynch was enraged that Liman would try to pressure him through Sorkin.

"Stay out of this," Lynch ordered. He had no intention of giving Levine any extensions. He wanted to keep the pressure on.

The showdown came in New York federal court on Thursday, May 22. Lynch stayed in Washington, and his deputy John Sturc argued the case. It was a crucial hearing; if a judge lifted Levine's asset freeze, he could easily finance a prolonged legal battle. He also might flee.

Sturc, in the most important argument of his career, painstakingly summarized the government's case, detailing in nine instances the pattern of Levine's insider trading. Liman, complaining about the "storm in the press which in my experience is unparalleled almost since Son of Sam," offered little evidence beyond old information about the companies Levine traded in. Much of it came from the same documents Levine had cooked up for the Bank Leu cover-up.

"There was literally an inundation of information about these companies," Liman insisted. Levine remained silent.

Federal Judge Richard Owen made short shrift of Liman's arguments. "It is quite clear," he said, "that being at the shoulder of people who are making the decisions is a vastly different story than being in a position to read 13-Ds or *The Wall Street Journal.*" He upheld the freeze of Levine's assets. The SEC had won its first major battle.

Liman called Carberry the next day, saying he wanted to meet in his office on Saturday, a time when the visit wouldn't be conspicuous. Carberry wasn't surprised. He assumed Liman would be trying to cut a deal, a plea bargain. Carberry thought that Levine was "dead" on possible tax evasion and perjury charges, not to mention insider trading.

Liman and Flumenbaum arrived on Saturday and met Carberry on the sixth floor. Despite Levine's boasts to Wilkis, Liman said Levine was prepared to plead if a deal could be worked out. He said Levine had information worth negotiating for: the identities of four other young investment bankers who participated directly in the insider-trading ring, as well as one other person "who's bigger," he said.

Carberry wasn't surprised. The trading patterns indicated that Levine must have had sources at other investment banks. *The Wall Street Journal* had published an analysis of Levine's deals, revealing a preponderance of transactions involving Lazard Frères and Goldman, Sachs. Carberry even thought he knew the name of one of the conspirators. He had gotten a call from Lawrence Pedowitz, a Wachtell partner who was a former head of the criminal division, who said he was representing Lazard Frères.

"We had a guy here named Robert Wilkis," Pedowitz said. "He was a close friend of Dennis Levine's. Dennis called him all the time. If there's a leak, he may be it."

Liman indicated that the four conspirators would be relatively straightforward cases involving direct tipping and sharing of profits, although Levine did not know the name of one of them. The lawyer also indicated that while the identity of the "bigger fish" would be immensely valuable to the government, he couldn't promise that Levine's testimony would result in his conviction.

Carberry was typically expressionless, displaying no great curiosity about the fifth man. And he wasn't interested in bargaining, preferring to lay his cards out on the table. He offered the Paul, Weiss lawyers a guilty plea of four felonies: one securities fraud count of insider trading, one perjury count, and two counts of tax evasion. In return, he expected full cooperation. He felt he was giving up almost nothing. With four felonies, the maximum jail term would be 20 years. Even if this was the largest insider-trading case ever, no one had ever been sentenced to as much as 20 years, no matter how many counts were involved. Cooperation would be in Levine's interest; it would be his main argument for leniency at sentencing.

After little more than an hour, Carberry and Liman had an agreement in principle. They went up to Giuliani's office, and Liman made what Carberry deemed a "hazy" proffer: the names of Levine's immediate co-conspirators and "an arbitrageur of some substance."

They all shook hands on the agreement. But Liman wouldn't name names yet, nor actually provide Levine's cooperation, until he was sure Levine also had an agreement with the SEC. The moment Carberry heard that the bigger fish was a prominent arbitrageur, however, he had a pretty good idea of his identity: the name of Ivan Boesky was prominent in the pages of Levine's pocket calendar.

An SEC agreement soon followed. In a series of phone calls and meetings, mostly between Flumenbaum and Sturc, who had been law school classmates, the SEC demanded most of Levine's assets. They agreed he could keep the Park Avenue co-op, the BMW but not the Ferrari, and, after considerable argument, the Citibank account. Levine had been adamant that he still had to have some "walking-around money." Most of that, the SEC lawyers assumed, would go for legal fees. The SEC agreement was contingent on Levine's cooperation with the U.S. attorney. Lynch expected the four members of the ring, but not much else; references to a more important person were still vague allusions.

Now all that remained was for Levine to deliver on his part of the bargain. When he arrived at St. Andrews Plaza with Flumenbaum, he was greeted by the government team: Robert Paschall, a postal inspector assigned to the case, Carberry and Doonan from the U.S. attorney's office, and Sonnenthal and Wang representing the SEC.

Carberry, instead of intimidating Levine, tried to make him feel like a member of the government team. He maintained a certain formality, always calling him "Mr. Levine" and emphasizing that he was trying to help Levine now. If he told the complete truth, Carberry said, it would impress the judge at his sentencing.

Carberry began the questioning by asking about Wilkis, and Levine seemed to hold nothing back, beginning with their first meeting at Citibank. Carberry was pleased that Levine made no attempt to minimize his own guilt: he freely admitted that he had been the one who lured Wilkis into the scheme, and said he'd also recruited Sokolow and Reich. He had a "sixth sense," Levine said, for knowing who would cooperate. Carberry was also impressed that Levine volunteered that Reich had refused his offers of money, and had dropped out of the scheme after he became a partner in the firm. Carberry didn't want a witness so eager to please the prosecutors that he'd exaggerate the culpability of others.

Levine told them about Cecola, noting that he'd gone "crazy" when he learned that Cecola had also opened an account at Bank Leu. He told the lawyers about the nighttime sweeps through Lazard Frères, and his and Wilkis's efforts to plant stories with the *Chicago Tribune* and *The New York Times.* Levine said he knew Sokolow had recruited a source at Goldman, Sachs—"Goldie"—someone who didn't work directly in M&A but in mortgages, he thought. Levine had never learned his name.

Then Carberry steered the interrogation to the unnamed arbitrageur, and Levine quickly confirmed their suspicions. He said he'd begun by mailing Ivan Boesky confidential documents on Boise Cascade and Elf Aquitaine, partly to try to push up the stock price, and partly to impress Boesky. Then he followed up with a phone call, openly offering a tip, and inviting Boesky for a drink, over which they worked out their tipping and compensation arrangement. Levine said he had been desperate to get to know Boesky both for the cachet and for the information.

Levine's lawyers had been careful not to overpromise with respect to the evidence Levine could give on Boesky. They never claimed it would be an easy case, or that Levine's evidence alone would produce a conviction. Carberry was impressed by Levine's apparent candor, however. The compensation agreement with Boesky, involving shifting percentages depending on the timing and effect of the information Levine passed, was too detailed for Levine to have fabricated it. It had inherent credibility, especially if Levine's tips could be matched with Boesky's trading records.

Carberry usually didn't concern himself with motives, but he couldn't resist asking Levine why he'd done what he did. Levine gave the same answer he'd often given Wilkis: that he wanted to start his own firm, to be an arbitrageur or merchant banker, hiring the "professionals" to serve him rather than being one himself. He'd wanted $20 million, he told the government lawyers; he'd intended to quit once he got it.

Levine also said that he, like Wilkis, Reich, and Sokolow, was bored with his work as an investment banker. This made an impression on the lawyers, who, like most everyone else at the time, had come to believe that investment bankers led glamorous, rich, exciting lives. The reality, Levine said, was far different. By contrast, insider trading was thrilling. Carberry doubted that Levine would ever have stopped, no matter how many millions he had earned. Once he'd reached $20 million he would have raised the ante to $30 million, then $40 million. There would never have been enough.

Levine's need for excitement and adventure, Carberry realized, made him a good candidate for undercover work. Despite his claims to Wilkis that he'd never cooperate, Levine seemed eager to help the government ensnare his fellow conspirators. Before they could begin, however, there was a brief period of anxiety after Carberry received a written death threat against Levine. This was more excitement than

Levine had bargained for, and he had to be whisked into the country-side under federal protection. The threat was quickly traced to a known crank. Levine returned to the city and agreed to place phone calls to Wilkis, Reich, Sokolow, and Boesky, and to have the conversations secretly recorded.

On Monday evening, June 2, just a few days after the conversation in which Levine had told Wilkis he "loved him like a brother," Wilkis got a call from Levine.

"Bob, you should cooperate," Levine began, and Wilkis knew immediately from Levine's voice that something had changed. "I know we're fighters," Levine continued. "But they know everything. Tell your lawyers to come in."

Wilkis was sure the conversation was being taped, and knew he should hang up and call his lawyer immediately. Yet he couldn't. He realized that on some level he still thought Levine would protect him, get him out of this mess unscathed. He talked and incriminated himself.

Levine didn't fare as well in his other calls. He called Boesky twice. The first time, Boesky sounded concerned but acknowledged nothing. "I'm sorry for your family," Boesky said. "I'm worried about your mental health. Remember, all things will pass." At the second call, Boesky hung up when Levine identified himself, saying they had no reason to be talking. Sokolow and Reich also hung up almost immediately. But the calls served a purpose; they put the suspects on notice that their identities were probably known to the government.

The very next day a lawyer for Sokolow called and began negotiating a plea. So, too, did a lawyer for David Brown, the Goldman, Sachs investment banker. Sokolow quickly confirmed that Brown, a close friend of his from Wharton business school, was "Goldie," the source he'd recruited at Goldman, Sachs. Each agreed to plead guilty to two felonies and pay substantial penalties to the SEC. Sokolow was later sentenced to a year and a day in prison; Brown was sentenced to 30 days.

Several days later, Wilkis was at home, still agonizing, when his apartment buzzer rang. "Mr. Randy is here to see you," the doorman announced. Wilkis knew it was Cecola and, despite his lawyer's advice, he went down to meet him. The two walked into Riverside Park. Cecola seemed overwrought.

"Randy, you should get a lawyer," Wilkis said, remembering with some bitterness how Levine had given him the opposite advice.

"There's something I never told you," Cecola said, obviously upset, "something about my girlfriend."

"Don't tell me," Wilkis insisted. "I don't want to hear." Cecola stopped. "You've got to be careful about what you say," Wilkis said. "They're taping conversations. The next time I call you on the phone, they may be taping."

"I'm going to Alan MacFarland at Lazard," Cecola continued. (MacFarland was a senior partner at the firm.) "I'm going to tell him I just went innocently to you for help on deals," he said, then paused to gauge Wilkis's reaction. "I'm not going to paint you in the best light."

Wilkis felt crushed, abandoned. "Do what you think you have to do," he said. "I'm dead anyway."

On June 5, with the government lawyers satisfied he'd given them all he could, Levine appeared in federal court and entered a plea of guilty to the four felony counts. The courtroom was packed with reporters, and television crews lined the stairs outside. Wearing a dark suit, Levine seemed calm and slightly thinner. He showed no emotion as he read a statement prepared by his lawyers.

"To contest the charges against me on technical grounds would serve only to prolong the suffering of my family. It would also convey the wrong message. I have violated the law and I have remorse for my conduct, not excuses." Levine's SEC agreement was made public; he agreed to disgorge $11.6 million, leaving him little more than his apartment and car, he claimed, and was permanently barred from the securities industry.

Wilkis was at his office at E. F. Hutton when he saw the news of Levine's plea. It seemed like his death knell, confirming his worst fears that Levine had turned against him. He rushed to Naftalis's office, begging the lawyer to work out a deal with the government. But Wilkis's procrastination had cost him what little leverage he might once have had. With the Levine deal in place, Wilkis had little to offer the government. Even though he considered himself far less culpable than Levine, Wilkis was given a take-it-or-leave-it plea offer of four felonies, the same as Levine. Naftalis told him he had little choice but to accept it, then try to impress the government with the level of his cooperation. Wilkis capitulated, and Naftalis accompanied him to St. Andrews Plaza. Wilkis wept in Carberry's office as he recounted his descent into insider trading.

Wilkis's principal value to the government was his potential ability to corroborate Levine's allegations about Boesky and Reich and to implicate Cecola. At Naftalis's behest, Wilkis had painstakingly reconstructed everything Levine had ever told him about "the Russian" and "Wally." Although Wilkis had never known their names, his memory, as Levine had feared, proved phenomenal, and the government seemed impressed. Wilkis corroborated key aspects of Levine's story.

Wilkis also dutifully went to Carberry's office and placed a recorded call to Cecola at his office at Dillon, Read. Not surprisingly, given the warning Wilkis had already given Cecola, the call produced nothing useful for the government. It was all too obvious that Wilkis had tipped Cecola, and Carberry was furious when he called Naftalis after the session.

"You idiot," Naftalis yelled at Wilkis. "You're trying to protect that kid. Don't you realize, they'll add four to five years to your sentence for that. You could lose the whole deal. Carberry hates you now. It's not good."

Barry Goldsmith, the government investigator working with Wilkis, told him the next day, "Carberry wants to kill you." Carberry told Wilkis he was nothing but a "commodity" to him, and he'd just devalued himself. "I know the difference between chicken salad and chicken shit," Carberry said. "What you've given me is chicken shit."

Wilkis nearly panicked, but reached again into his memory to make up for the damage. Cecola had once told Wilkis about trading in his girlfriend's name. Wilkis remembered her name and tracked her down at her job with People Express in Orlando. Wilkis took the information to Carberry as a peace offering.

"I'm sorry about the tape," he said ruefully. Two days later, the government obtained the girlfriend's trading records, and saw that Cecola had used her account for his insider trading. Confronted with the evidence, Cecola agreed to plead guilty to one count of tax evasion for failing to report his insider-trading profits, and settled the SEC charges, disgorging $21,800. He was sentenced to six years' probation. Harvard Business School suspended him with the right to reapply.

In July, Wilkis pleaded guilty to four felonies and settled the SEC's charges. He agreed to disgorge $3.3 million and the Park Avenue co-op he'd never had a chance to move into. It amounted to virtually everything he had. He was allowed to keep the West 78th Street apartment, his Buick, and $60,000. Wilkis wept as he was sentenced to a year and a day in prison and five years' probation.

Wilkis never spoke to Cecola again. "This kid will be angry at you," Goldsmith, the investigator, told him when he finally implicated Cecola. "But he'll never know what you sacrificed for him. I don't know why you let this guy do it to you. He was worse than Dennis Levine was at age 22."

That left only one member of the immediate Levine ring. Reich posed a more difficult challenge for the government. Unlike the others, he had taken no money. He hadn't traded himself. There was no paper trail. The case might be Levine's word against Reich's, and Levine had a record of lying under oath. Reich, by contrast, was an upstanding member of the bar, a partner in one of the city's most prestigious firms. But Carberry decided to enlist Levine for another try.

During the first week in July, nearly a month after Levine's plea, Reich was busy defending a hostile takeover attempt against a Wachtell, Lipton client, NL Industries, a conglomerate once known as National Lead. Since his suicidal episode in California, Reich had consoled himself with the knowledge that there was nothing concrete to link him to Levine's trading. If necessary, he would deny everything. He had distracted himself by throwing himself more frenetically than ever into his work, packing his wife and children off to the Hamptons for the summer.

When Reich returned to his office from an NL meeting, his secretary told him someone "bothersome" had called three times and wouldn't leave his name. At about 4:30 P.M. she buzzed him and said the caller was on the line, insisting Reich would know who he is. Reich picked up the phone, and heard what he considered a shadow of Levine's voice. "Hi, Ilan," Levine said weakly.

"How are you?" Reich asked.

"I'm at a phone booth," Levine said. "Go to a phone booth and call me here."

Reich was intensely suspicious. "I don't know what you're talking about," he said firmly.

"The government is putting pressure on me to tell about us, and I don't know what to say," Levine explained.

"I don't know what you're talking about," Reich repeated, and hung up. He went directly to one of his partners and told him about the call.

The Wachtell lawyers called both Lynch and Carberry, asking what Levine was up to. Was he free-lancing, still trying to falsely implicate others? The government lawyers were noncommittal. Then Herbert Wachtell, one of the firm's top partners, personally called them to find out what was going on. He reported to Reich that Carberry "didn't seem surprised" that such a call had been made, and that Lynch had remained silent. "Presumably, they knew what was happening," he said thoughtfully. Then he reassured Reich. "You did the right thing," he said. What he didn't tell Reich was that Lynch had recommended Reich retain an outside criminal lawyer.

On Friday of the same week, at about 3:45 P.M., the SEC's Peter Sonnenthal entered Wachtell, Lipton's reception area and demanded to see Reich or Wachtell. When the receptionist hesitated, he barged

into the corridor, looking for the lawyers' names on office doors.
Edward Herlihy, a partner at the firm and a friend of Lynch's, managed
to restrain Sonnenthal. He brought him into his office and got on the
phone to Lynch.

"What's this animal doing in here?" he demanded. Lynch explained that Sonnenthal's mission was to subpoena Reich. "We own
the guy now," Lynch said.

When Reich arrived at Herlihy's office, Sonnenthal was waiting
to hand him the subpoena. A shiver of fear went down Reich's spine.
Sonnenthal looked at him coldly.

The subpoena listed 102 deals, called for Reich's phone records,
credit-card charges, and brokerage accounts, and asked for information about a number of names. Wilkis was the only one Reich recognized.

From 9 P.M. to midnight Reich dictated his answers to the subpoena. He drew some confidence from the fact that he could answer
95% of the questions truthfully. He said he'd known Levine socially
for a number of years and had run into him working on several deals.
But he denied giving Levine any confidential information.

At 11 A.M. Monday, Reich was sitting idly with his feet propped
up on his nearly empty desk, having just overseen the release of an NL
press release. Pedowitz, the former prosecutor and a friend of Reich's,
called the young partner to his office and suggested they go to a
conference room. Three other partners were waiting: Bernard Nuss-
baum, Wachtell, and Allan Martin, all former prosecutors. As soon as
Reich saw them, he thought to himself: "Here comes the truth squad."

Reich disregarded their advice that he get his own lawyer though
he realized they wouldn't protect him under the attorney-client privilege. He was hurt by the lack of support. He said he wanted to hear the
facts as they knew them. As his partners began to summarize Levine's
allegations, Reich doodled furiously on a legal pad. He denied that he'd
given Levine any confidential information, even unwittingly. Levine's
trades, he insisted, had to be sheer coincidence. Then they told Reich
that another of Levine's conspirators had told the government he knew
Levine had a source at Wachtell, Lipton.

Reich was stunned. Levine had sworn that his identity would
never be revealed. He'd promised. How could Levine have betrayed
him? For the first time, Reich began to feel his world caving in around
him. He looked stricken, flustered, then began sobbing. The Wachtell
lawyers again urged him to get his own lawyer.

When he refused, they ordered sandwiches. Reich ate nothing.
Now his interrogators changed tack. Reich's partners reminded him
that they had staunchly stood by him for the past week. Their reputa-

tions were at stake if Reich were lying. Would he betray them—even his mentor, Lipton himself? Reich again began to sob. When he collected himself, he began rambling about his troubled adolescence, his difficulty at making friends. These partners were his friends. Finally he pulled himself together and said he wanted five minutes to think. On his pad, he tried to write down the pros and cons of telling the truth. He couldn't list any cons. Suddenly he couldn't bear the thought of lying to his partners any longer.

At about 2:30 P.M., after over three hours of interrogation and discussion, the story came pouring out. When he was through, his partners asked sadly why he'd done it. Reich mentioned friendship, loneliness, the money, but his voice drifted off. He didn't really have an answer.

Reich finally hired a criminal lawyer, Robert Morvillo, who'd also represented Carlo Florentino, the Wachtell, Lipton partner who had insider-traded years before. He resigned his partnership in the firm he'd come to love. If Wilkis had limited bargaining power, Reich had even less. He had no one else to implicate. He offered to explain "the deal world," as he put it, but the government's response was "So what?" No one seemed impressed by the fact that Reich had taken no money and had quit the scheme in 1984.

Alone among the conspirators, Reich testified before the grand jury and was indicted on two felony counts. A week after the indictment, on October 9, he pleaded guilty. To settle the SEC's charges, he agreed to pay $485,000. He was left with his West Side brownstone, an Oldsmobile, and $10,000. Like Wilkis, he was sentenced to a year and a day in prison and five years' probation. He and Wilkis entered Danbury federal prison together.

On February 20, 1987, hundreds of reporters, television crew members, and curiosity-seekers packed the street outside the federal courthouse in White Plains, a New York suburb where Levine's sentencing judge, Gerard Goettel, had been temporarily assigned. Police on horseback kept the crowd under control and cleared a path for the dark blue car bringing Levine, his lawyers, and his family to the sentencing. The courthouse was too small to accommodate the surge of public interest, and many reporters had to stand outside in the biting cold.

Liman appealed for mercy. "He is an outcast," Liman said of Levine, "a leper like I've never seen. Dennis Levine's name will always be remembered, Your Honor, as a synonym for this offense." Levine himself, wearing a conservative gray pin-striped suit, read a statement in flat tones: "I will never violate the law again"; "I have learned my lesson"; "I'm truly sorry and ashamed." There was also a tribute to his family. "It's been their love and support that has sustained me through this very difficult period," he said.

The lawyer appointed by the court to supervise Levine's assets, however, had his doubts. Sheldon Goldfarb had examined Levine's sources of income and assets acquired over the past six years, and several hundred thousand dollars couldn't be accounted for. Levine told him he'd lost the money gambling in the Bahamas. But Goldfarb was dubious. Levine's brother Robert, who had supposedly accompanied Levine on many of the trips, had no recollection of Levine losing any money, and was evasive. Levine himself had refused to answer questions about gambling losses under oath. In his final report to the court, Goldfarb expressed his suspicions that Levine had managed to conceal a substantial sum.

Prosecutors were now aiming higher than Levine, however, and Judge Goettel was more impressed by Levine's cooperation. "He pled guilty and he has cooperated and . . . his cooperation has been truly extraordinary," the judge said at Levine's sentencing. "Through the information he has provided, an entire nest of vipers on Wall Street has been exposed." The judge sentenced Levine to two years in prison and fined him $362,000 on top of the $11.6 million he was paying the SEC.

The "game" was over.

In late July 1986, a little more than two months after Levine's arrest, Boesky had flown to Los Angeles for a meeting with Milken. The two men sat beside Milken's pool. Levine's arrest had come as a shock to both of them; it suggested a level of securities enforcement that neither had previously believed existed. Milken warned Boesky that, given the media attention and government resources being focused on the markets, they had better limit their dealings. Boesky readily agreed.

They also talked about the $5.3 million payment that had been disguised as a consulting fee—the one piece of evidence that could cause them trouble. They agreed that they'd have to find a way to substantiate their phony explanation. Drexel could work up more documentation, showing the research it had done on Santa Barbara, Scott & Fetzer, and other deals that had never gone anywhere. But what about their accountants' records—the sheets Thurnher and Mooradian had worked up to reconcile their positions? Those would have to be destroyed.

Boesky, back in New York the first week in August, had called Mooradian at his lower Manhattan office.

"It's Ivan," he began in an uncharacteristically hushed tone. "You've got to come uptown and talk."

Mooradian wondered what this was all about. He talked to Boesky two or three times a day on the phone; they rarely needed to meet face to face. Even more peculiar, Boesky insisted that Mooradian meet him in the Pastrami 'n Things on West 52nd Street. It was the same place where Boesky and Siegel had often conspired.

Although the coffee shop was nearly deserted, Boesky led Mooradian to the downstairs level and chose a secluded booth. Speaking in a barely audible whisper, he told Mooradian that what he was about to say had to be kept in the strictest confidence. He was to tell no one. Mooradian nodded in agreement.

"Do you have the Drexel documents?" Boesky whispered. Mooradian thought the whispering was absurd, since no one else was in the room.

"Yes," he said in a normal tone.

"At home or in the office?" Boesky asked, continuing to whisper.

"At my office," Mooradian replied.

Boesky leaned over the table, his face close to Mooradian's. "Destroy them," he said.

By the middle of August, the annual exodus from Wall Street was nearly complete, with investment bankers headed in droves to the Hamptons, rural Connecticut, or Europe. Only skeleton trading and support staffs were left in the city. Both Lynch and Carberry felt that if there was a safe time for them to take vacations, this was it. Nothing important, they assumed, would happen in August. Carberry and his wife left for a long-planned trip to the English Lake District, where they were planning to stay in modest bed-and-breakfasts. Lynch packed up his family and drove to Friendship, Maine, a town on Penobscot Bay where they'd rented a small cabin for several previous summer holidays.

Lynch tried to unwind after the intense, tumultuous events that had begun even before Levine's arrest in May, but it was hard not to think about a potential case against Ivan Boesky. Boesky could become a bigger and more important case than Lynch had ever imagined. Like everyone else even remotely connected to the stock market, he knew the Boesky legend. Now he had learned a lot more. He and Carberry had been in contact by phone nearly every day since Levine had agreed to plead. They had read Boesky's book, *Merger Mania,* and they had done computerized searches and compiled every article that had been written about the arbitrageur, including the L.A. *Times* and *Fortune* magazine pieces that had caused Siegel such consternation. They had all Boesky's voluminous 13-D filings. The inquiries had been shrouded in secrecy, even within the U.S. attorney's office and the SEC.

Even with Levine's cooperation, Lynch knew that any case against Boesky would be difficult. Lynch had always thought arbitrageurs would be hard to convict on insider trading. Their business was trading on rumors and market intelligence. Boesky would be expected to have large positions in most takeover stocks. He would have masses of legitimate information that he could claim had motivated his purchases. Nonetheless, Lynch's instinct was to press forward with the investigation, even to try the case despite a likelihood of losing.

The commission members had approved going ahead with an investigation of Boesky. As a first step, earlier that month the staff had prepared and delivered a lengthy subpoena directed at Boesky and the various entities he controlled. It called for testimony and voluminous numbers of documents and trading records, and it was crafted with enough specificity that Boesky would know that Levine had implicated him. Boesky's response to the subpoena was due the week Lynch returned from vacation; perhaps something interesting would turn up. Lynch foresaw a long, drawn-out, expensive battle, however, probably unlike any the enforcement unit had ever undertaken.

On Tuesday, August 26, Lynch returned to his family's cabin and found a phone message from Harvey Pitt, Bank Leu's lawyer. He wondered, with some annoyance, how Pitt had managed to track him down in Maine, but he called Pitt back at his office in Washington.

Pitt apologized for bothering Lynch in Maine, but said, "We need to get together. It's important." This time, Pitt wasn't calling about Bank Leu. He was representing Boesky.

"Are you calling to negotiate the subpoenas?" Lynch asked. "Because if you are, I don't see why this can't wait. I'm on vacation."

But Pitt insisted. "We must get together now," he said. "We can't wait."

Lynch agreed to meet Pitt halfway, in Boston. "This had better be good," he said.

"I wouldn't waste your time," Pitt answered.

Pitt, in fact, had already interrupted his own vacation, stranding his family at the beach in Virginia for three weeks without telling them why. The matter was simply too explosive to confide in anyone—even his own wife—who didn't have an absolute need to know. At first Pitt had called his wife each day, saying he'd be away for another day, but perhaps would join her the day after. Finally she cut him off. "Please just tell me you're not coming at all. It's easier," she said.

Boesky had called Pitt the day he received the SEC subpoenas, saying they should talk. Pitt wasn't shocked; Boesky had been subpoenaed from time to time over the years, as had almost everyone who traded in such volume and filed so many disclosure reports. But something in Boesky's voice suggested that this was going to be different.

Pitt soon understood why: the subpoenas called for practically every scrap of paper Boesky's operations had ever produced, and the government was demanding a response in only a few weeks. This was no routine inquiry.

Pitt knew that the SEC had to have approved a formal order of investigation. He called the enforcement staff, and asked for a copy of the formal order. Much to his surprise, the staff refused. Never in his 18 years of practice had the SEC failed to produce a copy of a formal order of investigation. This, too, suggested something unusually serious.

Finally, the SEC staff told Pitt he could come over and read the order if he promised to make no copies. He went over to the SEC offices with three colleagues. Each memorized a page, then ran out and copied it from memory, giving Pitt a reasonably good facsimile of the original order. He drew two fast conclusions: Levine figured prominently in the allegations against Boesky, and this was going to be a massive investigation. Pitt thought it was prudent to bring in another firm to help. He called Theodore Levine, whom he had worked with years before at the SEC and who had shared the podium with Siegel at the early seminar on takeovers. Levine, now a partner at Wilmer, Cutler & Pickering in Washington, was also on vacation.

"Oh my God," Ted Levine said when told that Boesky was a target. He, too, interrupted his vacation and returned to Washington.

Within a week, Boesky called Reid Nagle, his chief financial officer, into his office to discuss several pending Northview deals, two of which were scheduled to close in little more than a week. "I've got some bad news," Boesky said. "We're canceling those transactions." Nagle had been working on some of these deals for more than a year; he couldn't believe it. When he pressed Boesky for an explanation, Boesky said, "It's a difficult time. We're being investigated even though there's no wrongdoing."

The following Sunday, Pitt, Ted Levine, and another Wilmer, Cutler partner, Robert McCaw, flew to New York and checked into the Grand Hyatt Hotel on 42nd Street. They were joined by Michael Rauch, Pitt's partner from the Bank Leu case. An American Bar Association convention was in progress at the hotel, so the presence of the lawyers wouldn't attract any attention. Boesky showed up the next morning.

He seemed thinner than ever, hesitant, nervous. Pitt introduced him to the Wilmer, Cutler lawyers, then got down to business.

"I can tell you what I think the government has got," Pitt began, "but only you know the truth. If what you tell us isn't truthful and complete, the advice we give you will be defective." He also warned Boesky that once he told his lawyers the truth, he couldn't change his story in the future on the witness stand. They would withdraw from representing him rather than let Boesky take the stand and lie.

Boesky needed little coaxing. Slowly, with some hesitation, he began to recount the dark side of his success. It was as if he were facing, for the first time, the often complex truth about himself.

Pitt felt a deep sadness. He knew he was watching the disintegration of one of the great careers in American finance. Pitt had known Boesky in his heyday, and he believed him to be tremendously talented.

Boesky's complete debriefing took two full weeks. Pitt moved their operations from the Grand Hyatt to the Helmsley Palace, and took over an entire floor of the expensive luxury hotel. Computers, copying machines, paralegals, and messengers were brought in. Masses of information, all potential evidence, had to be assembled and catalogued—all without attracting the attention of even the other lawyers at Fried, Frank.

As Boesky painstakingly took the lawyers through his dealings with Levine, Siegel, Milken, Mulheren, West Coast broker Boyd Jefferies, and many others, Pitt reached two broad conclusions: the government's insider-trading case, drawn from what Levine could tell them, was weak. Boesky could probably prevail. But there were worse things in Boesky's recital than insider trading.

Boesky was obviously terrified of Milken; he recounted his Milken dealings with an almost palpable sense of trepidation, as if he feared Milken were listening. Yet Boesky seemed to have little sense of the magnitude of what he was revealing. Pitt was stunned. Besides insider trading, Milken and Boesky were involved in a wide array of other crimes: 13-D violations, parking violations, and a broad conspiracy affecting the control of corporations. Boesky had done what Milken ordered him to do; even Boesky didn't know sometimes how his actions fit into Milken's grander schemes. These were historic revelations of criminal misconduct broader than anything Pitt had ever believed possible.

Pitt recognized almost immediately that Boesky would have to try to cut a deal with the government. The two most important variables in plea bargaining—the strength of the government's case and the target's ability to implicate others—were both working in Boesky's favor. Pitt knew he could "sell" Boesky and have the government lawyers salivating in anticipation. The information on Milken alone would have been enough.

"You have to understand the risks," Pitt told Boesky. "If you start the settlement process, you have risks. You're admitting to the government that they have a case, for one thing."

He pointed out that cooperation would be painful. Boesky would likely be vilified publicly, and his penalty was likely to be substantial. Pitt didn't want to sugarcoat his client's prospects. On the other hand, he told Boesky, the government clearly wasn't going to go away if Boesky decided to fight. His case would become the biggest in the country, one to which the government could devote its enormous resources. Boesky would be tried under the glare of publicity, an experience likely to extract a huge emotional toll.

Pitt emphasized that the clock was ticking. The favorable climate for settlement could evaporate instantly. Milken or Siegel might get to the bargaining table first. Then Boesky would become the big fish targeted for investigation and trial.

Boesky had three major questions: What would happen to his wife and children? (Their assets and trust funds, including those generated on their behalf by Boesky's illegal activities, would probably be unaffected since they were innocent bystanders.) What would happen to his employees and investors? (Boesky would probably be barred from the industry, so employees would lose their jobs, but investors probably wouldn't be hurt.) And, would he have to do jail time? (Probably, but far less than if he went to trial and were convicted. Each of the many securities crimes Boesky had admitted carried a maximum term of five years in jail.)

After extended discussions, Boesky paused, looking grave, and looked around the room at his lawyers. "I'm of the view we should settle," he said.

Pitt felt they hadn't a moment to lose. As soon as he got a good grasp of what Boesky could offer, he called the SEC and reached Lynch in Maine. On August 27, Sturc and another SEC lawyer flew to Boston from Washington; Pitt, Rauch, Levine, and McCaw flew in from New York. They all met Lynch in the windowless room that served as a library for the cramped regional SEC offices located above the Boston Garden, the home of the Celtics.

Lynch knew something big was about to happen when Pitt, skipping the usual pleasantries, insisted on an off-the-record conversation. Then he began to read from a prepared script. He told Lynch that Boesky couldn't respond to the subpoenas in the short time the SEC had allowed. But more important, Pitt argued, it wasn't in the government's interest simply to bring a case against Boesky.

"If we did a deal," he said, "the government would gain an insight into Wall Street practices that were comparable to the Pecora hearings that led to the passage of the securities laws." Boesky, he said, would be a "window on Wall Street. Assume Ivan can tell you about things, and not just as a casual observer."

Lynch was stunned but remained characteristically poker-faced, showing no emotion. He did not dare glance at Sturc.

"We realize the government will have to have certain things," Pitt continued, and laid out his negotiating parameters. Boesky would voluntarily withdraw from the securities business, he would agree to the payment of a substantial fine, and he would cooperate fully. In return, he wanted immunity from criminal prosecution.

Lynch told Boesky's lawyers that he couldn't speak for the U.S. attorney's office or Justice Department, and obviously there was no point in negotiating unless a plea agreement could be worked out. He said that he and his colleagues would do everything they could.

After Pitt and the other Boesky lawyers walked out, the SEC lawyers whooped out loud, slapped each other on the back, and all but got up on the table and danced.

Lynch couldn't wait to tell Carberry. He reached the prosecutor, just back from England, at his home over the Labor Day weekend. Lynch was afraid to say too much over the phone, so Carberry agreed to fly to Washington the next morning to meet with the SEC lawyers and Boesky's lawyers.

That same weekend, Boesky called Mooradian at home. "Did you destroy them?" Boesky asked. Mooradian knew he was referring to the Drexel documents, which he'd shredded just after the coffee shop meeting. "Yes," Mooradian said. "What the fuck are you talking about? Of course I did."

"Reconstruct them," Boesky ordered.

Mooradian was thoroughly confused. "Ivan, I can't possibly do that," he protested.

"You've got to," Boesky replied, and hung up.

Mooradian swore to himself, chalking this up as another one of Boesky's unreasonable demands. He didn't see how he could possibly remember all the stocks involved, let alone the exact positions. Then he remembered Maria Termine, the young woman who'd brought the folder down to Florida and had helped him when Boesky demanded that the amounts be reconciled with Milken's operation. She still had her worksheets. Mooradian also found a few fragments of underlying

documents he'd used in calculating the Drexel numbers. He and Termine began working together, trying to come up with what Mooradian
considered a reasonable facsimile of the original ledgers.

The Tuesday after Labor Day, Boesky's lawyers, the SEC lawyers, and Carberry met at Fried, Frank's offices on Pennsylvania Avenue. Pitt gave Carberry a presentation similar to the one he'd given
Lynch.

"Can we do a deal?" Pitt asked. Carberry said he had to confer
with Giuliani, but he was intrigued.

Back in New York, Giuliani gave Carberry five minutes. The U.S.
attorney was in the midst of the highly publicized political corruption
trial of Stanley Friedman, the former Bronx Democratic leader. Giuliani had decided to try the politically charged case personally, and a
success was essential for his political ambitions.

Carberry told Giuliani he was still a year or two away from being
able to try Boesky, and that even then he couldn't guarantee a conviction. In contrast, Boesky's cooperation, he argued, could lead to "interesting things."

With a minimum of discussion, Giuliani told Carberry to negotiate a plea. They agreed that immunity was out of the question: They
would demand a guilty plea to at least one felony. And they would want
a lot of money in fines and penalties. Carberry had recently noticed
that the SEC's annual budget was $105 million; he picked $100 million
as the figure he wanted from Boesky. It was a big, round number, one
that would dazzle the public—and he thought the comparison to the
SEC budget was impressive; it would demonstrate how worthwhile the
agreement was. Carberry knew that any deal that seemed too lenient
would generate a firestorm.

He also knew that secrecy was imperative if Boesky were to be
useful as an undercover operative. Carberry trusted Lynch and his top
aides, but he didn't know the SEC commissioners, with their political
agendas. When he called Lynch to tell him he'd gotten the go-ahead
from Giuliani, he emphasized the need for absolute secrecy. "I would
view any leak as an obstruction of justice," Carberry warned, "and I'd
seriously contemplate bringing charges."

Lynch restricted knowledge of the negotiations to only three
people in his office, and Carberry told only Giuliani and Howard
Wilson, head of the criminal division. Later, Carberry confided some
especially secret details of the operation to one other person, so that
there would be someone to carry on if he were killed or died suddenly.
All meetings were scheduled at Fried, Frank's offices, not at the SEC
or U.S. attorney's office, where the presence of the Fried, Frank and
Wilmer, Cutler lawyers might attract attention. To enhance secrecy,

Boesky was never referred to by name; his code name was "Igor" at the U.S. attorney's office, and "Irving" at the SEC.

The lawyers for Boesky and the government plunged into a frenzied round of negotiations. They were under intense time pressure, because one of Boesky's companies, Northview, faced a November 15 SEC disclosure filing. Any major development would obviously have to be disclosed then. They were hoping to enlist Boesky as an undercover agent, and this drastically narrowed the time in which he could operate.

Carberry said flatly at the outset of negotiations that he had to have a guilty plea to one felony count carrying a maximum prison term of five years. Boesky's lawyers offered little resistance, asking for an offense that carried a three-year maximum. Carberry was adamant, and they gave in. But there were prolonged discussions about which felony would be the subject of Boesky's plea. There was a wide array of five-year felonies from which to choose. Strategically, Carberry wanted something Boesky would likely be called to testify about. And he wanted to send the message that the case was about something bigger than insider trading. Conspiracy to commit securities fraud was settled upon as suitably all-encompassing.

The money issue was more complicated. Carberry and the SEC lawyers asked for the $100 million; they thought that $50 million was a reasonable ballpark estimate of Boesky's illegal profits, and an additional $50 million would be an appropriate penalty. They also thought that $100 million was in line with their own estimates of Boesky's net worth. Boesky's lawyers argued that $100 million was too much; that their own calculations showed that Boesky had profited by no more than $30 million from Levine's information, and since the Levine trading was all that the SEC knew about, Boesky shouldn't be penalized financially for volunteering more evidence of wrongdoing. Again, the government lawyers were adamant, insisting they had to have the $100 million.

Pitt knew it was a number Boesky could live with. The government had no way of knowing just how much money Boesky had made illegally; it wouldn't find out the full scope of Boesky's wrongdoing until the penalty was fixed. Nor was it free simply to seize everything Boesky owned. Penalties are supposed to be tailored to the wrongdoing. Later, however, the government did receive an accounting of Boesky's assets, and it turned out that the SEC's estimates weren't too far wrong. The confidential statement disclosed Boesky's net worth in January 1986 as $130,822,991, including cash ($2.7 million), securities ($115 million), real estate ($6.9 million), two Rolls Royces ($100,000), and art ($2.4 million). It disclosed annual income of $7 million, including a salary as chief executive of the Boesky entities of just $35,000. His estimated annual expenses of $6 million sealed the SEC's sense that he lived lavishly.

A crucial aspect of any plea negotiation is the "proffer," in which the defense formally tries to give the government an estimate of the value of a defendant's cooperation. At their first meeting in Washington, Pitt gave the government an oral proffer, an outline of Boesky's value as a witness that was more detailed than his earlier representations, but stopped short of naming names. At their last negotiating session, however, after all other aspects of the settlement had been worked out, Pitt produced a written proffer, which Lynch needed in order to get the commission's approval of the settlement.

That meeting, again at Fried, Frank's offices, seemed to go on forever. Finally, at nearly 4 A.M., Pitt unveiled the long-awaited document, and Lynch, Carberry, and the other government lawyers eagerly pored over it. Carberry felt his heart sink. It was much vaguer than he had expected. There were no names, only references such as "investment banker A," or "investment bank B." It was also cryptic about just what crimes Boesky's lawyers believed had been committed. Carberry looked up from the document, concerned.

"We can't tell whether we're getting Xerox operators or real players. This isn't good enough," he said.

"That's the best we can do until the SEC signs off," Pitt insisted, arguing that he couldn't expose Boesky any further. Lynch and Carberry left the room, convinced that they would have trouble selling the proffer to the commission, given Boesky's stature. They had to have more proof of what Boesky was giving them. There had to be bigger fish.

At nearly 6 A.M., Carberry hailed a cab and returned to what he considered a godawful hotel that didn't even have a desk clerk to let him in. It was all he could afford on his government allowance. He had barely gotten into bed when his phone rang. It was Lynch.

"They want one more shot at it," he said excitedly. "Pitt just called." But Carberry had had it.

"I don't care how many shots they want," he said. "I'm not doing anything before 10 A.M." He rolled over and fell asleep.

The next morning, Pitt threw caution to the winds. He offered to reveal orally the identities of everyone mentioned in the proffer, though he wouldn't put the names in writing. Then, to the amazement of the government lawyers, Pitt ticked off a list of some of the most prominent names in the world of finance: Michael Milken, the junk-bond king; Martin Siegel, Drexel's star investment banker; Boyd Jefferies, the prominent West Coast broker; and Carl Icahn, the corporate raider. He could have listed even more, but Pitt always liked to promise slightly less than he would ultimately deliver, ensuring that the government wouldn't claim that the terms of the proffer hadn't been honored. So he didn't mention Mulheren, for example.

There was suddenly no doubt that the SEC would approve the settlement. Boesky was offering a trove beyond the government's wildest imaginings. Just a few months earlier, the commission had thought it had cracked the insider-trading case of the decade when it nailed Dennis Levine.

Carberry took the proposed settlement back to Giuliani, who was still absorbed in the Friedman case, and quickly gained his approval. They couldn't pass up this opportunity. Lynch took the settlement to the commission on September 10. Since approving the formal order of investigation that summer, the commissioners had been told nothing. Even Chairman John Shad had been kept in the dark. They seemed stunned by the scope of the revelations, and the prospect of the reactions they were likely to trigger.

Based on Drexel's cooperation in the Levine case, Lynch and the commissioners were pretty sure that Drexel would immediately dismiss Milken and agree to cooperate. An institution like Drexel couldn't survive an SEC enforcement action of the scope outlined by Boesky, they felt. What legitimate businessperson would use Drexel if it tried to protect Milken? With both Boesky and Milken out of the market, they realized, a profound change in the economy would be wrought, one they would have to prepare for carefully. Boesky and Milken were the twin pillars of the takeover wave that had pushed the stock market to such heights.

Even after approving the settlement, Shad seemed to have trouble believing they had snared Boesky. He badgered Lynch almost daily, and seemed worried that the SEC wouldn't get its $100 million. "I'm sure Ivan is going to leave the country," Shad argued. "He could leave anytime. What's stopping him? What if we don't get our money? We've got to get him to pay now. We could freeze his assets."

Lynch tried not to show his impatience. "John, he's cooperating with us. We'll get the money. If we start to move against him, everyone will know. We've got to keep this buttoned down until the investigation is complete."

Lynch realized that secrecy would be increasingly hard to maintain as word of the settlement inevitably spread beyond the handful of people involved in the negotiations. Boesky's sister-in-law, Muriel Slatkin, co-owner of the Beverly Hills Hotel, had been told of the subpoenas, and the government's anxiety had soared when a small item appeared in the San Diego paper mentioning that Boesky had received a subpoena. Then Dan Dorfman, in a *U.S.A. Today* column that ran the first week in September, had also mentioned Boesky subpoenas. Every day, the government lawyers monitored the national press closely for signs of any leaks. Nothing further had appeared, but they knew they had no time to waste.

Boesky was formally enrolled as a government agent on Monday, September 17, when he signed his settlement agreement with the SEC. He signed his plea agreement with the Justice Department the next day. While he had been mingling with other guests at the Guterman party aboard the *QE2* on the evening of September 15, his lawyers had been working nearly around the clock to complete the final agreements. Pitt had had only two hours of sleep Sunday night.

Besides the provisions for the plea to one count and cooperation, the written agreement contained powerful incentives for Boesky to tell the truth:

> Your client must at all times give complete, truthful, and accurate information and testimony. . . . Your client agrees not to commit any other crimes whatsoever. Should your client commit any further such crimes, or should it be determined by this Office that your client has intentionally failed to give complete, truthful, or accurate information and testimony, or has otherwise violated any provision of this agreement, your client shall thereafter be subject to prosecution for any federal criminal violation of which this Office has knowledge, including but not limited to, perjury and obstruction of justice. Any such prosecutions may be premised upon any information provided by your client, and such information may be used against him.

The government got its first opportunity to test its new witness the following Sunday. Though Boesky had in many ways come to dominate their lives over the past four months, none of the government lawyers had ever met the arbitrageur. Lynch and Sturc flew to New York, as did the Boesky lawyers from Washington. Carberry and Doonan met them at the Westbury Hotel on Madison Avenue, where Boesky had rented a suite.

Since it was a Sunday, most of the lawyers, including Carberry, had dressed casually. Boesky was dressed in his usual black three-piece suit. He seemed tired. Throughout the session, he rubbed a small metal ball back and forth between his fingers. He was stiff, even rigid.

After everyone was introduced, Carberry began the session. "Your only obligation, Mr. Boesky," he said, "is to tell the truth. If you don't, we'll kill you at sentencing." Carberry encouraged Boesky to give the lawyers a narrative account of his crimes, beginning with Levine. He wanted to see how closely Boesky's version coincided with Levine's. Carberry was pleased that Boesky didn't try to downplay his own guilt. Except for a few details, his account closely matched Levine's.

Carberry steered Boesky to Siegel next, then to Jefferics, Icahn, and finally Milken. Carberry didn't interrupt with many questions, and didn't probe for details. He was content with an overview in Boesky's own words. His questioning took about an hour and a half. Doonan took notes, alert to opportunities to use Boesky for undercover investigation.

Lynch and Sturc took over from there. The wider scope of SEC legislation and the lower standard of proof for any civil case gave them a broader base for questioning. They adopted a deal-by-deal approach, walking Boesky through many of the major transactions that had figured in his illegal arrangements, such as Fischbach. They continued for about three hours.

Boesky didn't limit his remarks to subjects in the proffer. He told them not only about his visits to Gulf + Western with Icahn, a possible 13-D violation, but also about the manipulation of Gulf + Western's stock price involving Mulheren. He described Mulheren's other activities on his behalf. And he told them of dealings not mentioned in the proffer, such as his involvement in Britain's Guinness scandal. He also said he suspected that Goldman, Sachs's Bob Freeman was involved in insider trading.

Carberry began to have renewed respect for the wisdom of the securities laws, especially the seemingly technical provisions. What Boesky described reminded him of the 1920s—the secret pooling of interests, the manipulation of stock prices—but his revelations went even beyond that to include the creation of phony takeover threats and the putting of companies in play. He would never have believed that securities law violations were so prevalent or so varied.

The lawyers were also struck by the hierarchy of power and influence within Boesky's world. They had always thought that Boesky was a major player on Wall Street. Now, however, they reached the same conclusion that Boesky's lawyers had: Boesky was second-tier. He depended on Milken and Drexel.

Over and over, Boesky told Carberry and the other lawyers that Milken had become the most important man in his life. If Milken told him to do something, he did it, because Milken could make him rich, or destroy him.

The government debriefings continued for weeks. To preserve secrecy, they moved from hotel to hotel; most were located just outside of Manhattan in Westchester County, not far from Boesky's estate. Between sessions, Boesky commuted to his offices in Manhattan as usual, taking care not to alert even his own employees that anything major was afoot. Elaborate monitoring equipment was installed in Boesky's communications system, allowing the government to listen in and record every conversation.

At the government's behest, Boesky placed calls to everyone he'd implicated. Boesky was instructed not to press, not to try to put words in his targets' mouths, to behave as naturally as possible. At the same time, Carberry told Boesky that the more successful he was as an undercover agent, the less likely it was that he'd have to appear as a witness.

After two fruitless efforts, Boesky succeeded in getting Boyd Jefferies, head of Jefferies & Co., the West Coast brokerage firm, to make some incriminating remarks. Siegel was extremely wary, however, reluctant even to take Boesky's calls. Conversations with Milken were frustrating. Milken took Boesky's calls but was always in a hurry to finish. He limited the talk to issues of immediate concern. Milken also had a tendency to speak in sentence fragments, which, though meaningful to people around him, would be confusing and inconclusive for jurors. Finally, the government decided that Boesky would have to arrange a face-to-face meeting with Milken.

That summer, Boesky had attended a fund-raiser in Denver for the United Jewish Appeal; he stayed with Larry Mizel, the head of MDC Corporation, a Drexel client. Immediately after Boesky left, an FBI agent showed up and quizzed Mizel about who had been staying with him. When Mizel confirmed that Boesky had been his guest, he received a subpoena for his phone records. Mizel called Jim Dahl, the star Milken salesman.

"You won't believe this," he said breathlessly, "but the FBI just left my house." He explained that the agent had been asking about Boesky.

Dahl told Lowell Milken. Lowell pulled Michael off the trading desk, called him into his office, and made Dahl repeat the entire story. Michael Milken suddenly looked ashen, as if he'd seen a ghost, Dahl thought. From then on, Milken indicated, they should be careful in their dealings with Boesky, and assume that any conversations with him were being monitored. But when Boesky called, saying he wanted to get together with Milken in mid-October, Milken agreed.

Soon after, Cary Maultasch, the former Beverly Hills employee who had moved to New York but still handled Milken's trading, got a call from Charles Thurnher, who'd kept track of the Boesky scheme for Milken. Thurnher told Maultasch to get rid of any records relating to Milken's dealings with Boesky. Later, he called to get an "update" of the Boesky situation, and Thurnher assured him the records had been destroyed. Maultasch asked what was going on. Thurnher was cryptic, but mentioned that Milken had scheduled a meeting with Boesky at the Beverly Hills Hotel.

The next day Milken called Maultasch. "I think that's a horrible idea," Maultasch said of the plan to meet with Boesky. Milken told him not to worry. He said he'd be careful and would assume he was "speaking for the record."

In mid-October, Boesky and Tom Doonan, the investigator who was now assigned to handle him, met with Pitt in Pitt's small room at the Beverly Hills Hotel. They'd flown to Los Angeles separately so as not to attract attention.

Doonan asked Boesky to remove his shirt so he could attach a small battery pack and tiny microphone, but was disconcerted when he discovered Boesky wasn't wearing an undershirt under his expensive white dress shirt. Doonan didn't want to tape the microphone to Boesky's skin, so he shed his own clothes, offering Boesky his undershirt. Boesky hesitated. Doonan ordered him to put it on.

"Ivan breaks out in a serious rash if he puts anything that costs less than $250 next to his skin," Pitt quipped.

Boesky donned Doonan's T-shirt, and Doonan hooked up the microphone. It would broadcast from Boesky's suite on the first floor, where he was scheduled to meet Milken shortly after 1 P.M. Pacific time, into a tape recorder in Pitt's room.

"What happens if I get caught, if he figures out I'm taping?" Boesky asked nervously. He was still terrified of Milken, who had close friends in the casino industry. Boesky feared that someone might try to rub him out. "Get the hell out of there" if anything goes wrong, Pitt advised. "Just run out."

Boesky returned to his own suite. While they waited for Milken, Pitt asked Doonan if he wanted to order lunch from room service. Doonan was shocked that a hamburger at the Beverly Hills cost $16. Government regulations prevented him from accepting a meal paid for by someone else, and his modest per diem wouldn't cover anything on the menu, so he declined, even though he was hungry. He watched as Pitt ate a hamburger.

Boesky waited anxiously in his suite. A room-service waiter knocked, then wheeled in a table laden with food. Milken arrived moments later. Boesky greeted him, then paced nervously as the black-jacketed waiter fiddled with the dishes, silverware, and ice. They didn't have much time to spare. "That's fine, just leave it," Boesky finally said to the waiter. "Would you please get out of here?"

Boesky and Milken chatted briefly about the market. Boesky seemed himself. He was ordinarily so stiff and awkward that any nervousness at being wired seemed natural. Then Boesky turned the conversation to its real purpose.

"The SEC subpoenaed my records," he confided to Milken. The commission was "breathing down my neck." He indicated he was worried he was going to have to deal with the calculations of profits and losses on his "arrangement" with Milken, and wanted to make sure they had the same story.

"Well, my guy doesn't remember anything," Milken said, evidently referring to Thurnher. "Does yours?" Boesky took that as a veiled suggestion to have Mooradian destroy any records. Milken and Boesky went back and forth, with Boesky trying to get Milken to make a more explicit acknowledgment of their dealings.

"If we're asked, what will we say about the $5.3 million?" Boesky asked.

"We could say the $5.3 million outstanding was for investment banking services," Milken volunteered.

"What services can we say were included?"

Milken started mentioning some of the deals Drexel had explored for Boesky, but Boesky said he didn't have any documentation to back them up. Milken said he'd send Boesky some papers for his files. Then Boesky pushed the conversation a bit further, saying that he hadn't entirely made up for what he owed Milken with the $5.3 million payment. "You know, I'm still holding this for you," Boesky said.

"Keep it," Milken cagily replied.

Before Boesky could make further progress, Milken made a remark that startled him. "You've got to be careful," Milken warned Boesky. "Electronic surveillance has gotten very sophisticated." Boesky nearly panicked. Was Milken catching on? He quickly brought the meeting to a close.

Boesky was elated that he'd gotten through the session without being discovered by Milken. Nothing Milken said would be a "smoking gun" at any future trial, but the tape would be useful probative evidence. Milken had never denied the existence of their scheme; he'd never denied that Boesky owed him money. The discussion of the payment, and how it could be characterized as an investment banking fee, plainly suggested a cover-up. The whole discussion made little sense unless Boesky's version of the conspiracy were, in fact, true.

Doonan and the prosecutors were impressed by Boesky's finesse, and felt they'd gotten more from the meeting than they expected.

Milken had, of course, been forewarned by the call from Mizel, and the meeting only heightened his suspicions. After leaving the Beverly Hills Hotel, Milken called Joseph in New York. "Boesky's acting weird," Milken said. "I want him watched."

Time was running out for the government's undercover operation. On November 15, Northview had to make the SEC filing disclosing the fact that Boesky was under investigation. No one would talk to Boesky after that.

The SEC, in particular, was worried about how the stock market would react to any rumors of Boesky's imminent demise. The great bull market of the 1980s had been fueled in part by arbitrageurs like Boesky, who valued stocks in terms of their takeover value, not by the more conservative measures of earnings or book value. In an unusual step, the government decided that the Boesky news would be released after the market closed on Friday, November 14. That would give investors a weekend to digest the news before making any precipitous decisions.

Chairman Shad, in particular, remained concerned about safeguarding the SEC's $100 million, which in part depended on the value of Boesky's huge portfolio. The SEC also worried that having Boesky dump his stock all at once might, in and of itself, put the stock market into a tailspin. The commission therefore directed Boesky to begin liquidating some of his holdings during the two weeks preceding the announcement. He would continue overseeing the remainder of the portfolio for another 18 months. These steps, Lynch felt, would reassure the market and protect the government's financial interest.

The government lawyers also had to think about the future course of the investigation. They knew that the moment the Boesky agreement was made public, everyone he might conceivably implicate would begin to cover their tracks. The lawyers didn't want evidence destroyed, so they prepared a blitz of subpoenas for potential targets and witnesses. Once subpoenas were served, any destruction of evidence would be grounds for obstruction of justice charges. Process servers were poised to fan out through New York, in Los Angeles, and wherever else necessary, to deliver subpoenas to Siegel, Milken, Drexel, Jefferies, Icahn, and many others right after the market closed at 4 P.M.

All that remained was the big announcement. Giuliani in New York and Shad in Washington scheduled simultaneous press conferences for 4:30 P.M. on Friday, November 14. All was in place, Lynch and Carberry believed, for the law enforcement triumph of the decade.

That Friday afternoon, Mooradian was looking over the firm's net capital position. Something was wrong. Boesky only sold positions for two reasons: to profit (or cut losses) at the consummation of a merger, or to meet net capital requirements. But now Boesky had been whittling down the portfolio for months, and the selling had accelerated in the past two weeks. Their positions had actually peaked soon after March 21, the day of the Hudson Funding closing, at about $3.1 billion. Now it was down to less than $1.6 billion. Many of the positions were in big-capitalization stocks like Eastman Kodak and Time-Life, not in the takeover plays that Boesky usually favored. This wasn't like Boesky at all, Mooradian thought.

When Boesky's secretary, Ianthe Peters, called, telling Mooradian and several other people in the back office to be at 650 Fifth Avenue for a 3:15 P.M. meeting, Mooradian concluded that Boesky was going to wind up the partnership, as he had once wound up Ivan F. Boesky & Co. "This is it, we're going out of business," he gloomily told his colleagues at 11 Broadway, hoping he'd be proven wrong.

When Mooradian, Reid Nagle, and others in the downtown delegation arrived at Boesky's large conference room on the 34th floor, the room was already filled with other Boesky employees. There didn't seem to be any sense of impending doom. On the contrary, Davidoff, the head trader and a member of Boesky's executive committee, was joking and confidently predicting, "We're going to get an extra bonus. I know it, we've had a great year, plus we've got all the new Drexel money."

"Are you out of your fucking mind?" Mooradian interjected. Several people laughed.

At 3:20, the doors opened and Boesky appeared, looking tired and drawn, followed by a procession of 10 lawyers: Pitt, Theodore Levine, and the defense team from Fried, Frank and Wilmer, Cutler, as well as lawyers from two Boston firms representing Boesky's partnership investors. Wekili and Fraidin, the two people closest to Boesky, were absent. They had already been briefed, as had Boesky's wife, Seema, and his children. The family was in shock.

The minute they saw all the lawyers, Boesky's employees knew something was terribly wrong. Then Boesky began to read from a prepared statement. Boesky said it had been "very difficult" for him the past few weeks, when he had been unable to discuss anything with anyone and had avoided contact with them. He cautioned them that what he was about to say should not leave the room until after 4 P.M. and that they wouldn't be allowed to make any phone calls until 4:15

P.M. He paused, took a deep breath, then continued reading. It would be announced at 4 P.M., he said, that he had reached a settlement with the SEC in which he would pay $100 million, and that he had agreed to plead guilty to one count of conspiracy to commit securities fraud.

The government "justifiably holds me and not my business associates or business entities responsible for my actions," Boesky continued. "I deeply regret my past mistakes, and know that I alone must bear the consequences of those actions. My life will be forever changed, but I hope that something positive will ultimately come out of this situation. I know that in the wake of today's events, many will call for reform. If my mistakes launch a process of reexamination of the rules and practices of our financial marketplace, then perhaps some good will result," he concluded. He looked up at his stunned employees, then offered to take questions.

The room was silent. People were too numb to ask any questions. Finally someone asked if the firm was closing, and when. Boesky assured them he would have 18 months to wind up the operations, so there'd be no immediate dislocation. He offered to do what he could to help people find jobs at other firms. Finally, Johnny Ray, Boesky's longtime chauffeur, stood up and said, "Let's all go down with the ship!"

That broke the tension. People laughed, a few cried, and everyone lined up to shake Boesky's hand, or hug him, or just wish him well. Many had often thought of him as a tyrant, and he'd just thrown a wrench into all of their lives; but suddenly he seemed so frail, dependent on so many lawyers. He already seemed a shadow of the fierce trader they'd known. For most of the employees, it was hard to feel anything but pity.

The stunning news came across the ticker at 4:28 P.M. SEC CHARGES IVAN BOESKY WITH INSIDER TRADING, the headline read. "The Securities and Exchange Commission charged Wall Street arbitrageur Ivan Boesky with trading on inside information provided by Dennis Levine," the ticker copy began, and quickly reached the news that rocked Wall Street the most: "Boesky has agreed to cooperate with the SEC in its widening investigation of insider trading on Wall Street, SEC officials said. In addition, the United States Attorney in New York said Boesky entered into a criminal plea agreement in which he will plead guilty to one federal felony charge.

"The U.S. Attorney's office, which declined to identify the specific charge, said Boesky is cooperating in its continuing criminal investigation arising from the Dennis B. Levine insider trading case."

Almost everybody who counted had talked to Boesky at one time or another. Paranoia swept Wall Street.

. . .

Milken's traders and salesmen in Beverly Hills were winding down
after a busy week; Milken was still working at the trading desk when
Terren Peizer shouted, "Oh my God!" Everyone looked up, saw Peizer
riveted by the ticker, and hurried to see what was on the tape.

Milken got the news on his Quotron screen. He said nothing. He
stayed at his desk and answered the phone. His colleagues watched
closely for clues to his reaction. Milken seemed contemplative, but
otherwise acted as though nothing had happened. Everyone was
amazed at his self-control.

After three or four phone calls, Milken jumped up and walked
quickly into his brother Lowell's office. He shut the door and didn't
emerge for more than an hour.

Later, Fred Joseph called. He'd learned from Drexel's general
counsel that afternoon that subpoenas were out concerning Milken and
Drexel. They were subpoenas from the Justice Department, meaning
a criminal investigation was underway.

"There's nothing to worry about," Milken said firmly, sounding
unconcerned. Joseph relaxed. It was inconceivable that Milken had
done anything wrong. He had the best business in the country. He'd
been investigated before and everything had always turned out fine.
This would, too. Joseph left to attend a dinner for top Drexel officials
and their wives.

That weekend, Milken called Jim Dahl at home and asked him to
come to the office. Dahl drove in and settled in at his desk, waiting
impatiently for Milken to explain what he wanted. But Milken was
elsewhere in the office, talking with other people. Finally Dahl cor-
nered him.

"You called me," Dahl said. "What do you want?"

Milken walked silently into the men's room, motioning for Dahl
to follow. Inside, Milken turned on the tap water full blast and began
washing his hands. With the water running, he leaned toward Dahl.
"There haven't been any subpoenas issued," he said in a hushed tone,
though he must have known otherwise. "Whatever you need to do, do
it." Dahl wasn't even sure what a subpoena was, but he understood
what Milken meant: if he had anything incriminating, destroy it.

Milken set about eliminating other potential evidence, too. On
Monday, Terren Peizer was working at his desk when Milken asked
him about the blue ledger book he had told him to keep on the
arrangement with David Solomon. "Do you have that Solomon book?"
Milken asked, and Peizer nodded. "Why don't you give it to Lorraine
Spurge?"

The next morning, Peizer gestured for Spurge to meet him in the kitchenette off the trading floor. He'd noticed that everyone seemed to be having conversations with the water running, so he turned on the kitchen faucet, assuming the offices were bugged. He handed Spurge the blue notebook.

"Michael asked me to give this to you," he said. When Peizer got back to his desk, Milken asked, "Everything in that book had to do with Finsbury, right?" Peizer nodded yes.

The notebook was never seen again. Presumably, it was destroyed.

On Friday, after the Boesky news had hit the tape, Cary Maultasch booked a flight to Los Angeles and headed straight for Kennedy airport. He met with Milken the next day.

"You don't know anything about the $5.3 million payment," Milken flatly told him. Maultasch didn't know what to say. Milken's comment was a statement, not a question. But he did know about the payment. He asked Milken whether he'd been "careful" in his October meeting with Boesky at the Beverly Hills Hotel. Milken looked troubled. He said he thought he had been—but in retrospect, he wasn't sure he'd been "careful enough."

Milken scheduled a 4 A.M. meeting with Maultasch for the next day. When Maultasch arrived at the office, he was escorted into a conference room. He was alone with Milken in the room, and a guard stood at the door throughout the session. Milken had a stack of documents with him; Maultasch noticed the names of some of the Boesky stocks that had figured in the $5.3 million payment. Milken spoke only in hushed tones, and frequently wrote his questions on a small yellow pad rather than speak out loud. He erased them as soon as Maultasch answered. Milken spent the session quizzing Maultasch about what he knew about various stocks that figured in the Boesky conspiracy. When Maultasch wanted to discuss a specific stock, he used his pen to point at the stock's name on the list; he never mentioned it out loud.

When he left after about half an hour, Maultasch handed his entry pass back to the guard at Drexel's front entrance. The guard tore it up into small pieces. "Don't worry," the guard said. "You weren't here."

John Mulheren hadn't believed it when a friend called from Canada with the tip that Boesky was going to plead. Then the news came over the tape. Mulheren froze. Even before the text had finished clattering out, he called his Canadian friend back. "Son of a bitch, you were right," he said. "I still can't believe it." He called his wife Nancy, who'd taken the kids to Disney World. "You won't believe this," he said. "Ivan Boesky is a crook."

"I'm not surprised," Nancy said.

Mulheren's mood soon shifted. He'd defended Boesky many times against his critics, and now Boesky had made him out to be a fool. He felt Boesky had used him, and Mulheren hated to be used. It upset him that there were people like Boesky. It shattered his view of human nature. On some level, he felt he'd never be the same again.

A few days later, his lawyer called. "Boesky's lawyers called to say you should resign as a trustee for Boesky's children," his lawyer said. Mulheren flatly refused. "I'm not resigning unless Boesky calls me himself," he said.

But Mulheren decided not to wait. He called Boesky. "I've heard from your lawyers," Mulheren said. "But if there's ever a time your kids are going to need a trustee, it's now. I'm willing to do it."

"You don't want the litigation, the hassles," Boesky said, sounding remote, emotionally detached. "You should withdraw."

Mulheren felt betrayed, yet still willing to help. "This is going to be pretty difficult for you. You'll need psychiatric help. You'll need support."

"Thanks, thanks for calling," Boesky said, sounding eager to end the conversation. Finally Mulheren got angry.

"I'll never forgive you," Mulheren said, his voice rising. "I'll never forgive you for what you've done to the business and everyone in it. It will never be the same. How could you do this? How could you?"

Boesky showed no emotion. "This is a highly technical business, and there are gray areas," he said.

"Bullshit there are," Mulheren angrily replied.

No one in the government was prepared for the media blitz that unfolded the week after the Boesky announcement. Charles Carberry, never comfortable with the press, was besieged. Two news organizations tried to storm past the guards at the U.S. attorney's office. When Carberry declined to answer questions from a *New York Post* reporter, the reporter threatened to "blow your operation out of the water" unless he talked.

"Blow it," Carberry said.

After midnight on the Saturday after the Boesky announcement,

Carberry, suffering from a bout of insomnia, flipped on his television. There was Lynch on CBS, discussing the Boesky case. Everywhere he turned, he saw Boesky's face: on the covers of *Time* and *Newsweek,* in all the major papers, on network television, even in the middle of the night. It was as though the dark side of the booming eighties had finally been personified.

But to the dismay of the government lawyers, the press barely credited them with capturing Boesky. Instead it bashed them for not extracting punishment enough. Overwhelmed by the sheer volume of calls, lacking large public-relations staffs, both Carberry and Lynch decided to talk only to a handful of reporters, which meant their version of events often went unreported.

The story continued to escalate. On Monday, November 17, *The Wall Street Journal* ran a front-page story identifying Drexel, Milken, Icahn, Posner, and Jefferies as being named in subpoenas. The next day, the paper rocked Wall Street with the news that the SEC had targeted Drexel in a formal order of investigation. The story named 12 companies that figured in the SEC's probe. And one day later, the *Journal* reported that Drexel was the target of a criminal probe by a federal grand jury.

The stock market had shaken off the initial Boesky news with a 13-point drop on Monday. But Drexel and Milken were another matter. Traders knew that any threat to the Milken money machine was far more ominous than Boesky's removal from the securities business. On Tuesday, the day the *Journal* revealed Drexel to be a target, the Dow Jones Industrial Average dropped 43 points. There was carnage among arbitrage stocks rumored to be takeover targets. Junk-bond prices plunged. Some Drexel clients pulled out of pending deals; Ronald Perelman abruptly abandoned his Drexel-backed hostile bid for Gillette, causing further market turmoil and anxiety. False rumors abounded; the most popular—that Milken had resigned—swept the floor of the stock exchange on an almost hourly basis.

Arbitrageurs, highly leveraged and flush with takeover stocks, were particularly hard-hit, and they blamed the government. The idea took root that, in allowing Boesky to liquidate many of his holdings prior to making a public announcement, the government had helped Boesky commit the greatest insider trade of his career. The notion spread like wildfire within the tightly linked network of arbs.

They began working their phones, pressing the theory upon reporters and anyone else who would listen. Among those hawking the theory were arbitrageurs Sandy Lewis, who had once been eager for Boesky's downfall, and Robert Freeman at Goldman, Sachs, whose name also appeared on some of the Boesky subpoenas after Boesky told prosecutors his suspicions that Freeman was trading on inside information.

Finally the arbs got their revenge. Just a week after the Boesky announcement, on November 21, *The Washington Post* ran a front-page story headlined, WALL STREET LAMBASTES SEC ACTION: AGENCY REPORTEDLY LET BOESKY SELL OFF STOCKS IN ADVANCE. For the SEC lawyers, the story was a nightmare.

"Wall Street reacted with outrage yesterday to reports that the Securities and Exchange Commission allowed stock speculator Ivan F. Boesky to sell more than $400 million of stocks of takeover targets before it announced the insider trading case against him that sent stock prices plunging," the story began. " 'The SEC has unwittingly aided one of the largest insider trading scams in history,' said David Nolan, a chief stock trader for Spear Leeds & Kellogg"—who, the *Post* reporters had no way of knowing, was soon to be under investigation himself. "The SEC," the story continued, "aware that reports of Boesky's trading set off a tumult on Wall Street, said it had no comment on the matter. . . ."

The story was quickly picked up around the country by subscribers to the Washington Post News Service and by other papers, radio stations, and television reporters. Lynch, Sturc, and their colleagues were stunned. The idea had never occurred to them; now, with benefit of hindsight, they realized that it should have. They had allowed Boesky to wind down his position only to encourage market stability, and to guarantee that the government would get paid its $100 million. It had never occurred to them that it would be interpreted as helping Boesky trade in advance on his own inside information that he was going to plead guilty and settle SEC charges.

At the same time, Drexel and its sympathizers were pressing the view that Boesky was a traitor to Wall Street who had taped colleagues and served as a government stool pigeon. They hired a private investigator, Jules Kroll, to unearth damaging information about Boesky. They portrayed Boesky as a liar who couldn't be trusted, and as a far greater criminal than the government had admitted.

On Monday, November 24, with government lawyers still reeling from the previous Friday's *Post* story, *The Wall Street Journal* ran an article by Priscilla Ann Smith and Beatrice Garcia calculating that Boesky's actual illegal profits totaled $203 million from the Dennis Levine trading alone, suggesting that the SEC had failed to penalize him adequately. "The disclosure seems likely to spur further criticism of the SEC, which already has been widely denounced for having allowed Mr. Boesky to raise money to meet his $100 million penalty by quietly disposing of $440 million of securities ahead of the November 14 announcement," the story said.

This was unfair, since most of those profits had flowed to Boesky's investors. As unwitting beneficiaries of Boesky's wrongdoing, investors weren't required to disgorge the profits. Boesky's share of those profits was much smaller; his total assets at the time of his settlement were less than $200 million. The SEC could have pointed this out; instead, the story reported, "An SEC spokeswoman consistently declined to comment during phone calls late last week." Thus, the thesis that Boesky had actually illegally earned far more than his penalty was picked up by other news outlets and found its way into the popular consciousness. Published estimates of his unlawful gains soon soared to $300 million.

In its continuing efforts to shift attention away from itself and onto the government, Drexel constantly pressed the theme that government lawyers were improperly leaking damaging information to the press, especially *The Wall Street Journal*. Drexel offered nothing to substantiate this allegation. Nonetheless, the "leak" thesis was widely reported.

The barrage of negative press quickly triggered a chorus of further criticism, most of it directed at the SEC. New York Congressman Charles Schumer attacked the agency. Congressman John Dingell, chairman of the powerful House Oversight and Investigations Committee, demanded a formal explanation and held public hearings. He even called Brian Campbell, the former Merrill Lynch broker who had handled Bank Leu's trades to testify. Dingell hailed Campbell as a "26-year-old whiz kid" who "cracked the code and piggybacked over 20 of Mr. Levine's insider trades" at a time when the SEC, "despite all the wonder of the most modern technology . . . , could not make a case." Lynch was enraged that Campbell, a suspect himself, would be praised at the SEC's expense. Valuable government staff time was diverted from the investigation to calming Congress and responding to inquiries.

Worst of all was the loss of confidence within the agency itself. Shad, who had so looked forward to the Boesky press conference as the pinnacle of his career at the SEC, was devastated by the bad publicity. He seemed to blame Lynch. In Lynch's view, the commission began to delay approving his requests for additional subpoenas, which were crucial for continuing the investigation. He felt he was in danger of being crippled.

On November 24, the day of the *Journal* article suggesting that Boesky's illegal profits had vastly exceeded his penalty, Lynch called his demoralized troops into a conference room and tried to give them a pep talk. It wasn't easy. He likened the experience to having discovered the Salk vaccine, and then being criticized for killing monkeys in experimental trials. Lynch himself had been deeply depressed. He wasn't sleeping at night. He was thinking seriously of resigning.

But then he worried that no one else would pull through on the case, and the investigation would die. Knowing what he knew—the magnitude of the crime and the illegal profits, most of which were still going on—he couldn't let that happen. So he summoned every bit of determination he had. He warned his staff that, in all likelihood, there would be more bad publicity. They were only at the beginning of what was going to be a long, hard-fought war.

"We are engaged in what may be the most important thing we will ever do in our lives," he told his staff. "We have to fight and go on."

11.

Martin Siegel walked into his bedroom and tossed his suit coat on the bed. It was a relief to be home for dinner at a decent hour. It was just 6:30 P.M., October 29, 1986. He walked to his desk, by a large window that looked out over Gracie Square park, and gazed outside.

·Siegel felt better now than he had felt in months—since Dennis Levine's arrest. The day after the news of Levine's downfall and his panic in the airport phone booth, Siegel had gone to see his doctor. He hadn't felt well, and thought he was suffering from too much stress. Deep down, Siegel had wanted the doctor to ask why he felt so bad, so anxious. He'd wanted to unburden himself. Instead, the doctor gave him a quick examination and brushed aside his complaints. "It's just overwork," he said. "You'll be fine."

Perhaps the doctor had been right. Siegel and his wife had spent the previous weekend with friends in Key Biscayne. Out on the ocean on a catamaran, in a stiff breeze and blazing sunshine, Siegel had enjoyed himself.

He smiled at the view outside his window. Children clambered over the playground equipment. But the calm was interrupted by the telephone's ring. Siegel absentmindedly picked up the receiver, not waiting for Doris, the nanny, to answer. A man's voice interrupted his reverie.

"Is this Marty Siegel?"

"Yes, it is," Siegel replied.

"This is Bill." There was silence. On Monday, Doris had told Siegel that someone named Bill had called, leaving no number. The same thing had happened yesterday. Both days, Siegel had returned at his usual hour, about 8 P.M. He hadn't given the calls much thought; he didn't know, offhand, who Bill was.

"Bill who?" Siegel asked.

"You know," the voice said in an insinuating tone. "Bill."

"No, I don't know," Siegel answered, getting edgy. Was this a crank call? There was another pause.

"Did you get my letter?" Bill asked.

"No."

"You know, the letter I sent?"

Siegel didn't know why he didn't just hang up. "No, I don't know anything about a letter. Why don't you tell me?" There was another pause, then the voice dropped its bombshell.

"I mean, your relationship with the Russian."

Siegel closed his eyes, only to see an image of Boesky. He struggled to sound unconcerned. "I don't know what you're talking about," he said calmly.

"I sent a letter to you," Bill continued. "I told you in the letter, I want to meet with you."

"I don't know you," Siegel said.

"Oh come on, don't try to fool me," Bill said, his tone becoming menacing. "I know."

Siegel insisted again that he didn't know what the man was talking about, and then Bill clearly had a moment of anxiety. "Is this the Marty Siegel who worked at Kidder, Peabody and now works at Drexel?"

"Yeah, it is," Siegel said, deciding he'd had enough of this. "Don't bother me anymore. If you do, I'll go to the police."

"I doubt that," Bill replied sarcastically. Siegel hung up.

He reeled away from the desk, clenching his fists. He had feared his life would come to this. "So this is the way it all ends!" he cried aloud. His stomach heaved violently and he rushed toward the adjoining master bathroom.

Moments later, an anxious Jane Day came running into the room. She found her husband slumped over the toilet, vomiting. "Are you all right?" she asked anxiously as Siegel rose from the bathroom floor and tried to pull himself together.

"It must be a stomach virus," he told her. "It came on so suddenly."

As soon as he was alone again, he called Martin Lipton, the lawyer he felt closest to, both personally and professionally. Lipton's secretary at Wachtell said that her boss was in Houston that night, but gave Siegel a number where he could be reached.

"Marty, I'm being blackmailed," Siegel told Lipton, and gave him an outline of his conversation with the mysterious caller. Lipton urged Siegel to see Larry Pedowitz the next day. Pedowitz was the former chief of the criminal division at the U.S. attorney's office who'd handled the Ilan Reich affair for Wachtell.

Siegel met Pedowitz the next morning and gave him a detailed account of the exchange, mentioning that Bill had referred several times to a letter he'd sent him, seeking a face-to-face meeting. "Have you checked your mail in Connecticut?" Pedowitz asked.

Siegel realized that neither he nor Jane Day had been out to the Connecticut house for more than two weeks. When he drove out to the house, the letter was conspicuous in the heap of unopened mail. Siegel put on plastic gloves to protect any fingerprints; then, with trembling hands, he opened the envelope and hastily scanned the short letter. It said, briefly and enigmatically, "I know," and asked for money. If he wasn't paid off, Bill said, he'd turn Siegel in to the Internal Revenue Service. Siegel carefully placed the envelope and letter in a larger envelope, sealed it, and drove back to New York.

When Pedowitz saw the evidence, he was suspicious. He wondered out loud whether the letter and phone calls might not be an elaborate government attempt to entrap Siegel in a bribery scheme. It seemed unlikely, but in the wake of the Levine crackdown and government references to a continuing investigation, anything seemed possible. Still, Pedowitz suggested that Siegel wait and see if anything else happened.

The next week, Siegel got a call from Boesky, who suddenly seemed anxious to set up a meeting. Siegel said no and hung up, but was shaken by the call. Then, on November 10, special IRS agents showed up unannounced at Siegel's office. Siegel was out of town, but when he heard of this development, he called Pedowitz. This time Pedowitz said he thought he'd better contact the U.S. attorney's office.

"Go ahead," Siegel told him. "I want this thing cleared up."

That afternoon, Siegel heard from Pedowitz again. "You should come in first thing in the morning," Pedowitz said, sounding grave, offering no details.

"The U.S. attorney knows all about the letter," Pedowitz told Siegel the next morning. "They know all about you and Boesky." He didn't need to continue. Siegel's defenses were shattered. He put his head in his hands and began to weep.

"I did this," he said between sobs. "I'm guilty. I'm sorry. I want to do the right thing."

Pedowitz said he'd already spoken to his partners and they'd concluded that Wachtell, Lipton couldn't represent Siegel; the firm had represented too many clients in deals that might figure in any charges against him. But Pedowitz offered to help Siegel find another criminal lawyer. "Some lawyers fight, others work with the government," Pedowitz said. "Which kind would you prefer?" Siegel said he didn't want to make any decision until he'd spoken to his wife.

He took a cab back to his apartment. He knew he couldn't go any further without telling his wife, but it was the encounter he dreaded most. He was terrified that she might leave him. As the cab maneuvered slowly through midmorning traffic, Siegel fantasized about suicide: Instead of going up to the apartment, he would get the family's van out of its parking garage, leave the city, and drive east on Interstate 95 until he got to the Mianus River bridge. Then he'd drive off the edge. The prospect of death seemed abstractly inviting, but he blanched at the thought of a painful crash followed by drowning.

When he arrived at the apartment, the children's nanny told him that his wife had gone out to do some early Christmas shopping. Siegel paced the rooms. Everything, he knew, would soon be gone. His wife's 36th birthday was just two weeks away, and he was about to ruin it. Then he heard the front door open and went into the foyer. Jane Day, laden with packages, was surprised to see her husband at home, but began excitedly telling him about her purchases and her plans for the upcoming holidays. Siegel forced himself to cut her off.

"There's something I've got to tell you," he said as he led her into the living room. He closed the double wood-paneled doors as she took off her coat and sat down on the sofa. Siegel sat down next to her and took her hand. He took a deep breath and began: "You remember the letter I was so upset about, the one that arrived in Connecticut? There was something to it. I made a terrible mistake. I don't know how you'll ever be able to forgive me."

Jane Day immediately broke into sobs, realizing from her husband's tone and demeanor that something terrible was happening to them. Siegel pressed forward, quickly summarizing his insider-trading scheme with Boesky. He felt ill with anguish. Jane Day continued to sob, and Siegel saw with horror how he was hurting her. It was the worst experience of his life.

"What you did was horrible," his wife choked out. Her biggest problem, she said, was that she felt betrayed: that he'd kept this terrible secret from her. She said he had shattered her trust in him.

Yet even as she said this, she recognized her husband's suffering and despair and her own shock quickly yielded to fears that he might commit suicide. She gave him the crucial support he needed to go on. "You've been a good father and husband," she acknowledged, before dissolving again in tears.

At about 1 P.M., Siegel returned to the Wachtell, Lipton offices and met again with Pedowitz. "I don't want to fight," Siegel told him. "I want to get this over with, and make amends." Siegel ended up retaining Jed Rakoff, former head of the securities fraud unit in the U.S. attorney's office, and then a partner in Mudge Rose Guthrie Alexander & Ferdon. Rakoff came up from Mudge Rose's downtown offices and met with Siegel and Pedowitz. By the time he arrived, Siegel had received a subpoena from the SEC. The U.S. attorney's office, after the call from Pedowitz, had alerted the SEC that Siegel was at Wachtell, Lipton, so the subpoena was delivered there.

Rakoff was struck that, though obviously distraught, Siegel didn't try to minimize or deny his guilt. He quickly briefed Rakoff on the arrangement with Boesky, including the most damaging aspects, such as the cash payoffs. And the arrangement with Boesky wasn't all he'd done wrong, Siegel said. He told Rakoff briefly about his relationship with Freeman.

Siegel was particularly worried about his colleagues at Drexel, and his relationship to the firm. Under the circumstances, he couldn't keep working as though nothing had happened. He felt he had to talk to Joseph right away. Rakoff, on the other hand, wanted to preserve as much flexibility for Siegel as possible. He knew that Siegel might be valuable as an undercover operative. But Siegel was insistent that he would not go undercover at Drexel. None of his own wrongdoing had occurred there, he insisted, and he knew of no criminal activity at Drexel. So it wasn't fair to attempt to trap his Drexel colleagues. Rakoff agreed that Siegel could talk to Joseph, tell him about the subpoena, and ask for a "medical" leave while he dealt with the questions in the subpoena. Then he should meet again that evening with Rakoff and his partner, Audrey Strauss, at Mudge Rose's offices.

As Siegel was leaving Wachtell, Lipton's offices, he asked to see Lipton, who had now returned from Texas. Alone, he went into the senior partner's spacious office, which Siegel had visited so often during his investment banking career. Face to face with the man who'd done so much to launch and advance his career, Siegel again broke down. "I'm sorry," he stammered repeatedly. Perhaps Lipton had

lived through this nightmarish scene too many times: there had been
Florentino and Reich, two of his own partners; now it was Siegel,
someone who was almost like a son to him. Lipton offered Siegel no
comfort, no reassurance. To Siegel, he seemed as cold and remote as
stone.

After leaving Wachtell, Lipton, Siegel and Rakoff went to Rak-
off's office. Late that afternoon Pedowitz called and began to read to
Rakoff and Siegel the ticker report of Boesky's plea agreement and
SEC settlement. Suddenly the confusing sequence of events began to
make sense. "You have no idea of the magnitude of this," Siegel told
Rakoff and Strauss. "It's all going to come tumbling down."

Siegel finally reached his own office at Drexel late that afternoon,
and went straight to Joseph's office. Joseph had come down from the
strategy session after hearing the Boesky news. He thought Siegel
looked terrible, as if he'd had some terrible shock.

"I want to take a leave of absence," Siegel said. "I've gotten a
subpoena." Siegel was taken aback by Joseph's response. He laughed!
"Join the club," Joseph said cheerfully. "Ackerman's got one, so does
Milken. Everybody got one." Siegel, already dazed, was dumbfounded.
What was going on? What did all of these people have to do with him?
Absorbed in his own problems, he didn't stop to think that Boesky
might have implicated others besides himself.

"Is it an SEC subpoena or a grand jury subpoena?" Joseph asked.
Siegel said it came from the SEC. That seemed to alleviate most of
Joseph's concern. "Don't worry," Joseph said. "Just keep working.
There's no reason to take a leave. The firm will back you a hundred
percent."

While Siegel was meeting with Joseph, Rakoff had called Carberry. "I understand you want to serve a subpoena on Martin Siegel,"
Rakoff said. "I'll accept service. I'm Siegel's lawyer." He added that
he'd like to chat with Carberry about the case, and Carberry suggested
the next morning.

Rakoff knew then that he and Siegel would have to move fast.
He'd been Carberry's boss as head of the securities fraud unit, and
knew him as a no-nonsense guy who liked to hit potential white-collar
defendants fast and hard. Rakoff warned Siegel that if he were going
to cut a deal, he'd have to do it quickly, even though it meant accepting
the possibility of both criminal and civil penalties, possible disruption
of his marriage and family life, even potential bankruptcy. Rakoff also
offered to evaluate Siegel's defenses in the event he chose to fight.

"I want to plead, and I want to make amends," Siegel insisted.
"I'm not prepared to fight unless you tell me to."

Siegel and Jane Day came down to Rakoff's office the next morning, Saturday, November 15. Siegel felt much better than he had the day before. He had confided further in Jane Day the previous night, and he thought he had a commitment from her to support him, whatever happened. He felt a load had been lifted from him. He'd put his trust in the government. He'd do the right thing. He'd be punished, but then everything would be okay. He thought the government seemed a little like his parents; now the government would take care of him.

At one point, Audrey Strauss, Rakoff's partner on the case, cautioned him. "Marty, yesterday you were too down," she said. "Today you're too up."

Rakoff and Strauss briefed the Siegels further on the implications of a guilty plea, trying to reassure them, saying that things always look bleaker than they are, that the situation wasn't hopeless. Then Rakoff went over to see Carberry, who wasted no time getting to the point.

"We've got him," he said bluntly of Siegel. "We've got three witnesses: Ivan Boesky, the courier who dropped off the cash, and a witness to the transfer. We think Siegel can be of some help to us. We know about Freeman," he added, startling Rakoff with the one name he recognized immediately from Siegel's confession. Rakoff wondered if Carberry was bluffing.

"Assuming for the sake of argument that that's the case," Carberry continued, "I'm prepared to offer four felony counts."

Rakoff, trying to show no reaction, probed for more deal terms. What judge would be available? In Manhattan federal court, the same judge who accepts guilty pleas stays with a case through sentencing; Rakoff hoped that Siegel's plea could be timed so as to secure a lenient sentencing judge. Carberry said the government would try to be flexible, but Siegel would have to enter his plea when the government told him to. Would Carberry want Siegel to wear a wire? Yes, Carberry said.

Rakoff took the offer back to Siegel, who told him to cut a deal. Rakoff in turn gave Carberry an informal proffer, promising that Siegel could indeed provide incriminating evidence on the head of arbitrage at another major Wall Street firm, though he didn't mention Freeman by name. In return, Carberry offered to drop two of the felony counts. Rakoff said they had a deal, contingent on negotiating an SEC settlement.

With the criminal agreement in hand, Rakoff called Lynch at the SEC. Still smarting from all the bad publicity over the Boesky affair, the SEC was eager to parade Siegel as evidence of the value of Boesky's cooperation. It wasn't about to risk further criticism that it was too soft on Wall Street criminals. Rakoff asked what the SEC wanted.

"It's simple," Lynch replied. "We want everything except his two houses." ("Jesus," Siegel said later when Rakoff conveyed the news. "I only took $700,000" from Boesky.) Rakoff argued strenuously that the SEC was being unreasonable, that at the very least Siegel should be able to keep his earnings from Drexel, none of which were tainted by any wrongdoing. Sturc, handling most of the negotiations for the SEC, finally agreed, but Shad and the commission vetoed the agreement. They insisted on confiscating practically everything Siegel had. They knew they had Siegel over a barrel, and they were determined to overcome the earlier bad publicity. They'd allow Siegel to keep his pension plan contributions and the two houses, and that was it. Siegel would even have to forgo $10 million in stock and guaranteed bonus owed him by Drexel, which the agency wouldn't allow Drexel to pay him.

Rakoff thought he could fight the draconian terms, but Siegel told him he didn't want to. Now that it had come to this, Siegel was amazed at how little he cared about the money. When he'd been earning a six-figure income, money had seemed so important—but it had never been enough to confer the elusive sense of security he craved. Now he was ruined no matter how much money he had. So what did it matter if he had none at all?

He also thought the severe penalty would help assuage his guilt in the eyes of the public. If this was the price for making amends, so be it. If he had any lingering doubts, it was because his former Wall Street colleagues would view his plea bargain and SEC deal as a "bad trade." For a skilled dealmaker, that was embarrassing.

Though final details weren't worked out until mid-December, the SEC deal was largely in place within a week, and the plea bargain was quickly finalized. Now Siegel began life as a cooperating witness, as Boesky had done before him.

Late one evening during Thanksgiving week, Rakoff and Siegel slipped into a rear entrance of the massive federal post office located across the street from the World Trade Center in downtown Manhattan. The site and time—10 P.M.—had been chosen to preserve secrecy. Siegel was taken to the postal inspectors' offices, where he met Carberry for the first time.

Carberry's appearance confirmed his reputation as a "Columbo" type: Siegel couldn't help but notice ketchup stains on the shirt stretched over his considerable girth. Siegel also met Doonan, who he learned would be his "handler" during the undercover phase of his cooperation, and Robert Paschall. Siegel looked carefully at Doonan, who struck him as a tough Irishman. Something about Doonan seemed vaguely familiar, yet he was sure he'd never met him.

Carberry was impressed by Siegel, the first investment banker he'd met whom he considered "top-tier." Levine and Wilkis certainly weren't. Boesky was an arb. Siegel, by contrast, was good-looking, poised, charming, even when distraught.

"They want to look in your eyes to see if they can believe you," Rakoff had told him. "Answer their questions and tell the truth." Siegel took the prosecutors through all his deals with Boesky and Freeman. He tried to be as precise as possible, even though he was working from memory and would have liked to have reviewed some of his diary entries and trading records for precise details. Siegel talked that evening for about an hour and a half; a series of similar meetings followed. Some of the deals, especially with Freeman, were complicated: Unocal, for example, with its complex proration calculations, or the long saga of Storer.

Siegel made no attempt to suggest that his behavior had fallen into "gray" areas or that everyone on Wall Street did it. He made no excuses. Levine and Boesky had shown some remorse, but their primary sorrow seemed to be that they'd been caught. Siegel, the prosecutors thought, believed that what he had done was wrong and wanted to make amends.

SEC lawyers didn't attend any of the sessions. The chill between the U.S. attorney's office and the SEC was obvious to Siegel. The U.S. attorney's office was still smarting from the SEC's bad publicity. Siegel was told to reveal nothing to SEC lawyers, especially anything about Goldman, Sachs, for fear of leaks.

"Don't talk to them," Doonan told Siegel at one point. "They'll just screw things up."

Finally, in January 1987, the SEC said it had to have access to Siegel to corroborate some of Boesky's claims, and a meeting was arranged at a room at the Gramercy Park Hotel with Leo Wang and another SEC lawyer. But Siegel was allowed by the U.S. attorney's office to discuss only the Boesky aspects of his wrongdoing. Freeman's name wasn't mentioned.

When Siegel had agreed to cooperate, Rakoff had pressed him to face the fact that the life he had known in New York would soon be over. He had to accept the likelihood that every aspect of his present and former life would be subject to intense scrutiny. Rakoff wanted Siegel to see a psychiatrist or psychologist at the time he agreed to plead. But that was impossible; Goldman, Sachs might subpoena the therapist. Patient communications aren't necessarily protected from disclosure in federal courts.

Rakoff and Strauss urged Siegel to move his family out of the storm center as soon as possible, so that they would have time to adjust by the time Siegel's guilty plea became public. This was especially hard for Jane Day to accept; she loved the Connecticut house she and Siegel had designed, and the thought of leaving all her friends, pulling the children out of their schools, was devastating. Having agreed to stand by Siegel, however, she accepted the need to plan a new life somewhere else. They settled on Florida, a state whose homestead laws protect a defendant's home from seizure by creditors. Siegel put the Connecticut house and New York cooperative on the market, and spent several weekends touring various Florida cities, starting in Tampa, working his way down the West Coast and then up the East Coast, ending in Jacksonville. En route, Siegel had another suicidal impulse. Driving on I-95, he thought how easy it would be simply to shift the wheel and head into oncoming traffic. The thought of causing an accident, of hurting innocent victims, stopped him.

He settled on Jacksonville because Tampa/St. Petersburg was too sleepy; Miami too urban; tony Palm Beach would have sent the wrong message; and besides, he didn't want to run into all his former colleagues from Wall Street and corporate America. Siegel liked Jacksonville's healthy probusiness climate. He thought he could build a career there once he had put this ordeal behind him, assuming there ever would be such a time. And he found a beautiful house, a soaring, modern mansion directly on the beach in exclusive Ponte Vedra Beach. It had a three-car garage, a two-story living room with fireplace, and a third-floor turret with sweeping views above the master bedroom that would make a perfect home office. He also bought adjoining beachfront property, and had bedrooms for the children built on top of the garage. The house, the land, and improvements cost Siegel $3.5 million.

Siegel had no trouble selling the Connecticut house (for $3.5 million) and the apartment in the city, which was purchased by the first person who saw it (for $1.5 million). The Manhattan real estate market was still booming. Nearly all the proceeds were plowed into the Florida property, taxes and legal fees. No one knew the Siegels were moving to Florida, but inevitably, word leaked out that the they had sold their home; neighbors jumped to the conclusion that Siegel and Jane Day were getting a divorce. Siegel was infuriated that one of his neighbors called him, asking eagerly whether he'd be selling his jet ski.

Jane Day, Doris, Jessica, and the twins drove to Florida in mid-January. Siegel stayed in New York, trying to act as though nothing was happening. He wanted to be in Florida the day his family moved into the new house, but a heavy snow kept him from flying out of New York. "We're in the bush," Doris reported when Siegel reached them by phone at their new home. For six months, Scotty, one of the twins, would ask, "Where's the doorman?" whenever they drove up to his new home.

Siegel was lonely in New York, but somehow he kept up appearances, showing up for work, returning phone calls. Drexel hadn't pressed him for further explanations. The firm's lawyers at Cahill Gordon & Reindel had periodically called Rakoff, asking repeatedly for assurances that Siegel knew of no wrongdoing at the firm, and, initially, pressing for more information about Siegel's situation. Rakoff said only that there were "allegations" relating to Siegel's pre-Drexel career, but he refused to elaborate. Drexel took pains not to alienate someone who might be cooperating with the government. In January, Siegel received his $3 million bonus, which he turned over to the SEC.

Everyone who knew Siegel realized that something was terribly wrong. He had lost much of his energy, his enthusiasm, his sparkle. He stopped attending management committee meetings at Drexel and he wasn't generating any new deals. Both Siegel and Rakoff had been instructed by the government to lie if necessary to preserve his value as an undercover operative, but it rarely proved necessary.

"I hear you're cooperating," Joseph casually said one day. Siegel just shrugged and Joseph didn't press.

John Crudele, a reporter for *The New York Times*, called Siegel and asked him if he was in trouble.

"No," Siegel said.

At first Siegel resisted doing undercover work, but the government insisted, saying they wanted him to record DeNunzio and Tabor. They also told him they didn't want him to have any contact with Freeman.

"We don't want you getting anywhere near Freeman," Doonan said. They wanted to proceed cautiously, see how Siegel performed, and gauge the reactions of those he contacted. They didn't want to risk tipping Freeman.

One of the investigators' ideas was to wire Siegel and send him into a meeting with Ralph DeNunzio. Siegel would steer the conversation to Kidder, Peabody's arbitrage operations and the scheme with Freeman, trying to corroborate Siegel's claim that DeNunzio knew about the arrangement. Since DeNunzio hadn't traded himself, they needed more evidence; they wouldn't want to charge DeNunzio based solely on Siegel's word. But there were obvious problems. Siegel was reluctant. He didn't see how he could plausibly meet with DeNunzio after having abandoned the firm for Drexel.

The solution, hatched by Doonan and Paschall, was to have Siegel call his good friend Peter Goodson, now Kidder, Peabody's head of M&A. Siegel would tell Goodson that he wanted to come back to Kidder, Peabody because Drexel had been implicated in the Boesky scandal. He would ask Goodson to arrange a meeting with DeNunzio, which Siegel would attend wearing a wire. Siegel wasn't happy; Siegel was the godfather to Goodson's daughter. Goodson had been Siegel's best friend at Kidder, Peabody. But the government gave him no choice.

With Doonan at his side, Siegel called Goodson's home; he reached him on the third try. At first, Goodson seemed to swallow the story, and said he'd try to arrange the meeting. Ultimately, however, the gambit went nowhere. Goodson reported that DeNunzio had rejected the idea, and clearly hadn't yet gotten over Siegel's betrayal. DeNunzio's message to Siegel: "You made your bed, now lie in it."

The government showed scant interest in Wigton. He and Siegel had little in common in any event, and it was hard to come up with a plausible reason for Siegel to call him. Tabor, Wigton's former partner in arbitrage, was another matter. Doonan immediately saw him as a potential target.

Tabor had left Kidder, Peabody soon after Siegel. Much like Levine, he had parlayed his slender arbitrage experience into an impressive title and salary. First he had gone to Chemical Bank, where he was named head of arbitrage. He was going to launch the bank's new arbitrage department—but announcement of the move triggered a wave of bad publicity for Chemical. Clients were upset that the bank was going to try to profit from hostile takeovers. Chemical told Tabor he couldn't invest in hostile deals, an absurd restraint for any true arbitrageur. As a result, Tabor quit Chemical and became an arbitrageur at Merrill Lynch.

The government believed Tabor to be especially vulnerable to the threat of prosecution. After news of Levine's arrest broke, Tabor had called Siegel at Drexel. "Are we okay?" he'd asked, suggesting he knew Siegel could be a threat to him. Siegel had assured him he'd had no contact with Levine. Once at Merrill Lynch, Tabor had again called Siegel, who was then working for the Haft family in their Drexel-backed bid for Safeway. Merrill Lynch was representing the company in its defense. Tabor started giving Siegel what Tabor described as "Merrill Lynch's thinking" about the defense, including confidential information about the scheduling of board meetings. He was treading very close to inside information, and Siegel believed he was hoping to establish a relationship. Siegel had never taken the bait.

When Siegel called Tabor and suggested they get together to "talk about the good old days" at Kidder, Peabody, Tabor seemed puzzled. He put Siegel off. So Siegel tried another tack. Citing the

Boesky subpoenas at Drexel, he said he wanted to leave Drexel. "Maybe we could get together and set up our own thing," he said. That didn't bear fruit either, so Siegel called again. "Maybe I could talk to you about coming to Merrill Lynch."

Tabor must have wondered about Siegel's sudden desire to "get together." Their paths had rarely crossed when they were working together at the same firm. Doonan monitored all the calls, usually from a phone extension in his office.

On Wednesday afternoon, February 11, 1987, about 4:30 P.M., Doonan and Paschall showed up at Siegel's apartment, where he was still living pending the closing of its sale. That afternoon, Tabor had been fired from his arbitrage position at Merrill Lynch, an event which might weaken his resistance and increase his susceptibility to government cooperation. They were frustrated at Siegel's lack of success as an undercover operative and were getting impatient. They were also nervous about a recent gossip column item in a New York newspaper; the *New York Post*'s Suzy had mentioned that Siegel might be in trouble in the Boesky investigation. They knew this would only fuel suspicions of Siegel. Time was running out.

"This is your last chance," Doonan told Siegel sternly. "Get Tabor. Get a meeting with him." Siegel picked up the phone and called Tabor at home, trying to sound sympathetic to Tabor's having been fired, then raising again the prospect of Siegel setting up some kind of business with Tabor. Siegel suggested they meet to discuss the possibility. This time Tabor flatly refused, saying he was "too busy."

Doonan, monitoring the conversation from another phone, heard Siegel hang up, and then the click as Tabor hung up. But the line wasn't dead. He heard a male voice in Tabor's apartment. "Should I hang up now?" the voice asked. Doonan was annoyed. He realized immediately that Tabor had had his conversation monitored. He'd caught on.

"We're going to have to do this *our* way now," Doonan said ominously as he and Paschall stalked out of Siegel's apartment.

Siegel realized what "our way" might mean. He knew now what Doonan was capable of. Several weeks after their early debriefings, Doonan had spoken to Siegel for the first time on the telephone. Doonan's voice, isolated on the phone, had sounded eerily familiar. Suddenly Siegel had felt a chill. He had remembered. He was transported back to an autumn evening, to his bedroom; he was gazing at the playground, answering the phone.

"Is this Marty Siegel?" the voice had asked, ruining Siegel's life. "Did you get my letter?"

Doonan was "Bill."

About two weeks after the Boesky announcement, Milken again summoned Jim Dahl. Dahl still didn't really understand what was unfolding. All he knew was that, since their meeting in the men's room, Milken had been spending most of his time holed up with his brother Lowell.

"You need to get a lawyer," Milken said in a lowered voice. Dahl hadn't been subpoenaed, but given his importance in the high-yield area, and his direct dealings with Boesky, it was probably only a matter of time before he would be. Milken strongly urged Dahl to hire Edward Bennett Williams, the famed Washington criminal lawyer. Dahl didn't have to worry about Williams's fees—they'd be paid by Drexel, as would Milken's. Milken explained that he himself had retained Williams and assured Dahl he didn't need to worry. "The only one they want is me," he said.

Dahl wasn't sure it made sense for him to have the same lawyer as Milken. Wouldn't Milken's interests come first? He was still mulling things over the next week when Williams and a young lawyer from Williams & Connolly, Robert Litt, arrived in Beverly Hills for interviews with potential witnesses.

Dahl was dazzled by the crusty veteran of so many highly publicized battles. Williams was among the most famous of America's criminal defense lawyers, a Washington legend, unrivaled in criminal cases with political overtones. He had defended Senator Joseph McCarthy, Teamster boss Jimmy Hoffa, Lyndon Johnson protégé Bobby Baker, financier Robert Vesco, former Treasury Secretary John Connally, and former Congressman Adam Clayton Powell. As the owner of the Baltimore Orioles baseball team, and former part owner of the Washington Redskins, Williams understood business. He was also suffering from cancer.

"Listen, Jim, it's gonna pass," Williams said in his throaty voice. "All we have to do is hang together and fight this fuckin' thing. These government lawyers are no match for us." Williams continued in this vein, sprinkling his remarks with profanity. He and Litt assured Dahl that he wasn't a subject or target of the investigation; he was just a bystander, a potential witness to hurt Milken. "We'll beat these sons of bitches," Williams said, "but we have to remain on the inside of the tent pissing out."

It was crucial for Milken to keep potential witnesses under his control. Boesky could always be dismissed as an admitted liar and felon; his testimony alone would never convict Milken. Milken and his lawyers knew that, and so did prosecutors. A member of Milken's own team, however, could inflict a fatal wound, if any defected. That could not be allowed to happen.

Milken himself would never testify. Not for a minute did he consider pleading guilty, telling the truth, cooperating. Unlike Boesky and Levine, he had no one more important to turn in, and less to offer the government in return for leniency. He was the pinnacle, the most important person in American finance. There was no "bigger fish." And unlike Siegel, he apparently felt no remorse. He'd beaten back SEC inquiries in the past, and he seemed confident he'd defeat this one.

Unlike Pitt and Rakoff, Williams made no attempt whatsoever to get the truth from Milken, not in his initial interviews or at any time thereafter. Williams didn't want to know. Williams often said he had a cardinal rule: "Don't ask a question to which you don't already know the answer."

Milken had hired Williams almost immediately after the Boesky announcement on November 14, and seemed to treat him as an authority figure, to hold him in a kind of awe he displayed toward no one else involved in the investigation. He knew him through Drexel client Marvin Davis, the Denver oilman who, with the help of Milken's junk bonds, had transformed himself into a Hollywood tycoon and owner of 20th Century–Fox. Williams had long represented Davis, as well as Milken client Victor Posner.

Williams's partner, Litt, had been surprised when Milken hired Williams & Connolly. Litt knew Carberry from his own days in the Manhattan U.S. attorney's office, and had called Carberry earlier to congratulate him on the Boesky coup. Then, on the Sunday after the Friday announcement of Boesky's fall, Williams had called. "We're representing Milken," Williams had said gruffly. Litt then called Carberry to apologize for his earlier call, saying he hadn't realized Williams & Connolly would be involved.

The same weekend, Milken had also hired Arthur Liman and Martin Flumenbaum, the partners at Paul, Weiss, Rifkind, Wharton & Garrison who had also represented Dennis Levine. Despite the Levine case, Liman is known more as a corporate litigator than as a criminal defense lawyer. He represented Pennzoil in its monumental and successful fight against Texaco, and served as counsel for the Senate's Iran-Contra investigation.

Milken also knew Liman; Paul, Weiss had become the law firm of choice for many of Milken's clients, such as Nelson Peltz of Triangle

Industries and Ronald Perelman, who took over Revlon. Milken realized that Liman understood securities law and the world of hostile takeovers and junk-bond financing.

Williams insisted that he be lead counsel, and Milken agreed. Liman and Flumenbaum would be closely involved. What Liman sacrificed in ego, he and his firm would more than make up for in billings, since Paul, Weiss would contribute the bulk of the manpower, handling the voluminous, time-consuming, and often tedious SEC demands. Williams said from the beginning, "I don't give a shit about the SEC." He only wanted a small handful of lawyers from Williams and Connolly working on the matter. That was his style.

Paul, Weiss's style was to overwhelm. Known for its scorched-earth litigation tactics, Paul, Weiss could combat the government with the vast manpower of one of the country's largest firms. Drexel also had an army of lawyers. Drexel had retained its usual corporate counsel, Cahill Gordon & Reindel, another huge New York firm, as well as Peter Fleming, a noted criminal lawyer who had defended Hitachi in a well-known government sting operation.

The single most important lawyer in the Milken defense ranks, however, was probably the most obscure: Richard Sandler, Lowell Milken's boyhood friend who'd become the Milken family lawyer. He had been working from offices within Drexel's own Beverly Hills office building. Though Sandler had been closer to Lowell, he had always seemed to worship Mike Milken, on whom his practice and livelihood depended. His zeal went beyond the financial relationship; it was as though his own identity had fused with Milken's.

Sandler, unprepossessing but energetic, usually dismissed contemptuously by traders and salesmen in the office as "the real estate lawyer," was suddenly the most important person in Milken's orbit. He became the nerve center for information about the investigation, constantly in contact with potential witnesses and other lawyers. He immersed himself in the facts of the case—or, more precisely, the facts of the case favorable to Milken's declarations of innocence. He became nearly inseparable from Milken, traveling with him almost everywhere he went. Sandler's conference room seemed to become an oasis for Milken away from the trading desk, as he spent more and more time there. Sandler also oversaw construction of a second-floor conference room in the Beverly Hills office. Dubbed "the cone of silence," the soundproof room was swept for listening devices every week, and used for strategy discussions.

Not surprisingly, the Milken and Drexel lawyers agreed to cooperate, and signed a formal agreement known as a joint defense agreement. Such an agreement extends the attorney-client privilege to all the lawyers in the agreement, and provides for full disclosure of information within their ranks. Despite the agreement, however, the Milken camp didn't share everything with Drexel. From the outset, Williams told Milken and his lawyers that Drexel would eventually capitulate.

A securities firm, Williams predicted, couldn't survive in the shadow of prolonged criminal and SEC investigations. Drexel would become the enemy and was likely to give the government everything it had gleaned from Milken in the course of the investigation. None of this, of course, was communicated to Drexel officials or their lawyers.

Milken's lawyers had little respect for Drexel's. At an early meeting of all the lawyers at Peter Fleming's firm in New York, Thomas Curnin, Drexel's lead counsel, was leading a discussion when Liman arrived late. Liman began talking as he came through the door, interrupting Curnin, imperiously taking charge. Curnin smoldered in silence.

The Milken team also sometimes seemed an uneasy alliance. Despite the earlier agreement that Williams would be lead counsel, Paul, Weiss vied with Williams & Connolly for dominance. Early in the case, Williams learned that Flumenbaum had made what seemed an innocuous call to Carberry to discuss a subpoena matter. Williams, who deemed the U.S. attorney's office to be his turf and had a precise plan for communicating with prosecutors, hit the ceiling. He called Sandler and screamed, "If that fat little shit steps out of line again, I'll squash him like a bug. If he were at my firm, he'd be fired." Annoyed by what they deemed Flumenbaum's arrogant manner, the non–Paul, Weiss lawyers began to refer routinely to Flumenbaum as "the FLS."

The easiest way to keep everyone "in the same tent pissing out" was to have as many potential witnesses as possible represented by members of the Milken defense team. But the lawyers' Code of Professional Responsibility cautions against this, requiring that lawyers not represent defendants and witnesses, unless they have fully explained to each client all of the implications. Williams's pitch to Dahl arguably crossed this line, given the strong likelihood that Dahl would be asked to testify. But Dahl hadn't actually received a subpoena at the time, so Williams was free to go ahead, and the pitch worked. Dahl was awed by Williams and eagerly retained him and Williams & Connolly, as did Warren Trepp and another Beverly Hills official.

Williams, however, recognized that he couldn't represent employees already subpoenaed. These included Lowell, Maultasch, Thurnher, and Ackerman. Williams assured himself, however, that these witnesses—some potential targets—were in the hands of "friendly" counsel. The defense teams carefully went over the names of lawyers they might recommend to witnesses they couldn't represent themselves. The lawyers' skills and reputations were, of course, an element in the process, though hardly one that took up much time in the discussions. More important were the lawyers' track records in government cases. Williams and company wanted lawyers whose strong philosophical preference was to fight the government rather than cooperate with it.

Another factor played an important role: an elaborate network of dependence and obligation. Some of the lawyers ultimately approved had received so much business from Williams & Connolly, Paul, Weiss, or Cahill Gordon, that they could be counted on to share information and, within the limits of professional responsibility, cooperate with the lawyers representing Milken and Drexel. Mark Pomerantz represented one of Milken's assistants; he had been a Supreme Court clerk with Litt. Jack Auspitz represented another Milken witness; he had been an associate at Paul, Weiss. Seymour Glanzer represented Thurnher; he'd often received referrals from Liman. There were numerous other examples.

Finally, all of the prospective attorneys were interviewed personally by Sandler, whose fanatical loyalty to Milken further ensured the involvement of counsel likely to fight rather than counsel settlement.

The war began with a flurry of witnesses—including Dahl—before the SEC and the grand jury. Most simply invoked the Fifth Amendment and refused to answer questions. Dahl resisted this idea at first, feeling that he had nothing to hide. Invoking the Fifth, he thought, would make the government more suspicious. But at Litt's insistence, he exercised his right to remain silent.

Another witness, Milken's trader Warren Trepp, was concerned that Williams & Connolly was too close to Milken, and feared his own interests would suffer. Williams arranged for Trepp to be represented by William Hundley, a lawyer to whom he had often referred cases over the years. Trepp's defection caused an initial ripple of concern in the Milken camp, but it died away once he was in Hundley's hands, and after Trepp assured his colleagues he'd never turn against Milken. Over dinner at the Palm restaurant in Washington, Trepp told Hundley that he'd never testify against clients or colleagues. "I'm not the kind of guy who could ever be a fink," he said. "I don't have a reputation of being a fink lawyer," Hundley replied.

Within a matter of weeks, one of the largest and most expensive and comprehensive criminal defense teams in history had been assembled and the lines of defense were drawn. In many ways, they never changed. Henceforth, Milken was cast as the innocent victim of the despicable Boesky. He was to be portrayed as a genius, a treasure, a savior of the American economy, and a one-man engine of growth.

Privately, however, Williams warned some of his colleagues that this posture might need to be reconsidered as facts in the case unfolded.

Milken was now virtually surrounded by experts of one sort or another. But he was becoming more distant from almost everyone else. Fred Joseph was upset by the intense press coverage, especially *The Wall Street Journal* article of November 17 saying that Milken was being named in subpoenas. He wanted to get to the bottom of the matter himself; he wanted Milken's personal reassurance. Cahill's Tom Curnin and Peter Fleming, however, told Joseph they would interview Milken on his behalf. When they arrived, Milken's lawyers were already in place, and, despite all the lip service about cooperation, they refused to allow Milken to be interviewed alone by Drexel's lawyers.

Milken's lawyers told Curnin and Fleming that it was "common" in criminal investigations not to permit a company to interview an employee who might be a target of the investigation. Nonetheless, they assured the Drexel lawyers, Drexel had nothing to worry about. The Drexel lawyers passed the word back to Joseph. He didn't realize it, but this was a decisive moment in his leadership of the firm. Milken's lawyers were hardly telling the whole story when they insisted it was "common" to isolate an employee in Milken's position. On the contrary, many companies insist on immediately getting to the bottom of an employee's alleged unlawful conduct. If the employee refuses to be interviewed, or doesn't answer questions satisfactorily, he or she could be fired. Milken's lawyers took a calculated risk in refusing to permit Milken to be interviewed by Joseph or Drexel's lawyers. But they knew Milken's importance to the firm. Joseph believed Milken when he said he was innocent, and he also had to contend with other top Drexel officials who were even more dedicated to Milken. To suspend or dismiss Milken could have caused a civil war at the firm.

It was clear both from the subpoenas Drexel received on November 14, and from a set of grand jury subpoenas that followed in December, that Milken's relationship with Boesky was at the center of the investigation. The subpoenas were unusually lengthy and detailed, with appendices running to numerous pages. Almost all the deals in the Boesky/Milken conspiracy were identified, including Fischbach, Pacific Lumber, and Wickes. The $5.3 million payment figured prominently. The subpoenas called for the production of a vast quantity of documents, and gave Drexel only 30 days to respond.

Lawyers from Cahill launched an internal investigation immediately after the Boesky news, and spent the weekend of November 15 and 16 interviewing Drexel officials who had had any involvement with

Boesky or the transactions in question. Without access to either Boesky or Milken, it wasn't surprising that they couldn't find any immediate evidence of wrongdoing. When it came to the $5.3 million fee, there were plenty of witnesses, including David Kay, who could testify that Drexel had, in fact, done research for Boesky. Kay, in particular, liked to call Boesky a "tire kicker," someone who put Drexel through the motions but didn't follow through with a bid.

The Drexel executives eagerly embraced Milken's claim that the payment was for research. It was troublesome that Drexel ordinarily didn't bill clients for research. The events of March 21, the day of the payment, were also highly unorthodox. However much research had actually been done, the argument could be made that Drexel had been amply rewarded by the enormous fee it collected from Boesky in the Hudson Funding transaction. Still, none of that, however suspicious, necessarily made the payment a crime, the Drexel lawyers thought.

Drexel executives and lawyers pinned their hopes on a document Milken's lawyers showed them. It was a copy of handwritten notes by Thurnher dated "3-21-86," purporting to be contemporaneous notes for the Boesky junk-bond closing. It read:

Corporate finance $1,800,000.
Equity Research NY $2,000,000.
HY Dept. Research: $1,000,000.

This purported to be an allocation of most of the fee to departments that had done the Boesky research, and it "proved," the Milken lawyers insisted, that the $5.3 million was in fact an investment banking fee, as described in the invoice signed by Lowell and Donald Balser and provided at the time of the Boesky closing. The notes were meant to be an allocation of the fee to various parts of Drexel, for use in calculating credit for bonuses.

Curnin felt it was time to initiate contact with the SEC. He scheduled a meeting with Sturc at the SEC for the week of Thanksgiving, and offered to produce Joseph the following Saturday. Curnin didn't want to prolong the investigation if it could quickly be brought to a satisfactory resolution. Having represented the ill-fated E. F. Hutton in its massive check-kiting scheme, he had seen firsthand how bad publicity can hurt the operations of a respectable securities firm.

In Washington, Lynch, too, was hoping for a quick resolution. After the battering he'd taken in the press over the Boesky settlement, he was eager to show some results of the Boesky deal. If Milken and Drexel came right in and cooperated, he felt the commission could really blow the lid off the securities industry. He assumed Milken would be under considerable pressure. Lynch expected that Drexel would, at the very least, place Milken on a leave of absence and begin active cooperation. He didn't see that Drexel had much choice.

Rarely had the expectations of the SEC and a securities firm under its jurisdiction been so far apart. The discussions fell apart as soon as Curnin offered the opinion that the $5.3 million payment was an innocent payment for past services. The assertion seemed to enrage Sturc; it was, indeed, preposterous to anyone who'd heard Boesky's far more persuasive explanation. Curnin wanted to know what were the SEC's "concerns."

Sturc had no interest in helping Drexel if it was going to stonewall. The commission, he said coldly, "isn't yet prepared to share those concerns with you." When Curnin asked the SEC to "prioritize" what he deemed its unreasonably long list of documents to be produced, Sturc also refused. And when Curnin again offered to have Joseph come down to Washington, he was rebuffed. It was clear to Sturc that despite its claims to the contrary, Drexel was not in the least prepared to cooperate. For his part, Curnin was baffled by how upset the SEC had become over Drexel's explanation of the $5.3 million.

Finally, Curnin persuaded Lynch to meet with Joseph in Washington. If anything, the meeting was even more of a disaster. Lynch told Joseph that the case against Milken was "overwhelming," that the commission had contemporaneous documents and witnesses backing Boesky's version of events, and that Drexel "had to start cooperating immediately in its own interest." Lynch didn't know how much more strongly he could put it. Yet Joseph seemed to become indignant. "We've made our own inquiries," he said. "What you're alleging simply isn't true. Boesky is a liar and a convicted felon." Lynch was contemptuous of Drexel's so-called investigation. Joseph had acknowledged that Milken wouldn't talk to him or to Drexel's lawyers. That was an investigation? Then Joseph reiterated the theory of the $5.3 million fee, further angering Lynch. "Give us the evidence of violations," Joseph insisted. "We just want to know what we've done wrong."

Lynch interpreted this as a blatant attempt to fish for information from the SEC without offering anything in return. This was more than the normally unflappable enforcement chief could take, and he was furious. "You know what you did wrong," Lynch said, and the meeting broke up in recriminations.

"I can't believe they're doing this," Lynch told Sturc after the Drexel group left. "What they're saying is, 'We'll go down to protect Milken.'" Sturc nodded in baffled agreement. They'd known that Milken was the real power in the firm, but not that it had gone to these lengths.

Given the magnitude of Boesky's allegations, and without even a pretense of cooperation from Drexel or Milken, Lynch and Sturc concluded that they were likely to face litigation comparable in scope to that of the government's antitrust case that had led to the breakup of American Telephone & Telegraph. They quickly increased staffing on the case from 6 to 20 lawyers. It was the SEC's turn to prepare for war.

At the U.S. attorney's office, Carberry was hard at work to make sure that the case against Drexel would not depend solely on Boesky. He put two promising young assistant U.S. attorneys on the case: John Carroll, 31, a New York University law school grad who had clerked for New York federal district court judge Richard Owen; and Jess Fardella, 35, a Harvard Law graduate and former associate at a Boston law firm, Ropes & Gray.

Since his first interviews with Boesky, one of the things Carberry had found appealing about the case was the likelihood of corroboration. Boesky's and Milken's style had kept the full extent of their dealings to themselves, but they had relied on underlings to handle what they deemed the mundane tasks and recordkeeping functions. Carberry targeted several of Boesky's employees, especially Davidoff, the head trader, and Mooradian.

The Boesky employees quickly fell into the government's net. Davidoff, the highest-ranking of the Boesky employees implicated in wrongdoing, agreed to cooperate and plead guilty to one felony count of evading net capital requirements. He brought prosecutors a full arsenal of evidence on Boesky's dealings with Mulheren: the parking arrangements, the payback schemes, the details of conversations he had directly with Mulheren. Davidoff single-handedly fueled the Mulheren investigation. (Mulheren hadn't been one of the five targets cited in Boesky's proffer. Boesky had always soft-pedaled the value of his information about Mulheren. To the limited extent Boesky had real friends on Wall Street, Mulheren was his best friend.) Davidoff was of little use on the Drexel-Milken front, since he knew nothing about the secret arrangements beyond some of the trading he oversaw.

Mooradian, on the other hand, proved invaluable. On the Monday after the Boesky announcement, he had shown up for work at 11 Broadway as usual. The office had been swarming with SEC investigators, pulling documents out of filing cabinets, putting them in cartons, stamping them and sealing them. Mooradian had been clinging to a small hope that the firm would somehow survive. But now he saw it being literally torn apart. "We're history," he told his colleagues.

Later that morning, Mooradian got a call from Pitt. "Do you have a lawyer?" Pitt asked him. The question upset Mooradian, as did the fact that someone as important as Pitt was calling him. To him, that had to mean bad news.

"No," Mooradian said. "Why the hell would I want one? I don't know anything." Earlier, Pitt had spoken to Bob Romano, the Merrill Lynch official and former SEC enforcement lawyer who'd been involved with the anonymous letter from Caracas. Since then, Romano had left Merrill Lynch and gone into private practice. Pitt had told him he'd recommend him to Mooradian, one of four of Boesky's employees who Pitt believed would need their own counsel. "You'd better get a lawyer," Pitt told Mooradian, and recommended that he call Romano. Mooradian did, and then called his wife.

"This won't even take an hour," he predicted. "I don't know a thing about any insider trading."

Romano arrived at the Boesky office that afternoon. "What do you think the government wants to talk to you about?" Romano began. Mooradian, despite his claims that he knew nothing, started talking a mile a minute.

"You should know I've been in trouble before," he started, explaining his earlier suspension by the SEC. Now, he said, "I'm involved in the Drexel thing." He described the recordkeeping he did for Boesky, the efforts to reconcile the balances and his trip to Beverly Hills. And he told Romano all about the $5.3 million payment, the events of March 21, when Boesky had yelled at him for nearly upsetting the Drexel financing, and Boesky's subsequent orders to destroy the documents used to calculate the payment.

"Did you destroy them?" Romano asked.

"Yes," Mooradian said, and Romano saw a promising area of documentary corroboration vanish.

The next day Romano met with Carberry, who, as usual, went straight to the point, noting that Mooradian was implicated by Boesky in the falsification of records related to the Drexel scheme. Romano saw that he had little room to maneuver; Carberry already knew, from Boesky himself, most of what Mooradian had told him the day before. "How can Mooradian help you?" Romano asked.

Carberry ticked off a list: Drexel; Kidder, Peabody; Seligman Harris (Boesky's London broker); and Mulheren.

Romano returned to Mooradian's office and they did their best. Mooradian racked his memory, remembering details of how Boesky ordered documents destroyed. They combed through Mooradian's files, and Mooradian showed Romano the reconstruction of the Drexel reconciliation he'd done at Boesky's behest. But he had nothing to offer on Carberry's other targets.

When they met, and Mooradian said he'd come up empty-handed, Carberry told him that the U.S. attorney wanted him to plead to a felony. Mooradian was enraged.

"I am not a felon," he insisted vehemently. "I made no money on this." In his view, he had simply carried out Boesky's orders; everything he had done was routine on Wall Street.

Mooradian didn't want to be, as he put it, a "squealer," but Romano struck a deal with Carberry to the effect that the U.S. attorney would defer charging Mooradian or demanding a plea until after he had cooperated. Then they could evaluate Mooradian's effort. If they still felt he deserved a felony, so be it.

Mooradian was nervous at his first meeting as a cooperating witness with Carberry and other government lawyers. When he casually referred to Carberry as "Charlie," Carberry cut him off. "We use last names here, Mr. Mooradian," Carberry said. The audience seemed huge to Mooradian: five lawyers from the U.S. attorney's office and eight SEC lawyers. Gradually, however, he warmed to the task, leading them through the arrangement with Drexel and his role in it. When he got to the events of March 21, he hesitated, and then stopped altogether when asked what Boesky had said to him after he had nearly ruined the deal with his disclosure about the $5.3 million payment.

"What did Boesky say to you," one of the lawyers asked him. Mooradian looked anxiously at the two women lawyers in the room.

"Did he say 'fuck?' " the lawyer continued.

"Do you really want to know?" Mooradian asked apprehensively, before deciding he wouldn't be blamed for offending anyone. "He said, 'You stupid fucking bastard,' over and over," Mooradian stated.

Mooradian had destroyed, on Boesky's orders, what was becoming the single most important document in the investigation, the lengthy reconciliation of accounts leading to the $5.3 million payment. But he continued his effort to reconstruct the ledgers that began when Boesky changed his mind, working with Maria Termine and the scraps of underlying records he'd found in his files. He managed to re-create a reasonable facsimile.

Mooradian soon became an informal consultant for lawyers working on the case. Most of them knew almost nothing about financial markets and the workings of the securities industry, not even such basics as selling short or puts and calls—let alone the complex and sophisticated strategies employed by Boesky and Milken to carry out their schemes. They knew little about accounting. Mooradian spent hours teaching the lawyers, then poring over trading records showing how the data corroborated various strategies. He became a popular figure around the office, refreshingly down-to-earth, eager to please. Mooradian himself gradually came to understand and sympathize with Boesky's decision to cooperate. He realized that when your own life was on the line, you had a different view of cooperation. And he saw that it would have been fruitless for Boesky to lie. Too many other possible witnesses, including himself, knew the truth.

Buttressed by Mooradian's disclosures, the government soon gained the cooperation, such as it was, of Mooradian's counterpart at Drexel, Charles Thurnher, as well as that of Donald Balser. Both men were represented by Seymour Glanzer, a criminal lawyer in Washington recommended by Peter Fleming and Arthur Liman. At the outset, Glanzer had indicated his clients would invoke the Fifth Amendment if questioned.

Thurnher was an accountant by training, and faced possible charges for his role in the scheme. He was more valuable to the government, however, as someone with no ties or loyalty to Boesky, who could corroborate the arbitrageur's allegations. Thurnher had simply been carrying out Milken's orders. Balser's involvement had been even more minimal; he had been a mere bystander. When Drexel had needed to provide written justification for the $5.3 million, he had been dragooned by Lowell to sign the letter saying it was an investment banking fee.

Carberry felt that he could live with the prospect of immunity, and he granted it to both men; he had to start somewhere. The grant of immunity required both Thurnher and Balser to answer questions truthfully; they couldn't invoke the right against self-incrimination, since nothing they said could be used against them.

Still, to call this process cooperation would be an overstatement. In conversations with the Milken team, Glanzer made much of the fact that Thurnher's and Balser's testimony was being compelled by the government; they hadn't offered to implicate anyone. In sharp contrast to Mooradian, Thurnher volunteered little. Like Boesky, Milken had kept his employees largely in the dark. Milken had never told Thurnher why he was having him do various things, so he was of little use in figuring out Milken's motives and state of mind. Thurnher testified at one point that Milken hadn't even asked him to keep the list; on another occasion, he said Milken had described the list as "all a bunch of bullshit."

Thurnher walked a tightrope, trying to say as little as possible without lying. On more than one occasion, government prosecutors had to threaten him with a perjury indictment. Sandler was in constant contact with Glanzer, who boasted that Thurnher was doing nothing to help the government's case.

The government saw Thurnher's testimony differently, however. He may have been an unwilling witness, but he admitted that he had destroyed the computer disks used to compute the $5.3 million payment. While he didn't say he had done so as the result of direct orders from Milken, he made clear that he'd gotten the message to do so from Milken. He confirmed the dealings with Mooradian. Significantly, Thurnher testified that Milken personally dictated the amounts allocating portions of the $5.3 million fee to investment banking and high-yield—on the very document relied upon so heavily by Milken's lawyers in their efforts to persuade Drexel that Milken's version of the payment was correct. Thus, Thurnher couldn't say from his own knowledge that the allocation accurately reflected the purpose of the payment.

This was crucial information that might have affected Drexel's view of the evidence. But when Curnin met with Thurnher to find out what he'd told the government, Glanzer wouldn't let Thurnher answer most of his questions. Curnin was left with reassurances from the Milken camp that Thurnher hadn't done them any harm.

The pressures on Thurnher to avoid true cooperation were underscored by a joke that swept Drexel as soon as news leaked that Thurnher might be talking to the government. "Who's the highest-paid guy at Drexel? Thurnher's food taster."

Even though Thurnher's testimony didn't seem to be hurting Milken or Drexel, the continuing silence from those in Beverly Hills directly knowledgeable about the events covered by the subpoena began to worry Curnin. Then, on April 28, an article appeared in *The Wall Street Journal* focusing on the $5.3 million payment. In considerable detail, the article described how the payment was calculated, and reported that the invoice "was hastily produced after the payment was already made and only because Mr. Boesky's auditors questioned the lack of documentation for such a large payment." Both Curnin and Joseph were upset that reporters appeared to know more about the government's case than they did. They worried that the article might be correct.

No such doubts permeated the Milken camp, which heaped scorn on the press both within Drexel and to anyone else who would listen. Williams increasingly found himself to be the voice of caution, even as his hold over the case began to slip. In early 1987, Williams had surgery for cancer, which weakened him visibly. He didn't feel the case was at a point where any kind of negotiations should be considered, and he knew Milken wouldn't even entertain the possibility; but he knew it was prudent to keep lines of communication open at the U.S. attorney's office. As he'd confided in Litt, the government's case was likely to get stronger, not weaker, as time passed.

Not long after his surgery, Williams arranged a meeting in New York with Carberry, Howard Wilson, the chief of the criminal division, and another prosecutor working on the case. Williams came alone, without anyone else from the Milken defense team. After discussing the limited progress in the case, and after Carberry reiterated his reluctance to say much about an investigation that was still in the early phases, Williams finally asked, "How long is this going to take?"

Carberry estimated two years before an indictment. Williams paused, looking wistful. "I'll be dead by then," he said. "Can't you go any faster?"

After leaving Siegel's apartment on Wednesday afternoon, February 11, 1987, Doonan rushed to St. Andrews Plaza for a meeting with Carberry and Neil Cartusciello, the assistant U.S. attorney Carberry had assigned to the cases growing out of the Siegel investigation. With Tabor apparently tipped off to the existence of an undercover operation, time was running out. Doonan wanted to move against Freeman, Wigton, and Tabor the very next day, and he wanted Siegel to enter his plea that Friday. Carberry agreed.

Carberry thought the three suspects should be arrested, rather than subpoenaed (as Siegel and Boesky had been) or allowed to come in on their own. Freeman, already subpoenaed earlier as part of the Boesky investigation, had rebuffed any notion of cooperation, even though Carberry had heard from another lawyer that Freeman had been a "nervous wreck." Tabor also seemed vulnerable, having just been fired from Merrill Lynch. Carberry thought the pressure of a public arrest might lead one or more of them to capitulate and confess. He'd concluded that Wall Street types weren't strong in a criminal sense. They cared too much about respectability.

Carberry and Cartusciello went upstairs for a meeting with Giuliani and Wilson. Carberry believed that Freeman had engaged in a straightforward, illegal exchange of inside information. That he'd traded for information rather than cash made his offense even more destructive of market integrity. As for Wigton and Tabor, Siegel hadn't claimed that they were privy to his scheme with Freeman. But Siegel had mentioned Freeman as a source at least once, and Carberry believed they had to have known that Siegel had a source in Goldman,

Sachs. It was patently obvious from the trading patterns of Kidder, Peabody's arbitrage department.

"Let's arrest them," Carberry said. Giuliani agreed without any hesitation. There wasn't any discussion of the possible public reaction. Arrests were routine. They got the necessary arrest warrants, based on an affidavit signed by Doonan, taken from Paschall's notes of the Siegel debriefings. Then Doonan rushed off to Tabor's Upper East Side apartment building.

Matters began to go awry almost from the outset. Tabor was handcuffed and frisked in his building lobby, allowed to go back to his apartment for his coat, and then lodged in the Metropolitan Correction Center that night. The prosecutors hoped he might decide to confess and cooperate, but Tabor didn't cave in. Carberry may have misjudged the emotional makeup and loyalties of many on Wall Street. In their willingness to confess and cooperate, Boesky and Siegel were the exception, not the rule. Wall Street remains a small, closed world fueled by money, mutual favors, and strong loyalties. And perhaps Tabor had never figured out Siegel's relationship with Freeman, and had nothing to confess. If anything, his night in the MCC seemed to make him more defiant than he'd been the day before.

The next morning, with snow flurries whirling through the gray canyons of the financial district, Doonan and two other postal inspectors arrived at Goldman, Sachs's headquarters on Broad Street. "We have a warrant for the arrest of Robert Freeman," Doonan told a member of the building's security staff, and the shocked guard took them upstairs without protest.

Freeman's 29th-floor office was glass-enclosed, just off Goldman's large trading floor. Freeman stood up, looking startled, as the brigade entered his office. He had been busy trying to clear up some pending matters; he was scheduled to leave that afternoon to spend the long President's Day weekend skiing in the Rockies with his family.

"I have a federal warrant for your arrest," Doonan told him. "I'm now placing you under arrest." On Doonan's instructions, Freeman leaned forward and put his hands on his desk. Doonan frisked him, and removed everything in his pockets. Freeman said nothing. The incident created something of a commotion on the trading floor, as traders craned their necks to see what was going on.

Freeman asked to use the phone and called an in-house Goldman lawyer, who hurried into the office. The lawyer called Larry Pedowitz, who had been representing the firm since Freeman was named in the Boesky-related subpoena.

Pedowitz, who'd once worked with Doonan at the U.S. attorney's office, listened as Doonan explained the charges. He said he had a search warrant for Freeman's office and its vicinity. Then the two postal inspectors escorted Freeman to the elevators; once they reached the building's lobby, they handcuffed him. Doonan stayed behind, roping off a large area around Freeman's office, and began to sift through desk drawers and filing cabinets, piling documents into cartons.

As the agents hustled Freeman out of Goldman's headquarters, another federal brigade arrived at Kidder, Peabody's offices on Hanover Square. Richard Wigton looked up from his desk and saw a receptionist standing at his 18th-floor office door. "There's a Mr. Moreno here to see you," she said.

Wigton glanced at his calendar. He didn't see any entry for the morning of February 12. With the trading day in full swing, Wigton wasn't about to abandon his post. "I don't have time right now," he told the receptionist. "He doesn't have an appointment." Wigton wondered if this was a job applicant. College kids were so eager to work at investment banks that some of them were going around Wall Street, knocking on doors. Wigton went back to his work.

A few minutes later he looked up and saw that the receptionist had returned. She looked anxious. "They intend to see you this very moment," she said. "They said no ifs, ands, or buts about it." Wigton thought this was rude and highly unorthodox, but he decided to go out to the lobby to see what this meant.

He strode into the lobby near the elevators, the receptionist a few steps behind him. Two men were waiting. Suddenly they pulled out papers identifying them as U.S. postal inspectors and stated, "You're under arrest." Wigton stopped in his tracks. Was this a prank? One of them grabbed him by the arm, turned him around, then shoved him hard toward the wall. He caught himself. The postal inspectors quickly frisked him, then pulled his hands behind his back. They snapped a pair of handcuffs on his wrists.

The agents then led Wigton back to his office, crossing the trading floor in full view of the firm's employees. One of the traders, spotting the procession, immediately called John Roche, who came rushing into Wigton's office. "I'm the president of this company," Roche said with some indignation. "What's going on here?" The agents explained that they had just arrested Wigton on securities fraud charges. Wigton, still in shock, stood uncomprehending. "Hold on a minute," Roche told the agents, and picked up the phone to call Kidder, Peabody's counsel at Sullivan & Cromwell, Marvin Schwartz. "We'll get you the best criminal lawyer available," Roche assured Wigton.

The agents unlocked the cuffs to allow Wigton to don his suit jacket and overcoat. He called his wife, Cynthia. "Will you be home for dinner?" she asked anxiously.

"I can't say," he gravely replied. Then the agents snapped the handcuffs back into place.

Most of the traders had now dropped their phones and were following the action in Wigton's office, some standing for a better view. Then the agents again led Wigton onto the trading floor. As he walked toward the elevator, with agents on either side of him, Wigton began to weep. With his hands manacled, he couldn't brush away the tears.

After spending about an hour at the postal inspectors' offices in lower Manhattan where Siegel had been interrogated, Wigton and Freeman were taken separately to the federal courthouse for their arraignment, where they met Tabor. Tabor looked disheveled; he was wearing a white open-necked polo shirt, sneakers, and khaki trousers.

It was the first time the three men had ever been together. Freeman, at the pinnacle of the arbitrage world, had never bothered to return Wigton's calls.

"Hello," Wigton said.

"Hi, how are you?" Freeman answered. They all seemed at a loss for words.

The three men had lawyers inclined to urge them to fight. Soon after the Boesky announcement, in anticipation of the possibility that Kidder, Peabody would be drawn into the scandal, the firm's lawyers at Sullivan & Cromwell had retained Stanley Arkin, a noted criminal lawyer it often used for its criminal matters. Wigton was now handed over to Arkin, who, by temperament, prefers to fight the government. He, in turn, had recommended another lawyer, Andrew Lawler, for Tabor. As in the Milken case, the economic relationships among the lawyers meant that a core defense team—in this case dominated by Sullivan & Cromwell—would have great influence over the course of events. Kidder, Peabody would be paying all the legal fees. And Sullivan & Cromwell had been Kidder, Peabody's counsel throughout the events now being alleged to have been criminal. Pedowitz, representing Goldman, Sachs, recommended that Freeman retain Paul Curran, a former U.S. attorney and partner at Kaye, Scholer, Fierman, Hays & Handler. Wachtell, Lipton, Pedowitz's firm, had already done an internal investigation for Goldman, Sachs after Freeman's name had appeared on subpoenas flowing out of the Boesky plea agreement. Those subpoenas hadn't caused undue concern within Goldman, and the Wachtell investigation exonerated Freeman and his firm, finding no evidence of any wrongdoing.

By the time of the arraignment, at about noon on Thursday, the basement courtroom was only half-filled, mostly with reporters. In some ways, the news of the arrests was an even bigger bombshell than the Drexel and Milken allegations. While none of the men involved rivaled Milken in power and influence, their firms—Kidder, Peabody and Goldman, Sachs—represented the pinnacle of the Wall Street establishment. While Kidder, Peabody was known to have been struggling, Goldman, Sachs was probably, overall, the dominant firm on Wall Street. This was not a case involving upstart, greedy newcomers. Allegations of insider trading at this level had seemed almost unthinkable.

The manner of the arrests also added fuel to the fire. Unlike Levine, the arbitrageurs had been arrested in full view of other witnesses—Tabor in his apartment lobby, and Wigton and Freeman at their firms—ensuring that word of the arrests would course through Wall Street and the media. It did, including wild reports that the usually meek Wigton had decked one of the federal agents and had to be subdued to be handcuffed. Many on Wall Street were indignant that their colleagues were being treated like common criminals. There were repeated allegations that Giuliani, who had always courted publicity and was rumored to be eyeing a bid for public office, had tried to sensationalize the process for his own ends. Even though it was Carberry who had proposed the arrests, these charges fell on receptive ears.

By now, Wall Street was terrified. Many had been, to put it mildly, indiscreet with confidential information. Even before the latest rounds of arrests, many arbitrageurs and traders had been afraid of where the investigation might lead. They were horrified that the criminal provisions of the securities laws—even aspects they had long dismissed as technicalities, like the prohibition against "parking"—might actually be enforced. With two of the country's most prominent firms now implicated, many concluded that the investigation had gotten out of hand. It was threatening everyone's well-being.

The arraignment spurred even more rumors, speculation, and paranoia when the government identified the source of the charges against the three arbitrageurs as "CS-1." The designation stood for "confidential source one," implying there might also be a CS-2. The government said CS-1 had been a Kidder, Peabody official at the time of the events cited in the complaint. It refused to be more specific, saying only that CS-1's "reliability and trustworthiness" have been "amply established."

According to the charges made public, CS-1 had passed information about the KKR bid for Storer to Freeman, who, already having established a position in the stock, used the inside information to "determine an appropriate price at which to sell call options." The charges also alleged that Freeman had disclosed key information about a Unocal maneuver to defend itself against the bid by Boone Pickens in a telephone call to CS-1. CS-1, in turn, had passed the information on to Wigton and Tabor, who executed a sophisticated trading strategy involving Unocal put options to profit unlawfully on the information. The allegation involving Unocal was especially embarrassing for Goldman, Sachs, which had highlighted its Unocal defense strategy in its recently released 1986 annual report. The government added that the scheme had lasted from about June 1984 through January 1986, and involved "many specific significant corporate events in which such trading of material, non-public information occurred."

U.S. Attorney Rudolph Giuliani held a press conference shortly after the court proceeding. The arrests, he said, were just the beginning of "a very long and substantial investigation." In comments obviously aimed at Milken, Drexel, Freeman, Wigton, and Tabor, as well as others as yet unnamed who knew they were implicated, Giuliani said, "If they had common sense, and some sense of morality, what they would do is cooperate and try to help the U.S. government clean up this mess."

After the arraignment, Freeman returned to Goldman, Sachs for an emotional meeting with Robert Rubin, a former head of arbitrage himself, the same person who had shared the 1974 takeover panel with Siegel so many years before. Rubin hadn't been concerned by the subpoenas coming out of the Boesky case, but the arrests had changed things.

"This is all a lie," Freeman said.

Rubin, one of the heirs apparent to John Weinberg, the firm's chairman, had championed Freeman within the firm. He decided to take charge of the investigation, working closely with Pedowitz. When Rubin read the government's arrest warrant, the notion of a wide-ranging conspiracy didn't ring true to him. If Freeman and Siegel had been conspiring, then why had Goldman, Sachs actually lost money trading on some other Kidder, Peabody deals not mentioned in the government's charges? Rubin knew Freeman very well, and this simply wasn't the Bob Freeman he knew. Rubin was furious at Giuliani's public humiliation of Freeman and Goldman, Sachs. As a Democratic fund-raiser, Rubin didn't intend to allow the Republican Giuliani to gain politically at the expense of Goldman, Sachs.

There was an even more potent factor. When Rubin and Pedowitz had a chance to examine the charges more closely, they quickly concluded that the government was way off base. The Doonan affidavit describing the Unocal situation contained an error: it said the Unocal information had been passed by Freeman to CS–1. in April, rather than May, the date of the suspect trading.

Doonan, transcribing Paschall's notes, had simply made a mistake. The government might later argue, as it did, that it had made some purely technical mistakes with regard to timing, innocent mistakes caused by haste. But to minds disposed to believe in Freeman's innocence, and to suspect the worst of the government, such disclaimers understandably fell on deaf ears. In hardening attitudes at Goldman, Sachs, the errors damaged the government's case all out of proportion to the degree of the inaccuracy.

The Goldman, Sachs management committee met informally that afternoon, and decided unanimously to support Freeman. Meanwhile, Rubin told Pedowitz to continue his investigation, and said he wanted to get to the bottom of the question of whether Freeman had, in fact, done anything wrong. Nonetheless, the questions tended to focus on whether the government could "prove" a case beyond a reasonable doubt, not whether Freeman had done anything wrong. The investigation showed more interest in finding plausible alternative excuses for the trading in question rather than in determining whether Siegel actually tipped Freeman. This approach, too, was probably an inevitable by-product of the strong Goldman-versus-the-government mentality that took hold in the wake of Freeman's arrest.

Late that day, when he was finished with the lawyers, Wigton instinctively went back to his office at Kidder, Peabody. When his colleagues saw him come through the door, everyone on the trading floor jumped to their feet, giving him a cheering ovation. Wigton called his wife and reassured her that he would be home on time for dinner after all. At exactly 5:45 P.M., as he did every workday, Wigton met the two other members of his New Jersey car pool. They drove home, discussing that day's market activity and their plans for the holiday weekend. Out of deference to Wigton, his companions didn't mention the events that would soon figure prominently in network news programs. Wigton himself didn't bring the subject up, either. To do so, he thought, would show bad form.

Both Kidder, Peabody and Goldman issued public denials of wrongdoing the same day as the arrests and arraignment. A Kidder spokesman said that "the firm has a long-standing policy against trading on non-public information, and as far as we know, it has been strictly observed." Goldman was even more emphatic: "Based upon our own internal review, we have no reason to believe there has been any wrongdoing on the part of the head of our arbitrage department or our firm."

. . .

CS-1, of course, was Siegel. Early Thursday morning, Doonan had called him at his apartment. "Don't go to the office today," Doonan had ordered. "Go straight to Jed [Rakoff]'s office." On the ride downtown, Siegel sensed that he was going to be asked to enter his plea. Under his agreement with the government, he knew he would have to plead whenever the government ordered him to; he would not be allowed to "judge shop" by choosing the date of his plea.

When Siegel arrived at Mudge Rose's offices about 10:30 A.M., Rakoff confirmed that the undercover operation was being terminated and that he would be expected to enter his plea the next day. ("They'll probably make you plead on Friday the thirteenth," Rakoff had quipped weeks earlier; now his jocular prediction had proved true.) Siegel called his own number at Drexel to let his secretary, Kathy, know he wouldn't be in. Once again fated to be the bearer of significant tidings, Kathy was in a state of high excitement. "They've arrested Wigton and Tabor and Freeman," she said. "They handcuffed them." She had the ticker copy with the news in front of her, and read the account of the arrests. Kathy, of course, knew all three men: Wigton and Tabor from Kidder, Peabody, and Freeman from his frequent phone calls.

Kathy continued her account. "Everyone's excited here," she said of Drexel, explaining that people at the firm were practically rejoicing at the news. Siegel was momentarily puzzled, but Kathy quickly explained. After months of bearing the brunt of press reports about the course of the investigation, someone other than Drexel had finally been implicated. And not just anybody—Goldman, Sachs, the very firm that Drexel had most revered and had sought to supplant at the top of the Wall Street status pyramid.

To Siegel's amazement, Kathy gave no hint that anyone suspected he might be involved. He hung up when they finished talking, saddened that he was about to stun someone so steadfastly loyal.

Rakoff and Strauss walked Siegel through the events that would unfold the next day. Copies of the information to which Siegel would plead guilty and the government's press release arrived only late that night. It was obvious that the government was barely able to keep up with the rapid pace of events.

In discussing what the government would disclose about Siegel, a bone of contention was the amount of cash Siegel had actually taken from Boesky: Siegel insisted it was only $700,000, but Boesky had told the government it was $800,000. The prosecutors seemed exasperated by the discrepancy. They didn't want public speculation that one of their two star witnesses was lying, so they pressured Siegel to accept Boesky's version, which they wanted to include in the press release. Siegel steadfastly refused. He suspected that the cause of the different amounts was the skimming of the cash by the couriers—but that wasn't his concern. He had received $700,000 and he wasn't going to say otherwise, no matter how much pressure was applied. After years of living with a lie, he wasn't about to start again. The government backed down.

Now it was time for Siegel to begin what he feared would be the most difficult and draining aspect of his cooperation. During the undercover phase, he had been barred from telling anyone except his wife what was going on. Now he had to face the agony of telling the truth to his family, his closest colleagues, and his friends.

He reached his mother and father in Florida, where they were traveling in the RV Siegel had bought for them. He had both of them get on the phone. They had been upset a few weeks earlier, when Siegel had told them he wouldn't be able to make it down for their 40th wedding anniversary; they were hardly prepared now for news of this magnitude. Their son had succeeded beyond their wildest dreams; now this was worse than anything they'd ever imagined. His mother sobbed. Their main concern, however, was for their son's welfare. They wanted to see him immediately, but he dissuaded them. He tried to explain what would happen over the next few days, and to reassure them that he'd be all right.

Siegel continued down his list. He called his brother and his sister. He called Jane Day's parents. Shock, disbelief, tears ensued from nearly every call. Then he turned to the clients and colleagues who were closest to him. He tried to call Henry Kravis at KKR, but he couldn't be reached. He spoke instead to George Roberts, who told him how sorry he was, wishing him well. He reached Sam Heyman, his former neighbor and head of GAF. Heyman tried to be supportive; he said he'd known something was wrong, but hadn't wanted to press Siegel. He called Gershon Kekst, the corporate public-relations expert, and Stockton Strawbridge, another major client. "Now we'll find out if there's steel under there," Strawbridge told him. "There'd better be," Siegel grimly replied. And he called Peter Schwartz, a frequent cab driver for Siegel, who'd become a friend. "I'm sorry I let you down," Siegel said.

Finally he called Martin Lipton, the lawyer-mentor who meant so much to him. He still didn't know that Lipton and his firm were representing Goldman, Sachs. Siegel repeated his earlier apologies, said he was sorry over and over, and hoped desperately for some sign of compassion or forgiveness.

"I'll see what I can do for you," Lipton said finally. Siegel was encouraged by even that small chink in Lipton's cold façade.

Then Siegel again called Kathy, asking this time that she come over to Rakoff's office. When she arrived, Siegel led her into a conference room and closed the door. "I've made a terrible mistake," Siegel told her. "I've let you down." He felt as if he were confessing to his own daughter. Kathy still seemed not to understand. He told her that he was guilty of insider trading.

Kathy burst into tears. "Why?" she sobbed. "Why?"

Siegel couldn't answer her. He felt the anguish and pressure of the day burst within him. The two cried together.

Rakoff, worried still about Siegel's state of mind, picked him up in his car the next morning and drove him to the courthouse. He didn't want to risk the possibility that Siegel might have another bout of suicidal thoughts on the way to court. Siegel was brought in through a side door, then led into the large first-floor courtroom where motions and pleas are heard. He wore a dark gray suit, blue shirt, and red tie. Judge Robert Ward put Siegel last on the day's calendar, which meant he had to wait for nearly three hours.

Word that CS-1 would be identified and would be entering a plea had made its way through the media, and the courtroom—in contrast to the previous day, when Freeman, Wigton, and Tabor were arraigned there—was filled with reporters, including sketch artists who stared intently at Siegel throughout the proceeding. Television crews from all the major networks crowded the broad steps leading up to the main entrance and the imposing pillars of the federal courthouse. Finally Judge Ward called for Siegel to stand before him.

Siegel assured the judge that he wasn't taking medication and wasn't under the care of a psychiatrist. Judge Ward asked him what level of schooling he had achieved. Siegel paused momentarily. He was about to name Harvard Business School, his alma mater, but couldn't. He was too ashamed. "Graduate school," he finally replied. The judge read the charges in the criminal information, one count of conspiracy to violate the securities laws and another of tax evasion for failing to report the Boesky payments. Siegel hardly heard him. He brushed tears from his eyes.

"How do you plead?" He heard the words echoing in the large courtroom, then silence.

"Guilty, your honor," he said, softly but firmly. Judge Ward scheduled Siegel's sentencing for April 2, less than two months away.

Siegel was hustled into the holding pen, where he was fingerprinted along with a group of 27 drug dealers who had been arraigned that morning. He tried to slip out of the courthouse through a basement door, but a film crew from NBC was waiting. The cameras rolled as his lawyers rushed him to a car waiting to take him directly to the airport. He paused only to give Audrey Strauss a kiss on the cheek, then the car door slammed shut.

News of Siegel's plea and the arrests of Freeman, Wigton, and Tabor rocked Kidder, Peabody and its new owner, General Electric. Kidder's M&A administrator ran from the floor in tears upon hearing the news. Siegel still had many admirers, especially among the support staff. But sentiment within the firm hardened against him as the facts emerged, especially that he had accepted cash payments from Boesky. There had always been resentment about Siegel's departure for Drexel. It came quickly to the fore now.

Top GE officials learned the news as they were eating lunch in the company's Fairfield, Connecticut, headquarters dining room. They were stunned at the realization that their $650 million investment in what they believed was an eminent investment firm had been imperiled. A dinner that night at Manhattan's exclusive Le Bernardin restaurant, at which GE and Kidder officials were to celebrate the closing of a recent Kidder deal, turned into a wake.

There was some uneasiness between Kidder, Peabody officials and their new bosses, but the arrests drove a wedge between them. As Kidder officials such as Max Chapman came to Wigton's defense, GE officials took a more jaded view. At GE, they had had experience with criminal charges in the area of government contracting. In their view, the government didn't launch major investigations, let alone public arrests, without having some reliable evidence of wrongdoing. And with Siegel cooperating, they knew the government would have a strong case against Kidder, Peabody itself. A firm can usually be held criminally liable for the acts of its officials, and Siegel was admitting his crimes.

Since the acquisition, GE had left control of the firm in DeNunzio's hands and rarely interfered. Recognizing the potential gravity of the situation, however, Lawrence Bossidy, GE's vice chairman and the chief executive of GE Financial Services, the parent of Kidder, Peabody, took responsibility for the matter and put Joseph Handros, a GE deputy general counsel with criminal experience, in day-to-day charge of the matter. Bossidy, an imposing former professional baseball player of unimpeachable integrity, had no sentimental attachments to the "old" Kidder, Peabody, and was determined to move swiftly to repair any damage.

GE had already sent a team of its own auditors into Kidder, Peabody for a thorough examination of its financial performance and controls. GE immediately diverted the audit team into an investigation of the alleged insider trading. Kidder, Peabody put together its own task force, including John Gordon, Siegel's friend Peter Goodson, and the hapless in-house lawyer, Robert Krantz. As they began their work, fears, largely unspoken, swept the firm. Might Siegel implicate others, particularly DeNunzio? What was the story with arbitrage at Kidder, Peabody? Some officials were stunned to learn that the firm even had an arbitrage department. As it pored over trading records, the audit team would tally the number of trades it labeled "suspicious" and "questionable." Hal Ritch learned that the "suspicious" category had mounted to over 100 transactions in just a few days.

He and Gordon had other reasons to be worried. As they studied the government's allegations regarding Freeman, they recalled their own experiences in the SCA deal. Their suspicions at the time now seemed confirmed. They hated to admit it, but the government charges about Freeman rang true.

The day after Siegel's plea, a Saturday, the Kidder, Peabody team had been summoned to St. Andrews Plaza for a meeting with Giuliani, Carberry, Wilson, head of the criminal division, and Cartusciello, the prosecutor assigned to the Freeman case. Among the others attending had been the SEC's Lynch and Sturc, since any resolution of the Kidder, Peabody situation would have to include an SEC agreement. Sullivan & Cromwell partner Marvin Schwartz had taken the leading role for Kidder, Peabody; also present had been Krantz, Handros, and Gary Naftalis, Wilkis's lawyer, whom Handros had retained to represent GE.

"We've got you dead to rights," Giuliani began, but Schwartz immediately seized the offensive. "You should apologize," he told Giuliani indignantly, proceeding to denounce the office's handling of the arrests of Freeman, Wigton, and Tabor.

Carberry retorted by accusing Sullivan & Cromwell, Schwartz's firm, of a conflict of interest, since it had represented both Kidder, Peabody and Goldman, Sachs in other matters. Schwartz practically rose out of his chair, raising his voice, saying, "I don't need *you* to lecture *me* on conflicts. When I need advice on ethics, I assure you I won't turn to you."

The government lawyers could hardly believe it. They'd been suspicious of Sullivan & Cromwell and Kidder, Peabody ever since the

Winans affair, which had shown Kidder's obvious lack of controls and poor internal enforcement. Now Siegel, the firm's former star, had confessed to major criminal activity while representing the firm. And Kidder thought *the government* should apologize?

Krantz's aw-shucks manner didn't help. "What's the issue here? Help me," he said, looking around at the government lawyers, who were rendered speechless. "I just don't see what the violation is."

Giuliani remained calm. "Here's what our thinking is," he began. "You've got a problem. The sooner you resolve it, the better. And you're going to have to take some medicine." Then Carberry took over. He proceeded to review Kidder, Peabody's potential criminal liability for Siegel's acts and reminded them of their poor performance in the Winans affair, including some irregularities that had surfaced in a book written by Winans. Then Carberry dropped a bombshell: Kidder, Peabody's problems were by no means confined to Siegel's crimes. The government had other information of a stock parking scheme that involved Donald Little, Boesky's Kidder, Peabody broker in Boston; Kidder's co-head of equity trading; and, most astoundingly, Kidder's president, Jack Roche.

"We're going to indict you," Carberry said bluntly. Schwartz seemed flabbergasted. Giuliani lectured him on corporate liability for officers' crimes, and Schwartz lectured him on common sense. The talks quickly collapsed amidst further mutual recriminations. Schwartz angrily left the room, followed by the Kidder team, leaving Giuliani and his assistants enraged.

When Bossidy heard a report of the meeting from Handros, he was appalled. Sullivan & Cromwell, in his view, couldn't have adopted a worse stance. Something had to be done, fast. Bossidy had seen the devastating impact of an indictment on E. F. Hutton, and he believed that an indictment would destroy Kidder, Peabody's reputation even in the unlikely event that the firm ultimately prevailed.

The GE auditors stepped up their pace, reporting back to Handros and Bossidy. Their findings weren't encouraging. Some of the transactions under investigation, such as the General Foods trading, might be defended based on publicly available information. But what about Continental Group? Kidder's arbitrage department had displayed perfect timing in buying stock in that Goldman client just before the emergence of a white knight. And there were other, similar "coincidences." "One or two examples like this we could live with," Naftalis advised Handros. "But not five or six."

Nor were interviews with Kidder, Peabody's top officials all that reassuring. GE was willing to believe that DeNunzio didn't know about Siegel's scheme with Freeman—but DeNunzio had encouraged Siegel to advise Wigton and Tabor. He hadn't maintained even the pretense of a Chinese wall. He had abdicated control. His management of the firm, GE officials thought, had been abysmal; and if anything, they concluded, Roche, now under investigation himself, and Krantz were even less competent.

Two weeks after the Kidder, Peabody team's meeting with Giuliani and Carberry, Naftalis called Carberry. "GE wants to meet you," he told the prosecutor, "without anyone from Kidder or Sullivan & Cromwell." GE had decided to take control of the firm, and not just of the criminal investigation. Sullivan & Cromwell was dismissed from the case, replaced by Naftalis and his firm, Kramer, Levin, Nessen, Kamin, & Frankel. On March 7, Bossidy himself met with Giuliani and Carberry. He launched into a 15-minute presentation, in a tone dramatically different from that taken by Schwartz at their prior meeting.

Stopping just short of conceding that Kidder, Peabody was guilty of crime, Bossidy described GE's thorough examination—a sharp contrast to the whitewash the prosecutors believed the Goldman, Sachs investigation had been—and acknowledged that "serious problems" had been uncovered. He emphasized that GE had only recently purchased the firm, and had known nothing of the incidents that figured in the investigation. An indictment of the firm could put it out of business, costing the jobs of 7,000 innocent employees.

Then he offered concrete remedial steps: Kidder's top management, including DeNunzio, Roche, and Krantz, would be swept out, fired if necessary. Kidder, Peabody would abandon arbitrage entirely: Bossidy had concluded that an investment bank had no business being in arbitrage, and that no Chinese wall could guarantee against the improper use of confidential information. And the firm would work out an appropriate settlement with the SEC.

GE's candor and bold proposals made a favorable impression on the prosecutors. Giuliani told Bossidy that GE's approach was "a breath of fresh air" compared to what he was hearing from other firms implicated in the scandal, obviously referring to Drexel and Goldman. For the first time since the arrests, Bossidy and Naftalis saw a glimmer of hope that Kidder, Peabody wouldn't be indicted.

Just as events were taking a favorable turn with Kidder, Peabody, the government scored another victory. Boyd Jefferies, chairman of Jefferies Group, the big Los Angeles brokerage firm that pioneered off-market trading, pleaded guilty to two felonies in April 1987 and agreed to cooperate. Jefferies had "parked" stock for Boesky, much as Mulheren allegedly had, and the government had evidence of an incriminating $3 million payment from Boesky to Jefferies. The payment, described in the original invoice as being for "investment advisory services and corporate financial services," was in fact a reconciliation of parked stock positions—confirmation that Boesky had made use of phony invoices akin to that used in the $5.3 million Drexel payment.

More startling was Jefferies's revelation of a scheme that had nothing to do with Boesky. Jefferies admitted that, at the request of an unnamed co-conspirator, he had manipulated the price in a secondary offering of Fireman's Fund stock by American Express. The scheme had also involved the preparation of phony invoices when the conspirator reimbursed Jefferies for his losses incurred in driving up the price by buying large blocks of the stock. More than any others implicated, Jefferies was pleading guilty to acts that were all too routine on Wall Street. As Jefferies's lawyer told the government, "Boyd was accommodating customers. He grew up in the business accommodating customers. The rules are changing."

The conspirator who had asked Jefferies to manipulate the price of Fireman's Fund stock was none other than Sandy Lewis, the arbitrageur who had introduced Mulheren to Boesky at the Café des Artistes before falling out with Boesky. Eager for revenge, Lewis had virtually hounded Gary Lynch throughout the summer, urging him to pursue the investigation of Boesky. Now he had gotten his wish, and Boesky was ruined—but it was Boesky who had the last laugh. Lewis, who had always postured as Wall Street's high priest of ethical behavior, hotly denied that he was guilty. Few believed him. He was increasingly ridiculed for his hypocrisy. For all practical purposes, his career on Wall Street would soon be over.

But the euphoria at the U.S. attorney's office over these successes was short-lived. In the high-profile Freeman, Wigton, and Tabor investigation, the government seemed to be floundering. After moving to Florida, Siegel had finally seen the arrest warrants based on his debriefings, and he was immediately upset. In Unocal and Storer, the two deals the government had chosen to publicize in its charges, the government had staked out two of the most complicated transactions Siegel had described. Doonan had only interviewed Siegel once about both deals, while Paschall took notes. Siegel was dismayed when he read the Doonan affidavit. The gist of it was accurate, but, as Goldman, Sachs had already recognized, the details were garbled.

In Doonan's version, all the communications regarding the Unocal share buyback took place in the April phone conversation Siegel had had with Freeman in the Tulsa airport. That was, in fact, only part of the story. The affidavit had mistakenly telescoped into those phone conversations events that unfolded over days and weeks. Siegel knew that the actual trading records wouldn't support that version of events, and they didn't. The government also disclosed that Freeman had kept phony research files to cover his purchases, and Siegel was equally dismayed. He had told them that Boesky—not Freeman—kept such files. Rakoff knew that good defense lawyers would capitalize on the errors, embarrassing the government and raising doubts about the strength of the case. Siegel could see that he would undoubtedly—and unfairly—be blamed and accused of lying. Rakoff wished the government had asked him and Siegel to review the Freeman, Wigton, and Tabor charges before arresting them, but the prosecutors had been so concerned about preserving secrecy that they hadn't. It was too late now.

Rakoff called Carberry, with Strauss listening in. He wanted to make perfectly clear that Siegel wasn't to blame for the errors. Carberry acknowledged the mistakes and said the government would find an occasion to correct them. Rakoff was relieved that Carberry made no attempt to blame Siegel. Carberry didn't seem unduly concerned.

Freeman, Wigton, and Tabor were indicted on April 9, about seven weeks after their arrests. Without elaborating, the government did correct its mistakes, alleging that the Unocal trading by Kidder, Peabody had happened on May 15 and 17, 1985, not in April, and that the Storer trading had happened in April, not December, as previously alleged. But the government kept the indictments to the same two deals, charging each defendant with four felony counts.

Significantly, Kidder, Peabody itself wasn't charged, reflecting the understanding that GE officials had reached with Giuliani. In keeping with its vow to support the government, Kidder, Peabody promptly suspended Wigton without pay, stopped paying his lawyer's attorney's fees, and stopped paying for Tabor's lawyer. Unknown to most at Kidder, Peabody, GE had gone even further. GE lawyers met with Stanley Arkin, Wigton's lawyer, and told him bluntly that Wigton should fight the charges only if he were, in fact, innocent. If not, he should plead guilty and cooperate. Adding teeth to this recommendation, GE said that if Wigton fought the charges and was convicted, GE would sue Wigton to recover the $3 million it had already paid him for his Kidder, Peabody stock and would withhold the $3 million still owed him.

In contrast, Goldman, Sachs maintained its staunch support of Freeman, though it issued a statement taking a more moderate approach than it had earlier. "We know him and trust him," the firm said of Freeman. "Based on all we know now, we continue to believe he did not act illegally."

GE justified its measures as being consistent with a company policy to suspend employees who are indicted. The suspension also reflected the view of GE officials, who didn't really know Wigton or Tabor, that the government was probably correct in assuming that they had to have known Siegel was receiving inside information. The firm's withdrawal of support for Wigton enraged many at Kidder, Peabody, however, especially those still sensitive to the firm's loss of autonomy to a giant industrial corporation like GE. And the tactics made little impact on the unflappable Wigton. He held firm, hurt by the loss of the firm's support, but insisting on his innocence.

The grumbling at Kidder, Peabody over this turn of events was mild compared to the uproar that ensued a month later. On May 12, the two prosecutors handling the case, Cartusciello, looking exhausted, and another assistant U.S. attorney, John McEnany, appeared before the judge assigned to the case, Louis L. Stanton, and said they needed more time to prepare for trial. McEnany acknowledged that, "with the benefit of hindsight," the government might have waited to launch the highly publicized arrests, and admitted "we can be faulted for trying to proceed too fast."

It was a startling confession of bad judgment at a critical juncture, not only in the immediate case, but in other ongoing investigations, including the Milken case. Usually it is the defense that requests delays; but in this case, sensing that speed was on their side, the defense lawyers objected to any delay. The day after the government's motion, Judge Stanton sided with the defendants, citing the Sixth Amendment right to a speedy trial as he denied the government's motion. A spokesman for Giuliani told *The Wall Street Journal,* "I wouldn't characterize it as a defeat." But plainly, the defendants and their supporters had reason to be jubilant.

Now the onus was on the government. Should it go ahead and try the cases? Or should it consider what many believed to be nearly unthinkable, and walk away from the case, seeking to have the indictments dismissed? The debate raged within St. Andrews Plaza. Cartusciello and McEnany hadn't made the decision to launch the arrests, but they believed adamantly that the government had an obligation to go forward with the trial. Cartusciello, in particular, had been in the office for years, and had been trained in the traditions of Giuliani's predecessors. That tradition hardly sanctioned hasty arrests, but once the defendants had been subjected to that humiliation, Cartusciello took seriously their right to a speedy resolution of the cloud hanging over their reputations.

And both he and McEnany believed they had a case they could try without embarrassment, and with a good chance of success. They believed Siegel would be an excellent witness, highly credible. They had ample support for his claims in the voluminous trading records they'd gathered from Kidder, Peabody and Goldman, Sachs. But they lacked a good corroborating witness. No prosecutor was thrilled at the prospect of trying a case with only one major witness, let alone one who had just admitted felonies.

The head of the criminal division, Howard Wilson, opposed their view. He argued that the government shouldn't compound its earlier mistake by rushing forward now. He may have had other considerations as well: Part of Wilson's job was to protect his boss, Giuliani, and Giuliani's political future. Giuliani had had a remarkable string of highly publicized successes, including the conviction of Bronx Democratic leader Stanley Friedman, the case that had preoccupied him at the time of the Boesky agreement; he had tried the Friedman case himself, to considerable acclaim. He had reaped further praise for the Boesky plea agreement and his crackdown on Wall Street. Giuliani was on a roll, one that could easily propel him into New York City's mayoral mansion, or the state governor's mansion. His press had been almost uniformly laudatory. But what would now be worse? Dismissal of the case until a distant reindictment, when Giuliani might not even be in office, or a potentially embarrassing loss at trial that very summer, for which Giuliani would be blamed?

That left Carberry. He had suggested the arrests. He believed in the case. He wasn't a political animal. As a veteran prosecutor, he was reluctant to overrule the assistants with day-to-day responsibility for the case. He cast his lot with Cartusciello and McEnany, recommending that the case go forward.

For Giuliani, it was a difficult dilemma. For him to overrule the chief of his fraud unit would be devastating for Carberry. But Giuliani had backed Carberry on the arrests, and the results had been disastrous. Giuliani agreed with Wilson, and ordered the assistants to prepare a motion seeking the dismissal of the case.

By noon the next day, rumors were already circulating that the government was going to take the extraordinary measure of having the case dismissed. Rakoff called Siegel, and told him about the reports. "Could that be?" Siegel wanted to know.

"It's impossible," Rakoff replied, based on his years of experience in the office. He still believed that the arrests would never have happened without the government's having a corroborating witness. He assumed that the government would simply go to trial, even if it was sooner than the prosecutors wished. That, at least, would have been what happened while he was in the office.

But the "impossible" happened that very day. Cartusciello and McEnany went before Judge Stanton on May 13. In what was rapidly becoming the first major contested case of the insider-trading scandal, the courtroom was packed with reporters, lawyers for other potential defendants, and curious onlookers. Looking visibly pained—though more rested than he had the previous day—Cartusciello said that the government, faced with the choice of going to trial that Wednesday or asking that the charges be dismissed, "has concluded that the indictment must be dismissed." In an effort to blunt the impact of such an embarrassing step, he added that the indictment was "merely the tip of an iceberg" and vowed that the government would seek a new indictment expanding the insider-trading allegations from two to nine different stocks.

None of the defendants themselves had showed up for the proceeding, but their lawyers could barely contain their glee, even as they seized on the opportunity to blast the government. Arkin, Wigton's lawyer, called the government's maneuver a "cynical and transparent evasion of a right to a speedy trial." Tabor's lawyer, Lawler, said it "reflects badly on the strength of the government's case and on the strategy of making the arrests." Those themes, that the defendants had been badly mistreated and deprived of constitutional rights, were widely replayed in the press. In most pending cases, defense lawyers go out of their way to avoid offending the prosecutors, who retain enormous discretion in deciding the course of a prosecution. But in this war, every battle was fought to be won, as publicly and visibly as possible.

The bizarre turn of events did nothing for morale within Kidder, Peabody. Wigton's defenders were emboldened, and began clamoring for his reinstatement. There was even more outrage when, the day after the government's case was dismissed, GE carried out its own commitments to the prosecutors, ousting DeNunzio, Roche, and Krantz, and naming a GE director, Silas Cathcart, former chairman of Illinois Tool Works, as Kidder, Peabody's new chairman.

"I was thinking just the other day that what we need here is a good tool-and-die man," said a Kidder, Peabody official, his voice dripping with sarcasm. Speaking for GE, Bossidy said GE's investigation had revealed "substantial weaknesses" in Kidder, Peabody's financial, administrative, managerial, and information systems controls.

As a sop to Kidder, Peabody loyalists, Max Chapman, the one-time Siegel rival to become DeNunzio's successor as chairman, was made chief operating officer. But he was awarded only the title of executive vice president, reporting to Cathcart. "They've asked me to run the revenue side of the business, with Cathcart coming in, who is 61 years old," Chapman told *The Wall Street Journal*, getting in a dig at the aging Cathcart. There was no doubt that GE would now be exercising the control it had forsworn when it first acquired Kidder,

Peabody. It brought in GE loyalists for the top financial and administrative jobs, and installed a group of GE credit officials in the firm's
junk-bond and leveraged buyout areas. GE had a $600 million invest-
ment it was trying to protect. Its strategy became evident within a few
weeks, when the SEC announced it was settling charges with the firm
for $25.3 million. In a rare public affirmation, Giuliani announced
simultaneously that Kidder, Peabody would not be prosecuted.

There was no sentimentality about the outcome at GE. Bossidy
had achieved his overriding goal, which was to avoid indictment.
Kidder, Peabody had survived, which was more than could be said for
E. F. Hutton. From GE's vantage point, there was less a sense of loss
than one of bewilderment: How had an investment bank like Kidder,
Peabody, with its long and impeccable reputation, ever gotten so far
out of control? What remained of the firm was now free to resume its
business, out from under the prosecutorial cloud that had shrouded it
since the arrests in February.

But what remained? For many at the firm, Kidder, Peabody had
been transformed beyond recognition, into little more than a boutique
subsidiary to the giant GE Credit Corporation, itself only a subsidiary
of GE. The ouster of Wigton and GE's treatment of him had shattered
any lingering notion of collegiality. No one thought of Kidder, Peabody as "family" anymore. Among those leaving in a personnel exodus
that began almost immediately were Hal Ritch and, finally, even John
Gordon. They felt lost and alienated in an organization they no longer
recognized. In more reflective moments, however, they realized that
the Kidder, Peabody they'd known and loved had died long before.
The arrival of the big-money "star" system in the eighties had made
national celebrities out of Michael Milken, Ivan Boesky, and Martin
Siegel, even as it doomed the old-fashioned investment bankers like
themselves.

12.

Looking a bit stiff in dark suits and formal gowns, scores of assistant U.S. attorneys and Southern District alumni arrived at the massive crenellated towers of the 19th-century Park Avenue Armory, site of the 1987 Paul Curran dinner. An annual dinner reuniting lawyers who worked during a given U.S. attorney's tenure, in this case that of Paul Curran, is a long-standing tradition in the Manhattan U.S. attorney's office. The dinners help maintain the informal alumni network.

The 1987 Curran dinner was held on May 13, the day the government asked for the dismissal of its indictment against Curran's client Robert Freeman. The armory's large dining room buzzed with comments almost uniformly critical of the actions of their own office. Some laid blame on Goldman, Sachs, arguing that if the defendant were anyone less wealthy and powerful, there wouldn't be the uproar, and certainly not the media attention. But that was a distinctly minority view. The dismissal was at least an acute embarrassment; at worst, it reflected incompetence and damaged the office's reputation.

At one point during the evening, Jed Rakoff ran into Howard Wilson. "This is one of the great cases of all time, and you're fucking it up," Rakoff told him, only half in jest.

Wilson was quick to come to the defense of Giuliani. "What are you talking about? It's your guy's fault we have to get so much corroboration," he said, referring to Siegel.

Rakoff had hoped to keep the discussion friendly, but this angered him. "That's not fair," he retorted. "I always said, this is what he'll say. He's been totally honest. You made the decision to shoot first."

Within the U.S. attorney's office, it was Carberry who seemed to take the setback the hardest. He was, as usual, inscrutable, but he seemed to lose a certain enthusiasm. The bad publicity was painful.

Carberry was fundamentally so shy that he didn't even enjoy good publicity.

Not long after the Curran dinner, with Cartusciello and McEnany struggling to regain momentum and morale at a low ebb, Carberry stunned his colleagues by announcing his own resignation. Publicly, Carberry would say only that the two major investigations, Drexel and Freeman, were likely to drag on for years. Also, the Freeman investigation held little intellectual challenge for him. Unlike Milken's, it was a comparatively simple exchange of inside information; all it needed was routine corroboration. There were other reasons, too. Carberry felt he had already overstayed the office's usual tenure of three to four years when he accepted the position of chief of the fraud unit in 1986. He'd been in the U.S. attorney's office for eight years. His closest friends had already left. It was time for him to move on.

All of this was true, yet many of his colleagues didn't believe it to be the full explanation. It was clear to them that Giuliani had lost confidence in Carberry, even though Giuliani denied it. This loss of faith would have made the job untenable for anyone of Carberry's pride and professionalism.

Carberry didn't yet have a job offer. He dreaded the prospect of trying to sell himself to virtual strangers. Most important, however, his friends found it hard to believe that Carberry would abandon the Milken investigation. He was engaged in an enforcement action that had the prospect of reshaping fundamental attitudes on Wall Street and in the nation's financial markets for generations. Milken was the top of the investigative pyramid, the likely culmination of everything Carberry had set in motion when he first gained the cooperation of Levine. How could he step aside now?

Having made his decision, Carberry wasted no time. In August he was approached by Jones, Day, Reavis & Pogue, a large national law firm based in Cleveland, about launching a white-collar defense practice in the firm's New York office. Carberry didn't even know Jones, Day had a New York office. He flew to Cleveland, met his prospective partners, and, eager to end the search, accepted their offer without entertaining any other prospects. He left in October. What should have been a triumphal exit seemed more like a retreat.

Giuliani moved swiftly to try to shore up momentum and regain the initiative by naming Bruce Baird, one of his top lieutenants, to the securities fraud post. Baird had worked with Giuliani years before at the Justice Department, and, after joining the U.S. attorney's office in 1980, had successfully handled organized crime cases, including the Columbo investigation. He headed first the narcotics division and then

became chief of the criminal division. He knew something about securities law from his days as an associate at Davis Polk & Wardwell, the
prestigious firm representing Freeman along with Kaye, Scholer.

Whereas Carberry was fat with a wry sense of humor, Baird was
tall, thin, serious, and soft-spoken. He'd grown up in the Midwest and
graduated from the University of Wisconsin. If anything, Baird took
an even harder line than Carberry. Given his background in some of
the toughest areas of law enforcement, he wasn't troubled that Freeman, Wigton, and Tabor had been arrested and handcuffed. His clear-
cut view of right and wrong was closely akin to Giuliani's.

Baird accepted Giuliani's offer of the securities fraud job without
hesitation. He knew that he would be presiding over the two most
important cases in the office, those of Freeman and Milken, in the blaze
of publicity. He saw that Giuliani's political future, as well as the
credibility of the U.S. attorney's office, might turn on the outcome.
There was no higher-stakes assignment in the Justice Department. He
had to win.

Yet, as he set to work, the possibility of victory seemed remote.
The Drexel investigation, headed by Carroll and Fardella, seemed
stalled. The Freeman investigation was in shambles. Wall Street had
closed ranks around its own.

Baird was immediately struck by the similarities between the
insider-trading investigations and the Mafia cases he'd worked on. Like
organized crime, the Wall Street suspects prized silence and loyalty
over any duty to tell the truth and root out corruption. He assumed
that a Goldman, Sachs partner, for example, would go to jail rather
than implicate another partner at the firm. Also, as in organized crime
investigations, there were numerous interlocking cases, and not
enough investigators to pursue all the leads. Baird constructed a chart.
He wrote down the names of suspects and drew boxes around them,
then connected them based on interlocking relationships. When he was
done, he had nearly 20 boxes, arranged roughly in a circle. Not all
seemed to lead anywhere. Milken was at the top, Drexel near the
center.

In December, Baird and his colleagues stumbled upon some
valuable evidence against Milken. In a painstaking review of all the
documents collected from Boesky's operations, investigators had discovered a folder from Boesky's personal files marked "DBL arrangement." In the folder, apparently kept by Boesky's secretary, were what
looked like the very spreadsheets prepared by Mooradian, Boesky's
recordkeeper, and then destroyed at Boesky's orders. Carroll immediately called in Mooradian to review them.

"That's it!" Mooradian exclaimed when he saw them. "That's

what I did in Florida." Boesky had apparently forgotten that he had ordered his secretary to copy the Drexel positions before returning the originals to Mooradian.

Now Mooradian's effort to reconstruct the papers could be dropped. The government not only had an actual copy of the original—vastly more valuable as evidence—but the figures corroborated everything Mooradian had been telling them from memory.

The Mooradian papers were soon followed by what appeared to be another breakthrough—in both the Milken and Freeman cases. Soon after taking the post, Baird had sat down with Cartusciello and McEnany to discuss Freeman, who, Giuliani had made clear, was a top priority, given all the bad publicity. They were under pressure to live up to their vows that the withdrawn indictment was only the tip of an iceberg. But where could they get corroboration, additional evidence?

In the course of the Siegel debriefings, Cartusciello had made a mental note of a conversation Siegel remembered having with Freeman during the Storer deal. Freeman had assured Siegel that he knew Coniston Partners was accumulating the stock and was "serious" about forcing a major transaction. Siegel had asked Freeman how he knew. "I'm very close to the people buying the stock for Coniston," Freeman had replied.

Cartusciello had seized on Siegel's memory of the remark, which suggested that Freeman had a source of inside information apart from Siegel. But Siegel had remembered no name, and doubted that Freeman had even mentioned one to him. Some fast investigative work, however, had solved the mystery. Coniston had accumulated the Storer stock through a firm called Oakley-Sutton, whose officers happened to be the same people who ran Princeton-Newport Partners. The head of the operation, James Regan, had been Freeman's roommate at Dartmouth. Surely this was the person. Regan and Princeton-Newport had been subpoenaed about two weeks after the Freeman arrest and Siegel plea. Records revealed the expected trading in Storer stock, and phone records showed that, at the time of the deal, Regan and Freeman spoke often on the phone.

Baird thought that Princeton-Newport was likely to be a promising target for further investigation. Perhaps the firm's principals had conspired with Freeman; they might warrant prosecution themselves, or be candidates for a plea bargain or immunity grant in return for evidence and testimony against Freeman. Baird needed more information, however, and he didn't want to tip off the firm that it had become a target of the government's interest. So Baird turned to a classic investigative technique: Look for a disgruntled current or, more likely, former employee. He soon had a candidate.

Amid all the pressures of the Freeman investigation, Cartusciello had gathered the trading records of employees at Princeton-Newport, and had spent hours poring over them. The tedious work paid off: The records of one employee, William Hale, showed some suspicious pre-announcement trading in one of the stocks that figured in the investigation. When the prosecutors tried to locate the employee—another Dartmouth alumnus—they learned that he was no longer working at Princeton-Newport. He had been fired.

The prosecutors began by issuing Hale a subpoena, but the tactic was a failure. Hale retained a lawyer, and said he wouldn't come in voluntarily to talk with the government. With his lawyer, the prosecutors angled for some kind of deal, hinting that they'd be receptive to a proffer, especially if Hale could implicate anyone at Princeton-Newport. The answer came back: Hale refused to make any kind of proffer. Almost as a last resort, the prosecutors decided to call Hale before the grand jury, forcing him to testify with a grant of immunity. It was a risk. They knew that they might want to prosecute Hale later, but felt they had no alternative.

Hale arrived for his testimony in November 1987. He was young, tall and gangly, with sharp features and dark blond hair. He didn't seem nervous. Baird handled the questioning. As he had expected, the exercise seemed almost pointless, with Hale evasive and reluctant. Then Baird shifted to a seemingly innocuous question, asking Hale why he'd left Princeton-Newport. Hale hesitated only slightly before answering matter-of-factly, "I didn't leave. I was fired."

"Why?" Baird asked, instinctively following up on this sudden burst of candor. But nothing in his career as a prosecutor had prepared him for the startling answer.

"I couldn't stand all the crimes they were committing," Hale said.

Baird could hardly contain his mounting excitement as Hale plunged into an account of wrongdoing at Princeton-Newport. It went beyond anything the prosecutors had imagined. Not only did it appear that the government would now have a case against Princeton-Newport and its top officials, but, according to Hale, the firm's principal co-conspirator was none other than the Beverly Hills office of Drexel. Suddenly the obscure New Jersey operation looked like the previously missing link between the fraud unit's two biggest cases.

According to Hale, Princeton-Newport routinely "parked" securities with Drexel as well as Merrill Lynch, creating phony losses with which to cheat the Internal Revenue Service. The usual contact at Drexel was Bruce Newberg, the Beverly Hills trader who had once chewed his way through the phone cord. To generate the phony tax loss, Princeton-Newport would "sell" securities to Drexel's high-yield department at a loss, then "buy" them back soon after at the same or slightly higher price. Hale said the transactions were really a sham, because Drexel didn't bear any risk of ownership. Drexel was doing Princeton-Newport the kind of favor designed to make it a captive client, one willing, even eager, to buy junk bonds when Drexel salesmen came calling.

Hale explained that Paul Berkman, his boss at Princeton-Newport, had assigned him to handle what were known as the "tax parks," which had worried him because of the obvious potential legal problems. But Berkman hadn't shared Hale's concern. At a meeting attended by other Princeton-Newport officials, Berkman had blithely said that the IRS "didn't have the manpower to sort out these types of trades and didn't have the intelligence" to figure them out, either. Berkman instructed Hale to "camouflage" the scheme by repurchasing the securities at slightly different prices from those at which they were sold, and told Hale to keep track of the positions and the prices on a list he referred to as "the parking lot."

When Hale had balked at carrying out this scheme, he was fired, he told Baird.

Although Hale couldn't enlighten prosecutors on Regan's relationship with Freeman, he was suddenly shaping up to be the most serendipitous witness in the investigation. And he had even more leads for the prosecutors to pursue. At Drexel, he said, there couldn't be any doubt that Newberg was a knowing participant. He also had an assistant, Lisa Ann Jones, who could probably corroborate much of Hale's account, since she often handled transactions for Newberg. Moreover, Hale revealed, there was a good chance that conversations about the parking scheme had been unwittingly recorded. Hale explained that Princeton-Newport maintained a recording system that routinely recorded the firm's traders, though not its top officials. Such systems are common at many firms, usually kept in order to resolve any disputes with customers about orders and their execution.

Baird and Cartusciello decided that it was important to move swiftly on Hale's information, before word leaked that he'd been granted immunity and had testified. Fortunately, his firing had left Hale estranged from his former colleagues, so there was little risk that Hale himself would describe his cooperation. Information, however, had a way of spreading among defense counsel. The prosecutors were especially concerned about the tapes. Hale thought they were routinely destroyed after six months; that process might be accelerated if the firm knew of Hale's disclosures.

Despite the bad publicity over the government's handling of the

Freeman, Wigton, and Tabor arrests, the prosecutors weren't deterred by the prospect of another show of force. Using Hale's disclosures, they quickly obtained a search warrant for Princeton-Newport's offices, citing suspected tax evasion but making no mention of Drexel or Freeman. In a telling measure of Baird's approach to law enforcement, the prosecutors acted as though the problem with the earlier arrests of the arbitrageurs had not been that the government had acted too harshly, but rather that the government hadn't been forceful enough to intimidate the suspects into pleading guilty and cooperating. As a mafia and drug prosecutor, Baird had learned that his targets understood the language of force. With Giuliani's approval, he planned a search that would make the Freeman, Wigton, and Tabor arrests look tame.

Several weeks after Hale's grand jury appearance, in mid-December, several vans pulled up to the inconspicuous, vaguely colonial-style office complex in the center of Princeton, New Jersey, that housed Princeton-Newport. Christmas decorations brightened the adjacent shop windows on the street, which led, just a short distance away, to the main entrance of Princeton University's tranquil campus. Out of the vans poured fifty United States marshals, armed and wearing bulletproof vests.

The marshals crowded into the elevators, then pushed their way through the glass doors of Princeton-Newport's offices. After showing their warrant, they swarmed through the offices as terrified employees froze at their desks. No one was allowed to leave until the marshals completed their work. They pulled open filing cabinets and desks, emptying the contents into cardboard boxes. By the end of the afternoon, they had carted off more than 300 boxes containing documents, records, and—most important—all the tape recordings they could find.

Baird and Cartusciello had also enlisted their top investigator, Tom Doonan. The day of the Princeton-Newport raid, Doonan flew to California, then drove to a modern apartment complex north of Los Angeles, the home of Drexel's Lisa Jones, arriving at her door just before 10 P.M.

Jones was a 1980s embodiment of a Horatio Alger hero. At the age of 14, she had run away from her New Jersey home, heading west to California and landing a $5,000-a-year job as a bank teller by lying about her age. She earned a high school degree by attending an equivalency program. Now, still only 25 years old, she was earning $117,000 a year as a trading assistant in Drexel's Beverly Hills office, working for Bruce Newberg, just one step away from Milken himself. She arrived at work every morning at 5:30 A.M., and spent the day writing up orders for Newberg and placing them on various exchanges, sometimes working three phones at once. She worked hard, and she had realized a level of comfort and security she'd never known before. She was the kind of person Milken liked to hire and promote.

Doonan rang her doorbell, and Jones, a short, curly-haired brunette, answered the door. "Can I speak to you?" Doonan asked politely, explaining who he was and that he had a federal subpoena with him. Jones invited him into her living room, and Doonan quickly outlined the trades between Drexel and Princeton-Newport, showing that he already had considerable knowledge of the situation. The interview was promising at first, with Jones truthfully confirming various details of her relationship to Newberg and Princeton-Newport. Then Doonan got to the crux of the matter.

"Were you parking for them?" Doonan asked.

"Yes, I was," Jones replied hesitantly.

"Was it for tax purposes?" Doonan continued. Jones suddenly seemed apprehensive.

"No, it wasn't," she began, but then her voice trailed off. "I want to talk to a lawyer," she said. Doonan sighed, but didn't press her.

"We were hoping you would be willing to cooperate with us in this investigation," Doonan said, almost sadly. He left her with a grand jury subpoena. Jones, suddenly fearful that her phones were tapped, rushed to a pay phone to call the only lawyer she knew.

Back in New York, investigators began cataloging the seized materials and reviewing the tapes. Much of it was routine, of no use to the government. But then Cartusciello made an extraordinary discovery: for some reason, apparently involving a client dispute, tapes covering several days in December 1984 hadn't been destroyed. As he listened, several conversations practically jumped out at him. Cartusciello rushed to get Baird.

Soon they had organized about 20 of the conversations onto a single tape. Baird called in prosecutors from the Freeman and Drexel-Milken cases, and as the tapes played, their excitement quickly mounted. It was just like being in the Princeton-Newport offices as the scheme unfolded. Most of the significant tapes captured conversations between Newberg and Charles Zarzecki, a trader and general partner of Princeton-Newport; but an unexpected bonus was an incriminating tape of Drexel's Cary Maultasch, apparently handling some matters in Newberg's absence. This might be the evidence that would crack Maultasch's stalwart resistance to any notion of cooperation with the government.

Drexel prosecutor John Carroll was home with the flu that day, but his colleagues couldn't resist calling him repeatedly about the lucky discovery. They even put some of the tapes on the phone so he could hear.

In one of the tapes, Regan is bickering with Newberg about the cost of "carrying" the parked stock positions. "I've carried plenty of positions for you, in case you haven't been realizing it," Newberg says. "I've been charging you my cost to carry."

In what seems a clear acknowledgment that Drexel stock was parked with Princeton-Newport, Regan replies: "What I carry on my books now is your position."

It was an extraordinary find, the biggest break the prosecutors had had since the indictments were dismissed six months earlier. The tapes were irrefutable evidence of wrongdoing that went beyond what Hale had divulged. Besides the parking to create phony tax losses for Princeton-Newport, the conversations revealed that Princeton-Newport had performed illegal favors at Drexel's behest: parking stock of toymaker Mattel Inc. in 1985, and embarking on a stock manipulation scheme. The tapes showed that Drexel had enlisted Princeton-Newport to manipulate the price of an over-the-counter stock, C.O.M.B., a Minneapolis-based merchandiser for which Drexel was handling a securities offering. The prosecutors wondered: if this was what went on at Princeton-Newport and Drexel during a random few days, what other crimes might have been committed at the firms? Baird recognized almost immediately that Drexel could probably be convicted on the strength of the taped conversations alone. Fred Joseph had said repeatedly that he wanted some evidence of wrongdoing—now he could hear it for himself.

But of all the taped conversations, two made a deep impression on the prosecutors. They stood out not just because of their value as evidence—neither, standing alone, was proof of any crime—but because of what they revealed about the state of mind that prevailed on Wall Street in the mid-eighties.

In the first of these, Freeman is talking with Zarzecki. In an almost wistful tone, Freeman tells Zarzecki that he'd recently been to Atlantic City and that when he was younger, he loved to go to Las Vegas and gamble. But now, he says, he doesn't like casino odds. "It's not fun anymore. I guess I've been in this business too long," he says. "I'm used to having an edge." In the second conversation, Zarzecki is talking to Newberg in Beverly Hills. After arranging one of their sham sales, Newberg tells Zarzecki, "You're a sleaze bag."

"You taught me man," Zarzecki responds. "Hey listen, turkey . . ."

Newberg interrupts with a sardonic chuckle. "Welcome to the world of being a sleaze."

Despite the unfolding scandal, the great bull stock market of the eighties had rolled on. On May 12, 1986, the day Levine was arrested, the Dow Jones Industrial Average had topped 1800. Few had seen any portent in the arrest of an obscure investment banker. By November, when Boesky agreed to plead guilty, the Dow stood at nearly 1900. After some initial tremors, mostly in deal stocks and arbitrage plays, the stock market resumed its ascent. If anything, the resistance of Freeman and Milken, Goldman, Sachs and Drexel, had reassured investors that the engine of the takeover boom would continue.

Drexel had done everything it could to shore up that impression. Despite the shadow of the government's investigation, the firm was able to draw on the loyalty of its clients to sustain its business and market share at near-record levels. Drexel may have been uniquely positioned on Wall Street to withstand attacks on the legality of its business. After all, it had stood by many of its largest clients, like Posner, when they were in trouble and no one else wanted to be associated with them. Now it was Drexel's turn.

And the clients responded. Despite the possibility that Drexel might be charged or indicted at any time, the firm completed an impressive series of massive junk-bond deals. The government could not count on client pressure to encourage Drexel to cooperate. On the contrary, the clients were, in many cases, as defiant as Milken. Given his continuing power over many of them, they had little option.

New business suffered, however. The firm lost its incredible momentum. It had to abandon plans for its own skyscraper at 7 World Trade Center; Drexel's hated rival Salomon Brothers took the tower instead. And the Drexel-backed hostile tender offer lost its psychological power. Perelman's withdrawal from his Gillette bid and Icahn's failure to take over USX were perceived as Drexel failures. But Drexel was eager to distance itself from its controversial role in hostile takeovers. It didn't back any during most of 1987.

Soon after the Boesky revelations, Joseph had hired Ira Millstein, a senior partner at Weil, Gotshal & Manges, a large and prominent New York firm, to serve as his personal lawyer. Millstein had quickly concluded that Joseph had no personal exposure to criminal liability. On a personal rather than a legal level, however, he warned Joseph that he believed Milken might be in serious trouble, and that the best course for Joseph would be to resign from Drexel. Joseph had been

startled by the suggestion. The prospect was unthinkable. He insisted
to Millstein that it was nonsensical to think that a man of Milken's vast
wealth would stoop to crime.

In the weeks that followed, Joseph seemed determined to tie his
and the firm's fate even more closely to Milken. Even before the
Boesky scandal broke, Joseph had hoped that G. Christian "Chris"
Andersen's New York-based investment banking group might develop
into an East Coast client-getting group comparable to Milken's. It
hadn't happened. So Milken insisted on bringing back Don Engel, the
Milken loyalist Joseph had fired for what he considered ethical lapses,
to rejuvenate Drexel's client-getting capability.

Joseph initially resisted. There was strong opposition from the
Bachelor-Andersen faction. Milken emphasized, however, that in
tough times, "relationships" were what counted. Milken said his own
relationships were keeping the firm afloat, and—in an obvious slap at
corporate finance officials Bachelor, Andersen, and their East Coast
allies—he added that Engel seemed to be the only other person at
Drexel who understood how to cultivate client loyalty.

In this as in other respects, Joseph cast his lot with the Milken
camp. "Mike wants you to do this," Joseph told Engel. "We need
you." Engel agreed to come back in January 1987 as co-head of the
investment banking group. He also managed to keep his compensation
agreement, and insisted that he report directly to Joseph—not to
Bachelor or Andersen, his nominal equals.

No sooner had Engel made his triumphal return than he rechristened the investment banking group the "relationships group"—without consulting Andersen. Andersen barged into Joseph's office and
threatened to resign. Stephen Weinroth, who had opposed Engel's
return from the outset, also threatened to leave, and other members of
the East Coast faction followed suit.

Less than a month after Engel's return to the firm, Joseph persuaded him to withdraw and resume his status as a consultant. After
all, Engel was still in charge of the Predators' Ball, which had now
assumed unprecedented importance as a show of strength in the wake
of the government's investigation.

As the 1987 conference got underway, the first week in April,
there was fear in the air. There were daily rumors of a massive government raid, a prospect made all the more plausible by the Freeman,
Wigton, and Tabor arrests. Engel, however, was undaunted, rising to
the challenge. The 1987 high-yield conference was the biggest ever, a
display of client loyalty that drew more than 2,500 participants.

Plainly, the real audience for the conference wasn't in Beverly

Hills, but in Congress and the nation at large. The tone of this year's event changed dramatically. The freewheeling, muscle-flexing sense that anything was possible was gone—along with the exhilaration. Engel's bungalow party, again a stag affair, and the ensuing dinner at Chasen's, were staid in comparison to prior years. The glitzy rock-backed videos were replaced by a quasidocumentary entitled "Drexel Helps America," featuring emotional testimonials in praise of junk bonds from employees of big Drexel clients.

The film was propaganda. When a Stone Container employee said he'd like to "shake the hand" of whoever had championed junk bonds for his company, a cynic in the audience blurted out, "How much did we pay that guy?" At the end of the film, the narrator sounded Drexel's new investigation-inspired theme: "High-yield financing and Drexel Burnham Lambert—they help America work!" The audience burst into thunderous applause.

Milken sounded similar themes, and began to promote his new image as a "national treasure." In his opening remarks, he made no mention of hostile takeovers, concentrating instead on how junk bonds had promoted the growth of midsize companies and kept America competitive. Boone Pickens had planned a rousing defense of take-overs and shareholder democracy for his keynote address. After Drexel reviewed his proposed remarks, he substituted a numbingly dull talk on economic conditions in the oil and gas industry.

The tone of the conference was meant to suggest that the government's investigation was of no concern to Drexel and Milken. Yet clearly, combined with the bad publicity, it was exacting a toll. Joseph looked haggard; Maultasch looked even worse. In contrast, everything about Milken—his energy, his demeanor, his constant presence—conveyed reassurance. Milken "hasn't been hampered by any guilty conscience that I can see," one participant told *The Washington Post*. "I figure that means he's either not guilty or he doesn't have a conscience."

As usual, the press was barred from the conference sessions, but many showed up at the Beverly Hilton anyway. The reporters weren't ejected, but were followed closely and barred from entering rooms where meetings were scheduled. Only designated participants, such as client William Farley, head of Fruit-of-the-Loom, were allowed to make comments to the press, and those were carefully scripted by Drexel to underline the conference's themes.

This was just one component of the biggest media offensive ever mounted by a private defendant in a criminal investigation. Much of it was intended to deflect attention from Milken's alleged misdeeds and shore up his national stature. It would be an unprecedented test of the degree to which public opinion could be used to shape the outcome of a criminal investigation.

Soon after the junk-bond conference, Drexel launched a two-week-long, firm-wide celebration of junk bonds, including sporting events, lectures, and films touting the glories of junk bonds and their contributions to America. In a policy shift first announced at the conference, Drexel abandoned its long-standing efforts to replace the word "junk" with "high-yield" in popular parlance. Instead, it decided to embrace "junk." Employees were given pins with the message, JUNK BONDS KEEP AMERICA FIT. One of the videos featured Joseph and firm chairman Robert Linton lip-synching the lyrics, "When the going gets tough, Drexel gets going."

Full-page newspaper ads showed alleged beneficiaries of junk-bond largesse: not, of course, people like Milken himself, or Milken satellites like Carr or Spiegel, but a wholesome young man, his pregnant wife and their child standing in front of a soon-to-be-completed new home. What linked this scene of happy domesticity to junk bonds? Hovanian, the home's builder, was a Drexel client that, with junk bonds, had been able to "provide 50,000 people with a living room and 20,000 people with a living," the ad claimed. A $4 million network television campaign was similarly sentimental, showing an energy plant in Vidalia, Louisiana, built with Drexel junk bonds, that had supposedly lowered unemployment in the impoverished Louisiana town. Many at Drexel were furious when *Wall Street Journal* reporter Laurie Cohen pointed out that the television commercial wasn't even filmed in Vidalia, that most of the plant's workers lived elsewhere, and that the Louisiana Department of Labor disputed the ad's claim that the plant had lowered unemployment.

The television campaign was only one part of the media blitz. Richard Sandler and other Milken allies at Drexel began to assert control over every aspect of Milken's portrayal in the media. Every journalist covering the story was "analyzed," and reporters were "graded" on how favorably disposed they seemed to be toward Milken and how easily manipulated they might be. The Milken camp placed reporters in two broad categories: the ideologues, who could be counted on to support the Milken line because they held similar political views, and the pragmatists, who needed help from the Milken camp because they were failing to break any stories on their own.

The Milken team's favorite ideologue was Edward J. Epstein, a *Manhattan inc.* columnist, who had been among the first to write that Milken was being unfairly hounded by prosecutors. Epstein sounded themes that resonated powerfully with supporters of Reagan-era deregulation and supply-side economics. After passing muster with Williams, Epstein was granted the first personal interview with Milken. He wasn't allowed to ask about the investigation.

The *Wall Street Journal*'s editorial-page writers became the most potent exponents of the pro-Milken line. This camp seemed to favor the antiestablishment "creative destruction" that they believed Milken had spawned, and showed a barely disguised contempt for the securities laws as needless government limitations on innovation and entrepreneurship.

As the hot summer of 1987 wore on, an uneasy calm descended on Wall Street. The period of cooperation, which culminated in the Boesky and Siegel plea agreements, was obviously over. New indictments of Freeman, Wigton, and Tabor seemed ever more remote. Except for those immediately caught up in the continuing investigation, the scandal seemed to recede into recent history.

Arbitrageurs were once again celebrating. Most had more than recouped their losses from the brief plunge in stocks that followed the announcement of the Boesky plea. They were leveraged more than ever, throwing money at real and contemplated takeover stocks. The market surged ever higher, topping 2,700 in early August. There was talk of a 3,000 Dow Jones Industrial Average by the end of the year.

Joseph tried to caution Drexel officials about the rising euphoria, especially the incredibly high prices shareholders were being offered in takeovers and leveraged buyouts. That fall, he met with Milken and his Beverly Hills contingent and told them that Drexel had to be prepared to let its enormous junk-bond market share shrink. "Let others do these deals," Joseph urged. "You've got to be able to let a real order, a real client, go somewhere else." Everyone seemed to nod in agreement, including Milken, though the notion of "letting" a client go was anathema to him.

The stock market soon imposed its own discipline. The first tremors came on October 14, with rumors from Washington of pending legislation designed to limit the deductibility of interest incurred in financing hostile takeovers. The prices of a host of stocks had been driven to exorbitant levels on expectations of takeover bids; these now seemed in jeopardy. A sell-off began, slowly at first, as some arbitrageurs stepped in to buy stocks at lower prices, but then more rapidly as institutions began to sell swiftly in order to lock in unrealized profits. On Thursday and Friday, October 15 and 16, the market dropped more than 100 points each day.

Milken was at his trading desk both days, reassuring Drexel

clients that existing junk bonds wouldn't be affected directly by the proposed legislation, and continuing to make markets. Yet he was indirectly responsible for the market's tremors—since he, more than anyone else, had shown that takeovers could be financed at prices never before thought possible. More than any other single person, Milken had been behind the massive revaluation of stocks that had carried the Dow Jones average above 2,700.

Then, on Monday, October 19, the stock market crashed, dropping more than 500 points in the worst one-day loss in its history. A selling frenzy developed as computerized program trading translated investor sentiment into sell orders faster than had ever before been possible. Virtually every stock was caught in the plunge, takeover targets and the most secure blue-chip companies alike. The market itself came close to breakdown, especially on Tuesday, October 20, when it plunged again before rallying in the afternoon. Many market-makers on the New York Stock Exchange lacked the capital to absorb the selling onslaught. The Federal Reserve had to flood the system with cash to stave off disaster.

Unlike the great crash of 1929, Black Monday 1987 didn't usher in a nationwide recession. It was a psychological breakdown, rather than an economic one. Corporate earnings remained strong. Main Street America continued spending. And even the shaken market itself began an extended rally from its new lows. Junk bonds, after plunging initially in a widespread flight to safer treasury bonds, recovered even faster, in part because of Milken's tireless proselytizing that they remained sound investments. Indeed, he told his major clients to step in and buy more, and they did. Milken's influence over his vast network of bond buyers made him uniquely positioned to restore confidence in the market.

Yet the market's plunge left real devastation in its wake. Small investors suffered heavily, and many were so alienated by the experience that they never returned to trading. Already suspicious of the market's integrity, these investors were now convinced that the stock market was a rigged game for professionals. In time, this attitude would seriously impair the country's capital-raising structure—just as the drafters of the original securities laws had feared.

Wall Street was littered with victims. To a profound degree, the mood changed overnight. People no longer made as much money, and they didn't expect to again. It wasn't as much fun to come to work.

The arbitrageurs were the first victims of a decade of leverage. In imitating Boesky, no other group had embraced the notion of leverage with such abandon, and no other paid so heavily for it. In the demise of the arbitrageurs lay one of the great lessons of the crash: that high returns aren't necessarily market anomalies, but measures of far greater risk. This should have been obvious to junk-bond buyers, who had also enjoyed returns that seemed out of proportion to the risk. Yet most remained dazzled by their sun king in Beverly Hills.

There were isolated warnings. Warren Buffett, chairman of Berkshire Hathaway in Omaha, who is considered one of the country's most astute investors, warned repeatedly of the perils of junk bonds. "When you insure substandard drivers, you get paid more than when you insure standard drivers," he told *The Washington Post*. "Some have done very well doing that and some have gotten killed."

On December 20, with the arbitrage world he had known still in shambles from the crash, a gaunt and uncharacteristically pale Ivan Boesky appeared in Manhattan's federal court. Police barricades had to be erected to hold back the hundreds of reporters, photographers, television camera crews, and curious onlookers packing the courthouse steps. The courtroom was packed with reporters and lawyers, with access controlled by court marshals. The crowd became hushed, and strained to hear as Boesky himself stood and addressed federal judge Morris Lasker.

"I am deeply ashamed and do not understand my behavior," Boesky began, speaking in a soft voice. "I have spent the last year trying to understand how I veered off course," he continued. "I would like the opportunity as I go forward to redeem myself and leave this Earth with a good name. That is what I want."

It was Boesky himself who had begged to be sentenced that day. Ordinarily, cooperating government witnesses, as a guarantee of their continued cooperation, aren't sentenced until they have completed their testimony for the government; Boesky was slated to be the star witness in the government's Milken case. Yet prosecutors allowed Boesky to be sentenced; it looked as though a Milken trial might be years away and, if he had to go to prison, Boesky wanted to go soon. He was growing increasingly anxious that his own safety was in danger. He was tired of biding time with charitable work at the Cathedral of St. John the Divine and studies at the Jewish Theological Seminary. These endeavors had had little impact on public opinion.

Allowing Boesky to begin his sentence was a decision prosecutors would live to regret, but at the time, the loss of some leverage seemed a small price to pay for all that he had given them. At a presentencing hearing, prosecutor John Carroll described Boesky's cooperation as the "most remarkable in the history of the securities laws." He added that "the larger crimes in our view are the crimes that Mr. Boesky has engaged in largely at the behest of others. There we are dealing with a very systemic type of problem. A systemic corruption that undermines the financial world, and that is not, unfortunately, an exaggeration." Given the subsequent defiance of others on Wall Street, Boesky's honesty had come to seem all the more remarkable.

Judge Lasker praised Boesky's cooperation, hailing it, as did the government, as "unprecedented." He showed some sympathy, noting that "there is no doubt that Boesky has been humiliated, vilified, and cut down to size in a degree rarely heard of in the life of a person who was once regarded favorably as a celebrity."

As a result of pleading guilty to only one felony, Boesky faced a maximum term of five years in prison. As suspense mounted in the courtroom, Judge Lasker meted out a term of three years. While immediately attacked by Milken forces as excessively lenient, the sentence was more than half of the maximum he could have received. It was also the most severe sentence imposed so far in the still-developing scandal.

"The signal must go out," Judge Lasker concluded, plainly disturbed by what he had learned about the scope of illegal conduct on Wall Street. "The time has come when it is totally unacceptable for courts to act as if prison is unthinkable for white collar defendants. . . . To preserve not only the actual integrity of the financial markets but the appearance of integrity in those markets, criminal behavior such as Mr. Boesky's cannot go unchecked."

Boesky had hoped to elude the press by leaving the courthouse through a rear entrance. As he reached the sidewalk, however, waiting camera crews stampeded, swarming over parked cars, crushing their hoods and roofs. Papers the next day were filled with close-ups of Boesky looking terrified as he slipped into a waiting limousine.

February 18, 1988, was a cold, gray Thursday with snow threatening in northern New Jersey. John Mulheren's mood was dark as he emerged from the front door of his sprawling Victorian mansion and placed a gym bag on the back seat of his car. In the bag Mulheren had placed a loaded, .233-caliber Israeli Galil assault rifle, purchased two weeks before, and a set of army fatigues. He also had a chest pack of 300 rounds of ammunition. Already in the car were a 9-millimeter semiautomatic pistol, a .357 Magnum pistol, and a 12-gauge pistol-grip shotgun—a veritable arsenal.

The pressures of the government's investigation had been building, and Mulheren had reached the breaking point. He was deeply depressed. He hadn't slept at all the previous night, staying up to watch a continuous stream of movies on television, movies whose names he didn't even remember. He had stopped taking his lithium. The day before, his lawyer had told him he was about to be indicted. Even more dispiriting was the fact that his lawyer also told him he should plead guilty.

Mulheren got behind the wheel, started the car, and began backing it down the long, curving drive toward North Ward Avenue. His mission: to kill the one man behind all his torment, someone he'd once counted among his closest friends: Ivan Boesky. Then the "headhunt," as he later called it, would be over.

Perhaps it was inevitable, even within the confines of a white-collar scandal, that violence would erupt. The money and power at stake were immense; many have killed, and been killed, for less. Siegel had feared Boesky would have him killed; Boesky feared Milken would have him killed; now Mulheren had actually set out to kill Boesky.

Mulheren's mental condition had been deteriorating almost steadily since the Boesky plea agreement had shattered his view of human nature. That was even before he learned that Boesky, whom he still considered a friend, might be implicating him—"ratting" on him, as Mulheren put it.

The previous January, Mulheren had received a Boesky-related subpoena clearly covering the string of alleged parking arrangements, beginning with Unocal, that Mulheren had done for Boesky in 1985. "So what?" had been Mulheren's reaction. Who cared about a few favors he'd done? Surely that wasn't a crime.

Mulheren just couldn't believe that Boesky or Davidoff would say anything bad about him; but he'd heard that Mooradian was cooperating. The inflated invoices Mulheren had used to reimburse Boesky for some of the gains on the allegedly parked stock figured prominently in the subpoenas. Mulheren had guessed that Mooradian was probably pointing those out to the government.

In February 1987, Mulheren had gotten another subpoena covering the maneuvering in Gulf + Western stock at the time Boesky and Icahn teamed up to threaten the company. That didn't bother Mulheren either. He couldn't understand when his lawyer, Kenneth Bialkin, refused to let him testify. "This is a witch hunt," Bialkin had warned, and insisted that Mulheren consult a criminal lawyer whom Bialkin recommended, Otto Obermaier.

But not everyone was as nonchalant as Mulheren himself. Some of his investors were worried, and asked bothersome questions about what their "exposure" might be. The lawyers were around constantly,

and Mulheren had no great love of lawyers. But the year wore on with
no visible progress in the government's investigation.

Financially, Mulheren had been having a tremendous year as he
headed into October. Boesky's absence from arbitrage had increased
his profit opportunities, because there was less competition. After the
first nine months of 1987, Mulheren had gains on paper of $120
million. He was actually doing better than when Boesky had been
feeding him tips.

Then came October 19. Like other arbitrageurs, Mulheren was
hard hit, losing $80 million in the crash. Unlike many of his colleagues,
he seemed excited by the action, turmoil, and panic around him. As the
market plunged, he jumped up and down on the trading floor, laughing
and exclaiming, "We'll make it all back!" He was exulting that the
crash gave him a new challenge, a new opportunity to make yet more
money and to outperform his rivals. Even to people accustomed to
Mulheren's outbursts, his reaction seemed inappropriate to what was,
after all, a loss of $80 million. True to his word, however, Mulheren
plunged back into his work with newfound enthusiasm, boldly investing his remaining capital even as rival arbitrageurs were folding the
tents. He finished the year up 18%, a remarkable gain.

Yet even during December, with his business recovering nicely,
Mulheren continued to behave in odd ways. One Saturday night during
this period, Mulheren had dinner with his friend Bruce Springsteen,
who'd just finished work on another album. He and Mulheren excitedly
planned Springsteen's concert tour to accompany the release of the
record. Then Mulheren mentioned that he'd seen Panama strongman
Manuel Noriega on the cover of *Time* magazine. "Noriega's a victim"
of U.S. oppression, Mulheren said. Springsteen looked puzzled. Then
Mulheren mentioned the Singer case in Utah, in which state police
surrounded the home of a suspect in a Mormon church bombing. "The
state is oppressive," Mulheren said. Springsteen chose to ignore these
provocative remarks.

Soon Mulheren began carrying a loaded weapon everywhere. The
police, he had now concluded, were in league with the government
prosecutors trying to ensnare him in the Boesky scandal. Mulheren felt
he should be armed in case a policeman tried to kill him. He became
so convinced that all policemen were trying to kill him that he would
cross to the other side of the street whenever he saw a policeman
approaching.

One Friday in December, Mulheren failed to show up at his office.
When his colleagues checked, they learned that he had left for work on
schedule in his helicopter and had been dropped off at the Battery Park
helipad in lower Manhattan. Then, apparently, he'd disappeared.

Mulheren, clad in his usual khakis and T-shirt, without a coat, had spent the day walking from Battery Park, at the southern tip of Manhattan, to Harlem and Washington Heights at the northern tip of the island. Mulheren himself couldn't explain why he was doing this. Nothing like it had ever happened before. He'd stopped taking his regular dose of lithium because of physical side effects. He felt suicidal. He recognized what might be the onset of the four-year cycle of "black moods" that periodically interrupted his usual manic highs.

Still, Mulheren seemed to recover from that escapade. Then, in January 1988, the news broke that Davidoff had agreed to cooperate and plead guilty to one felony. Now Mulheren had to face the likelihood that Davidoff was implicating him. And he learned through his lawyer that Boesky had implicated Davidoff, which meant that Boesky had probably turned on him as well. Even worse, the felony to which Davidoff had pleaded guilty was evading net capital requirements through a parking scheme—and parking was the very charge that Mulheren continued to insist couldn't be deemed a crime.

Mulheren again plunged into despair, brooding over this latest and most serious betrayal by his former friends. He would never do this himself. He was, in fact, under pressure to testify against friends and former colleagues at Spear Leeds, where he'd once worked, as well as against the Belzbergs. He'd said nothing.

On Monday, February 15, Mulheren had been in such a dark mood that he didn't go into the office. On Tuesday, his emotions had swung to the other extreme; he was excited and overanimated. He went to the dentist in the morning, and arrived at the office in ebullient spirits. He told his colleagues that they'd been working hard and deserved a break. Mulheren ordered five helicopters for the following Monday, and told his staff that after the market closed, he'd fly them to Atlantic City, where they could gamble and party as late as they wanted. They'd fly back the next morning in time for the market opening. It would all be at Mulheren's expense. It was an outsize gesture, even by Mulheren's standards.

On Wednesday, February 17, Mulheren was again depressed; he screamed at his dentist that his teeth were hurting and he got a codeine prescription. Unbeknownst to Mulheren, he was about to learn of the most ominous development yet in his troubles with the government.

After taking over from Carberry, Baird had assigned the Mulheren case to Robert Gage. An experienced prosecutor in the office, Gage had joined the fraud unit the year before as part of the effort to beef up the division. The Mulheren case, unlike Freeman's or Milken's, was considered one of the most straightforward cases coming out of the Boesky agreement, and a comparatively easy one to try. The government had two major cooperating witnesses in Boesky and Davidoff. During January, Boesky had given the grand jury an incriminating account of his dealings with Mulheren, including the parking allegations and numerous instances of stock manipulation and of stock tips suggesting insider trading. For example, Boesky had testified that he had told Mulheren to "push up the price" of Gulf + Western, and that Mulheren had replied, "I understand what you're saying."

Most of Boesky's grand jury testimony stuck closely to the elements of the various crimes for which Mulheren was being investigated; but at one point on January 13, Gage probed Boesky's motives, asking why he'd embarked on these illegal activities with Mulheren. Boesky's answer captured the peculiar dynamics of Wall Street during the heyday of the eighties, when criminal activity seemed to have insinuated itself into the very fabric of human relationships.

Boesky had seemed slightly surprised by the question, and answered more slowly than usual. "There had been many, many years of friendship," Boesky said of himself and Mulheren. "Doing for one another, enriching each other when possible, saving each other when necessary and interested in each other's families, charities." He paused thoughtfully, and then summed up quite simply, "We were friends." In Boesky's world, money and favors—especially the exchange of information—were the measure of friendship. This was true in his relations with Siegel and Milken, and especially so with Mulheren.

Late on the afternoon of Wednesday, February 17, while Mulheren was still suffering from a toothache, his criminal lawyer, Obermaier, came down for a meeting in Mulheren's baronial office. Earlier in the afternoon, Gage had called Obermaier with ominous news: He was close to asking the grand jury for an indictment of Mulheren on parking and market-manipulation charges. The government, he had said, now had ample evidence to support the charges. In addition to Boesky's grand jury testimony, the government had documentary corroboration, including the damaging evidence of the inflated invoices. Gage had emphasized that, if Mulheren hoped to get any favorable treatment from the government, now was the time to plead, before any indictment was made public. But Gage had made it clear that a plea to at least one felony would be required. Immunity wasn't an option.

Obermaier had apparently concluded that, in Mulheren's own interest, he had to get him to consider seriously pleading guilty. The facts alleged by the government weren't in serious dispute; trading records confirmed all the stock transactions. Mulheren could testify to his own state of mind—that he believed he bore the risk for the stock allegedly "parked" by Boesky, and that he knew nothing of Boesky's interest in boosting the price of Gulf + Western—but a jury would have to believe Mulheren over Boesky and Davidoff, and the circumstantial case was strong.

After laying out the substance of his talk with Gage, and briefly reviewing the strengths and weaknesses of the government's case, Obermaier brought up the possibility of settlement, something Mulheren had thus far stoutly refused to consider. "Why not get this over?" Obermaier asked, trying to keep his tone fairly light, as though this wouldn't be the end of the world. "Go in and plead. If you don't they'll ruin your life." Mulheren listened in disbelief.

"I didn't do anything," Mulheren yelled angrily. He'd maintained consistently that all he'd done was a few favors for Boesky.

"Put your principles in your back pocket," Obermaier advised, which really drove Mulheren wild.

"I'm not pleading guilty!" Mulheren all but yelled. "I don't care what they do to me." The very idea of bowing to government pressure tapped Mulheren's deep-seated resentment of authority, and his reaction was intensified by his manic condition.

"Going to jail isn't so bad," Obermaier continued, evidently heedless of Mulheren's mounting fury. "You could use a vacation from your kids."

That did it. Mulheren leapt to his feet, screaming and yelling. He told Obermaier he was firing him and called him names, concluding with, "Otto, why do I need you scumbag lawyers?" Mulheren stormed out of the office.

Shortly after Obermaier left, an agitated Mulheren called Ken Bialkin, the lawyer who had first suggested Mulheren retain a criminal law expert, and who had stayed involved in the case. Bialkin tried to calm him. This further angered Mulheren. "You fucking lawyers are all the same," Mulheren yelled, saying he was firing Bialkin, too. Then Mulheren slammed down the phone. His lawyers were so upset by Mulheren's behavior and mood that they tried to reach Mulheren's psychiatrist that night. But he was vacationing in the Caribbean, and couldn't be reached.

Mulheren didn't sleep at all that night, staying up and watching movies on television. He felt he was going over some kind of edge; his life was being ruined. He was a victim.

The next day, February 18, Mulheren's mental state continued to deteriorate. He became increasingly restless and belligerent, raving about his betrayal by Boesky and Davidoff. He said he wanted to kill them. Finally, his wife Nancy called the local police, saying she was concerned about her husband's emotional state and his access to firearms, and that he seemed agitated and upset about Boesky. The police dispatched a patrol car, which parked near the entrance to the Mulheren compound on North Ward Avenue.

Soon thereafter, Mulheren emerged from his house, got into his car, and drove toward the entrance. The policeman pulled his car forward, cutting off the entrance gate from the street. He got out of the car and came over to Mulheren, immediately spotting the pistols in the backseat. He seized the weapons, but didn't arrest Mulheren, since he had a permit and since he hadn't taken the weapons off his property. Mulheren seemed agitated but drove back to the house.

It was later that afternoon that Mulheren came out of the house and hurried to his car, carrying the gym bag with the assault rifle and the fatigue clothes. This time he gunned his car down the driveway and pulled out into the street before the police could block the entrance. As Mulheren sped off, a second car was called. After a brief pursuit, the police managed to bring Mulheren to a stop.

"Do you want it to start here?" Mulheren yelled as the police converged on his car.

Mulheren knew both of the local police officers, and launched into a rambling denunciation of Boesky and Davidoff, saying that "without Boesky and Davidoff the headhunt would be over." He ranted that he'd lost faith in the justice system and would "take care of things in my own way." He claimed he'd staked out Davidoff's house the previous day, hoping for an opportunity to kill him. Now he was on his way to get Boesky. Questioned by police about his mental state, Mulheren said he was "smart enough" to feign insanity and, once released, he would again try to kill Boesky and Davidoff. The officers arrested him, charging him with carrying the assault rifle off his property without a permit.

Mulheren wasn't charged with attempted murder. Given his mental state, it's hard to know just what he did intend. It's plausible that he wanted to get caught; perhaps he longed for the comparative safety of jail. Mulheren hadn't hidden the assault rifle, and he acknowledged that he was breaking the law by carrying it off his property. Indeed, Mulheren himself suggested the charge as the police officers tried to figure out what he should be arrested for. Despite his claim that he'd staked out Davidoff's house the previous day, Mulheren later said he hadn't; he was just bragging to be provocative, in what he said was a characteristic of his severe manic-depressive episodes. Yet Mulheren's actions couldn't be entirely dismissed as the results of a crazed mind. He had been implicated by Boesky and Davidoff, and they were likely to be witnesses against him. Had he set out to kill them, it would have been a crime with ample precedent.

The police took Mulheren to the Monmouth County jail for the night. They also notified the Manhattan U.S. attorney's office, where Boesky was being debriefed. Boesky gasped when he was told of the bizarre developments. Already concerned about his safety, he became even more frightened. He asked if he could begin his sentence immediately; he thought he'd be safer in prison.

The next morning Mulheren was led into a makeshift New Jersey courtroom, his left wrist shackled to a line of a dozen other prisoners. Nancy and his parents watched as he was charged on two weapons counts and bail was set at a comparatively modest $17,500. The same day, after the U.S. attorney's office obtained a warrant charging him with threatening and attempting to threaten a witness in a federal case, Mulheren posted bail in New Jersey and was brought to the Metropolitan Correction Center. Within days of his arrest, his firm, Jamie Securities, whose name had once awed Wall Street and whose investors included the Tisch and Belzberg families, began the formal process of dissolution. Whatever the outcome of the legal proceedings, Mulheren's meteoric career on Wall Street seemed over.

Unlike Levine and Tabor, Mulheren wasn't released after just a one-night stay in the MCC. The government argued strenuously against granting bail, claiming that Mulheren remained a danger to Boesky and Davidoff, and he stayed locked up. "This case is as severe a case of an attempt to obstruct justice as could possibly exist," Gage, the prosecutor, told the judge. The bail hearings dragged on for days. Mulheren was brought in under heavy security, managing occasional waves and wan smiles for his wife and members of his extended family, who packed the courtroom every day.

In the Metropolitan Correction Center, Mulheren was glad he was tall and heavyset, and that he had been working out with Springsteen. He was surrounded by hard-core criminals, including members of New York's Westies and Monsanto gangs. There wasn't a cell available for him, so he had to sleep in a cot in the hallway, where he felt especially vulnerable. Each morning except for Sundays he was awakened at 5:30 A.M. for washing up, then placed with other prisoners in the so-called holding pen until he was needed for a court appearance, usually about 9:30 or 10. As Mulheren resumed taking his medication and his depression eased, he became popular with many of the prisoners he met in the holding pen, often playing cards with them and chatting to pass the time. He soon became a favorite of Anthony "Fat Tony" Salerno, the alleged mafia don, and he struck up a relationship with Mushulu Shakur, a self-styled revolutionary and a defendant in the Brinks robbery case. Mulheren listened intently for hours to Shakur's radical left-wing political theories, and to his claims that he'd used the proceeds from the Brinks theft to feed the poor. Mulheren told him he admired his dedication.

Each day Mulheren remained locked up, the pressure to plead guilty intensified. Obermaier angered him by continuing to recommend that he give in and plead. The government was willing to drop the weapons and witness charges if Mulheren pleaded to parking and cooperated. Mulheren refused; if anything, his mental state made him more adamant against admitting a crime he didn't believe he committed. Finally, after Mulheren had been in jail for nearly two weeks, Obermaier worked out an arrangement whereby the government agreed to release him to the maximum-security wing of the Carrier Facility, a private, highly regarded psychiatric institution in New Jersey.

Before Mulheren left the MCC, Salerno came over to him to offer his best wishes. "You're all right," Salerno said, patting Mulheren affectionately on the back. "You're the only guy on Wall Street who's not a rat."

"But I don't know anything. I don't have anything bad to tell them," Mulheren protested.

"Oh, yeah," Salerno said, chuckling and rolling his eyes with exaggerated sarcasm. "Right."

13.

On March 24, 1988, a scared Ivan Boesky arrived at Southern California's Lompoc Federal Prison Camp to begin his three-year sentence. The minimum-security facility, though hardly a "country club," does have its own tennis courts and outdoor patios. It was Boesky's own choice; his plea bargain allowed him that perk. With Boesky behind bars and Mulheren safely lodged in the Carrier facility, an uneasy calm descended on the investigation.

Gary Lynch at the SEC grew restless. He and his staff had been banished from the Freeman investigation and, after the fiasco of the government's withdrawal of the indictments, were glad they weren't involved. Even so, they remained under tremendous pressure—from the commission itself, from oversight committees in Congress, from the public, and from Drexel. Still reeling from the bad Boesky publicity, they were eager to demonstrate the value of Boesky's assistance by moving against their biggest targets by far, Drexel and Milken.

By late spring 1988, however, their investigation had stalled. Drexel's resistance had been fierce and infuriating. Drexel's lawyers protested that producing the subpoenaed documents was an overwhelming task, but Lynch thought they were dragging their heels. Subpoena enforcement actions had to be threatened repeatedly. The SEC's fundamental distrust had been hardened by Drexel's public-relations barrage. Drexel employees, the SEC staff believed, were primarily interested in protecting Milken. Many invoked the Fifth Amendment, refusing to answer questions. Some, such as Peter Gardiner, were even willing to commit perjury.

Gardiner, red-haired, balding, in his 30s, was a Drexel salesman who had replaced Cary Maultasch when Maultasch moved to New York in 1985. He worked for Alan Rosenthal, one of Milken's closest allies, on the convertible securities desk.

As a result of an earlier inquiry begun by the SEC's Chicago enforcement staff, the commission had zeroed in on what appeared to be suspicious trading in securities of Viacom, a large cable and entertainment company based in New York. In 1986, Viacom's management had decided to retain Milken and Drexel to finance a proposed leveraged buyout; Milken had dealt personally with Viacom's chief executive. At the time Milken learned that Viacom might launch a leveraged buyout, Drexel had had a short position in Viacom of nearly 300,000 shares—betting that the price of Viacom shares would drop. Almost immediately after Milken's conversation with Viacom's chief executive, Drexel had eliminated its short position and established a long one. To the SEC, it was obvious that Drexel, using Milken's inside information, had bet heavily that Viacom stock would rise. It did— more than $5 a share in a single day—when the leveraged buyout proposal was announced just six days later. It looked like classic insider trading.

Gardiner was the Drexel trader in Beverly Hills who had ostensibly handled the Viacom trading that day, so the SEC was naturally eager to question him. Under oath, Gardiner initially said that he didn't remember the specific trading in Viacom, dismissing his actions as simply the routine hedging of a position. When the SEC discovered from the trading records that Drexel had actually been covering a short position and establishing a long one, Gardiner changed his testimony. He acknowledged the shift, but said he did it on his own, knew nothing about any proposed LBO, and hadn't spoken to Milken about it.

Then the SEC learned that Gardiner hadn't even been in Beverly Hills when the trading took place. He had left for a vacation in England that day. Gardiner said he'd stopped in New York en route to London, and had done the trading there. But he couldn't produce any travel or expense records from New York, and couldn't identify anyone at Drexel's New York office that he'd seen or spoken to. He had no explanation for the sudden decision to switch from a short position to a long one.

The SEC staff thought Gardiner was a brazen liar. The staff was convinced that the Viacom trading was done either by Milken or by someone other than Gardiner, acting on Milken's orders. Even so, Gardiner was useless. He obviously was doing nothing to further their investigation against the main targets, and there was little the SEC could do. Lacking the power to grant immunity, it could only refer him to the U.S. attorney's office for a possible perjury prosecution. Even then, any subsequent testimony by Gardiner, even if true, would be so weakened by his apparent perjury as to be worth very little.

Despite such obstacles, Lynch felt that with Boesky's testimony, the outlines of a solid case against Drexel and Milken were in place. Lynch wanted a complaint filed in a federal court, so that a federal judge would oversee the continuing investigation and could regularly enforce subpoena compliance and threaten contempt if it wasn't forthcoming. Lynch had begun this process that January 1988, offering the Drexel and Milken lawyers the opportunity to make a so-called "Wells submission," a formal effort to persuade the SEC not to file charges. The teams had made a voluminous submission, and succeeded in persuading the SEC to drop its investigation into alleged violations in connection with the leveraged buyout of Safeway Stores, a KKR deal financed largely by Drexel. That left numerous other charges, including all those related to Boesky. Drexel continued to infuriate the SEC staff with its insistence that the $5.3 million was an investment banking fee, and that Boesky was a habitual liar.

Drexel's defense continued to puzzle Lynch. The Wells notice is often a signal to begin serious settlement talks. Until charges were filed, Drexel could maintain, as it had, that it was the subject of irresponsible reporting and leaks from an investigation likely to lead nowhere. But the actual filing of charges would show that the investigation was complete and that an important regulatory body had reviewed them and found that the charges had merit. It was a step most firms would go to great lengths to avoid, and yet Drexel and the SEC remained miles apart. In a feisty speech broadcast to the firm, Joseph told Drexel employees, without acknowledging any talks, that Drexel couldn't settle with the SEC for anything like the amount of money the SEC wanted. To do so would be perceived as admitting guilt. Milken loyalists were cheered.

With few options remaining, Lynch took the SEC's proposed 160-page complaint to the commission on June 1, and obtained its unanimous approval to file charges. In an unprecedented step, however, the SEC decided not to file the complaint immediately, as it usually does, but to hold off indefinitely. The SEC made no public disclosure of the move, but Drexel reacted predictably, reasserting its innocence and blaming Boesky, a "convicted felon and admitted liar." The firm waited uneasily for a public filing of charges, a blow that it knew was now all but certain. But speculation flourished that the SEC was trying to give Drexel one last chance to settle and cooperate.

In fact, the unorthodox delay was the result of a serious split between the SEC and the Manhattan U.S. attorney, one that could have had devastating consequences on the course of the investigation. Lynch's frustrations over the pace of the SEC's Drexel investigation were mild compared to those brewing in Giuliani's office in Manhattan. After the euphoria of the discovery of the Princeton-Newport tapes, morale had suffered as one lead after another led to brick walls. Everything became more confusing: investigations that had seemed discreet had become intertwined, and Baird had to keep drawing in new lines on his chart connecting the various cases. Princeton-Newport, it was now clear, led to Freeman through the Storer trading and, more importantly, to Milken and Drexel through James Regan, Bruce Newberg, Lisa Jones, and Cary Maultasch. All these connections had been captured on the tapes.

In February, *The Wall Street Journal* had run a front-page article relating the results of its own investigation into Freeman's conduct. In a level of detail that startled the prosecutors, the *Journal* reporters had uncovered many of the same transactions they were investigating and had found information even the prosecutors didn't know. Deep in the story, the Beatrice transaction was described, with Freeman seeking confirmation from Siegel that terms of the deal were being modified. "In a call from Mr. Freeman to Mr. Siegel," the story said, "Mr. Siegel told Mr. Freeman, 'Your bunny has a good nose.' "

Baird was startled as he read and reread the mysterious passage. Despite Siegel's prodigious memory, he had never mentioned such an incident. At Baird's behest, Rakoff questioned Siegel. Siegel said he didn't remember saying those exact words. But it did remind him that he had talked to KKR, which had confirmed Bunny Lasker's informa-

tion. Freeman had called shortly thereafter, having also talked to
Lasker, and it was then, Siegel thought, that he might have said, "Your
bunny has a good nose."

It seemed yet another example of insider trading. It was too bad
Siegel's memory seemed shaky, but Baird had a hunch the *Journal*
account was true. He would seek confirmation from other potential
sources.

Still, the seemingly impregnable walls around Milken and Freeman held fast. James Regan, the head of Princeton-Newport, was brought
in by prosecutors to hear the tapes for himself; Baird thought there was
a good chance that, when confronted with such damaging evidence, he
would capitulate and cooperate. On the contrary, Regan displayed a
cavalier attitude. He arrived for the session wearing casual clothes and
a baseball cap emblazoned with the words, SHIT HAPPENS. He listened
to the tapes and left without showing any reaction. His lawyers told the
prosecutors to go ahead and file charges. Baird threatened to indict
Princeton-Newport under RICO, the Racketeer Influenced and Corrupt Organizations Act, aimed at organized crime and providing for
heavy damages. Regan seemed unfazed, vowing to fight to the end.

Regan told colleagues that he was innocent, that he was being
pressured only because he knew Freeman and Milken, and that his case
was "too complicated" to be understood by a jury. He was confident
he'd be acquitted. He refused to consider cooperating; he wasn't about
to turn against a Dartmouth roommate like Freeman. At Drexel's 1988
Predators' Ball, Regan was a minor celebrity, shaking hands and accepting congratulations from Milken loyalists thrilled at his defiance in
the face of government pressure. The threat of using RICO against
Princeton-Newport was eagerly seized upon by Milken's public-relations team as a new theme of government heavy-handedness that could
be used to influence public opinion against the prosecutors.

Newberg and Maultasch continued to invoke the Fifth Amendment, refusing to cooperate or testify. Lisa Jones, however, did testify
before finally invoking the Fifth Amendment. Because she was so low
on the ladder of responsibility, the prosecutors opted immediately to
grant Jones immunity, forcing her to testify. They assured her that as
long as she told the truth, she couldn't be prosecuted for any other
crime. It was the same tactic that had worked so well with Will Hale.

Jones's only risk was perjury. Yet, despite assurances from the
prosecutors, and despite her earlier admission of parking to Doonan,
she flatly denied the existence of various trades, denied ever discussing
"parking" or related fees with Newberg or anyone, and denied keeping
records of parked securities. (Jones did not know that the government
had tapes of her Princeton-Newport conversations.) During a break in

her testimony, the prosecutor handling her questioning, Mark Hanson, warned her lawyer that she was committing perjury. He happened to be from Cahill Gordon, the firm representing Drexel. As concerns mounted, Joseph and the Cahill lawyers urged her to tell the truth. On February 23, she received a letter warning her that she was likely to be indicted for perjury. At this point Drexel hired another lawyer for her. Blinded by loyalty to Newberg and Milken, she still refused to come clean.

Like Jones, the rest of the Drexel ranks held firm in the face of some of the strongest weapons in the prosecutor's arsenal. In part this was a measure of the extraordinary loyalty generated by Milken among his employees. But in all likelihood, it also reflected their shrewd calculation of their financial interests. In January of that year, when Milken had his compensation meetings, potential witnesses had discovered that their compensation was expected to soar. Dahl, for example, had been promised a mere $10 million in 1986—the best year by far for high-yield department profits; now he was allocated an astounding $35 million.

Despite her obvious perjury, Drexel kept Jones on the payroll, paid all her legal expenses, and gave her a generous bonus. Even Joseph worried that Milken's 1988 bonus payments to potential witnesses within the high-yield department might make it look like Drexel was buying their cooperation; but he decided that under Drexel's compensation system, it was Milken's money to distribute, as it had been in prior years, and there wasn't any reason for him to interfere.

As of mid-1988, the U.S. attorney's investigation had all but stalled, even as pressure mounted from the SEC and elsewhere. Giuliani was quietly eyeing the possibility of running for political office—probably mayor of New York, for which an election would be held in November 1989, little more than a year away. To mount a campaign, he would have to resign from the U.S. attorney's office by the end of 1988 or soon after; the political advantages of guilty pleas or at least solid indictments against Freeman, Wigton and Tabor, Drexel, and Milken were obvious.

There were also the cooperating witnesses to worry about. Siegel, exiled in Florida, unemployable, with nothing to do but wait with the scepter of a prison sentence hanging over him, begged to be sentenced, as Boesky had been. But Baird kept promising that a new indictment of Freeman was all but imminent, and that Siegel's testimony would stand him in good stead at his sentencing. Baird didn't want to lose the leverage over Siegel that the government had sacrificed with Boesky.

Baird also kept insisting to Lynch at the SEC that his investiga-

tion needed just a little more time. He and Giuliani were anxious to
prevent the SEC from going forward. They feared that the Milken and
Drexel legal teams would use the court process to discover the government's evidence, zeroing in immediately on the Boesky testimony.
Premature disclosure of investigative matters, they felt, could be devastating to the government's continuing investigation. Baird and Giuliani resisted the pressures to rush. They hadn't yet tried the tactic
of offering immunity to top members of the Milken entourage. Without promises of genuine cooperation in advance, they didn't want to
risk another Lisa Jones experience. And they were wary of a backlash
should they inadvertently immunize someone who later turned out to
be a major criminal. Instead, they continued to pressure witnesses low
on the ladder that led to Milken.

Baird and Giuliani repeated their arguments to Lynch, as pressure on him from the commission and Congress mounted. Drexel kept
pressing the point that it wasn't being given a chance to defend itself
in court. Lynch countered Giuliani's arguments, saying the the U.S.
attorney could always obtain protective orders for information it didn't
want to disclose in discovery, and that the delays only seemed to be
solidifying Drexel's ability to resist and the perception that the government didn't have a strong case. Lynch also continued to be angered by
Liman, especially by secondhand reports that Liman was lobbying
Giuliani to block the SEC's complaint, claiming that Lynch and Sturc
were "wild" and had to be restrained. But Lynch kept backing down,
agreeing to give Giuliani and Baird another month. Then the month
would pass, with little progress evident, and the arguments would start
again. Finally, in late July 1988, Lynch called Giuliani to announce that
the SEC had decided to go forward without Giuliani's consent, and the
whole government investigation came close to self-destructing.

"You can't do this," Giuliani yelled angrily into the phone.

"We're going to," Lynch insisted.

Giuliani hated defiance, and the impetuous side of his nature took
over. "If you file, we'll throw our lot in with the defendants," Giuliani
threatened. "We'll support a motion to dismiss your action."

Lynch could scarcely believe what he was hearing. Could Giuliani
really be willing to join Drexel and Milken in urging a court to dismiss
their case? Lynch had delivered Levine and Boesky to Giuliani, and
had taken the heat on the Boesky settlement while helping to launch
Giuliani's reputation for cracking down on Wall Street. How could
Giuliani turn on him now? Lynch slammed down the receiver.

In the face of such a dire threat, the SEC decided to back down,
agreeing that Giuliani could have another month. They decided they

couldn't do anything that might provoke Giuliani into hurting their
case against Drexel and Milken. Giuliani calmed down and tried, in his
own way, to apologize to Lynch. He told Lynch that he had misunderstood, that Giuliani would never throw in his lot with the Milken camp
against the SEC. Relations were soon restored between the prosecutors
and the SEC staff. But Lynch would never forget Giuliani's threat.

As the government's effort floundered, Milken stepped up his counterattack. In March 1988, at Arthur Liman's suggestion, he hired an
aggressive young PR firm: Robinson, Lake, Lerer & Montgomery.
Linda Gosden Robinson, the firm's head, had become the PR embodiment of the eighties. The Southern California–bred daughter of Freeman Gosden, the actor who played Amos in "Amos 'n' Andy," Robinson had bounced on the knee of actor Ronald Reagan as a young girl.
An attractive blonde who worked as an acupuncture therapist in the
seventies, she had helped in the 1980 Reagan campaign and had then
worked for Transportation Secretary Drew Lewis. When Lewis moved
to Warner Amex Cable, she had gone with him, becoming close to the
joint venture's chief executives: American Express chairman Jim Robinson and Warner Communications chairman Steve Ross. She had
ultimately married Robinson, and moved the offices of her own PR
firm into Warner's New York headquarters building. She knew Liman
through Ross, a Liman client, and he saw her work firsthand when she
represented Texaco in its long-running battle with Pennzoil, another
Liman client. In her mid-30s, she was already a force to be reckoned
with, both as an appendage to powerful men—her husband, Liman,
Ross—and in her own right.

Robinson brought Republican-style "attack" and negative campaign tactics to corporate public relations. She is smart, bold, and
tough, a worthy adversary for even the best reporters. While she can
easily turn on the charm, those who cross her, especially if they happen
to be lower than she on the social and power scale, find her difficult,
imperious, and unpleasant. She required two secretaries to keep track
of her crowded social and business calendars, including coordinating
the helicopter rides for her and her husband to their Connecticut
home, maintaining fresh flowers in their luxury co-op in Manhattan's
Museum Tower, reminding her of birthdays of celebrity friends like
Frank Sinatra, or tending to the needs of her three King Charles
spaniels (named for characters in "Amos 'n' Andy") or her numerous

horses. She'd often simply take the latest Bergdorf Goodman catalogue, circle what she wanted, and send one of her secretaries to do the shopping. Turnover among her employees was high.

Edward Bennett Williams had been adamantly opposed to hiring her—or any other PR counsel, for that matter. He was openly contemptuous of "flacks," and his own approach to public relations had always served him well. He usually shunned the press. He was even rude if necessary. He rarely talked to reporters, either on his own behalf or for a client. But Liman twisted his arm, and ultimately Milken himself insisted that Robinson be hired.

Robinson flew down to Washington to meet with Williams. He brought her into a conference room at Williams & Connolly and sat her at one end of the long table while he sat at the opposite end. Williams told her bluntly that he considered PR a waste of time and money. He supposed it wouldn't hurt for her to handle questions about Milken and Drexel's business. But then, despite his illness, he glowered and jabbed his finger in her direction. "Stay goddamn away from the criminal case," he shouted. Robinson sputtered and protested, but Williams wouldn't budge. She left clearly shaken by the encounter.

Still, she had a foot in the door. Soon a team from Robinson, Lake, led by Robinson's chief partner, Kenneth Lerer, who had worked for her at Warner Amex, arrived in Beverly Hills to plot strategy. Robinson had previously confined her work to respectable corporate clients. Lerer had run the Senate campaign of former Miss America Bess Myerson, who later became embroiled in the New York City government "Bess Mess" affair, in which Myerson had been charged with improperly trying to influence the judge handling the divorce of her paramour.

Lerer and his colleagues sat down with Milken in Beverly Hills and asked the financier to list his principal achievements, things that could be used to "position" him with the American public. Milken took a legal pad and red felt pen. He began to write, starting with the first grade. He mentioned winning a dance contest in fifth grade. He continued in that vein, climaxing with his being voted most popular, and being elected prom king in high school. Then he stopped. He hadn't written a word about Drexel or junk bonds.

Two of the Robinson, Lake officials looked at each other and rolled their eyes. But it was clear Milken was serious. They realized that turning Milken into a nationally recognized hero was going to be an even greater challenge than they had anticipated. Lerer smiled weakly, then suggested that they were looking for something more directly related to his work at Drexel. "You really are a national resource," one of the PR executives said. "Look at all you've accomplished. That's how you should be positioned." Lerer added that the theme he saw in Milken's work was "creating value." Maybe they could work that into something.

Milken showed no reaction. He simply looked blankly at them, as though such notions had never occurred to him, even though his lawyers had long been describing him as a national treasure. The others, however, were enthusiastic. "You are a national resource," Sandler repeated. Someone else mentioned that Milken really was a "genius." Milken demurred, saying he knew people smarter than he was; he just worked harder. Sandler, Lerer, and the others brushed aside such modesty, and gradually Milken seemed to come around, nodding in agreement as he seemed to ponder the concepts. Soon, "creating value" were buzz words of the Milken defense effort.

The firm of Robinson, Lake insisted that Milken could no longer remain a recluse, that he had to grant some press interviews. Milken was leery of the prospect—he had, after all, gone so far as to buy up the copyrights to all wire service photographs of himself. Sandler too was averse to the idea at first, fearful that Milken was too naïve about press relations to risk interviews with anyone other than carefully screened ideologues like Edward Epstein. Once they were assured that interviews would be strictly controlled, however, and used as an opportunity both to "humanize" Milken and to project themes favorable to his defense, Sandler and Milken agreed to test the waters.

Robinson and Lerer set about arranging strictly controlled personal interviews with selected reporters. Any questions about the investigation were off limits; nonetheless, Lerer boasted that reporters were "salivating" for access. The quid pro quo was that the coverage must be deemed "fair" by Milken or all future access would be denied. A parade of reporters came to California, including David Vise from *The Washington Post*, Kurt Eichenwald from *The New York Times*, and Scott Paltrow from the *Los Angeles Times*. To them Milken expounded on the importance of family, the merits of junk bonds, the need to keep America competitive, and the issue of Third World debt.

Lerer would call these reporters frequently, working the phones as he played Nintendo in his office, or calling from his car, planting story ideas worked up by members of his staff. Occasionally he dribbled bits of "exclusive" information to his current favorites. Lerer once called it "breast-feeding" the reporters. Lerer encouraged his staff by telling them they were "trying to turn a battleship in the water," and, in another metaphor, to be content with hitting "singles and doubles." Every once in a while they hit what they considered a "home run," such as the time *Business Week*'s Chris Welles criticized the SEC for leaking to *The Wall Street Journal*.

By contrast, *The Wall Street Journal* news pages and *Fortune* magazine were considered anathema. Robinson herself made a personal pilgrimage to meet with editors and reporters at the *Journal*, threatening that when Milken and Drexel were exonerated, as they undoubtedly would be, the news might have to be leaked to the rival *New York Times* in retaliation for the *Journal*'s unfriendly coverage. The Milken camp also tried, unsuccessfully, to cultivate a Los Angeles-based *Journal* reporter in an effort to split the paper's reporting ranks. *Fortune* was banished after referring to Milken's public-relations effort as "inept."

Robinson, Lake had a much easier time dealing with the nation's op-ed pages. With a ready supply of willing Milken clients at their disposal, the public-relations staff began churning out think pieces endorsing various pro-Milken themes, such as "junk bonds make America competitive." These would be signed by Milken clients and published under their names. Thus, commentary and letters to the editor purporting to have been authored by, for example, Reginald Lewis, head of Beatrice International, William McGowan, the chairman of MCI, and Ralph Ingersoll, chairman of Ingersoll, were actually crafted by Robinson, Lake, often reviewed by lawyers at Liman's firm, Paul, Weiss, and edited by Milken himself.

The public-relations staff also churned out lists of what were called "talking points," short, pithy pro-Milken pronouncements that loyalists should insert into interviews, and "tag words," even shorter sound bites like "creating value" and "national treasure."

Yet some efforts inevitably went awry. After Lerer spent considerable time on an op-ed submission for Warner chairman Steve Ross, Ross refused to sign it, despite his personal friendship with Robinson.

Especially embarrassing was a "Nightline" television appearance by Ralph Ingersoll, chosen for his loyalty to Milken and his willingness to go on national television. Everything Ingersoll was supposed to say was carefully scripted by Robinson, Lake and reduced to about 20 "sound bites." Ingersoll's key line was "What kind of society do we live in that indicts a man it should be adulating?" Ingersoll had no trouble with it in rehearsals. But when he got on the air, the Robinson, Lake team watched, horrified, as he fumbled phrases and talking points, garbled sound bites, and appeared to forget his key line altogether. Ingersoll was easily outmaneuvered on the show by Giuliani.

The Robinson, Lake campaign was intended to ensure that the nation received a constant barrage of the same words and phrases, achieving much the same effect as an ad campaign. The goal, Robinson and Lerer told their staff, was to turn public opinion from outrage to neutrality to acceptance, and finally to admiration. The campaign was remarkably effective. The SEC staff and assistant U.S. attorneys, hobbled by severe restrictions on what they could say to the press and intimidated by allegations that they were leaking, watched dismayed as the pro-Milken line gradually built into a chorus.

The entire public-relations effort was enormously lucrative for Robinson, Lake, which demanded a $150,000-a-month retainer and often exceeded it in actual billings. When partner Walter Montgomery expressed concern that representing a prominent alleged criminal might tarnish the firm's reputation with the blue-chip clients it hoped to cultivate, he was ignored. Just as in the Milken legal defense, the possibility that Milken might have done something wrong was never discussed. The very idea was heretical. Robinson would occasionally spring what staffers deemed to be Milken "loyalty tests." One afternoon, David Gilman, an employee working on the Milken account, was conferring with Lerer when Robinson marched into Lerer's office and stared intently at Gilman.

"Is Milken innocent or guilty?" she demanded.

"Innocent, of course," Gilman promptly replied. Robinson didn't look satisfied, so he repeated with even more conviction, "He is innocent."

"Right," Robinson answered.

The 1988 Predators' Ball, at the Beverly Hilton in April, had largely been a public-relations showcase for Milken. At Robinson, Lake's behest, the press had been invited to hear Milken's thoughts on Third World debt and public education. There were frequent testimonials to Milken from devoted clients like Steve Ross and Nelson Peltz.

But less than two weeks later, Milken confronted his first hostile audience: the U.S. Congress. Representative John Dingell, the Michigan Democrat known for his intrepid investigative staff, convened a session of the House Oversight and Investigations subcommittee, which he chaired, to probe Drexel's private partnerships, such as Otter Creek, the vehicle for Drexel's investments in National Can. The subcommittee issued congressional subpoenas to both Milken and Fred Joseph.

It was Milken's first direct confrontation with the government he had come to disdain, and it was deeply unsettling. The reclusive financier who had so prized anonymity was all but mobbed as he, Williams, and the ubiquitous Richard Sandler made their way up the steps of the Capitol building and into the high-ceilinged hearing chamber. Milken managed a wan smile as flashbulbs popped continuously during the half-hour wait for the proceedings to begin.

Williams's first official pronouncement was to invoke a rarely used congressional rule to demand that the room be cleared of all cameras and recording devices. Dingell, showing deference to the visibly ailing Williams, obliged, banishing all film crews and photographers.

The mood changed quickly when Dingell began by asking Milken if he had a financial interest in Otter Creek. Milken invoked the Fifth Amendment. A second question met with the same response. "He doesn't intend to answer any of your questions if he follows my advice," Williams stated.

Dingell adjourned, then held a press conference unveiling the committee's suspicions: that the Drexel partnerships engaged in widespread self-enrichment at the expense of Drexel's clients. "There have been questions raised about whether . . . this complies with, among other things, the law relating to insider trading, front-running and . . . what might be defined as market manipulation," Dingell said.

Drexel quickly issued a statement. "Mike Milken has our full support," the firm said. "He is a colleague, a friend and an individual who has made an enormous contribution to financing this country." But nothing Drexel could say could undo the damage of Milken's invoking the Fifth Amendment. It was his constitutional right, of course, just as it was the public's impulse to wonder why Milken would invoke it if he were as innocent as he claimed.

That night, the Milken team fixed its attention on Joseph, who was scheduled to testify the next day. Joseph wouldn't be invoking the Fifth Amendment. He didn't believe he had any risk of prosecution, and wanted to avoid any further loss of public confidence in Drexel. Unfortunately, Joseph was functioning under a severe handicap: he knew virtually nothing about the operations of the Milken-led partnerships. In some cases, he didn't even know they existed. In his preparations for testimony, the Milken representatives kept him up past 2 A.M., badgering him with hypothetical questions and feeding him canned answers. Joseph was even asked to submit a statement to the committee containing information he believed to be false.

While Milken had looked fresh for his appearance, Joseph looked haggard and tense as the hearing convened the next morning. Dingell quickly took command of the questioning, and made mincemeat of Joseph. Focusing in part on the Beatrice deal, Dingell and his colleagues charged that Drexel had favored its own employee partnerships over Drexel clients and engaged in self-dealing by having clients buy bonds from the partnerships at inflated prices. At one point Joseph had to admit, "I think I am confused," about the applicability of various securities laws. One congressman summed up the day by saying to Joseph, "The public perception is that what you have done doesn't pass the smell test."

Joseph felt humiliated, and was furious with his lawyers. Looking back on the events leading up to the hearings, he began wondering about the advice he'd been given. Had he been set up? Whose interests were the Milken lawyers really serving? And what *had* gone on in the Milken-led partnerships? For the first time, Joseph felt the beginnings of doubt about Milken and his motives. Alone among Joseph's advisors, Ira Millstein, his personal lawyer, had been warning him that Milken might be convicted. Millstein had been so angry over Joseph's refusal to heed his advice that he had threatened to quit. Perhaps, Joseph now thought, Millstein had been right.

Sitting in the front row of the congressional hearings, just a few feet from Milken, wearing a bright yellow dress, was Connie Bruck, the reporter who'd written the Boesky profile in the *Atlantic*. She was now working on a book about Drexel Burnham and Milken. In February 1986, Bruck had told Milken her plans, and asked for his cooperation. "I do not want it to be done," Milken had replied before proposing to buy out her book contract. "Why don't we pay you the commitment fee that your publisher would have paid you, except we'll pay it to you to not write the book. Or, why don't we pay you for all the copies you would have sold if you had written it?"

By the summer of 1988, Bruck's manuscript was completed. Under an earlier agreement with Bruck, Joseph was allowed to read it and comment on the facts, but not make copies. He knew immediately that there would be trouble. Titled *The Predators' Ball: The Junk Bond Raiders and the Man Who Staked Them*, the book was a thorough, sober study of Drexel, Milken, and several of their clients, a groundbreaking examination of Milken's junk-bond empire.

The book reported that Drexel had hired prostitutes for the Predators' Ball, that in his early days at Drexel Milken had worn a miner's helmet on the commuter bus so he could read prospectuses in the dark, and that the junk-bond king himself had tried to buy Bruck out of writing the book. Worse, the book left the strong impression that Boesky's allegations were entirely consistent with the values and culture spawned by Milken.

Despite security precautions at Simon & Schuster, Bruck's publisher, Liman soon managed to obtain a copy of the manuscript, and had it quickly reproduced on Paul, Weiss copy machines. The Milken defense machine began planning an all-out counterattack. Finally, it seemed, the enormous defense apparatus had something concrete to attack, even if it was a book rather than a grand jury indictment.

A high-level meeting was convened at Paul, Weiss. Present were Robinson, Lerer, and several others from Robinson, Lake, as well as Liman, Flumenbaum, Sandler, and Milken himself. Liman and Milken arrived late, and while the others waited, they perused copies of the manuscript. Sandler was quickly incensed. "There was no miner's cap," he exclaimed, then quickly modified his denial. "It was a gift. It was an eye doctor's thing. He never wore it; he only wore it once."

When Liman and Milken arrived, Milken sat down and started reading. He began shaking his head, glowering. "This book is turning me into a geek," he said angrily. Complaining that the book made him seem self-centered and obsessed, that no one ever called him "the king," he concluded angrily, "I want this stopped."

Some advisors warned him that anything they did would generate publicity and attention for the book, and that no one would probably read it anyway. ("Americans aren't readers," Lerer assured him.) They also reminded him that he'd refused to talk to Bruck, so he couldn't really blame her if his views weren't represented. Milken would hear none of this. He wanted the book stopped, preferably before it was published. Despite private doubts, Liman and Robinson were supportive. Liman had had success in the past attacking books, notably biographies of client William Paley, chairman of CBS. And an attack strategy was consistent with Robinson's view of publicity. The team plunged into a massive campaign to discredit Bruck and her book, ignoring the likely positive impact on book sales.

At Liman's and Robinson's direction, the Robinson, Lake staff dutifully began compiling a line-by-line analysis of the book, citing certain facts as "misstatement," "mischaracterization," or one of two lesser categories of transgressions. The plan was to send a list of "errata" to every book reviewer in the country, hoping to destroy the book's credibility. "The errata will be longer than the book itself," Lerer exclaimed. "That's great!"

Several Robinson, Lake staff members spent a full month trying to discredit the book. Unfortunately, the "truth squad," as it came to be dubbed, found it increasingly difficult to disprove many of Bruck's assertions. For example, despite Milken's insistence, some of his own clients did refer to him as "the king," even in conversations with the Robinson, Lake employees trying to disprove that very fact. But the staff was afraid to bring that to Milken's attention. The list of errata had to be padded with alleged inaccuracies that were patently trivial.

This didn't give Milken any pause. Not content with the plan to discredit the book's accuracy and fairness, he still wanted it blocked. Liman called Drexel's chief lawyer, Tom Curnin, saying the book was "extremely damaging" to Milken, who wouldn't be able to get a fair trial if it were published. "Take steps to prevent its publication," Liman ordered, "either through contacts" at Simon & Schuster, "or in court." Curnin was startled by the request; surely Liman knew that prior restraint of the press is granted only in exceedingly rare and compelling circumstances.

Cahill Gordon partners and noted First Amendment lawyer Floyd Abrams joined Curnin in advising Liman that they could never persuade a judge to enjoin the book. Liman seemed furious, threatening to tell Joseph that Cahill "isn't supportive of Milken and Drexel." Still, they held their ground. "If we want this, we should get it," Liman said, arguing again that Milken's desires should come first.

Curnin advised Joseph that he thought such a suit would harm Drexel. Joseph agreed. He thought it a preposterous idea, another example of Liman's putting Milken's interests ahead of Drexel's. It was revealing, Joseph thought, that when all was said and done, Milken and his lawyers weren't willing to file the suit on their own. Liman was too smart for that.

Ultimately the campaign had little effect. *The Predators' Ball* was published on schedule. Reviewers were baffled; they aren't fact-checkers. On the face of things, few of the Milken allegations were persuasive. The campaign led to immense prepublication publicity for the book, including a front-page article in *The Wall Street Journal*.

When Edward Bennett Williams warned the prosecutors that he wouldn't live to see the end of their investigation of Milken, he had known that he was probably beginning his last bouts with cancer. Robert Litt had known Williams was gravely ill when, just before an SEC appearance together, Williams turned to Litt and said, "You'd better be prepared to talk." Litt was taken aback. Williams always did the talking. When the day arrived, Williams could barely walk down the SEC hallway.

In early 1988, Williams had asked Vincent Fuller, a prominent Williams & Connolly partner, to begin getting involved in the Milken case. But Fuller and Milken never seemed to reach a rapport. Milken revered Williams, and felt that no one could take his place. With the onset of Williams's illness, Liman, Flumenbaum, and Paul, Weiss lawyers quickly shouldered aside their colleagues at Williams & Connolly. Whatever influence Williams's thinking might have had on Milken was lost.

Williams rallied somewhat for the Milken congressional hearings, even though he looked pale and drawn. But it was his last public appearance on Milken's behalf. He died four months later, on August 13. Milken flew to Washington. During the funeral, he covered his face with his hands and wept.

During the first week in August 1988, Bruce Baird and his prosecutors invited Lisa Jones and her new lawyer, Brian O'Neill, to their offices. Wasting no time, they turned on a tape machine and watched as Jones and her lawyer listened, for the first time, to the young woman's voice arranging illegal trades with Hale at Princeton-Newport. Jones blanched.

After the meeting, O'Neill quickly drafted a letter to the government; hearing the tape had "refreshed" Jones's memory. Under her grant of immunity, she was now willing to admit that she had engaged in the trades and had conversed about them with Hale. The prosecutors were unimpressed. Amazingly, Jones was still refusing to admit anything other than what had appeared on the tape. She had lied before, and was obviously still lying, they believed. Prosecutors rightly view perjury as a serious crime that undermines the judicial process. A message had to be sent. Despite her youth, her hard early life, and her low-level status at Drexel, Jones's immunity was revoked.

At the same time, prosecutors stepped up the pressure on Princeton-Newport. Baird revealed that the government was prepared to ask the grand jury for an indictment under RICO. It was the first time the statute would have been used against officials of a securities firm.

RICO was the most serious weaponry the government could throw into the case. Passed in 1970 to combat organized crime and drug operations, the law provides that any person or organization that commits two or more related felonies as part of a "pattern" of criminality can be charged with racketeering. The law carries severe penalties, including prison terms of up to 20 years and the confiscation of property and earnings. RICO has a civil legislative counterpart that allows private plaintiffs to sue for triple damages.

Though potentially ruinous to Princeton-Newport, the threat of a RICO indictment had little effect on the potential defendants. The company was a shell, one of numerous interlocking entities; its assets could simply be shifted out of the partnership, allowing Princeton-Newport to collapse. James Regan remained defiant; his lawyer, Theodore Wells, attacked the potential use of RICO as "frightening," but insisted on his client's innocence and determination to fight the government. "It seems clear that Mr. Regan is being used as a pawn in a chess game being played on a much larger board," he observed.

In that regard, Wells was correct. Though its immediate intent was to pressure Regan and Princeton-Newport, the real message of the potential RICO charge was aimed at Drexel. If a small firm like Princeton-Newport faced RICO charges for its trading, then Drexel, with many more transactions under suspicion, was even more vulnerable.

Final attempts to reach settlement agreements proved fruitless. On August 4, the grand jury indicted Lisa Jones on charges of perjury, and charged Regan, Zarzecki, other Princeton-Newport principals, and Drexel's Newberg, with racketeering. The first indictments of the government's two-and-a-half-year investigation had finally been issued, the opening shots fired in what promised to be a long war.

To alert observers inside the Milken inner circle that August, there was a conspicuous and alarming omission in the defendants named in the Princeton-Newport suit: Cary Maultasch.

Like Newberg, Maultasch had been captured on the tapes. He had protested vigorously that it wasn't fair to target him, since he'd only been filling in for Newberg the day the calls were recorded—but no one thought prosecutors would find that persuasive. Indeed, just the day before the indictment, Maultasch had been notified he would be included in the charges.

That meant he faced the possibility of two indictments: one for the Princeton-Newport dealings, and another for his dealings with Milken and Boesky. Maultasch, rightly perceived by prosecutors as one of the weakest members of the Milken entourage, was already wavering. He'd shown up one afternoon earlier that year in the office of a Washington defense lawyer, Reid Weingarten, and said he wanted Weingarten to replace Charles Stillman, the lawyer he'd hired at the suggestion of the Milken camp. Maultasch said he worried that Stillman was too close to Milken. Weingarten discouraged him, saying he knew Stillman to be an outstanding lawyer, but Maultasch persisted. "I want independent counsel."

Weingarten took the case, and was struck almost immediately by the arrogance of the Milken defense team. He soon began talks with the U.S. attorney's office, but made little progress. Giuliani wanted a guilty plea to two felonies from Maultasch. But the dialogue was constructive.

On the eve of the Princeton-Newport indictment, Weingarten had managed to persuade the government to hold off naming Maultasch. Maultasch would cooperate. Then the government could evaluate his assistance and decide whether they needed a guilty plea. It was similar to the arrangement that had been reached with Mooradian's lawyer. In part because the prosecutors trusted Weingarten, they decided to permit the arrangement.

Though he was never an enthusiastic witness, Maultasch began in August talking to the government, describing his role in the $5.3 million payment, corroborating Boesky's version of the payment, and describing his summons to Beverly Hills and his meeting with Milken after news of Boesky's fall. He gave also them valuable information about Thurnher, the accountant who'd also worked on Milken's records of the $5.3 million payment, enabling the government to pry more testimony from that reluctant witness.

At Weingarten's insistence, Maultasch decided to resign quietly from Drexel. He complained bitterly that he was forgoing at least $2 million in bonuses, but he did meet with Joseph to announce his decision to leave. He was vague about his reasons, saying nothing about any agreement with the government. Instead, he spoke of his obligations to his family, his wife. . . . Joseph barely listened. It all sounded so familiar after similar testimonials from Levine and Siegel. He called Curnin at Cahill Gordon as soon as Maultasch left. "Maultasch is cutting a deal," he said.

Jim Dahl could hear the phone ringing as he fumbled with his keys and luggage at his front door in Beverly Hills. It was the beginning of September 1988, and Dahl was even more tan and blond than usual, feeling reinvigorated after his annual vacation at the beach near Jacksonville, Florida, close to his hometown. The phone kept ringing as Dahl got into the house, and he managed to answer it.

It was his lawyer at Williams & Connolly, Bob Litt, and the call dashed Dahl's good spirits. "I don't know how to tell you this," Litt said, "but you got a target letter. I'm shocked."

Dahl was more than shocked. Litt and the Williams & Connolly lawyers had reviewed every trade Dahl had done and had concluded he had nothing to worry about. Dahl had been assured repeatedly that Milken was the target, not him. Litt and Williams had warned him early on that the day would come when the government would try to squeeze him, but he'd never expected to face an indictment.

The prospect was frightening. Dahl did have something to worry about. At the end of each year, at Milken's direction, Dahl would execute parking arrangements with Milken's friend and client Tom Spiegel at Columbia Savings, generating phony tax losses for the giant thrift, one of Milken's biggest captive clients and purchasers of junk bonds. Dahl had given the matter little thought, and had made no effort to conceal the trades within the office. He had kept a ledger on his desk to keep track of the positions parked with Columbia. The ledger now covered a five-year span of possibly illegal trading, written corroboration of any alleged wrongdoing. In all likelihood, others in the Beverly Hills office knew what he had been doing.

For the first time since the investigation began, Dahl wondered whose interests his lawyers really represented: his or Milken's. Would Milken protect Dahl the way Dahl, so far, had been willing to protect Milken? He wasn't so sure.

As soon as he hung up, Dahl called a close friend in Florida, a lawyer named Steve Andrews. The son of a judge, Andrews had been Dahl's fraternity brother at Florida State and now practiced law in Tallahassee. While Andrews wasn't really a securities lawyer, he knew the field. He had a tax degree from New York University and he'd once been a principal in a small Florida securities firm. Most important, the six-foot-three, heavyset lawyer had the common sense of someone far outside the Manhattan/Washington/Beverly Hills triangle and the world of Milken. Dahl felt he could trust him.

Andrews needed to hear only two facts: that Dahl had received a target letter in the Milken investigation, and that he had the same lawyers as Milken himself. "Get yourself a new lawyer," Andrews ordered. "Now." Dahl wanted to hire Andrews. Andrews agreed, but insisted that Dahl also retain a lawyer in New York.

Dahl called Litt back to break the news: He wanted another lawyer, someone who wasn't also representing Milken. Litt immediately recognized the potential significance of a Dahl defection. He insisted that Dahl didn't need another lawyer, that they were all better off sticking together. This time, especially without Williams to back up the message, Dahl wasn't persuaded. That strategy hadn't kept him from getting a target letter.

Litt stalled, saying he'd put together a list of counsel Dahl might consider. But no list was forthcoming; it was almost as if Litt hoped Dahl might change his mind. So Dahl called one of his major bond customers, Carl Lindner. Lindner recommended his own lawyer, Peter Fishbein at Kaye, Scholer in New York, the same firm that was representing Freeman. Only when Dahl told Litt that he was going to talk to Fishbein did Litt's list of potential new lawyers for Dahl appear. Not surprisingly, it consisted only of defense lawyers securely in the Paul, Weiss, and Williams & Connolly fold, including lawyers already representing Don Engel and Milken client Fred Carr. Dahl interviewed them, and came away with heightened suspicions that their loyalties might be compromised. He decided to retain Fishbein.

Fishbein and Andrews flew to California immediately to meet with Dahl. Both lawyers were worried about their client's potential exposure. They assumed that Spiegel at Columbia Savings was also under investigation, given his close ties to Milken, and they worried that Spiegel would turn on Dahl, implicating him as part of a plea bargain, before Dahl could reach any agreement with the government. Dahl didn't trust Spiegel to protect him.

Dahl's confidence in Milken was also severely shaken. When Dahl and his new lawyers finally reviewed the government's target letter, they were surprised to discover that it did not cover Dahl's Columbia Savings trading. Rather, it covered a series of equity trades with Boesky that appeared in Dahl's records—trades that had been part of the reimbursement scheme that had culminated in the $5.3 million payment. Dahl had no memory of any such trades, and he thought they seemed peculiar, because Dahl handled only bond trading for Boesky, never equity trading. That was handled by Milken himself.

Further investigation showed that none of the handwriting on the targeted trading tickets was actually Dahl's. On the dates shown on two of them, Dahl hadn't even been in Beverly Hills. One of the tickets had the initials "M.M." at the bottom. When he saw the tickets, Dahl was sure what had happened: Milken had simply had Dahl's trading assistant enter the trades in Dahl's records. Dahl concluded that the government was focusing on the wrong person, that he could prove he wasn't involved. He felt sure Milken would back him up.

Dahl went immediately to Litt. "I didn't do the trades—Mike did," Dahl told him. He expected Litt to be excited at the news that Dahl should be exonerated. "There's nothing wrong with those trades," Litt insisted. "There's nothing to worry about." Dahl pressed on, suggesting that Milken simply sign an affidavit that he had done the trades. Once the government saw that, Dahl felt sure, they would drop their investigation of him. If the trades were innocent, as everyone said, then Milken had nothing to lose. Litt seemed less than enthusiastic about Dahl's line of reasoning, but he said he'd talk to Milken. Andrews pressed the case with Richard Sandler, who also insisted the trades were harmless. "If that's the case," Andrews countered, "why can't Mike just say he did them?"

A week later, Litt returned with Milken's response: Milken had refused to sign any affidavit or to acknowledge that he had done the trades. Moreover, Dahl's trading assistant had had a memory lapse; she didn't remember anything about the trades, so she couldn't back him up either. Dahl was stunned. "Mike knows he did those trades," he exclaimed. "Boesky knows Mike did those trades. Tell the government to ask Boesky who did those trades."

Litt replied that it wasn't his place to tell the government what to ask its witnesses. "If you keep quiet and hang tough, the problem will go away," Litt insisted again, urging that Dahl and his new lawyers say nothing to the government about whether Dahl did or did not handle the suspicious trading.

With Dahl clearly wavering, the Milken camp stepped up the pressure on him. Milken called Dahl aside one day and told him he was getting bad advice from Andrews, that he really ought to get another lawyer. Dahl said he wouldn't, that he trusted Andrews and wanted to keep him. Then Milken and Sandler tried another tack, suggesting that Andrews move his practice to Beverly Hills and open up an office with Sandler in Drexel's building, implying that the arrangement would be far more lucrative for him. Andrews saw that tactic as a thinly disguised effort to buy his loyalty, and rebuffed the approach.

Unclouded by any loyalty to Milken's interests, Andrews and Fishbein recommended that Dahl approach the U.S. attorney's office—fast. The decision was a difficult one for Dahl, even though he felt Milken had betrayed him by refusing to acknowledge his part in the Boesky trades. He didn't want to hurt Milken, who, after all, had made him a millionaire many times over. But Dahl didn't want to go to jail or be indicted for something he hadn't done. And, much as Boesky had beaten Milken to a plea bargain, Dahl didn't want Spiegel getting there first. He authorized his new lawyers to approach the government.

At about the same time, in September 1988, Fred Joseph arrived in Beverly Hills for an annual dinner with top officials of the firm. The guests included Milken and nearly everyone in the Beverly Hills office. In a tribute to the high-yield department, Joseph read the names of every trader whose performance had strengthened the firm during a difficult year. Joseph had never liked Dahl, and the lawyers had warned him that Dahl was wavering. Joseph couldn't bring himself to praise him. Dahl's name was omitted from Joseph's citation.

It was a tactical mistake. Dahl was angry and hurt. He had been the office's top performer, and he'd given everything he had to the firm. Drexel's official position had been that he should tell the truth, and that's all he was contemplating. He concluded that Joseph didn't deserve his loyalty.

Later that month, a courier arrived at St. Andrews Plaza with a five-volume submission prepared by Fishbein and his staff, containing documentary proof that Dahl hadn't performed the trades being questioned by the government. Dahl and his lawyers waited anxiously for the government's reaction, but heard nothing for a week. Finally, John Carroll called Fishbein. "I'm persuaded," he said; he now believed Dahl hadn't done the trades. But the conversation didn't stop there. Fishbein was still concerned about Dahl's exposure for his savings and loan dealings, such as the Columbia trades. Fishbein suggested, without making any explicit promises, that Dahl could be valuable to the government in other ways, if he received a sufficient inducement to cooperate.

Carroll took the bait. As Milken's top salesman, Dahl could provide the government with immensely valuable information about the workings of the Milken operation. Dahl was intimately familiar with how Milken worked. He was even more important to the government for psychological reasons; the prosecutors knew that the wall of silence around Milken, once breached, would likely collapse.

The prosecutors also realized that immunizing Dahl carried large risks. If it turned out that Dahl was guilty of significant crimes, and that he'd be able to keep the many millions of dollars he'd earned, the public reaction against the government could be severe; this would undoubtedly be heightened by the Milken publicity machine. Yet the government had found no convincing evidence that Dahl was guilty of any crime. Prosecutors had looked closely at the Staley Continental situation, when Dahl had tried to force the company into a leveraged buyout. They had found Dahl's threats distasteful but not necessarily criminal. Fortunately for Dahl, the prosecutors as yet knew nothing about the Columbia transactions; and in any case, they had to focus on their ultimate objective. Dahl was a major stepping stone toward Milken, and this outweighed all other risks. In October, Dahl received his grant of immunity; shortly thereafter, he arrived at St. Andrews Plaza for the first of his many debriefings.

The Milken "tent," so carefully erected and sealed by Williams & Connolly and Paul, Weiss, had blown open.

News of the Dahl defection sent tremors through the Milken and Drexel defense camps. Officials and lawyers were caught between insisting that Dahl had nothing to tell the government (because Milken, of course, had never done anything wrong) and trying to intimidate Dahl. Dahl, perhaps naïvely, had planned to keep trading at Drexel. But he was moved off the fifth-floor trading room in Beverly Hills and banished to the second floor. Drexel justified the move by saying it couldn't guarantee Dahl's safety from the wrath of fellow traders. Later, Drexel sharply reduced Dahl's pay, from the $23 million he received for 1988 to $5 million for 1989. Lowell Milken stopped speaking to him.

Such countermeasures proved fruitless: Dahl became the first truly cooperative Drexel witness the government had. Ever the master salesman, he quickly charmed the prosecutors as he had countless bond buyers. He was even more useful than the government had hoped, giving an eyewitness account of the insider trading in the Diamond Shamrock/Occidental Petroleum deal, and describing the running-water-in-the-bathroom scene. His detailed knowledge of Milken's dealings with savings and loans opened up an entirely new dimension in the case. Dahl held nothing back, patiently guiding Carroll and Jess Fardella through the mysterious, little-understood world of junk-bond trading.

As the government had hoped, Dahl's defection triggered a stampede of other witnesses now eager to cooperate. Prosecutors shrewdly issued another half dozen subpoenas and target letters in the wake of Dahl's agreement to cooperate. Recipients included Milken aides Terren Peizer and Warren Trepp.

Targeting Peizer proved to be one of the government's luckiest maneuvers. Positioned as he was at the center of the illegal arrangement with David Solomon, Peizer had been the custodian of the incriminating blue binders turned over to Lorraine Spurge. He was an even more important potential witness than Dahl, though the government had no way of knowing this. Peizer was also singularly susceptible to government pressure. He was relatively new to the firm, having been hired in 1985. As the salesman with the least seniority, he feared he would be the first person implicated if Milken ever decided to talk. Despite the "high fives" he gave Milken and his other efforts to curry favor with him, Peizer had to think of his own interests first.

As soon as he received his subpoena, Peizer hired a Washington lawyer, Plato Cacheris, a former partner of William Hundley, Trepp's lawyer; Cacheris had recently represented Fawn Hall in the Iran-Contra scandal. Peizer met with Cacheris in Washington, bringing with him a cache of documents from Drexel's Beverly Hills office. "I have these documents that are really damaging and I want to make a deal," Peizer said, displaying an unusual conviction and sense of purpose. "Why?" Cacheris wanted to know. Peizer said he was convinced that if he didn't turn on Milken first, Milken would turn on him.

As Cacheris examined Peizer's papers, he realized they were a treasure trove for the government. Among them were papers with what Peizer said was Lowell Milken's handwriting reconciling accounts between Solomon and Drexel. According to Peizer, the whole Solomon arrangement—including the Finsbury scheme—had been overseen by Lowell. And Peizer could link Milken to the scheme as well. When Peizer had questioned Milken about the arrangement, Milken had said, "Go ask Lowell, he'll explain it to you." Peizer had met with Lowell two or three times—and had kept notes of the conversations. Peizer had nodded in agreement when Milken asked him if the blue notebook had all the Solomon transactions. But he had shrewdly kept some of the most damaging evidence.

Peizer also recalled an incriminating conversation with Milken. "What are you doing?" Milken had asked one afternoon as Peizer went through his file drawers. "Complying with document subpoenas," Peizer had replied. As Peizer watched, Milken opened his own file drawers. They were empty. "If you don't have any documents, you can't comply," Milken said. Peizer hadn't turned over the most damaging material to Drexel's lawyers, but neither had he destroyed it. He could now offer it to the government.

Cacheris immediately contacted the U.S. attorney's office, unveiling Peizer's documents. Peizer was in a position to testify to the entire scheme between Milken and Solomon—a criminal scheme that was wholly independent of anything Boesky had revealed. For the prosecutors, Peizer was almost too good to be true. He got immunity almost instantly.

Peizer, too, was now removed from his seat near Milken and exiled to another floor. Like Dahl, he was stripped of all his client responsibilities. While Dahl gradually stopped showing up for work, however, Peizer was more dogged, refusing to accept his fate. Every morning he showed up on time and called Trepp. "Do you have anything for me today?" he'd ask.

In contrast to Peizer, Trepp, one of Milken's earliest lieutenants, continued to resist government pressure, and maintained his early loyalty to Milken. Yet he had his limits; he wouldn't commit perjury on Milken's behalf, and had invoked the Fifth Amendment when questioned by the government under oath in early 1988. "I don't understand why Warren wouldn't testify," Sandler had complained to Hundley, Trepp's lawyer. For his part, Hundley tried to get the Milken camp to face up to the mounting evidence of parking, knowing that if Milken capitulated, the pressure on Trepp would probably vanish.

"Well, Bill, Michael just doesn't see the parks the way the government does," was Sandler's reply.

As his employees defected, Milken seethed with bitterness and a sense of betrayal. His mood darkened. While he made no direct mention of Dahl's or Peizer's cooperation, he faulted nearly everyone else he dealt with. In late September 1988, Dahl was in New York planning to fly back to Los Angeles when Milken called him at his hotel room. Milken told Dahl that he was in Washington; if Dahl flew down, he suggested, they could ride back to Los Angeles on Milken's plane. Thinking some kind of reconciliation might be at hand, Dahl accepted.

When Dahl arrived at the airport, he and Milken went to the hangar and boarded Milken's Gulfstream IV jet, equipped with butler service and a large movie screen. Milken said virtually nothing to Dahl, who became uneasy. After takeoff, Milken selected a movie, *Raiders of the Lost Ark,* and turned the volume so high that Dahl's ears hurt. "Mike, if we're not going to talk, would you at least turn that thing down?" Dahl asked. Milken ignored him and continued to watch the film at an ear-splitting decibel level. For the rest of the flight, Milken said nothing to Dahl. He didn't even look at him. It dawned on Dahl that the trip had been staged to make one point: As far as Milken was concerned, Dahl had ceased to exist.

14.

By August 1988, Joseph had listened to Milken's lawyers and all their reassurances for nearly two years. He'd listened to Peter Fleming, the criminal lawyer he'd brought in to advise Drexel. He'd listened to Sandler, to Linda Robinson. Everyone had assured him that Milken was innocent, that Boesky was a liar, that Drexel had nothing to worry about except overzealous prosecutors envious of Milken's success. And Joseph had believed. He'd told his top people—Leon Black, Peter Ackerman, John Kissick, the board—that he'd never allow Drexel to turn against Milken as long as he believed Milken to be innocent.

Now Joseph developed a nagging cough that he couldn't seem to shake. At summer's end, he seemed pale and haggard. He was having trouble sleeping. Even at his farm in northwestern New Jersey, far from Wall Street, he couldn't seem to escape a mounting sense of doom. His lawyer, Ira Millstein, had again recommended that he resign from Drexel. Joseph no longer rejected the suggestion out of hand. But now he could think of no one else to take the helm in his absence. His fate and that of the firm now seemed inseparable.

On September 7, 1988, the SEC filed its long-expected lawsuit against Drexel. The 184-page complaint named Drexel, Milken and Lowell Milken, Maultasch, and another high-yield employee, Pamela Monzert, as well as the Posners, Milken's clients in Fischbach. In addition to the expected array of Boesky-related charges, including the alleged Fischbach conspiracy, the complaint cited two other instances of insider trading, including the Viacom trading Gardiner had been involved in.

Drexel did its best to prepare its employees and clients, outwardly welcoming the development as the firm's chance to get its day in court. Speaking for Milken, Paul, Weiss's Martin Flumenbaum issued a statement saying, "The complaint is based almost entirely on the false accusations of Ivan Boesky. It is obvious that Mr. Boesky was motivated to lie and make false accusations." Increasingly, however, this seemed obvious only to Flumenbaum and others in the immediate Milken circle. What was clear was that the government had not been dissuaded by Drexel's concerted efforts to persuade the SEC that the charges had no merit. Such a case, with so much at stake, wouldn't be undertaken lightly.

Drexel's day in court quickly degenerated into a petty exercise by the Drexel-Milken lawyers to disqualify federal district court judge Milton Pollack, who was already presiding over some private civil suits against Boesky and was therefore familiar with many of the underlying issues. The 81-year-old judge summarily rejected their requests, at one point characterizing Liman's arguments as "nonsensical"; Judge Pollack later said he was "thunderstruck" by the behavior of the lawyers for Milken and Drexel.

The strategy not only angered the judge (his decision was upheld on appeal), but the tactics enraged the SEC lawyers and, more important, the SEC commissioners who would ultimately have to approve any Drexel settlement. Many observers wondered: If Milken and Drexel were innocent and eager for their day in court, why weren't they contesting the merits of the allegations instead of attacking the integrity of an elderly, respected judge?

Giuliani's office still hadn't acted, and Joseph and his lawyers stepped up their efforts to dissuade the prosecutors from pursuing criminal charges against the firm. One evening, about 8:30 P.M., after a strenuous session in which Joseph and Curnin tried to convince Baird that the SEC charges didn't make sense, Baird interrupted. "You asked to see some evidence of wrongdoing," Baird said. "I think we're prepared to show you something."

Joseph and Curnin, not knowing what to expect, followed Baird, Carroll, and Fardella into the courthouse and into one of the judge's chambers equipped with audio equipment. They were offered headphones. The prosecutors played about 15 minutes of excerpts from the Princeton-Newport tapes, leaving Curnin and Joseph with the phrase "Welcome to the world of sleaze" reverberating in their ears.

"What do you think?" Baird asked Joseph. "Aren't you disturbed?"

Curnin ordered Joseph not to respond. "Do you have others?" Curnin asked. "Do they involve other Drexel people?"

"Yes," Baird replied.

"Lisa Jones?" Curnin asked. The prosecutors didn't reply.

Joseph was badly shaken. He and Curnin discussed the development into the night. There was no arguing with the tapes. Joseph knew now exactly what had been going on, and he knew it was a crime. He told Curnin, "Newberg wouldn't go to the bathroom without Milken knowing about it." It was clear to him that Milken had to be behind the scheme.

The tapes also raised new doubts about Milken's candor. Through his lawyers at Paul, Weiss, Milken had insisted that his only accuser was Boesky, and that in any contest of credibility, Milken won over Boesky hands down. Yet the Princeton-Newport arrangement had nothing to do with Boesky.

The next morning, when Drexel's lawyers asked Milken's for an explanation of the tapes, Paul, Weiss insisted that Milken knew nothing about Newberg's activities. Newberg, under indictment in the Princeton-Newport case, wasn't talking. Milken's lawyers also assured Joseph that the documents the government believed backed up Boesky's version of the $5.3 million payment were "reconstructions" that would be easily discredited in court. But when the government invited him to look at the documents. Joseph was staggered to find copies of original documents, Mooradian's records. Worse, the documents plainly showed calculations that made sense only in the context of a parking arrangement.

Curnin called Flumenbaum with these latest revelations. "It's what we thought it was," Flumenbaum responded smugly, showing no concern.

"What about the carrying charges? What about the fact that these are originals?"

"It's what we expected," Flumenbaum repeated.

If so, Curnin thought angrily, Milken's lawyers had known more than they ever shared with Drexel and had breached their joint defense agreement. Curnin and Fleming insisted on a meeting with Liman and

Flumenbaum. Every damaging point Curnin raised was airily dismissed as "meaningless," "not harmful," "benign," "as we expected," or something Milken knew nothing about. As for the cost-of-carry, Flumenbaum insisted, "That's just part of the accounting mechanism here." Curnin cut off the meeting before he lost his temper.

That fall, in the offices he shared with Richard Sandler in Beverly Hills, Craig Cogut was growing uneasy about some of the Milken-led partnership payouts he was expected to make. In particular, he was concerned about MacPherson Partners. Milken had created the partnership to hold warrants to buy Storer stock as part of the LBO deal that had figured so prominently in the fortunes of Siegel, Freeman, KKR, Milken, and Drexel.

KKR had given the warrants to Drexel, in care of Milken, as an additional inducement for Drexel's clients to buy the Storer junk bonds. Yet Cogut could see that the warrants hadn't ended up in the hands of Drexel's clients. The MacPherson participants seemed to be Milken himself, his family members, and, even more worrisome, various mutual-fund managers who bought junk bonds from Milken. Now that KKR had sold Storer's cable television stations at a big profit, the warrants were supposed to be cashed in and the proceeds distributed to the participants. Cogut felt queasy. The MacPherson payments looked like they might be examples of Milken self-dealing, or worse, bribes to the fund managers.

Cogut had joined Milken's in-house law firm in 1984, and it was rechristened Victor, Cogut & Sandler. He had never been under any illusions that this was a law firm in the true sense; Milken and his family were the sole clients, and the firm's offices were on the third floor of the Drexel office building owned by the Milken brothers. Cogut had hoped that he'd end up working on Drexel venture capital and tax deals, but he'd ended up doing much of his work for Lowell Milken, who oversaw all the partnership activity.

After news of the Boesky agreement, Cogut had agreed to be represented by New York criminal lawyer Michael Armstrong, Lowell's lawyer. But like Maultasch and Dahl, Cogut had become uneasy about his attorney's possible conflict of interest. Lowell's interests were too close to Mike Milken's. Cogut's concern had increased when, earlier in 1988, Armstrong came to him with an affidavit he had prepared for Cogut to sign. Its intent had been to exonerate Lowell, based on assertions of fact by Cogut. Cogut read it over and had only one problem: the facts weren't true. He angrily refused to sign, and began looking for new lawyers, eventually hiring Los Angeles lawyers Tom Pollack and Ted Miller.

In early November, in Drexel's offices in New York, Cogut ran into Joseph as Joseph was hurrying into the men's room. Cogut said he wanted to talk to him and Joseph motioned for him to follow.

"There's a partnership I don't think you know about," Cogut said in hushed tones. Joseph looked at him, puzzled. "You're not going to like it," Cogut added.

"Why?" Joseph asked.

"Fund managers were given warrants," Cogut replied. "Mike's kids got warrants."

"Did the fund managers buy the deal?" Joseph asked.

"Yes."

"We'd better get the lawyers," Joseph said, recognizing with alarm that bribery might be involved. At the very least, the partnership violated Drexel's own internal regulations.

For years, Milken had come to Joseph for advice and guidance about whether certain trades were ethical. They usually were. Such exchanges had given Joseph confidence that Milken himself was scrupulously careful. Suddenly Joseph sensed that it might have all been a carefully crafted illusion; that Milken might have come to him on the close calls to camouflage any blatant wrongdoing.

Joseph went straight into Drexel chairman Robert Linton's office, telling him what he'd just learned from Cogut. "Oh shit," Linton replied. Joseph immediately called the lawyers at Cahill Gordon.

"Get on this this second," he ordered.

Cogut and his new lawyers also explained to Liman and Flumenbaum that they planned to volunteer the MacPherson information to the government. "No!" Flumenbaum all but exploded. "You can't do this. They'd never find out about this." But Liman restrained him. "Let them do what they feel they have to do," he said to Flumenbaum with a tone of resignation.

Joseph's belief in Milken's innocence, and the elaborate defense he'd built on that foundation, collapsed one rainy night in late November. Curnin had called late that afternoon, saying it was important that they talk privately. Joseph was due at a formal dinner in midtown, so he suggested he pick Curnin up in a Drexel radio cab, and the two could ride uptown together. Joseph, clad in black tie and tuxedo, rode the few blocks to Cahill Gordon's offices and picked up Curnin as the rain turned into a torrent. They were soon mired in traffic.

"It looks like the guys on the coast did some things they shouldn't have done," Curnin said. He ticked off the recent troubling developments, culminating in his review of trading records that corroborated the Solomon allegations. He wanted Joseph to recognize that there was evidence of wrongdoing, that it was mounting, that it was material, and that it was not related to Boesky. Now that the wall of silence among Drexel employees had been broken, there would likely be more defections. And Drexel didn't even yet have the whole story— nor would it get it from its erstwhile allies in the Milken camp.

Joseph asked some questions, and thanked Curnin for his analysis. When he reached his destination, the Marriott Marquis hotel in Times Square, he stepped out into the pouring rain. He was now convinced that Drexel and its 10,000 employees had been betrayed by Milken, the man on whom he'd built the firm he'd always dreamed of. He had been willing to do anything for Milken as long as he believed him to be innocent. But he couldn't say he believed that anymore.

Joseph wasn't the only one who'd lost faith in Milken. In Los Angeles, Dahl had a meeting with Litt at the Four Seasons Hotel. "Mike's gonna have to plead guilty," Dahl told him, mentioning his own damaging evidence. "Somebody's got to tell him." Litt didn't insist, as usual, that Milken was innocent.

"I'm not going to be the one to do it," Litt said.

Nor, apparently, was anyone else. Litt's position on the Milken defense team was precarious. So was Williams & Connolly's. After Williams's death, Paul, Weiss had assumed the dominant role, pushing Williams & Connolly aside. Vincent Fuller, who'd been brought in to replace Williams, hadn't had a chance to establish any rapport with Milken or Sandler, who relied instead on Liman.

But Fuller decided someone had to undertake the unpopular option of plea negotiations. Someone had to at least sound out the government on what it would demand. In discussions involving Carroll, Fardella, Baird, and eventually even Giuliani, Fuller found the prosecutors to be surprisingly reasonable, given the resources that had been expended on the case and the attendant publicity. They tossed out the idea of a joint settlement between Milken and Drexel for a total of $1 billion—a large number, to be sure, but one that would be easily paid by Milken, especially if at least half were paid by Drexel, as it surely would be. But money had never been the real issue. The plea was the real issue. Fuller argued first for a plea of nolo contendere, then offered a plea to a single felony. The prosecutors indicated that they could probably live with a relatively modest plea to two felonies.

Cautious optimism set in at St. Andrews Plaza. Finally there was hope that a deal would be worked out. Milken, it was believed, would plead, and cooperate—taking the investigation onto another plane entirely. There was only one problem: the prosecutors couldn't tell whether Fuller had the backing of the other Milken lawyers, let alone Milken himself. There was certainly nothing in Milken's public posture that suggested any willingness to compromise or admit guilt. And the public-relations campaign was continuing, infuriating prosecutors working on the case; there had never before been anything comparable undertaken on behalf of a potential defendant.

Liman was kept informed, but Robinson, Lake wasn't told about Fuller's negotiations, and continued to deny emphatically that such a course was even under consideration. Since the *Predators' Ball* fiasco, the campaign had broadened its objectives, focusing on Milken's charitable activities (including production of an expensive calendar highlighting the Milken foundation's beneficiaries) and attacking the use of RICO against Drexel. A spate of anti-RICO letters and op-ed pieces drafted by Robinson, Lake began appearing in publications around the country. They were shrewdly drafted to generate sympathy for Milken, arguing that RICO deprives a defendant of assets before any trial. Robinson, Lake also drafted speeches for Milken to deliver to business groups, and continued to make him available for trusted members of the press—as long as no questions were asked about matters under investigation. Milken was with a *Time* reporter when he heard that he and Drexel had been officially charged by the SEC.

Any Manhattan jury would likely have a large contingent of black jurors, and Milken began to recruit black support. His public-relations effort began to focus more on the local newspapers, the *New York Post*, the *Daily News,* and the *Amsterdam News,* papers more likely to be read by blacks than *The Wall Street Journal* or *The New York Times.* Former Los Angeles mayor Tom Bradley; Reginald Lewis, the head of Beatrice International and a Milken junk-bond client; and Percy Sutton, former Manhattan borough president, were Milken's key links to black organizations. They helped make sure Milken gained an introduction to Jesse Jackson. Bradley (who, according to the *Los Angeles Times,* had received over $70,000 in Milken campaign contributions) had praised Milken as "that man of genius, that man of courage, that man of vision, that man of conviction" soon after Milken was implicated in the scandal by Boesky.

Though Milken had shown scant interest in civil rights issues in the past, he held a party for a group of black junior high school students in Los Angeles. "I'd like to introduce you to a close friend of mine," Milken said, and in walked Jesse Jackson. At a conference in New York, Jackson and Warner chairman (and Liman client) Steve Ross both praised Milken. Robinson, Lake arranged photo opportunities with handicapped and underprivileged children, most of them

black and Hispanic. Robinson even hired a black public-relations specialist, Mary Helen Thompson, a former press secretary for Representative Louis Stokes of Ohio. Thompson focused pro-Milken efforts on
the congressional black caucus. Milken was honored by the One Hundred Black Men Society, a national organization of successful black
men, including Sutton. Milken and Robinson, Lake each bought tables
at the event.

In what became Milken's most celebrated foray into image
remaking, he took 1,700 underprivileged, largely minority children to
an afternoon Mets game at Shea Stadium in September 1988. Though
the Milken forces later insisted that the event wasn't meant to be
publicized, Drexel chairman Linton just happened to mention it at
luncheon with members of the press present (some invited by Robinson, Lake). At the game, television cameras rolled as the junk-bond
financier, sporting a jaunty baseball cap, did his best to look relaxed.
"We haven't added a single public event to his calendar, not one
thing," Lerer told *The Wall Street Journal* after the event.

Soon, the Milken public-relations forces had a fresh target: Giuliani himself, who announced plans to leave office and run for mayor
of New York. A political campaign, with the media hungry for Giuliani
stories, would be an ideal opportunity to stir up criticism of his handling of the Milken investigation. It also meant a new and uncertain
regime at the U.S. attorney's office.

The time was propitious for a settlement. Giuliani recognized the
obvious political benefits to wrapping up his tenure with the conviction
of the most powerful financier in America. The Freeman arrest was a
cloud on his record, but a Milken guilty plea, in all likelihood, would
eclipse that mistake. Giuliani, Baird, Carroll, and Fardella began seriously to contemplate accepting Fuller's proposition of a guilty plea to
a single felony.

Many details of the agreement—such as how Milken's brother
Lowell would fare, and whether Milken would cooperate—still hadn't
been worked out. They could have been, had Milken and his lawyers
moved quickly; but they didn't. Fuller had obviously never gained the
backing of his client, and his co-counsel at Paul, Weiss didn't support
the notion of settlement. As Fuller disclosed the negotiations to a wider
circle within the Milken camp, he was all but branded a heretic. Paul,
Weiss lawyers opposed any plea, as did Sandler.

Soon the opportunity for a plea to a single felony vanished. As the
fruits of Dahl's and Peizer's cooperation were gathered and the case
against Milken grew proportionately stronger, the prosecutors dropped
the idea as too favorable to Milken. Baird felt that a single-felony plea

would rightly be criticized as a victory for Milken, and would fail to deter others in the securities industry. To Giuliani's credit, his duty as a prosecutor took precedence over his ambitions as a politician. If he had to resign with the Milken and Freeman cases both still pending, so be it.

As for Fuller, he largely washed his hands of the case, leaving his partner Litt to deal with Williams & Connolly's co-counsel duties. Sandler and Liman had seized full control of the Milken defense. There was little risk now that Milken would hear anything but an echo of his own increasingly isolated view of reality.

Even as the secret plea negotiations foundered, Wall Street's attention was diverted by the biggest, most tumultuous leveraged buyout battle of the decade: the $25 billion conquest of giant RJR Nabisco by Kravis and KKR. With a cornucopia of multimillion-dollar fees at stake, practically every major firm on Wall Street entered the fray as a three-way battle emerged between groups advised by Shearson Lehman Brothers (with Linda Robinson busily maneuvering behind the scenes) and Salomon Brothers; Goldman, Sachs and First Boston; and, for KKR, Wasserstein Perella & Co., Morgan Stanley, and Drexel.

For Drexel, RJR was not just the deal of the decade. It was a life-or-death struggle to prove to the world that the firm would survive the government's investigation. KKR was a traditional Drexel client, and a huge piece of business. If Drexel lost the financing assignment, its market share in junk bonds would plunge for the year, and its franchise would be destroyed in the eyes of Wall Street.

For Joseph, RJR would also be a crucial test of Drexel's ability to survive the loss of Milken—which Joseph now recognized as inevitable. Already, the dynamics of Drexel's high-yield operation in Beverly Hills had changed radically. Milken, once completely dominant, was increasingly absent, busy with his public-relations campaign and his lawyers. The mantle of leadership had fallen uneasily on Peter Ackerman, the smooth-talking Ph.D. who was strong on client contact but lacked genius as a trader. Joseph himself had assumed much of the burden once shouldered by Milken. In the midst of some of the most damaging developments in the government's investigation, he called personally on Kravis to convince him to retain Drexel.

Kravis took almost no persuading, mainly because he remained loyal to Milken, even though it would once have been unthinkable for any respectable client to entrust a $5 billion bond offering to a securities firm being charged with securities fraud and other offenses by the

SEC. But times had changed, and Kravis owed much of his empire to Drexel and Milken. Drexel had brought him Storer. It had raised $2.5 billion to conquer Beatrice. Results were what counted.

Joseph assured Kravis that, even if Drexel were indicted, it would complete the deal for KKR. Although a Drexel "highly confident" letter had always been enough before, Drexel agreed it would provide a $1.5 billion bridge loan if necessary—a commitment of its own capital to the deal. At a Saturday meeting to complete arrangements for the RJR bid and its financing, Kravis asked Joseph only one question: "Fred, do we have your assurance that Drexel will complete the financing?" "Yes," Joseph replied. KKR engaged Merrill Lynch as a co-manager of the offering, just in case. But Joseph vowed that Merrill Lynch would stay on the sidelines.

Drexel launched the most ambitious capital-raising effort in its history. It scheduled 20 elaborate sales meetings, known as road shows, for potential buyers from Tokyo to Zurich. It wooed wealthy individuals and institutions, this time offering equity stakes to the buyers rather than keeping them for Milken-led partnerships. No effort was too small to be spared. Drexel even doled out RJR Nabisco products—shredded wheat, Planter's peanuts, Oreo cookies, Carefree chewing gum—and RJR T-shirts and sweatshirts. Joseph knew that the future of the firm hinged on the deal.

Despite his assurances to KKR, Joseph had concluded that Drexel could not, in fact, survive a criminal indictment, let alone an ensuing lengthy and damaging trial. Shortly after his cab ride with Curnin, he stepped up the pace of meetings with members of the Drexel board and top Drexel officials. Without elaborating or providing any details, he began to convey the message that he had ceased to believe in Milken's innocence.

In late November 1988, the Justice Department approved the filing of RICO charges against Drexel and Milken, the last step before indictment. Drexel would have to post a bond with the government immediately after the filing of any charges. Much to Joseph's fury, Baird and his colleagues refused to tell Drexel how much the government would demand. Joseph recognized that the financial uncertainty could cripple Drexel. Large securities firms like Drexel depend on their ability to obtain short-term loans and to issue commercial paper, mostly to large banks. In preliminary talks, Drexel's banks warned that they wouldn't be able to extend credit to a firm under the cloud of a RICO indictment. Drexel boasted over $1 billion in capital above regulatory requirements, and a litigation reserve of over $500 million. But the firm's chief financial officer reported to Joseph that the company could survive a RICO indictment for—at most—one month. Joseph conveyed this dire forecast to top officials and stockholders.

Their reactions reflected their financial self-interests. The firm's emphasis on cash compensation and bonuses rather than equity stakes had left ownership largely in the hands of its European partner, Groupe Bruxelles Lambert, and senior officials, like Burnham and Kantor, who had little role in the firm's recent success. Their top priority was to protect their equity interest by making sure Drexel survived. They favored settling the charges.

Pitted against them were officials like Leon Black, who cared little about the value of his equity stake but seemed obsessed with maintaining his huge income stream—$20 million in 1989. He made it quite clear that he cared little about Milken's ultimate innocence or guilt; he simply wanted the engine of the firm's cash flow to keep running as long as possible. Black and his allies favored any strategy that would delay Milken's departure, and opposed anything that would require his dismissal.

Finally, there were the ardent Milken loyalists—Ackerman, Kissick, and Fred McCarthy, a managing director based in Boston—who wouldn't entertain any proposal that might weaken his defense. Far from dreading Drexel's demise, they seemed to welcome it, reasoning that Giuliani would be blamed for the firm's collapse. They believed that the attendant outcry would weaken the government's determination to prosecute Milken. This group's motto: "Death Before Dishonor."

The split posed serious problems. While the old guard controlled the board, and could be persuaded to support a settlement, the Milken loyalists were the key to the firm's future success and survival. If they defected, there would be little at Drexel worth saving.

After a troubled Thanksgiving at his New Jersey farm, Joseph and Drexel's lawyers plunged into a hectic series of negotiations with Giuliani, Baird, and others at the U.S. attorney's office. The parameters were simple: Drexel would plead guilty as long as Joseph and his advisors thought the firm would survive. That meant, in essence, two things: Drexel could not be perceived by its top employees as turning against Milken, and the financial burden couldn't be so crushing as to extinguish the firm. In that event, Drexel might as well go ahead and be indicted and be forced into bankruptcy.

Joseph tried to get prosecutors to understand the delicate dynamics of the firm—but the years of defiance and bad publicity aimed at the government now took its toll. The prosecutors had little but contempt for the Milken loyalists. It infuriated them that, even on the eve of capitulation, Drexel still insisted on soft-pedaling Milken's guilt. Drexel refused to admit publicly that the $5.3 million payment was part of the illegal Boesky arrangement—because Milken insisted that it was not. It didn't want to fire Milken. It still wanted to pay Milken more than $200 million in compensation that was due him that year.

In a heated exchange, Baird banged his fist down and said, "Stop talking about money. I'm talking about justice."

Joseph erupted. "I'm not representing a church. Ten thousand people are clothed and fed off our payroll."

A Drexel guilty plea began to look inevitable. On Thursday, December 1, Joseph issued a memo to all Drexel employees. "I want to bring you up to date on the status of the investigation. In recent weeks, we have had discussions with the government which are now reaching a critical stage. If we do not agree to settle with the U.S. Attorney, we believe that he intends to indict the firm (as well as certain of our employees), and to include in such an indictment so-called racketeering charges ('RICO'). We expect that one of these two alternative scenarios will unfold within a short time."

Astute readers realized that the memo dwelled on the hazards of indictment and the virtues of settlement. An indictment "will put pressure on the firm and its businesses. We will also face a long, drawn out battle in the courts (and, unfortunately, in the press) before any final resolution of the matter. . . . If we settle, we can put this constant attack on the firm behind us. But to do so will require a guilty plea."

For the first time, Joseph attempted to quantify the cost to Drexel of the investigation: "We believe Drexel has lost some $1.5 billion of potential revenues and has spent over $175 million in direct expenses during the past two years because of the investigation. The toll on our people has been high. . . . We would like to put the trauma of the past two years behind us, but not at an unfair cost to the firm and its employees."

Not surprisingly, the memo's implications were clear to Milken loyalists, who were horrified at the drift of events. Foremost among them was Don Engel, who was kept informed of almost every development by Fred McCarthy, his chief ally on the board. In early December, the board held a Sunday meeting, and McCarthy called Engel at home immediately afterward with an ominous message. "I get the feeling they'll sell out Mike," McCarthy reported.

Engel's fears deepened when he and Black met with Joseph the next week. Engel knew Joseph liked to reach a consensus by tossing up trial balloons, and at the meeting Joseph said he was worried about the individuals who might be indicted if Drexel didn't settle. "How would you feel if the two of you, Ackerman, Kissick, were all indicted?" Joseph asked.

"Fuck it, let them indict us," Engel said, and Joseph realized he meant it.

Baird was now threatening to have the grand jury indict the firm at any moment. He gave Joseph an ultimatum: Drexel was going to have to plead guilty to six felonies, and pay a whopping fine. Joseph read with anguish the disclosure in *The Wall Street Journal* on December 14 that Drexel had set aside a $700 million contingency fund— far more than the government realized Drexel had. Baird immediately boosted his demand from $450 million to $750 million. But at this point money wasn't the issue. Drexel could survive a payment of that size. Even at this late stage, the most important figure in the negotiations was still offstage: Milken.

To placate Milken's allies, Joseph was still fighting to avoid turning evidence related to Milken over to the government, to prevent him from being fired, and to pay him the hundreds of millions of dollars he was still owed. He was even trying to avoid mentioning the $5.3 million.

On Friday, December 15, Joseph undertook a last round of diplomacy to gain support for the settlement. Late that afternoon, about 5 P.M., Joseph arrived at Paul, Weiss to meet with Liman. After that, he planned to meet with Engel. Even though Engel wasn't on the board and wasn't even officially part of the firm, Joseph had pegged him as the ringleader of the pro-Milken faction.

By the time Joseph reached his office, Liman was well aware of the latest developments. Joseph did his best to explain what he thought was Drexel's hazardous choice, emphasizing the dire credit situation if Drexel were indicted and what he was doing to try to safeguard Milken. Liman didn't seem impressed. Instead, he began lecturing Joseph on principles of justice, philosophy, notions of right and wrong. Then he stunned Joseph by comparing his decision to the Nazi persecution of the Jews. He argued that Joseph was depriving Milken of his rights prior to trial. "That's the first step towards concentration camps," Liman argued. "No man can deprive another of his freedoms."

Joseph could hardly listen. He was too shocked by the unfairness of Liman's charge and the attempt to manipulate his emotions. "Mike did what he did," Joseph responded. "What we do won't have any affect on the proceedings against him. I'm not here to try Michael Milken."

Joseph said his own decision was final, but he couldn't speak for the board. Perhaps he'd be voted down. Liman, abandoning the Nazi angle, seemed disappointed but resigned. Then, as he prepared to leave, Joseph added, almost as an afterthought, "Mike is going to plead guilty anyway." This really aroused Liman's indignation. "Never," he said firmly, showing Joseph to the door. "Absolutely not."

Within minutes, Liman was on the phone to Engel to report on his meeting with Joseph. "Donny," Liman reported in grave tones, "he's selling him out."

Joseph went from Liman's office to Engel's spacious coop apartment at 570 Park Avenue. He arrived about 7 P.M. The two men sat down with drinks in Engel's library. To Engel, Joseph had aged markedly; he was coughing. But in spite of all that, and despite an outward civility, Engel was spoiling for a fight, and he got it.

As Engel launched an impassioned defense of Milken, Joseph cut him off. "I know you're loyal," Joseph said. "I appreciate loyalty." Then his tone shifted. "But get your fingers out of my eyes."

Engel retorted that he had had no choice but to turn against Joseph and rally others to Milken's defense. "He's our brother," Engel said. "You've got to fight. A mafia lawyer wouldn't act like this," Engel said, indignant over what he saw as Joseph's weakness.

"We're not a mafia company," Joseph responded. "Donny," he continued in a more conciliatory tone, "don't do anything hasty. Remember, we have to think of 10,000 people." Engel practically leaped from his chair in rage and indignation. "What the fuck are you talking about?" he yelled. "We don't have 10,000 people to think about. We have one person."

On Saturday, December 17, Engel flew to California for Milken's son's bar mitzvah, seizing the opportunity to plot strategy with Peter Ackerman and Leon Black, who also attended. Joseph hadn't been invited. At the party, Engel managed to maneuver Ackerman into a conversation about Milken and Joseph. "The little bastard is selling him out," Engel said. "There's only one way to stop this." Then he unveiled his trump card: "You've got to stand up on your desk on Monday and say, 'No RJR.' The salesmen will not sell another bond." It was a bold gamble that could have crippled the deal on which Drexel's future—with or without Milken—depended. Engel believed that the threat alone would force Joseph to end all talk of settlement.

"Let it play out, Donny," Ackerman replied enigmatically. But Engel insisted. "You're the only person who can do this," he emphasized.

Word of the bar mitzvah meeting among Black, Engel, and Ackerman swept the firm, along with rumors of threats to defect if Drexel settled with the government. Robinson, Lake officials, even Robinson herself, fanned the flames, planting stories with reporters that rebellion was brewing in opposition to any settlement with the government. Milken loyalists even suggested that Joseph had negotiated his own immunity from prosecution as part of the deal, putting his interest ahead of the firm's and Milken's. The story, patently false, found its way into print. Joseph was never a target, and his immunity had never been discussed. Joseph had been secretly taped when he visited the Beverly Hills office in September, pledging to back Milken. Now Lowell's lawyer, Michael Armstrong, threatened to release transcripts. Joseph was appalled that his own employees had taped him.

Taken together, the desperate efforts to sabotage any settlement showed how ugly the Milken camp's attacks on Joseph were becoming. Millstein was so concerned that he called Liman, speaking to him as one dean of the New York bar to another. "I certainly hope this isn't going to turn into a PR contest," he said. Liman refused to acknowledge that there had been any PR campaign directed at Joseph; nonetheless, the attacks eased off after Millstein's call.

Black and Ackerman stopped short of actually threatening to quit if Drexel pleaded guilty, but they left the possibility hanging. Joseph ultimately guaranteed their loyalty to the firm the only way he could: he bought it. Ackerman's price: $100 million, which Joseph pledged would be his reward for the RJR deal. Black and Kissick were also promised outsize bonuses.

Ackerman also told Joseph about Engel's RJR threat. Joseph was in a fury when he reached Engel on the phone on Monday. "You're inciting," he practically shouted at him. "I want this stopped." Engel was equally angry. "Have you told the government we're going bankrupt? If you haven't, then you can't negotiate. You've got to say, 'Here are the keys. The place is yours. It's your responsibility.' Have you said that?" "No," Joseph answered, and Engel slammed down the phone.

Drexel's board met that afternoon, and again rejected the government's proposed settlement as too harsh. Engel and his allies believed they had prevailed. That evening, Drexel's corporate finance officials, with their spouses and dates, hurried through the revolving doors of New York's Waldorf-Astoria and into the hotel's grand ballroom for the department's annual Christmas party. With the balconies decked in greenery, Christmas trees twinkling, and champagne flowing, it seemed, at least for an evening, like the brash, confident Drexel of old.

Drexel's chairman, Robert Linton, took to the stage for a rendition of "Rudy the Red-Nosed Reindeer," attacking Giuliani in verse.

Then Joseph moved to the podium and, with Linton at his side, announced that the board had met that afternoon and voted unanimously to reject the government's settlement offer. "We're going to fight!" he exclaimed as hundreds jumped to their feet, yelling, cheering, clapping, and beating on the tables in an ovation that seemed as though it wouldn't stop.

But the euphoria was short-lived. "They had parties in Berlin right before the end of the war, didn't they?" asked one Drexel vice president after the party. Even as some Drexel officials were nursing their hangovers the next morning, Curnin got a call from the U.S. attorney's office in what was termed a "sanity check." Curnin and Carroll agreed that perhaps they could live with a further compromise. That night they closed the gap slightly: Drexel wouldn't have to admit Milken's guilt. The firm would be allowed to say that it "couldn't disprove" the government's allegations against him and itself. Drexel wouldn't have to waive its attorney-client privilege. But it would have to cooperate against Milken. It would have to plead guilty to six felonies—including numerous Boesky-related offenses—and it would have to pay $650 million. And on one final point the government remained adamant: Drexel wouldn't be allowed to pay Michael and Lowell Milken their bonuses, and the brothers would have to leave the firm, either voluntarily or by being fired.

Carroll made clear that this was the government's final offer, that Drexel's brinksmanship would produce no further concessions and would have to end. He told the firm that, if the government heard nothing further, it could expect to be indicted at the grand jury session the next afternoon. Around Drexel that week, Joseph wore a large lapel button that read STRESS: THAT'S WHAT HAPPENS WHEN THE MIND OVERRIDES THE BODY'S NEED TO KICK THE SHIT OUT OF SOMEONE WHO JUSTLY DESERVES IT.

Joseph convened another board meeting at noon on Wednesday, December 21. The choice, while agonizing, seemed clear. Drexel would collapse within a month if subjected to a RICO indictment. Curnin estimated that the firm would have to post a crippling $1 billion bond, and credit would evaporate almost immediately. On the other hand, the settlement, while harsh, wouldn't cripple the firm if its people rallied behind the decision. Curnin recommended accepting the settlement, as did Irwin Schneiderman, the Cahill Gordon partner who had long been the firm's principal outside counsel, and Millstein, Joseph's personal lawyer.

Peter Fleming, however, broke ranks, casting his lot with the Milken loyalists. Joseph and Curnin knew that Fleming had been drifting closer and closer to the Milken camp for some time. Sounding much like the Milken lawyers, he claimed that none of the evidence amassed by the government was all that damaging. In fact, he was already angling to become part of the Milken defense team in the event that Drexel settled. As a criminal rather than corporate lawyer, he didn't accept the premise that a RICO indictment would destroy the firm. He argued to the board that Drexel should reject the settlement, allow itself to be indicted, and then see what happened.

Black, Kissick, and Bachelor quickly lined up behind Fleming. Black, volatile under ordinary circumstances, seemed increasingly distraught at the prospect of Drexel's abandoning Milken. At 4 P.M., with debate still raging, Carroll called and spoke to Curnin. "You're about to be indicted," he said.

News that the grand jury was, even then, beginning to vote sent panic through the ranks of the directors. Burnham himself, trying to salvage the remnants of a firm that bore his name but whose dynamics he now barely understood, called, almost hysterically, for an immediate vote.

Sixteen of the firm's directors voted for the settlement, including Linton, Kantor, Burnham, and all six board representatives of Groupe Bruxelles Lambert. Kissick, Black, Bachelor, and two others voted against the settlement. With the outcome already decided, Joseph cast the last ballot. Although he had been the architect of the settlement, he made one last, transparently insincere attempt to bridge the looming chasm between himself and the Milken loyalists. He voted against the plea bargain.

As the directors filed out of the conference room in glum silence, Joseph returned to his office and placed the hardest call of his career: he called Milken in Beverly Hills, and they spoke for about 10 minutes. When Joseph broke the news of the board's vote, Milken said he had already heard it from his lawyers. "Aren't I innocent until proven guilty? Isn't this a free country?" Milken asked aggressively.

Joseph had vowed he wouldn't be diverted by another discussion of Nazi Germany or morality. "I'm sorry, Michael," Joseph said. "The board has voted. It's final. I hope you'll understand."

Even though Edward Bennett Williams had warned him long ago that this day would come, Milken seemed shaken and said he was deeply disappointed to lose the firm's support. "I guess I'll have to fight my own battles and make my own decisions," he said.

It took several days for final details of the elaborate plea agreement to be worked out, but the pact was finally sealed and the news broke just before Christmas. The specific counts to which Drexel would plead guilty weren't disclosed, nor were any terms of the agreement relating to Milken's future. But, in a crucial concession extracted by the government, Drexel acknowledged it would cooperate in the continuing investigation. The significance for Milken was obvious. As Alan Bromberg, a securities law professor at Southern Methodist University, remarked to *The Wall Street Journal*, "This is a very shrewd prosecution by Giuliani. It is a classic case of turning the screws on one defendant to get incriminating information on higher-ups."

In at least two respects, Joseph's judgment was vindicated: Drexel survived the initial blow of the guilty plea, and none of the top performers resigned. Ackerman was offered a seat on the board, joining Kissick and Black, and the three plunged into the still-pending RJR junk-bond deal. RJR now loomed as a test for a post-Milken Drexel. Drexel began its U.S. road show with a presentation for investors in San Diego on January 18; hundreds of potential buyers later packed the ballroom at the Helmsley Palace hotel in New York for a breakfast presentation. By the end of January, exultant Drexel officials were able to term the offering a resounding success. The firm had obtained so many commitments—more than $5 billion—that the offering had to be increased. Drexel earned more than $250 million in fees. And like the Drexel of old, it had shut Merrill Lynch out of the offering altogether.

Even Engel, dismayed though he was by the Drexel plea, agreed to assume his customary role organizing the 1989 Predators' Ball. He continued to insist that Drexel would have been better off going bankrupt than turning against Milken, but the success of the RJR offering seemed to placate him.

Engel flew back to Beverly Hills to meet with the conference committee and plan the first Predators' Ball at which Milken wouldn't be present. He insisted that no one try to fill Milken's shoes, not even John Kissick, whom Joseph had designated as Milken's heir apparent after passing over Ackerman as too divisive, and Trepp as lacking the necessary demeanor and management abilities. (Unlike Kissick, the two other candidates also remained under investigation; Joseph didn't want yet another indictment to disrupt the Beverly Hills operation.) Engel decreed that no one would deliver the customary speeches that Milken had used to set the tone for each day of the conference. Instead, the conference would feature videos in which the spirit of Milken would predominate. Indeed, the high point of the conference was to be a lavish and emotional filmed tribute to Milken.

Then Joseph enraged the committee by issuing a memorandum ordering that Drexel employees were to have no further contact with Milken. He also banned the Milken video from the conference. It was too much for Milken's assistant Lorraine Spurge, who became nearly hysterical over the video issue. She, Robert Davidow, a high-yield department official, and Harry Horowitz, Milken's boyhood friend, threatened to sabotage the conference unless Joseph allowed the video. Joseph held firm, anxious that nothing at the conference upset the SEC at a delicate stage in their negotiations.

In March, a glum conference committee—Engel, Horowitz, Davidow, and Spurge—gathered in the fifth-floor conference room in Beverly Hills. Their planning efforts had proceeded in a desultory fashion. Engel couldn't muster any enthusiasm; he barely wanted to go on, and was thinking of quitting. Suddenly the door opened and Milken himself came in, bursting with vitality and ideas. He sat down at the table and began talking almost immediately, focusing on the conference as though nothing had changed, as though he'd be leading the sessions, taking the stage to introduce the year's surprise celebrity. He reeled off the latest detailed financial statistics on key Drexel clients, focusing in particular on the recent success of MCI Communications and 20th Century–Fox, and how they should be presented to participants.

As suddenly as he'd come in, Milken left. Somehow, Engel knew that it was the last time Milken would help them plan a conference. He felt tears well up in his eyes. He looked around the table and saw that the others, too, were trying to keep their emotions in check. But their cause had been renewed. They would show the world. The conference would go on. They would show their video, no matter what Joseph said. They would do it for Milken's clients. They would do this for Mike.

Drexel's plea agreement with the U.S. attorney's office was contingent on the firm's reaching a settlement of the SEC case. In Washington, it was time for the commission, still smarting from the Drexel-generated bashing after the Boesky agreement and all that had ensued, to extract its revenge.

Joseph, stung by criticism from Engel and others within Drexel that he'd been outnegotiated by Giuliani and Baird, assembled a new team to handle the SEC negotiations. He replaced Curnin and Fleming, who'd generated so much resentment over the SEC case—Lynch was candid in acknowledging that he "hate[d] their guts"—with another Cahill Gordon partner, Gerald Tannenbaum. And he added John Sorte, a mild-mannered corporate finance executive untainted by any of Milken's transgressions. Unfortunately, Joseph also included Leon Black, who quickly drove the SEC lawyers to new plateaus of rage.

When the Drexel negotiating team arrived in Washington in January, Lynch, Sturc, and others at the SEC expected them to have finally adopted the posture of supplicants seeking mercy. After all, the firm had just admitted six felonies and agreed to the largest fine in the history of the securities laws. At the outset, Lynch made clear that no settlement would be reached unless Drexel admitted wrongdoing. Yet Black, speaking in his usual nasal whine, asserted, "I don't know that there have been any problems" at Drexel. The SEC lawyers were dumbfounded. Black repeated several times that he didn't see any evidence of wrongdoing and added, arrogantly in the SEC's view, that "we" would need much more proof from the SEC before reaching any agreement.

Black's posture enraged not only the enforcement staff but the commissioners. The SEC retaliated by insisting, on top of their other demands, that Milken and Lowell be fired, that Drexel be barred from any junk-bond underwritings for two years, and—a demand that enraged Black—that the Beverly Hills office be closed and moved to New York. With the exception of the firing of Milken, Lynch himself hadn't originally cared about these provisions; he had simply seen them as bargaining chips. But the commissioners were now so angry that they dug in and refused to drop any of the demands.

Black continued his obstreperous ways, and the SEC became convinced that his mission was to sabotage any possibility of an SEC settlement—which would, in turn, cause Drexel's criminal plea bargain to unravel. Joseph wasn't so sure; the tactics struck him as Black's usual negotiating style, which was to be as offensive as possible to the other side. But with negotiations near collapse, he went to Washington to meet Lynch.

Joseph was at his most reasonable. He was tired of all the fighting; he wanted to put the nightmare behind the firm. "Gary," he began, "you've got to tell me honestly. Do you want to shut Drexel down? Or are you trying to set new compliance standards, ones that could be a model for the whole industry? Because if you're determined to shut us down, we won't settle with Rudy Giuliani. We'll get RICO'd. Let it be. But if you want to set a compliance model, that's our goal, too. So what's the game?"

"The latter," Lynch replied. "We're not trying to put you out of business. We're not trying to punish you further." Joseph agreed to remove Black from the negotiations and work hard toward an agreement. Relations between Lynch and Joseph now seemed so reasonable and constructive that each wondered how differently the whole affair might have gone had they adopted this posture two years ago, before their first negotiations had collapsed in acrimony.

With Lynch's and Joseph's new rapport, and with Black gone, the negotiations regained a modicum of civility. Sorte and Tannenbaum were able to convince Lynch and his colleagues that the internal situation at Drexel was volatile; that any sense of vindictiveness toward Milken could rupture the fragile support for the firm's settlement. The SEC agreed to drop its demands that the Beverly Hills office be relocated and that Drexel be barred from junk-bond underwritings. It wouldn't relent, however, on the fate of the Milken brothers: they had to be gone before the SEC would entertain any settlement. On this front, Joseph took matters into his own hands, recognizing that the moment had come to break the news to Milken. As he had done the day of the board vote on the guilty plea, Joseph reached Milken in Beverly Hills by phone.

Milken began by telling Joseph he was going through tough times, that his kids had been beaten up at school, that they were being taunted for having a criminal as a father. At this point, Joseph didn't know whether to believe Milken or not. "Michael, I know you've got a lot of concerns," Joseph said, but then he got to the crux. "From my point of view, I'd rather you resign than have to terminate you. But it's your choice. How do you want to handle this?"

Milken seemed startled, even though his departure had plainly been a condition of the plea bargain. He sounded wistful. "I thought I'd work here forever," he said softly. But he agreed that he and Lowell would take a leave of absence and eventually resign, sparing Joseph the task of firing them. The lawyers could work out the details, they agreed, and then hung up. It was their last conversation.

At the U.S. attorney's office, change was in the air, and a new sense of urgency. Giuliani, on his way out of office, wanted to resolve the Freeman and Milken cases. He was immensely frustrated, he told Baird, that the Freeman case hadn't made more progress. Freeman's lawyers were pressing hard for a settlement that would involve dropping the criminal charges in return for settling related SEC charges, and Giuliani warned Bruce Baird that he was seriously considering that approach. A loss on the Freeman front could be outweighed by a Milken conviction.

Cartusciello, Carroll, and others working on the cases had misgivings. Princeton-Newport still hadn't gone to trial; success for the government in that case might finally pressure Regan, Newberg, and the other defendants to capitulate and finally cooperate. That meant that the Freeman investigation had yet to exhaust all possibilities for a breakthrough. But on the Milken front, Carroll agreed to approach the Milken camp again, despite its continued public defiance. He contacted Litt at Williams & Connolly and began some preliminary talks; he was encouraged when Liman stepped into the negotiations. That meant Milken, possibly for the first time, was taking the negotiations seriously.

But the talks stalled when Milken insisted that Lowell be granted immunity as a part of any settlement. Giuliani was deeply disappointed. To his credit, he put the brakes on hasty efforts to resolve matters before his departure. Without a Milken conviction to soften the impact, there was no further thought of abandoning the Freeman case. Giuliani left office at the end of January 1989, and was immediately attacked by the Milken public relations forces for his handling of the cases. As the campaign unfolded, they became the most publicized blots on a largely outstanding record of convictions.

Word of the Milken negotiations leaked out to *The Wall Street Journal* even as Milken's lawyers continued to insist to Joseph and Curnin that no settlement talks were underway. Milken's lawyers released a statement: "Discussions between prosecutors and defense attorneys are routine in any criminal case, especially where the Department of Justice has authorized a [racketeering] prosecution. In this case, the prosecutors approached us and made certain proposals, which we rejected. There are now no discussions between us and the U.S. Attorney. Mr. Milken and his attorneys are preparing his defense. If Mr. Milken is indicted, he will plead not guilty and defend himself vigorously."

But with a new interim U.S. attorney in place—Benito Romano, a former Giuliani aide who returned from private practice at Giuliani's behest to take up the post—Milken's lawyers resumed plea bargaining almost immediately, testing the new regime's resolve. Incentives for a plea bargain were strong on both sides. Despite their confidence, the prosecutors, exhausted by the long two-and-a-half-year investigation, were facing the prospect of a long, complicated trial. This type of complex financial fraud case had never been tested before a jury. For Milken, if he were going to plead, doing so before indictment had obvious advantages. It would enable him to put the case behind him before being subjected to public disclosure of the full scope of the government's case. Carroll again called Litt at Williams & Connolly to start the process.

Weeks of talks ensued. The prosecutors knew the Milken camp was serious when Sandler himself flew in from the West Coast and met with Baird at St. Andrews Plaza. Baird was curious about Sandler's role. Even though Milken had both Paul, Weiss and Williams & Connolly—two of the most sophisticated criminal law firms in the country—representing him, Sandler seemed to be calling the shots. He said little at the meeting and seemed to be trying to gauge Baird's strength and sincerity more than the merits of the government's case. He acted as if he suspected that the government's entire investigation and threat to indict Milken were some kind of subterfuge. Baird did his best to convey to him that a settlement offer wasn't a sign of weakness—that if it were rejected by Milken, the government would obtain his indictment.

By late March, the prosecutors had put an offer on the table. Many details remained to be resolved, such as the amount of any fine. But Milken had never shown any concern about the money; that could easily be negotiated. Given the recent testimony by Peizer and Dahl, the offer was a favorable one for Milken: a guilty plea to just two felony counts, three if the deal also included immunity for Lowell. But, as is routine in most plea agreements, Milken would have to admit wrongdoing and agree to cooperate with the government.

Baird, Carroll, and Fardella, the prosecutors most involved in the case, agonized over the deal. They had genuine concerns that it was too favorable to Milken. They still had investigative leads worth pursuing. But they made the offer, and Milken's lawyers indicated that they had a deal. Even though Flumenbaum and Sandler apparently continued to insist on Milken's innocence, both Liman and Litt seemed to be favoring a plea bargain. Still, until Milken's formal consent was obtained, nothing could be certain. Milken was given a deadline of 3 P.M. on Wednesday, March 29, after which he would be indicted.

The day arrived with no word from Beverly Hills. Copying machines at the U.S. attorney's office began to whir as the huge, 98-count Milken indictment was reproduced and press releases announcing the indictment were prepared. The most startling thing about the indictment wasn't its length or its contents. It contained most of the same charges as in the SEC's complaints, focusing on the Boesky scheme and the $5.3 million payment, as well as the Princeton-Newport scheme. It omitted all of the Dahl and Peizer revelations, most of which were still under investigation. What was eye-popping were the dollars involved. The indictment revealed, for the first time, that Milken had earned as much as $550 million in a single year from what it termed a "racketeering enterprise," and the government demanded that a $1.2 billion bond be posted under the racketeering statute.

That Thursday afternoon, Carroll and Fardella arrived in Romano's office in St. Andrews Plaza to wait for the expected call from the Milken forces. The grand jury waited in the courthouse, standing by for the 3 P.M. deadline. As time passed with no word, Fardella left to join the grand jury at the courthouse. The jurors had already heard the government's remaining evidence, and Fardella had reviewed the case for them. All that remained was a vote.

Expecting that the case would end that day with a Milken settlement, Litt had planned a trip to Disney World with his family. He sat by his phone, waiting for news. Liman had scheduled a trip to France. He, too, waited for word from Beverly Hills. As the morning wore on, Milken stopped taking phone calls. He was described as closeted in a room with his wife.

Litt watched the clock move past noon; phone lines hummed as he talked to co-counsel, trying to figure out what was going on. He spoke to Carroll, who warned that there would be no reprieve. Finally he got through in Beverly Hills and Milken came to the phone.

"I can't decide," Milken said. "I've got these concerns . . ."

Litt cut him off impatiently. "You've got to decide. They're going to the grand jury." Milken continued to waver. Finally, as the 3 P.M. deadline passed with no decision, Litt despaired. He called Romano's office, saying it looked like they had failed to reach a deal.

Carroll was crestfallen. Tired but resigned, he left to convey the news in person to Fardella, who finally asked the grand jury for a vote. It voted to indict Milken.

Still, the government did nothing. A press conference at St. Andrews Plaza was scheduled for 4 P.M., then postponed. Late that afternoon, as copies of the indictment were being readied for distribution and the press conference was about to begin, Baird joined Romano in his office to discuss plans for the next steps in the case. Romano's phone rang. It was Liman. He was breathless, calling from a pay phone at Kennedy International Airport, where he was waiting for the departure of his flight to France.

Milken had finally made up his mind. "He's ready to reach an agreement," Liman said.

"I'm sorry," Romano responded after a pause. Without even conferring with Baird, he added, "It's too late."

15.

Milken had just made the worst trade of his career. Romano and Baird marveled at the turn of events, even as they wondered what could possibly have been going through Milken's mind. Perhaps, as a trader, Milken had simply believed a better deal could be extracted by defying the deadline.

The two prosecutors were relieved that the deadline had passed. They had worried that the plea bargain was too lenient, and had agreed that morning that the offer would be withdrawn after the deadline. They wouldn't reconsider. Still, they said nothing of Liman's call, not even to their own colleagues. Nor did Liman inform the Milken entourage.

When the press conference finally convened, at about 5:15 P.M., Romano announced that Milken had been indicted on 98 counts, including RICO charges. He noted that the bond was the largest amount ever sought by the government against an individual defendant. Milken, as he had agreed, began his leave of absence from Drexel and issued a statement. "In America, an indictment marks the beginning of the legal process, not the end. After almost 2½ years of leaks and distortions, I am now eager to present all the facts in an open and unbiased forum. I will plead not guilty to the charges and vigorously fight these accusations. I am confident that in the end I will be vindicated."

Milken pleaded not guilty two weeks later, secretly entering the U.S. courthouse in Manhattan three hours before his scheduled arraignment. It was his first meeting with the judge assigned to his case, Kimba Wood, a recent Reagan appointee with a gentle manner, a keen mind, and flowing dark hair. There was little in her record to suggest how she would approach a major securities fraud case.

Milken, tanned and looking relaxed, stood before Judge Wood with Liman and Flumenbaum on either side. His wife, Lori, sat with

Sandler in the first bench behind him, along with a capacity crowd of hundreds, mostly reporters. "How do you feel today, physically?" Judge Wood asked. "Okay, Your Honor," Milken replied. "Are you under the care of a physician or psychiatrist?" "No, Your Honor," he replied. Indeed, his lawyers thought his spirits seemed better than they had been for weeks. The indictment itself had come as something of a relief, particularly since it still relied heavily on the Boesky allegations. Milken, once again, believed he was going to win at trial. "How do you wish to plead?" Judge Wood asked. "Not guilty, Your Honor," Milken replied firmly.

Milken had now inherited the notoriety once reserved for Boesky. A phalanx of helmeted New York City policemen had to hold back the crowds of onlookers and television crews as he left the courthouse and hurried into a waiting limousine. Hundreds of supporters organized by Robinson, Lake wore T-shirts and baseball caps that read MIKE MILKEN: WE BELIEVE IN YOU. In an unprecedented display of business support for a charged felon, major Milken clients took out full-page newspaper ads in *The Wall Street Journal, The New York Times,* and other papers, repeating the refrain, "We Believe in You."

But Milken's public-relations effort was diverging ever further from the truth. In the wake of the indictment, a new wave of witnesses against Milken cut deals with the government. David Solomon was probably the most damaging; he provided complete disclosure of the illegal arrangement between him and Milken in the Finsbury and MacPherson matters, as well as other crimes. Reed Harmon, another Beverly Hills employee involved in the Boesky transactions, obtained immunity and testified. Milken's dealings with Columbia Savings and Loan, including the illegal tax trades, were now under intense investigation.

In March 1989, the government began its first courtroom test of a case arising from the Levine and Boesky allegations: the trial of Lisa Jones on perjury charges. Her lawyer, Brian O'Neill, could do little except appeal to the jury's sympathies for the young former runaway. Jones took the witness stand and, weeping, told the jury, "I was scared in the grand jury room" and "I just think I answered inaccurately because I couldn't remember." The jury took just four hours to convict Jones on all counts: five of perjury and two of obstruction of justice. Jones sobbed as the verdict was read. In an obvious message to other likely witnesses, Romano added that the Jones case demonstrates that the government takes perjury charges "very seriously."

A far more important test loomed, however: the trial of Regan and his co-defendants in the Princeton-Newport case. The Milken forces had often said they didn't think a jury could understand such complicated financial cases. The trial began in June and lasted for five weeks of often tedious, complicated testimony. The jury listened to dozens of the tapes seized by the government in its raid of Princeton-Newport's headquarters. Both Will Hale, the dismissed Princeton-Newport employee, and more significantly, Fred Joseph, testified. As a government witness, Joseph explained Drexel's own rules restricting trading in clients' securities.

The jury spent barely two days deliberating, a relatively short time given the complexity of the 64 separate felony counts. Defendants took that as a sign that they would be vindicated; James Regan, in particular, had never wavered in his belief that no jury would convict him. As Cartusciello had put it in his closing arguments, the defendants were guilty of an "arrogance that everything is so complicated and so clever that no one will be able to piece it together."

On July 31, as the jurors filed back into the courtroom, Zarzecki, who had been featured so prominently in the tapes, smiled broadly and made a thumbs-up gesture toward spectators. The mood changed abruptly as the foreman delivered the verdict: guilty on 63 of the 64 counts. The wives of many of the defendants wept.

There was gloom in the Robinson, Lake offices. Ken Lerer, in particular, seemed devastated by the verdict. He'd been prominent among those confidently predicting an acquittal or, at worst, a mistrial.

For the prosecutors, however, the sweeping guilty verdict didn't produce the immediate breakthroughs they'd hoped for. Despite renewed pressure, Newberg and Regan, the two defendants probably in the position to give the government valuable information about Milken and Freeman, refused.

With Regan still recalcitrant, almost every investigative avenue in the Freeman case had been exhausted. Cartusciello and McEnany were making little headway. No one within Goldman, Sachs broke ranks, a reflection in part of an institutional culture that had placed the firm ahead of its individual partners for generations. The prosecutors had pursued the Beatrice lead from the *Journal* article, questioning Bunny Lasker about his call to Freeman. Lasker claimed he didn't remember it. Increasingly desperate, the prosecutors went so far as to offer Tabor immunity in return for any testimony that could further implicate Freeman. But Tabor, sensing the government was making no progress, refused. Wigton was all but forgotten.

Siegel, isolated in Florida, was growing increasingly desperate to be sentenced. Freeman, Goldman, Sachs, and Drexel had hired private detective Jules Kroll, and the detective's investigators were shadowing all Siegel's moves. Once, while working on setting up a computer camp for children in Jacksonville, Siegel was in the office of a potential donor when the phone rang. The caller identified himself as "Phil Spence," a free-lance reporter for the Associated Press. He told the businessman that he was doing a story on "Ivan Boesky's relationship with Martin Siegel." He asked him whether Siegel had a "hidden interest" in the man's company. When "Phil" refused to further identify himself or leave a number, the businessman hung up. He also pulled out of Siegel's computer project.

Siegel and Rakoff complained to Cartusciello, who pursued the matter and found there was no Phil Spence at the AP. The caller was actually a Kroll operative. The same person called all of Siegel's former neighbors in Connecticut. When Siegel visited a friend in New York, "Phil" called the friend. "I know you're hiding money for Marty Siegel," he began. "We know this." Later, a man showed up at the friend's apartment and identified himself as a New York Police detective, showing a badge. The friend let him in, and he looked around. Later the friend called the police—and learned that no such detective existed. From the man's license plate, the U.S. attorney's office was able to trace the detective to Kroll Associates.

The prosecutors were so angry they threatened to charge Kroll with obstruction of justice and harassment of a federal witness. Kroll agreed to stop. Then Kroll operatives started contacting parents in the Siegels' children's car pool. An investigator bribed their 16-year-old baby-sitter with $50, asking her whether Siegel paid her in cash and whether she'd seen Siegel smoke marijuana. The Siegels were constantly interrupted by phone calls in the middle of the night; they had to change their phone number three times. Prosecutors warned Kroll again, and the incidents tapered off.

Although unpleasant for Siegel, the $1.5 million Kroll effort produced laughably insignificant results. Still, Siegel wondered how much more he could take. Every time the Freeman case was mentioned in the press, Siegel was pilloried as a liar. In January he met with Baird in New York and all but begged to be sentenced. Baird again talked him out of it.

Freeman's lawyers, Robert B. Fiske, Jr., of Davis Polk and Wardwell and Paul Curran, of Kaye, Scholer, and Goldman, Sachs's Pedowitz, were also effective in their continuing meetings with the government. Unlike Milken's lawyers, they never claimed that Freeman was innocent. They never insulted the prosecutors' intelligence and judgment by claiming that everything Siegel said was a lie or that Freeman was a national treasure. Instead, they produced voluminous research demonstrating possible alternative sources for Freeman's and Siegel's trading information. They didn't claim that these were the actual sources; they simply emphasized that they could raise doubts in the minds of any jury. Their efforts demonstrated the difficulty of proving an insider-trading case against any professional arbitrageur, even with a cooperating witness like Siegel.

Still, Baird and his colleagues were prepared to present the case to a jury. They thought they could rely on a strong performance by Siegel and corroborating documentary evidence. Then, finally, came a lucky breakthrough.

In a last effort to corroborate Siegel's testimony, the prosecutors immunized Frank Brosens, one of Freeman's top aides in the Goldman, Sachs arbitrage department, and brought him before the Freeman grand jury. At first, Brosens provided nothing new or of value. Then, on the point of giving up, McEnany asked him, "Is there anything else you remember?" Brosens seemed uncomfortable, and asked if he could confer with his lawyer. A brief recess was called.

When Brosens returned, he answered the question: "Yes." To the amazement of the prosecutors, he acknowledged that Freeman had called Siegel during the Beatrice deal. Freeman hadn't been able to resist repeating Siegel's confirmation of Bunny Lasker's tip: "Your bunny has a good nose." It proved a fatal indiscretion.

At last, the government had obtained a shred of corroboration. It produced more startling effects than expected. Brosens was immediately debriefed by the Goldman, Sachs and Freeman lawyers, and repeated his damaging admission. They were alarmed. When *The Wall Street Journal* article containing the "bunny" quote had appeared more than a year earlier, they had assumed that government prosecutors had leaked the information to the *Journal* in order to pressure Freeman. That meant, they reasoned, that the government had to have a source—presumably Siegel—who could testify to the exchange with Freeman.

Yet Siegel had not been questioned by the prosecutors about the "bunny" quote until June 1989, when he was again brought before the grand jury. Asked about the Beatrice incident, and the "bunny" remark, Siegel recalled talking that day to Henry Kravis and to Freeman. But the best he could say about the actual quote was that it sounded like something he might have said. He didn't remember it, and he didn't remember giving Freeman inside information about Beatrice.

Freeman's lawyers fell into the same trap that had snared Milken's and Drexel's: they simply couldn't believe that reporters could have obtained their information from anyone but the government. They failed to consider the possibility that the government had known nothing about the "bunny" exchange before the *Journal* article. They assumed that Siegel would testify to his end of the conversation, and they now concluded—erroneously—that the government had two witnesses, not just Brosens.

Bob Rubin, Freeman's longtime supporter and now co-chairman of Goldman, Sachs, was finally swayed in his view of the case. He had always thought Freeman had a "triable" case, one he had a good chance of winning. Yet research into the makeup of any potential jury hadn't been encouraging. The public clearly held all arbitrageurs in low esteem, and Freeman had earned huge amounts of money. The Princeton-Newport verdict had confirmed Rubin's fears that the public was ill-disposed toward wealthy Wall Street executives.

Moreover, Freeman didn't dispute the facts about Beatrice; he had never denied receiving the "bunny" tip, or having traded on the basis of the information. And the Princeton-Newport verdict had been particularly hard on Freeman. One lawyer thought "the fight just went out of him" after Regan was convicted.

Rubin himself now decided that Freeman had made an "error in judgment," as he told his colleagues at Goldman, Sachs. If the vast conspiracy once alleged by the government could be boiled down to a single communication, "Your bunny has a good nose," Rubin was confident that the case could be disposed of with minimal damage to Goldman, Sachs. Indeed, the government would probably seem a laughingstock.

The Freeman forces approached Baird and the prosecutors and indicated a willingness to consider a guilty plea to one count of insider trading based on the Beatrice incident. A battle erupted immediately among the prosecutors. Cartusciello and McEnany, adamantly opposed to such a favorable deal for Freeman, were willing to go ahead and try the case. Baird, however, thought the deal had much to recommend it. It would be an admission of guilt, it would remove Freeman from the securities business, and it would subject him to a possible prison term; the SEC could deal with the loose ends in a civil suit.

Baird didn't think he could keep putting Siegel off; he'd been waiting to be sentenced for over two years. In addition, unlike Milken's, Freeman's case wasn't growing stronger with age. Baird had vowed to see the Freeman case through, but he was anxious to leave the U.S. attorney's office for private practice.

For Romano, the settlement was also an opportunity to serve his friend and mentor Giuliani, now caught up in the heat of the mayoral campaign. Disposing of the case that summer would eliminate it as a continuing electoral issue, demonstrating that the man Giuliani had arrested had in fact been guilty of a crime and not the innocent victim Giuliani's critics were holding up. Romano sided with Baird. Though the younger prosecutors continued to grumble, they were finally won over with a promise that they could introduce evidence of all of Freeman's other transgressions at his sentencing hearing.

On August 17, Freeman appeared in federal court and agreed to plead guilty to a felony. He simultaneously resigned from Goldman, Sachs, the firm that had been "an integral part of my life" for 19 years, he said. In his letter of resignation to Goldman, Sachs senior partner John Weinberg, he admitted his guilt in Beatrice but didn't apologize. He insisted he wasn't guilty of any other wrongdoing in his entire career and, saying the investigation had been "a nightmare for me and my family," implied that he was pleading guilty largely to end the investigation. The plea didn't require Freeman to cooperate with the government, and he never did.

Goldman, Sachs tried to minimize the impact, seizing the opportunity to attack the prosecutors rather than a partner who had just admitted a felony. In a statement distributed to everyone at the firm, Goldman, Sachs said, "Bob has been subjected to an arrest that the prosecutors have since characterized as a mistake, a withdrawn indictment, the promise of new charges in record time followed by a grueling two-year investigation, and a series of highly-publicized formal allegations and innuendoes that far exceed anything he actually did."

But some at Goldman, Sachs were deeply disturbed by the admission that accompanied Freeman's plea. Freeman described a world in which, as Goldman, Sachs's top arbitrageur, he had routinely gained market information denied other investors. In the Beatrice situation, for example, he acknowledged that he had talked to Henry Kravis about the deal; that he had learned that Richard Nye was selling his Beatrice stock because Goldman, Sachs handled Nye's trading; that he had spoken to Nye; that Lasker had called him reporting problems in the Beatrice deal; and that he had then called Siegel.

Even if it weren't criminal, the free swapping of confidential information unavailable to other investors was scandalous, showing the hazards of allowing a large investment bank to engage in arbitrage trading. Nonetheless, unlike Kidder, Peabody, which volunteered to get out of arbitrage after concluding that it represented an inherent conflict of interest, Goldman, Sachs's arbitrage department remains one of Wall Street's most active and lucrative.

The investigation of Wigton and Tabor was closed. Wigton showed remarkably little bitterness over his earlier handcuffing, displaying to the end the stiff upper lip of the Kidder, Peabody he had known. As the Freeman plea hearing began, and the prosecutors announced that his ordeal was over, Wigton was on an exercise bike at his health club; he'd left word he didn't want to be disturbed. After absorbing the news, he proceeded to play his usual round of golf at the country club. He said later that he felt the prosecutors had been "gentlemen."

Siegel was sitting in his kitchen, having completed the day's shopping in his role as househusband, when the phone rang and his lawyer Audrey Strauss broke the news of Freeman's plea. Siegel was stunned. He couldn't believe he'd gone through such an ordeal only to have it collapse in a single felony plea. He'd actually begun to look forward to testifying. He knew he was telling the truth, and he was sure a jury would believe him. Finally he'd get the vindication he felt he deserved. The public would see that he had tried to do the right thing.

The end of the case shattered Siegel's remaining faith in the government, which he had once assumed would make everything work out. Even worse, he still couldn't be sentenced, because now he was being held in reserve as a possible witness at Freeman's sentencing hearing. Siegel complained bitterly to Cartusciello, who told him he'd tried to hold out for a Freeman plea to at least two felony counts. "I can't say this in open court," Cartusciello told Siegel and Rakoff, "but we totally mishandled this."

A week after Milken's indictment, as more than 3,000 participants packed the Beverly Hilton for the 1989 Predators' Ball, his loyalists again confronted Joseph about the Milken tribute video. Led by Lorraine Spurge, they met with Joseph in his hotel suite and told him they'd walk out of the conference if he didn't allow the video to be shown. Joseph was once more thrust into the impossible task of managing a Milken-dominated firm. As he had so often, he relented. On Thursday evening, the emotional tribute ran, complete with Milken voice-overs and stirring music. Even in absentia, Milken was the star of the Predators' Ball.

Hovering over the proceedings was a giant banner that read DREXEL BURNHAM PRESENTS HIGH-YIELD CITY 2089; under it was a model of a revolving space station featuring products of Drexel clients. But Don Engel had a premonition that this Predators' Ball would be the last. Even the surprise entertainer—singer Sheena Easton— seemed second-rate. At the RJR presentation, Engel felt lonely and isolated without Milken at his side. When the session was over and the participants had left the room, Engel lowered his head and wept.

Shortly after the conference ended, Drexel at last concluded its

SEC negotiations and the terms of the settlement were announced. In a sweeping consent decree, the SEC all but took control of Drexel. Most startling was the announcement that John Shad, the recently retired SEC chairman, would become chairman of Drexel. Joseph would remain chief executive. SEC-approved Drexel officials would be required to scrutinize all of Drexel's continuing activities. Drexel won its battle to keep its high-yield operations in Beverly Hills, but the settlement still included a condemnation of Milken and Lowell, and required that Drexel buy out their equity in the firm and have no further contacts with them.

"Assuming these agreements are approved in due course," Joseph told the firm's employees, "we can get along with the rest of our lives and careers. I think we can all be proud of how we've come through. Ninety-six percent of the most important people in the firm are still here. I think that's an extraordinary performance."

Drexel agreed to pay Milken $70 million for his equity stake in the firm. Milken announced that he had formed a new company, International Capital Access Group. He issued a press release, drafted by Robinson, Lake, that said the new company would devote its resources to "the creation of ownership opportunities for employees, minorities, and unions." Lerer denied that Milken was trying to appeal to potential blue-collar and minority jurors.

Pro-Milken dissent was still an issue at Drexel. To keep top performers, Joseph continued to buy their loyalty with lavish bonuses. He guaranteed that everyone's 1989 compensation would be at least 75% of what they earned in 1988—regardless of the profitability of the firm. Black, for example, was to be paid $20 million; Kissick, $11 million. Kissick took charge of the former Milken empire and Black became co-head of corporate finance. They were replaced on the firm's underwriting assistance committee, the group that reviewed the quality of potential deals, by junior employees with neither the experience nor stature to question senior officials, no matter how risky some of the deals appeared to be. It was a recipe for disaster.

Black and Peter Ackerman seemed bent on doing deals and generating up-front fees no matter what the future risks or consequences, in a campaign they had begun even before the Drexel agreement to plead guilty. In fall 1988, at Black's insistence, Drexel had agreed to back a hostile takeover for West-Point Pepperell by Milken loyalist William Farley, whose Fruit of the Loom was already heavily leveraged with Drexel-backed junk bonds. In early January 1989, Ackerman brought in a deal proposed by former Boesky investor Meshulam Riklis, a $175 million buyout of Trans Resources, a company that owned the Haifa Chemical Co. in Israel.

Stephen Weinroth, the member of the underwriting assistance committee who had argued against financing Boesky, was appalled by both the West-Point and Trans Resources deals. Weinroth's objections were shouted down by Black and Ackerman. The more junior members of the committee sat meekly as Black and Ackerman forced the deals through. Disgusted, Weinroth stopped bothering to attend the meetings. He couldn't get Joseph's attention; the chief executive was too busy dealing with the government and trying to restructure a firm that could survive the settlement.

The new deals showed that without Milken to sell the bonds—bribing buyers if necessary—the Beverly Hills sales force couldn't find a market for them. The era when Milken could force-feed product to captive clients had vanished. Potential buyers actually began scrutinizing the terms of Drexel-backed bond deals and, in some cases, they were appalled. Drexel ended up having to buy most of the junk paper out of its own capital, which left the firm with a growing portfolio of its own bonds. The firm was stuck with $250 million in Farley loans alone—nearly a quarter of Drexel's equity capital. By the end of the summer, the firm had a huge portfolio of junk bonds in companies such as Resorts International, Braniff, Integrated Resources, SCI Holdings, Gillett Holdings, Simplicity Pattern, Consolidated Oil and Gas, Hillsborough, and Southmark—all highly leveraged Drexel deals.

Joseph was alarmed. He managed to prevent Black from financing a ruinously high bid for Prime Computer by Drexel client Bennett LeBow, and he tried to rein in Ackerman after a disastrous private placement for Paramount Petroleum that cost Drexel $50 million. Ackerman was furious, and despite his $100 million guarantee, quit working for all practical purposes. He moved to the London office, ostensibly to develop business opportunities in Europe. Instead, Ackerman told colleagues, he planned to begin work on a book. In Beverly Hills, a cartoon circulated depicting Ackerman escaping over a wall at night with a large bag of money.

Despite the large bonus promises, Ackerman wasn't the only problem. Lorraine Spurge and Bob Davidow, still angry over Joseph's attempt to suppress the tribute to Milken, quit the firm, withdrawing their equity stakes. Other Milken loyalists also defected, and many parts of the firm suffered, especially the retail brokerage network. As individual investors troubled by the guilty plea left, Drexel had to offer its brokers higher and higher salaries to stay. Even with the large salaries, the number of brokers shrank from about 1,400 to 1,200. It was impossible to recruit new brokers—no one wanted to work at Drexel. And as expenses rose, economies of scale declined. Joseph projected a loss in the retail system of $40 to $60 million in 1989 alone.

By the time of the Predators' Ball bond conference in April, Joseph had known that a drastic restructuring was imminently necessary. The brokerage system, once the foundation of the firm, would have to be slashed. Joseph felt terrible. Throughout the investigation, he had called on the loyalty of Drexel's brokers, and most had given it without question. Joseph had pledged repeatedly that Drexel would stay in the retail brokerage business "forever." In a mid-April speech, however, he said, "The world has changed for Drexel. We're reviewing all our businesses." The audience of brokers gave him a standing ovation anyway, and Joseph couldn't understand why.

A few days later, on April 8, Joseph announced that Drexel was abandoning the retail brokerage business, as well as municipal bonds and foreign stocks. It was the end of Joseph's dream of building a full-service firm to rival Goldman, Sachs. The 10,000 employees he had so often invoked to justify the settlement with the government were now slashed to just over 5,000. Brokers, suddenly thrown out of work, were bitter at what they considered a betrayal. For Joseph, the choice had been painful but clear: the firm's survival was at stake.

As Joseph wrestled with mounting administrative problems, more threatening trends appeared in Milken's vast junk-bond empire. In the past, whenever Drexel's large bond issuers had begun to threaten default on the bonds, Milken had simply arranged an exchange offer, restructuring the debt, usually with even more leverage. The process, resembling a pyramid scheme, had masked credit problems and given Drexel's bonds an enviably low default rate. Now the Beverly Hills sales force found it impossible to roll over weak debt into new bonds. Any crack in the junk-bond façade had dire potential, because Milken's big clients—from savings and loans like Columbia to insurance companies like Executive Life—were already so loaded with junk paper that any decline in the value of their junk portfolios would curb their ability to absorb more.

The crack, when it came, was an earthquake. Just days after Milken's formal resignation in June, Integrated Resources, a seller of tax-shelter partnerships that had diversified with $2 billion in Milken-financed junk bonds into a $15 billion insurance and real estate empire, defaulted on its interest payments. The quintessential Milken success story, Integrated had loyally issued junk bonds, invested in them, and become one of Milken's biggest captive clients. Integrated had attracted millions of dollars, the savings of unwitting investors, in its financial products. Its stock price had soared from $7 in 1981 to $46 in 1983. Even though the tax reform act of 1986 had curbed its profits on sales of tax shelters, Milken debt had propelled it into new lines of business. Top executives and major owners—members of the Zises family—had paid themselves huge salaries.

But with its underlying business eroding, Integrated was a house of cards, a microcosm of the whole junk-bond empire. Infusions of new debt could mask its financial deterioration for only so long. Recognizing that, Milken himself had been arranging an equity infusion and acquisition of control by another captive client, ICH Corporation, a Louisville-based insurer (which eventually did buy out the Zises' interests) in December 1988. It was a typical Milken maneuver to prop up a deteriorating junk issuer, but the pressures of the investigation and Drexel's guilty plea intervened. The ICH deal was never completed. Without Milken, the Beverly Hills sales force couldn't hope to sell more Integrated junk debt, and the company lurched inevitably toward a cash crisis.

In February 1990, Integrated would file for bankruptcy, wiping out the value of all of its junk bonds, including a sizable position held in Drexel's own inventory. Among the victims were thousands of investors, policyholders, and employees—a broad cross section of Americans, most of whom never knew Integrated had any connections to Drexel.

The collapse of Integrated caused alarm in the financial community, especially among the many former Milken clients who had to write off the value of their Integrated bonds. Alarm changed to panic in September, when giant retailer Campeau Corporation disclosed a liquidity crisis that meant it couldn't meet obligations on the billions in junk bonds it had issued to acquire first Allied Department Stores and then Federated (with such high-profile names in retailing as Bloomingdale's). The Campeau crisis was startling because the nation's economy was still growing. What might happen to the bonds of leveraged companies in a slow-down or recession?

It was as if the nation's investors had awakened from a decade-long dream and recognized finally that high returns could not be realized without increased risk. Even though Drexel wasn't involved with Campeau—the deal had been the brainchild of star investment banker Bruce Wasserstein and First Boston—investors now rushed to dump junk bonds at almost any price. Values across the board cascaded, affecting Drexel's most credit-worthy customers. It devastated the value of Drexel's own junk-bond portfolio, which couldn't be sold without flooding the market and further driving down prices. And Drexel's portfolio of junk bonds made up a dangerously high percentage of its assets.

Drexel's capital was further weakened when it paid the government $500 million, the bulk of its $650 million settlement payment. Its capital was also drained by payments to Milken and Lowell for their Drexel stock, as well as to Milken loyalists who were quitting and selling their equity stakes in the firm. To stem the defections, Joseph refused to allow firm officials to withdraw all their equity interest at once.

Joseph took one other symbolically significant step: he reined in Milken's and Lowell's legal expenses. As he had with Milken's skyrocketing compensation, Joseph felt he had to honor their original agreement: Drexel would pay Milken's legal costs. Even after Drexel's guilty plea, the firm had continued to pay all of Milken's legal fees, including his Robinson, Lake fees which were funding, among other things, the public-relations firm's efforts to sabotage the Drexel settlement. Milken's bills were running at a clip of $3 million a *month.* Payments to Paul, Weiss totaled about $2 million a month. When Joseph questioned the size of the billings and asked Paul, Weiss to itemize the fees and disbursements, Liman flatly refused.

Joseph, while not reneging on the agreement to pay for Milken's defense, put a cap on the fees of $1.25 million a month. As he put it, Milken might be entitled to the best legal defense money could buy, but he wasn't entitled to *all* the legal defense that money could buy. Liman was irate, telling a reporter, "The quality of Michael Milken's representation will not be affected by Drexel's nickeling and diming their lawyers."

Soon Joseph was also wrangling with Milken over what he was still owed by the firm. In the wake of the guilty plea, Joseph had recalculated the bonus pool for the year, charging Milken's high-yield operation with a pro rata share of legal defense costs. Though he was no longer at the firm; though payment was being held up by the government, and though he presumably had weightier matters at hand, Milken still fought the cost allocation with tenacity. Drexel and Milken's lawyers never reached an agreement.

As internal bickering mounted, Drexel's capital was plunging, from $1.5 billion in January 1989 to less than $700 million by October. In mid-October, another event beyond Drexel's control battered the firm. UAL Corporation, the parent of United Air Lines, announced that it couldn't complete a leveraged buyout that had pushed the company's stock above $200 a share. The UAL failure crystallized the symbiotic relationship between the health of the junk-bond market and the ability to mount the takeovers that had so pushed up prices in the stock market. Wary buyers were no longer willing to invest in junk bonds; without that market, stocks couldn't command stratospheric prices. The bubble burst on October 13, 1989, in a smaller-scale rerun of Black Monday. With takeover stocks leading the plunge, the market dropped nearly 200 points, In terms of points, it was the the second-largest drop ever.

The October "minicrash," as it was quickly dubbed on Wall Street, proved a more long-lasting harbinger of trouble than the dramatic October 1987 crash. Beginning with Integrated and Campeau, and then continuing with alarming regularity, junk-bond issuers began to default on their obligations. Payment terms in highly leveraged deals, especially those completed in the frenzied days prior to the 1987 crash, had managed to disguise the underlying folly of the investments, often through the issuance of so-called "zero-coupon" bonds, "payments in kind," and "re-sets" which required no payments whatsoever for several years. Eventually the piper had to be paid. Like Integrated, the whole junk market began to tumble as companies admitted they couldn't fulfill the promises they had been so eager to make just several years before.

By the time the financial data for 1989 were collected and analyzed, a growing suspicion of many participants in the junk-bond market, even of some Milken loyalists, was confirmed: Milken's oft-repeated premise that "investors obtained better returns on low-grade issues than on high-grades" was false. It was the criminals who earned astronomical returns. During the decade ending in 1990, Lipper Analytical Services reported, money invested in the average junk-bond fund grew 145%. That was, in fact, worse than returns on the same amount of money invested in stocks (207%); investment-grade corporate bonds, so often ridiculed by Milken (202%); U.S. treasury bonds (177%); and equal to returns from low-risk money market funds. During the decade's last year, junk bonds returned a negative 11.2%.

With benefit of hindsight, Milken's "genius" seemed his ability to make so many believe his gospel of high return at low risk. As David Scheiber, a junk-bond portfolio manager at Far West Financial Services and a big Milken customer, told The Wall Street Journal in 1991, "Some people believed whatever Mike Milken said." But the way things turned out, "Bondholders got all the risk and very little of the upside."

Data also undercut the vigorous Robinson, Lake claims that Milken-raised capital had been the savior of entrepreneurs and small businesses. Of the 104 small firms involved in public issues of nonconvertible Drexel junk bonds since 1977, 24% had defaulted on their debt or were bankrupt by mid-1990—five times the default rate of comparable firms, according to Dun & Bradstreet.

With astonishing speed, some of Milken's biggest boosters began to collapse under the weight of the debt burdens they had embraced with such enthusiasm. Ralph Ingersoll lost control of his U.S. newspaper empire when he failed to make payments on his Drexel-generated bonds. William Farley couldn't complete the West-Point Pepperell acquisition. Even Tom Spiegel, the Milken apostle at Columbia Savings, was ousted and his savings and loan taken over by government regulators. Eventually, nearly every savings and loan that was a major player in Milken's ring of purchasers was declared insolvent and placed in the hands of government receivers.

Could Drexel itself survive? Joseph knew how grave the situation had become. He had already faced the possibility of the loss of Drexel's independence. In September—even before the October debacles in the junk-bond and stock markets—he had secretly begun a series of phone calls to top executives at every other major Wall Street firm, seeking an equity infusion or even a merger partner. It was a humiliating experience for the chief executive of the firm that had once terrorized the very firms he was calling. Many didn't even return his phone calls, and those that did dismissed the possibility, citing Drexel's still-unresolved liability in investors' civil lawsuits as an uncertainty that would prohibit any thought of merger. The truth was probably even worse: Drexel's reputation and admission to felonies made it anathema to its rivals, even if they still coveted the remnants of Drexel's junk-bond prowess. Joseph quickly learned the cost of Drexel's years of arrogance, its insistence on dominating offers, its refusal to share underwriting fees. Drexel had no friends on Wall Street.

Even as the firm's plight was becoming desperate, Joseph faced the prospect of making good on his promise that 1989 bonuses would be no less than 75% of those of 1988. The promise now looked foolhardy, but Joseph felt that if he reneged, he would lose all credibility and mass defections would destroy the firm. Instead, he began a series of meetings to persuade top performers to take a portion of their 1989 bonuses in Drexel preferred stock rather than cash. For the first time, Joseph asked employees to put the survival of the firm ahead of their own immediate financial interests. After all, he thought, no one among Drexel's top officials truly needed more cash. They were already rich.

Amazingly, Joseph had misunderstood the ethic of the Drexel culture, the mindset fostered by the firm and embodied in Milken: Drexel was nothing but a corporate vehicle for personal gain. When Joseph asked his stars to accept lower bonuses, howls of protest rose from Black and his allies. Ultimately Joseph persuaded Black to accept some preferred stock, though they fought bitterly over the exact amount. Kissick was more amenable, and he got the Beverly Hills group to agree. Joseph took all of his own $2.5 million bonus in preferred stock. Still, he could get his people, on average, to accept only 18% of their bonuses in stock. Drexel saved only $64 million in cash, as it paid out over $200 million of its desperately needed capital.

As 1990 began and the scope of Drexel's problems became more apparent, Drexel's short-term lenders refused further financing. The firm couldn't sell short-term commercial paper. As previous short-term loans came due, it had to make the payments out of its dwindling capital and couldn't refinance the debt. By February 1990, Drexel had paid out $575 million to cover commercial paper alone.

Joseph believed the firm still had $1 billion in capital, admittedly in investments like unsaleable junk bonds and equity interests in leveraged buyouts. He began planning some kind of an equity infusion, perhaps through a packaging and sale of the firm's best LBO stakes, as well as a shift of $300 million in capital from its regulated broker-dealer subsidiary into the Drexel holding company.

But it was the end of the road. On Friday, February 9, the SEC and New York Stock Exchange notified Drexel that it would not be permitted to reduce the capital of its regulated subsidiary. Joseph was stunned—he believed Kidder, Peabody had been allowed to go far below the regulatory minimums prior to its cash infusion from GE. But Kidder, Peabody had had the promise of the GE deal. The regulators considered Joseph's schemes for raising capital to be pipe dreams, and they valued Drexel's assets at far less than Drexel did. Once again, Joseph had underestimated how much damage the firm's fierce resistance and guilty plea had done with regulators. Unlike Drexel, Kidder, Peabody had cooperated. No one was inclined to do anything that even hinted at favorable treatment for Drexel.

Drexel collapsed with unnerving speed. Bankruptcy lawyers descended on the firm that weekend. On Monday, February 12, Joseph called Gerald Corrigan, the powerful head of the Federal Reserve Board of New York, desperately hoping that Corrigan would pressure the big New York banks he regulated to extend emergency loans to Drexel. Representatives of a group of banks convened in Drexel's Broad Street offices at 4 P.M. as Drexel made a plea for loans. Given the haste of the rescue effort, Joseph was ill prepared for their questions, and even though he discounted the value of Drexel's portfolio to a new low—$850 million—he failed to persuade them that it would yield substantial value over time. The banks left without making any commitments.

Joseph called Corrigan that night at about 11 P.M. Wasn't the Fed doing anything to help? Corrigan replied enigmatically that, while he wasn't telling Joseph how to run his business, "If I were you I'd talk to the chief executives of some of these banks directly." Joseph, grasping at any straw, took that as an indication that Corrigan must have pressured them.

He began an immediate series of calls, but got nowhere. When Joseph pressed the bankers on whether the Fed had encouraged them to help Drexel, he got no encouragement. Gradually he realized that the Fed had done nothing.

Now frantic, Joseph again called Corrigan, about midnight. "Is there some misunderstanding?" Joseph asked. "The banks aren't doing anything."

Corrigan sighed, and then replied, "Call Treasury. I'm afraid we have a different agenda."

Joseph knew he was doomed. The Secretary of the Treasury was none other than Nicholas Brady, the former head of Dillon, Read, who, Joseph believed, had never forgiven Drexel for the hostile raid on one of his largest clients, Unocal.

At 1 A.M. Corrigan called Joseph back. They were linked by conference call to Bush's new SEC chairman, Richard Breeden, and Corrigan told Joseph they spoke for Treasury Secretary Brady as well. Corrigan got directly to the point. "We see no light at the end of the tunnel here," he said. If Drexel entered voluntary bankruptcy proceedings, he added, the government would not have to step in and seize control of the firm and liquidate its remaining assets. They wanted Joseph's answer by 7 A.M.

Joseph hastily convened a meeting of the board at 6 A.M. As he told the gloomy and despairing gathering, "The four most powerful regulators"—Brady at Treasury, Corrigan at the Fed, Breeden at the SEC, and Phelan at the Stock Exchange—"have told us to go out of business." The board voted unanimously to file for Chapter 11.

Joseph recognized that everything he and the board had fought for the last three years, and everything they'd spent their careers building, was about to be gone. Drexel's guilty plea had bought the firm another year of life, but in the end, Milken, the man who made Drexel what it was, had also destroyed the firm.

At 11:15 P.M. on Tuesday, February 13, 1990, Drexel filed for bankruptcy protection.

By the spring of 1990, Milken had outlasted them all. Levine, Siegel, Boesky, Freeman, Regan, even the great Drexel, were gone from Wall Street.

The two top government officials in the Milken case were gone, too. During the previous summer, Bruce Baird at the U.S. attorney's office and Gary Lynch at the SEC had announced their resignations, Lynch after the Drexel settlement was hammered out, and Baird after the Freeman plea.

Both were exhausted, especially Lynch, who had devoted himself to the case with hardly a break since the beginning of the Bank Leu investigation more than four years earlier. Both had undergone grueling public attacks from well-armed opponents and had stayed in their low-paying government jobs long beyond the usual call of duty. New regimes were arriving to take charge of their respective offices, and the opportunity to shift to private practice would never be better.

Even though their biggest target, Milken, remained at large, the two lawyers knew what few others did: Milken had already capitulated once, his lawyers were again seeking a plea bargain, and sooner or later he would be convicted. The case was ready. Most of their work was done. With little public fanfare, they stepped aside, leaving the cases to John Carroll, Jess Fardella, and Baird's successor at the U.S. attorney's office, Alan Cohen. John Sturc at the SEC agreed to stay on for the duration of the case even though he was passed over for promotion to Lynch's position as chief of enforcement.

The Milken team continued to produce propaganda. Robinson, Lake employees were summoned for a crash project ordered by Milken: a book, to be published and distributed by Milken, featuring company success stories that depended on Milken's junk bonds. But no sooner would the writers finish a chapter on a company such as Ingersoll Communications, than the company would threaten to default. Even Lerer began to despair over the project.

The desperation of the Milken forces was perhaps best exemplified by their handling of a letter from a Lompoc prison inmate, sent to both Liman and Thomas Puccio, Mulheren's lawyer and former U.S. attorney in Brooklyn. In lurid detail, the letter claimed that Boesky had been bribing prison officials, was allowed to have a male lover in prison, was engaging in sex with other prisoners, and was having women imported into the prison for further sexual escapades. Despite the fact that the letter had been written by a convicted felon, Liman called Puccio, intrigued by the revelations and their potential for use in cross-examining Boesky, still expected to be the government's star witness. When Puccio questioned the relevance of Boesky's alleged sexual preferences or promiscuity—not to mention their accuracy— Liman brushed his objections aside. Paul, Weiss hired an expensive Los Angeles detective firm comprised of former prosecutors to investigate the letter's allegations. No expense was spared. Puccio, too, tried to confirm the letter's contents independently. Predictably, the allegations couldn't be verified.

Even Liman apparently now realized that Milken's trial wouldn't depend heavily on Boesky's testimony. Prosecutors had added even more cooperating witnesses in the early months of 1990. They were threatening to bring a new indictment, one that focused much more on deals unrelated to Boesky: Milken's alleged manipulation of thrifts, the bribing of fund managers, the excessive spreads and cheating of Drexel. The new indictment would be a far more damning portrait of a thoroughly corrupt operation. The prosecutors took a far tougher position in the negotiations than they had the prior year, when they were willing to offer just two felony counts. Now they wanted six, and a payment of over $600 million.

Even though a plea to six felonies exposed Milken to a potential prison term of nearly 30 years (conviction at trial on even more counts would increase the exposure accordingly), Milken's lawyers minimized to him the likely length of any prison term. Liman convened a meeting of Milken lawyers that included Flumenbaum, Sandler, Armstrong, and Litt, and asked each lawyer to estimate Milken's likely prison sentences if he went to trial and were convicted, and if he pleaded to the six felonies. Except for Litt and Flumenbaum, the stiffest estimate was for a 1-year term—if Milken went to trial and were convicted. Flumenbaum estimated 5. Litt attracted glares when he estimated 15 to 20 years if Milken went to trial, and 3 to 10 years if he agreed to plead. "No way he does less than Boesky," Litt muttered.

The plea negotiations were as cantankerous and difficult as they had been the year before. Liman's and Flumenbaum's relations with Carroll and Fardella were so strained that they brought in another lawyer, Steve Kaufman, to deal with the U.S. attorney's office. Negotiations were at an impasse throughout the fall and winter of 1989–90, even as the world Milken had created crashed into ruins. Finally a compromise was struck: the U.S. attorney agreed it wouldn't prosecute Lowell—despite an overwhelming amount of evidence—and it would allow that Milken's interviews with prosecutors—his "cooperation"— would begin only after he was sentenced. Dropping the charges against Lowell was the most difficult decision for the prosecutors. It was justified on the rationale that he had been little more than a lieutenant, faithfully carrying out Milken's master plan.

As for cooperation, it meant little if the defendant still intended to resist, as Milken gave every sign he would do. But in a departure from precedent, the prosecutors agreed that Milken's plea bargain would stand even if he lied during the cooperation phase. By contrast,

Boesky's and Siegel's plea bargains were revocable if they lied—giving their versions of events inherently more credibility than Milken's.

In return, the prosecutors extracted a concession that was vitally important to them: Milken would admit publicly that what he had done was wrong. They weren't going to allow Milken to claim a moral victory.

Carroll and Fardella made their final offer of six felonies, a $600 million fine, no charges against Lowell, and no cooperation until after sentencing. They gave Milken a deadline of 3 P.M. Friday, April 20. Employees at Robinson, Lake knew something was afoot when Lerer and Robinson, looking grim, disappeared behind closed doors the night of the 19th. Sandler, who had never accepted Milken's guilt, was devastated.

The day of the deadline was an eerie replay of the previous year. Carroll and Fardella expected an agreement, but they had learned to take nothing for granted. As the deadline approached, they heard nothing.

Milken was again at home with his wife Lori. They had been talking together since the early hours of the morning, taking no phone calls. She advised him to maintain his innocence. His brother Lowell had told him not to plead guilty for his sake. His mother, too, told him not to give in.

Liman, Flumenbaum, Litt, Sandler, and the other Milken lawyers gathered in New York in the conference room next to Liman's office, waiting for the call. Only Litt had advised a guilty plea. Privately, many of them thought Milken couldn't hold up under the stress of a trial. Lately, cut off from his trading desk, he had seemed a broken man.

Just before 3 P.M., Carroll and Fardella joined Cohen in his office, sitting across from the desk where Levine had been frisked over four years earlier. Wearily, they began to contemplate the prospect of gathering the grand jury to vote on the new Milken indictment.

Finally the phone rang at Paul, Weiss. Liman took the call in his office as other lawyers got on the extensions. Milken had reached a decision. "I'll do it," he said, his voice flat.

Liman placed the call to St. Andrews Plaza. Cohen put him on the speaker phone so Carroll and Fardella could hear. "He'll plead," Liman began. The prosecutors barely heard the rest of his message. It was over. Carroll and Fardella jumped up and, in a rare display of emotion, hugged each other.

The following Tuesday, April 24, hundreds packed the Manhattan federal courthouse's largest courtroom and hundreds more gathered around the building, congregating on the broad front steps along with television crews. Milken arrived in a dark limousine, and, in contrast to his earlier back-door appearances, walked up the main steps as police held back the crowds. He looked pale. He seemed to have lost weight, and his eyes appeared sunken.

Inside, the courtroom had the improbable air of a reunion. It was packed with supporters of Milken, including family members and Don Engel, who had rallied former colleagues and clients. There was a large contingent of government lawyers who had devoted much time to the case, and reporters crowded the jury box and spilled out into the audience. Many knew each other well after four years of covering the story.

There were titters when Judge Kimba Wood told Milken that the court would appoint a lawyer for him if he couldn't afford his own counsel. Then the mood turned somber, as Milken began to read a detailed confession to the six felonies: conspiracy with Boesky; aiding and abetting the filing of false statements in connection with the Fischbach scheme; aiding and abetting the evasion of net capital rules; securities fraud for concealing the ownership of MCA stock; mail fraud for defrauding investors in Finsbury; and assisting the filing of a false tax return, for the tax scheme with David Solomon.

Still, Milken clung to the public image he had tried so hard to nurture. He argued that his admission of guilt was "not a reflection on the underlying soundness and integrity of the segment of the capital markets in which we specialized and which provided capital that enabled hundreds of companies to survive, expand and flourish." Then he reached his conclusion.

"I realize that by my acts I have hurt those who are closest to me," Milken said, beginning to have difficulty with his words. "I am truly sorry. . . ." His voice choked and he started to fall forward. Liman and Flumenbaum rushed to his side. As they supported him, he covered his face in his hands and sobbed. Under the high, coffered ceiling of the courtroom, he suddenly seemed very frail.

That night, far from the television cameras and talk shows, the government lawyers who had made it all possible convened at the old-fashioned, inexpensive Harvey's Chelsea Restaurant on West 18th Street for their first and only celebration. Some had never actually worked together. Carberry, Lynch, and Baird all came back, joining Carroll, Fardella, Sturc, Cohen, Cartusciello, and other veterans. Neither Giuliani nor Romano were there. This was a party for those who'd never been in the limelight.

The Milken-led PR attacks had forged an unusual level of cama-

raderie. Morale in the U.S. attorney's and SEC offices is usually buoyed
by two convictions: that the government's cause is just, and that the
government will win. In the Milken case, both those beliefs had come
under intense attack. Inevitably, there had been moments of doubt.
The lawyers had had only each other for support.

When the check came, the lawyers who were now in private
practice picked it up. Even though their collective efforts had raised
well over $1 billion in fines and penalties for the U.S. Treasury, the
taxpayers couldn't pay for a celebratory dinner, not even a modest one.

Milken's sudden capitulation took the spotlight, but not the pressure,
off John Mulheren, the last major target still awaiting trial. Mulheren
had again rebuffed offers of a plea to a single felony, and his trial on
multiple parking, tax fraud, evading net capital requirements, and
stock manipulation counts began in May, with Boesky slated to be the
star witness.

On May 22, Boesky, dressed in his black suit and white shirt, with
neatly trimmed hair, made his courtroom debut as a witness, a role for
which he had been preparing since he agreed to plead guilty in 1986.
He performed abysmally. He was stiff, awkward, and evasive. His
memory was terrible. Events that he had remembered with considerable clarity when he was first debriefed by prosecutors now escaped
him. By allowing him to complete his prison term—Boesky had been
released from Lompoc to a Brooklyn halfway house in December 1989
after completing 18 months of his prison sentence, and left the halfway
house four months later—prosecutors had lost most of the leverage
they once held over him. Puccio could easily have challenged Boesky's
credibility on cross-examination based on his deviations from his earlier statements to prosecutors—but, in nearly every case, his earlier
testimony had been more damaging to Mulheren.

Boesky avoided looking at Mulheren, who was in the courtroom,
dressed in jeans or khakis and his signature polo shirts. Boesky testified that he had once considered himself a "close friend" of Mulheren.
This led to speculation that Boesky was still doing his best, short of
committing perjury, to protect Mulheren. If so, the effort made little
impression on Mulheren.

"When you hear my testimony, you'll realize he wasn't much of
a friend," Mulheren remarked to a reporter during one of the breaks.

Puccio's eagerly awaited cross-examination did nothing to damage Boesky's already shaky credibility. Despite the Kroll investigation
commissioned by Milken's lawyers (and turned over to Puccio), and
despite years of probing Boesky's affairs, lawyers for those implicated

by Boesky had found nothing particularly damaging. Puccio was left to review Boesky's crimes and the numerous occasions he admitted having lied, all of which were already known.

In any event, as would have been the case in a trial of Milken, Boesky wasn't the pivotal witness. Far more damaging to Mulheren was testimony by Davidoff and by a witness from Mulheren's own firm who had cooperated with the government.

Conspicuous by his absence was the once formidable raider Carl Icahn, who figured so prominently in the Gulf + Western manipulation charges and who had been included in Boesky's initial proffer to the government. Icahn was never charged with a crime, and the investigation of him had become moribund. Prosecutors had never been able to prove that Icahn and Boesky had acted as a "group," within the meaning of securities laws, when they joined to threaten Gulf + Western, even though their behavior had had virtually the same effect as if they had.

Mulheren testified in his own behalf, cheerfully admitting some of the most damaging facts, such as the agreement to reimburse Boesky through inflated invoice payments. "I increased the bills," Mulheren said, "to get them back a favor." But he insisted it wasn't part of an illegal parking arrangement and that he believed he bore the risks in the positions he took at Boesky's behest. He also testified that he had felt victimized by the Gulf + Western deal, that he hadn't been trying to push up the stock price and hadn't known Boesky was trying to use him to get out at a higher price.

Of all the defendants to take the stand in the insider-trading scandal, Mulheren was the most credible. Yet, after six and a half days of deliberations, the jury found him guilty of conspiracy and securities fraud, ruling that he had manipulated Gulf + Western's stock price. It said it was hopelessly hung on the 26 counts of parking, and the judge declared a mistrial on those counts on July 22. Mulheren, however, still faced sentencing on the other charges, and the government reserved the right to retry him on the parking charges. Mulheren seemed stoic as the verdict was read. "I was quite surprised it ended like this," he said. But if nothing else, he had stood on principle.

That summer, Martin Siegel finally ended his long exile, returning in June to Manhattan federal court for his sentencing. Prosecutors had spent much of the year after Freeman's guilty plea squabbling about whether they could introduce the evidence of further wrongdoing by

Freeman at Freeman's sentencing hearing. The judge in the case had finally rejected the idea, even though such procedures are not uncommon. He ruled that Freeman's lawyers were so likely to overwhelm the court with evidence that the sentencing hearing could end up taking many months.

Since February 1987, Siegel had been held in reserve as a potential witness. Finally, on April 13, 1990, Freeman had been sentenced on his single felony count. He was given a relatively light sentence of four months in prison and a fine of $1 million. "The trading of inside information has become a watchword or standard practice of arbitrage," Judge Pierre Leval commented.

Ultimately, all the delays worked to Siegel's advantage. Over the years of the investigation, the prosecutors had concluded that Siegel, almost alone among all those caught up in the scandal, had displayed true remorse. He had done his best to tell the truth, spending countless hours explaining the workings of the market and guiding the government through reams of complicated trading records. He had seemed, in fact, almost like part of the team of prosecutors.

In a presentencing hearing with the presiding judge, Robert Ward, Rakoff made his case for a lenient sentence, and Ward seemed sympathetic. Cartusciello also came through for Siegel. In a sentencing report that seemed unprecedented in the annals of St. Andrews Plaza, the prosecutors' presentation was, if anything, *more* favorable than the one prepared by Rakoff. The government praised Siegel as a "credible and reliable" witness who cooperated despite "an intense campaign of villification."

On June 18, Siegel flew to New York from Jacksonville and appeared in Manhattan federal court. He and Jane Day still made a handsome couple; both were tanned. She wore a simple navy dress and a strand of pearls. He was still fit and trim, wearing a dark business suit. He looked anxious and contrite as he stood before Judge Ward.

The judge lectured at length on the importance of Siegel's cooperation, and the need to reward such forthrightness if law enforcement is to succeed. Nonetheless, he insisted on the need to impose a prison term to deter white-collar crime. "After Mr. Boesky received a three-year sentence, I began to think about Mr. Siegel," Judge Ward said. "At that time, I was of the view that a [prison term] of eighteen months to two years would be reasonable." But he considered Siegel's cooperation and the fact that Freeman, who didn't cooperate, had received a light sentence. He had concluded, he said, that Siegel should serve "a sentence less than imposed on Mr. Freeman."

Judge Ward sentenced Siegel to two months in prison and five years' probation, working on the computer camp for children he had been setting up in Jacksonville. It seemed to take a moment for the brevity of the prison term pronounced by Judge Ward to dawn on Siegel. Then Jane Day threw her arms around him and they hurried, relief evident on their faces, from the courtroom.

By November 1990, despite all the efforts of the Milken team, public opinion had turned against Milken with a vengeance. It was as if all the negative publicity Robinson, Lake had managed to stave off had been unleashed at once. Milken was blamed, often unfairly, for all of America's failings. A recession had begun that summer, ending the economic boom of the eighties. The savings and loan debacle, in which junk bonds had played a significant role, was growing worse by the week, costing taxpayers billions of dollars. Milken had now supplanted Boesky as the embodiment of a decade of greed.

On Wednesday morning, November 21, 1990, Milken returned to the same courtroom where he had entered his guilty plea. His wife, his mother, his brother Lowell, Ken Lerer, and Richard Sandler sat behind him in the first row. As Milken sat listening, occasionally brushing away tears, Liman read at length from letters favorable to Milken and asked the court for leniency. Fardella, representing the government, urged that Milken be sentenced to a prison term as a deterrent to other potential criminals. In their sentencing memo, the prosecutors excoriated Milken for "a pattern of calculated fraud, deceit and corruption of the highest magnitude" and argued that "Milken's crimes were crimes of greed, arrogance and betrayal," part of a "master scheme to acquire power and accumulate wealth."

Suspense mounted as Judge Wood began to speak in calm, measured tones. She emphasized the "extraordinary interest" in the proceeding and said she wanted to dispel several misconceptions, among them that Milken should be punished for the economy's and the savings and loan industry's ills. She also rejected leniency on the grounds of Milken's role in the economic boom. She noted the "legitimate" principle "that everyone, no matter how rich or powerful, obey the law," and "that our financial markets in which so many people who are not rich invest their savings be free of secret manipulation. This is a concern fairly to be considered by the court."

Judge Wood's gracious demeanor did not mask the fact that, as she spoke, she demolished one plank of the Milken platform after another. She stated unequivocally that overzealousness on behalf of clients was no excuse; that Milken's avoidance of more brazen crime might indicate "you were willing to commit only crimes that were unlikely to be detected." She said that she had found evidence that he had obstructed justice. On the other hand, evidence that, as Milken claimed, the vast majority of his business was honest, "is sparse and equivocal."

Milken seemed to be in a daze as he listened, even as Judge Wood's remarks became more pointedly judgmental. "When a man of your power in the financial world, at the head of the most important department of one of the most important investment banking houses in this country, repeatedly conspires to violate, and violates, securities and tax laws in order to achieve more power and wealth for himself and his wealthy clients, and commits financial crimes that are particularly hard to detect, a significant prison term is required in order to deter others," she continued. "This kind of misuse of your leadership position and enlisting employees who you supervised to assist you in violating the laws are serious crimes warranting serious punishment and the discomfort and opprobrium of being removed from society."

"Mr. Milken," Judge Wood commanded, "please rise."

Milken got to his feet, and Liman and Flumenbaum moved to his side, Liman taking Milken's elbow in support. "You are unquestionably a man of talent and industry and you have consistently shown a dedication to those less fortunate than you," Judge Wood began, looking directly at Milken. "It is my hope that the rest of your life will fulfill the promise shown early in your career. . . .

"However, for the reasons stated earlier, I sentence you to a total of ten years in prison"—a gasp rose from the courtroom—"consisting of two years each on counts two through six to be served consecutively. . . . You may be seated at this point."

As the judge rose and left the courtroom, Milken showed no reaction—but his family and friends looked grief-stricken. They rushed to his side, shielding him from curious reporters, and moved him quickly toward the door at the rear of the courtroom leading to the judge's antechamber.

When Milken and his entourage had gathered in the corridor outside, the heavy door to the courtroom was firmly closed, blocking access. Milken had still said nothing, and looked confused and disoriented. Then he turned to Liman. "How much did I get?" he asked, as if he hadn't heard Judge Wood. "Two years?"

There was a moment of stunned silence. His lawyers suddenly realized that Milken, hearing he was being sentenced to two years on each of the various counts, hadn't understood he'd been given *consecutive* sentences. Liman broke the news. "Ten years, Michael," he said gently. "The sentence is ten years."

The blood drained from Milken's face. He took Lori's arm and the two disappeared into a small witness's waiting room off the corridor, closing the door behind them.

Moments later, first Lori, and then Milken, emitted bloodcurdling screams. Sandler burst into the room as Milken collapsed into a chair, hyperventilating, struggling for breath. "Oxygen!" someone yelled, as a federal marshal raced for help.

Epilogue

Could it happen again?

Perhaps one man and one market will never again dominate the financial world like Milken and junk bonds. Wall Street, suffering from layoffs and recession, has given every sign of being chastened. Securities prosecutions have declined, and the perception, at least, is that insider trading and other more devious forms of securities fraud have become far less prevalent.

Yet history offers little comfort. The famed English jurist Sir Edward Coke wrote as early as 1602 that "fraud and deceit abound in these days more than in former times." Wall Street has shown itself peculiarly susceptible to the notion, refined by Milken and Boesky, that reward need not be accompanied by risk. While the junk-bond market will likely recover and take its place among other useful but stodgy capital-raising alternatives, a pied piper will surely emerge in some other sector.

The financial markets have shown remarkable resilience and an ability to curb their own excesses. Yet they are surprisingly vulnerable to corruption from within. If nothing else, the scandals of the 1980s underscore the importance of the securities laws and their vigorous enforcement. The Wall Street criminals were consummate evaluators of risk—and the equation as they saw it suggested little likelihood of getting caught.

The government's record on appeal has done little to change the sense on Wall Street that most securities crimes are beyond the reach of law enforcement. Part of the Princeton/Newport verdict, including the RICO convictions, was reversed on appeal, and Mulheren's conviction was entirely reversed. Mulheren's securities manipulation charges were dismissed in an opinion that concluded "no rational trier of fact could have found the elements of the crimes charged here beyond a reasonable doubt." His year-and-a-day prison term and $1.5 million fine were set aside.

The Mulheren result wasn't surprising. It seems obvious from the events themselves that Boesky manipulated Mulheren, not that Mulheren manipulated the market. If Mulheren was guilty of anything, it was the parking charges on which the jury couldn't reach a verdict. The Princeton/Newport and reversals in other securities cases were largely technical. Still, confronted with Wall Street crime on an unprecedented scale, prosecutors were desperate to convict on practically any grounds. In some cases, they overreached.

These results don't change the fact that there was massive wrongdoing on Wall Street, nor that the principal criminals were caught and stopped through guilty pleas. But they do call into question the wholesale criminalization of the securities laws. Congress should enact a tough but precise criminal securities code that targets the most serious versions of securities fraud while leaving enforcement of matters like net capital requirements to the SEC.

At the very least, Congress should enact a statutory definition and prohibition of insider trading, and should define a "group" as part of a criminal ban on fraudulent disclosure practices. Securities firms should be barred from engaging in arbitrage; self-policing has clearly failed, as Kidder, Peabody recognized when it withdrew from arbitrage. And courts should continue to define mail and wire fraud broadly; fraud has proven itself to be, as Lord MacNaghten predicted at the turn of the century, "infinite in variety."

Ilan Reich and Robert Wilkis reported to the federal penitentiary at Danbury, Connecticut, on the same day, March 27, 1987. They had met for the first time only after the collapse of the Levine ring, and the shared experience might have launched a friendship. But they reacted differently to prison. Reich became progressively more listless and withdrawn. Wilkis fraternized with other prisoners and threw himself into an exercise program.

The two men were released after serving eight months of their year-and-a-day sentences. They haven't met since. Reich began work for a New York real estate developer. Wilkis found a new career in the entertainment industry, helping to put together a deal to finance Radio City Music Hall's "Easter Spectacular," starring the Rockettes.

Set Mooradian was granted immunity for his cooperation; he settled SEC charges and was banned from the securities industry for a year. He had trouble finding work. He was divorced in the spring of 1990 and had to sell his house in New Jersey. He bought a used IBM personal computer from the Boesky organization when it dissolved, and has been teaching himself to use it.

James Dahl quit the securities business after leaving Drexel, even though his agreement with the government didn't include any suspension. Most of his time has been spent cooperating with prosecutors and with lawyers for the Federal Deposit Insurance Corporation in its lawsuit against Milken and Drexel. He remains a multimillionaire and is building a new house on a large tract of land near Jacksonville, Florida, not far from Siegel. He plans to open a camp for underprivileged children. His California home is for sale.

Even before his conviction was reversed, Mulheren had had no difficulty raising capital from major investors like the Belzberg and Tisch families. He formed Buffalo Partners and continues his splashy investment style from new offices on Broad Street in downtown Manhattan, commuting from his New Jersey estate. While his SEC agreement prevents him from trading on his own behalf, he simply trades through Merrill Lynch and Bear, Stearns.

Robert Freeman served his four-month sentence and was released on August 30, 1990. His guilty plea didn't call for cooperation with prosecutors. He remains an active investor, and outwardly, little has changed. In the summer of 1991, he and his friends, James Regan and Henry Kravis, attended a golf outing hosted by Granite Capital. Granite is an investment partnership formed by Freeman's former colleague at Goldman, Sachs, Lew Eisenberg, which plans to acquire broadcast properties with KKR.

Dennis Levine complained that he was ostracized as a "squealer" at Lewisburg, a federal prison in central Pennsylvania. He worked in the landscaping crew and appeared at occasional court hearings looking tan, thin, and healthier than he had seemed in years. He completed his sentence in a Manhattan halfway house and was released on September 8, 1988.

Levine founded his own financial advisory firm, Adasar Group, and has assiduously courted further publicity. Despite a New York law that seeks to prevent felons from further profiting from their crimes, Levine published an account of his experiences in the May 19, 1990, issue of *Fortune* magazine, and, with a ghostwriter, has written a book, scheduled for publication in the fall of 1991. Having failed to get his picture on the cover of *Newsweek*, he realized an even greater ambition when "60 Minutes" began work on a segment about him scheduled to air in September 1991.

Though the government believed it had seized the bulk of Levine's assets, he has continued to live the life of a wealthy investment banker. He has been seen lunching at the expensive Four Seasons restaurant in Manhattan. He spent two weeks in February 1991 in Vail, Colorado, skiing with his family. The SEC has inquired into the source of his apparent affluence.

Ivan Boesky completed his term in Lompoc prison on December 15, 1989, and was released from a Manhattan halfway house three-and-a-half months later, after serving two years of his three-year term. While in prison, he grew a flowing white beard and shoulder-length hair. He acknowledged during testimony in the Mulheren trial that he paid other inmates to do his laundry. Like Levine, he was ostracized as an informant. Inmates tacked cartoons making fun of him on the prison bulletin board.

Since his release, Boesky has tried to keep a low profile. He lives in France, dividing his time between his apartment in Paris and his house on the Côte d'Azur, where he has been seen in the company of Wekili. Boesky has separated from his wife Seema, who continues to live at the Mt. Kisco estate.

As was the case with Levine, Boesky's fines and penalties don't seem to have made any dent in his luxurious standard of living. He arrives at meetings in chauffeured limousines and has been seen dining at expensive Manhattan restaurants. He is again clean-shaven, neatly groomed, and wearing black three-piece suits. He has approached potential investors about launching a new offshore investment limited partnership. Unlike Mulheren and Freeman, however, who didn't implicate others on Wall Street, Boesky has been given a cold shoulder by wealthy investors. Friends say he now realizes his notoriety precludes another financial career.

Michael Milken entered the federal prison in Pleasanton, California, outside San Francisco, on March 3, 1991. He will first be considered for parole in March 1993; Judge Wood recommended that he serve a minimum of 36 to 40 months. He puts in a 37-hour work week in maintenance and construction. He wears a baseball cap; prison regulations don't permit a hairpiece. His chief complaint has been boredom.

Milken has told some former colleagues that pleading guilty was a mistake and that he no longer believes he did anything wrong. He has hired celebrity criminal defense lawyer Alan Dershowitz to consider among other strategies a motion to undo his guilty plea. He faces scores of civil suits and has said he looks forward to testifying in them. Milken has spent hours with government lawyers as part of his agreement to cooperate. So far, he has provided incriminating information about James Dahl, Terren Peizer, and David Solomon—all of whom testified against him and have immunity. Prosecutors are despairing that any further cooperation from Milken will prove of substantial value to law enforcement.

Much of Milken's time apparently is spent pondering how to influence history's verdict. Lorraine Spurge is now president of an organization, "Working for the American Dream," whose purpose is to burnish Milken's image. Board members include Milken apologists George Gilder, the economist; Peter Magowan, chairman of Safeway; and Jude Wanniski, a commentator.

The book about Milken's clients that so troubled Robinson, Lake's employees was finally published in June 1991 as *Portraits of the American Dream*. Spurge and her organization have written letters seeking financial contributions to the Milken cause. "People like Michael Milken are living proof that compassion not greed dominated the decade," one such letter says.

Martin Siegel entered the federal prison at Jessup, Georgia, on July 1, 1990 and was released on August 24. He painted lines on the prison parking lot and helped computerize the prison library.

Phil Donahue, once Siegel's next-door neighbor in Connecticut, recently bought Siegel's former home in Greens Farms for $4.75 million. Donahue plans to level the house to expand his own grounds.

While waiting to be sentenced, Siegel created a computer camp for underprivileged Jacksonville high school students. The program has grown from 8 to 150 participants and is being run by Siegel with the support of local businesses under the auspices of Florida Community College Jacksonville. As part of his sentence of two years' community service, Siegel now works full-time on the project.

Siegel has had a recurring dream. Dressed like an investment banker in a conservative suit, he walks into the law office of his former mentor, Martin Lipton. In the dream, Lipton gets up and walks toward Siegel. Lipton embraces him, and then says, "I forgive you."

Chronology

MAY 1986   The SEC and federal prosecutors accuse Dennis Levine of making $12.6 million in insider-trading profits.

NOVEMBER 1986   Ivan F. Boesky agrees to pay a $100 million penalty to settle SEC charges of insider trading. Prosecutors reveal he has been cooperating in an undercover investigation. Drexel Burnham Lambert and Michael Milken receive subpoenas.

FEBRUARY 1987   Levine is sentenced to two years in prison.

FEBRUARY 1987   Robert Freeman, Richard Wigton, and Timothy Tabor are arrested on insider-trading charges. Martin Siegel admits insider trading and is identified as cooperating in the government's investigation.

MAY 1987   The indictments of Freeman, Wigton, and Tabor are dismissed. Prosecutors vow to seek a new indictment.

OCTOBER 1987   The stock market crashes.

DECEMBER 1987   Boesky is sentenced to three years in prison.

FEBRUARY 1988   John Mulheren is arrested on weapons charges for allegedly trying to kill Boesky.

SEPTEMBER 1988   The SEC accuses Drexel, Milken, and others of insider trading, stock manipulation, fraud, and other violations of federal securities laws.

DECEMBER 1988   Drexel agrees to plead guilty to six felonies, settle SEC charges, and pay a record $650 million.

MARCH 1989   Milken and his brother Lowell are indicted on 98 counts of racketeering and securities fraud.

AUGUST 1989   Freeman pleads guilty to one count of insider trading. The investigation of Wigton and Tabor is dropped.

OCTOBER 1989   The junk-bond market collapses.

FEBRUARY 1990   Drexel files for bankruptcy-court protection.

APRIL 1990   Milken agrees to plead guilty to six felonies and pay $600 million.

JUNE 1990   Siegel is sentenced to two months in prison.

JULY 1990   Mulheren is convicted; the conviction is later reversed.

NOVEMBER 1990   Milken is sentenced to ten years in prison.

Notes and Sources

Though I didn't realize it at the time, my reporting for this book began the afternoon of Dennis Levine's arrest, May 12, 1986, and has continued since then. As a *Wall Street Journal* reporter, I worked nearly full time on the stories of Levine, Boesky, Siegel, Drexel, Milken, and their associates until September 1988, when I became the *Journal*'s page-one editor. Since then, I have continued my reporting and have written several stories for the paper covering aspects of the scandal. As a reporter I worked closely with fellow *Journal* reporter Daniel Hertzberg, whose outstanding work helped make this book possible. After I became an editor, Laurie P. Cohen became the *Journal*'s chief reporter on the story and a researcher for this book. She conducted numerous interviews and became a vital part of the reporting process.

Nearly every person named in this book was interviewed or was asked for an interview and given an opportunity to comment. Numerous other persons with knowledge of the story were interviewed but not named. Many of the interviews were conducted on a not-for-quotation basis, but with the understanding that the text could reflect their states of mind and quotations they or others recalled. No anonymous quotations are used in this book. States of mind came from the person identified, either directly, in an interview, or from sworn testimony or notes taken by lawyers. Quotations came from the speaker, someone who heard the remark, or from transcripts and notes. In disputed cases, I accepted the speaker's version (even in a few cases where there was sworn testimony to the contrary).

In instances where differing accounts of events couldn't be reconciled, I have included the dissenting account in these notes and a brief explanation of why I chose the version that appears in the main text. Most of these discrepancies occur between Milken's and Boesky's versions of events. My reporting found that Boesky's version was consistently more accurate. After making his plea agreement, Boesky's only obligation was to tell the truth; indeed, his plea bargain would be revoked if he lied. In many instances, he testified under oath, and while his memory wasn't flawless, his recollections were largely corroborated by Siegel, Mulheren, Jefferies, and others implicated by him, with the exception of Milken. In contrast, Milken didn't testify under oath, even at his presentencing hearing, and during the investigation he repeatedly invoked the Fifth Amendment. Milken's accounts have also changed substantially during the course of the government's investigation, from his early protestations of innocence to his ultimate admission of guilt to six felonies.

In my reporting career, I have never before encountered a story so shrouded in secrecy. Nearly all of the participants either faced or still face potential criminal and civil charges or are likely to be witnesses in criminal or civil proceedings. Hundreds of civil suits are pending, involving billions of dollars in potential damages. In view of this, it isn't surprising that so many felt precluded from speaking on the record. The U.S. attorney's office and the SEC banned their employees from commenting except under extremely confining circumstances, in keeping with their usual practices. Employers also banned many from commenting. General Electric even went so far as to threaten a former Kidder, Peabody employee with termination of his pension benefits if he told his story.

Despite such obstacles, numerous people involved in every aspect of the story did agree to be interviewed. For many, this took exceptional courage and a dedication to the truth. In some cases, their cooperation was extraordinary, involving many days, repeated phone calls, and the sharing of documents and diaries. In over four years of stories for the *Journal,* these unnamed sources have proven their reliability and accuracy on countless occasions, despite intense campaigns to discredit the stories at the time they appeared. The passage of time has confirmed the accuracy of their statements, and I have continued to rely on them in reporting for this book.

In addition to interviews, I reviewed thousands of pages of court documents, including transcripts of court proceedings and, in a few instances, grand jury testimony and documents introduced as evidence. Many of these documents are cited in these notes.

Many participants were debriefed extensively by government lawyers, defense counsel, and other lawyers, and in some cases I had access to these lawyers' notes. I never relied solely on personal recollections when I could obtain documentary evidence. In many cases, however, interviews supplemented the written sources, and thus the sources cited here may not contain all the detail that appears in the main text. Among the published sources cited, two stand out: *The Predators' Ball* by Connie Bruck (New York: Simon & Schuster, 1988) and *Levine & Co.* by Douglas Frantz (New York: Henry Holt, 1987). Bruck's seminal work on how Milken and Drexel conducted their business remains essential reading. Frantz's account of the Levine scandal is especially good in its detailed account of Bank Leu's role.

Prologue

page 13 Thayer was sentenced to four years in prison after pleading guilty to lying to SEC officials. He settled insider-trading charges, agreeing with his co-defendants to pay $1 million. Andy Pasztor, "Thayer, Friend Are

Sentenced to Four years," *Wall Street Journal*, May 5, 1985. Pownall was preparing for Thayer's parole hearing in May 1986 when Siegel visited.

page 14 The ticker announcement of Levine's arrest appeared at 2:46 P.M. on May 12, 1986. The full text was obtained through Dow Jones News Retrieval.

Book One. Above the Law

Chapter 1
page 22 The history of Kidder, Peabody is set forth in Vincent P. Carosso, *More Than a Century of Investment Banking: The Kidder, Peabody & Co. Story* (New York: McGraw-Hill, 1979).

pages 22–23 The Pecora hearings are recorded in U.S. Senate, Committee on Banking and Currency, 73rd Cong., 2nd session, "Stock Exchange Practices: Hearings" and a resulting "Report of the Proceedings," 1934.

page 26 Participants in the takeover panel are identified in the program.

page 27 The history of the Morgan era and Morgan's anti-Semitism are reported in Ron Chernow, *The House of Morgan* (New York: Atlantic Monthly Press, 1990).

page 28 The profile of Siegel was "Takeover Target's Defender," *Business Week*, May 16, 1977, pp. 160–162.

page 34 A description of Boesky's life and career appears in *U.S.* v. *Ivan Boesky*, Defendant's Memorandum on Sentencing (hereafter cited as "Boesky memo"), pp. 38–40.

page 35 "Wrestling and arbitrage . . ." and "There are times . . ." quotes taken from Connie Bruck, "My Master Is My Purse," *The Atlantic*, December 1984.

page 35 Boesky's experience in Iran is discussed in a report prepared for Drexel Burnham Lambert by Kroll Associates, a private detective agency. Drexel turned the report over to the government.

page 35 Acquaintances of Boesky when he lived in Detroit were interviewed in 1986. Boesky's early life is also discussed at some length in Bruck, "My Master Is My Purse."

page 36 In a short sale, an investor agrees to sell a given stock at a given price on a designated future date. The difference between the price agreed upon and the market price on the designated date is profit (or loss) to the investor. The SEC requires that short sellers own or have guaranteed access to the stock they have promised to sell. The most common practice is for investors to make a short sale of stocks they don't actually own; instead they "borrow" the stocks from a third party, who guarantees that those stocks will be available for the investor to buy on the day of the transaction. The investor is betting that the price will drop, so that the borrowed stock will cost less than the price agreed upon in the short sale.

pages 40–44 Milken's background is discussed at length in *U.S.* v. *Michael R. Milken*, SS 89-CR-41, Sentencing Memorandum of Michael R.

Milken (hereafter cited as "Government's Milken memo"), pp. 3–28. The backgrounds of Burnham, Milken, Joseph, and Drexel are described in Bruck, *The Predators' Ball*, pp. 23–40.

page 45 W. Braddock Hickman, *Corporate Bond Quality and Investor Experience* (Princeton University Press, 1958). The book sold just 934 copies.

page 48 Black's father, Eli, committed suicide in 1975. The scandal received widespread publicity, including the front-page story: Mary Bralove, "Giving Up," *Wall Street Journal*, Feb. 14, 1975.

page 54 Milken's salary was disclosed in *U.S.* v. *Michael R. Milken*, SS 89-CR-41, Government's Sentencing Memorandum ("Government's Milken memo ") p. 20, n. 8.

page 54 Robert Ludlum, *The Matarese Circle*, 1980 Bantam edition, p. 446.

Chapter 2

pages 58–59 The backgrounds of Dennis Levine and Robert Wilkis are discussed at length in *U.S.* v. *Dennis B. Levine*, 86-CR-519, Sentencing Memorandum on Behalf of Dennis B. Levine, 1989 (henceforth cited as "Levine sentencing memo"), pp. 1–10.

page 60 Levine's father is discussed in *U.S.* v. *Dennis B. Levine*, First and Second Reports of the Receiver (hereafter cited as "Levine receiver's reports").

page 61 Levine's and Wilkis's accounts of how they began insider trading are sharply at odds. Levine claims that Wilkis "opened" his eyes "to the concept of insider trading" when he intercepted a coded telex at Citibank in 1978 and urged Levine to buy stock in a takeover target. He maintains that Wilkis sought inside information from him while he was in Paris and that Wilkis opened a Swiss account on a visit to Paris in the spring of 1979 (Levine sentencing memo, pp. 12–14). Wilkis denies this account. Wilkis disclosed all his banking transactions as part of his plea bargain; there was no record of any Swiss account opened in Paris. For these and other reasons, the text reflects Wilkis's version of events.

page 63 Hill's relationship with Levine is summarized in *SEC* v. *Dennis Levine*, 86 Civ. 3726, Declaration of J. Tomilson Hill III, 1986.

page 66 Though Levine often boasted to Wilkis that "everyone" was insider trading, including Hill, there isn't any evidence to support his claims. Significantly, Levine didn't implicate anyone other than his immediate conspirators when he had every reason to do so in order to enhance the value of his cooperation.

page 68 The code names are discussed in Frantz, *Levine & Co.*, p. 53.

page 69 The meeting between Reich and Levine is described in Steven Brill, "Death of a Career," *American Lawyer*, December 1986.

page 70 Reich's background is described in Sentencing Memorandum on Behalf of Ilan K. Reich (hereafter cited as "Reich sentencing memo"), pp. 4–12.

page 73 Copies of Levine's original Bank Leu documents were produced by the SEC in response to an FOIA request.

page 73 Details of Levine's trading in Jefferson National and other stocks referred to on subsequent pages, as well as calculations of his profits and losses, were disclosed by the SEC in appendices to its filings in *SEC* v. *Dennis Levine A/K/A Mr. Diamond et al.*, the SEC's civil injunctive action, and supporting motions and papers, pp. 5–21. A chart showing the trading and profits also appeared in *The Wall Street Journal*, May 16, 1986.

page 76 Levine's American Express receipts while at Smith Barney were produced to the SEC, which disclosed them in its FOIA response.

page 78 The charges against Florentino received widespread press coverage; e.g., *The Wall Street Journal*, Aug. 17, 1983.

page 79 Fraysse recorded his meetings with "Mr. Diamond" in memos to the bank's files, which were produced to the SEC and disclosed with the FOIA material.

Chapter 3

page 81 Mulheren described his first meeting with Boesky at the Café des Artistes in *U.S.* v. *John A. Mulheren, Jr.*, 89-CR-452, transcripts of proceedings, testimony of John Mulheren (hereafter cited as "Mulheren testimony"), June 13, 1990, pp. 2471 ff.

page 81 Mulheren described his background and career in detail during his testimony in *U.S.* v. *Mulheren*.

page 83 The origins of the takeover boom in the eighties are explored in detail in Roy C. Smith, *The Money Wars* (New York: E.P. Dutton, 1990).

page 89 Mulheren discussed the Boesky rescue in detail in his court testimony. Quotations are from Mulheren testimony, June 13, 1990, p. 2477.

page 89 The quotations are from Mulheren testimony, p. 2478.

page 91 The tennis outing and Boesky's arrival in a Rolls Royce were first described in James B. Stewart and Daniel Hertzberg, "Unhappy Ending," *Wall Street Journal*, Feb. 17, 1987.

pages 93–94 Boesky described the beginnings of his insider-trading scheme with Siegel in *U.S.* v. *Mulheren*, transcripts of proceedings, testimony of Ivan Boesky (hereafter cited as "Boesky testimony"), May 22, 1990, p. 418. Siegel also described their relationship in numerous government debriefings. Their accounts don't differ in any material respect.

page 95 Siegel's starring role in the Martin Marietta/Bendix battle was described in detail in Hope Lampert, *Till Death Do Us Part: Bendix vs. Marietta*.

page 96 Boesky's profits from Siegel's information were disclosed in *SEC* v. *Martin A. Siegel*, Complaint for Injunctive and Other Equitable Relief (hereafter cited as "Siegel complaint"), pp. 5–14.

page 97 Most details of the cash payments have never before been revealed. They were first mentioned in Siegel complaint, p. 6, and further described in Stewart and Hertzberg, "Unhappy Ending."

Chapter 4

page 99 Boesky's ownership of the Beverly Hills Hotel is discussed in Bruck, "My Master Is My Purse."

pages 99–100 The history of the Beverly Hills Hotel is described in Laura Landro, "Show Business Deals Can Go Swimmingly If the Setting Is Right," *Wall Street Journal*, Apr. 15, 1985.

page 101 A "Chinese wall" in an investment banking firm generally refers to an information barrier between investment bankers and traders, including arbitrageurs. It is intended to prevent a firm's traders from acting on confidential information entrusted by clients to the investment bankers.

page 102 The background and career of Posner are reported in Michael Allen, "Troubled Raider," *Wall Street Journal*, July 14, 1987. Posner's relationship to Drexel is also discussed in Bruck, *Predators' Ball*, pp. 119–125.

page 103 Ronald Perelman was head of MacAndrews & Forbes and launched a hostile takeover of Revlon. Nelson Peltz, head of Triangle Industries, acquired National Can and then bought American Can from Primerica. He sold American National Can to Pechiney, the French packaging company. Gerald Tsai was chairman of Primerica, which he reshaped into a financial services concern which owns Smith Barney, the brokerage firm. Irwin Jacobs is a corporate raider based in Minneapolis. The Hafts became corporate raiders, launching an unsuccessful bid for Safeway Stores. The Pritzker family owns Hyatt Hotels Corporation and invests in numerous other ventures.

page 104 Carr has denied being part of any scheme to free Posner from the standstill agreement.

page 104 While based on independent reporting, the text's account of the Fischbach transaction closely parallels that set forth in Government's Milken memo, pp. 30–37 (redacted). Carr denied being part of any Milken-led scheme involving Fischbach.

page 108 Although Milken pleaded guilty to a felony count of conspiracy for his role in Fischbach, he disputes some of the key facts that were alleged by the government and that appear in the text based on independent reporting. Milken insists that he didn't instruct Boesky to buy Fischbach stock or guarantee him against loss at the time of Boesky's original purchases of Fischbach. Thus, Milken argues that Boesky's actions in Fischbach weren't part of a broader Milken-led scheme to free Posner from the standstill agreement (Milken's sentencing memo, pp. 80–82). This version assumes that the timing of Boesky's purchases vis-à-vis the standstill was sheer coincidence and offers no motive for Milken's having agreed to protect Boesky from loss, as Milken concedes he did in at least some Fischbach instances. For these and other reasons, the text largely reflects Boesky's version of events.

page 110 The Otter Creek trading in National Can was first disclosed in James B. Stewart, "Dubious Deals," *Wall Street Journal*, July 15, 1988. The trading records were disclosed by the House Subcommittee on Oversight and Investigation. A Milken spokesperson denied any impropriety, arguing that Milken didn't know that National Can was contemplating a buyout prior to the public announcement (even though Drexel was handling the buyout financing and met with National Can officials.)

page 111 The quotations are from the New York Stock Exchange's confidential report on its investigation provided to the House Oversight Subcommittee.

page 112 Engel denies Joseph's allegations, and has never been charged with any wrongdoing in connection with the incident.

page 112 Engel's dismissal was reported in Bruck, *The Predators' Ball*, pp. 337–339.

page 116 The 1985 Predators' Ball was the subject of Anthony Bianco, "The Growing Respectability of the Junk Heap," *Business Week*, Apr. 22, 1985.

page 118 Bruck reported the presence of prostitutes at the 1985 Predators' Ball, quoting participants such as Fred Sullivan, chairman of Kidde Inc. (Bruck, *The Predators' Ball*, p. 15). Joseph and Engel deny the assertion.

page 118 The quotation is from Peter Dworkin, "The Inside Story on the High Tech of Finance," *San Francisco Chronicle*, Apr. 4, 1985. The full quotation is " 'You have to be pretty impressed by the aggressiveness and acuity of these fellows,' said Tully Friedman, a partner in the San Francisco investment firm of Hellman & Friedman. 'What you don't know is if you have a watershed in American business or a South Sea bubble,' he said, referring to one famous speculative binge."

Chapter 5

page 119 Levine's receipt from the River Cafe was included in the expense receipts disclosed by the SEC.

page 121 Ken Auletta, *Greed and Glory on Wall Street: The Fall of the House of Lehman* (New York: Random House, 1986).

page 124 Reich's effort to distance himself from Levine, and his re-ensnarement, are described in Reich sentencing memo, pp. 18–21.

page 127 Cecola ultimately pleaded guilty to two counts of tax evasion, and has denied engaging in any insider trading. He was dismissed from Harvard Business School.

page 129 The quotations are from *In the Matter of Transactions in the Securities of Textron, Inc.*, File No. HO-1677, transcript of deposition of Dennis B. Levine, Nov. 14, 1984, pp. 15–17.

page 131 Levine's spending is described in Levine receiver's reports.

page 132 A copy of Hadley Lockwood's "Candidate Presentation" for Levine, marked "confidential," was produced to the SEC and disclosed as part of its FOIA response.

page 133 The terms of Levine's employment at Drexel are set out in an internal Drexel memorandum dated Jan. 18, 1985, from Herbert Bachelor to

Tom Lee, and in a letter dated Jan. 9, 1985, from David Kay to Levine, both produced by the SEC.

page 133 The purchase of the Ferrari is described in Levine receiver's reports.

page 134 In May 1990, Levine said he first met Boesky at the 1985 Predators' Ball and they began speaking on the phone afterward (Dennis B. Levine, "The Inside Story of an Inside Trader," *Fortune*, May 21, 1990). Earlier, he claimed that Boesky first called him seeking information in Feb. 1985, "the first of countless telephone calls from Ivan Boesky" (Levine sentencing memo, p. 24). The text reflects Boesky's version, suggesting that Levine called Boesky in Feb. 1985, which is consistent with Levine's long-standing desire to cultivate Boesky, rather than vice versa.

page 134 Details of Boesky's trading in ANR and in other transactions discussed here were taken from his voluminous 13-D filings, obtained from the SEC.

page 135 Boesky's earnings from Levine's tips were disclosed in the SEC's complaint in *SEC* v. *Ivan F. Boesky et al.*

page 136 The terms of the Boesky/Levine arrangement are also disclosed in the SEC's complaint in *SEC* v. *Ivan F. Boesky et al.*

page 136 There is no evidence to support Levine's claims about Gleacher or Wasserstein, and neither has been charged with any wrongdoing. See note to p. 66.

page 137 Biographical details of Sir James Goldsmith are from James B. Stewart and Phillip Revzin, "Nimble Financier," *Wall Street Journal*, Nov. 21, 1986.

page 138 The meeting at Sir James's townhouse was described in the SEC's deposition of Roland Franklin. The luncheon is also described in Frantz, *Levine & Co.*, pp. 134–136.

Chapter 6

page 140 The Natomas transaction is described in Siegel complaint, pp. 7–8.

page 141 The Texaco/Pennzoil/Getty battle, including Siegel's role, is the subject of Thomas Petzinger, *Oil and Honor* (New York: Putnam, 1988).

page 143 Boesky's and Siegel's accounts of the amount of cash delivered differ. Boesky was apparently unaware of the "skimming"; the text reflects Siegel's sworn statements to government investigators.

page 143 Boesky's success in the Gulf deal is described in detail in Bruck, "My Master Is My Purse."

page 145 On the Carnation deal: Siegel complaint, pp. 6–8.

page 146 The SEC termed Carnation's comments denying knowledge of any reason for its stock activity "materially false and misleading" and issued new guidelines for company disclosures. *Wall Street Journal*, July 9, 1985.

page 148 The article that so troubled Siegel is Gwen Kinkead, "Ivan Boesky, Money Machine," *Fortune*, Aug. 6, 1984.

page 149 Biographical material on Robert Freeman is from Richard B. Stolley, "The Ordeal of Bob Freeman," *Fortune*, May 25, 1987.

page 150 The article referred to is Bruck, "My Master Is My Purse."

page 152 The quotation "Don't you love me anymore?" was first reported in Stewart and Hertzberg, "Unhappy Ending."

page 152 Freeman has denied engaging in any criminal activity other than the one instance of insider trading with Siegel to which he pleaded guilty. The government, in a presentencing memorandum, argued that Freeman had engaged in numerous instances, presumably including many of the transactions described in the text of this book. It also alleged additional criminal activity that Freeman engaged in with others besides Siegel. At Freeman's request, this document was sealed by the sentencing judge, as was Freeman's reply memorandum. Thus, Freeman's defense, if any, to the specific incidents described in the text isn't known. *The Wall Street Journal* moved to obtain both the government's memo and Freeman's reply; the motion was denied by Judge Leval. The decision was appealed, and the appeal was pending as this book went to press.

page 153 The Brant-Winans scandal is the subject of R. Foster Winans, *Trading Secrets: Seduction and Scandal at The Wall Street Journal* (New York: St. Martin's Press, 1986).

page 153 Krantz's role in the Winans scandal, and his performance as a witness in the Winans trial, are the subject of Stephen J. Adler and Donald Baer, "Afraid to Blow the Whistle," *American Lawyer*, June 1985. The article concluded that Krantz "ended up as an ineffective cop who let the bad guys run wild on his beat."

page 154 Wigton's background is described in Steve Swartz and James B. Stewart, "Justice Delayed," *Wall Street Journal*, Aug. 21, 1989.

page 154 The creation of the Kidder, Peabody arbitrage department and DeNunzio's role was first disclosed in Stewart and Hertzberg, "Unhappy Ending."

page 156 Wigton denied being privy to the phone call about Continental.

page 157 Details and timing of the bidding for Continental were obtained through Dow Jones News Retrieval.

page 159 Details of trading by Freeman and Goldman in this book were obtained from copies of actual trading records obtained by the author. Some of these trades were first disclosed in James B. Stewart and Daniel Hertzberg, "Suspicious Trading," *Wall Street Journal*, Feb. 12, 1988. Freeman and his lawyers declined comment on the trading, and have never challenged the accuracy of the records.

page 165 The backgrounds of Coniston Partners, Princeton-Newport, and James Regan are described in James B. Stewart and Daniel Hertzberg, "Insider Focus," *Wall Street Journal*, Apr. 6, 1988.

page 167 See note to p. 159.

page 168 *Selling short* is the sale of a security or commodity futures contract that is not owned by the seller, a technique used to take advantage of an anticipated decline in the price or to protect a profit in a long position. An investor borrows stock certificates for delivery at the time of short sale. If the seller can buy that stock later at a lower price, a profit results; if the price rises, however, a loss results.

Selling a call is the short sale of a call option. A call option is the right to buy 100 shares of a particular stock at a predetermined price before a preset deadline, in exchange for a premium. Purchase of a call represents a bet that a stock price will rise; selling a call is a bet that it will fall. Buying a put achieves the same strategy.

page 169 The Unocal transaction is described in the indictment in *U.S. v. Robert Freeman*. Other deals for which Freeman was investigated were first disclosed in James B. Stewart and Daniel Hertzberg, "Wall Street Inquiry Focuses on 11 Stocks," *Wall Street Journal*, May 22, 1987.

page 171 Boesky disclosed another source for the Macy information within Goldman's real estate department in interviews with prosecutors.

page 172 The quotation "Your bunny has a good nose," was first disclosed in Stewart and Hertzberg, "Suspicious Trading," and later was the subject of Freeman's guilty plea. In a statement released at the time of his plea, Freeman gave this account of the conversation: "I told Mr. Siegel that I had heard there was a problem with the Beatrice LBO. He asked from whom I had heard that. When I answered Bunny Lasker, Martin Siegel said, 'Your bunny has a good nose.' " Further details of the Beatrice situation are reported in James B. Stewart and Steve Swartz, "Abrupt Confession," *Wall Street Journal*, Aug. 18, 1989.

page 172 In its original November 1985 bid for Beatrice, KKR offered $43 in cash and $7 in preferred stock per share. In January 1986, KKR modified its offer to $40 in cash and $10 in preferred stock, a bid the Beatrice board accepted in February. Although the face value of the offer remained $50 per share, or a total of about $6.2 billion, the market value of the bid dropped because of the uncertainty of the higher percentage of preferred stock (*Wall Street Journal*, Feb. 3, 1986).

Chapter 7

page 176 Details of Mulheren's career, including the rescue of his son, were reported in James B. Stewart and Daniel Hertzberg, "How a Wealthy 'Arb' Enmeshed in Scandal Turned to Violence," *Wall Street Journal*, Feb. 22, 1988.

page 177 The quotations are from Mulheren testimony, p. 2489. These quotations and those on the succeeding pages reflect Mulheren's version of the Unocal "parking" charges. Whether Mulheren believed he was at risk or not was a major issue at his trial on parking charges, and neither Boesky nor Davidoff recalled Mulheren's comments to the effect that he wouldn't trade if he wasn't at risk. Nor is the payback scheme, which Mulheren didn't contest, consistent with Boesky bearing the risk. Prosecutors contended that Mulheren lied. Since the jury wasn't able to reach a verdict on the parking charges, however, I have accepted Mulheren's account in the main text.

page 177 Net capital requirements were established by the government after the 1929 crash to protect investors in securities operations like Boesky's from excessive speculation. Boesky's borrowing through Drexel also carried net capital requirements intended to protect debt-holders. Net capital is measured as the value of equity (gross capital) minus debt, and under the requirements it may not fall below a mandated safety margin.

page 178 The quotation is from a copy of an internal memo from Stephen J. Conway to Ivan F. Boesky dated June 18, 1985. It was introduced as government exhibit no. 34 in *U.S.* v. *Mulheren*.

page 178 The quotations are from Mulheren testimony, p. 2503.

page 178 The quotations are from Mulheren testimony, pp.2509–10.

page 180 The account of the Diamond Shamrock/Occidental Petroleum insider trading in the text is based primarily on interviews with participants, but it is largely consistent with the account contained in Government's Milken sentencing memo, pp. 65–70 (redacted). (The government memo was heavily redacted at the request of Milken's lawyers, and thus the text is riddled with references to "John Doe." In all cases, the actual names were determined through independent reporting, and appear in the main text.) The government version has Boesky calling Milken; as the text indicates, witnesses recall Milken placing the call.

In his sentencing memo, Milken didn't address the government's allegations to which he didn't admit guilt, but generally Milken has insisted that he committed no crimes other than the six to which he pleaded guilty. Diamond/ Occidental was not part of the Milken plea; these charges were dropped as part of the agreement, even though they seem the most clear-cut example of insider trading by Milken. Nor did Milken address the facts of the Diamond/ Occidental trading in his reply sentencing memo, arguing only that if Milken had routinely insider traded with Boesky, Boesky wouldn't have had any reason to deal with Levine. See *U.S.* v. *Milken*, reply sentencing memo of Michael R. Milken, p. 65.

page 183 The Golden Nugget/MCA transactions were the subject of count three in Milken's plea agreement. The facts are set forth in detail in Government's Milken sentencing memo, pp. 37–41. Milken doesn't dispute the facts, but argues that purchasers of MCA stock were "victims" of Boesky's rush to sell rather than their scheme (Milken's sentencing memo, p. 86).

page 184 The tax trades and the repayments scheme are described in Government's Milken sentencing memo, pp. 70–77. Milken denies that the trades were "shams" for tax purposes (Milken's reply memo, pp. 86–87).

page 185 The MGM/UA dealings are described in Government's Milken sentencing memo, pp. 84–89. The quotations from *The New York Times* and *The Wall Street Journal* are as cited by the government. Milken denies the government's account (Milken's reply memo, p. 96, fn. 44).

page 185 The Pacific Lumber takeover is described in Government's Milken sentencing memo, pp. 82–84. In his reply memo, Milken doesn't specifically address this or other aspects of the Boesky conspiracy alleged by the government, other than to deny generally that he insider-traded or tried to influence corporate events. Milken's lawyers stated that "it is obviously impossible for us to refute in this memorandum the government's narrative as to each and every transaction which Boesky now claims was tainted with illegality" (Milken's reply memo, pp. 96–97).

page 186 Harris Graphics is described in Government's Milken sentencing memo, pp. 79–82.

page 188 The Milken-Boesky recordkeeping scheme was first described in James B. Stewart and Daniel Hertzberg, "Drexel's Michael Milken Called a Focus of Probe of Suspected Boesky Scheme," *Wall Street Journal*, Feb. 5, 1987. Milken has consistently denied the existence of a recordkeeping scheme as alleged by the government.

page 192 The Beatrice warrants are described in Smith, *The Money Wars*, pp. 234–235.

page 192 The source of Rosenthal's quotation is "What's News," *The Bawl Street Journal*, June 6, 1986.

page 193 Ivan Boesky, *Merger Mania* (New York: Holt, Rinehart & Winston, 1985). In a review for *The New Republic*, James J. Cramer wrote, "Boesky's legend will live because he spotted the Gettys, CBS and Gulfs early and he wagered it all," a typically adulatory comment about Boesky. Cramer later bemoaned his naïveté in "All My Heroes Turned Out to Be Crooks," *M inc.*, June 1991.

page 194 The Boesky quotation is from David Vise, "Q and A: Ivan Boesky on the Art of Arbitrage," *Washington Post*, June 23, 1985.

page 197 Boesky described the Gulf + Western dealings with Icahn in *U.S.* v. *Mulheren*, Boesky testimony, pp. 614 ff. Icahn has never testified publicly on the subject.

page 199 Boesky's run at CBS received widespread press coverage; see, e.g., David Carey, "CBS Sues One of Its Biggest Shareholders," *Financial World*, May 15, 1985.

page 200 The quotation is from Boesky testimony, p. 628.

page 201 The investors in Boesky's partnership were disclosed in Robert J. Cole, "Drexel-Boesky Tie for Some Investors," *New York Times*, Nov. 19, 1986.

page 203 The suspicious circumstances of the $5.3 million payment were first disclosed in *The Wall Street Journal* (see note to p. 188). In his reply memo, Milken continued to assert that the $5.3 million was an investment banking fee (Milken's reply memo, p. 105). Drexel itself, however, no longer disputes the government's characterization of the fee. Mooradian's role was the subject of Daniel Hertzberg, "The Informer," *Wall Street Journal*, Oct. 11, 1990.

page 206 The quotation is from a copy of the letter obtained by the author.

page 206 In its complaint against Milken and Drexel, the SEC described the invoice for the $5.3 million as follows: "To conceal the true reason for the $5.3 million payment, Boesky, Drexel, Milken and Lowell Milken falsely described it in a confirmation to auditors, in an invoice, and in offering documents as a payment for 'consulting services' " (SEC complaint, p.11). The Milkens and Boesky initially denied the allegations, and later settled without admitting or denying guilt.

Chapter 8

page 209 Drexel's aggressive posture was the subject of Ann Monroe, "Drexel Burnham, Rivals Duel on Buyouts," *Wall Street Journal*, April 21, 1986.

page 210 The quotations are from the complaint in *Staley Continental Inc.* v. *Drexel Burnham Lambert et al.* filed in U.S. District Court for the Northern District of Illinois. The suit and its contents were reported in Jeff Bailey and Daniel Hertzberg, "Drexel Burnham Is Sued by Staley Continental Inc.," *Wall Street Journal*, Feb. 20, 1987. Dahl has denied threatening Staley.

page 211 Kidder, Peabody's deteriorating finances and the sale to GE were described in James B. Stewart, "Cashing In," *Wall Street Journal*, May 5, 1986.

page 216 The discussions at the Water Club were described in Frantz, *Levine & Co.*, pp. 318–320.

page 218 Drexel's contributions to politicians are the subject of Brooks Jackson and Thomas E. Ricks, "Lobbyists, Speaking Fees, Contributions Didn't Keep Milken from Capitol Hill," *Wall Street Journal*, Apr. 28, 1988. The attendance of various senators at the 1986 Predators' Ball is described in Bruck, *The Predators' Ball*, p. 259.

page 220 Milken's relationship with David Solomon is the subject of counts four and five of the Milken plea agreement. The Finsbury transactions are described in detail in Government's Milken sentencing memo, pp. 45–51. While the facts aren't in dispute, Milken rejects the government's assertion that Milken's motive was to induce Solomon to purchase securities sold by Drexel. "We steadfastly dispute that assignment of motive and any other suggestion that Michael Milken improperly induced [Solomon] to do business with Drexel. [Solomon] did business with Drexel because Drexel was the principal market maker and underwriter of high yield securities, [Solomon's] specialty" (Milken's sentencing memo, pp. 88–89). The text reflects Solomon's version, which seems amply corroborated by circumstantial evidence.

page 220 The account of the blue notebook is from Peizer's testimony in the Milken Fatico hearing (see note to p. 442). Lowell Milken's lawyer, Michael Armstrong, has denied that Lowell was involved in any illegal scheme.

page 223 The quotation is from Kathleen Pender, "The World According to Boesky," *San Francisco Chronicle*, May 19, 1986.

page 223 The circumstances of Boesky's invitation to give the commencement address are described in David Vogel, "How Boesky Advanced the Cause of Equal Opportunity in Scandal," *San Francisco Chronicle*, Dec. 15, 1986. Boesky described the speech in *U.S.* v. *Mulheren*, Boesky testimony, p. 727.

page 224 The Stone Container and Wickes transactions are described in Government's Milken sentencing memo, pp. 94–101. Milken denied the allegations,

page 225 Boesky's renovation project is reported in Al Gordon, "Boeskys' Dream House Exceeding Their Grasp," *Newsday*, Dec. 16, 1988.

page 225 The quotation is from a copy of the letter obtained by the author.

pages 225–226 The description of the Guterman bar mitzvah is from Georgia Dullea, "Coming of Age on the Ocean," *New York Times*, Sept. 16, 1986.

page 227 The date of Boesky's surrender to federal authorities appears in *U.S.* v. *Mulheren*, Boesky testimony p. 630.

Book Two. The Chase

Chapter 9

page 231 A copy of the Caracas letter was obtained from Merrill Lynch.

page 231 The account of Merrill Lynch's handling of the letter is from interviews with Merrill Lynch officials involved.

page 234 The Fedders affair was the subject of Brooks Jackson, "Storm Center," *Wall Street Journal*, Feb. 25, 1985. Fedders resigned after the article was published.

page 236 The Campbell deposition is discussed in James B. Stewart, "Tracing a Scandal," *Wall Street Journal*, July 15, 1987.

page 236 The quotations are from the transcript of Campbell's three day deposition, released by the SEC.

page 237 The involvement of the Bank Leu officials Meier and Pletscher is discussed in considerable detail in *SEC* v. *Dennis B. Levine*, 86 Civ. 3726 (RO), Memorandum in Support of Plaintiff's Application for a Temporary Restraining Order (hereafter cited as "SEC memo"), pp. 8–10, and Supplemental Memorandum of Plaintiff SEC in Support of Application for a Preliminary Injunction (hereafter cited as "SEC supplemental memo"), pp. 17–19. SEC lawyer Leo Wang elaborated in a deposition released by the SEC. Pletscher also gave two days of depositions on his and Meier's involvement.

page 238 The quotation "you are the smart guys . . ." is from Pletscher's deposition transcript, second day, p. 5.

page 242 Levine's instructions to destroy the records were described in Pletscher's deposition and in Frantz, *Levine & Co.*, p. 195.

page 242 The quotations are from Pletscher's deposition.

page 243 The Knopfli quote is from Pletscher's deposition.

page 245 The SEC roundtable discussion is described in *Frantz, Levine & Co.*, pp. 233–235. The quote is from a transcript of the proceedings released by the SEC.

page 249 The case involving the Morgan Stanley investment banker is *U.S.* v. *Newman*. Stockbroker James Newman was convicted of insider trading in 1983, and the decision, which established the "misappropriation" theory of insider trading, was upheld on appeal. Newman's co-conspirators, Morgan Stanley investment banker Jacques Courtois and Kuhn, Loeb investment banker Adrian Antoniu pleaded guilty.

page 251 The circumstances of the wire transfer were first reported in Stewart, "Tracing a Scandal."

page 252 Levine's presence at the *Top Gun* screening was described in Frantz, *Levine & Co.*, p. 328. The engagement appears on his appointment diary released by the SEC.

page 253 Levine's attempts to transfer his funds are described in *SEC v. Levine*, SEC memo, pp. 9–10, and SEC supplemental memo, p. 19.

page 260 Reich's reaction to Levine's arrest and his trip to Los Angeles are described in Brill, "Death of a Career."

Chapter 10

page 262 The Flumenbaum quote is cited in *SEC* v. *Dennis Levine*, transcript of proceedings, May 22, 1986, p. 72.

page 268 Levine's guilty plea was described in "Levine Pleads Guilty," *Wall Street Journal*, June 6, 1986. The resolution of the SEC case is set forth in SEC Litigation Release No. 11117, June 5, 1986.

page 269 The Cecola plea to two counts of filing false tax returns was reported in *The Wall Street Journal*, Dec. 23, 1986.

page 269 Wilkis's guilty plea to four felonies was reported in *The Wall Street Journal*, Dec. 23, 1986.

page 271 Reich's interrogation by his partners is described in Brill, "Death of a Career."

page 272 Levine's sentencing was reported in *The Wall Street Journal*, Feb. 23, 1987.

page 273 The receiver's suspicions are set forth in *U.S.* v. *Levine*, Second Report of the Receiver.

page 273 Boesky's poolside meeting with Milken is described in Government's Milken sentencing memo, p. 101.

page 274 The discussions between Boesky and Mooradian were described in Hertzberg, "The Informer."

page 281 Boesky's assets are described in a copy of the Boesky accounting obtained by the author.

page 284 Copies of the government's plea agreement with Boesky, Sept. 18, 1986, and the SEC's settlement agreement, Sept. 17, 1986, were released by the government.

page 285 Boesky's disclosures about his role in Guinness, passed on by the SEC to British authorities, rocked the London financial world. Boesky revealed that he had helped Guinness PLC, the giant brewer, manipulate stock prices during its 1986 bid for Distillers PLC. Ernest Saunders, former chairman of Guinness, was sentenced to five years in prison for what the judge called "dishonesty on a massive scale." Among those implicated was Boesky's friend and investor, Gerald Ronson, who was sentenced to a year in prison. See *The Wall Street Journal*, Aug. 29, 1990.

page 288 The transcripts of the Boesky-Milken discussions have not been disclosed, and the quotations in the text are based on the memories of participants or of people with access to the transcripts. The government has provided this description: "In that conversation, Milken was intent on providing Boesky with a false explanation for the $5.3 million payment. Milken and Boesky also assured each other that their subordinates would be reliable in the face of a governmental investigation" (Government's Milken sentencing memo, p. 103, fn. 39).

page 290 The text of Boesky's remarks to his staff was released by his lawyers when his agreement was announced.

page 291 The Nov. 14 ticker copy was obtained through Dow Jones News Retrieval.

page 292 Peizer's reaction to the Boesky news was described in his Fatico testimony (see note to p. 442). Milken's reaction was described by Peizer and Dahl in their testimony. Milken's spokespeople dispute the timing of Milken's reaction, insisting that Milken didn't go into Lowell's office until approximately 4 P.M., two and a half hours after the Boesky announcement.

page 292 Dahl testified to the running water incident in his Fatico testimony (see note to p. 442).

page 293 Peizer described his disposal of the blue ledger in his Fatico testimony (see note to p. 442). Spurge's role in any destruction of evidence has been the subject of government inquiry, but she hasn't been charged with any wrongdoing.

page 293 Maultasch's trip and his exchange with Milken were described in Maultasch's Fatico testimony (see note to p. 442).

pages 295 The *Wall Street Journal* stories discussed are James B. Stewart and Daniel Hertzberg, "Spreading Scandal," Nov. 17, 1986; "SEC Is Probing Drexel on 'Junk Bonds,' " Nov. 18, 1986; and "Grand Jury Is Said to Be Probing Drexel," Nov. 19, 1986. More than any others, these stories triggered a Drexel and Milken campaign to discredit the *Journal*'s reporting and to accuse the government of leaking to the *Journal*—a campaign which continued even after Drexel and Milken had filed guilty pleas.

page 296 The article quoted is David A. Vise and Michael Schrage, "Wall Street Lambastes SEC Action," *Washington Post,* Nov. 21, 1986. The investigation of Nolan and Spear Leeds was disclosed in *The Wall Street Journal,* Jan. 14, 1988. Neither Nolan nor the firm has been charged with any wrongdoing.

page 296 The estimate of Boesky's profits that so upset the SEC appeared in Priscilla Ann Smith and Beatrice E. Garcia, "Boesky Apparently Reaped at Least $203 Million in Illicit Profits with Levine's Inside Information," *Wall Street Journal,* Nov. 24, 1986.

page 297 The Dingell comment on Campbell's testimony was reported in Stewart, "Tracing a Scandal."

Chapter 11

page 302 Siegel's subpoena at Wachtell, Lipton and the ensuing events were first described in Stewart and Hertzberg, "Unhappy Ending."

page 304 Attorneys' efforts to have defendants plead before a lenient judge—a practice known as "judge shopping"—were once common in the Southern District of New York. Judges sat for two-week periods hearing pleas, and defendants were routinely granted a six-week period in which to plead; this guaranteed defense lawyers a choice among at least three judges. The six-week period has since been eliminated.

page 305 The SEC announced its settlement with Siegel in Litigation Release No. 11354, Feb. 13, 1987. It simultaneously filed its charges, *SEC* v. *Martin A. Siegel*, Complaint for Injunctive and Other Equitable Relief.

page 306 Prosecutors pressed Siegel to see if he would implicate others, including Henry Kravis. But Siegel refused, saying he wouldn't exaggerate his value as a witness and knew of no wrongdoing by Kravis.

page 307 Many states have a homestead provision, protecting a resident's home from seizure by creditors up to a certain dollar amount. Florida is one of the few states that protect the home no matter how great its value, and as a result has become a haven for those seeking to protect assets from creditors by buying expensive property.

page 310 Merrill Lynch said it fired Tabor because of large losses in its arbitrage operation, and not for anything related to the government's investigation.

page 311 Williams's life and career are described in a front-page obituary in *The New York Times* by Albin Krebs, Aug. 14, 1988.

pages 312–313 Milken's hiring of criminal lawyers was first reported in *The Wall Street Journal*, Dec. 8, 1986.

page 313 Liman's career is discussed in Christopher Knowlton, "The Man Asking Iranscam's Tough Questions," *Fortune*, June 8, 1987.

page 313 Fleming represented Hitachi after the U.S. conducted a massive "sting" operation designed to uncover the illegal export of American companies' technology. Officials of the giant Japanese conglomerate were videotaped in 1982 as they tried to take delivery of stolen IBM equipment for export to Japan. Hitachi was charged with conspiracy to transport stolen property and eventually pleaded guilty.

page 317 A copy of the handwritten Thurnher document was obtained by the author.

page 317 E. F. Hutton pleaded guilty in 1985 to 2,000 counts of mail and wire fraud and agreed to pay a $2 million fine after admitting that its employees had concocted a check overdrafting scheme. Hutton never recovered from the scandal, and was later taken over by Shearson Lehman Brothers.

page 319 Davidoff's plea and cooperation were first reported in *The Wall Street Journal*, Jan. 29, 1987. He was later sentenced to probation.

page 323 Thurnher's cooperation was first reported in *The Wall Street Journal*, Feb. 5, 1987.

page 323 Thurnher's account of the $5.3 million payment was described in Milken's reply sentencing memo, p. 101.

page 323 The article described is James B. Stewart and Daniel Hertzberg, "U.S. Accumulates Evidence Supporting Case Against Drexel, Milken," *Wall Street Journal*, Apr. 28, 1987.

page 325 Freeman's and Tabor's arrests were also described in James B. Stewart and Daniel Hertzberg, "Street Bombshell," *Wall Street Journal*, Feb. 13, 1987.

page 325 When Siegel asked Pedowitz to represent him, Pedowitz had told Siegel that he couldn't because Wachtell, Lipton had represented too many clients that figured in the Siegel–Boesky deals, and that this might give rise to a conflict. Curiously, however, although Wachtell, Lipton had also represented clients involved in the Freeman-Siegel deals, Pedowitz did agree to represent Goldman, Sachs. Pedowitz also had had an attorney-client relationship, however briefly, with Siegel, which could have created a further conflict in the event Goldman, Sachs accused Siegel of lying. Pedowitz declines comment.

page 331 Siegel was first identified as CS-1 in Stewart and Hertzberg, "Street Bombshell," see note p. 325.

page 333 The Siegel plea was described in Stewart and Hertzberg, "Unhappy Ending."

page 334 General Electric's reaction to the arrests was described in James B. Stewart and Janet Guyon, "Damage Control," *Wall Street Journal*, June 8, 1987.

page 336 The involvement of Roche and Little in an alleged stock parking scheme was reported in *The Wall Street Journal*, June 9, 1987. At the time, Roche declined comment and Little said, "I'm stuck in the middle of this thing. I had nothing to do with this parking thing." No charges were filed, and the investigation ended when Kidder settled SEC charges.

page 337 Jefferies's guilty plea and settlement of SEC charges was reported in *The Wall Street Journal*, Mar. 20, 1987.

page 338 Lewis was identified as Jefferies's co-conspirator in *The Wall Street Journal*, Mar. 23, 1987. Lewis later pleaded guilty to three felonies (see *Wall Street Journal*, Aug. 31, 1989).

page 341 The decision to drop the charges was widely reported. See, e.g., *The Wall Street Journal*, May 14, 1987, which includes the "tip of the iceberg" quote from Cartusciello.

page 342 The "tool-and-die" quote, obtained by reporter Steve Swartz, appears in a *Wall Street Journal* article, May 15, 1987. In the same article, DeNunzio denied that his ouster had anything to do with the scandal and denied any wrongdoing with respect to Siegel's activities at the firm.

page 343 The Kidder, Peabody settlement is reported in *The Wall Street Journal*, June 5, 1987.

Chapter 12

page 348 Hale testified on Mar. 14, 1989, in the government's trial of the Princeton-Newport officials and Newberg.

page 349 The Princeton-Newport raid was described in James B. Stewart and Daniel Hertzberg, "Insider Focus," *Wall Street Journal*, Apr. 6, 1988.

page 350 Jones's life story is the subject of Stephen J. Adler, "Working Girl," *Wall Street Journal*.

page 352 Transcripts of the taped conversations between officials of Drexel and Princeton-Newport were introduced as evidence in the Princeton-Newport trial. All quotes are from the transcripts.

page 352 The transcript of the conversation between Freeman and Zarzecki has been made public as government exhibit T-1 in the Princeton-Newport trial.

page 352 The quotes are from Princeton-Newport government exhibit T-1, page A-1627.

page 354 Engel's return to Drexel, and subsequent departure, is discussed in Bruck, *The Predators' Ball*, pp. 338–342.

page 355 The Drexel video at the 1987 Predators' Ball was described in Steve Coll, "Drexel's Faithful Sing Praises of Junk Bonds," *Washington Post*, Apr. 5, 1987. The quotation, "How much did we pay that guy?" is from that article.

page 355 The "guilty conscience" quote is from Coll, "Drexel's Faithful."

page 356 The quote "When the going gets tough . . ." and description of the junk-bond celebration are from Bruck, *The Predators' Ball*, p. 348.

page 356 The article described is Laurie P. Cohen, "Drexel's New Television Ad Tugs at the Heart but Fudges the Facts," *Wall Street Journal*, Dec. 8, 1987.

page 357 For examples of *Wall Street Journal* editorials, see "Junk Prosecution?" July 12, 1988 ("The case against Drexel may be more risky than a high-yield bond"); "Drexel: Prosecution and Fall," Feb. 15, 1990 ("It is a mockery of due process that Mr. Milken has not had his day in court after more than three years of investigation. . . . No serious person is arguing that the government's charges amount to a claim that Mr. Milken built the junk bond on some crooked scheme").

page 358 The 1987 stock market crash is the subject of James B. Stewart and Daniel Hertzberg, "Terrible Tuesday," *Wall Street Journal*, Nov. 20, 1988.

page 359 The Buffett quote is from David A. Vise, "Despite Setbacks, Drexel Still Calls Shots in 'Junk Bond' Revolution," *Washington Post*, Apr. 17, 1988.

page 359 The Boesky sentencing was described in *The Wall Street Journal*, Dec. 21, 1987. In materials made public in connection with Boesky's sentencing, his psychiatrist offered this explanation of his wrongdoing: Boesky "has begun to recognize that he suffered from an abnormal and compulsive need to prove himself, to overcome some sense of inadequacy or inferiority that is rooted in his childhood. He was driven to work without any limit of time or effort. He sacrificed closeness with family and friends without realizing that it was happening . . ." (Boesky memo, p. 40).

page 360 The quotes from Judge Lasker are from *U.S.* v. *Boesky*, transcript of the sentencing hearing, Dec. 20, 1987.

page 360 The events of Feb. 18, 1988, are described in detail in Stewart and Hertzberg, "How a Wealthy Arb . . . Turnéd to Violence."

page 364 The grand jury testimony quoted is from a transcript disclosed by the government in connection with *U.S.* v. *Mulheren*.

page 366 Mulheren's quotes are from the police report, introduced in evidence in *U.S.* v. *Mulheren*.

page 367 Jamie's dissolution is discussed in *The Wall Street Journal*, Feb. 23, 1988.

Chapter 13

page 368 Lompoc is no longer a minimum-security facility.

page 369 In its complaint, the SEC charged Milken and Drexel with insider trading in connection with the Viacom trading. The charges are described in detail in *SEC* v. *Drexel Burnham Lambert et al.*, Complaint for Injunctive and Other Equitable Relief, pp. 166–171. Milken has said he knew nothing about the Viacom trading and that, in any event, it was a routine hedging procedure and wasn't insider trading. After receiving immunity, Gardiner testified about his various inconsistencies in the Fatico hearing (see note to p. 442).

page 370 Drexel's Wells submission was reported in *The Wall Street Journal*, Jan. 26, 1988.

page 371 The article that captured Baird's attention was Stewart and Hertzberg, "Suspicious Trading."

page 373 The Jones perjury charges are the subject of Adler, "Working Girl."

page 375 Robinson was the subject of a front-page article, Joann Lipman, "Power Broker," *Wall Street Journal*, Dec. 5, 1988.

page 379 The Dingell hearings are described in Thomas E. Ricks, "Milken Refuses to Testify in House Probe," *Wall Street Journal*, Apr. 28, 1988.

page 381 Milken's attempt to buy Bruck out of her book contract is described in Bruck, *The Predators' Ball*, p. 359.

page 383 Liman has denied that he urged Drexel or its lawyers to try to block Bruck's book.

page 383 The article referred to is Laura Landro, "Junk Bond People Think Book on Them Is So Much Trash," *Wall Street Journal*, May 19, 1988.

page 385 The indictments were reported in *The Wall Street Journal*, Aug. 5, 1988.

page 386 Maultasch's cooperation was first reported in Laurie P. Cohen, "Senior Drexel Trader Is Witness," *Wall Street Journal*, Dec. 7, 1988.

page 390 Dahl's cooperation was reported in *The Wall Street Journal*, Oct. 5, 1988.

page 392 Peizer testified about the desk drawer conversation with Milken, and the Solomon arrangement, at the Fatico hearing (see note to p. 442).

Chapter 14

page 394 The SEC's complaint is summarized in the SEC's Litigation Release No. 11859, Sept. 7, 1988. The 184-page complaint contains the most detailed account of the government's version of Milken's criminal enterprise. See note to p. 369.

page 396 Cogut testified in the Fatico hearing (see note to p. 442). The MacPherson situation was also described in Laurie P. Cohen, "About Face," *Wall Street Journal*, Apr. 23, 1990.

page 398 The existence of plea negotiations was first reported in *The Wall Street Journal*, Jan. 27, 1989.

page 399 The quotation "That man of genius . . ." is from Glenn F. Bunting, "How Drexel Made Itself Welcome with Politicians," *Los Angeles Times*, May 7, 1989. The article, a detailed report on Drexel's political contributions, also reported that Bradley intervened on Drexel's behalf with the SEC and tried to enlist the help of California Representative Tony Coelho.

pages 399–400 Milken's public-relations campaign aimed at blacks is the subject of Mary G. Gotschall, "The Machine Behind Michael Milken," *Regardies*, January 1991.

page 401 The fight for RJR Nabisco is the subject of Bryan Burrough and John Helyar's best-selling *Barbarians at the Gate* (New York: Harper Collins, 1990). Robinson's role is described in detail in the book.

page 402 Drexel's effort to sell the RJR bonds is the subject of Randall Smith, "Capital Coup," *Wall Street Journal*, Mar. 3, 1989.

page 402 The events that led to Drexel's settlement are described in Steve Swartz and Laurie P. Cohen, "Executive Anguish," *Wall Street Journal*, Dec. 16, 1988.

page 404 The text of Joseph's memo appeared in *The Wall Street Journal*, Dec. 5, 1988.

page 405 Liman has acknowledged having had a broad philosophical and historical discussion about Drexel's decision to plead guilty with Joseph, but has denied that he meant to compare Drexel's conduct to the Nazi persecution of the Jews.

page 408 The events leading to Drexel's demise are the subject of Laurie P. Cohen, "The Final Days," *Wall Street Journal*, Feb. 26, 1990. Additional details appear in Brett Duval Fromson, "The Last Days of Drexel Burnham," *Fortune*, May 21, 1990.

page 410 The RJR road show is described in Smith, "Capital Coup."

Chapter 15

page 417 The indictment and press conference are described in Laurie P. Cohen, "The Other Shoe," *Wall Street Journal*, Mar. 30, 1989, which contains the quote, "In America . . ."

page 418 The Jones trial is described in Adler, "Working Girl."

page 418 The Princeton-Newport trial and verdict were reported in *The Wall Street Journal*, Aug. 1, 1989. The Court of Appeals reversed the convictions in part, including the RICO and tax charges, but upheld the securities and conspiracy convictions (see *Wall Street Journal*, July 1, 1991). The appellate decision had little practical impact on the defendants.

page 424 The 1989 Predators' Ball is described in Jaye Scholl, "Skeleton at the Feast," *Barron's*, April 10, 1989.

page 425 Details of the Drexel settlement were reported in *The Wall Street Journal*, Apr. 14, 1989.

page 425 Drexel's first choice for the chairman's post was former Tennessee senator Howard Baker, who reportedly declined the job because he thought he would be a mere figurehead. Though Drexel was perceived as trying to buy respectability by hiring Shad, Shad insisted at the time that he would be an "active chairman" and not window dressing. Shad added, "I wouldn't have accepted this position but for my confidence in and my respect for Fred Joseph." See *The Wall Street Journal*, Apr. 17, 1989.

page 427 The crisis at Integrated Resources is the subject of Linda Sandler, Randall Smith, and Joan Lebow, "Limited Resources," *Wall Street Journal*, June 23, 1989.

page 429 The controversy over Milken's legal fees was reported in Laurie P. Cohen, "Drexel Is Putting Milken's Attorneys on a Strict Budget," *Wall Street Journal*, Oct. 4, 1989, which contains the quote from Liman.

page 429 The collapse of the UAL deal is the subject of Jeff Bailey, Asra Nomani, and Judith Valente, "Flawed Portent," *Wall Street Journal*, Oct. 16, 1990.

page 430 One of the harshest indictments of Milken's business is Benjamin J. Stein, "Was Drexel/Milken the Biggest Scam Ever?" *Barron's* Feb. 19, 1990. "Drexel/Milken, a critic charges, was a vast Ponzi scheme. There never was a Wizard of Oz or nerd/genius, but only Michael the Cheerleader," was how *Barron's* described the piece in its table of contents. The article enraged the Milken camp, but quickly became the most talked-about survey of Milken's economics.

page 430 The statistics on the performance of junk bonds and other investments are from George Anders and Constance Mitchell, "Junk King's Legacy," *Wall Street Journal*, Nov. 20, 1990.

page 430 The quotation is from Anders and Mitchell, "Junk King's Legacy."

page 431 Ingersoll's mounting debt woes were the subject of Patrick M. Reilly, "Deadline Squeeze," *Wall Street Journal*, Mar. 26, 1990.

page 431 The seizure of Columbia Savings and Loan by federal regulators was reported in *The Wall Street Journal*, Jan. 28, 1991.

page 436 Nearly all plea agreements approved by the Justice Department are revocable in the event the defendant lies subsequent to entering into the agreement, as Boesky's was. But not Milken's. In paragraph six of the Milken plea agreement, dated Apr. 22, 1990, four events are cited that render the agreement revocable. Subsequent false testimony isn't cited. (The government did reserve the right to charge Milken for perjury, but such cases are notoriously difficult to prosecute, the Jones conviction notwithstanding.) This provision was a remarkable concession, suggesting the government's desperation to reach a plea. The provision undercuts the value of Milken's cooperation, since it is all but a license for Milken to lie.

page 439 The Mulheren verdict was reported in *The Wall Street Journal*, July 13, 1990.

page 439 Siegel's sentencing was reported in *The Wall Street Journal*, June 8, 1990.

page 441 Milken's role in the collapse of various savings and loans is the subject of pending lawsuits filed by private plaintiffs, including Columbia Savings & Loan, and the Federal Deposit Insurance Commission. In its complaint, the FDIC alleges that Milken, Drexel, and other defendants defrauded numerous S&L's of unspecified millions. Milken and Drexel have denied the charges.

page 442 Prior to Milken's sentencing, two weeks of hearings were held at Judge Wood's direction, beginning Oct. 11, 1990. At the time of Milken's plea, prosecutors obtained an agreement from Milken's lawyers allowing them to introduce evidence of additional crimes by Milken for consideration at sentencing. Milken's lawyers subsequently demanded the right to contest the government's allegations, and Judge Kimba Wood ordered the government to pick no more than six additional charges and present evidence, giving Milken's lawyers the right to rebut them. Such hearings are known as "Fatico" hearings, named after the case that established a defendant's right to contest such allegations. The hearings proved anticlimactic. Boesky wasn't called as a witness (the prosecutors had been dismayed by his performance at the Mulheren trial) and none of the Boesky-related charges, about such deals as Diamond Shamrock and Pacific Lumber, were presented. Evidence for some of the charges presented seemed inconclusive (see, e.g., Laurie P. Cohen and Wade Lambert, "Prosecutors Fail to Tie Milken to Trades," *Wall Street Journal*, Oct. 12, 1990). Judge Wood ultimately disregarded the additional charges, though she said she was persuaded that Milken had attempted to obstruct justice.

page 442 Excerpts from Judge Wood's statement at the Milken sentencing appeared in *The New York Times*, Nov. 22, 1990.

Acknowledgments

This book couldn't have been written without the extraordinary support and patience of my colleagues at *The Wall Street Journal*. I will always be indebted and grateful to Norman Pearlstine, the *Journal*'s executive editor, who backed my reporting at every step and encouraged me when I most needed his support. He has given this book his enthusiastic backing and has been a sensitive and perceptive editor.

Paul Steiger, the *Journal*'s managing editor, has been a staunch defender of my reporting and I have benefited on numerous occasions from his advice, maturity, and good judgment.

Daniel Hertzberg was my collaborator on many stories during the scandal. His talent and dedication inspired me on countless occasions, and much of what appears in this book would not have been uncovered without him. In the additional reporting I did for this book, I tried to emulate the high standards he always insisted upon.

The *Journal*'s Laurie P. Cohen acted as a researcher and reporter for this book. Her contributions far exceed those of the usual research assistant, and she was instrumental in gaining the cooperation of many sources. Steve Swartz provided valuable advice and served as a sounding board throughout the reporting and writing process. Fred Saez did much of the fact-checking and computer research. The *Journal*'s computer experts, Richard Schuster, Cathy Fiducia, and Jim McDonald, rescued me from technological crises.

The talented editors who work on page one—Jane Berentson, Dan Kelly, John Brecher, John Bussey, Jane Mayer, Paul Martin, Henry Myers, David Sanford, Tim Smith, and Chuck Stevens—bore the brunt of my absences and distractions. Along with news assistant Christine McAuley, they responded with hard work and good spirits. I am also indebted to the *Journal*'s bureau chiefs and reporters for their patience and understanding.

At Simon & Schuster, Alice Mayhew has been a superb editor at all stages of this project, our third collaboration. George Hodgman also did outstanding editing on the text. Simon & Schuster has provided enormous support; I am especially grateful to Richard Snyder, Charles Hayward, Jack McKeown, Eric Rayman, copy editor Michael Cain, and photo researcher Vincent Virga.

My agent, Amanda Urban, has been enthusiastic and diligent from the beginning of this project. I also owe thanks to Joni Evans, who encouraged me to do this book while she was at Simon & Schuster.

Probably none have suffered through the reporting and writing of this book more patiently and with better spirits than my family and friends, the people I love. I hope that I can repay them in the years ahead, and that this book will somehow begin to compensate them for my at times inexcusable absorption in my work.

Above all, I am grateful to my parents. At their hands I learned the moral lessons of this book long before I knew anything about the riches and power of Wall Street.

Photo Credits

1. Joyce Ravid, Onyx
2. Steve Smith, Onyx
3. Arty Pomerantz, *The New York Post*
4. Robert A. Cumins, Black Star
5, 12, 13, 32. UPI
6, 9, 10, 11, 14, 15, 16, 17, 18, 20, 21, 28, 29, 30. Wide World Photos
7. Tom Fenton
19. Women's Wear Daily
22. Roger Sandler, Black Star
23. Roger Sandler
25. Michael Garland, Onyx
31. Faye Ellman

Other photos used courtesy of private sources.

Index

About the Author

James B. Stewart, front-page editor of *The Wall Street Journal*, is the author of *The Partners* and *The Prosecutors*. He was awarded the 1988 Pulitzer prize with Daniel Hertzberg for their stories on the 1987 stock market crash and the insider-trading scandal. He lives in New York City.